CHURCHILL AND THE
DARDANELLES

CHURCHILL AND THE DARDANELLES

CHRISTOPHER M. BELL

OXFORD
UNIVERSITY PRESS

OXFORD
UNIVERSITY PRESS

Great Clarendon Street, Oxford, OX2 6DP,
United Kingdom

Oxford University Press is a department of the University of Oxford.
It furthers the University's objective of excellence in research, scholarship,
and education by publishing worldwide. Oxford is a registered trade mark of
Oxford University Press in the UK and in certain other countries

First Edition published in 2017

Impression: 1

Published in the United States of America by Oxford University Press
198 Madison Avenue, New York, NY 10016, United States of America

British Library Cataloguing in Publication Data
Data available

Library of Congress Control Number: 2016945385

ISBN 978–0–19–870254–2

Printed in Great Britain by
Clays Ltd, St Ives plc

For Alex and Matthew

Acknowledgements

I began my previous book, *Churchill and Sea Power*, by explaining why I had chosen to publish a new work about Winston Churchill, surely one of the most studied historical figures of the twentieth century. Four years later, I find myself in the curious position of having written another volume about Churchill, and on a topic that I had already addressed in the earlier book. This new project was inspired by a sense of unfinished business. *Churchill and Sea Power* devoted around twenty-five pages to the opening months of the First World War and the Dardanelles campaign, which was barely enough to do justice to such a rich and complex subject. In the limited space I had to work with, there was no room to delve into the details of the naval operation and explore precisely why things had gone so badly wrong. I could give only the basic outlines of the Britain's chaotic decision-making process and Churchill's role in it. And there was little scope to examine the complicated relationship between Churchill and his naval advisers, especially Jacky Fisher. All I could do was sketch out those aspects of the campaign relevant to the subject of the book I was writing— Churchill's development as a naval strategist over the course of half a century.

And even that was a demanding task. The Dardanelles campaign was probably the most challenging subject I covered in *Churchill and Sea Power*. Before I could get to grips with what had happened, I first had to strip away layer after layer of myth, and a century's worth of controversy. Countless drafts were needed to get things right. And at the end of it all, I was struck by how much I had had to leave out. The biggest disappointment was that I had not been able to follow the story of the Dardanelles past May 1915. How did this failure affect Churchill's subsequent political career? Why did the campaign become so heavily mythologized? What part did Churchill play in shaping popular perceptions of the campaign? How did he contribute to the myth-making? As I reflected on these questions, it struck me that they could only be answered by first revisiting the campaign itself. The myths and misconceptions surrounding the failed naval offensive were now so firmly embedded in the story that a monumental debunking effort was essential. Only then would it be possible to deconstruct the myths of the Dardanelles and explore their place in the 'Churchill Legend'.

On a more personal level, I wanted to satisfy myself that I had at last worked out how the Dardanelles fit into Churchill's legacy. As an impressionable undergraduate, I had absorbed Churchill's case for the campaign. His memoirs of the First World War, *The World Crisis*, seemed persuasive and plausible. And I have to admit, I wanted to believe that the figure whose heroic defiance of Nazi Germany I admired had, in fact, been right about this as well. Churchill's case for the Dardanelles was validated by enough historians that it did not seem safe to dismiss it lightly. But it was also obvious that most of these historians were not authorities on the Royal Navy. And many of them were obviously predisposed to accept Churchill's claims uncritically, making a degree of scepticism seem warranted. Yet even as my doubts about Churchill's version of events grew, I still nurtured hopes that an exhaustive study of the evidence would one day reveal that he had been right to launch this campaign—that it actually was a brilliant concept that might have succeeded if not for the mistakes of lesser figures. This is not what happened though. As I delved deeper into the archives, I had to admit that Churchill had made mistakes. Many of them. Some of them quite serious. Churchill was not, after all, the hero of this particular story. Nor was he a victim. But it was also clear that his failures did not automatically make him the villain of the piece. He had not been wrong about everything. In fact, there was a great deal he got right. And he was by no means the only one to make mistakes. Many of the recurring criticisms that have been levelled against him over the years are distorted, exaggerated, or wrong. My goal, as I worked on this project, has been to get as close to the truth as possible. It was clear early on that this study would not produce a simple thumbs-up/thumbs-down verdict about Churchill that would please either his admirers or his critics. The past, unfortunately, is seldom that simple. Sometimes we have to be satisfied with 'it's complicated' for an answer.

I am indebted once more to the many helpful and knowledgeable individuals at the archives and libraries I have used. Particular thanks are due to Allen Packwood and the staff of the Churchill College Archives Centre in Cambridge; the National Museum of the Royal Navy, Portsmouth; The National Archives in Kew; the Imperial War Museum; the National Maritime Museum; the British Library; the Sir Basil Liddell Hart Archives Centre at

King's College, London; Nick Mays and Anne Jensen at the News UK Archives and Records Office; the Parliamentary Archives; the West Sussex Records Office; the Australian War Memorial; Elizabeth Garver and the Harry Ransom Center at the University of Texas at Austin; Lesa Davies at the Isle of Wight County Record Office; the University of Leeds Library; the National Army Museum; the Institute of Commonwealth Studies; Phyllis Ross and the Killam Library, Dalhousie University; and the National Library of Australia. I am grateful to these institutions for permission to examine and quote from papers in their possession. Documents in The National Archives and all other material under crown copyright are cited by permission of the Controller of Her Majesty's Stationery Office.

I would also like to thank the friends and colleagues who have offered advice and assistance over the last few years. In Halifax, I have been fortunate to discuss this project at various stages with David Campbell and Todd McCallum. Carla Pass shared her extensive knowledge of the Mass Observation Archive, and unearthed a mountain of useful material for me in British newspapers. I am grateful to the Australian War Memorial and the Australian National University for inviting me to speak at the Gallipoli Centenary Conference in Canberra; to Antoine Capet for bringing me to Paris for the Winston Churchill Conference at the Sorbonne in 2015; and to Brunel University London's Department of Politics and History, where I was given the opportunity to address their Research Seminar and annual PhD Student Conference in 2016. I was greatly impressed by the hospitality extended to me by all of these institutions. As usual, there is a long list of people who kindly answered queries, helped me to track down documents, or just listened while I rambled on. Many thanks to Len Barnett, George Cassar, Ronald Cohen, Rhys Crawley, Richard Dunley, Martin Folly, Simon Harley, Alex Howlett, Thornton McCamish, Ann Moyal, Paul Ramsey, Duncan Redford, John Stubbs, and Richard Toye. The Churchill Centre has provided encouragement and support for my work for many years. Richard Langworth and Lee Pollock in particular have both gone above and beyond the call of duty. John Moorehead and Caroline Moorehead generously supplied the photograph of their father with Winston Churchill in 1956. John Ferris, Andrew Lambert, and Graham Clews read the manuscript and made many excellent suggestions. My greatest debt, as always, is to my wife, Rae, and my sons Matthew and Alex.

Table of Contents

List of Illustrations

List of Maps

List of Abbreviations

AIF	Australian Imperial Force
ANZAC	Australian and New Zealand Army Corps
BEF	British Expeditionary Force
CID	Committee of Imperial Defence
CIGS	Chief of the Imperial General Staff
DMO	Director of Military Operations
DNI	Director of Naval Intelligence
DNO	Director of Naval Operations
MEF	Mediterranean Expeditionary Force
NID	Naval Intelligence Division
RNAS	Royal Naval Air Service

Churchill and the Dardanelles

A Riddle Wrapped in Myths
Inside a Legend

From the vantage point of the early twenty-first century, the story of Winston Churchill and the Dardanelles campaign does not actually begin in June 1940, but it does takes a sharp detour there. It is almost impossible today not to view the failed naval offensive of February–March 1915 through the lens of Britain's 'Finest Hour'. In Britain's national mythology, Churchill single-handedly changed the course of the Second World War. He inspired the nation to carry on the fight against Nazi Germany, sustained the morale of the British people at the lowest point of the war, and ensured Hitler's ultimate downfall. Today, Churchill dominates the historical stage and towers over his contemporaries. A. J. P. Taylor famously described him as 'the saviour of his country', and it would be not just unwise but counterproductive to pretend that the 'baggage' attached to Churchill's name can simply be ignored.[1]

This historical 'baggage'—known today as the 'Churchill Legend'—has in recent years become a subject of study in its own right, and deservedly so, for it has done much to shape popular understanding of the twentieth century. The immense fame and prestige Churchill acquired during the Second World War magnified in the decades after 1945, as he was transformed into the embodiment of Britain's war effort, the greatest Briton of the era, and a titan on the world stage. And while this reputation was founded on a mixture of truth and myth, there can be no denying its impact and longevity. It was a reputation, moreover, that Churchill himself had always aspired to. He once suggested that the past should be left 'to history, especially as I propose to write that history myself', and through the pioneering work of historians like John Ramsden and David Reynolds we know just how much effort Churchill put into crafting his legend for posterity.[2] He had no intention after 1945 of leaving his legacy to chance, and he achieved remarkable success in selling his version of the war to an eager and receptive public through his monumental six-volume memoir-history of the Second World War.

Myth-making and legend-building were hardly new pursuits for Churchill. In the decades before the Second World War he had worked hard to create a heroic public persona for himself. And he had failed. Despite his best efforts to influence how the British people saw him, he could never overcome the unflattering reputation that was crafted for him by his enemies—that of an erratic, reckless, and egocentric adventurer. This image was all the more frustrating for Churchill because it was based in large measure on his record in the First World War, a conflict he had expected to showcase his unique talents and establish his reputation as an inspiring leader and gifted strategist. Of all the episodes in the Great War to attract criticism, none was as damaging to Churchill as the failed attempt in 1915 to force a passage through the defences protecting the Straits of the Dardanelles. The accepted version of events is that Churchill was driven from office in disgrace due to the failure at the Dardanelles offensive, although this is not entirely accurate. The Dardanelles was, to be sure, the cause of his break with Admiral of the Fleet Lord Fisher, the First Sea Lord. But in May 1915 there was as yet no widespread perception of the Dardanelles as a serious defeat, let alone a disaster. The doubts harboured by the British press and public about Churchill at this time stemmed mainly from rumours about his domineering behaviour at the Admiralty, not the Dardanelles operation specifically. Churchill's colleagues in Herbert Henry Asquith's Liberal government were initially content to see him remain at the Admiralty when the political crisis that brought down the government first broke in May 1915. It was only Asquith's decision to bring the Conservative party into a coalition that ensured Churchill's fall from power—and the Conservatives would have demanded Churchill's sacrifice no matter what had happened at the Dardanelles.[3]

There could be little doubt, however, that Churchill left the Admiralty in 1915 under a cloud. His widely publicized clash with Lord Fisher was enough to ensure that. Before long, the idea took hold that he was personally responsible for launching the unsuccessful naval attack on the Dardanelles *and* the even more costly campaign that followed on the Gallipoli peninsula. The British public assumed that land operations had flowed seamlessly and inevitably from the naval assault. As the former came increasingly to be perceived as a costly and ill-conceived failure, criticism of Churchill mounted. It is hardly accurate to suggest that he was simply made a scapegoat, as he *had* been the driving force behind the original naval attack, which set everything in motion. And this was widely known. If the attack on the Dardanelles had succeeded, he would have received most of the credit. When it was judged a failure, the blame naturally attached to him. It did not help Churchill's position that the Dardanelles was easily represented by his critics as the latest in a series of wartime blunders by an impetuous and overbearing politician perpetually at odds with his naval advisers. But Gallipoli and the Dardanelles were the costliest failures directly linked to Churchill during the war, and these campaigns, more than any other misfortunes, discredited him in the eyes of the British public—and nearly destroyed his political career.

Controversy has raged around the Dardanelles since 1915, and the campaign still casts a long shadow over Churchill's reputation. Two competing narratives have emerged. In one, Churchill was to blame for everything. He was an amateur strategist who conceived the idea of a naval attack on the Dardanelles, ignored warnings from Fisher and other admirals that it was doomed to fail, duped his Cabinet colleagues into supporting the scheme, and suppressed opposition until the campaign was finally overtaken by disaster. In this version, the idea of forcing a passage through the heavily defended Straits without the support of troops never offered any prospect of success. In the other narrative, the Dardanelles offensive was one of the war's few creative strategic concepts, an alternative to the futile slaughter on the Western Front, and a tragic missed opportunity. The failure was in the execution, not the conception. The admirals in charge were half-hearted and timorous. The operation was called off at the first setback, even though it was actually on the verge of complete success. If the attack had been renewed, the enemy's defences would have collapsed in short order, allowing the Allied fleet to reach Constantinople, knocking the Ottoman Empire out of the war, saving Russia from defeat (and ultimately from revolution), and fatally weakening Germany.

As this study will show, neither perspective holds up under scrutiny. The first step towards achieving a balanced view is to eject unnecessary baggage. To start with, it must be recognized that the main framework of the cases both for and against Churchill were established between 1915 and the mid-1920s, long before the Churchill Legend existed to complicate things, but also long before the official records of the war were open to scholars. The case against Churchill was actually established *during* the First World War, when few details about the higher direction of the war were available to the public. Its broad outlines were already in place by the time Churchill left the Admiralty in 1915, the product of Whitehall gossip, unconfirmed rumours, and calculated leaks to the press. The earliest public attacks on Churchill over his part in the Dardanelles campaign were therefore highly speculative and often inaccurate, since wartime restrictions on the disclosure of information limited the ammunition available to his critics. But the early criticisms stuck. Later attacks on Churchill followed along the same lines, but were now supported with information released by the Dardanelles Commission, which had been established by Parliament in 1916 to examine the inception and conduct of the naval and the military campaigns. Its influential first report, published in 1917, was relatively favourable to Churchill, but the evidence it reproduced was fragmentary. Churchill's multi-volume memoir-history of the First World War, *The World Crisis* (1923–31), placed additional documents in the public domain, although the record was still far from complete. It would be another forty-five years before historians had full access to the surviving official government records about the Dardanelles, by which time the battle lines were firmly entrenched.

The nature of the early evidence available to critics also distorted the first attempts to write the history of the Dardanelles campaign. With official documents in short supply, the testimony gathered by the Dardanelles Commission was relied upon to fill the gaps. This created obvious problems. First, the Commission's initial report reproduced only a tiny fraction of the testimony it gathered over the course of twenty-one days from interviews with thirty-five different individuals, the transcripts of which run to hundreds of pages. From this mass the commissioners selected just a handful of quotes to illustrate particular points they wished to make. The testimony they reproduced did not always reflect the range of opinions they had heard. Objectivity and misrepresentation were also problems. When the Commission interviewed witnesses in late 1916, the Gallipoli campaign had already ended in failure: the public was looking to apportion blame, and participants were ducking for cover. Everyone implicated in the inception of the campaign and its mismanagement had a strong motive to conceal their mistakes, shift responsibility, and present their involvement in the best possible light.

To complicate things further, many of the Commission's witnesses colluded over their testimony. Liberal Cabinet ministers, including Churchill, coordinated their evidence to their mutual advantage with the assistance of the Secretary to the War Committee, Maurice Hankey. The generals who had fought on the peninsula also worked together behind the scenes, as did civilian and military officials at the War Office. Churchill and Fisher arranged to tailor their evidence so as not to incriminate or contradict one another, and Fisher may have tampered with documents to strengthen aspects of his own case. Some of the witnesses consulted had not even been personally involved in launching or conducting the operations, and naturally took the position that if they *had* been consulted, they would, of course, have predicted failure. This is not to suggest that nobody ever told the truth to the Commission, but everyone who testified had an agenda of some kind. This applies equally, of course, to those who later published their memoirs. Historians have mined these records without always making sufficient allowances for their limitations, often treating evidence that supports their argument as completely reliable while dismissing or ignoring contradictory testimony that might undermine their position.[4] This problem is frequently compounded by the tendency to forget that even contemporary documents must be used with caution. The positions taken by individual decision-makers could change radically on a day-to-day basis, making it dangerous to draw generalizations about anyone's views over an extended period.

The myths of the Dardanelles campaign are now firmly entrenched. The idea that the naval offensive was the great missed opportunity of the First World War has endured in part because it has become embedded in the Churchill Legend that grew up after the Second World War. Charges that Churchill foisted a hopeless plan on his advisers and colleagues have been embraced with equal fervour by those who wish to challenge or subvert the Churchill Legend. In both cases, the failed offensive of 1915 is seemingly of interest only to the extent that it can be used to shed light on Churchill's leadership during the Second World War. This episode in his early career provides fodder for his admirers and critics alike. It can easily be made into the first manifestation of Churchill's remarkable gifts as a war leader and strategist—or an unheeded warning of his erratic judgement and recklessness. Both sides of the debate naturally gravitate towards the interpretation that best suits them.

This study divides naturally into two parts. The first, focusing on events from the outbreak of the First World War to Churchill's ejection from the Admiralty in May 1915, employs contemporary documents to establish a record that is, as far as possible, undistorted by the claims and counter-claims made later in full knowledge of the campaigns' failure. Information and opinions drawn from the Dardanelles Commission and post-war sources are used cautiously and sparingly at this stage, and not as a means to establish definitively any individual's actions or motives. Fortunately, the range of contemporary sources available a century after the campaign is extensive, if not always complete. A careful look at the documentary record shows that many aspects of Churchill's involvement in the Dardanelles campaign have been misunderstood or misrepresented. The naval offensive, to begin with, is seldom treated as a distinct campaign in its own right. It was eclipsed almost immediately by the fighting on the Gallipoli peninsula, and understandably so—the latter campaign lasted longer, involved vastly larger forces, and produced far more casualties. As a result, the naval attack is often represented as little more than a short and futile prelude to the inevitable battles on the Gallipoli peninsula. This, in turn, suggests that the inception of the naval assault is sufficient explanation for everything that followed. But the decision to land troops was taken separately, weeks after the naval assault was approved. It was not initially considered a necessary or inevitable step, and Churchill was not the leading actor in bringing it about.

Another piece of baggage that needs to be jettisoned is the widespread assumption that Churchill completely dominated the decision-making process at the Admiralty and in the Cabinet and War Council. This has been a problem almost from the beginning. There were already suggestions in the British press in April 1915 that Churchill had somehow forced his plans on both the Admiralty and the government. Cabinet ministers and admirals alike were supposedly helpless to resist his overwhelming powers of persuasion and dominating personality. The tendency to single out Churchill as virtually the only decision-maker who mattered has increased over time. The debate over the merits of the Dardanelles strategy was always highly personalized, in large part because Churchill himself was so active after the war in promoting his version of events. But the problem became even more pronounced with the growth of the Churchill Legend. Over the last half century, most British politicians, statesmen, and warriors of 1914–18—many of them household names in their time—have virtually disappeared from public memory, even as Churchill's prominence has steadily risen. To understand Churchill's part in Britain's strategic decision-making process it must be recognized that he was never anything like a dictator. He may have *wanted* to dominate and control the process, and he certainly felt himself qualified to do so, but he never wielded the kind of arbitrary power often attributed to him. His colleagues, including such formidable figures as Asquith, Field Marshal Lord Kitchener, and David Lloyd George, were important and powerful actors in their own right.

At the same time, it would be a mistake to assume that Britain's machinery for managing the war in 1914–15 was rational and efficient. The decision-making system that developed over the first months of the war was haphazard, chaotic, and amateurish to a degree that is now difficult to believe. Ministers did not meet regularly; they seldom understood all aspects of the strategic options under consideration; and they were inadequately briefed by the fighting services. Information was invariably funnelled through the two service ministers, Churchill and Kitchener, who too often gave a partial or misleading picture to their colleagues. Churchill was well aware of the deficiencies of the system and attempted to manipulate it to his advantage. The lack of formal oversight and systematic consultation helped him to advance his own agendas. He did not create the dysfunctional system by which the government and the armed services coordinated strategy, but he certainly contributed to its defects.

The relationship between Churchill and his naval advisers has always been the most difficult aspect of the Dardanelles campaign to untangle, and here, again, many misconceptions permeate the literature. The problem stems in large part from the paucity of contemporary written evidence. Very little was committed to paper when the naval operation first came under consideration at the Admiralty, leaving a large hole where evidence is most needed. Fisher, whose views are the most important and controversial, wrote almost nothing about the project during this period. We know that the subject was discussed by Churchill and his advisers on numerous occasions in early January 1915, but no minutes were taken at these meetings. All we have to go on are the vague, self-serving, and contradictory recollections the various participants offered to the Dardanelles Commission over a year and a half later. These have been used selectively over the years to support different versions of the story, but not always with a critical eye. The reality is that we simply cannot say with a reasonable degree of certainty exactly what advice Churchill received from his naval advisers when the Dardanelles scheme was first mooted.

The mystery surrounding Fisher's views on the Dardanelles is a historical problem in a class of its own. It is probably not true, as many accounts suggest, that he was *always* strongly against the project. His level of support fluctuated from January to May 1915, although it would be fair to say that he was never, or almost never, enthusiastic about it. But when did he finally and decisively turn against it? And why? The answers are usually assumed to be self-evident. He was against it from the beginning—one only needs to look at his disparaging remarks in April and May 1915 to see that. And he turned against it because he knew it would fail. None of this is necessarily untrue, but it is not the whole truth either. The paper trail the First Sea Lord left for historians is a veritable minefield. Fisher 'always has a motive behind his opinions', Margot Asquith commented in May 1915, 'so I never value them so very much'.[5] The Admiral was notoriously inconsistent in the views he expressed. He spoke and wrote in colourful and bombastic terms, in keeping with the brash, outspoken, and resolute persona he sought to cultivate, yet as First Sea Lord in 1915 his bold words often belied a timid and hesitating disposition. He repeatedly shrank from direct confrontation with Churchill and other politicians even as he boasted privately of his fear-less opposition to their plans. Fisher's personal letters and remarks to friends cannot be taken at face value, as he was quick to exaggerate his opposition to the Dardanelles when he thought he had a sympathetic audience. And he evidently found it difficult to articulate the reasons why he disliked the scheme, probably because his opposition was more intuitive than reasoned. The explanations he did offer were inconsistent and contradictory. He told the Dardanelles Commission in 1916 that he was afraid that operations in the eastern Mediterranean would prevent him from launching an audacious naval offensive in the Baltic Sea. This was in keeping with the public image he wished to project, but in January 1915 he had protested against doing anything in the eastern Mediterranean because it might jeopardize the navy's defensive and largely passive strategy in home waters.

Churchill himself struggled to understand Fisher's views on the Dardanelles. It is often claimed that he was aware from the start that the admiral disliked the project, and simply ignored or suppressed his objec-tions. The evidence shows, however, that Churchill was often left guessing where Fisher stood. There is a real possibility, moreover, that Churchill was telling the truth when he later claimed that he thought Fisher had initially supported the operation. The First Sea Lord did not always express his views to his chief clearly; and he sometimes did not express them at all. At one point he actively concealed his opposition to the scheme from Churchill. Nor was Churchill the only one confused about Fisher's position. Asquith and other members of the government were also in the dark much of the time. The Dardanelles Commission post-mortem did little to clarify things, and probably only added to the confusion. Fisher's testimony was colourful but patently unreliable. The commissioners rightly ignored much of his evidence. A century later, Fisher remains an enigma. He was by nature volatile, emotional, duplicitous, secretive, and inconsistent. Sweeping generalizations about what he thought and felt about the Dardanelles inevitably break down when they come up against the fact that much of what he said or wrote about the campaign cannot be treated as reliable.

This study also highlights an aspect of Churchill's fall from power that has received little attention: his difficult relationship with the British press in 1914–15. Churchill himself had few illusions as to the harm done to him by the newspapers, although he seldom referred to it in his public writing and speeches. In November 1916, C. P. Scott, the editor of the *Manchester Guardian*, recorded a private remark by Churchill that his biggest mistake in the war had been 'in not allowing enough for the power of the press, at a time of suspended party activity, to attack and ruin an individual'.[6] Churchill was thinking of the bitter campaign against him during the first nine months of the war by H. A. Gwynne, editor of the *Morning Post*, a popular Conservative newspaper. By May 1915, the influential Northcliffe press (which included *The Times* and the *Daily Mail*) had joined in the attacks. What Churchill did not know was that this press criticism was fuelled by the indiscretions of Admiral Fisher and leaks to the Conservative press and politicians by Whitehall insiders, including Henry Wilson, one of Britain's top generals and a future Chief of the Imperial General Staff (CIGS). It would be wrong to suggest that Churchill was brought down by a conspiracy, but there undoubtedly were influential figures in April–May 1915 intriguing for his removal from the Admiralty. These press attacks illustrate Churchill's inability to protect his public reputation during the early stages of the war, a fact made painfully clear to him by the speed and completeness of his fall from power in May 1915.

The second part of this book continues the story of Churchill's association with the Dardanelles after he was driven from the Admiralty. It is well known that the campaign nearly wrecked his career, but his efforts to reshape public perceptions of the campaign in his favour have received only cursory attention from scholars. Churchill's earliest attempts at damage control in mid-1915 were clumsy and ineffectual. By the end of the year it was clear that the road to vindication would be long and arduous. Given how low his reputation had sunk by then, it is a testament to his resilience and determination that he did not shrink from the challenge. This study reveals just how much time and energy he devoted to reversing opinion on the Dardanelles in the years that followed. The first opportunity to sway public opinion on a large scale came with the Dardanelles Commission in 1916–17, and Churchill was determined to make the most it. He developed a formidable defence of his actions in 1915, based on an exhaustive study of the documentary record. 'Winston's method, accuracy and knowledge of his subject are amazing', one observer remarked after seeing Churchill's preparations. 'He knows where to find every paper and what every paper contains.'[7] Churchill left nothing to chance. He coordinated his case with his former colleagues in the Liberal government, who might easily have cast him overboard; with Lord Fisher, who had caused his downfall; and with a few well-placed sympathizers in the navy. He did everything in his power to manipulate the proceedings to his advantage. And he came down hard on witnesses who threatened any element of his case.[8]

Churchill's campaign to clear himself of blame for the Dardanelles was renewed with vigour during the 1920s, even after it seemed that his political career had safely revived. It is during this period that Churchill came into his own as a self-propagandist. The main vehicle was *The World Crisis*, but this was not the only means at his disposal to influence public opinion. He also appealed to the public directly through his journalistic writings and speeches, and indirectly by supporting sympathetic treatments of the Dardanelles by friends, allies, and fellow travellers. These efforts were supplemented by behind-the-scenes manoeuvring in his role as Cabinet minister to secure a favourable representation of the Gallipoli and Dardanelles campaigns in official government publications. Churchill was clearly motivated in all this by self-interest, and the elaborate defence he constructed is no less problematic than many of the disparaging claims that had been made against him. Examining the evolution of Churchill's defence from 1915 through the early 1930s serves several purposes. First, it shows how the myth of the Dardanelles as a brilliant short-cut to victory was crafted by Churchill himself over the space of several years. Second, it reveals precisely where and how he manipulated and distorted evidence to support his view of the campaign. Finally, it suggests that Churchill honestly believed the case he made. He was willing at times to concede minor points to his critics, but his natural predilection was to embrace and trumpet the evidence that supported his case, to discount any that did not, and to throw everything he had into his defence. At no point does he appear to have doubted the rectitude of his actions or the wisdom of launching the Dardanelles campaign.

How far Churchill was successful in his efforts to justify the Dardanelles is, of course, impossible to measure, but popular opinion did gradually shift in his favour in the two decades before the Second World War. And Churchill's personal campaign to reshape perceptions undoubtedly played a part in this, even if he cannot be given all the credit. But changing public opinion was only ever a means to an end. For Churchill, the real measure of success was whether the legacy of the Dardanelles stood in the way of his political career. By the late 1920s, the Churchillian narrative of the Dardanelles campaign had obtained enough support to ensure that the failures of 1915 were no longer the dominant factor in his public reputation. Given the strength of popular feeling against him in 1915–16, this was a major accomplishment. However, the real test came in May 1940. At the start of the Second World War, Churchill had not yet decisively won the battle over the memory of the Dardanelles. Nor could he be confident that his earlier reputation as a dangerous amateur strategist was safely behind him. This is where his efforts to recast the eastern campaigns of 1915 paid off. Not only had he found supporters on the Dardanelles question, he had also, and more importantly, created a plausible case that his record in the previous conflict should not bar him from high office in a new war. For Churchill, the legacy of the Dardanelles was finally laid to rest when the British public decided that, despite his baggage, he was a safe replacement for Neville Chamberlain as war leader.

I

Stalemate and Frustration

The First Months of War

Winston Churchill was a rising star in the Liberal Party when he became Britain's First Lord of the Admiralty, the political head of the Royal Navy, at the remarkably young age of thirty-seven. His arrival at the Admiralty in October 1911 was initially received by the navy with some apprehension. Just a few years before, Churchill had been prominent among the 'economists' within his party who fought against heavy expenditure on the Royal Navy. However, by 1911 his outlook had changed. The steady growth of Germany's navy posed a direct threat to Britain's security, while Germany's menacing posture towards its continental neighbours pointed to other sinister intentions. Churchill took up his new appointment in 1911 convinced that Britain must prepare for war. An intensification of the German shipbuilding programme in 1912 spelt the end of any lingering hopes Churchill may have had of achieving economies in the naval estimates. Nor was Germany the only challenge to be met. Britain might have to defend its maritime interests and sprawling empire against Germany's allies, Austria–Hungary and Italy, who were significant naval powers in their own right. Maintaining Britain's preponderant naval position against such a formidable array of potential enemies during a time of rapid technological advances and heightened competition in armaments required a massive and steady programme of naval construction by British shipyards. The Royal Navy had to ensure that it was neither outnumbered nor outclassed by its potential enemies.

All this was expensive. Technological advances were relentlessly driving up the cost of new warships. The revolutionary 'dreadnought' battleships of the previous decade were being eclipsed in the pre-war years by even more powerful and expensive 'super-dreadnoughts'. Naval estimates were inflated

Figure 1.1. Winston Churchill and David Lloyd George, 1916.
Topham Picturepoint

further by the need to supplement the traditional battle fleet and far-flung cruiser squadrons with new types of warship, particularly submarines, and with a new naval air service. Churchill was characteristically determined to meet these challenges head on, and he quickly gained a reputation as a forceful and eloquent advocate for the navy, both in Cabinet and in Parliament. Against formidable opposition, much of it from within his own party, he ensured that Britain maintained its supremacy at sea. Between 1911 and 1914, naval spending increased by a massive 25 per cent, ensuring that, in 1914, Britain's navy was larger and, in virtually every respect, more powerful than Germany's.[1]

The pre–war years were attended by much controversy, however, most of which was initiated by Churchill. The new First Lord regarded himself, with some justification, as a progressive, modernizing figure fighting against the forces of reaction to drag the navy into the twentieth century. And, like most men of his era, the young Churchill had great faith in technology as a force for progress. He was receptive to the idea that new weapons like the aeroplane and submarine would revolutionize naval warfare. And he was an early and enthusiastic proponent of naval aviation—so much so that he took the highly unusual step of learning how to fly himself, much to the displeasure of his wife. He also publicly voiced the radical view that these new weapons might one day render Britain's powerful battleships obsolete. Churchill was not afraid of these changes. On the contrary, as First Lord he was eager to funnel money into research and development to ensure that Britain remained at the cutting edge of naval science. His record of achievement in other areas is also impressive. He established the navy's first general staff organization; he secured long-overdue pay increases for the Lower Deck; he instituted a system to allow sailors from the Lower Deck to obtain commissions as officers; and he completed the navy's conversion from coal to oil.

Yet despite his many accomplishments, Churchill's relationship with his naval advisers was often strained, largely as a result of what would now be termed his 'management style'. Churchill was an unconventional First Lord. He arrived at the Admiralty in 1911 eager to master the inner workings of the navy. He visited warships and dockyards around the country, and questioned officers, both senior and junior, about all aspects of their profession. If he had to ignore the traditional chain of command to get the information he wanted, he did not hesitate to do so, even if it upset senior officers, which it usually did. Churchill was also eager to immerse himself in highly technical matters like ship design and naval strategy—areas that were usually avoided by civilian ministers, and that were regarded by naval officers as their own special preserve. But what troubled the service most was that as Churchill's knowledge and confidence grew, he involved himself more and more in technical and professional decisions. Civilian ministers normally deferred to their naval advisers on these matters, but Churchill did not accept that admirals always knew best. Naval officers, on the other hand, resented what they saw as 'interference' and 'meddling' by a civilian minister who, no matter how gifted, would always be regarded as an amateur in the realm of complex naval subjects.

Churchill's forceful personality did not help the situation. He could be impatient and domineering. As a rule, naval officers were neither trained nor experienced in the art of debate, putting them at a disadvantage when they had to argue their case against such an articulate, forceful, and determined politician as Churchill. Captain Thomas Crease, Lord Fisher's naval secretary, offered a typical mixed assessment of the First Lord. Churchill 'had wonderful qualities', he wrote, 'and his energy, determination, decision and willingness to take responsibility were invaluable to the Admiralty'. On the other hand, 'there is no doubt whatever that he was a difficult man to work with. His methods were extraordinarily irritating, and there was no detail of Naval business, however technical, into which he would not plunge with utmost confidence!'[2] But difficult as he undoubtedly was, Churchill was hardly the tyrant he is sometimes made out to be. If the admirals were determined to oppose him, and especially if they maintained a united front, he would almost invariably back down. But the process could be exasperating, and Churchill's relationship with his senior admirals was often stressed.

The pressures of war would eventually strain this relationship to the breaking point, but Churchill was confident in 1914 that he was the right man to lead the Royal Navy to war. Indeed, the prospect of doing so excited him. Late on the evening of 28 July 1914, the day Austria-Hungary declared war on Serbia, and Russia began mobilizing its army, he confided to his wife that Europe's rapid descent towards war had left him 'interested, geared-up & happy'. This was not, he realized, a sentiment that would have met with general approval. And he possessed enough self-awareness to appreciate that his reaction might point to some defect of character. 'Is it not horrible to be built like that?', his letter continued. 'The preparations [for war] have a hideous fascination for me. I pray to God to forgive me for such fearful moods of levity.'[3] This was not a passing mood. Even after the fighting had dragged on for months and a bloody stalemate had set in, Churchill's enthusiasm for the war was undiminished. 'I think a curse should rest on me', he told Violet Asquith, the daughter of the Prime Minister, in February 1915, 'because I *love* this war. I know it's smashing & shattering the lives of thousands every moment—& yet—I *can't* help it—I enjoy every second I live.'[4]

Churchill found the First World War exhilarating. 'My God!', he exclaimed to Margot Asquith, the Prime Minister's wife, 'this—*This* is living History. Everything we are doing and saying is thrilling. It will be read by 1000 generations—think of *that*!!'[5] Across the Continent, the clash of great armies numbering in the millions was deciding the fate of all Europe and the British Empire. As First Lord of the Admiralty, Churchill delighted in being at the centre of these momentous events. Not given to self-doubt, and supremely confident in his abilities as a strategist, he was determined from the outset to play a leading part in guiding Britain to victory. No one was surprised when the energetic young Cabinet minister thrust himself into the centre of the decision-making machinery. Colleagues who had distrusted his judgement in peacetime remained wary, but even his critics within the government had to concede that Churchill possessed an intuitive understanding of modern warfare that they lacked. He had, after all, spent years immersed in the business of preparing the Royal Navy for war with Germany. And he had both studied war and experienced it first hand, giving him an authority that was in short supply in the Liberal government that led Britain in August 1914.

The only other Cabinet minister with personal experience of war was Field Marshal Lord Kitchener, one of Britain's most popular and experienced generals, who was rushed into the government in August 1914 to serve as Secretary of State for War. Asquith's Cabinet took the momentous decision in the first days of war to send the small British Expeditionary Force (BEF) to France to bolster the French Army, but Liberal ministers were generally content during the first months of war to leave the day-to-day management of the fighting services to their respective ministers, Churchill and Kitchener. There was as yet little conception within the government of the heavy demands that industrialized mass warfare would make on Britain in the years to come. Indeed, it was not yet clear, despite warnings from

Figure 1.2. Herbert Henry Asquith.
Library of Congress

Figure 1.3. Field Marshal Horatio Herbert Kitchener, 1st Earl Kitchener. Library of Congress

Kitchener, that the war would last for years. The government's philosophy during the first months of the conflict was popularly summed up by the expression 'Business as Usual'.[6] Most Liberal leaders believed that the war could be waged with minimal disruption to the economy and the lives of the British people. Britain, an island nation, was thought to differ fundamentally from the great powers on the Continent. In wartime, its strength would rest on its financial and industrial resources, backed by the Royal Navy, rather than on the strength of its army. In 1914, most of Britain's leaders hoped to play to their nation's strengths and fight a war of limited liability. France and Russia, with their large conscript armies, would bear the brunt of the fighting on land, while Britain, with its far smaller, professional army, would contribute a modest expeditionary force to strengthen the French Army in the west. Few expected this force to make a decisive contribution to the conflict. The nation's main weapon would be the Royal Navy. By dominating the seas, Britain would maintain its trade, credit, and industry, while simultaneously weakening the German economy and propping up its allies.

The Royal Navy was in a strong position to fulfil this role. Britain had maintained a commanding numerical lead over Germany in modern capital ships. At the start of hostilities, Britain possessed twenty-two modern battleships (including two semi-dreadnoughts of the Lord Nelson class) and nine battlecruisers, compared to Germany's sixteen modern battleships and five battlecruisers. And as the war progressed, Britain's margin of superiority was set to improve still further. The Admiralty expected to add another fifteen dreadnoughts to the fleet by the end of 1915, compared to only two or three for Germany in the same period.[7] These powerful warships were concentrated in a 'Grand Fleet' under Admiral Sir John Jellicoe, which would prove more than adequate to the task of neutralizing its counterpart across the North Sea, the German High Seas Fleet. Both sides assumed that, in a straightforward trial of strength, the larger British force would prevail. German leaders had no desire to risk a fleet action that would almost certainly end in their defeat, so they adopted a cautious strategy. Their main fleet was kept safely in home waters and waited for opportunities to even the odds by engaging weaker British forces on favourable terms.

With the German Navy in no position to challenge Britain directly for command of the sea, the Royal Navy could afford to adopt a cautious strategy. There was no need to accept battle on unfavourable terms. Jellicoe's Grand Fleet, the foundation of Britain's dominant position in the North Sea, was therefore kept a safe distance from enemy shores, always ready to respond to sorties by German heavy forces but relatively secure from torpedo attack by enemy submarines or destroyers. Under the cover provided by the Grand Fleet, British cruiser squadrons and flotilla forces had a relatively easy time establishing a cordon around the North Sea and clearing the high seas of German surface raiders and merchant ships. The Admiralty assumed that the resulting dislocation of Germany's overseas trade would gradually weaken the enemy's war economy and might, in time, persuade the Germans to take greater risks with their fleet, but naval leaders understood that it might be years before the two fleets met in battle, if they ever did, and that economic pressure alone was unlikely to have any immediate impact on Germany's war-making capacity.[8]

The Royal Navy quickly established its dominance in the early months of the war. An aggressive raid into German coastal waters on 28 August 1914 brought a clear victory over the Germans in the Battle of Heligoland Bight, where the enemy lost three light cruisers and one destroyer. The German merchant fleet was immediately driven from the trade routes. And at the Battle of the Falkland Islands in December, the German East Asia Squadron was destroyed, removing the last significant threat to British trade on the high seas. There was every reason, therefore, to be satisfied that naval war

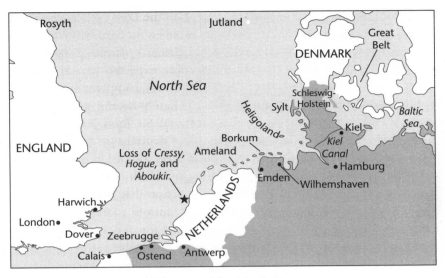

Map 1.1. The North Sea.

was, despite a few inevitable slip-ups, off to a good start. Churchill, never-theless, found this state of affairs frustrating. He wanted the Royal Navy to seize the initiative, and he craved immediate and tangible results. What most concerned him was the passive nature of British naval strategy, something he had tried to address before the war began. Prior to 1911, the navy's war plans had had a more pronounced offensive element than they did in 1914. Planners then had hoped to seize an island near Germany's North Sea coast to serve as an advance base from which British flotilla forces could maintain an 'observational blockade' of the enemy's coastline. However, new weapons were making the navy's traditional blockade strategy increasingly dangerous. By the time Churchill arrived at the Admiralty it was generally accepted that British naval forces operating near German bases would be constantly at risk from submarines, torpedoes, mines, and aircraft. With inshore operations along the enemy coast becoming prohibitively danger-ous, naval opinion shifted to the idea of establishing a 'distant blockade' of Germany, the strategy Britain implemented in 1914. This was a sensible response to new operational realities, but there were obvious disadvantages. Drawing British naval forces back from the German coast would make it much easier for enemy warships to leave their ports and traverse the North Sea undetected, making it entirely possible that all or part of the German fleet might appear along the British coast or in the English Channel with little or no warning.[9]

Churchill was among those at the Admiralty who chafed at the idea of conceding so much of the initiative to the enemy. In February 1913, a few months after the distant blockade strategy was accepted by naval planners, he complained to Prince Louis of Battenberg, the First Sea Lord, that it would be 'impossible by a purely passive defensive to guard against all the dangers which may be threatened by an enterprising enemy'. If the Germans were prepared to run risks with their ships, they could conceivably interrupt Britain's sea communications with France, bombard targets along the British coast, or even land troops on British shores. 'Along the whole line from the Shetlands to the Straits of Dover', Churchill warned Prince Louis, 'we shall be dispersed, anxious, weak and waiting: the only question being where are we going to be hit.'[10] Prior to the outbreak of war, the Admiralty was finalizing plans to place fast cruiser squadrons in the North Sea to detect the movement of German forces towards Britain or the Channel, but Churchill yearned for more aggressive measures to contain the German fleet. In early 1913 he proposed that, when hostilities broke out, the navy should dispatch nearly all its available light forces to the German coast in order to obtain an 'overwhelming flotilla superiority' over the German Navy for the first week of the war. This would ensure that the Germans would be bottled up in the Heligoland Bight and unable to interfere with the transportation of the BEF to France. 'There lies the true protection for the transports in the Channel', he proclaimed. However, he was no less eager to ensure that the navy would engage enemy forces at the first opportunity. Inflicting an early defeat would, he proclaimed, allow the British to establish their 'moral superiority' over the German Navy.[11]

This was not the limit of Churchill's ambitions. Ideally, he hoped to establish a strong flotilla presence in the Heligoland Bight on a permanent basis. He stubbornly refused to accept the naval staff's view that it was no longer possible to seize an island near the German coast. However, his pre-war efforts to revive plans for establishing British flotillas in the Heligoland Bight ran into strong opposition from his naval advisers, who were adamant that the risks involved were too great. Among those who disparaged Churchill's ideas was the Director of the Operations Division at the Admiralty, Captain George Ballard, who noted that even if Britain sent all its available destroyers into the Bight, Germany would still have a superiority of torpedo craft in the region. Captain Herbert Richmond, Ballard's

Assistant Director, predicted that half the destroyers sent on such an 'absolutely impracticable' operation would probably be lost.[12] A less determined First Lord would have accepted the nearly unanimous opposition of his uniformed advisers on such a technical subject, but Churchill was unwilling to drop the idea. Instead, he attempted to circumvent the naval staff by establishing his own ad hoc planning group to investigate the feasibility of seizing a German or Dutch island.

The central figure on this body was Rear-Admiral Sir Lewis Bayly, who was presumably chosen to lead the investigation because he could be counted on to give the project a sympathetic hearing. Asquith later observed that Bayly was 'an admiral after [Churchill's] own heart'. The First Lord reportedly described him as one of the 'Yes school' of naval officers—those who were eager to take the offensive even if heavy risks were involved.[13] The result of this investigation was exactly what Churchill hoped for. Bayly's group concluded that an expedition to capture a German or Dutch island *could* be mounted with a good chance of success. This view was not welcomed by the Admiralty War Staff, however. In the face of strong and united opposition from the navy's leading planners and strategists, Churchill was induced to let the matter drop—but only temporarily. In June 1914 he attempted to revive the scheme by enlisting the support of Admiral Jellicoe, the future Commander-in-Chief of the Grand Fleet, whose endorsement would carry considerable weight within the service. Jellicoe was given a copy of Bayly's report to examine before departing for a holiday in France, but he was not impressed with what he read. On 27 July 1914 he reported that the cost of seizing an island was not justified, since Britain could achieve its main objectives from existing bases just as effectively, and with little risk. 'I am distinctly of the opinion', Jellicoe concluded, 'that the enterprise is not worth the sacrifices involved.'[14]

Churchill, however, was still not convinced. Just four days after Jellicoe submitted his report, and with war now imminent, the First Lord sent a copy of Bayly's plans to Asquith, but without mentioning the strong body of naval opinion against the project.[15] He nevertheless urged the Prime Minister, who was temporarily acting as Secretary of State for War, to have the plans studied by qualified officers at the War Office so that 'military and naval action can be coordinated & concerted in harmony'.[16] If any further information was required on the naval aspects of the plans, the War Office was instructed to consult Rear-Admiral Arthur Leveson, who had recently replaced Ballard as Director of Operations. Notably, Leveson had been a member of Bayly's planning group, and was therefore one of the few senior officers at the Admiralty who could be expected to support the project. Britain's entry into the war a few days later prompted Churchill to press ahead with preparations for amphibious operations before the army's views had been received. On 9 August he instructed Battenberg and Admiral Sir Doveton Sturdee, the Chief of the Admiralty War Staff, to begin drawing up plans for the occupation of Ameland, one of the Dutch Frisian islands.[17] Captain Richmond recorded in his diary that, when he discussed the subject with Churchill that day in the Admiralty's Chart Room, it was clear that nothing would be gained by arguing against the project. The First Lord, he recorded, 'was vehement in his desire to adopt an offensive attitude. I saw that no words could check his vivid imagination & that it was quite impossible to persuade him both of the strategical & tactical futility of such an operation.'[18]

While Churchill was eager to promote this scheme as a means of pushing the German fleet to action, he was also excited about the opportunities that would open up if British forces along the German coast succeeded in destroying the fleet or blocking the Kiel Canal. Britain could then send warships and transports into the Baltic Sea, a move that had regularly featured in the navy's war plans only a decade earlier. This would increase the economic pressure on Germany by cutting its iron ore imports from Sweden, but the real attraction, from Churchill's perspective, was that the Royal Navy could cover the landing of Russian troops on the German coast less than 100 miles from Berlin.[19] Here was an opportunity, it seemed, for the Royal Navy to exert a direct and possibly decisive influence on events on land. But Churchill first had to overcome opposition to his plans to maintain British forces near the German coast to contain the German fleet. Richmond produced a memorandum the next day emphasizing the political arguments *against* seizing a Dutch island. He told his wife afterwards that he 'met Winston in the passage, & he hadn't seemed best pleased with his paper about the Dutch scheme. W. said "I wanted your opinion of how to do it not a criticism of the scheme." '[20] A new obstacle to Churchill's ambitions appeared on 11 August, when the army officer detailed to examine Bayly's plans also declared against the project. He told Admiralty officials what most of them already knew, that the potential 'advantages to be gained' by seizing a forward base were not 'commensurate with the risks incurred'. Britain lacked the troops to capture German fortified islands, he noted, while islands like Ameland were so close to the mainland that they would be exposed to long-range artillery fire after being captured, rendering them useless as naval bases.[21]

Opinion at the Admiralty consistently ran against Churchill's offensive schemes. And his advisers had good reason to question them. As long as the Grand Fleet remained intact and afloat, Britain's command of the sea was secure. The German Navy would be hard pressed to threaten any vital British interests. Naval leaders were therefore committed to a risk-averse strategy. Britain had little to gain by exposing its naval forces to heavy losses, and potentially stood to lose everything if it suffered a crushing defeat. Even the gradual attrition of British strength in minor operations could be disastrous. 'It is suicidal to forego our advantageous position in the big ships by risking them in waters infested by submarines', Jellicoe told Churchill in September. 'The result might quite easily be such a weakening of our battle fleet and Battle Cruiser strength as seriously to jeopardise the future of the country by giving over to the Germans the command of the open seas.'[22] The navy's leaders believed it would be irresponsible to risk their numerical superiority in operations that could not substantially improve Britain's strategic position. 'We have the game in our own hands if we sit tight', Richmond recorded in his diary, 'but this Churchill cannot see.' The First Lord's shortcoming, he concluded, was that 'He must see something tangible & can't understand that naval warfare acts in a wholly different way from war on shore. That Fleet in the north dominates the position.'[23] Richmond, one of the navy's most intellectual officers, was also dismissive of Churchill's plan to send British flotilla vessels into the Heligoland Bight, which he labelled, in his characteristically caustic manner, 'an amateur piece of work of a mediaeval type'. Such a force was unlikely to inflict much damage on the enemy, he concluded, and was 'far more likely to bump into a superior force & be cut off itself. It serves no purpose and merely loses men & ships.'[24]

Churchill had difficulty hiding his irritation. 'I can't stand these fellows who oppose me', he told Lieutenant-Colonel A. H. Ollivant, a general staff officer attached to the Admiralty.[25] Captain Cecil Lambert, the Fourth Sea Lord, warned Richmond that he would now be regarded by the First Lord as 'one of the obstructionists...well, you won't be consulted again'.[26] The tug-of-war between Churchill and his naval advisers over inshore operations in the Heligoland Bight was temporarily settled at a conference on Jellicoe's flagship, *Iron Duke*, at Loch Ewe, on the west coast of Scotland, on 17 September. Churchill led a delegation from the Admiralty, which included the Chief of the War Staff and the Director of Naval Intelligence (DNI), to

meet with Admiral Jellicoe, his chief of staff, and senior officers of the Grand
Fleet. Churchill was undoubtedly eager to take this opportunity to obtain
backing for his offensive plans, but Jellicoe was probably no less determined
to kill the idea. The conference's first casualty was a proposal to capture
Heligoland, a fortified island near the German mainland. This was a pet
project of Admiral Sir Arthur Wilson, a former First Sea Lord who returned
to the Admiralty after the outbreak of war to serve as an unofficial adviser.
'Naval opinion was unanimous', the final report on the conference recorded,
that such an operation 'would involve far more serious losses in capital ships
than would compensate for any advantage gained.' The admirals then turned
to Churchill's plans to send a British force into the Baltic. Once again, the
First Lord was outgunned by his uniformed advisers. The only naval officer
to support the idea of an attack on the Kiel Canal was Bayly, who attended
the conference in his capacity as Commander of the Grand Fleet's 1st Battle
Squadron.[27]

   The official record of the Loch Ewe conference suggests that Churchill
raised another idea he was toying with around this time—the creation of a
second 'grand fleet'. Churchill recognized that as long as the German High
Seas Fleet remained active, Jellicoe's fleet would be tied to the North Sea, and
British heavy forces could not be detached for service in the Baltic, where
they risked being overwhelmed by a superior German force. But the situation would change if the Austrian fleet were destroyed, thereby freeing
French ships for service in northern waters. It would then be possible for
Britain and its allies to maintain two separate fleets in northern waters, each
superior to the full strength of the German High Seas Fleet. Jellicoe's fleet
could then remain safely in the North Sea, as the ultimate guarantee of
British naval dominance, while Allied warships no longer required in the
Mediterranean provided the core of a multinational fleet for the Baltic.
Depending on circumstances, the new fleet might include ships from Britain,
France, Russia, Italy, Greece, and Japan.[28] The advantage of this force, from
Churchill's perspective, was that it could be used offensively, even at great
risk, since its loss would not jeopardize Britain's naval dominance. The admi-
rals assembled for the conference probably had little interest in this plan, but
since it was unlikely ever to be implemented they agreed—probably as a sop
to the First Lord—that the proposal would be 'thoroughly investigated'.[29]

   Churchill does not appear to have taken this latest setback well. Britain
had now been at war for six weeks and the Royal Navy had seemingly
contributed little to the Allied cause. What frustrated him most was that

the navy had done little fighting thus far, and might not do much for the foreseeable future. Britain's naval preponderance in the North Sea was so pronounced that the German fleet might conceivably *never* come out to fight, as the Grand Fleet's margin of superiority would steadily increase. Churchill knew, of course, that it was unrealistic to expect a great Trafalgar-like battle of annihilation in the first weeks of war, but he could not shake the feeling that the navy should still be doing more than it was.[30] However, his efforts to take offensive measures against the Germans had been frustrated at every turn by his professional advisers. He found little consolation in the knowledge that economic warfare might eventually produce major results. Economic pressure could not cripple the German war machine quickly, and there was no certainty that it would *ever* have a significant impact. German shipping had virtually disappeared from the high seas by September 1914, but Churchill was acutely aware that Germany continued to import goods from overseas through neutral ports like Rotterdam in the Netherlands.

The decisive rejection of his offensive schemes by the officers of the Grand Fleet therefore came as a heavy blow. Upon returning to London, Churchill's wife, Clementine, observed that he was 'gloomy & dissatisfied' with his current position. 'It is really wicked of you', she wrote, 'not to be swelling with pride at being 1st Lord of the Admiralty during the greatest War since the beginning of the World.'[31] Churchill had no difficulty defending the navy against charges of inactivity when called upon to do so, but his heart was not really in it. His restless nature made him temperamentally ill-suited to preside over a predominantly passive naval strategy, especially when epic land battles were taking place across Europe. So great was his dissatisfaction at this point in the war that Clementine had to dissuade her husband from leaving the Admiralty altogether. 'You know the sailors can't do anything alone', she wrote, '& just because your preparations are so perfect that for the moment there seems little to do, this is not the moment to hand over the whole concern to another or to allow the sailors who have been tutored & bent to the yoke for the last 2 years to take charge.'[32] Churchill's frustration was also apparent to his colleagues at the Admiralty. After dining with the First Lord in October, Richmond, who was temporarily back in favour, noted that his chief was 'in low spirits... rather oppressed with the impossibility of *doing* anything':

The attitude of waiting, threatened all the time by submarines, unable to strike back at their Fleet, which lies secure behind the dock gates of the [Kaiser

Wilhelm] Canal, Emden or Wilhemshaven, and the inability of the [Naval] Staff to make any suggestions seem to bother him. I have not seen him so despondent before.[33]

At the same time, Churchill was fascinated by the fighting on the Continent, which seemed to offer more scope for the action and initiative he craved. Arthur Balfour, a Conservative politician and former Prime Minister, noted on 22 September that, 'Winston for the moment, unfortunately, is much more anxious to rival Napoleon than Nelson, and thinks more of the Army than the Navy.'[34]

Churchill's fascination with military matters was more than just a by-product of his combative personality and impatience. He appreciated from the outset that the First World War would ultimately be decided by events on land rather than by anything the Royal Navy could do at sea, which made Britain's 'limited liability' strategy potentially risky. The BEF had helped to halt the German advance into France in the first weeks of the war, but the possibility had to be faced that Britain's allies might not be up to the task of beating the German Army on their own. By mid-September, an Allied victory was far from certain. In the east, the Germans had inflicted major defeats on the Russians at the Battles of Tannenberg and the Masurian Lakes. In the west, they rapidly overran and occupied most of Belgium and parts of northern France. Churchill was well aware of the limitations of sea power in a predominantly continental struggle. And he was not the only one. While most members of the Cabinet were content in 1914 to provide a small force to fight on the Continent, Kitchener took a radically different view. The new Secretary of State for War predicted that the war would last for years; and he believed that Britain must raise a mass army capable of taking a full share of the fighting.[35] Such a force would take time to raise, equip, and train, but Kitchener believed it would be ready to throw into the fighting just as the continental powers, friend and foe alike, were reaching their breaking point. The new British Army would therefore be in a position to make a decisive contribution to Germany's final defeat on land *and* to secure Britain's position at the peace conference afterwards.

This was not what most members of the Liberal Cabinet had in mind, but having brought Kitchener into their ranks with great fanfare, his resignation would have been politically disastrous. The field marshal was therefore allowed to begin a massive recruiting campaign for the expansion of the British Army into a continental-size force. The recruiting stations were flooded with applicants. By the end of 1914, over a million men had volunteered for service. Churchill enthusiastically supported Britain's transformation into a land power. The navy was a vital part of this process, in his view. It would enable the transformation to take place. But he also assumed that the army would ultimately become the nation's most powerful means to strike at the enemy. Speaking at the National Liberal Club on 11 September, Churchill declared that: 'The sure way—the only way—to bring this war to an end is for the British Empire to put on the Continent and keep on the Continent an army of at least one million men.'[36]

Few expected the Royal Navy to contribute anything more to the land war than the safe transportation of the BEF to France, but Churchill could not resist the urge to involve his service directly in the opening battles in France and Belgium whenever possible. The obvious means were at hand in the Royal Marines, and the Admiralty hastily organized four battalions of this service into a new Royal Marine Brigade. Churchill decided to supplement this force with two additional 'naval brigades'—new infantry formations manned with a mixture of surplus naval reservists, new recruits, and volunteers from the fleet. These formations were to be combined with the Royal Marine Brigade to create an entirely new entity, the Royal Naval Division. To his critics, Churchill appeared to be creating his own private army. And they were not entirely mistaken. The diversion of naval personnel for service ashore was widely condemned at the time, especially within the navy. Richmond, for example, wrote in his diary on 20 August: 'I really believe Churchill is not sane.'

> What this force is to do, Heaven only knows.... A special uniform has been designed by Winston of khaki colour & seamanlike shape. It was brought here yesterday & the Lords of the Admiralty called in to look at it, Winston as pleased as Punch! This is the beginning of a great war in which our whole future rests upon the proper use of the Navy!! It is astounding.... [H]ow the Board [of Admiralty] can permit him to indulge in such foolery, without a word of serious protest, I don't know.[37]

Some of these troops were successfully employed for several weeks in August and September to defend Ostend, an important port along the Belgian coast. Their success there probably encouraged Churchill and the government to commit most of the division to the defence of an even more important Belgian port, Antwerp, when reinforcements were urgently needed there.

At the beginning of October 1914, the Belgian government warned its allies that Antwerp could not be held much longer and its defence might soon be abandoned. The British and French governments were both eager to retrieve the deteriorating situation there, if possible by augmenting the Belgian defences with Allied troops. Elements of the new Royal Naval Division were rushed to the city as an interim measure. At the same time, Churchill decided, largely on his own initiative, to visit the city himself. He departed on 2 October, ostensibly to communicate with the Belgian government, stiffen the defenders' resolve, and report back to London on the situation. Remarkably, once he had persuaded the Belgians not to abandon the city, he threw himself into the task of organizing its defences rather than returning immediately to London. For several days, Churchill's colleagues were left in the dark, not knowing when, or even *if*, the First Lord intended to return to his post. At the Cabinet meeting on 5 October, Kitchener expressed his doubt that Churchill would return. 'The first big <u>naval</u> engagement between Allies & Germany will not take place', he observed, 'on Belgian <u>land</u>.'[38] But after two months of relative inaction and frustration at the Admiralty, Churchill was now where he most wanted to be: directing troops in the midst of battle. Kitchener was correct in thinking his colleague had no desire to return. On the morning of 5 October, Churchill cabled Asquith offering to trade his office as First Lord for the command of Allied forces defending Antwerp.[39]

At the time, plans were in motion to send a large relieving force to bolster the Belgian and British forces in the city. The British were committed to supplying the remainder of the Royal Naval Division and two army divisions, while the French had offered a territorial division.[40] Churchill badly wanted to command this substantial force himself. He suggested to Asquith that he should be 'given necessary military rank and authority, and full powers of a commander of a detached force in the field'.[41] Asquith described this episode as 'a bit of tragi-comedy', and recorded that the offer was received by the Cabinet 'with a Homeric laugh'. The Prime Minister was one of Churchill's strongest supporters, but even he found the proposal absurd. Winston 'is an ex Lieutenant of Hussars', he observed privately, 'and would if his proposal had been accepted, have been in command of 2 distinguished Major Generals, not to mention Brigadiers, Colonels &c: while the Navy were only contributing its little brigades'.[42] Asquith's daughter Violet, a close friend and admirer of Churchill, also questioned her friend's judgement. In her memoirs she recalled her shock at 'the sense of proportion (or lack of it) revealed by Winston's choice':

> His desire to exchange the Admiralty, in which for years he had invested all his treasure and which was now faced with its first test and greatest opportunity, for the command of a mere major-general, one of many, in the field seemed to me to be hardly adult. It was the choice of a romantic child. In terms of scope and power the two jobs were not comparable. He would be abdicating his part in the grand strategy of the war which he had always seen in world-wide terms, in order to play a personal part in a small part of it.[43]

The Prime Minister diplomatically declined Churchill's proposal, saying that he was needed at the Admiralty, but it remained unclear when the First Lord would return to his duties. After meeting with Battenberg, Asquith complained that the First Sea Lord 'had no more idea than I have of when we might look for the return of the First Lord'. As a precaution, Asquith instructed that all important Admiralty decisions should be run by him (Asquith) for approval.[44] Churchill finally returned to London on the morning of 7 October, more eager than ever to abandon the Admiralty if a suitable military command could be found for him. He met later that day with the Prime Minister, who recorded that the First Lord 'implored me not to take a "conventional" view of his future':

> Having, as he says, 'tasted blood' these last few days, he is beginning like a tiger to raven for more, and begs that sooner or later, & the sooner the better, he may be relieved of his present office & put in some kind of military command. I told him he could not be spared from the Admiralty, but he scoffs at that, alleging that the naval part of the business is practically over, as our superiority [in capital ships] will grow greater & greater every month. His mouth waters at the sight & thought of K[itchener]'s new armies. Are these 'glittering commands' to be entrusted to 'dug-out trash', bred on the obsolete tactics of 25 years ago—'mediocrities, who have led a sheltered life mouldering in military routine &c &c'.

Churchill went on to declare that 'a political career was nothing to him in comparison with military glory'.[45] The prospects of securing a high military command were remote, however, and he resigned himself to remaining at the Admiralty. His frustration persisted. In late November, Balfour's private secretary remarked on 'Churchill's desire for more active service' to Admiral Sir Francis Bridgeman, a retired First Sea Lord and no admirer of Churchill. Bridgeman noted at the time that Commodore Charles de Bartolomé,

Churchill's newly appointed naval secretary, had remarked 'in an unguarded moment that "Churchill seemed bored now, & could talk of nothing but what the army was doing, his thoughts were impressed with the operations in the field"!'[46] Admiral Jacky Fisher remarked later that Churchill's 'heart is ashore, not afloat! *The joy of his life is to be 50 yards from a German trench!'*[47]

There was little for Churchill to do, however, but resume his duties at the Admiralty, where he promptly resumed his campaign for a naval offensive in the North Sea. If he was stuck at the Admiralty, he was determined the navy would make a more significant contribution. On 8 October, the day after he returned from Antwerp, Churchill reminded Jellicoe of his view that British naval operations should be directed towards securing 'the eventual command of the Baltic'. He instructed the admiral to examine how this could be achieved once it was certain the High Seas Fleet could no longer interfere.[48] The naval staff, however, continued to resist the idea of operations along the German coast, a necessary prelude to any large-scale Baltic expedition. As First Lord, Churchill was not expected to initiate naval operations, but he pressed on regardless. Just a few weeks earlier, he had committed himself publicly to bringing about the destruction of the German fleet, telling an audience in Liverpool that if the enemy was unwilling to leave their ports and accept battle, 'they will be dug out like rats in a hole'.[49] This colourful phrase struck many, including the King and several naval officers, as undignified.[50] When reminded of it in 1916, even Churchill admitted 'It was a very foolish phrase, and I regret that it slipped out.'[51]

After three months of war, Churchill was feeling pressure not only to deflect criticism of the navy's inactivity, but also, and more importantly, to reassure the British public about his competence as First Lord. Churchill's popularity peaked at the beginning of the First World War, in large part because the Royal Navy was mobilized and at its war stations when Britain declared war against Germany on 4 August 1914. This owed more than a little to luck. As the states of Europe began their descent to war in late July, the Royal Navy was nearing the end of a trial mobilization that had been organized months before. Rather than allow the fleet to disperse as planned at the end of the month, Churchill and Battenberg kept it together. Churchill later confided to Bonar Law that he 'had to mobilise the fleet without legal sanction and contrary to a Cabinet decision'.[52] This took some courage on Churchill's part, as many of his Cabinet colleagues were determined at the time to avoid any provocative action that might result in Britain being drawn into the war. But once Britain entered the conflict, his action was universally applauded. In the weeks that followed, Churchill also benefited from the initial surge of patriotic support for the Royal Navy. But this spontaneous goodwill would not last forever. The public expected the navy to cover itself with glory, and soon became frustrated by the fleet's passivity. When Britain began to suffer reverses at sea, Churchill, a politician, was an obvious target for criticism.

The first serious blow to British naval prestige occurred in September 1914, when three old Bacchante-class armoured cruisers, *Cressy*, *Aboukir*, and *Hogue*, were sunk in rapid succession by a single German submarine. The ships were part of a regular patrol maintained off the Dutch coast in an area close to the German border known as the 'Broad Fourteens'. They were placed there to intercept German light forces moving south towards the English Channel, but their isolated position and proximity to German submarine bases made them an easy and obvious target. Within the Grand Fleet, they were reputedly nicknamed the 'live-bait squadron'. On 22 September the squadron was patrolling without a destroyer screen. *Aboukir*, the first to be torpedoed, sank rapidly. The other two cruisers closed in to rescue survivors, making them easy targets. Both were promptly sunk. Over 1,400 British sailors lost their lives. This disaster was clearly avoidable, and the public wondered why these ships had been exposed to such obvious risks in the first place. Churchill was immediately singled out for blame. 'It never should have happened', wrote Thomas Gibson Bowles, a former MP and well-known writer on naval affairs, in the *Candid Quarterly Review*. 'It never would have happened had the First Lord of the Admiralty heeded the repeated warnings of his own Admirals and recalled the cruisers.'[53]

The claim that Churchill was personally responsible for the loss of the ships was accepted by many, even though they were not justified. Churchill had actually played only a minor role in this episode. And to his credit, he had realized the risk to these ships and a few days earlier had recommended that they be withdrawn from their exposed position near the German coast. These cruisers, he wrote on 18 September, 'ought not to continue on this beat. The risk to such ships is not justified by any service they can render.'[54] The decisions that led directly to the loss of the ships were taken by Admirals Battenberg and Sturdee. Churchill had appointed both men, and must share in the blame for their mistakes, but there is no basis for the claim that he had ignored clear warnings of impending disaster or overruled his professional advisers. Bowles' criticisms were, nevertheless, widely reported in the British press. It did not help Churchill's position that he had delivered his boastful 'rats in a hole' speech the day before the three British ships were lost.

A more humiliating loss occurred several weeks later. Shortly after the outbreak of war, the German East Asia Squadron crossed the Pacific to attack British trade off the west coast of South America. The German force consisted of two modern armoured cruisers and three light cruisers. This presented the local British commander, Rear-Admiral Sir Christopher Cradock, with a dilemma. He could concentrate the ships available to him, including the old battleship *Canopus*, into a squadron that could theoretically outgun the German force. But the *Canopus* was so slow that the Germans would have no difficulty avoiding action. If, on the other hand, he employed only his faster ships—two old armoured cruisers, a more modern light cruiser, and a converted merchantman—his squadron might hope to catch the enemy, but it would be heavily outgunned if it succeeded. Cradock chose to detach *Canopus* from his squadron and seek out the enemy with his remaining ships. The result was the one-sided Battle of Coronel, off the coast of Chile, on 1 November. Cradock's two armoured cruisers were both destroyed by the Germans, with the loss of nearly 1,600 British sailors, including Cradock himself. The other two British ships escaped under cover of darkness. The damage to the German cruisers was negligible. Churchill was again widely criticized for his part in the disaster, but in this instance also he was largely blameless. He had expected Cradock to keep *Canopus* with his other ships so as to avoid precisely this outcome.[55] When news of the defeat reached London on 4 November, he told the Cabinet that Cradock had 'disobeyed orders not to engage enemy without Canopus in company'.[56] This is not strictly accurate, as muddled staff work at the Admiralty prevented any clear orders to this effect being sent to the admiral, but Churchill appears to have genuinely believed that Cradock would not divide his forces.

Churchill and the navy would come in for further criticism in December 1914 when a German battle-cruiser squadron evaded detection and raided the British coast. The towns of Scarborough, Hartlepool, and Whitby were all shelled, causing over seven hundred casualties, most of them civilians. But by far the harshest criticism of Churchill during the first months of the war arose from the unsuccessful defence of Antwerp in October. The attack was led by a Conservative newspaper, the 'aggressively right wing' *Morning Post*.[57] After just two months of war, the *Post*'s editor, Howell Arthur Gwynne, had concluded that Churchill was so great a menace as First Lord that it was his patriotic duty to see him removed from office. Gwynne had been particularly outraged by the use of the Royal Naval Division in the defence of Antwerp, as this formation contained many new and hastily trained recruits. He wrote privately to Lady Bathurst, the newspaper's proprietor, that:

> This man Churchill gathered from all the ends of England a force which he called the Naval Reserve Volunteer Force [*sic*]. It consisted of old men and

Figure 1.4. Howell Arthur Gwynne, editor of The Morning Post (drawing by Bernard Partridge, *Punch*, 1929).
Author's Collection

youths, men who had not fired a rifle in their lives, officers who had not been
trained and had just come from the Officers' Training Corps. The consequence
was that they were led to perfect slaughter.... The whole thing was a horrible
blunder which deserves not only the severest condemnation but which ought
to bring about the resignation of Churchill.[58]

In fact, the battle was not the 'perfect slaughter' Gwynne imagined it to be.
His informants had mistakenly reported that British casualties were around
8,000–9,000, when in fact only 60 had been killed and another 138 wounded.
Even taking into consideration the British soldiers taken prisoner (over
900) and the large number (around 1,479) interned in the Netherlands after
the battle, British losses were still far below Gwynne's numbers.[59] He was,
nevertheless, convinced that Churchill bore the full brunt of the blame
for this setback to British arms. As he explained to Bathurst, 'The whole
adventure [i.e. Antwerp] was one which in my opinion deserves the severest
condemnation inasmuch as it was, as far as I can make out, wholly a Churchill
affair and does not seem to have been considered or thought over, or
consented to, by the Cabinet.'[60]

The Conservative press had patriotically suppressed its criticisms of
the Liberal government since the outset of the war, but on 13 October an
editorial in the *Morning Post* called the attempt to relieve Antwerp 'a
costly blunder, for which Mr. Winston Churchill must be held responsible on the present evidence'. Gwynne, its author, went on to claim that
the First Lord had used 'the resources of the Admiralty as if he were personally responsible for naval operations', and, in doing so, had misused
'his position of civil authority to press his tactical and strategic fancies
upon unwilling experts'.[61] This outspoken attack—the first on a Cabinet
minister since the war began—was reprinted the next day by other
Conservative newspapers, including Lord Northcliffe's *Daily Mail*, and
attracted considerable attention in both the British and the international
press. The attack was immediately denounced by Liberal newspapers,
where it was widely noted that the *Post* had not produced any evidence
to back up its charges. But the idea that Churchill had been solely responsible for the failed defence of Antwerp was widely accepted by Churchill's
Conservative critics.

The decision to prolong the defence of Antwerp had been supported by
both the British and French governments and was not taken by Churchill
alone, but Churchill's prominent role in organizing the city's defence
ensured that the First Lord would be closely linked in the public mind to

any military setback suffered there. A week after Gwynne launched his attack, the story that Churchill was solely to blame was given additional credence by the *New York Times*. The American newspaper provided an even less accurate account of the origins of British involvement at Antwerp under the headline: 'It Was Churchill's Own Personally Conceived Idea, Carried out Against Kitchener's Advice'. The newspaper mistakenly reported—based on accounts by allegedly 'well-informed persons'—that Churchill's proposal to send British troops to Antwerp had been rejected by both Kitchener and General Joffre, the Commander-in-Chief of the French Army. It claimed that Churchill, 'on his own initiative, hurriedly assembled some naval reserves and others, the greater part of them half-trained men, and rushed them off to Antwerp'.[62]

Churchill told his friend Sir George Riddell, the proprietor of the *News of the World* and the chairman of the Newspaper Proprietors' Association, that he did 'not mind what they say' in the newspapers, as his work at the Admiralty would 'speak for itself'. He added: 'I have plenty of enemies. I do not intend to waste my time replying to Press criticism. I have too much else to do.'[63] But Churchill was more bothered by the incident than he was willing to let on. His first reaction to the *Morning Post*'s attack was to call for official action to be taken against the newspaper. On the same day Gwynne's damning leader was published, Churchill summoned Sir Stanley Buckmaster, the Solicitor General and the government's recently appointed chief censor, to the Admiralty. According to Buckmaster's account, Churchill 'said that he did not mind criticism but that this was unfair because he had a complete answer to it which the public interest prevented him from revealing. He wanted to know if I had done anything to the paper or to stop the repetition of this class of work.' Buckmaster believed his mandate extended only so far as the censorship of military or naval information that might be exploited by the enemy. He was therefore unwilling to suppress press reports criticizing the government or individual ministers. He told Churchill that he 'could not stop matter merely because it was unjust. [Churchill] then said "Will you not do anything?" and I replied that I could not.'[64]

Buckmaster wrote to Gwynne that same evening, gently suggesting that in future he might show greater restraint in criticizing ministers who were not free in wartime to respond to allegations made against them. Gwynne was at once conciliatory and unrepentant. His reply the next day rehearsed his complaints about Churchill's despatch of poorly trained troops, and also censured Churchill for his frequent absences from the Admiralty. 'Within the last month', he noted, Churchill 'has left his work at the Admiralty to pay visits to the Army Headquarters in France, to Dunkirk, and to Antwerp. He was under shell fire at Antwerp. He took part in the details of the expedition and so, in my opinion, must have neglected the high office which he holds.'[65] Churchill's Cabinet colleagues would have agreed with this complaint. Gwynne insisted that he had an obligation to speak out when he saw 'things going absolutely wrong':

> I want you to understand that in this or in any other criticism I shall be guided only by what I consider to be the needs of the nation. Of course, there may be two opinions as to the necessity of this, but I think in this present case I could prove to you conclusively not only that I am quite justified in the criticism I have made about this Antwerp affair, but that as an Editor, with a sense of responsibility which is sometimes overpowering, it was my bounden duty to make it.[66]

Churchill decided there was nothing to be gained by pressing Buckmaster on this issue, but his frustration did not soon abate.[67] On 22 October he complained to Riddell that, in wartime, the press should not be allowed to criticize the government at all. 'War is a horrid thing', he said. 'Disasters will occur. You cannot avoid them. It is very difficult to conduct warfare under conditions which permit free criticism.'[68] In the weeks that followed, he attempted to wrest greater control over censorship for the Admiralty, but his efforts were unsuccessful.[69] Churchill's lobbying of Buckmaster may have been a factor in Gwynne's decision not to publish a new (and probably even more critical) article he was preparing on Antwerp, but the *Morning Post* continued to criticize Churchill.[70] The complaint most often voiced was that Churchill routinely ignored his naval advisers. The result, according to one editorial, was that 'Mr. Churchill has gathered the whole power of the Admiralty into his own hands, and the Navy is governed no longer by a Board of experts, but by a brilliant and erratic amateur.'[71]

The controversy created by the *Morning Post*'s attack took weeks to die away. On 11 November, Churchill's role in the Antwerp expedition was raised by the Conservatives in both Houses of Parliament—by Lord Selborne, a former First Lord of the Admiralty, in the House of Lords, and by Andrew Bonar Law, the leader of the party, in the Commons.[72] Speaking for the government, Asquith replied, 'in the clearest and most explicit terms, that the responsibility for what was done there was the responsibility not of any individual Minister, but of the Government as a whole, that, in particular, the Secretary of State for War was consulted, and that everything that was done was done with his knowledge and approval'.[73] This clear statement brought the public debate on the subject to a close for the time being, but Churchill remained frustrated. On Christmas Day 1914, he prepared a detailed statement for the press on the circumstances leading to the Battle of Coronel. This communiqué paid generous tribute to Cradock's gallantry and devotion, but left no doubt that he could have avoided disaster by keeping all the ships at his disposal, including *Canopus*, concentrated. 'The Admiralty', Churchill wrote, 'have no responsibility for Admiral Cradock's decision.' The navy's chief censor, Rear-Admiral Douglas Brownrigg, later related that this document had already been issued to the Press Bureau when it was urgently withdrawn after the First Sea Lord threatened to resign if it were published.[74]

Unable to respond publicly to attacks in the British press, Churchill concentrated on achieving high-profile results in the war at sea. His main preoccupation in the final months of 1914 was finding the means to take the war to the German coast. Since the key obstacle to operating in the Heligoland Bight was technological—mines, torpedoes, and submarines—Churchill instinctively looked to technology for a solution. He was immediately attracted by the possibilities of big-gunned warships known as monitors. These heavily armed but slow vessels had been ignored by the navy before the war, but their value as coast assault weapons soon became evident. Their shallow draught allowed them to operate close inshore, and they could be built with 'bulges' in the hull to offer protection against torpedoes and mines. In August 1914, the Royal Navy acquired three such vessels, armed with a mixture of 6-inch and 4.7-inch guns, which had recently been built in Britain for use by the Brazilian Navy on the Amazon River. Brazil had defaulted on payment for these ships, and the Royal Navy purchased them on the outbreak of war to ensure that they were not acquired by a neutral power and resold to Germany. In the months that followed, these monitors frequently demonstrated their worth along the Belgian coast, where they provided valuable fire support for Allied operations ashore without suffering any losses.[75] Churchill was so pleased with their performance that, in early November, he decided to begin construction of four new monitors using 14-inch gun turrets supplied by the Bethlehem Steel Corporation in the United States. A month later he was eager to build even more. What was required, he wrote on 11 December, were ships 'which can certainly go close in shore and attack the German fleet in its harbours'. By expediting the construction of these ships, he hoped that Britain could have as many as twelve new monitors, with guns

ranging from 13.5 to 15 inches, by mid-1915. If the German fleet had not
been destroyed by then, he looked forward to these 'special vessels' giving
Britain 'the power of forcing a naval decision at the latest in the autumn of
1915'.[76] 'It is with this fleet', he later told Bayly, 'that I propose to "dig the rat
out of his hole"'.[77]

While British shipyards began to work on a 'digging out' capability for
the navy, Churchill kept up his efforts to block the German Navy in its
harbours by establishing a flotilla base along the German coast. In November,
he asked Vice-Admiral Sir Cecil Burney, Commander-in-Chief of the
Channel Fleet, to review a plan drawn up in September by Admiral Wilson
for the seizure of Heligoland. Burney, one of the few senior officers afloat
who had not already rejected the project, was also unimpressed. Wilson's
proposal would put valuable ships at risk, in his view, and would almost
certainly fail. Naval gunfire was unlikely to destroy the forts on the island or
neutralize the garrison defending it. And even if a small force of marines did
somehow manage to establish itself ashore—Wilson detailed just a single
battalion for this purpose—they were unlikely to hold it. The Germans
would probably recapture the island the next day, he predicted. The plan,
Burney concluded, was 'impracticable. I even go further and say that I think
the scheme if carried out would result in a national disaster.'[78] This report is
probably what subsequently induced Churchill to identify Burney as one
of the 'No school' of naval officers.[79] However, it seems to have at least
persuaded Churchill that Heligoland was not a promising target.

The First Lord secured a potential ally at the end of October when public opinion and press agitation forced the German-born Battenberg to
relinquish his office. Prince Louis had not distinguished himself as First
Lord. Churchill had found him an agreeable adviser, however, because he
seldom opposed the First Lord's ideas and allowed him a greater degree of
control over naval policy than would have been possible under a stronger
First Sea Lord. When it became clear that Battenberg would have to go,
Churchill decided to bring Admiral of the Fleet Lord Fisher out of retirement to serve again as First Sea Lord. One of the obvious attractions of
Fisher was the prospect of pursuing a more aggressive naval strategy. He had
been a strong proponent of Baltic operations during his previous tenure as
First Sea Lord, and had inspired Churchill's idea of using the Royal Navy to
land Russian troops on the Pomeranian coast for a march on Berlin. The
appointment was received with apprehension in many quarters, however.[80]
As First Sea Lord in 1904–10, Fisher had been a dynamic reformer and

innovator, but his abrasive methods and combative personality had created many enemies within the service. When he retired in 1910 he left behind a navy riven with factionalism. Fisher himself was not one to let go of a grudge, and Churchill had hesitated to bring him back out of concern about reopening old controversies. But the First Lord was a friend and admirer of the admiral, and he seems to have assumed—naively, as it turned out—that their good personal relationship would translate into a harmonious working partnership. He also thought that the septuagenarian Fisher would be easy to manage. This may, in fact, have been Churchill's main consideration in bringing him back. Before making the controversial appointment, he described Fisher and Wilson, who would soon be the two highest-ranking admirals at the Admiralty, as 'well-plucked chickens' of 74 & 72'.[81]

Churchill's desire to keep control of naval policy in his hands was obvious to Richmond, who complained that 'Tug Wilson & Jacky [Fisher] are so old...that they will really be under Winston's thumb.'[82] At the same time, Fisher's reputation as a dynamic and forceful personality fuelled speculation that the two men would eventually clash, and probably in a spectacular fashion. Fisher himself was evidently eager to establish that he had no

Figure 1.5. Admiral of the Fleet John Arbuthnot 'Jacky' Fisher, 1st Baron Fisher of Kilverstone.
Library of Congress

Figure 1.6. Admiral of the Fleet Sir Arthur Knyvet Wilson.
Library of Congress

intention of letting Churchill have everything his own way. Within days of returning to the Admiralty, the admiral announced to Captain Philip Dumas, the Assistant Director of Torpedoes, that he (Fisher) had been 'having b—y rows all round & finished by speaking of "that d—d fellow with a red pencil [Churchill used red ink on Admiralty minute sheets] at the end of the passage" which doesn't look happy for his future relations with Winston!'[83] However, the new leadership at the Admiralty worked together smoothly at first, and Fisher was less confrontational than many expected. It was not long, in fact, before Richmond began complaining that Fisher was too compliant. He told his wife in mid-November that 'Winston is virtually running the show now, as apparently Jacky gives in to him, or agrees with him I don't know which. I don't quite understand how this is for when J. first came he is reported to have said "if one of us has to go because he can't get his own way, it will be that jackanapes with the Red Pencil, not me" (meaning W.).'[84]

But Fisher was far from subservient to Churchill, and did not immediately fall in with the First Lord's plans for naval operations in the North Sea. Shortly after taking up office, Fisher enlisted Sir Julian Corbett to prepare a memorandum outlining the major strategic project he preferred, a naval offensive in the Baltic. Corbett, a civilian, was Britain's pre-eminent naval strategist. He had taught the Royal Navy's Senior Officer War Course before the war, and in 1911 published *Some Principles of Maritime Strategy*, an officially sanctioned treatise on national strategic doctrine. Fisher was eager to use Corbett's historical knowledge and skill with the pen to make his case for a Baltic operation. Corbett had been employed since the start of the war in the Committee of Imperial Defence's (CID's) Historical Section, and he was eager to assist. In late December he completed a memorandum entitled 'On the possibility of using our Command of the Sea to influence more drastically the Military Situation on the Continent'. Like Churchill, Fisher and Corbett were not certain that economic pressure applied through sea power would be sufficient to cripple Germany. In the event that the Royal Navy's blockade did not seem to be producing results, they concluded that '*risks must be taken to use our Command of the Sea with greater energy*'. Drawing on the Seven Years' War for inspiration, Corbett and Fisher proposed that a decisive stroke might be delivered against Germany by maintaining a British fleet in the Baltic. This would allow the Allies to land Russian troops along the German coast and threaten Germany's communications on the Eastern Front.[85]

This is precisely the sort of offensive spirit Churchill had been hoping for, or so it seemed. The difficulty was that the British fleet deployed to the Baltic would have to come from the North Sea. Churchill believed the German High Seas Fleet must be neutralized before such a movement could take place, lest the Germans exploit the absence of a British fleet in home waters to strike a powerful blow in that theatre. He therefore insisted that the German fleet must be blocked into its harbours by British forces operating from a forward base near the German coast. Only then would it be safe to enter the Baltic in force. Fisher, however, proposed to neutralize the German fleet by '*sow[ing] the North Sea with mines on such a scale that naval operations in it would become impossible*'.[86] The feasibility of this scheme was open to challenge. Corbett immediately saw the weak spot in Fisher's proposal—if British mines could deny the North Sea to the German fleet, German mines could presumably deny the Baltic to the British.[87] Churchill doubted that North Sea mining would be sufficient to contain the German fleet. He preferred Arthur Wilson's idea of aggressive inshore operations by the Royal

Navy to mine the German coast.[88] Oliver also had serious doubts about Fisher's project: 'How the Fleet would pass the Great Belt [a narrow strait running through Danish waters] in single line ahead, with the German battle fleet deployed and crossing its T, did not interest him [Fisher] or how the fleet could be supplied in the Baltic.'[89]

In the short term, however, what mattered most to Churchill was that his top professional adviser was receptive to the idea eventually to send a British fleet into the Baltic, which Churchill regarded as the culminating stage of British naval strategy. He therefore raised the idea of seizing an island near the enemy coast at a meeting of the Cabinet's War Council, a new ministerial committee charged with overseeing the broad direction of the war effort, on 1 December. This is the first time Churchill had attempted to gain explicit political backing for his scheme. If Fisher had reservations about it, he did not voice them. His main contribution to the discussion was to urge that some offensive action be taken by the navy. 'The present defensive attitude of the fleet', he announced, 'was bad for its *moral[e]*, and did not really protect it from the attacks of submarines.' Typically, Churchill had no desire to dwell on technical objections to the project. He restricted himself to outlining the potential benefits of occupying a suitable island. Britain could then establish a forward base for flotilla forces to maintain a constant watch on the German fleet, and air raids could be launched 'every few days'. In these circumstances, it would be almost impossible, he explained, for the Germans to mount a successful invasion of the British Isles.[90]

Kitchener raised doubts about the availability of troops for such an operation, but the politicians were sufficiently impressed by the project's potential that the Admiralty was encouraged to investigate it further. Nor was Kitchener inclined to dismiss the idea out of hand. He asked Major-General Charles Callwell, the War Office's Director of Military Operations (DMO), to investigate the possibility of an attack on the Dutch Frisian islands. 'I suppose', Callwell complained to a colleague, that 'Winston has been talking to him.' Callwell was clearly unimpressed with the idea. 'I think we can put a stopper on this', he wrote, 'thanks to talk about mines, shallows, batteries and so forth. All this sort of thing however takes up one's time and that such projects should be entertained even for a moment shows the extraordinarily mistaken idea which intelligent people sometimes entertain with regard to elementary principles of war.'[91]

Churchill set to work the next day sketching out a plan for the capture of Sylt, one of the northernmost German islands. The operation he envisioned would begin with a bombardment of the island's defences by a naval force consisting of four old battleships, three monitors, and twenty destroyers. After approximately two hours, he proposed to land around 5,000 troops on the northern end of the island. Additional forces, including nine battalions of the Royal Naval Division, would be held in reserve, and the Grand Fleet would be nearby in case the German fleet attempted to interfere with the operation. Once the island was secure, he believed it could be protected by the large force of submarines and destroyers that were to be maintained there permanently. Any attempt by the Germans to retake the island would work to Britain's advantage, he maintained, since it would expose German ships to destruction.[92] That Churchill would begin drafting the plan himself is surprising, as this was a task normally delegated to naval staff officers. But by laying out his view that the scheme was both feasible and beneficial, he presumably hoped to ensure that Admiralty planners got on with the task of solving any technical problems they encountered, rather than dwelling on the reasons the scheme should not be adopted. Churchill's tendency to overlook or brush aside the obstacles involved in the schemes he promoted was noted at the time by Arthur Balfour, who had been invited to attend meetings of the War Council. After discussing the project with Churchill at the Admiralty he was concerned that the First Lord was so eager to launch an attack that he 'refuses to recognize even the most obvious difficulties'.[93]

Balfour was, nevertheless, sympathetic to the idea of seizing an island base. On 3 December, he sent a memorandum on the subject to Maurice Hankey, the Secretary to the War Council, in which he concluded that this was 'the most effective way of crippling the movements of the enemy's fleet, and parrying any attempt at invasion'.[94] Churchill's proposal failed to develop any momentum within the Admiralty, however. Nearly three weeks after outlining his plan for the capture of Sylt, he complained to Fisher that he could not 'find anyone to make such a plan alive & dominant'.[95] One of the main obstacles was Fisher himself. The First Sea Lord remained committed in principle to the idea of one day establishing a British naval presence in the Baltic, but he had little interest in seizing a base near the German coast, which Churchill believed was an essential first step in any such scheme. The First Lord tried to persuade the admiral to support his plan, telling him on 22 December that he was 'wholly with you about the Baltic. But you must close up this side first. You must take an island & block them [i.e. the Germans] in à la Wilson; or you must break the canal or the locks, or you must cripple their Fleet in a general action.' Churchill bluntly rejected the alternative favoured by Fisher. 'No scattering of mines', he wrote, 'will be any substitute for these alternatives.'[96]

Despite Fisher's lack of enthusiasm, Churchill was undeterred. He succeeded in having Admiral Burney moved to the Grand Fleet in order to free Bayly for command of the Channel Fleet, the force that would be responsible for implementing any offensive operation in the Heligoland Bight. Asquith noted on 24 December that Churchill was 'now meditating fearsome plans of a highly aggressive kind to replace the present policy of masterly inactivity'.[97] But with little support for such an operation at the Admiralty, Churchill evidently decided that he needed to obtain strong and explicit backing from the War Council to move his plans forward against professional opposition. His first step was to secure the support of the Prime Minister. He wrote to Asquith on the 29th to lay out the case for a more vigorous naval policy. It was now clear that no rapid decision could be expected on the Continent. By the end of 1914, the war of manoeuvre in the west had been replaced by static trench warfare. Modern firepower gave such a marked advantage to the defensive that neither side could hope to launch an offensive without suffering prohibitive casualties for little gain. The new armies being raised by Kitchener would see action after all. But where? Churchill argued against committing these forces to bloody and futile attacks on the Western Front. 'Are there not other alternatives', he asked, 'than sending our armies to chew barbed wire in Flanders?'[98]

Churchill suggested to Asquith that Britain should exploit its superior sea power to open a new front against Germany. One of the possibilities he raised was the landing of British troops in Schleswig-Holstein, along Germany's Danish frontier, which would enable Britain to threaten the Kiel Canal and possibly win Denmark over to the Allied cause. Alternatively, Russian troops might be deposited on Germany's Baltic coast. By opening a new northern theatre of operations, he maintained that the Allies would be able to impose a heavy burden on Germany's resources, thereby hastening its collapse. But to achieve any of this, it would first be necessary to deal with the German High Seas Fleet. For this purpose, the 'capture of a German island for an oversea base' would be 'indispensable'. Rear-Admiral Henry Oliver, the new Chief of the War Staff, had recently identified Borkum as the most promising target, and Churchill now proposed to make it, rather than Sylt, the navy's target. He sketched out for Asquith the benefits of mounting an attack on the island. If the German fleet came out to defend it, the navy's long-sought-after fleet action would finally take place. In this event, the defeat of the High Seas Fleet was taken for granted. And if the Germans did not contest the attack, Churchill predicted that their fleet would be driven into its harbours and held there by minefields protected by British flotilla forces operating from their new advance base. The navy would then be free to enter the Baltic.[99]

Churchill believed that the plan could be implemented in April or May 1915, around the time the navy's new monitors would be ready for action, but he insisted that the project could only move forward if Asquith threw his support behind it. This proposal was well timed, as the Prime Minister received two other memoranda on similar lines in the final days of December. The first came from Hankey, a former officer of the Royal Marine Artillery who had served as Secretary of the CID before the war and became

Figure 1.7. Maurice Hankey, Secretary to the War Council.
Library of Congress

Secretary to the War Council in November 1914. Hankey, an energetic and especially able civil servant, was also deeply impressed by the futility of launching new offensives on the Western Front. And, like Churchill, he believed that the right course was to use 'our sea power and our growing military strength to attack Germany and her allies in other quarters'. He proposed, however, to strike at the Ottoman Empire, which had entered the war on Germany's side at the end of October, rather than at Germany. 'Has not the time come', he asked, 'to show Germany and the world that any country that chooses a German alliance against the great sea power is doomed to disaster?' By opening a new front against the Ottoman Empire, Hankey believed the Allies could unite the Balkan states and join them to the Allied cause. The commitment of three British Army corps to this theatre along with Greek and Bulgarian troops should be sufficient, he predicted, to capture Constantinople and drive the Turks out of Europe. At the same time, Russia, Serbia, and Romania could combine forces for a decisive attack on Austria-Hungary.[100]

David Lloyd George, the Chancellor of the Exchequer, had also started looking for an alternative to the deadly stalemate on the Western Front. Like Hankey, he proposed that the right course was to commit Britain's new armies to operations against Germany's allies. By launching simultaneous attacks on Austria-Hungary and the Ottoman Empire, the Chancellor suggested to Asquith that Germany could be brought 'down by the process of knocking the props under her'. Lloyd George also assumed that it would be a simple matter for Britain to forge a Balkan coalition. Committing large British forces to the region would persuade the Balkan states to put aside their differences, confident in the knowledge that they would all gain territory at the expense of Germany's allies. Britain, he calculated, could initially contribute over half a million troops to the region, and its new Balkan allies might contribute a million more for a devastating attack on Austria's southern flank. This operation would coincide with an offensive against the Ottoman Empire. The Chancellor proposed to land 100,000 British troops in Syria to cut off the retreat of Ottoman forces moving south against the Suez Canal. 'Unless we are prepared for some project of this character', he concluded, 'I frankly despair of our achieving any success in this War. I can see nothing but an eternal stalemate on any other lines.'[101]

These memoranda made an apparently compelling case against committing Britain's new armies to the Western Front, the course preferred by Britain's military leaders. Asquith was won over. 'The losses involved in the trench-jumping operations now going on on both sides are enormous', he observed, '& out of all proportion to the ground gained.'[102] By the end of 1914, a consensus was emerging within the War Council that the time had come to exploit the strategic flexibility offered by sea power.[103] The Prime Minister informed his colleagues that the matter would be examined by the War Council during the first week of the new year. If the decision were taken to open a new front, the obvious question to be settled was where to strike. At the end of December 1914, Churchill, who is usually identified as the driving force behind the decision to attack the Ottoman Empire, was firmly focused on his bold but unrealistic plan to attack Germany via the North Sea and the Baltic. It was initially Hankey and Lloyd George who ensured that there were other options on the table, including operations in the Balkans and Middle East.

2

The Origins of the Naval Offensive

The frequent and sometimes heated debates over British grand strategy during the First World War are often characterized as a simple clash between two opposing schools of thought, 'Westerners' and 'Easterners'. The 'Westerners' were those who wanted British resources committed primarily to the campaign in France and Flanders, which they regarded as the decisive theatre of the war. This was the only place where the German Army could be finally beaten, they correctly pointed out. And a major Allied defeat there could not be risked, since this would mean ultimate victory for Germany. The 'Easterners', on the other hand, preferred to avoid the costly stalemate in the west, committing only enough forces there to avoid defeat while using the rest of Britain's available resources to achieve tangible results against weaker opponents in the Balkans or the Middle East. Churchill's advocacy of an assault against the Ottoman Empire in 1915, together with his vigorous defence of the operation during and after the war, has led many historians to conclude he was a leading member of the 'eastern' school. However, at the beginning of 1915 Churchill did not fit easily into either group. He *was* eager to find a peripheral theatre in which to fight, which certainly distinguished him from the generals and others who wished to concentrate on the Western Front, but he preferred a 'northern' campaign against Germany to an 'eastern' one against either Austria–Hungary or the Ottoman Empire.

In Churchill's view, however, major operations in the North Sea and the Baltic did not preclude the possibility of minor or subsidiary operations in the Middle East. Even before hostilities formally commenced between the Allies and the Ottomans, Churchill was willing to risk a new war in this theatre by violating Ottoman neutrality. In August 1914, the German battle

cruiser *Goeben* and the cruiser *Breslau* eluded British warships in the
Mediterranean and sailed to safety through the Dardanelles Straits. The
German government, knowing that the ships had little chance of escaping,
offered them as a gift to the pro-German government in Constantinople, an
arrangement that did not sit well with the British. The ships were subsequently incorporated into the Ottoman Navy and given Turkish names,
although they retained their German crews. Their escape had been a serious
embarrassment for the Admiralty, and Churchill was, consequently, in
'his most bellicose mood' when the matter was taken up by the Cabinet on
17 August. With little regard for the possible consequences, he argued that
a flotilla of British destroyers should be sent through the Straits to sink
the two ships. Nothing came of this idea, however, as Kitchener and other
ministers feared that the British Empire's Muslim population would be
alienated if Britain appeared to be launching an unprovoked attack against
the Ottoman Empire.[1]

The British, nevertheless, suspected that the Ottomans would eventually
enter the war on Germany's side, and Churchill was eager to strike immediately if they did. However, his primary goal in 1914 appears to have been
a relatively modest one—ensuring the destruction of the *Goeben* and *Breslau*.
To achieve this, British warships would have to pass through the Dardanelles
Straits, a heavily defended waterway approximately 40 miles long, separating
the Aegean Sea and the Sea of Marmara. This could only be accomplished,
he suggested in early September, by seizing control of the Gallipoli peninsula, a narrow strip of land flanking the Straits on the western side. But
even if there had been troops available for such an operation, Churchill
had no desire to turn this into a major *British* campaign. On 31 August,
he arranged with Kitchener for officers from the War Office and Admiralty
to meet the following day to work out a plan by which the *Greek* Army
might seize the Gallipoli peninsula in order to allow a British fleet to pass
through the Dardanelles Straits.[2] Greece, it should be noted, was then a
neutral power. Major-General Callwell, the principal War Office delegate,
informed Admiralty officials (including Richmond and Cecil Lambert) on
1 September that he 'did not regard it as a feasible military operation &
that he believed this to be the War Office view'. This might have ended the
matter, but Callwell was subsequently recalled to the Admiralty for another
meeting on either 2 or 3 September, and this time both Churchill and
Battenberg were in attendance. After the matter was 'thrashed out again',
Callwell produced a slightly more optimistic appraisal.[3] Any such operation

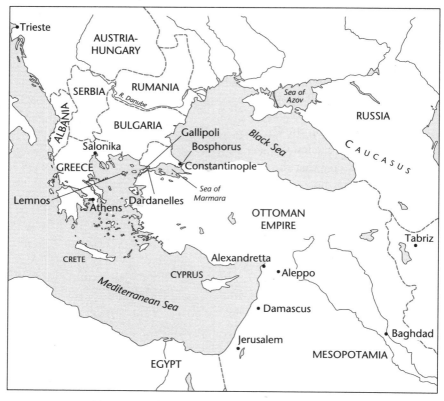

Map 2.1. The Ottoman Empire and the Balkans.

by the Greeks, he wrote on 3 September, would be 'an extremely difficult operation of war'. The Ottomans would be able to rush in strong reinforcements, making it necessary to land no fewer than 60,000 men on the peninsula.[4]

This was enough encouragement for Churchill, who instructed Rear-Admiral Mark Kerr, the head of the British Naval Mission in Greece, to begin devising plans for a combined Anglo-Greek campaign. 'The right and obvious method of attacking Turkey', Churchill wrote, 'is to strike immediately at the heart.'

To do this, it would be necessary for a Greek army to seize the Gallipoli Peninsula under superiority of sea predominance, and thus to open the Dardanelles, admitting the Anglo-Greek Fleet to the Sea of Marmora, whence the Turco-German ships can be fought and sunk, and where in combination with the Russian Black Sea Fleet and Russian military forces the whole situation can be dominated.[5]

If Greece would not contribute the necessary forces, Churchill proposed that Russian troops could be sent to the Gallipoli peninsula instead, an unlikely prospect given that they would have to be transported to the Mediterranean from a distant Russian port such as Archangel in the far north or Vladivostok on the Pacific coast. Typically, Churchill did not dwell on the potential obstacles. On the contrary, he reassured Sir Edward Grey, the Foreign Secretary, that the occupation of the Gallipoli peninsula would not only allow the destruction of the two German ships, it would also be such a devastating blow that the Ottoman Empire might be knocked out of the war entirely. 'The price to be paid in taking Gallipoli wd no doubt be heavy [for the Greeks or the Russians!]', he told Grey, 'but there wd be no more war with Turkey. A good army of 50,000 men & sea-power—that is the end of Turkish menace.'[6]

The *Goeben*, now renamed *Yavuz Sultan Selim*, bombarded the Russian Black Sea port of Sevastopol on 29 October on the initiative of its German commander, Admiral Souchon. When the British Cabinet met the following day, Churchill was keen to declare war on the Ottoman Empire immediately, prompting Grey to remark that Churchill 'want[ed] a new war with someone once a week'.[7] But with no army immediately available from any source to land on the Gallipoli peninsula, Churchill had to shelve his ambitious idea of a combined multinational offensive. Instead, he instructed British naval forces in the eastern Mediterranean to bombard the forts protecting the entrance to the Dardanelles Straits. This operation, conceived as a one-off, was carried out successfully on 3 November, before Britain had formally declared war. Over the next two months, the prospects of finding a Greek, Russian, or British Army did not improve, and Churchill showed little interest in promoting an expedition to capture Gallipoli.[8] His hopes for a major new offensive were, by now, fixed firmly on the North Sea. When Hankey proposed at the end of December 1914 to open a new front against the Ottomans, Churchill played down the idea, reminding the Prime Minister that it would be difficult to obtain Kitchener's support for a new land campaign.[9] Fisher, however, told Hankey that Churchill had been not just dismissive of the idea but hostile. 'I went for it "tooth & nail"!', he told Hankey. But Churchill was 'against it! He says it's too far from the main theatre of war.'[10]

Fisher remained enthusiastic about Hankey's plan, however. He told
Churchill on 3 January, in his characteristically effusive manner, that
'I CONSIDER THE ATTACK ON TURKEY HOLDS THE FIELD!—
but ONLY if it's IMMEDIATE!'[11] The First Sea Lord, elaborating on
Hankey's ideas, wrote to both Hankey and Churchill, proposing to force the
Dardanelles with pre-dreadnought battleships. At the same time as the fleet
moved up the Straits, he suggested that Bulgaria, then a neutral power (and
later a German ally), would take Constantinople; the Greeks, who were *still*
not at war, would seize the Gallipoli peninsula; and 75,000 seasoned British
troops and additional Indian forces drawn from the BEF would be embarked
at Marseilles and landed directly on Turkey's Aegean coast at Besika Bay.[12]
This scheme never stood a chance, as there was little prospect of Greece and
Bulgaria being persuaded to put aside their mutual animosity, and even less
chance of such an ambitious plan being implemented rapidly, as Fisher
demanded. Churchill was also reluctant to commit himself to a major diversion of British land forces to the Mediterranean, which would decrease the
chances of launching a major new operation against Germany in the North
Sea or the Baltic. 'I wd not grudge 100,000 men [for an attack on the
Ottomans] because of the great political effects in the Balkan peninsula', he
told Fisher on 4 January, 'but Germany is the foe, & it is bad war to seek
cheaper victories and easier antagonists.'[13]

There were also good reasons for Churchill to question whether British
or Indian forces would be available for such an operation, since British generals and the French would inevitably fight any attempt to reduce their
strength on the Western Front. The new armies being raised by Kitchener
were not yet ready. But the possibility of action in the east was given additional impetus on 1 January when the Russians, who were under pressure
in the Caucasus, appealed to the British for a military or naval demonstration
against the Ottomans. What could be done? The Secretary of State for War
informed Churchill the following day that there were no troops available 'to
land anywhere'. The army, in his opinion, would 'not be ready for anything
big for some months'. The only chance of taking pressure off the Russians,
Kitchener suggested, would be a naval 'demonstration' at the Dardanelles,
especially if it appeared that Constantinople was threatened.[14] Churchill was
intrigued by the idea of launching a purely naval action against the Ottomans,
but he was also wary about being dragged into a major commitment of
British forces in the Near East. And since the Fisher–Hankey scheme for a
major offensive against the Ottomans was clearly a non-starter, Churchill

continued to focus on his Borkum project. This scheme had the obvious advantage of striking directly at Germany, the main enemy; it did not rely on the cooperation of unpredictable Balkan states; and it would require fewer troops—only a single infantry division was to be committed.

With the War Council preparing to consider alternative theatres for the employment of British forces, Churchill decided that the time had come for the Admiralty to formulate concrete plans for the capture of a German North Sea island. On 3 January he instructed Fisher, Wilson, and Oliver to begin work on the project, which he hoped to launch as early as March or April 1915. Typically, he could not resist offering detailed suggestions as to what the plan should look like. He was eager, for example, to see the navy's new monitors employed in the operation, and he advised that careful consideration should be given to fitting the bombarding ships and specialized landing craft with strong protection against enemy fire. And, as usual, he was quick to brush aside the potential difficulties. 'A resolve to have the island at all costs', he pronounced, 'coupled with exact and careful preparations, should certainly, with our great resources, be successful within three days of fire being opened.'[15]

Churchill also renewed his efforts to enlist Jellicoe's support. He wrote a personal letter to the admiral the following day, spelling out at length the advantages of his plans, and reassuring him that under no circumstances would the Grand Fleet's numerical superiority over the Germans be jeopardized by a more aggressive policy in the North Sea.[16] Around the same time, he asked Captain Roger Keyes, until recently the commodore of the navy's submarine service, to report on whether torpedo craft could be expected to defend the island once in British possession. Churchill was clearly eager to secure a positive response, and instructed Keyes to assume that Borkum would *not* be subjected to German artillery fire and that enemy warships in the port of Emden would be blocked in. With these problems conveniently removed, the offensive-minded Keyes provided the sort of optimistic assessment Churchill wanted. 'I do not think', the naval officer wrote, 'the defence of Borkum *from seaward* would be a difficult matter provided a sufficient number of submarines, destroyers, trawlers and aircraft can be maintained there in an efficient condition.'[17]

While preparations for the seizure of Borkum were moving forward, Churchill reflected on Kitchener's suggestion that the navy might undertake a 'demonstration' in the Dardanelles. He may have been genuinely concerned about Russian difficulties in the Caucasus, or have simply seen, finally, an opportunity to destroy the *Goeben* and *Breslau*. Whatever the reason, to have any value—in his opinion—the navy's action must consist of something more ambitious than the bombardment of the Dardanelles' outer defences on 3 November. Fisher's letter of 3 January introduced an important new element into the equation. Churchill had hitherto assumed that it would be necessary to take the Gallipoli peninsula before ships could be sent through the Straits into the Sea of Marmara, but the First Sea Lord had raised the possibility that pre-dreadnought battleships could force a passage through the Dardanelles on their own. Churchill was also probably impressed by Fisher's enthusiasm for Hankey's proposal, and by his note of urgency. Churchill had been struggling for months to find a scheme that his naval advisers would back without reservation. The idea of an eastern diversion also seemed to have Kitchener's support, which would ensure approval when the matter came before the War Council. If both Kitchener and Fisher were willing to support an attack on the Ottoman Empire, Churchill was not going to miss the opportunity to take action.

He nevertheless proceeded cautiously. The First Lord told Fisher on 4 January that he wanted more feedback on the 'Turkish plans' before reaching any decision. But what he now had in mind was not a joint army–navy operation, as Fisher and Hankey envisioned, but a purely naval assault to force a passage through the Straits. The day before, Churchill had written to Vice-Admiral Sir Sackville Carden, commander of the navy's Eastern Mediterranean Squadron, to ask if he thought 'the forcing of the Dardanelles by ships alone' would be 'a practicable operation'. His hopes were probably not high. He had recently observed that Carden 'has never even commanded a cruiser Sqn. & I am not aware of anything that he has done wh[ich] is in any way remarkable'.[18] But Carden was not only the man on the spot, he might also be the officer charged with carrying out the operation, making his support important. Churchill was undoubtedly trying to move the project forward, and sought to encourage a positive response by noting that the assault would only employ older battleships 'fitted with minebumpers...preceded by Colliers or other merchant craft as bumpers and sweepers'. The 'Importance of results', he concluded in his telegram, 'would justify severe loss.'[19]

It is often said that Churchill framed his query in a deliberately leading manner, so that Carden would feel compelled to suppress his doubts and support the operation. And some accounts go much further, suggesting that Carden was somehow 'coerced' into going along with Churchill's wishes.[20] When challenged two years later by the Dardanelles Commission, Churchill

Figure 2.1. Vice-Admiral Sir Sackville Carden.
Library of Congress

did not deny that he had hoped for a positive response. 'I do not think it is wrong', he observed, 'to cast a telegram in a way which shows that action, if possible, would be very desirable. I think you may say that it certainly shows that we should have been very glad if he had had a good plan.' Churchill disagreed, however, with the suggestion that a high-ranking naval officer would meekly go along with an idea he disliked simply because it had originated with the First Lord. After four months of war, Churchill was accustomed to his recommendations being shot down or obstructed by his naval advisers. Jellicoe, for example, had resisted his Borkum scheme at every step. Churchill pointed out in 1916 that, in the 'overwhelming majority of cases', naval opinion was against any new proposal for offensive action. 'The negative tendency is enormously powerful', he maintained, 'far more powerful than the positive tendency; in fact, the negative tendency is supreme.'[21] Carden, it should be noted, told the Commission that he did feel at the time that Churchill wanted a positive answer, but he denied that this had any influence on the reply he sent.[22]

One of the unanswered questions at the heart of the Dardanelles controversy is whether Churchill's naval advisers supported the idea of a naval attack on the Dardanelles when it was first raised. There is no hard evidence

Figure 2.2. Rear-Admiral Henry Oliver, Chief of the Admiralty War Staff (portrait by Francis Dodd, 1917).
Topham Picturepoint

Figure 2.3. Admiral Henry Jackson (portrait by Francis Dodd, 1917).
Mary Evans Picture Library

from which to draw a conclusion. On the basis of later testimony, it seems safe to say that Churchill did discuss the matter with members of the Admiralty 'War Group'. This informal body included the First Lord, the First Sea Lord, the Chief of the Admiralty War Staff (Oliver), Arthur Wilson, Admiral Sir Henry Jackson (attached to the War Staff as an adviser on overseas expeditions), and Commodore Bartolomé, Churchill's naval secretary. The 'War Group' emerged after the outbreak of war as the main body at the Admiralty overseeing naval strategy and operations. Churchill *may* have been encouraged by his advisers to send his telegram to Carden, but it is also possible that he approached Carden in hopes of obtaining a positive response that could be used to win support for the proposal within the Admiralty. This was a method Churchill often employed when faced with (or when anticipating) what he regarded as 'obstruction'.

Churchill's naval advisers were by now familiar with his methods—not just his desire to initiate offensive plans, but also his readiness to dismiss opinions he disliked. Oliver, for example, complained that it was 'no good contradicting or opposing him—it only makes him worse'. By early January, Churchill's relationship with Fisher was also beginning to deteriorate. Richmond noted on 3 January that 'Winston & Jack have tremendous rows at intervals.'

> Two days ago Jack found that W. had approved the moving of a number of destroyers from one place to another without his having been consulted. He was furious & said he wd resign if things that so vitally affected his control of affairs were to be settled without his knowing anything about it 'I shall resign. I won't stand it. I won't stay in the office.' However, Winston got out of it by lying, and pretending he hadn't approved the orders. Of course if one of them has to go, it would be Winston. Public opinion wouldn't stand Jacky's being turned out because he didn't get on with W. It would have to be the other way about.[23]

Fisher's dissatisfaction with Churchill's methods is evident in a letter he wrote to Balfour on 4 January. He stated:

> I've been within an ace of leaving, but this is absolutely between ourselves. Like Lord John Russell Winston feels competent to command the Channel Fleet! and certainly he has amazing courage! But I have had a big explosion yesterday and possibly things may be better but it's difficult for the leopard to change his spots or the Ethiopian his skin! And I really don't contemplate a long stay where I am! (as I said before this is absolutely personal to yourself!).

Fisher also urged Balfour to consider the merits of Hankey's plan for an attack on the Ottoman Empire, which suggests that he was still thinking in terms of a combined operation.[24]

But Churchill was by now eager to follow up the idea of a strictly naval attack. Besides writing to Carden, he sought the opinion of two other admirals, Jackson and the offensive-minded Bayly, now Commander-in-Chief of the Channel Fleet and the designated commander of any future operation along the German coast. Carden was the first to weigh in. 'I do not consider Dardanelles can be rushed', he wrote on 5 January. But he suggested that, 'They might be forced by extended operations with large numbers of ships.'[25] Jackson, however, was more ambivalent. His detailed appreciation, submitted the same day, concluded that a naval force *could* be rushed through the Straits—the course rejected by Carden—but at a heavy cost in ships. The first step, according to Jackson, would be the destruction of the heavy guns at the entrance to the Dardanelles. This would be relatively easy to accomplish, he concluded, since the guns of the fleet had greater range. Once these defences were neutralized, the bombarding squadron, preceded by minesweepers, could begin its rapid passage through the Straits. Jackson predicted that the approach to the 'Narrows', a distance of about twelve miles, would take around an hour, during which time all the unarmoured minesweepers would probably be sunk and the battleships themselves would suffer heavy damage.

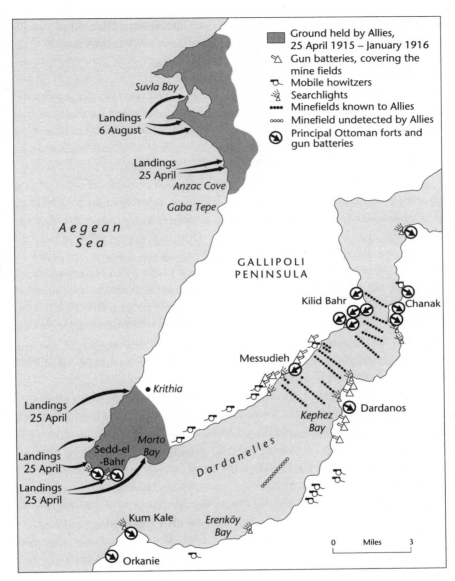

Map 2.2. Gallipoli and the Dardanelles.

Further losses were predicted once the squadron reached the Narrows, the most heavily defended part of the Straits. The fleet could pass through this area in around ten minutes, suffering additional damage along the way. What was left of the squadron could expect to enter the Sea of Marmara around twenty-five minutes later.

Jackson estimated that an attempt to rush the Straits in this manner with a squadron of old battleships would end with six of the eight capital ships out of action, and the remaining two badly damaged. Any cruisers or unarmoured vessels with the squadron would suffer even more heavily. It would therefore be necessary, he advised, to send a second squadron of battleships close behind the first one in order to have sufficient force on hand to deal with the *Goeben* and the rest of the Ottoman fleet, which might be waiting to engage British forces as they emerged from the Straits. Jackson's memorandum only dealt briefly with the possibility that the forts in the Narrows might be weakened by deliberate long-range fire before an attempt was made to rush ships through. This would involve a much larger expenditure of ammunition, but the attacking force would probably suffer less damage on its final charge through the Narrows if the defences could be reduced first. Would such heavy losses be justified? Jackson was not prepared to reject the scheme outright. He acknowledged that a British fleet entering the Sea of Marmara might have far-reaching *political* effects, but he pointed out that it would probably not influence military operations in the Caucasus. In fact, he questioned whether the fleet could accomplish *anything* other than the destruction of the Ottoman fleet. Without troops to occupy Constantinople, Turkish resistance could not be easily overcome. British battleships 'might dominate the city and inflict enormous damage', he observed, but this 'would probably result in indiscriminate massacres'.[26]

This was not an optimistic assessment by any means, but Churchill never needed much encouragement. What probably struck him about the memorandum was that Jackson believed a British fleet *could* reach the Sea of Marmara. The admiral was clearly unenthused about the prospect of heavy losses, but even he admitted that the costs might be reduced by adopting a slower advance through the Straits, as Carden's telegram had suggested. In any event, the possibility of sunk or damaged warships did not alarm Churchill the same way it did his naval advisers. The pre-dreadnought battleships he contemplated using in any such operation were too old to be used against modern German battleships in the North Sea. Britain could therefore afford to lose them without risking Jellicoe's margin of superiority over the German High Seas Fleet in the decisive theatre. And many of these old vessels were due to be scrapped soon anyway—why not let them go down fighting instead? In Churchill's eyes, these ships were *expendable*. He thus wanted to see them doing something—*anything*—to make a positive contribution to the Allied war effort.

On 6 January, Churchill sent a telegram to Carden assuring him that 'high authorities here' agreed with his view that the Dardanelles could be forced by 'extended operations'. He later suggested that the 'high authorities' in question were Jackson and Oliver. Carden was instructed to elaborate on his proposal that a fleet might force a passage through the Dardanelles.[27] Fisher's views are unknown. He may not have been consulted about this telegram. Churchill knew of the admiral's preference for a combined operation, and might have avoided raising the issue with Fisher until he had found supporters. But Fisher's attention may also have been focused elsewhere. On 6 January, the First Sea Lord was greatly worked up by the threat of German Zeppelin raids on London, and threatened to resign if the Cabinet did not agree, as one minister noted, 'to tell Germany that if they do this we will shoot all German prisoners here!'[28] Fisher may not have realized that Churchill was beginning to gather professional support for a purely naval assault on the Dardanelles.

As Carden began drawing up a detailed plan, Bayly's views arrived at the Admiralty. Bayly was predictably enthusiastic about a naval offensive—*any* offensive—and probably hoped to command it himself using ships from the Channel Fleet. Like Jackson, he assumed that a British squadron of pre-dreadnought battleships would attempt to pass through the Straits as quickly as possible. The most serious obstacle, he accurately predicted, was not the Turkish forts but the minefields. The fleet would therefore have to be preceded by destroyers and fast steamers fitted as minesweepers. Like Churchill, Bayly preferred not to dwell on potential difficulties. If he expected to incur heavy losses passing through the Straits, he kept this detail to himself. Once a British squadron had broken through, the admiral advised against any attempt to occupy Constantinople using men from the fleet. The navy, he suggested, should concentrate instead on destroying the Ottoman fleet, stopping the movement of troops between Europe and Asia, keeping the Dardanelles open for the passage of ships, and possibly transporting Russian troops across Black Sea.[29]

There is no record of Churchill's reaction to these proposals, but it is hard to imagine that such unqualified support for a Dardanelles offensive did not fuel his interest in the project. Notably, however, he did not press his advisers to adopt Bayly's plan. Nor did he mention it in his memoirs. He may have appreciated the advantages of a slow, methodical advance through the Straits, or he may simply have assumed that Carden's more cautious approach stood a better chance of winning support from Fisher and the naval staff. Whatever the reason, he was undoubtedly influenced by the fact that Bayly's star was now falling fast. In the early hours of 1 January, the old battleship HMS *Formidable*, part of the Channel Fleet, had been torpedoed and sunk by a German submarine in circumstances that reflected badly on the Commander-in-Chief. Bayly was soon relieved of his command, which effectively killed his hopes of leading an expedition either to capture Borkum or to force a passage through the Dardanelles.

While it is often suggested that Churchill was determined to attack the Dardanelles from the moment he asked for Carden's views, his support for the project actually developed gradually and was initially overshadowed by his strong preference for the capture of Borkum. When the War Council met for the first time in the new year—on 7 January—the First Lord did not mention the Dardanelles scheme at all. Instead, he appealed to his colleagues to support the capture of an island on the German coast. He approached the matter cautiously. The explicit backing of the War Council would help him circumvent the ongoing obstruction by the naval staff, but he did not see any advantage in presenting Borkum to his colleagues as the first step in a larger scheme that would end with British troops in Schleswig-Holstein or a fleet in the Baltic. He therefore emphasized, as he had in December, the immediate benefits of establishing a forward base, particularly the ability to prevent a German invasion or raid by maintaining a constant watch on the German coast. He also insisted that he was only looking for authorization for the Admiralty to begin *planning* the operation, which did not commit the War Council to carrying it out. Fisher, who also attended the meeting, did not voice any objections, noting only that the navy would need two or three months to prepare such an operation. With the First Lord and First Sea Lord seemingly in agreement about the project, the Council concluded that the attack was '*approved in principle, subject to the feasibility of the plan being worked out in detail*'.[30]

The War Council took up the possibility of alternative theatres for the British Army when it met again the following day. Kitchener was seemingly unenthusiastic about the idea, and read out a letter from General Sir John French, the Commander-in-Chief of the BEF, suggesting that a stalemate was likely to emerge in any new theatre just as it had on the Western Front. The War Minister suggested, however, that if an attack were launched in the Mediterranean, the Dardanelles would be 'the most suitable objective', since an attack there could be supported by the British fleet. If successful, he noted, Britain could re-establish communications with Russia; settle the Near Eastern question; draw in Greece and, perhaps, Bulgaria and Romania;

and release wheat and shipping now locked up in the Black Sea. Hankey added that success would also give Britain access to the Danube, which would enable an Allied offensive against Austria-Hungary.[31] Lloyd George also spoke in favour of attacking Austria-Hungary and the Ottoman Empire. Surprisingly, given his recent interest in the Dardanelles, Churchill contributed little to the discussion, and only agreed that these proposals should be carefully studied. He did *not* mention that he had, for several days now, been investigating the possibility of an attack by the navy alone, probably out of concern that his Borkum scheme would be dropped if any consensus emerged behind military operations in the eastern Mediterranean. The minutes of the meeting record that Churchill, rather than backing an eastern operation, 'urged' that his colleagues 'not lose sight of the possibility of action in Northern Europe'.[32] He reaffirmed his commitment to making war against Germany a few days later when he wrote to General French that he was strongly opposed to 'deserting the decisive theatre & the most formidable antagonist to win cheaper laurels in easier fields'.[33] The 'decisive theatre' in this case was not, as French understood it, the Western Front, but the war against Germany.

Even with the explicit backing of the War Council, the Borkum project failed to gain traction within the navy. Jellicoe was one of those ill-disposed towards the scheme. He wrote to Churchill on 8 January explaining—for the third time in less than a year—his objections. Borkum probably *could* be captured, he admitted. But since the island was strongly fortified, heavy losses would be incurred in the process. Once taken, the waters around the island would be infested with German submarines, which would inflict steady losses on the British ships operating there. Worst of all, the losses would ultimately be for nothing, since the proximity of the island to the German coast meant that the enemy would probably have little trouble recapturing it.[34] Churchill was not swayed by any of this, however. On 11 January he answered Jellicoe with a long defence of his proposal. Capturing the island might be a costly operation, he conceded, but there was no doubt in his mind that Borkum could be held. The key, he maintained, was to transform this new base into 'the most dreaded lair' of submarines 'in the world, and also the centre of an active mining policy'. Yet, despite his confidence that British submarines could inflict serious losses on the enemy in the Heligoland Bight, the First Lord was seemingly unconcerned about the corresponding threat to British surface ships from German submarines, which, as Jellicoe pointed out, would be operating near their own bases. 'This is the only aggressive policy which gives the Navy its chance to apply its energy and daring', Churchill insisted, 'and in six weeks of fierce flotilla fighting we could beat the enemy out of the North Sea altogether.'[35] But there was nothing new here to sway the admiral. These were the same arguments Churchill had been making for months, and he could have had little hope that Jellicoe would be suddenly converted by this latest appeal.

The only senior admiral to consistently support the idea of operations in the Heligoland Bight was Bayly, but the loss of *Formidable* effectively removed him from the debate. Nothing could be done to save him from the loss of his sea-going command, as even Churchill had to admit that the admiral had 'outraged every principle of prudence and good seamanship without the slightest military object'.[36] Churchill was nevertheless determined to press forward. He insisted that the Admiralty should begin serious planning for the operation. Oliver was against the idea, but Wilson was evidently willing to begin working out the details. The task was eventually delegated to Richmond in the Operations Division, who was aghast at the idea. In his diary, he complained that the whole concept was '*quite mad*':

> The reasons for capturing [Borkum] are NIL, the possibilities about the same. I have never read such an idiotic, amateur piece of work as this outline [by Churchill] in my life. Ironically enough it falls to me to prepare the plans for this stupendous piece of folly. . . . I sincerely hope I shall not be invited to take any part in the enterprise.[37]

Richmond confided to his wife that he intended to undermine the project by putting 'the requirements of ships & men so high that they will be considered impossible'. So serious were his doubts that he also proposed to voice his objections to Hankey, in hopes that the Secretary to the War Council would convey them to the Prime Minister. In Richmond's opinion, the fact that plans were being prepared at all was a severe indictment of both Fisher and Wilson, whom he expected to oppose Churchill's 'wild schemes'.[38]

Richmond's spirits improved the following day, 5 January, when he was told by Captain Thomas Crease, Fisher's naval secretary, 'that the 1st Sea Lord didn't intend to have the Borkum business done . . . Crease said they can go on getting out their plans as much as they like, but Jacky is simply not going to do them in the end'. Richmond was relieved, telling his wife afterwards that 'he felt quite happy & worked away at the plans with quite a light heart, now he knew they wouldn't be carried out!'[39] This incident says a great deal about how dysfunctional the decision-making process at the

Admiralty was in early 1915, and about the methods employed by Fisher. The First Sea Lord was evidently content to allow the naval staff to waste time planning operations he had no intention of allowing; he did not warn Churchill that he intended to prevent the project being carried out; and, most remarkably, when Churchill advocated the scheme at the War Council on 7 January, he did not voice any objections and appeared to give the scheme his tacit support. Fisher could easily have killed the Borkum project simply by declaring his firm opposition, but for reasons unknown he decided against this course, preferring to keep both the naval staff and the First Lord in the dark as to his real intentions.

This duplicity did not go unnoticed. Richmond was surprised and dismayed four days later to learn that the War Council had endorsed the idea of capturing Borkum. Hankey explained to him that both Fisher and Wilson had attended the meeting, but that the two admirals 'had sat absolutely mum only looking grumpy, while Winston dilated on his plan'. Moreover, they had 'allowed Winston to persuade everybody else'. Richmond was indignant, complaining afterwards that 'Fisher talks very big in his own room about putting his foot down and not having it, but when it comes to the point, he says nothing & lets Winston have all his own way.'[40] Oliver, the Chief of the War Staff, was also opposed to the Borkum scheme, but Richmond held out little hope that this would make a difference, as Oliver was seemingly powerless to impose order on the Admiralty's decision-making process. As Richmond told his wife:

> Oliver says himself that his time is wholly taken up with trying to manage 'two stupid old men & one raving lunatic'. He says 'I play them off against one another'—& his efforts to prevent any of their stupid or wild schemes to be put into execution really occupies him to the exclusion of anything else. It doesn't sound an ideal system to be running a great war on—when the junior member of the Board of Ad[miral]ty is solely occupied in preventing the other members from bungling things![41]

The chorus of complaints from senior members of the naval staff points to a 'system failure' at the Admiralty by early 1915. The responsibility for this state of affairs rests primarily with Churchill, who had constructed the system and selected the individuals who filled the senior posts. At the root of the problem was his desire to dominate the central decision-making process and initiate major operations himself, even when he encountered opposition from senior officers. The Second World War would show that Churchill's energy and imagination could be effectively harnessed for the benefit of the war effort when he was surrounded by strong and capable advisers who knew how to deflect him from dangerous projects. The situation was very different in 1914–15. The two senior admirals at the centre of the system, Fisher and Wilson, were not effective at 'managing' their political chief. Nor did they provide effective guidance to the Admiralty staff. The result, all too often, was confusion and friction.

And yet Churchill encountered enough opposition from his subordinates that he never succeeded in achieving anything approaching complete control over naval policy and strategy. Despite the War Council's support for the Borkum project in early January, Churchill realized that he would have difficulty pushing the scheme through the Admiralty or obtaining the cooperation of Jellicoe and the Grand Fleet. He was therefore probably in a receptive frame of mind when Carden's plans for a systematic and deliberate assault on the Dardanelles crossed his desk on the morning of 12 January. Carden proposed to subject the forts inside the Straits to heavy direct and indirect fire, beginning with the outer forts and proceeding by stages to the strong defences at the Narrows. Good aerial reconnaissance was essential, and a massive amount of ammunition would be required. During each phase of the operation, the bombarding ships, preceded by minesweepers, would gradually close to 'decisive range' to effect the final destruction of the opposing forts. This would be accompanied by the progressive sweeping of the minefields until a passage was cleared and the fleet could proceed to the Marmara. Depending on the state of the enemy's morale and weather conditions, Carden predicted that the attacking force 'Might do it all in a month about.'[42]

This was everything Churchill could have hoped for. Carden, a vice-admiral with recent experience in the eastern Mediterranean, raised no doubts about the feasibility of the project or the losses that might be suffered, and he avoided the awkward question of what a fleet could accomplish once it had passed through the Dardanelles. Churchill now threw his weight behind the new project. Carden's telegram was discussed that day by members of the Admiralty 'War Group', although no minutes were taken of the meeting, making it impossible to know for certain what happened. Churchill always maintained that both Fisher and Oliver 'seemed favourable' to Carden's plan.[43] This appears to be accurate. Oliver never concealed in later years that he had supported the Dardanelles scheme. Fisher, on the other hand, had probably given the matter little consideration in the days before Carden's plan arrived, and may have simply been carried along by his chief of staff's favourable views. In the event, there is no record of any member of the War Group objecting. The offensive plans Churchill had previously backed for operations in the North Sea had all been met by obstruction or indifference from his naval advisers, and if Admiralty officials had wished to kill this new project they could easily have employed the same tactics. But instead of obstructing the scheme, Oliver helped it gain momentum by suggesting that Britain's latest super-dreadnought, HMS *Queen Elizabeth*, should be assigned to the operation. Fisher evidently agreed. He wrote that same day to Oliver supporting the idea that this new battleship, which was about to begin its gunnery trials, should direct its fire at the Dardanelles forts rather than 'uselessly into the ocean at Gibraltar'.[44] When Admiral Jackson was instructed to evaluate Carden's proposal, his response, submitted a few days later, began with the statement: 'Concur generally in his plans.' Jackson's main concern was the huge supply of ammunition that would be required to silence all the Turkish guns lining the Straits. He was, nonetheless, committed to proceeding with the first stage of the operation, the reduction of the outer forts, 'as the experience gained would be useful'.[45]

The absence of evidence of dissent at this stage has not stopped many historians from claiming that naval opinion was strongly if not unanimously against a purely naval attack on the Dardanelles. And if this claim is accepted, the only explanation for the operation proceeding must be that Churchill overrode Fisher and his other advisers. According to Geoffrey Penn, for example, Fisher had 'little option' but to go along with the project. The decision was taken 'by the First Lord, using his ultimate power of veto. Fisher had been overruled. He would never have agreed.'[46] In fact, Fisher did have options. If he truly disliked the proposal at this stage he could have refused to support it! Churchill could not have forced his consent. And it does not appear that he had to. After discussing the Dardanelles plan with members of the War Group on 12 January, Churchill prepared a minute for Fisher and Oliver that would have reflected the conclusions they had previously reached. This document made no attempt to persuade the two admirals of the scheme's feasibility, which suggests that there was, in fact, a tacit consensus that the Carden plan was worth pursuing. Churchill's minute moved directly to the question of which ships should be allocated to a Dardanelles offensive. On this point, he felt it necessary to reassure his advisers, and Fisher in particular, that nothing would be done to weaken the Grand Fleet. Of the fifteen British capital ships he tentatively earmarked for the offensive, only four would be taken from home waters, and these, he noted, were old ships 'already ordered to be dismantled'.

Another interesting feature of this document is Churchill's apparent assumption, which clearly influenced Jackson's subsequent appraisal, that the bombardment of the outer forts did not commit the navy to subsequent operations *inside* the Straits. 'It is not necessary', Churchill wrote, 'to develop the full attack [on the inner defences] until the effect of the first stage of the operation has become apparent.'[47] He was clearly alive to the possibility that the initial attacks might not go as planned, in which event he envisioned the remainder of the project being abandoned. Fisher and Oliver were therefore advised that the full fleet allocated to the operation should not be assembled at the outset. Some of the battleships required for the attack inside the Straits should be deployed elsewhere at first, Churchill suggested, so as not to 'accentuate failure, if the [outer] forts prove too strong for us'. He also proposed that the initial naval assault should be combined with an operation to seize the Turkish port of Alexandretta. As he later informed Kitchener, if the Dardanelles attack had to be abandoned, it could then be represented 'as a mere demonstration to cover the seizure of Alexandretta'.[48]

These sensible proposals were the extent of Churchill's 'meddling' in the early stages of planning the Dardanelles offensive. Over the first six months of the war the First Lord had frequently instructed his professional advisers on how to seize an island along the German coast, but in January 1915 he was content to accept Carden's plan and let the naval staff work out the details, presumably because no effort seemed to be required on his part to ensure that operational planning would proceed. There is some truth, therefore, in his later claims that 'Right or wrong, it was a Service Plan.... At no point did lay or civilian interference mingle with or mar the integrity of a professional conception.'[49] It should also be noted that Churchill's sudden enthusiasm for a Dardanelles offensive did nothing to diminish his interest in capturing Borkum. It has often been suggested that Churchill was so enamoured of this new project that he immediately forgot the old one, but this is wrong.[50] One of the attractions of Carden's plan for Churchill was that the operation was only expected to last around four weeks. There was no possibility of a combined operation in the North Sea until the weather improved and the new monitors were ready, which would take several months. Churchill therefore assumed that the Dardanelles project would not interfere with a northern offensive in April or May 1915. The Dardanelles campaign was to be a *prelude* to operations in the North Sea and Baltic, not an alternative to them. Indeed, a successful campaign against the Ottomans would help Churchill overcome opposition to the Borkum project by demonstrating to sceptics that offensive naval operations *could* be undertaken in enemy–controlled and heavily defended waters.

With few exceptions, historians have not appreciated that Churchill initially expected the Dardanelles campaign to be a short and relatively minor operation.[51] This misconception arises in large part from Churchill's deliberate misrepresentation of his views after the war. An accurate appraisal can be found in an early draft of *The World Crisis*, where he explained that the difficulty he faced with the Borkum scheme in January 1915 was that 'many months would be required before any decision other than preparation and study need be taken':

> Meanwhile the naval operation at the Dardanelles, which was a far smaller and less formidable business, would either fail or succeed.... If it succeeded, we should gain the prestige, which alone would enable so terrific and deadly a business as the storming of Borkum...to be carried out.... [E]ven while the Dardanelles was on I always regarded it as [long] as I was in power only as an interim operation, and all the plans for the Borkum-Baltic project were going forward.[52]

But Churchill had second thoughts about revealing his true motives, and this passage was dropped before the volume was published. The reasons are not difficult to surmise. He could not risk giving the impression that he had gone into the Dardanelles campaign with his attention focused elsewhere, or that he badly underestimated its requirements. The Borkum project was therefore abruptly dropped from his narrative, creating the misleading impression that it had been at first overshadowed and then quickly replaced by the Dardanelles.

This is not to suggest that Churchill was in any way half-hearted about the Dardanelles. Once he concluded that his naval advisers were on board, he threw himself into the project with all his characteristic zeal. This was, after all, precisely the sort of offensive project he had been chasing since the war began, and he was determined to make the most of the opportunity. Selling the idea to the War Council did not prove difficult. When this body met on 13 January, the First Lord, accompanied by Fisher and Wilson, presented Carden's scheme in a favourable light. Since the guns of the fleet could outrange the heavy guns of the Ottoman forts, there appeared to be virtually no serious risk to the ships from enemy gunfire. The dangers would be further minimized by employing mostly old (i.e. expendable) battleships, although three modern, heavy-gunned ships would also be on hand to destroy the larger and more modern Turkish guns. Two battle cruisers (necessary to catch and destroy the

Goeben) and the *Queen Elizabeth* were initially allocated to the operation. The new battleship would not, however, be sent through the Straits. Churchill reassured his colleagues that this large squadron could be assembled in the eastern Mediterranean without impairing Britain's critical margins in the North Sea. Once the forts had been systematically neutralized, the minefield could be swept, and there would be nothing to stop the fleet proceeding to Constantinople and destroying the *Goeben*.[53]

A frequent criticism of Churchill is that he withheld critical information from the War Council on 13 January and supressed his advisers' doubts about the feasibility of the operation. It is worth emphasizing, therefore, that there is no evidence that Fisher had expressed any dissent prior to the War Council. Nor did he raise any objections while Churchill was unfolding his proposal to his political colleagues. The most that can be said with certainty about this meeting is that Churchill glossed over or ignored the issues we know Jackson had raised in his memorandum of 5 January. However, by this time some of the admiral's concerns had, in fact, been addressed. First, the fleet was only to undertake a slow, methodical advance rather than a 'rush' through mined waters. Second, the operation was to be called off if it did not go as expected. This considerably reduced the likelihood that heavy losses would be incurred. But Jackson had raised two other concerns that should have received greater attention at this stage than they did. The first was what the fleet could hope to accomplish if it got through. The second was the possibility that the Ottoman defences would remain intact after the fleet reached the Sea of Marmara.

Churchill preferred not to raise these issues, and he does not appear to have attached much weight to them. He would have been content if the operation only resulted in the destruction of the *Goeben* and *Breslau*, so he was not necessarily concerned at first about what else the fleet might do once it entered the Sea of Marmara. But he was nonetheless optimistic that passing a fleet through the Straits would have far-reaching political repercussions. Churchill had a low opinion of the Ottoman Empire. He did not regard it as a first-rate military power; he had doubts about its political stability; and he expected its morale to collapse at the first sign of defeat. The appearance of a British fleet at Constantinople would probably be sufficient, he thought, to knock the Ottomans out of the war entirely. British victories were also expected to transform the diplomatic situation in the Balkans. New allies would flock to the Allied cause, and Greek or Bulgarian armies would rush to finish the job started by the British fleet.

Churchill was therefore disinclined to dwell on the seemingly remote possibility that a British fleet, having passed through the Dardanelles, would have to fight its way back. It is worth noting that he also downplayed the obstacles posed by enemy minefields, concealed field guns, and howitzers. In this case, however, his optimism reflected the views of his advisers, who badly underestimated these obstacles during the early stages of planning the operation.

The War Council was impressed by Churchill's presentation. Hankey, the secretary, recalled in his memoirs that: 'The idea caught on at once. The whole atmosphere changed. Fatigue was forgotten. The War Council turned eagerly from the dreary vista of a "slogging match" on the Western Front to brighter prospects, as they seemed, in the Mediterranean.'[54] Ministers accepted the First Lord's optimistic forecast of the fleet's chances of breaking through the enemy's defences, which appeared to have the support of both Fisher and Wilson. No one felt it was necessary to ask the admirals for their views. One of the chief attractions of the scheme, and a critical consideration for Kitchener in particular, was that the naval bombardment could easily be broken off if it proved ineffective or the fleet suffered a reverse. Nor would it be necessary to worry about finding troops for the operation. The War Council was still divided over the wisdom of using the British Army to open a new theatre of operations somewhere in the east. A purely naval campaign in that theatre would allow the Council to defer any decision on this contentious issue. Sir Edward Grey later recorded that 'the attack on the Dardanelles was agreed to on the express condition that it should be a naval operation only; it was under no circumstances to involve the use of troops.... If the attack on the Dardanelles did not succeed, it was to be treated as a naval demonstration and abandoned.'[55]

Here, then, was a seemingly low-risk venture that might produce far-reaching results. Churchill's colleagues shared his disparaging view of the Ottoman Empire.[56] They also believed that a successful naval offensive had the power to transform the diplomatic and strategic landscape in the Balkans and Middle East. The War Council of 13 January therefore concluded with a decision that the Admiralty should begin preparing *for a naval expedition in February to bombard and take the Gallipoli peninsula, with Constantinople as its objective*.[57] This did not guarantee that the operation would be launched, but it certainly improved the chances. Churchill was naturally eager to maintain this momentum. In a minute prepared for Fisher and Oliver immediately following the War Council, he declared that the Dardanelles operation was 'regarded by the Government as of the highest urgency and importance'.[58] This was probably meant to impart a sense of urgency to the preparations, although he may also have wanted to silence actual or potential objections to the plan within the Admiralty. But contrary to what many accounts suggest, Churchill did not have to bulldoze his way through strong naval opposition from the minute the Dardanelles operation received the War Council's blessing. It is easy, on the basis of testimony provided after the operation had failed, to suggest that Churchill's advisers were against the idea and had to be overborne by the First Lord. But the documents that survive from mid-January 1915 suggest that Admiralty officials continued to give their cautious support. Oliver and Bartolomé believed the concept was sound, while Jackson, as noted earlier in this chapter, presented his view on 15 January that the navy *should* launch an exploratory attack on the forts defending the entrance to the Straits. Even the hypercritical Richmond was receptive to the idea. His diary entry for 16 January criticized Churchill for adhering to 'his silly Borkum scheme', but expressed optimism about the Dardanelles project. 'With our modern long heavy guns we can outrange the Turkish forts', Richmond wrote, '& a useful bombardment can be carried out. If we can force the passage, we have Constantinople open, & the result will I hope be a revolution in Turkey.'[59]

Churchill was probably just as inclined in later years to exaggerate his naval advisers' support for the failed project as they were to distances themselves from it, but the fact remains that their reservations at this time were not so strong that they came out openly against the enterprise. Naturally, they had concerns. But their objections appear to have been held in check at this stage by the understanding that operations inside the Straits would not proceed unless the attack on the outer forts was successful. Naval opinion regarded this first phase of the operation as being relatively free of risk, so there was little disincentive to launch what was generally regarded as a tentative and exploratory attack. The naval staff therefore busied itself working out plans for the offensive. Jackson's comments on the Carden plan, prepared on 15 January, were optimistic about the prospects of neutralizing the four forts at the entrance to the Straits, a view influenced by the deceptively encouraging results of the brief bombardment on 3 November 1914. On that occasion, four capital ships, two British and two French, had each fired eight rounds at the Ottoman forts. One shell hit a magazine in Fort Sedd-el-Bahr, causing a tremendous explosion and temporarily putting the fort out of action.[60] Jackson calculated from this that it would require just ten rounds per naval gun to knock out each of the enemy's heavier guns (6-inch or greater). Given that there were an estimated 200 such guns, some of which would be concealed from view, he concluded that it would be unwise to attempt the operation with fewer than 3,000 rounds of ammunition for the fleet's heavy guns, and a comparable number for the ships' secondary armament.[61]

This was a drastic underestimation. A post-war technical study of the Dardanelles operation concluded that, at a range of around 12,000 yards, just 2–3 per cent the shells fired by the fleet's heaviest and most accurate guns could expect to hit an enemy gun positioned 'end on' (that is, pointed directly towards the ships, thereby offering the smallest possible target). And this was under ideal conditions, with the bombarding ship 'at anchor, with perfect conditions and perfect spotting'. In the actual conditions prevailing in the Straits, where ships were constantly under way, it concluded that the chances of scoring direct hits on guns 'was very remote'.[62] A 'best case' estimate of the fleet's ammunition requirements based on these figures suggests that around 10,000 rounds would be required to destroy all of the enemy's heavy guns. And as historian Robin Prior has pointed out, it would have been prudent to allocate 20,000 rounds— considerably more than the 3,000 estimated by Jackson.[63]

In the week and a half after Jackson completed his memorandum, the War Staff began preparations to assemble a large fleet in the Eastern Mediterranean, including Queen Elizabeth, the modern battle cruiser Inflexible, ten pre-dreadnought battleships, four light cruisers, sixteen destroyers, one seaplane carrier (HMS Ark Royal) with nine seaplanes, twenty-one trawlers for minesweeping, and various other vessels.[64] On 25 January, Churchill informed members of the government that preparations were now well advanced and the operation could begin on 15 February. On the same day, Carden was instructed to let the Admiralty know what else he would need that could not be provided from forces already in the Mediterranean.[65] So far, Churchill appears to have had no reason to think that his advisers were not on board. He had encountered opposition to his plans before, and this was not what it looked like.

The first overt resistance he encountered was not from his naval advisers, but from the French. With planning for the Dardanelles moving ahead smoothly, the First Lord officially informed Britain's allies that an attempt would be made the following month to force a passage through the Straits. The Russians were invited to contribute a naval force to prevent the Goeben and other Ottoman warships escaping through the Bosphorus into the Black Sea; and the French were asked to provide a squadron of battleships for the advance through the Dardanelles.[66] The Russians were enthusiastic about the proposal, but, to Churchill's surprise, it went over badly in Paris. Naval authorities there were annoyed that the British had initiated a major operation in the Mediterranean without first consulting them, in violation of an earlier agreement that the French would have the dominant voice in this theatre. They were also alarmed to learn about the developing British plan to seize Alexandretta. The French hoped eventually to control this area themselves, and the French Minister of Marine, Victor Augagneur, was suspicious of British motives for establishing a presence in the Levant.[67] Churchill was indignant about the prospect of the French taking control of operations at the Dardanelles. 'I only suggested French co-operation out of loyalty and politeness', he complained to Grey when he learned of the French objections.[68] But both sides realized that a compromise was essential. Augagneur met with Churchill at the Admiralty the following week and the matter was amicably resolved. The French accepted British control of the Dardanelles operation, while the British agreed to shelve the idea of an expedition to capture Alexandretta.[69]

Churchill accepted this concession in part because Grey insisted it was necessary to preserve good Anglo-French relations. But he had also been informed by Kitchener that an expedition to take Alexandretta could not be arranged in time to coincide with the attack on the Dardanelles.[70] The British would therefore no longer have an alternative operation they could point to if they needed to disguise failure at the Dardanelles. However, this was evidently no cause for alarm at the Admiralty. The Dardanelles bombardment could still be called off if it failed to achieve the expected results. The naval staff continued working out plans for the Dardanelles as an Anglo-French naval campaign. But even as this crisis was being resolved, another was developing: the First Sea Lord's support for the operation collapsed.

3

'A Great Experiment'

The Dardanelles Plan Approved

When Fisher first championed the idea of a major maritime offensive to capture the Gallipoli peninsula, occupy Constantinople, and force the Dardanelles Straits, he could not have predicted that Churchill would embrace only the naval part of the project. There is no reason to think he was pleased by the unexpected direction the project took, although Ruddock Mackay, Fisher's biographer, suggests that Fisher was so preoccupied with other matters in the first week of January that he probably paid little attention to Churchill's initial efforts to promote a naval attack on the Dardanelles. This would certainly explain why there is no written record of Fisher's opinions at this time. The absence of documentary evidence to the contrary tends to support Churchill's claims that Fisher did not voice strong objections to the project in the critical days before the War Council meeting. As the professional head of the Royal Navy, Fisher had an obligation to represent his opinions clearly and forcefully to the responsible minister. The project could easily have been shut down by the First Sea Lord on 12 January when Carden's plan was discussed by senior officials at the Admiralty. But there is no contemporary record to show that he objected to the Dardanelles offensive when it first came up for discussion. Nor could the other members of the War Group recall any protests when questioned by the Dardanelles Commission in 1916. If the First Sea Lord voiced doubts at this time, they could have made little impression on his colleagues.

This does not necessarily mean Churchill thought the First Sea Lord was *enthusiastic* about the new project. But there are signs that Fisher was initially a willing participant. He had backed the idea of adding the *Queen Elizabeth* to the assaulting force; he approved Churchill's minutes calling for the naval staff to study and prepare for the operation; and he sat alongside the First

Lord when the plan was first pitched to ministers on 13 January. His silence on this occasion is difficult to explain if he really believed the project would end in disaster, as many historians claim. Some have explained this away as another instance of the all-powerful First Lord silencing his helpless professional advisers. Fisher himself always maintained that he did not speak up because he felt it was inappropriate for him to undermine his chief at the War Council. But even if this is true, it does not explain why he did not make these views known to Churchill *before* he took it to a Cabinet committee for approval. Churchill appears to have pressed ahead with preparations for an assault on the Dardanelles believing that his principal naval adviser backed the idea. This is supported by a letter he received from Fisher on 18 January, in which the First Sea Lord enthused about the possibility of landing 750,000 troops in the Netherlands to outflank the German Army in Belgium. He noted, however, that in putting forward this scheme he had 'no wish whatever to cold-douche any projects for our being troublesome to the enemy', and specifically that he was 'not minimizing the coming Dardanelles operation'.[1] This communication would have raised no concerns on Churchill's part that Fisher's commitment to the Dardanelles might be wavering. Indeed, it seems to have been intended to reassure Churchill of his support for an operation for which the naval staff was now busy preparing.

Fisher clearly did have doubts about the wisdom of the project, even if he was not yet ready to articulate them. And these doubts mounted in the week following the arrival of Carden's plan. He first revealed his concerns in a personal letter to Jellicoe on 19 January, in which he worried that the Dardanelles offensive might denude the Grand Fleet of ships '*urgently required at the decisive theatre at home!*' He expressed particular concern about the dispatch of three modern capital ships and a flotilla of destroyers to the eastern Mediterranean. This was a complaint that Jellicoe, who strongly opposed any diminution of his strength, was sure to welcome. The remarkable feature of Fisher's letter, however, is the strength of his opposition. Despite expressing his tacit approval of the Dardanelles to Churchill only a day before, the First Sea Lord now proclaimed 'There is only one way out, and that is to resign.'

> But you say '*no*', which simply means I am a consenting party to what I absolutely disapprove. *I don't agree with one single step taken*, so it is fearfully against the grain that I remain on in deference to your wishes.[2]

This may have been Fisher's view about the Dardanelles all along—and historians often assume this to be the case—but his suggestion that resignation was his only way out has created a misleading impression that he had exhausted all other means to stop the scheme. In fact, he had done nothing. Churchill was seemingly unaware at this time that the First Sea Lord was opposed the scheme at all.

Fisher's campaign against the operation only began in earnest with his letter of 19 January to Jellicoe. The next step might have been a strongly worded letter to Churchill outlining his objections to the project, but Fisher preferred not to confront the First Lord directly. This is how he had dealt with the Borkum project, which was strongly disliked by the naval staff, and he employed the same methods now with the Dardanelles, a project that had achieved some measure of support from his naval colleagues. The only difference is that, in this instance, he talked 'very big' to friends and colleagues outside the Admiralty, but not to those inside it. After telling Jellicoe that he was strongly opposed to the project, he set out to undermine it by expressing strong doubts to another confidant, Maurice Hankey. This is often treated as a case of the admiral 'venting' his frustrations to a sympathetic friend, but Fisher was a seasoned intriguer who almost certainly had another audience in mind.[3] As Secretary to the War Council, Hankey had unique access to the Prime Minister and other leading ministers, who generally held his views in high regard. If Fisher intended to influence Asquith, he was not disappointed. On 20 January, the Prime Minister recorded that Hankey had been to see him 'to say—*very privately*—that Fisher . . . had come to him in a very unhappy frame of mind':

> He likes Churchill personally, but complains that on purely technical naval matters he is frequently over-ruled ('he out-argues me'!) and he is not by any means at ease about either the present disposition of the fleets, or their future movements. Of course, he didn't want Winston, or indeed anybody to know this, but Hankey told him he shd pass it on to me.

Asquith knew Churchill well enough to realize that his domineering personality might be creating problems at the Admiralty. 'Tho' I think the old man is rather unbalanced', Asquith concluded, 'I fear there is some truth in what he says . . .'[4] Hankey also hinted to Arthur Balfour, another member of the War Council, that there might be trouble at the Admiralty. Fisher 'frequently disagrees with statements made by the First Lord at our War Council', he confided on the 21st. 'I wish he would speak up.'[5]

Fisher's complaints also made their way to both Kitchener and Lloyd George. The War Minister learned about Fisher's reservations after the admiral revealed his views to Colonel Oswald Fitzgerald, Kitchener's military secretary.[6] Lloyd George learned of his dissent either from Fisher directly, or via Hankey. Frances Stevenson, the Chancellor's private secretary and mistress, recorded in her diary that Fisher had been complaining that Churchill:

> [O]verrules everyone at the Admiralty, even those who have far more experience than he, and that even Admiral Jellicoe is beginning to get uneasy at the orders he receives from Winston. The latter now wishes to take some of the finest ships in the North Sea for operations in the Mediterranean & Jellicoe says if he does this the Grand Fleet will be inadequate for the North Sea. Fisher says they try to argue with him at the Admiralty, but he simply overrides them and talks them down. If he continues in his domineering course they fear there may be a catastrophe.[7]

Surprisingly, Churchill seems to have been unaware of the admiral's campaign to undermine him and the Dardanelles operation.

Hankey's remarks to Asquith suggest that the admiral's determination to avoid a confrontation with his chief stemmed, at least in part, from the admiral's own insecurities, which seem to have been increasing with age. Fisher's frame of mind around this time was described in unflattering terms by Richmond, who had frequent opportunities to observe the First Sea Lord. The admiral, he complained, 'does nothing: he goes home & sleeps in the afternoon. He is old & worn out & nervous. It is ill to have the destinies of an empire in the hands of a failing old man, anxious for popularity, afraid of any local mishap which may be put down to his dispositions. It is sad.' He had complained to his wife two days earlier that 'Jacky hasn't done a hand's turn of work since he came to the Adty. It seems he goes to bed all the afternoon always.'[8] J. A. Spender, editor of the *Westminster Gazette* and a friend of Fisher, later recalled the admiral's own account of the difficulty he had dealing with Churchill:

> 'I am sure I am right. I am sure I am right', he [Fisher] kept repeating, 'but he [Churchill] is always convincing me against my will. I hear him talk and he seems to make the difficulties vanish, and when he is gone I sit down and write him a letter and say I agree. Then I go back to bed and can't sleep, and his talk passes away, and I know I am right. So I get up and write him another letter and say I don't agree, and so it goes on.' Fisher was not quite the unsophisticated seaman in the hands of the dialectician that this narrative might suggest. He had wiles of his own which on his best days made him the equal of any politician that ever lived. But Churchill's wiles and his were on different

planes and Churchill dazed and dazzled him and produced a mental confusion which he was painfully aware of, but unable to clear up.[9]

Asquith later told the Dardanelles Commission that Fisher had told him ' "you know, I am constantly overborne in argument" ' by Churchill. 'He complained of the superior facility of the First Lord in language.' Asquith expressed doubts, however. He reportedly told Fisher that ' "You are quite old enough to take care of yourself. I have sat for nearly ten years on the CID and have never known you to hesitate to express your opinion freely, and cogently and picturesquely." '[10] But while Fisher could still be outspoken at times, Hankey was right about the admiral being reluctant to express his views at meetings of the War Council.[11] This was especially true if they might lead to disagreement with Churchill. When addressing his friends and supporters, Fisher's inclination, as Richmond had noted, was to 'talk very big'. But he appears to have had little confidence in his ability to defend his case against such a forceful and skilled debater as Churchill. And in 1915 he was prepared to go to great lengths to avoid doing so. Where Churchill was concerned, Fisher preferred subterfuge to confrontation.

Fisher's activities over the next few weeks suggest that he hoped to undermine the Dardanelles project by encouraging supporters such as Hankey to work against the scheme behind the scenes, rather than by raising his objections privately with Churchill or openly in the War Council. And he continued to leave the First Lord in the dark about his growing opposition. On the strength of the Grand Fleet, the immediate source of his disquiet, Fisher expressed only mild concern to his chief. On 20 January he wrote to Churchill to convey Jellicoe's concerns about the adequacy of the forces allotted to him. Fisher suggested that the Commander-in-Chief, who seemed to be suffering from a 'temporary depression', should be given additional ships before his anxieties began to spread through the Grand Fleet. Remarkably, however, Fisher told Churchill that, after reviewing the relative positions of the British and German fleets, he believed Jellicoe's strength in 'Battleships, Battle Cruisers and Cruisers...to be overwhelming'. He suggested that the Grand Fleet would benefit from an increase in light cruisers, but the only serious deficiency he noted was in destroyers, where Jellicoe was 'undoubtedly weak'.[12] When Churchill promptly agreed to supply the Commander-in-Chief with much of what he wanted, Fisher agreed that the case he put forward had been met. His reply to Churchill carefully avoided any suggestion that Fisher himself was alarmed about the strength of the Grand Fleet. He recommended to Churchill that the cruiser *Blenheim* and the destroyer flotilla allocated to the Dardanelles be replaced by French destroyers, but even this measure was represented as a means to placate Jellicoe, rather than a matter that Fisher himself regarded as vitally important.[13]

The First Sea Lord struck a completely different note, however, when he wrote to Jellicoe the next day. 'I just abominate the Dardanelles operation', he declared. And he was just as willing to mislead the Commander-in-Chief as he had been Churchill. The First Sea Lord claimed that he had fought 'tooth and nail' against the diversion of modern capital ships and a flotilla of destroyers for the Dardanelles operation, which he labelled 'a serious interference with our imperative needs in Home waters'. To explain why the operation was still going forward, he insisted that the decision had been taken by the Cabinet on political grounds, which made it difficult for him to resist. But he assured Jellicoe that he had not been won over. The only way he could be induced to support the operation, he concluded, would be if it was converted into a joint venture and the army supplied 200,000 troops.[14] It is not clear, however, why Fisher would assume that Jellicoe would be any happier risking British naval supremacy in the North Sea for a combined operation in the eastern Mediterranean than for a purely naval operation.

A few days later Fisher was effusing over the prospects of another combined operation that had been under consideration for several weeks by the War Council: a major drive by the BEF, with naval support, along the Belgian coast all the way to the Dutch frontier. The obvious advantage of this operation from a naval perspective was that the Germans would be denied the use of the Flanders coastline as a base for submarines and flotilla forces. Fisher told Churchill on 23 January that 'really we should fight to the death over this matter [i.e. in the War Council]', but there were doubts there about the wisdom of giving French enough troops to make such an operation feasible. If the army was not assigned this task, the possibility remained that Zeebrugge would be periodically bombarded by the navy alone, an option that held little appeal for Fisher.[15] The prospect of the navy embarking on not one but two coastal operations without support from the army was too much for the admiral, who finally decided he would take a stand. To this end, he enlisted the aid of Hankey and Corbett, who drafted a lengthy memorandum stating his position. On

25 January, his seventy-fourth birthday, Fisher sent Churchill a copy of this document, with a request that it be circulated to the War Council. In a brief covering note, he stated that he had 'no desire to continue a useless resistance in the War Council to plans I cannot concur in'.[16]

Fisher's memorandum was Churchill's first clear indication that his principal naval adviser had developed serious objections to the Dardanelles project. The document began by setting out the principles that Fisher felt should guide British naval strategy in the war against Germany. 'The pressure of sea power to-day is probably not less but greater and more rapid in action than in the past', he proposed, 'but it is still a slow process and requires great patience.' Above all, Britain had to maintain a commanding lead over the enemy in the vital North Sea theatre. 'We play into Germany's hands', he warned', if we risk fighting ships in any subsidiary operations such as coastal bombardments or the attack of fortified places without military co-operation.' It was therefore 'imperative', he wrote, 'and indeed vital, that no operation whatever should be undertaken by the British Fleet calculated to impair its present superiority'. As long as the navy maintained its position in the North Sea, Britain could enforce and gradually strengthen its blockade of Germany. He did not suggest that the resulting pressure would be decisive in itself, but it should, he suggested, eventually force the enemy to accept a fleet action. Since there was nothing to do but wait for the Germans to come out to fight, Fisher insisted that: 'Ours is the supreme necessity and difficulty of remaining passive, except in so far as we can force the enemy to abandon his defensive and expose his fleet to a general action.' He concluded:

> Being already in possession of all that a powerful fleet can give a country we should continue quietly to enjoy the advantages without dissipating our strength in operations that cannot improve the position.[17]

Hankey told Corbett the next day 'how angry our memo. for Fisher had made Winston'.[18] The depth of Fisher's opposition to the Dardanelles project undoubtedly came as an unpleasant surprise to Churchill, who had been under the impression that preparations were proceeding smoothly. The day Fisher's memorandum arrived, the First Lord had sent the Prime Minister, Kitchener, and Grey the final list of ships that Oliver and the naval staff had detailed for the Dardanelles operation.[19] Churchill was also caught off guard by Fisher's desire to take his case directly to the War Council without first discussing it with him. Fisher may have now been armed with a forceful and eloquent statement of his position, but he clearly preferred to let the politicians kill the project for him and not be drawn into a debate with his formidable chief. However, he had not counted on Churchill's resourcefulness. The First Lord had no desire to air his differences with the admiral in the War Council. Hoping to resolve the matter quickly and quietly, he proposed instead to send Fisher's memorandum, along with his response, only to the Prime Minister.[20] A meeting was hurriedly arranged for the three men on the morning of 28 January, immediately before the next War Council, but Fisher had no desire to attend. He warned Churchill that he planned to go instead to his home in Richmond, Surrey.[21] He also sent Hankey with a letter to Asquith the morning of the meeting, informing him of his intended absence. 'I am not in accord with the First Lord', he explained, 'and do not think it would be seemly to say so before the Council.'[22] This was a curious position for Fisher to adopt, given that he was eager to present his dissenting views to the War Council in a memorandum. Fisher also hinted to both Asquith and Churchill that he intended to resign, since there appeared to be no prospect of agreement.

Churchill immediately informed the admiral that both he and the Prime Minister considered his presence at the War Council 'indispensable', a reasonable position given that there was a war on and Fisher was First Sea Lord![23] Fisher relented. Twenty minutes before the War Council was due to convene he arrived for a private meeting with Churchill and Asquith at 10 Downing Street. Both politicians were aware of Fisher's position from letters he had sent them that morning, which clearly stated his bottom line. He would not agree to either the Dardanelles or the Zeebrugge operations *unless* the army cooperated on a large scale. The loss of ships in either venture could only be justified by significant gains on land—the army must permanently occupy either the Dardanelles forts or the Belgian coast up to the Dutch frontier. He now insisted, moreover, that neither the *Queen Elizabeth* nor the proposed two battle cruisers could be spared from the North Sea. His letter to Asquith implied that he was more concerned about the absence of these three modern capital ships from Jellicoe's fleet than he was about the potential loss of pre-dreadnought battleships. 'What will our officers and men say to me', he asked the Prime Minister, 'if I agreed to those 15-inch guns [of the *Queen Elizabeth*] being in Asia Minor when at any moment the great crisis may occur in the North Sea and the German High Sea Fleet be driven to fight by the German Military Headquarters...?'[24] Notably, however, he did not state, either in his memorandum for the War

Council or his letters that morning to Asquith and Churchill, that he had doubts about a British fleet being able to force a passage through the Dardanelles.

Churchill replied to Fisher with a carefully constructed memorandum of his own. He made no attempt to challenge the admiral's position that Britain must not take risks in the North Sea. This was, in fact, an argument that Churchill had made himself on numerous occasions since the outbreak of war. He was fully alive to the consequences of a defeat in the critical theatre. His only difference from the First Sea Lord was over how large a margin of superiority Jellicoe needed. Fisher now seemed to believe that no margin was too large, but this was not a view Churchill was willing to accept. In a letter to Jellicoe the day before, he had tried to dispel the idea that Britain depended solely on numbers for its advantage over the Germans. Even with a superiority of just 5:4 at the recent Battle of Dogger Bank, he noted, the Germans had 'no thought but flight, and . . . a battle fought out on that margin could have only one ending'. Churchill insisted that he would 'not feel the slightest anxiety at the idea of' Jellicoe meeting the enemy fleet with equal numbers.[25] In his response to Fisher, Churchill dismissed the idea that numbers were a problem. To this end, he provided a detailed account of the vessels added to the Royal Navy since the war began, which amply supported his view 'that the strength of the Grand Fleet, which was originally sufficient, has now been greatly augmented and will continually increase'. There was therefore no question, he insisted, of depriving Jellicoe of ships he would need to defeat the German High Seas Fleet if and when it accepted battle. But once the Grand Fleet had been given enough ships to ensure victory, he maintained that other vessels should be treated as 'surplus', especially older battleships that could not fight their modern German counterparts. Those ships, and any others not required for critical tasks like trade defence (he was thinking in particular of the monitors then under construction), must be available, he insisted, 'for special services and for bombarding as may be necessary from time to time in furtherance of objects of great strategic and political importance'.[26]

Fisher might have been able to shake Asquith's confidence in the Dardanelles project had he attacked it on technical grounds, but his argument that excessive risks were being run in the North Sea failed to sway the Prime Minister. In light of the reassuring figures provided by Churchill, the suggestion that the temporary absence of two or three modern capital ships would threaten British dominance in home waters seemed unduly alarmist, as it was. And if Fisher was prepared to denude the Grand Fleet of some ships for a combined operation in the Mediterranean, then the situation might not actually be as bad as he was making out. Asquith was also well aware that Fisher had threatened resignation on numerous other occasions. 'He is always threatening to resign', Asquith remarked on 28 January, '& writes an almost daily letter to Winston, expressing his desire to return to the cultivation of his "roses at Richmond".'[27] If the Prime Minister had realized the full extent of Fisher's opposition to the Dardanelles he probably would have allocated more than twenty minutes to resolving the issue. But the meeting was wrapped up surprisingly quickly, which can be attributed to the fact that Asquith had already sided with Churchill before the discussion began. Fisher, who had previously gone to great lengths to avoid a face-to-face debate with Churchill, probably had no desire to argue it out with not one but two eloquent politicians. At the end of the meeting, Asquith was evidently under the impression he had worked out a compromise by which Churchill would abandon any idea of a naval bombardment of Zeebrugge, and Fisher would withdraw his opposition to the Dardanelles.[28]

The three men went immediately to the meeting of the War Council, where Churchill promptly sought his colleagues' support for the Dardanelles operation, which, he acknowledged, would 'undoubtedly involve some risks'. To encourage their support, he announced that the project was enthusiastically supported by the Russians, and that the French had promised to participate in the attack. The Admiralty's preparations were now far enough advanced, he reported, that the operation could begin in mid-February. Fisher, however, had clearly not accepted Asquith's proposed compromise. According to the minutes, the First Sea Lord interjected to say that he 'had understood that this question would not be raised to-day. The Prime Minister', he stated, 'was well aware of his own views in regard to it.' Asquith pointed out that preparations were now too far advanced for the operation to be 'left in abeyance'.[29] Fisher might have expressed his opposition to the attack at this point, but instead rose silently from the table and moved to leave the room.[30] He was intercepted by Lord Kitchener, who realized that the admiral did not intend to return to the meeting. Fisher recounted the episode to the Dardanelles Commission, recalling that he 'felt so bloody-minded' he began leaving the room. 'I was by the window, and Kitchener got up and came after me and he said "What are you going to do?" I said "I am going to resign; I am never going back to that table."'

Lord Kitchener then urged on Lord Fisher that he (Lord Fisher) was the only dissentient, that the Dardanelles operation had been decided upon by the Prime Minister, and he put it to Lord Fisher that it was his duty to his country to carry on the duties of First Sea Lord...Then he turned on a lot of hot air and said I was the only fellow who could do it, and so on. Then he said 'Look at me where I am—I am not going; you ought to stick to the thing.' He went on with further appeals to me, and it did have an effect upon me.[31]

In his memoirs, published in 1919, Fisher recalled that Kitchener 'was so earnest and even emotional that I should return' that he 'reluctantly' agreed to take his seat again.[32]

Asquith noted afterward that 'old 'Jacky' maintained an obstinate and ominous silence' for the remainder of the War Council.[33] The admiral must have realized by now that he could expect no support. One by one, ministers spoke in favour of the Dardanelles operation. Kitchener stated that the naval attack was 'vitally important. If successful, its effect would be equivalent to that of a successful campaign fought with the new armies.' Balfour, consistently one of the operation's strongest supporters, was excited about the advantages that would flow from an Allied victory:

It would cut the Turkish army in two;
It would put Constantinople under our control;
It would give us the advantage of having the Russian wheat,
     and enable Russia to resume exports.
This would restore the Russian exchanges, which were failing
     owing to her inability to export, and causing great embarrassment;
It would open a passage to the Danube.[34]

'It was difficult', he concluded, 'to imagine a more helpful operation.' Grey also expressed his confidence that success would have a decisive impact on the attitude of neutral states in the Balkans.[35] It was Churchill, rather than Fisher, who turned the Council's discussion to the feasibility of the naval attack. He emphasized that the operation had the support of the admiral responsible for carrying it out, and that the operation was only expected to take 'from three weeks to a month'. Moreover, there appeared to be no danger of the fleet encountering enemy submarines in the eastern Mediterranean. Churchill reported that he 'did not anticipate that we should sustain much loss in the actual bombardment, but, in sweeping for mines, some losses must be expected'. He was referring here only to the first phase of the operation, the attack on the defences at the entrance to the Straits.

'The real difficulties', he continued, 'would begin after the outer forts had been silenced, and it became necessary to attack the Narrows.'[36]

Given how frequently it is suggested that Churchill won the War Council's support by suppressing or misrepresenting the views of his naval advisers, it is worth noting that the overview he provided to the War Council on 28 January accurately reflected the plans being drawn up by the naval staff at this time. There was, as Churchill suggested, little concern at the Admiralty about the attack on the outer forts, which even Jackson thought would entail few risks. Nor did he conceal that the attack on the Narrows might entail 'real difficulties'. Churchill undoubtedly underestimated these difficulties, but ministers were clearly aware that warships would certainly be lost in the attack. However, they were still confident that the operation could easily be called off if it proved more difficult than expected. The only important question that does not seem to have been discussed that day is what would happen if the fleet succeeded in reaching the Sea of Marmara. Churchill was still confident that, at the very least, *Goeben*, *Breslau*, and the rest of the Ottoman navy would be destroyed. And he continued to assume that the appearance of the British fleet at Constantinople would solve any other difficulties that might arise. His colleagues shared this view. If the naval attack went well, there were hopes that enemy's morale might collapse before the Anglo-French fleet even reached the Sea of Marmara. Grey, for example, told the War Council that 'the Turks would be paralyzed with fear when they heard that the [Dardanelles] forts were being destroyed one by one'. If this did not drive the Ottomans out of the war, the arrival of Allied warships at Constantinople was expected to spark a revolution and lead to a hasty surrender. The absence of British troops was not necessarily a problem either. The success of the naval attack would spark a virtual feeding frenzy in the region, as the Balkan states rushed to attack the Ottomans and secure a share of the spoils when the empire disintegrated.

British ministers were so dazzled by these possibilities that they thought the only real challenge would be getting ships through the Dardanelles. But if the Ottomans did not immediately surrender, the guns defending the Straits would remain in place and the minefields would presumably be replenished, making it almost impossible for unarmoured ships to use the passage. In this scenario, the fleet would eventually run short of fuel, ammunition, and supplies, forcing it to fight its way back into the Mediterranean. This was what worried Fisher and Jackson. Churchill did not raise this possibility at the War Council on 28 January. Fisher did not offer his views, nor was he asked for them. If he had spoken up, uninvited, ministers were so confident about the impact of a successful naval assault that they would not necessarily have been alarmed by the prospect of continued Ottoman resistance, which seemed an unlikely contingency. But if Fisher had protested strongly, they would undoubtedly have taken his warnings seriously.

During a break in the War Council's deliberations Churchill met privately with Fisher to firm up his support. 'I had noticed the incident of his leaving table', Churchill later told the Dardanelles Commission:

> After lunch I asked him to see me in my room, and we had a talk. I strongly urged him to undertake the operation, and he definitely consented to do so. I state this positively. (Well I state everything positively, but I state this super-positively.) I mean I would never have set out on this business unless he had definitely agreed to do it, it being recognised that he was not in favour of it as to policy, but he agreed definitely to put it through.[37]

By the end of this private meeting, Churchill was confident enough of the admiral's support that, when the War Council reassembled that evening, he announced—with both Fisher and Oliver at his side—that the Admiralty had definitely decided to 'push on with the project...to make a naval attack on the Dardanelles'. As a concession to Fisher, he also informed the Council that the idea of a purely naval assault on Zeebrugge had been abandoned, although he hinted that the project might be revived once the navy had taken delivery of its new monitors.[38]

Churchill now received the War Council's permission to launch the Dardanelles operation, and he immediately threw himself into the task of seeing that all the necessary preparations were made. But Fisher's heart was still not in it. In the weeks to come, his support was never more than grudging and half-hearted. More importantly, he did not feel bound by any pledges he had made to support an attack by the navy alone. His covert campaign to undermine the Dardanelles project resumed the day after the War Council approved it. The First Sea Lord still reposed great hope in the memorandum Corbett and Hankey had drafted for him, and on 29 January he sent copies to two members of the War Council, Balfour and Lloyd George. In his covering note to Lloyd George, Fisher wrote that the memorandum 'contains the convictions of my life time as regard sea fighting'. To justify his unconventional approach to a Cabinet minister behind the back of both Asquith and Churchill, Fisher hinted that he was being deliberately silenced. He asked that the Chancellor of the Exchequer not mention he had seen the memorandum, as 'no doubt the Prime Minister has some good reason for suppressing it and I am only a cipher!'[39]

Lloyd George replied the next day that the document was 'very impressive—but distinctly disquieting'. He suggested that his 'views ought to be brought to the attention of the War Council', although he showed no interest in taking up the cause on Fisher's behalf, which is undoubtedly what the admiral had wanted.[40] Nor was Balfour moved to take action. The Conservative politician was completely in agreement with Fisher about the need to maintain the superiority of the Grand Fleet, but he shared Churchill's view that Jellicoe already had ample strength and that the navy's surplus forces would be better employed in secondary operations than in over-insuring Britain's position in the North Sea. He was still enthused, moreover, by the benefits that would flow from a successful passage of the Dardanelles. 'The advantages of success—military, political, economical—would be enormous', he wrote a few days later in an uncirculated memorandum. Balfour also felt that the risk to British warships in the Straits was relatively small, given that the fleet's guns could outrange those of the Turkish forts. And even if a ship was lost 'by a lucky shot', he assumed that most of the crew could be saved.[41]

Having failed to win over either Lloyd George or Balfour, Fisher made one more attempt to raise opposition. On 31 January he sent a copy of his memorandum to Andrew Bonar Law, the leader of the Conservative Party. Unlike the previous recipients, Bonar Law was not a member of the War Council. Again, Fisher asked for secrecy, noting pointedly that Asquith had decided against circulating the document. 'Why he has suppressed it is beyond my comprehension', he wrote. 'Anyhow he is the Prime Minister and there's the end of it!'[42] In a postscript, however, Fisher suggested again that he was being deliberately silenced: 'I sent a paper last February to the Prime Minister warning him that German submarines would sink our merchant ships off Liverpool and I was flouted. That paper also suppressed! This is very secret.' Fisher probably calculated that Bonar Law was more likely than Balfour to exploit a rift between the First Sea Lord and members of the Liberal government for political gain, but this approach also failed to produce any immediate results. Fisher wrote to Bonar Law again in March attempting once more to stir up trouble. This time, he sent the politician the memorandum he had written shortly before the war about the submarine threat. Fisher suggested that he should ask Lord Lansdowne, leader of the Conservatives in the House of Lords, to study the document. Again, he hinted that his views were being suppressed. 'As the Prime Minister decided in his discretion not to circulate the enclosed', he wrote, 'I must ask you to keep them secret and not quote them. The vacillations and procrastinations drive me mad! It's a war of "lost opportunities". Our Army should now be at Gallipoli.'[43]

Fisher's most industrious and effective ally was Hankey, who used his position as Secretary of the War Council to ensure that ministers heard the case for allocating troops to the Dardanelles operation. The CID had examined the question of attacking the Ottoman Empire through the Dardanelles in 1906–7, and had decided, after considering the views of both the War Office and the Admiralty, that there were too many risks involved to justify the idea, even as a joint assault. Hankey circulated the minutes of the CID's deliberations to the War Council on 24 January, possibly in hope of casting doubt on the idea of *any* attack on the Dardanelles.[44] The following week, by which time the naval assault had been approved, he refocused his efforts on converting the operation into a combined venture. On 2 February he sent a letter to Asquith, subsequently circulated to the entire War Council, stating that he had been 'immensely impressed' by the scattered statements throughout the Council's recent deliberations that, taken collectively, pointed to the need for '*military* action in the Dardanelles'. Hankey then made the case for troops that Fisher had only hinted at. The strongest argument, in his opinion, was the need to open up a secure line of communications through the Dardanelles and Bosphorus so that Russia could be provided with the supplies it needed to take the offensive. Hankey also pointed to the possibility that the commitment of British troops would draw in Romania, Bulgaria, and Greece, who could collectively contribute over a million troops to the Allied cause. Britain could then use its sea power in the Danube, which raised the possibility of British troops operating against Austria-Hungary. Finally, Russian wheat would again be available for export, which, among other benefits, would reduce the danger of food shortages in Britain and help to keep prices down. The underlying assumption in all this was that Ottoman resistance would *not* collapse when the fleet reached Constantinople. Hankey concluded by drawing attention to Churchill's admission that a successful naval assault could 'open the Dardanelles and Bosphorus to warships, which are more or less impervious to field gun and rifle fire, but they cannot open these channels to merchant ships so long as the enemy is in possession of the shores'.[45]

Hankey launched a second salvo two days later. This time, he enlisted the aid of Corbett, who was asked to prepare a memorandum on the Royal Navy's attempt to force a passage through the Dardanelles in 1807. In his diary, Corbett recorded that the goal was 'to convince K[itchener] & others [that the] fleet must not attempt it alone'. But Hankey instructed Corbett not to reveal in the document that he was aware of its real purpose.[46] Corbett supplied a letter to Hankey the same day, recounting how a British fleet successfully passed through the Dardanelles in 1807 but was unable to reach Constantinople on account of the wind suddenly dying away. The Turks immediately began strengthening their defences and the British admiral was forced to withdraw before the Straits became impassable. Heavy losses were suffered on the return passage, and British prestige was badly damaged. The lesson here was obvious: the operation had failed because the fleet attempted to reach Constantinople without an army to support it.[47] Hankey later told Corbett that he had submitted the memorandum 'at [the] right moment to get [the] War Council to consent to troops going to help the fleet'.[48]

While Hankey used his influence to persuade the War Council to change the plan, Churchill pressed on in the belief that the operation would be carried out as it had been approved—as a purely naval assault. French support had already been secured in principle, but the Admiralty had not yet provided its ally with much in the way of details. Augagneur, the French Minister of Marine, confirmed French participation in the attack on 31 January, albeit without having asked his naval advisers for their views on the operation. The main concern in Paris, it seems, was to ensure that French interests in the region would be protected if the operation succeeded—and that the British could be blamed if it failed.[49] On 2 February, the French were finally provided with an overview of the operation by Admiral Oliver, who was overseeing the planning process at the Admiralty. The chief of staff was committed to a cautious approach. The outer forts were initially to be bombarded by ships anchoring outside the range of the enemy guns. To minimize the expenditure of ammunition, firing would only take place in good weather and light conditions. Once it was certain that the enemy's heavy guns were no longer capable of replying, older battleships would move in and complete the forts' destruction using their secondary armament. Minesweepers operating inshore would be protected from enemy fire by old battleships and various smaller vessels. The fleet could then begin its advance through the Dardanelles.

The challenges during this phase of the operation were not as easy to foresee, but it would clearly be much riskier. Oliver expected the attack to develop along the same lines as did Churchill, as a sort of long-range gunnery duel between the fleet and the Ottoman forts. He was confident that the forts could be systematically destroyed by the guns of the fleet employing a combination of direct fire (i.e. when gunners could see their target) and indirect fire (i.e. when gunners could not observe the target and relied on 'spotters' to guide their fire). Like the politicians, the chief of staff had a low opinion of Ottoman resolve. 'It is expected', he wrote, 'that the slow, irresistible destruction of the forts by vessels which cannot be reached effectively by their fire will have a great effect on the morale of the garrison of those forts which have yet to be attacked.' Furthermore, the fleet's steady progress would 'go far to shake the confidence of the Turks in their German advisers, and it may possibly result in an overthrow of the German rule in Constantinople'.

At this stage of the planning, Oliver did not give careful attention to the problem posed by the enemy minefields, which would prove to be the most difficult obstacle to overcome. This represents probably the most serious failure in planning by the Admiralty. A post-war study by the naval staff concluded that:

> The belief that sweeping a clear channel was a simple task and could be carried out by anyone was then [in February–March 1915] a general one. Under the exceptionally trying circumstances [in the Dardanelles] it would have required high-speed sweepers with efficient gear and a very highly trained personnel to perform the work with any real degree of efficiency.[50]

It is true that the Royal Navy had little wartime experience in sweeping mines along a hostile coast, but concerns had been raised at the Admiralty about the adequacy of the service's minesweeping force. One operation in particular had received close attention. On 23 November 1914, two British pre-dreadnought battleships had bombarded the German-occupied port of Zeebrugge. Eight slow minesweeping trawlers were allocated to the bombarding force. On six of these boats the sweeping gear broke down before the operation began. On the final pair the gear broke down during the bombardment. The admiral commanding the operation was not impressed. He reported afterwards that the 'point in connection with these operations which forced itself upon me most strongly was that mine-sweeping trawlers of the type sent to act with me were practically useless as a protection to my ships'. He recommended that 'faster and better vessels should be employed when acting in conjunction with battleships in any similar operations'.[51] Leveson, then Director of the Operations Division, and Oliver drew the obvious conclusion: that fast minesweepers—often referred to as 'fleet minesweepers'—would be necessary for such operations. The report was seen by Churchill, Fisher, and Wilson [52] The importance of fast minesweepers was ignored or forgotten, however, when the naval staff began planning the Dardanelles operation.

Admiral Carden also badly underestimated the problem of clearing mines in the Dardanelles. He initially calculated that he would need just '12 minesweepers including perhaps 4 fleet minesweepers'. This proved to be far short of the mark. During the first months of the war, the British had lost one minesweeper for every five mines swept.[53] With such a high attrition rate to be expected from mines alone, a force of twelve minesweepers was clearly insufficient to clear the 300-plus mines protecting the Dardanelles. Heavier losses could be expected in the Turkish Straits, moreover, as the minesweepers would also be operating under continuous fire. To make matters worse, the fast 'fleet minesweepers' Carden requested could not be supplied. There were only six of these vessels available to the entire navy when the war began, all of which were urgently needed to support Jellicoe's Grand Fleet. The navy's modest force of fast minesweepers consisted, at this time, entirely of old gunboats at the end of their normal service life. These were supplemented in December 1914 by eight converted fast merchant steamers designated as 'auxiliary sweepers'. One of these was promptly lost, and none proved to be very efficient. The rest of Britain's minesweeping force consisted of slow, heavy draught fishing trawlers like the ones used in the Zeebrugge bombardment in November 1914. In early 1915, these boats were fully occupied in clearing German mines laid in British waters.

The need for fast minesweepers had become obvious in the first months of war.[54] And the Zeebrugge operation had revealed to officials at the Admiralty the inherent limitations of fishing trawlers. 'Trawlers are too slow for sweeping with battleships', Oliver noted at the end of December 1914, just days before the idea of a naval assault on the Dardanelles was first raised. The chief of staff recommended that the Admiralty's initial order for twelve new purpose-built fast minesweepers should be increased to thirty-six. 'Any operations by battleships on the enemy's coast [will] involve extensive mine-sweeping by vessels which can sweep at 10 knots speed', he concluded, 'otherwise they will be sunk by gun-fire. As it is, a considerable loss must be anticipated from mines. Successful operations on the enemy's coast will require large numbers of fast small vessels.'[55] Oliver was thinking, at this time, of inshore operations against Germany, but the accuracy of his remarks would be fully borne out by operations in the Dardanelles. Churchill and Fisher both read and commented on Oliver's minute, so they must have had some idea of the limitations of the existing minesweeping force. And all three knew that the first new fleet minesweepers would not be ready until April 1915, long after the Dardanelles offensive was set to commence.

No one at the Admiralty, including Churchill and Oliver, was seemingly alarmed in February 1915 by the shortage of minesweepers available for despatch to the Dardanelles, or the acknowledged shortcomings of the converted trawlers. Their low opinion of the Ottoman Empire was probably a factor. It is difficult to imagine slow trawlers with relatively inexperienced reservist crews being deployed against an integrated system of coastal defences in German waters, yet no objections were raised to their employment in the Dardanelles. Nor was this the extent of the Admiralty's planning failures. Oliver foresaw that the minesweeping trawlers would come under fire from the many field guns and howitzers lining the Straits and the batteries covering the minefields, but he and the naval staff also underestimated how dangerous this fire would be. They assumed at this stage that the enemy's guns could easily be located by seaplanes and destroyed by naval gunfire. Both calculations were flawed. The Ottoman guns were sited where they could not be hit by the guns of the fleet. The relatively flat trajectory of naval gunfire was little or no use against targets behind hills and promontories or other obstructions. Given that the Ottoman defences along the Straits had been designed specifically to foil a naval attack, planners should have made allowances for this fact. Gunnery experts in the army, who would have had a better understanding of these issues, were not consulted.

The Ottoman guns were also difficult to locate even with good aerial reconnaissance, which was seldom available. At the beginning of 1915, the Royal Navy had only a handful of vessels capable of operating seaplanes— three converted tenders, with just three seaplanes each, and HMS *Ark Royal*, which carried six seaplanes and four aeroplanes. *Ark Royal*, considered too slow for operations with the Grand Fleet, was assigned to the Dardanelles operation. At this stage of the war, the navy had no practical experience using aircraft to spot for ships' guns. It was known that the army had enjoyed some success on the Western Front with air control of gunfire, but in January

1915 the navy could only speculate that seaplanes 'might prove of great value' in spotting for the fleet.[56] On 16 January, Oliver urged that pilots and observers from the *Ark Royal* be sent immediately to the Western Front to gain some practical experience observing artillery fire before the carrier was despatched to the Mediterranean around the end of the month.[57] The ability of the Royal Naval Air Service (RNAS) to provide effective spotting for the fleet was therefore largely a matter of faith at this stage of the planning.

The Admiralty War Staff and Carden's staff in the Mediterranean both seriously misjudged the difficulties that would be encountered clearing the minefields and neutralizing Ottoman defences ashore. Oliver optimistically predicted that the fleet and its minesweepers could expect to reduce the enemy's defences and advance at the rate of 'perhaps a mile a day, perhaps more, perhaps less'.[58] The Admiralty's operational orders, finalized on 5 February, provided Carden with additional details. The destruction of the outer forts was still regarded as a simple and straightforward task, and the Commander-in-Chief was admonished to conserve ammunition and minimize the wear on *Queen Elizabeth*'s valuable guns. The new battleship was nevertheless expected to take a leading part in this stage of the operation, and Carden was reminded that the ship must, under no account, be risked in waters that had not been swept for mines. Oliver predicted that its 15-inch guns would be as accurate and devastating as the German 38-cm howitzers that had destroyed the forts at Antwerp in 1914. The problems that would be encountered sweeping a channel through the minefields continued to be underestimated. The minesweepers were expected to attract considerable fire from concealed guns and enemy troops on both sides of the Straits, but Oliver still assumed that aerial reconnaissance would enable the fleet to lay down effective suppressing fire.

Once the entrance had been cleared of mines, the fleet would begin its advance. This was to be deliberate, methodical, and cautious. 'It is not expected or desired', Oliver wrote, 'that the operations should be hurried to the extent of taking large risks and courting heavy losses.' What the Admiralty envisaged was a 'slow relentless creeping forward of the attacking force mile after mile'. Two battalions of Royal Marines were to be on hand in case landing parties were needed to destroy particular targets ashore. These troops were also to be used cautiously. Carden was told that they 'should not be landed against superior forces or entrenched positions in circumstances where they cannot be efficiently supported by the ships' guns'.[59]

Churchill and Oliver were clearly in accord as to how the operation should proceed. The only significant point over which they appeared to differ was the size of the Royal Marine force to provide landing parties. Churchill was adamant that two battalions were sufficient, while Oliver wanted to draw on the Royal Naval Division to provide a larger contingent. Richmond recorded in his diary on 9 February that he believed Carden:

> [O]ught to have 4000 marines for operations of landing & destroying forts which had been knocked out by ships, torpedo stations, mine directors & cables, searchlights, & so on. Winston refused to send more than 2000. Oliver suggested that it was 'about time the Naval Division earned its keep' & should go out en masse for the business. They are pretty rotten, but ought to be good enough for the inferior Turkish troops now in the Gallipoli peninsula...But no, not one of them will the 1st Lord allow to go. It is hopeless trying to make war with men like these.[60]

Despite these misgivings, Oliver remained a believer in the naval attack. The efforts by Hankey to transform the operation into a combined operation had so far failed to have an impact. The War Council remained committed to an attack by ships alone, and ministers appear to have been cautiously optimistic about the operation's prospects. Asquith was probably expressing the view of most of his colleagues when he wrote on 9 February that: 'I can't help feeling that the whole situation in the Near East may be vitally transformed, if the bombardment of the Dardanelles by our ships next week...goes well. It is a great experiment.'[61]

Churchill's optimism never wavered in the weeks leading up to the attack. If anything, his confidence increased as the execution approached. Violet Asquith later recalled that she had 'rarely seen Winston more completely happy and fulfilled' than after the War Council approved the operation. 'He was wholly pervaded by the plan and talked of little else', she recorded. 'Its possibilities seemed limitless.'[62] His excitement was unmistakable on 16 February when he informed the full Cabinet of the impending assault, now just days away. According to one of the ministers present, the First Lord explained that the Queen Elizabeth:

> [A]nd a large squadron of old battleships armed with new guns are to lie off the town, well beyond the range of the forts' guns, and to batter to pieces at their leisure each fort in turn, until the way through to the Black Sea is clear. No risks are to be run, and the operation may take a fortnight or 3 weeks.... We are promised a military rising and ultimate revolution on the fall of the first fort.

Compared to Churchill's cautious description to the War Council on 29 January, these optimistic predictions bordered on reckless. But the statement he would probably come to regret the most was saved for the end of his presentation, when he declared that the attack had been 'decided at War Council and *he would take all responsibility*'.[63]

4

'I Will Find the Men'

The Plan Remade

Despite the political consensus behind a purely naval assault on the Dardanelles, the idea of employing troops refused to die away. The War Council's decision on 13 January to allow the Admiralty to begin preparing an assault on the Dardanelles did nothing to resolve the thorny question of where Kitchener's new armies should be employed when they were ready. Churchill recoiled from the prospect of using them in futile frontal assaults on the Western Front, but he was nonetheless receptive to the idea of joint army–navy operations along the Belgian coast, a favourite scheme of Field Marshal French. The idea nearly foundered on 7 January when the War Council concluded that there were insufficient forces available to launch such an operation, but the subject was reopened at its next meeting the following week. French, who attended the discussion, insisted that he could both capture and hold the position, although Lloyd George questioned whether any great advantage would be obtained even if the operation succeeded. The Chancellor still believed that better results could be achieved by sending British forces to the Balkans instead. With no troops immediately available for either option, the War Council temporized. Ministers agreed that preparations should begin for an offensive along the Belgian coast, but stipulated that a final decision would not be taken until February. They also decided that a special subcommittee should be set up to investigate alternative theatres for a British offensive in the event, as seemed likely, that the stalemate on the Western Front continued into the spring.[1]

These issues were allowed to drift without any decision for over two weeks, but a consensus gradually emerged in favour of Allied action in the Balkans. The catalyst was a growing fear that Germany and Austria-Hungary were preparing a joint offensive to crush Serbia once the winter weather had passed. Serbia's defeat would be a serious blow to Allied prestige, and would likely destroy any possibility of rallying neutrals to the Allied cause. But bringing the Balkan states into the war was a more difficult proposition than British leaders seemed to realize. Because Greece, Serbia, Montenegro, and Bulgaria had recently fought together against the Ottoman Empire in the First Balkan War (1912–13), there was a tendency to assume a new coalition could easily be formed in the region by holding out the prospect of significant territorial gains for all parties. However, the Balkan states had fallen out after their victory over the Ottomans, and in the Second Balkan War (1913), Greece, Serbia, and Romania had all fought Bulgaria, their former ally. Lingering animosity between Bulgaria and its recent enemies created a serious obstacle to any new Balkan coalition. And with a revanchist Bulgaria standing in the wings, Greece and Romania both had a strong incentive not to commit their armies to war against either the Austrians or the Ottomans. British decision-makers were optimistic, however, that the commitment of British troops to the region would be enough to induce some or all of the Balkan states to enter the war. By mid-January, Asquith, Lloyd George, and Grey were all prepared to send British troops to aid Serbia. Asquith was so alarmed by the future of Britain's ally that, on the 21st, he suggested the creation of a new Balkan front should take priority over the other operations then under consideration, including Zeebrugge and the Dardanelles.[2]

The War Council subcommittee that had been charged with considering alternative theatres did not gather until 28 January, by which time ministers were leaning solidly towards the eastern option. Kitchener chaired the meeting, which was attended by Churchill, Balfour, Lloyd George, General James Wolfe-Murray (the CIGS), and the ubiquitous Hankey, who acted as secretary. Everyone agreed in principle that, as a first step towards aiding Serbia, British forces should be sent to the port of Salonika, on the Aegean coast of Greece. It was generally assumed that this would be sufficient to induce the Balkan states to set aside their differences and enter the war against Austria-Hungary. Failing that, the presence of British troops would encourage Greek participation by acting as a guarantee of Bulgarian neutrality. The only questions that remained were how many men would be available, and when they could be sent. Kitchener held out the possibility that half a million British troops might eventually be deployed to the region, but he warned that, in the short term, the army had little to spare unless it was prepared to withdraw men already committed to the Western Front, which no one considered a serious option. Churchill, who was still lukewarm about the idea of opening a major commitment in the Balkans, suggested that it might only be necessary to commit a single brigade, around 3,000 men, which would provide 'an earnest of our intention to send more'. Such a force would serve a purely political purpose, he maintained, and would not even have to leave Salonika to achieve its goal. Kitchener and Lloyd George believed it would be necessary, however, to follow up this token commitment with a larger force as soon as possible. There was no choice, therefore, but to create the new army from formations that would otherwise have been sent to augment the BEF. French's Zeebrugge offensive was now effectively dead.[3]

The War Council realized this news would not be welcomed by the Commander-in-Chief, but a bigger concern was how the French government would react when it learned that Britain had decided to divert, to the Balkans, troops that had already been earmarked for the Western Front. Lloyd George complained to Churchill the next day that, since Britain had already provided the French with three times as many soldiers as they had been promised before the war, France was not entitled to say where other British troops could be deployed, 'as if we were her vassal'. 'It would be criminal folly', he stated, 'if we allowed it to compel us to look on impotently while a catastrophe was being prepared for the Allies in the Balkans.'[4] Fisher also complained around this time that Britain seemed to be raising its new mass army 'to be the tool of a silly jealous France!'[5] But the fact remained that Britain could not afford to alienate its closest ally. The French were firmly committed to the primacy of the Western Front, and the initial reaction from Paris was not encouraging. The British were able, however, to persuade French leaders that a relatively modest commitment of forces to the Balkans might have far-reaching results. Before the matter was reviewed by the War Council on 9 February, the French had been converted, and even raised the possibility of a joint expedition to Salonika, with Britain and France sending one division each.[6] The War Council was therefore optimistic that a new front could be opened, especially as the Greeks appeared to be willing partners. Although still formally neutral, the pro-Allied government of Eleftherios Venizelos in Athens had agreed to allow the Allies to use the island of Lemnos as a base from which to stage the assault on the Dardanelles. Asquith was confident that the landing of an Allied force at Salonika would bring Greece and possibly Romania into the war, by neutralizing the threat of a Bulgarian attack. Kitchener, who believed that first-rate troops would be required, was even prepared to commit the British

29th Division to the operation. This was a regular army force, previously destined for France, comprised of professional soldiers rather than recent volunteers.[7] All that remained was to secure formal Greek approval.

Britain thus committed itself to two separate operations in the east: a naval assault against the Ottoman Empire and a land campaign against Austria-Hungary. The Prime Minister expected the Salonika operation to begin in March, by which time the Dardanelles offensive would be under way. If all went smoothly, it was assumed that a successful naval attack on the Ottomans would make the Balkan states more amenable to the idea of joining the Allies against Austria-Hungary. Asquith was therefore eager to launch the naval operation as soon as possible.[8] Throughout these deliberations, no thought was apparently given to whether a single combined operation against one enemy would be preferable to separate naval and military campaigns against two foes. And there were so many obstacles to finding the troops for Salonika that ministers appear to have given little thought to how they might find even more men for the Dardanelles. What thought they did give this matter was probably the result of Hankey's memoranda to the War Council during the first week of February. These documents had failed to produce the desired result, but the Secretary to the War Council was not easily dissuaded. Over the next week he continued his efforts to turn the Dardanelles into a combined operation by lobbying individual members of the War Council. On 10 February, he informed Balfour that he was:

> [C]onvinced that an attack on the Dardanelles is the only extraneous operation worth trying. From Lord Fisher downward every naval officer in the Admiralty who is in the secret believes that the Navy cannot take the Dardanelles position without troops. The First Lord still professes to believe that they can do it with ships, but I have warned the Prime Minister that we cannot trust to this.[9]

At the Admiralty, Oliver seems to have remained optimistic about the prospects of a naval attack, but by mid-February there undoubtedly were growing concerns over the absence of troops for the operation. The most prominent critic was Jackson, who had never been more than a cautious supporter of the plan. On the 15th, he produced a long memorandum for Carden containing detailed recommendations for overcoming the Ottoman defences lining the Straits. At the end of the document, Jackson advised Carden to have transports and military forces ready at short notice to participate in the operation. Jackson now seemingly contemplated a very different type of attack to the one the naval staff had spent the last month planning. He advised that the Ottoman forts could only be destroyed by putting ashore 'strong military landing parties with strong covering forces'. He was presumably thinking that more would be required than just a few battalions of Royal Marines. To ensure the operation's success, he maintained that it would be necessary to do more than just knock out the guns in the Turkish forts—troops would also have to occupy the Gallipoli peninsula so that unarmoured vessels would be able to use the Straits. Carden, who had no control over the military forces assigned to the operation, could not have been heartened by Jackson's conclusion that the 'naval bombardment' he was about to launch was not 'a sound military operation, unless a strong military force is ready to assist in the operation, or, at least, follow it up immediately the forts are silenced'.[10]

Richmond independently came to the same conclusion. He had prepared a memorandum the day before that also argued for troops to ensure the operation's ultimate success. He did not dispute the idea that ships might be able to force a passage through the Dardanelles, but he questioned what this would accomplish. The fleet 'may pass into the Black Sea and so give Russia the command there', but he warned that 'we shall have performed our task incompletely and shewed the Turks the real limitation of sea power divorced from military power'. The best course, he suggested, would be to send out a strong British Army to attack the Ottomans in conjunction with Greek and Russian forces.[11] Richmond gave a copy of this memorandum to Fisher and Hankey. Both were impressed. Hankey described it as 'absolutely A1', and suggested that, in sending his memorandum to the First Sea Lord he was 'preaching to the converted, although it may help to ginger him up'. Fisher replied the same day that 'Your paper is excellent!'[12]

Hankey was hopeful by now that his campaign to obtain troops for the Dardanelles was bearing fruit, and he assured Richmond that 'things are much better than you think'.[13] The reason for his optimism was that Asquith was coming round to the idea that troops should be found for the Dardanelles. On 13 February, the Prime Minister had revealed to Venetia Stanley, a friend of his daughter with whom he had become infatuated, that he had:

[J]ust been having a talk with Hankey, whose views are always worth hearing. He thinks very strongly that the naval operations...should be supported by the landing of a fairly strong military force. I have been for some time coming to the same opinion, and I think we ought to be able without denuding [Field Marshal] French to scrape together from Egypt, Malta & elsewhere a sufficiently large contingent [for the Dardanelles]. If only these heart-breaking

Balkan States could be bribed or goaded into action, the trick wd. be done
with the greatest of ease & with incalculable consequences.[14]

Asquith evidently had no desire at this time to divert troops from the Balkan
expedition for the Dardanelles, but this began to change as his plans for an
expedition to Salonika began to crumble. The cautious Greeks were not as
eager to join the war as Allied leaders had thought, and the offer of two
Allied divisions was not enough to win them over. On 15 February, Greece
informed the British and French that it was remaining neutral. The plan to
send Allied troops through Salonika to aid Serbia had to be dropped.

The impact on British strategy was immediate. The War Council had
initially backed the idea of a purely naval assault on the Dardanelles on the
assumption that no troops were available to support the operation. However,
by mid-February, ministers had not only learned that forces could be spared
from the Western Front, but that the War Office was ready to send a full
division of regular troops to open a new theatre in the eastern Mediterranean.
When the planned expedition to Salonika was suddenly abandoned,
Hankey's persistent lobbying ensured that attention turned to the possibility
of employing these forces at the Dardanelles. Asquith was the driving force
behind this fateful change of strategy. On the afternoon of 16 February, the
Prime Minister met informally with one or two of his ministers. Hankey,
who was not present, recorded later that other ministers were 'subsequently
called in' to take part in the discussion. Six of the ten members of the War
Council ultimately participated in Asquith's impromptu meeting, including
Churchill, Fisher, Kitchener, Lloyd George, and Grey. No minutes were
taken. By the end of the discussion, a decision had been reached, notwith-
standing the absence of nearly half the Council's members, that a military
force would be assembled 'in case of necessity' to back the naval assault on
the Dardanelles, this force to include the British 29th Division, Australian
and New Zealand troops then stationed in Egypt, and the Royal Marine
battalions already allocated to the operation.[15]

It was unusual for the War Council to reach such a big decision so quickly,
but the informality of the process is typical of how the British government
was still directing its strategy six months into the conflict. Churchill's precise
part in this momentous decision is not recorded. He would later claim that
he had not been responsible for the commitment of troops to the operation,
which is not entirely true. He may not have been the driving force behind
it, but he was undoubtedly present when the decision was taken, and it is
unlikely that he expressed any dissent. The commitment of British and

imperial land forces by an informal meeting of the truncated War Council represented an important turning point in the evolution of the Dardanelles campaign, and the tacit abandonment of Churchill's original plan for a purely naval offensive. The army was now committed to the theatre, which all but ensured that troops would eventually be employed in some capacity. But the War Office had not recently examined its requirements for a land campaign against the Ottoman Empire in support of the navy. And no thought was evidently given by anyone as to whether the naval assault should be held up so that the army might seize the Gallipoli peninsula in conjunction with the navy's passage through the Straits. This would have entailed a delay of several weeks at least while the necessary troops were dispatched to the eastern Mediterranean and shipping was assembled to carry them to the enemy's coast. The navy, however, had been preparing its attack for weeks, and was only days away from starting. Rather than hold everything up, the naval operation was to proceed as originally planned.

Churchill seems to have welcomed the decision to provide troops, and particularly relished the idea of using elements of the Royal Naval Division. Violet Asquith recorded in her diary that her friend was 'thrilled at prospect of the military expedition & full of plans for landing them in Gallipoli when the teeth of the situation had been drawn by the ships—marching them into Constantinople "That will make them sit up—the swine who snarled at the Naval Division." '[16] But while Churchill was undoubtedly excited about the prospect of having troops on hand, he remained confident that the navy could force the Straits without military assistance. The army was only needed, in his opinion, to exploit the navy's victory. He told Kitchener on 18 February, the day before the naval assault began, that an army of 50,000 men should be gathered 'either to seize the Gallipoli peninsula *when it has been evacuated* [of Ottoman forces], or to occupy C'nople if a revolution takes place'. He did not mention the possibility that the army might be used to secure the fleet's passage, and had probably given it little thought. But he clearly recognized that, even if the naval operation prospered, there were some things that the ships could not do, such as occupy a city. 'We shd never forgive ourselves', he told Kitchener, 'if the naval operations succeeded & the fruits were lost through the Army being absent.'[17]

What the politicians on the War Council expected the army to contribute is not known. But Kitchener, like Churchill, envisioned the campaign unfolding in two distinct stages: a naval assault followed by the landing of troops to consolidate the navy's victory. 'You get through!', he reportedly told Churchill,'I will find the men.'[18] The two service ministers were agreed at this stage that the army was not needed to ensure the fleet's passage through the Straits. But controversy quickly developed over the employment of the British 29th Division. If troops were only needed to occupy abandoned positions or garrison the capital of an already-defeated enemy, Kitchener did not believe that regular forces were essential. When the War Council met on 19 February, he proposed to substitute Australian and New Zealand troops in Egypt, equivalent to an army corps, for the elite British 29th Division. Kitchener did not rule out the possibility that the latter might *eventually* be committed to the operation, but he was alarmed by recent heavy Russian losses, which raised the possibility that the Germans might rapidly transfer forces west for a big attack in France or Belgium. He therefore preferred to hold back the 29th Division until it was certain that reinforcements were not urgently needed for the BEF.

Churchill was upset by this development. If a division of British regular troops could be spared from the Western Front, he wanted them for the Dardanelles. The presence of these first-rate troops in the east might, he suggested, make the difference between success and failure, but the absence of just one division from France was unlikely to have much impact. Churchill received some support from Asquith, Lloyd George, Grey, and Balfour, who were all eager to see the Dardanelles operation succeed, but Kitchener refused to budge—and his colleagues were not willing to overrule him. The field marshal insisted that he was willing to send the 29th Division later if its presence appeared to be critical, but he held that the Australian and New Zealand forces should be sufficient in the meantime. As usual, Kitchener had his way. At the end of the meeting, it was agreed that the Commonwealth troops were to be despatched to Lemnos, and no final decision was taken on the 29th Division. At Churchill's suggestion, however, the preparations for carrying this force to the Mediterranean were to continue so that no additional time would be lost if the decision was later taken to send it. In four or five days, he noted, the situation in the east should be much clearer.[19]

While the fate of the 29th Division was being debated in London, Carden's attack on the outer defences of the Dardanelles was getting under way. The admiral had a significant force at his disposal, including the *Queen Elizabeth*, two modern battle cruisers, fourteen pre-dreadnought battleships, and a French squadron of four pre-dreadnought battleships. The objective on the first day of the offensive was to destroy the four forts defending the entrance to the Straits, two on the Asiatic side and two on the tip of the

Gallipoli peninsula. Planners had always assumed that the outer defences would be the easiest to deal with, and their hopes were not disappointed. Conditions for this phase of the operation were everything Carden could have hoped for. As predicted, the big guns of the battleships outranged the guns of the forts, so there was no danger of ships being hit during the opening stage of the bombardment. The absence of mines and submarines outside the Dardanelles meant that warships not only had complete freedom to manoeuvre during this phase, they could also drop anchor and remain stationary while firing, which considerably improved their accuracy. The initial attack therefore got off to a promising start. Each of the bombarding ships positioned itself to fire on one of the enemy forts, while another ship, at right angles from the target and at a safe distance, spotted its fire and signalled the necessary corrections. The Allies were able, as expected, to shell the enemy forts at long range without encountering any return fire. After several hours, the bombarding ships moved in to lay down even heavier and more accurate fire using their secondary armament. This brought them within range of the enemy guns, and it was no longer possible to remain stationary while firing. Everything continued to go according to plan. By late afternoon, one of the forts on the Asiatic shore, Kum Kale, appeared to be completely out of action, and the other forts had taken numerous hits. But when Allied warships moved in to 'decisive range' to effect their destruction, they were subjected, for the first time, to heavy return fire.[20]

This was the first clear indication that ships would have to do more than hit the enemy forts to silence them. To ensure the guns were destroyed, each one would need to be knocked out individually. But these were very small targets, and scoring a direct hit on each would be a time-consuming process requiring a massive expenditure of ammunition. Still, when the first day's operation was suspended on account of failing light, the results were encouraging. The enemy's defences had been shelled without interruption all day, at least one fort had apparently been demolished, and, most importantly, not a single Allied warship had been hit by Turkish fire. All that appeared necessary to complete the destruction of the outer forts was more time. Adverse weather prevented the attack being renewed for several days, but Churchill had no reason to be dismayed by these results. Although suffering from a bout of influenza, he threw himself into the business of arranging the transportation of troops to the Allied base at Lemnos. The fate of the 29th Division was still in the air, but Churchill was hopeful that it would eventually be made available. On 23 February, he calculated that the Allies might have as many as 109,000 troops within striking distance of the Dardanelles by the end of March, a figure that included, in addition to elements of the Royal Naval Division and the Australians and New Zealanders, a division recently promised by the French, two British divisions (the 29th Division and a territorial division), and (unrealistically) a Russian brigade. This would be sufficient, he suggested, to occupy Constantinople, isolate Ottoman forces in Europe, and begin rallying the Balkan states to the Allied cause.[21]

In the Mediterranean, Carden was understandably confused about when and how he was expected to use troops to support his operation. While he waited for the weather to improve, he discussed with the general commanding British forces in Egypt the possibility of landing 10,000 troops to take and hold the southern end of the Gallipoli peninsula. But this was not the sort of operation that either Churchill or Kitchener had in mind at this time. The War Office promptly ruled that the occupation of this territory was 'not necessary for the reduction of the forts'. The obvious concern was that if the peninsula had not already been evacuated, such a small force was in danger of being overwhelmed by enemy troops.[22] Churchill also preferred not to commit troops during the naval assault. He wired immediately to tell the admiral that his original instructions for forcing the Straits were unchanged. 'It is not proposed at this stage', he wrote, 'to use military force other than parties of Marines landed to destroy particular guns or torpedo tubes.' Churchill still believed that the troops being assembled in the theatre would only be needed *after* the naval assault had succeeded, in order 'to reap the fruits'. All that he would concede was that the first contingent of 10,000 troops would be available to the admiral if he made faster progress than expected through the Straits. But Churchill insisted that they should not 'be employed in present circumstances to assist the Naval operations which are independent and self-contained'.[23]

When the War Council met on 24 February it soon became evident that Carden was not the only one confused about the role to be played by the army. Ministers should have discussed all the implications of committing the army to the Dardanelles operation at their meeting of 16 February, but they clearly had not done so. Churchill and Kitchener both believed troops would only be called on after the fleet had broken through the Straits, but their views were starting to diverge on other points. Kitchener was not yet thinking about how the Allies could exploit to the fullest an Allied naval victory over the Ottoman Empire; and he evidently assumed that there was no need to land troops to drive the enemy out of the Gallipoli peninsula. He told his colleagues on the War Council that, when the fleet broke through into the Marmara, 'the [Ottoman] garrison of Gallipoli would probably be withdrawn. Otherwise they would run the risk of being cut off and starved out.' Moreover, he predicted that a naval victory would induce the Turks to withdraw their troops from Europe and abandon Constantinople.

Churchill had predicted similar scenarios himself in the lead-up to the attack, but he was now optimistic that even more could be accomplished if a large military force was available to press home the Allied advantage. He therefore continued to lobby for the release of the 29th Division. To win over his colleagues, he outlined a plan to assemble over 100,000 men in the theatre by the end of March. Kitchener was surprised. This was considerably more than the two divisions (one British, one French) that the War Council had contemplated sending to Salonika, and was probably more than anyone had suggested sending to the Dardanelles when it was decided to commit troops there instead. When the field marshal asked whether the Admiralty 'now contemplated a land attack', Churchill hedged his bets. Despite having just told Carden that troops were not meant to help the fleet get through, he now admitted to his colleagues that 'some local military operation' might, after all, be required if the fleet encountered a temporary setback. This prompted Kitchener to ask what such a large force was expected to do. Besides occupying Constantinople, Churchill suggested that the troops could be used in a variety of ways to influence the situation in the Balkans, including landing at Salonika or advancing up the Danube.

Lloyd George evidently sensed that Churchill was wavering with regard to the idea that the naval offensive would be called off if it ran into difficulties. He asked the First Lord whether he now 'proposed that the Army should be used to undertake an operation in which the Navy had failed'. Churchill denied this was his intention, but he would not rule out a scenario in which the navy was close to success, 'but where a military force would just make the difference between failure and success'. The Chancellor was still committed to the idea of opening a new theatre of operations in the east, but he did not believe this necessarily had to be at the Dardanelles. If the naval operation there stalled, he told the War Council that he 'hoped that the Army would not be expected to pull the chestnuts out of the fire for the Navy'. Lloyd George evidently still believed it was possible to call off the naval attack if it was not achieving the desired results, but his colleagues were now beginning to question whether this could be done without badly damaging British prestige in the east.

Some blame has been directed at Churchill for this development. On the day after Carden's attack began, the Admiralty had issued a statement to the press announcing the first day's operation, even naming the ships that had taken part in the bombardment.[24] Churchill was the driving force behind this. According to Richmond

> Winston had written it himself, putting in a lot of detail and giving all the names of the ships engaged. He had sent for Oliver & shown it to him, & Oliver had been very indignant and said it was giving much too much information to the enemy to say all that.... He succeeded in making Winston modify his despatch a little, but in the end W. sent it down to the Press room with orders that it was to be published as it was; and there was very little change in it.

Fisher also questioned the wisdom of providing such a detailed statement to the press, but neither admiral expressed any concern that this would make it more difficult to call off the operation if it faltered.[25] However, there were some concerns about this within the War Council. Lloyd George complained to Frances Stevenson several months later that Churchill 'broke faith with his colleagues & caused the announcement to be made in the Press with great eclat that we had begun the bombardment of the Dardanelles forts, & intended to force the Straits. Thenceforth it was of course impossible for the Government to withdraw.'[26] Hankey was also concerned, and recorded in his memoirs that members of the War Council felt themselves now fully committed to the operation by the Admiralty's announcement.[27]

These claims need to be treated with caution, however. The text of the Admiralty statement did actually not state, as Lloyd George later suggested, that the Allied fleet 'intended to force the Straits'. The Chancellor appears to have confused the Admiralty press release, which dealt only with the first day's bombardment, with commentary on the attack provided by the press, and in particular by Charles à Court Repington, the military correspondent for *The Times*. Repington wrote on 22 February that the Dardanelles attack, 'having begun, ... must be successfully carried through at all costs'.[28] One historian has recently confused the issue further by also treating the Admiralty press statement and *The Times*' commentary as if they had both emanated directly from Churchill.[29] But Churchill had not announced that the Allies intended to force a passage through the Dardanelles, or even that operations there would be protracted. There is no real basis, therefore, to suggest that Churchill's press release was responsible for all the disasters that followed by making it impossible to call off the offensive, and by ensuring troops would have to be employed when the naval attack failed. Nor can Churchill's press release be blamed for warning the Ottomans that the Allies intended to continue their offensive, as historian Tom Curran recently suggested.[30] The appearance of a large Allied fleet attacking the outer defences of the Dardanelles was surely sufficient in itself to alert the enemy to the possibility that the Allies might be attempting to force the Straits!

Even if no press announcement had been made, Allied prestige was bound to become a factor in the decision-making process. Additional attempts to reduce the outer forts would inevitably reveal that the Allies were, in fact, committed to a major operation, especially once the fleet began its assault on the inner defences. The further the ships advanced, the more difficult it would be to conceal that the Allies were attempting to force a passage into the Sea of Marmara. As long as the offensive was going well, there was no reason to call it off, leading to further operations and a greater commitment of British prestige—and this, in turn, made it more difficult to draw back when a setback did occur. Thus, while the Admiralty press release was clearly ill-judged, ministers were already beginning to realize that it would not be as easy to call off the naval attack as they had initially thought. The Admiralty press release, and the speculation it generated in *The Times*, merely drew attention to the problem. In Grey's words, 'failure [by the fleet] would be morally equivalent to a great defeat on land'. Even Kitchener, who continued to resist committing first-rate troops to the attack, was worried about the impact of a naval defeat on British prestige. If the fleet could 'not get through the Straits unaided', he informed the War Council that 'the army ought to see the business through. The effect of a defeat in the Orient would be very serious. There could be no going back.'[31] This was an important admission on Kitchener's part, although nobody was thinking yet of calling off the operation. Nor was there any apparent sense of urgency—bad weather had temporarily halted the naval assault, and everything so far seemed to be proceeding according to plan. The War Council broke up on 24 February without any decision being reached as to the fate of the 29th Division.

The main difference between Churchill and Kitchener at this stage was whether a local victory over the Ottomans could be exploited to further Allied aims in the Balkans. Churchill was optimistic that it could, but only if there were sufficient troops on hand. In effect, he hoped to merge the

Dardanelles naval assault with the abandoned expedition to Salonika. This was clear to Balfour, who prepared a memorandum after the War Council on the 24th, outlining the key issues at stake. Victory over the Ottomans alone would have far-reaching implications, he observed, but even greater prizes could be won in the Balkans, as the Allies might 'unite the whole of the South-East of Europe with Britain and France in a combined action against the Central Powers'. This, he suggested, could have a decisive impact on the war in Europe. But he questioned whether 100,000 Allied troops would be enough to tempt the Balkan neutrals into the war. Such a force might be too small to have much impact. On the other hand, 40,000 troops might not be enough to ensure that the Dardanelles offensive was successful. And since it was impossible to foresee what resistance the army might encounter after a naval victory had been won, he hoped to commit enough troops to prevent any setbacks.[32] Churchill, however, remained fixated on the fate of the 29th Division. He prepared a memorandum for his colleagues the following day in which he restated his case for releasing the formation for the Mediterranean. If the fleet was being held up, the army could ensure it got through. And if the fleet got through on its own, a large force would be available immediately to exploit any opportunities in the Balkans.[33]

When the War Council reconvened on 26 February, Churchill ensured that the discussion remained focused on the 29th Division. He found a useful ally in Lloyd George, who hoped to send every available man to the eastern theatre. But Churchill's frustration with Kitchener now began to cloud his judgement. Asquith noted afterwards that: 'Winston was in some ways at his worst—[despite] having quite a presentable case. He was noisy, rhetorical, tactless & temperless—or full.'[34] Kitchener was adamant throughout the meeting that he would not agree to dispatch his only significant reserve formation until he had a better idea what would happen both on the Russian front and at the Dardanelles. Churchill, however, was more determined than ever to have the 29th Division released immediately for the east, and worried that delaying a decision could prevent troops being available when they were finally needed. 'We should avoid the risk of finding ourselves with a force inadequate to our requirements', he warned his colleagues, 'and face to face with a disaster.' Ideally, he wanted to send not just the 29th Division to the Dardanelles but also a territorial division. Kitchener effectively undermined Churchill's position by drawing attention to the weak point in his argument: the fate of the Dardanelles campaign was unlikely to hinge on the availability of just a single division, around 16,000 men. As Asquith told the Council, the issue seemed to be whether 'the difference between 69,000 men and 85,000 men would prejudicially affect the operation'. In response to the Prime Minister, Churchill clearly overstated his case. '85,000 men *were* enough', he stated, 'and 63,000 were not.'[35] Asquith, for one, was not impressed. '[T]he difference', he told Stanley, 'between sending to the Dardanelles at once 60,000 troops (which we can certainly do) & say 90,000 cannot, I think, for the moment at any rate be decisive.'[36]

When Kitchener would still not budge, Churchill announced that he wished to place 'on record that he dissented altogether from the retention of the XXIXth Division in this country. If a disaster occurred in Turkey owing to insufficiency of troops, he must disclaim all responsibility.' When this failed to produce any result, he accused Kitchener of inconsistency. The field marshal had been willing to send the formation to Salonika only two weeks previously, he noted, 'in order to entice Greece into the war. In fact', he continued, 'this Division had been hawked round the Balkans. Now that a real and decisive opportunity for using it had arisen Lord Kitchener declined to send it.'[37] This tactless outburst also failed to move the Secretary of State for War, who insisted, as ministers already knew, that the deteriorating situation on the Eastern Front created an important factor that had not existed two weeks earlier. There was, in fact, considerable concern within the War Council about the situation in the east at this time. Lloyd George, for example, stated that 'in his opinion, the collapse of Russia was so imminent' that immediate action was needed to draw the Balkan states into the war. These fears tended to bolster the case for holding reserves at home until the situation was clearer. 'We accepted K[itchener]'s view as right for the immediate situation', Asquith noted afterwards, 'to Winston's immense & unconcealed dudgeon.'[38]

Churchill spilled out his frustrations in a letter to his brother John, complaining that he had 'had many difficulties in trying to keep people up to the scratch'. The problem with his colleagues, he suggested, was that the 'capacity to run risks is at famine prices. All play for safety.' But he found comfort in the fact that the naval offensive had resumed. The delay caused by bad weather had been 'vy vexatious to me, & hard to bear', he confided.[39] Carden had renewed his bombardment of the outer forts on the morning of 25 February, and everything still appeared to proceed according to plan. British and French battleships again poured their fire into the enemy defences, and were themselves subjected to heavy, and sometimes accurate, fire throughout the morning. No serious damage was sustained by the fleet, however, and by midday the Turkish forts had virtually ceased firing. The warships were able to close to within 2,000 yards to complete their mission. Admiral Guéprette, the commander of the French squadron, pronounced that it had been: 'An excellent day, allowing us to augur well for the success of the campaign.'[40] There were ample grounds for optimism. After just two days of active operations, the four outer forts were out of action, and the fleet could now begin its passage through the Straits. Churchill was also optimistic about the day's results, telling his brother that 'so far everything shows the soundness of the plan'.[41]

Carden informed Churchill on the morning of 27 February that the second phase of the operation had begun the previous day. Again, there seemed to be no cause for concern. Minesweepers had not located any mines in the first four miles of the Straits, and British battleships were able to begin their long-range bombardment of the first of the inner forts. Demolition parties had also been successfully landed on both the Asiatic and European shores to ensure that the enemy defences at the entrance to the Straits were permanently destroyed. This, too, appeared to go well. Carden reported that three of the four outer forts were now completely demolished, and the other one was partially demolished. British casualties for the day amounted to only one killed and three wounded.[42] Churchill was so confident about the fleet's progress that he now warned the Russians to be ready at short notice to participate in the offensive by launching their own naval attack against the Turkish defences at the Black Sea entrance to the Bosphorus. 'Although the hardest part of the task is not yet begun', he told the Russian Grand Duke Nicholas, Commander-in-Chief of the Russian Army, 'progress may be quicker than we expected.'[43] He also made another plea to the War Council to release the 29th Division, telling his colleagues again that the forces so far committed were not sufficient for the tasks that might be required of them, and warning that the absence of regular troops would expose the naval battalions and Australian troops 'to undue risk'.[44]

Churchill's continued preoccupation with the 29th Division stemmed from his belief that Ottoman opposition might collapse sooner than expected, and possibly *much* sooner. The fleet's initial successes only fuelled his optimism. On 28 February he told Grey that it was 'now likely' that the fleet would get through the Dardanelles. Fisher, Oliver, and Jackson were told, as a matter of urgency, to begin investigating how Carden's fleet should go about destroying the Bosphorus defences after crossing the Sea of

Marmara.[45] But even though the naval assault seemed to be going according to plan, Carden's early reports were overly optimistic in some important respects. The demolition parties that had been put ashore on 26 February had encountered little opposition from Ottoman forces, but they were only able to reach two of the four outer forts that day. The fleet had inflicted extensive damage to the Orkanie fort, on the Asiatic side, but at Sedd–el–Bahr, on the tip of the Gallipoli peninsula, it was discovered that naval gunfire had not been as effective as initially thought. Only two of this fort's six heavy guns had been destroyed. The remaining four were wrecked by the landing party, but this meant that only two of the forts could rightfully be counted as 'demolished'. The next fort was not examined until 1 March, when a demolition party reached Kum Kale, on the Asiatic side. Again, it was found that naval gunfire had not been responsible for silencing the fort. Seven of its nine guns were in fact still undamaged.[46] The outer forts, in other words, had been silenced because the Ottomans had deserted them, *not* because the fleet had demolished them.

Figure 4.1. Ottoman fort Sedd–el–Bahr, showing damage sustained in the bombardments of February 1915.

National Library of France

Figure 4.2. British soldiers examining a 9.4 inch coastal defence gun of the Cape Helles battery, which was dismounted by a direct hit believed to have been fired by HMS *Queen Elizabeth* on 25 February 1915.
National Museum of the Royal Navy

The obvious conclusion to be drawn from this was that heavy naval fire, even at 'decisive' range, could temporarily suppress the fire from Ottoman forts, but was unlikely to put their guns permanently out of action. To achieve this, the fleet would have to expend even greater quantities of ammunition than planned for, or continue to land demolition parties to complete the process. The latter requirement had been foreseen, but the difficulties had been underestimated, and not just by Churchill. The first landing parties were small groups, covered by no more than fifty Royal Marines, hastily assembled from the companies of the bombarding ships. Their initial success was attributable to the fact that Ottoman troops offered only slight resistance. This would not continue for long, however. On 4 March, a demolition party was landed on each side of the Straits, each supported by a full company of Royal Marines, to destroy any remaining guns covering the entrance. The Ottomans now had additional forces on hand to meet them. British troops were successfully landed on both shores

NAVAL LANDING PARTY COMING TO KUM KALEH (DARDANELLES)   3454-13

Figure. 4.3. Royal Marines landing at Kum Kale, 4 March 1915.
Library of Congress

that day, but these forces met such heavy resistance that they were unable to reach their objectives and had to be withdrawn.[47] Even with naval guns supporting them, landing parties now ceased to be a feasible option. To make matters worse, other unexpected obstacles began to emerge as soon as the fleet began to operate inside the Straits. But none of this was obvious yet in London, where March 1915 began on a decidedly optimistic note.

5

'Groping Round without a Plan'

The Offensive Stalls

Churchill and his naval advisers had known all along that the Turkish forts defending the entrance to the Straits would be relatively easy to put out of action, but the fact that they had been neutralized so quickly, after just two days of bombardment, and with barely any damage to the Anglo-French fleet, raised unrealistic hopes in London that the inner defences could be overcome just as easily. No one was more optimistic than Churchill, who informed the Cabinet on 2 March that the situation at the Dardanelles was 'very good', and that if the weather continued to cooperate 'we may get through in 4 or 5 days'.[1] Hopes also ran high throughout the Admiralty. Writing to his son on 1 March, Admiral Sir Frederick Hamilton, the Second Sea Lord, commented that Carden was 'a lucky chap' to be in charge of the operation, 'I would have given a lot for that job.' He suggested that there would be 'no difficulty' in knocking out the remaining forts 'by long range fire...then all is plain sailing as the Bosphorus forts all face North so that we can attack them in rear and destroy them'.[2] Richmond was also reportedly 'enchanted at the success of the Bombardment up to now'.[3] He was so confidant of success that he lobbied hard to be sent east to take part in the operation, only to be told by an equally optimistic Oliver on 4 March that 'it wd be useless to send anybody out now, as the business ought to be over practically before one cd get there which would be in ten days at the earliest'.[4] There were also signs of optimism at the War Office. General Callwell, the army's Director of Military Operations and Intelligence, wrote on 1 March that 'the Dardanelles affair is getting on very nicely and, if the Navy will only go very cannily and not rush things, I believe the Turks will drift off out of the Gallipoli Peninsula and its occupation will be a fairly simple matter and well within the competence of the 40,000 men' already gathered in the theatre.[5]

Even the cautious Hankey concluded that the time had come to think seriously about what would happen after Carden's fleet had passed through the Straits, an issue that both the War Council and the Admiralty had so far tended to gloss over. On 1 March, the Secretary to the War Council prepared a detailed memorandum entitled 'After the Dardanelles: The Next Steps', in which he reminded ministers that the ultimate objective of the offensive was to induce the Balkan states to enter the war against Austria-Hungary. To this end, he urged them to consider a recent proposal by Lloyd George to send a special emissary to the region. Neutrals were most likely to join the conflict, Hankey suggested, if the Allies demonstrated their intention to commit forces to the region. He therefore recommended the prompt dispatch of a British naval flotilla capable of operating on the Danube, which would serve as 'an earnest of our intention to intervene effectively'. To secure Britain's immediate objectives, Hankey recommended that Carden, after passing into the Sea of Marmara, should ensure the destruction of the enemy's fleet, prevent the evacuation of troops from the Gallipoli peninsula, capture or destroy Turkish dockyards and arsenals in the vicinity of Constantinople, and isolate the city by cutting its railway and telegraph lines. Once these things had been done, Hankey suggested the time would be right to present Allied terms.[6]

British hopes reached new heights after encouraging news arrived the same day from Athens. The Greek Prime Minister had also been impressed by the progress of the Allied fleet, and he informed London that he was making two important recommendations to the King of Greece, backed by the threat of his own resignation. First, that Allied troops be allowed to land at Salonika in order to aid Serbia. Second, that Greece provide an army corps of three divisions to cooperate with the Allies in the seizure of the Gallipoli peninsula.[7] All the optimistic predictions that success at the Dardanelles would transform the strategic landscape in the Balkans now appeared to be on the verge of fulfilment. Violet Asquith recalled in her memoirs the electrifying effect the Greek offer of troops had on Churchill. 'I was sitting with Clemmie at the Admiralty', she wrote, 'when Winston came in in a state of wild excitement and joy. He showed us, under many pledges of secrecy, a telegram from Venizelos promising help from the Greeks.'[8] And Churchill was not the only one whose hopes were raised. If Greece was prepared now to enter the war against the Ottoman Empire, it was easy to imagine the other Balkan states soon following suit. There were already rumours circulating that Bulgaria, which had seemed to be moving towards an alliance with Germany just days before, was now mobilizing for an attack on Turkey.[9]

When the War Council assembled on 3 March, an Ottoman collapse was taken as virtually certain. The main topic of discussion that day was how the spoils would be divided among the victors. The proposed addition of Greek troops to those already committed by Britain and France—and the prospect of additional military support from Bulgaria and Russia—seems to have convinced Churchill that the Allies would have little difficulty expelling the Ottomans from all their European territories. He told his colleagues that when Carden passed through the Dardanelles, his first objective would be the destruction of the Ottoman fleet, followed by an assault on the defences along the Bosphorus. Once Britain controlled this waterway, he was confident that the Ottomans would be unable to reinforce the European part of their empire. With the Balkan states now seemingly on the verge of entering the war, Churchill was so confident of the outcome that he resumed his earlier efforts to *minimize* Britain's commitments in the Balkans. 'We ought not to employ more troops in this theatre of war', he advised, 'than are absolutely essential in order to induce the Balkan states to march.' He informed his colleagues that the Admiralty was still building monitors for use on the Danube, but he preferred to leave the fighting in this theatre to Britain's expected new allies. Unlike Lloyd George, Churchill had no desire to turn this into a major *British* campaign. Once the Ottomans had been defeated, the 'proper line of strategy', he advised, would be in the North Sea and the Baltic. In other words, he still hoped to launch a naval offensive to seize an island along the German coast. All that was required, in his opinion, was the completion of additional monitors and the successful conclusion of war with the Ottoman Empire. 'The operation in the East', he concluded, 'should be regarded merely as an interlude.'[10] He informed Jellicoe a few days later that additional monitors should soon be ready, and that he hoped to launch an assault on Borkum in mid-May.[11]

Despite his immediate preoccupation with the Dardanelles, Churchill still had the North Sea very much on his mind. The Germans had initiated unrestricted submarine warfare against Allied trade on 18 February, and inshore operations along the German coast might enable the navy to block the exit of German submarines.[12] On the day the War Council met, Churchill proposed to Fisher that Admiral Wilson be asked to study the capture of Borkum.[13] The following day, Churchill suggested to Oliver that, at the conclusion of the Dardanelles operation, a squadron of Queen Elizabeth-class battleships might be sent to the Baltic.[14] And several days after that he informed Jellicoe that the Borkum operation would be going forward. This was prompted by a message from Jellicoe offering his congratulations on the early success of the Dardanelles offensive. The fleet's 'progress so far is so encouraging', the admiral admitted, 'that it seems as if we shall get through without nearly so much loss as one might have expected'.[15] Churchill may have sensed that Jellicoe would now be willing to reconsider his opposition to the Borkum project, or he may simply have decided that success at the Dardanelles would allow him to sweep aside his naval advisers' opposition. Either way, he clearly no longer felt the need to persuade Jellicoe of the Borkum scheme's merits. Not a single ship had been lost so far in the Dardanelles operation, and Churchill was more confident than ever that the navy could undertake inshore operations along an enemy coastline without suffering prohibitive losses. He informed Jellicoe that the Admiralty was making 'extraordinary exertions' to complete six new monitors by 1 May, which would allow the attack to 'take place on or about the 15th of May'. He explained that the assault would involve six new monitors, armed with guns ranging from 12–15 inches, supplemented by a squadron of eight to ten older battleships modified to provide additional protection against submarine attack. Twelve thousand troops would be landed using 'unsinkable transports'. It would take just three days to capture the island, Churchill predicted, and another six to turn it into a base for naval and air operations. And just as the Dardanelles offensive was expected to bring the Balkan states into the war, he predicted that a successful North Sea operation would draw in Denmark and the Netherlands.[16]

But success at the Dardanelles was still far from certain. The prospect of Greek assistance was thrown into doubt shortly after Venizelos' telegram arrived. The Russians expected to be given Constantinople when the fighting was over, and had no intention of allowing the Greeks to occupy the city, fearing that they would be unwilling to relinquish it. The Allied ambassadors in St Petersburg were warned that Russia would not condone Greek participation in the city's capture. British ministers were indignant at the Russian attempt to veto the acquisition of a valuable new ally—especially since this new ally might make the difference between success and failure. But they also recognized that they could not resist too strongly without alienating Russia. Churchill's instinct, however, was to defy the Russians.

He drafted a note to Grey on 6 March, urging him to take a strong stand. 'If Russia prevents Greece helping', he wrote, 'I will do my utmost to oppose her having Cple.' Russia, he suggested, needed British and French support too badly to risk a rupture. 'She is a broken power but for our aid', Churchill concluded, '& has no resource open but to turn traitor—& this she cannot do.'[17] Before this advice was sent, however, news arrived that the King of Greece had rejected his Prime Minister's advice about Salonika and the Dardanelles, and that Venizelos had consequently resigned.[18] The Russian veto no longer mattered: there was no longer any prospect of Greece intervening against the Ottoman Empire.

This did nothing to diminish Churchill's confidence in the naval assault. The news from Carden so far had been reassuring. On 4 March, Churchill informed Kitchener that the admiral predicted he would need just fourteen more days of good weather to complete his passage through the Straits.[19] But Carden's telegrams, though optimistic in tone, increasingly revealed the serious obstacles the fleet still faced. The cornerstone of the Ottoman defences inside the Straits was the approximately 344 contact mines located in multiple lines in and around the area known as the Narrows. The fleet's collection of small, unarmoured minesweepers could only do their job after the guns defending the minefields had been neutralized. But it was becoming obvious that Carden and the Admiralty had badly underestimated the difficulties. It was already known from the bombardment of the outer forts that the Ottoman guns could only be put out of action permanently by a direct hit. Even under the ideal conditions prevailing in the initial bombardment, only a handful of guns had actually been destroyed by the fleet in this manner. Inside the Straits, conditions were more challenging. The first serious problem to emerge was the number of field guns and howitzers along both sides of the Straits. These were able to fire from concealed positions, and many of them were mobile, so that even if they could be detected and attacked they would soon be moved to a new location. One source reports that, by mid-March, the Ottomans had 82 guns in fixed positions defending the Straits and another 230 mobile guns and howitzers.[20] These guns were unlikely to sink armoured battleships, but they could and often did damage their superstructures, and they were lethal to minesweepers. Allied warships in the Straits found themselves under continuous fire from these guns, even when out of range of the Turkish forts. This prevented them dropping anchor, and reduced further the accuracy of their fire.

An attempt was also made to demolish the Ottoman forts in the Narrows with indirect fire across the Gallipoli peninsula from the modern 15-inch guns of the *Queen Elizabeth*. This took place over two consecutive days, 5–6 March. Ottoman howitzers were active on the western side of the peninsula as well, and the battleship was gradually driven back to a position 21,000 yards from its targets.[21] Great hopes had been placed on the ability of the *Queen Elizabeth* to smash the Turkish forts, but indirect fire depended on good spotting, since the ship's gunners could not see the targets themselves. Battleships had been assigned to spot the fall of shot from inside the Straits, but these ships had to keep their distance from the target and were constantly under fire and in motion, which considerably reduced their effectiveness as spotters. The obvious solution to the spotting problem was aircraft, but the British were badly unprepared in this respect. The one seaplane carrier allocated to the attack, HMS *Ark Royal*, carried only six seaplanes and four aeroplanes. The latter could not be used, however, as no suitable locations had been found near the Dardanelles for the construction of an airfield.[22] The seaplanes fell far short of expectations. Besides being mechanically unreliable, they had difficulty taking off when the water was either too rough or too calm. On many days, adverse weather conditions prevented them flying at all. They were also vulnerable to rifle fire at low altitudes, and had considerable difficulty reaching a safe height. Commodore Roger Keyes, Carden's chief of staff, recorded, for example, that seaplanes were completely ineffective on the first day of the *Queen Elizabeth*'s indirect bombardment. One of the machines assigned to the task, he recalled, 'had engine trouble and fell into the sea, the pilot and observer being seriously injured. Another was forced to return, her observer being wounded by a bullet, and the third only succeeded in giving one spotting correction.'[23] No aerial spotting was provided at all the following day, as the seaplanes were unable to get into the air.[24]

The limited and unreliable air support available to the fleet was a constant hindrance. These problems were compounded by the inexperience of everyone involved. As one source notes, 'aerial observers and warship gunnery officers at the Dardanelles had to devise an *ad hoc* system of signalling and coding on the spot under combat conditions, with no experience or precedents to guide them, complicated by the fact that the wireless sets could transmit but not receive'.[25] The experiment with indirect fire across the peninsula was called off after the second day, by which time Carden had asked for, and received, permission to move the *Queen Elizabeth* inside the Straits. The results there were no better. None of the British or French battleships achieved significant results in the week that followed. There was only a small chance of scoring a direct hit on the forts' guns at distances exceeding 12,000 yards, and even when ships succeeded in silencing the forts while the gunners took shelter, the minefields prevented ships closing to medium ranges to press their advantage. Until the mines were cleared, Allied battleships could not hope to achieve a 'decisive range' of 2,000–3,000 yards—and even if they had, there was no longer any prospect of putting ashore demolition parties to ensure that any surviving guns were destroyed. Ships were also virtually powerless to silence the enemy's mobile howitzers. Without effective aerial reconnaissance these guns could seldom be located, which meant they could not be fired upon. The fleet was thus unable to eliminate the main obstacle in the way of the minesweepers. And this, in turn, prevented the battleships closing on the Ottoman forts.

The Allied fleet was also poorly prepared to cope with the minefields, a problem that could have been foreseen. The converted fishing trawlers from the North Sea, manned by 'hostilities only' reservists, were slow vessels lucky to manage 5 knots. This was barely adequate against the strong currents they

Figure 5.1. British minesweeping trawlers.
National Library of France

encountered inside the Straits, which reduced their progress to as little as 1–2 knots, making them easy targets for the Ottoman gunners. To make matters worse, the navy had little experience sweeping mines under fire at this stage of the war, and the severity of the problem only revealed itself gradually. To protect the minesweepers from the enemy's guns, they were initially instructed to do their work at night, something that had not been attempted before. These efforts were a complete failure. The Ottomans skilfully used searchlights to illuminate the minesweepers as they approached their objectives, and the boats were exposed to heavy fire from batteries on both shores. The warships that accompanied them were unable to knock out either the searchlights or the gun batteries. The minesweepers' crews were reputedly prepared for the possibility of hitting a mine in the course of their work, but were unwilling to accept the additional risk from gunfire, and usually turned back as soon as shots were fired. The first attempts to sweep mines, on 1 and 3 March, were both abandoned before the sweepers even reached the first line of mines in the formidable Kephez minefield, which guarded the approach to the Narrows.[26]

Another attempt was made to clear mines on 9 March, but it too was called off before a single mine could be swept. If Carden was concerned about this problem, he did not let on. His telegrams to the Admiralty tended to contain only the bare details of the previous day's operations, and Churchill was frequently frustrated by the sparsity of information. Carden's telegrams were drafted for him late in the evening by Keyes and another staff officer, Captain William Godfrey of the Royal Marines. Keyes told his wife that at the end of the day's operations 'Carden read a novel or dozed' while he and Godfrey 'made a report to telegraph—generally about midnight to one a.m.'. Once a draft was ready, Keyes 'would take it to C[arden] who would argue over every word until I wanted to yell'.[27] Carden's report on 6 March mistakenly stated that the minesweepers had been prevented from sweeping by the *forts* at the Narrows—it was, in fact, the minefield batteries that had harassed the minesweepers—and he reassured the First Lord that this obstacle would eventually be eliminated by the guns of the fleet. A channel could then be swept through the mines, he predicted, 'in a few hours'.[28] The problem was far more serious than he realized, however. Another attempt to sweep mines that evening was also abandoned before the Kephez minefield was reached.

The shortcomings of the minesweeping flotilla were, by now, clear to Keyes, but he had difficulty impressing his concerns on Carden. Rear-Admiral John de Robeck, the second in command, was more receptive to the commodore's pleas for a vigorous effort to clear the minefields. On 10 March, by which time it was obvious that mines, not guns, were the main obstacle to the fleet's advance, Keyes and de Robeck learned that no attempt was to be made on the minefield that evening. All that was planned was a reconnaissance by two picket boats. According to the record Keyes made at the time, de Robeck 'said that we must get on, there was not time to arrange for that night, but we must do better the next. Then, I began "Why not time? It could be arranged. We must not waste another night...".'[29] These efforts had the desired effect, and a concerted effort was made to clear mines that evening. This was the minesweepers' *seventh* attempt to reach the Kephez minefield, and for the first time they succeeded. The results were not impressive. The first pair of trawlers managed to sweep two mines, but another soon struck a mine and was lost. The remaining trawlers now came under such heavy fire that they did not even attempt to deploy their sweeping gear and promptly retired. Another effort the following evening also ended prematurely when the crews abandoned the operation after the first shots were fired. The lesson belatedly drawn from this was the reservist crews would have to be replaced with regular naval personnel.

Carden must have appreciated by now the full extent of the problem he faced. The fleet could not ease the way for the minesweepers until the minesweepers had first cleared a path for the fleet. But battleships clearly could not knock out either the forts or the minefield batteries.[30] The admiral was evidently in no hurry to reveal his concerns to London, even though Keyes was eager to act. The latter urged his chief to provide a more detailed description of the situation to the Admiralty, and confided to his wife on 8 March that, though he liked Carden 'very much', he found him 'very slow'. Keyes, a great optimist, firmly believed that victory was possible, but he realized by now that 'it is a much bigger thing than the Admiralty or anyone out here realized, and I am insisting as much as I can [on] the absolute necessity of telling the Admiralty by wire the exact position and what it all means'. Keyes and Godfrey were already working on a long and detailed telegram for the Admiralty, but Carden, he complained, 'wants to cut it about and go to bed on it!!'[31]

It was only on 10 March that Carden despatched a detailed account of the obstacles he faced. The most serious impediment, in his eyes, was still the guns in the Ottoman forts. He suggested that an attack using both indirect fire by the *Queen Elizabeth* across the peninsula and direct fire by battleships within the Straits might provide better results than those obtained so far, but he did not have high hopes. 'The methodical reduction of the forts is not feasible', Carden bluntly told Churchill, 'without expenditure of ammunition out of all proportion to that available.' After observing that the Ottoman forts could only be neutralized permanently by landing demolition parties, he highlighted the problems posed by concealed howitzers, poor aerial reconnaissance, and an inability to clear the minefields.[32] Carden was clearly out of ideas, but his frank appraisal stopped short of suggesting the naval offensive should be called off. His telegrams to Churchill gave no indication that he questioned his orders to force a passage through the Straits unaided, although he may have been pinning his hopes on the army, which would soon be in a position to support his advance. By 20 March there were expected to be as many as 60,000 Allied troops available for operations in the theatre, and Carden had been thinking for some time about how these might be used to his advantage.

Shortly after the naval attack on the outer forts had commenced, Kitchener instructed General Sir John Maxwell, the officer commanding British forces in Egypt, to consult with Carden about how the army might support the naval operation.[33] Unfortunately, Carden had only a vague idea what to request. He had proposed a landing on the southern tip of the peninsula near Sedd-el-Bahr, followed by an advance east.[34] Maxwell, who obviously expected more guidance from the naval Commander-in-Chief, was unimpressed. Carden's telegram, he complained to Kitchener, had been 'so helpless that I feel that unless the military authorities take the initiative, no progress is likely to be made'.[35] Kitchener promptly sent another general from Egypt to confer with Carden. Major-General William Birdwood, commander of the formation that would soon be known as the Australian and New Zealand Army Corps (ANZAC), was also unimpressed. Carden, he wrote, was 'very second rate, lacked initiative and imagination'.[36] After observing conditions in the Dardanelles during the first week of March, Birdwood concluded that Carden's predictions were 'too sanguine'. He informed Kitchener that he doubted the naval offensive would succeed, and certainly not within the timeframe contemplated by the Admiralty.[37] Carden was now interested in landing troops at Bulair, at the base of the peninsula, but Birdwood suggested instead a landing at Cape Helles, on the southern tip, followed by an advance northward to take the Ottoman forts on the European side of the Straits in reverse.[38]

Nothing came of these discussions, however, since Kitchener and Churchill had separately advised their respective subordinates against any major commitment of land forces. The disadvantage of landing troops on the peninsula, of which both Kitchener and Birdwood were acutely aware, was that the only Allied forces that could be sent in the short term would be exposed to attack by the much larger Turkish forces in the region. The Allies still had fewer than 10,000 troops at Lemnos ready to commit to the offensive, while the enemy possessed an estimated 30,000–40,000 men on the Gallipoli peninsula alone. Kitchener therefore proceeded on the understanding that the Allied force being built up in the theatre would only be used to occupy Constantinople after the fleet had broken through. Kitchener told Birdwood on 4 March that he could use his troops to assist the fleet by seizing forts or other positions, provided this could be done without undue risk.[39] Local landings might therefore be launched, provided they were well covered by the guns of the fleet and did not attempt to hold ground permanently. But Birdwood was not to risk having his troops overwhelmed by superior forces. The field marshal was impressed by Birdwood's pessimistic appraisal of the naval operation, however, and accepted in principle that the army would have to assist the navy if it could not get through on its own. In this event, he contemplated a major operation that would require more than the 60,000 men then allocated to the theatre. Birdwood was told that if a major operation on the peninsula became necessary, which was not yet certain, he would have to wait until more troops could be sent.[40]

Carden was still reluctant, it seems, to recommend to the Admiralty that troops be committed, but his increasingly pessimistic telegrams and the slow progress being made by the fleet began to break down even Churchill's enthusiasm. The First Lord provided the War Council with an upbeat account of naval operations on 10 March, and announced that the Admiralty still believed the fleet could get through unaided. At the same time, he admitted that 'they were glad to know that military support was available, if required'.[41] Kitchener, probably inspired by Birdwood's pessimistic forecasts, announced at the same meeting that he was finally prepared to release the 29th Division for the Mediterranean. Allied forces in the theatre were now expected to reach as many as 130,000, provided Russia made good on its commitments. This news, combined with Carden's gloomy telegram of 10 March, seems to have dispelled any doubts Churchill had about the desirability of landing troops to aid the fleet's passage. At the Admiralty, Jackson also came down firmly in favour of military intervention in the near future.

'The position', he wrote to Oliver, 'has changed considerably recently; there are now ample forces ready at short notice for cooperation with [Carden].' In his view, 'the time has come to make use of them'.[42]

The situation at the Dardanelles was discussed on 11 March by the Admiralty's 'War Group'. If Churchill's account is to be trusted, an unusual degree of harmony existed within the group that day.[43] The most likely explanation for the spirit of cooperation is that Churchill was now coming round to the view advocated by his advisers that troops should be committed to help the fleet get through, although he did not acknowledge this in his memoirs. He did emphasize, however, that his chief naval advisers supported his goal of pressing ahead with the naval attack. At first glance this seems surprising, given that Carden's recent report left no doubt as to the severity of the obstacles the fleet still faced. But there were alarming signs that either the Germans or the Austrians might soon dispatch submarines to the eastern Mediterranean, which might shut down the entire operation. This pointed to the need for haste. At the same time, the increasing likelihood of military support for the fleet would have provided reassurance that further naval setbacks could be redeemed. And the fact remained that the Allies had so far lost no ships, or even suffered serious damage. No one, including Fisher, was thinking of calling the operation off at this point. On the contrary, the War Group approved a new, and more ambitious, set of instructions for Carden, which were despatched that day.

The Commander-in-Chief was commended for adhering to his instructions to proceed cautiously, and told that the time had now come to take greater risks. The Admiralty telegram proposed for his 'consideration that a point has been reached when it is necessary . . . to overwhelm the forts at the Narrows at decisive range by the fire of the largest number of guns, great and small, that can be brought to bear upon them'. This would overcome the current impasse in the Straits, it was hoped, by neutralizing the forts long enough to land demolition parties and begin clearing the mines. 'This operation might', the telegram continued, 'have to be repeated until all the forts at the Narrows had been destroyed and the approaches cleared of mines.' Churchill clearly wanted to proceed along these lines, but he realized it was unwise to suggest that Carden had no say in the matter. 'We do not wish to hurry you', he continued:

[O]r urge you beyond your judgment, but we recognise clearly that at a certain period in your operations you will have to press hard for a decision, and we desire to know whether you consider that point has now been reached. We shall support you in well-conceived action for forcing a decision, even if regrettable losses are entailed.[44]

The admiral could have had no doubt what reply was expected of him.

The Admiralty was also beginning to take the problem of air support more seriously. On 25 February, it allocated two additional seaplanes to the *Ark Royal*, which would bring the ship's complement to eight.[45] The following day, the decision was taken to move an experienced RNAS squadron (including fourteen aeroplanes) from France to the Dardanelles to supplement the fleet's modest supply of seaplanes. However, suitable landing grounds had still not been found on the British-held islands near the theatre of operations. Churchill could not understand why some means could not be improvised to get the *Ark Royal*'s four aeroplanes into service immediately. He wrote to Carden on 8 March to suggest that use might be made of the nearby island of Imbros.[46] Carden reassured the Admiralty the following day that every effort had in fact been made to find a suitable landing ground. He also pointed out that the *Ark Royal*'s aeroplanes could not carry an observer, making them of little use for spotting. The telegram concluded with an appeal for the dispatch of more than just two additional seaplanes.[47] The Admiralty continued to focus on the problem of employing aeroplanes. Commander Robert Clark-Hall, the Commanding Officer of the *Ark Royal*, was therefore asked whether men from the fleet could:

> [B]e landed to clear and stamp down sufficient area of ground for aeroplanes to arise and alight. This has been done successfully with very rough ploughed fields in France. As an alternative could not aeroplanes be sent off deck of Ark Royal and be given buoyancy bags for landing in shallow water.

This query was drafted by Commodore Murray Sueter, the Director of the Air Department at the Admiralty. The final version of the message concluded with a short passage probably added or instigated by Churchill: 'You are expected to solve this difficulty in one way or another... the reputation of the Naval Wing depends upon the Fleet being fully served by aerial reconnaissance' prior to the arrival of the new squadron of aeroplanes.[48]

While Churchill waited for Carden to respond to his proposal for a more vigorous offensive, he also became absorbed in the problem of securing military assistance for the fleet. The main obstacle, as usual, was Kitchener. The War Minister still did not want an offensive on the peninsula unless it became absolutely necessary. The decision to dispatch the 29th Division necessitated the appointment of a senior British general to take charge of the expanded force now being assembled in the eastern Mediterranean, and the post fell to General Sir Ian Hamilton, a long-time friend of Churchill's. Hamilton's instructions from Kitchener before he departed for the Dardanelles made it clear that Kitchener had decided, without explicit sanction from the War Council, that the army might have to be landed on the peninsula to ensure the naval attack succeeded. 'Having entered on the project of forcing the Straits', he wrote, 'there can be no idea of abandoning the scheme.' But he emphasized that, if the fleet required his assistance to get through, Hamilton must not attempt major operations to neutralize Ottoman defences until all his forces had been assembled, including the 29th Division, which had not yet left England.[49] Kitchener also explained his position to Churchill, who was informed that large-scale operations could not be contemplated in the short term unless it was found that Ottoman forces on the peninsula were much weaker than thought.[50] Other than minor and local operations to help the navy secure some immediate objective, Hamilton could not support the fleet for around a month. This was not what either Churchill or his naval advisers had in mind. Admiralty opinion now favoured immediate action. Before Hamilton departed, Churchill tried to persuade him to ignore Kitchener's instructions and use the approximately 40,000 troops that would soon be available in the theatre to launch an attack on the peninsula as soon as possible.[51] Hamilton may have been sympathetic to the idea but, not surprisingly, he adhered to his instructions.

This difference in opinion between Churchill and Kitchener might have resulted in another clash at the War Council, but the prospects for a naval breakthrough seemed to improve the next day and the question of military support was temporarily pushed into the background. On 13 March, codebreakers in 'Room 40', the Admiralty's cryptanalytic bureau, solved an important message from authorities in Berlin to the German officer overseeing the Ottoman defences at the Dardanelles. It stated that 'Everything conceivable' was being done in Germany 'to arrange for the supply of ammunition' for the Ottoman defences. The DNI, Captain William 'Blinker' Hall, took the telegram immediately to Fisher. In his unpublished memoirs, Hall records that he found the First Sea Lord in Churchill's office:

> Lord Fisher took the message, read it aloud and waved it over his head. 'By God', he shouted, 'I'll go through tomorrow!' Mr Churchill, equally excited, seized hold of the letter and read it through again for his own satisfaction.

'That means', he said, 'they've come to the end of their ammunition.' 'Tomorrow', repeated Lord Fisher, and at that moment I believe he was as enthusiastic as ever Mr Churchill had been about the whole Dardanelles campaign. 'We shall probably lose six ships, but I'm going through.' The 1st Lord nodded.

The German telegram contained one other important piece of information: neither the Germans nor the Austrians had yet sent a submarine to aid the Ottomans, although the possibility was 'being seriously considered'.[52] Even after making allowances for Hall's embellishment, there is little doubt that Churchill and Fisher were both excited about the telegram, from which they inferred that the enemy's ammunition situation was becoming critical. However, this was not explicitly stated in the telegram. All that could be known for certain was that the Germans were eager to supply the Ottomans with more ammunition. Churchill and Fisher nevertheless informed Carden that 'we have information that the Turkish forts are short of ammunition and that the German officers have made desponding reports and have appealed to Germany for more'.[53]

In light of this new information, Fisher and Churchill were both eager to press on with the naval offensive. The admiral was evidently so confident of an imminent breakthrough (or had so little confidence in Carden) that he proposed to go to the Mediterranean himself to take over command of the naval offensive. 'It was "touch & go" yesterday', he told Jellicoe on 15 March, 'whether I would not go off to the Dardanelles this morning but it was decided otherwise.'[54] But when the German message reached Hall, Carden had not yet responded to the Admiralty telegram of 11 March urging him to consider more aggressive action. The fate of the naval offensive was in the air for several days. A new telegram from Carden on the morning of 13 March provided a brief account of the previous day's operations, but still no response to the Admiralty's proposal. To make matters worse, the news from the eastern Mediterranean was not encouraging. Carden reported that the fleet had not attacked the Turkish forts that day, and that the latest attempt to sweep mines was 'not satisfactory owing to heavy fire, no casualties'.[55]

Churchill was annoyed by the apparent inactivity of the fleet, which had seemingly been 'brought to a standstill', and even more by the failure of the minesweepers to persevere with their operations. 'I do not understand', he wrote to Carden, 'why minesweeping should be interfered with by fire which causes no casualties. Two or three hundred casualties would be a moderate price to pay for sweeping up as far as the narrows.' He therefore encouraged the admiral to go ahead with his proposal to call for volunteers from the fleet to man the minesweepers. What he really wanted, however, was an answer to his telegram proposing an escalation of the naval offensive, especially in light of the news of possible Ottoman ammunition shortages. Churchill's message of 13 March to Carden made it plain that he was eager for operations to be:

> [P]ressed forward methodically and resolutely by night and day the unavoidable losses being accepted. The enemy is harassed and anxious now. Time is precious as the interference of submarines would be a very serious complication.[56]

Carden finally replied the following day, agreeing that a stage in the operation had been 'reached when vigorous sustained action [was] necessary for success'. There could have been little doubt by this time that something new had to be tried. The bombardment of the inner forts had, in fact, been suspended for several days now. Nothing was being achieved any more except using up valuable ammunition and wearing out the heavy guns of the battleships. As Keyes noted on 9 March, 'we are standing easy for a bit' while attention was given to the minesweeping problem.[57] The fleet's discomposure was also obvious to the Germans. Admiral Guido von Usedom, the chief German technical adviser at the Straits, reported to authorities in Berlin that, after 7 March, 'a noticeable alteration occurred in the activity of the enemy':

> Days went by on which nothing was attempted in spite of the finest weather. A bombardment by night of the outer batteries, a fleeting appearance of single ships in the entrance by day, were the sole proofs of the presence of a hostile fleet. The whole affair gave the impression of groping round without a plan and gave rise to the belief that the settled plan of the enemy had been frustrated.[58]

The situation had not improved by 12 March. Carden was preparing to make one more attempt to sweep at night now that naval personnel had been put on the trawlers. If this failed, the only way to move the fleet forward would be to eliminate the guns lining the Straits, which would then allow the minefields to be swept. Churchill and his advisers were thinking of a big effort by the fleet to overwhelm the enemy's defences, but it is hard to imagine that Carden could have been optimistic about the prospects of another bombardment given the meagre results obtained so far. But still he kept any doubts to himself. Instead of admitting that the naval offensive had stalled, he suggested that it was so close to success that it was now time to commit troops. 'In my opinion', he wrote, 'military operations on [a] large scale should be commenced immediately in order to ensure my communication line immediately Fleet enters [the] Sea of Marmora.'[59]

Carden was probably unaware that opinion at the Admiralty now favoured the idea of using troops to help see the fleet through. Churchill and Fisher were both eager to meet his wishes. Churchill was attracted to the idea of a major landing by Allied forces to occupy the Kilid Bahr plateau, opposite the Narrows, which would allow the Allies to dominate the forts and batteries protecting the Kephez minefield. Action by the army, he wrote to Carden, might prove to be 'be less costly than a Naval rush' through the Straits.[60] However, this was precisely the sort of operation Kitchener had repeatedly told his generals to avoid, and his opposition would have to be overcome. The First Lord wrote immediately to the War Minister, hoping to put his proposals in the best possible light. Churchill wisely avoided any suggestion that a major commitment of troops *must* take place, contrary to Kitchener's instructions, but he noted that the request had now been made by Carden, and intimated that the decision should be left to Hamilton, who was due to arrive in the theatre soon. As a first step, which would not commit anyone to an occupation of the peninsula, Churchill proposed that all of Birdwood's troops still in Egypt should be sent to Lemnos as soon as possible to join up with the forces already there and the French division that was due to arrive in a few days. He also hinted that Kitchener's opposition would be received badly by the navy. Fisher, he wrote, was 'very insistent, and I agree with him', that these preliminary steps should be taken.[61]

Fisher felt strongly about the need to launch a military operation. On 15 March he wrote to Churchill proposing a special meeting of the War Council to reach an immediate decision. 'Delays now may have vital consequences', he wrote. 'HOURS *now count.*' He was also eager that leaders of the Conservative Party be invited to participate. If both major parties agreed that it was desirable to take Constantinople, 'military co-operation' should be pushed, he insisted, 'with all speed'. 'Everything points to instant action by a collective vote & decision of the War Council with the Opposition joined in.'[62] Churchill, however, did not share Fisher's sense of urgency. The War Council had consistently sided with Kitchener in previous disputes, and they would probably do so again if the field marshal stood his ground. Churchill therefore proposed to take a different course. 'I don't think we want a War Council on this', he wrote to Fisher the same day. 'It is after all only asking a lot of ignorant people to meddle in our business.' He suggested that the best course was to wait until Hamilton reached the eastern Mediterranean and could report on the situation there. If Hamilton backed the idea of military operations, which he evidently thought was possible, Churchill predicted that Kitchener 'will do what we want...if you & I see him together'.[63]

Churchill's decision to wait for Hamilton's report meant that no decisive steps would be possible in the next few days. Meanwhile, preparations for an escalation of the naval offensive continued. Carden informed the Admiralty on 14 March that the latest attempt to sweep mines at night, using regular naval personnel rather than reservists to man the trawlers, had also failed. Once again, the minesweepers were unable to pass through the minefield undetected, and the ships supporting the operation failed to knock out either the Turkish searchlights or the minefield batteries. Keyes, the driving force behind the reorganization of the minesweepers, wrote afterwards:

> The enemy were very much on the alert. They let the seven sweepers and five picket boats get right into the middle of the minefield on the way up, only firing a single gun occasionally—then all the searchlights went out—a minute later they all flashed on again, and concentrated on the sweeping flotilla. The enemy then opened a heavy fire which followed them up to the turning point, after they had turned, and while they were sweeping down. All except two were so damaged that they could not get their sweeps out, kites were smashed, wires cut, and winches destroyed by gunfire. They were hit with projectiles ranging from six-inch to shrapnel from field guns.[64]

None of the minesweepers was lost in the operation, but four trawlers and one picket boat were badly damaged, and seventy casualties were suffered, including twenty-seven killed. A few mines were reportedly destroyed, but the operation only proved, in Carden's opinion, that the minefield defences were 'so well organised' that 'efficient sweeping by night is impossible'.[65] Given the importance of clearing the minefields to the success of the operation, the decision to proceed without an adequate force of fast and efficient minesweepers is a serious indictment of naval staff work. By the time it was realized that no progress would be made sweeping at night, eleven separate attempts had been made to sweep the Kephez minefield. On nine of those occasions, the minesweepers had turned back before even reaching the minefields. Their efforts on the other two occasions resulted in the destruction of around 4 of the roughly 350 mines blocking the Straits.[66]

There was nothing left but to try sweeping the mines by day under cover of the fleet. Up to this point, Carden had only used a few battleships at a time to bombard the inner forts. He now began preparing for an attack using a larger proportion of his fleet to suppress the enemy's guns long enough for the minesweepers to begin clearing a path. This, it was hoped, would enable the battleships to begin moving further up the Straits, where their fire would become increasingly effective. Nobody expected this to be a fast process, but Churchill was eager that no time should be wasted. There was certainly no question in his mind of delaying things for even a few days, by which time a large number of troops would be available at Lemnos for a combined operation—provided, of course, that Kitchener gave his consent. Nor was Churchill prepared to wait to see if Hamilton recommended using troops immediately to take the Gallipoli forts in reverse. The First Lord's instructions to Carden stated that the Admiralty wished the operation 'to be pressed forward without hurry but without loss of time', although he continued to emphasize that no attempt was to be made to *rush* the Turkish defences.[67] Carden appears to have been ready to continue, for the time being, with a purely naval assault, albeit on a larger and more ambitious scale than before. All that remained, he reported to the Admiralty on the 16th, was to ensure that the areas the fleet would traverse during the bombardment were thoroughly swept for mines. The attack was scheduled to begin the following day.

6

From the Dardanelles
to Gallipoli

On the eve of Carden's big push in the Dardanelles, most decision-makers in London had some idea, albeit an exaggerated one, as to what the attack might accomplish if it succeeded, but only a vague understanding of how it would proceed or the obstacles it might encounter. At no point had detailed memoranda about the operation been submitted to the War Council by either the War Office or the Admiralty, and neither the First Sea Lord nor the CIGS generally expressed their views unless directly asked, which seldom happened. Ministers were content to let Churchill and Kitchener represent the opinions of the Admiralty and the War Office respectively. The War Council therefore received very little in the way of unfiltered information from the services about the military and naval operations under consideration, or even those in progress. To further complicate matters, the Dardanelles plan had been in a state of near-constant flux from mid-February onwards. The original idea of a naval offensive had been supplanted, after somewhat cursory discussion, by a new plan that envisioned troops consolidating a naval victory, but by mid-March this arrangement was also beginning to unravel. Churchill and his naval advisers now regarded soldiers as at least desirable, and possibly necessary, to ensure that the fleet could pass through the Dardanelles. The admirals hoped to employ troops as soon as they were ready, but Churchill was prepared to proceed with a navy-only assault while he waited for support to emerge for a combined operation. Rather than push for a clear decision, which would open his plans up to scrutiny, he preferred to make arrangements directly with Kitchener and hope that Hamilton might take the initiative. Meantime, the War Minister had accepted in principle that the army would help the fleet get through, but he was not prepared to commit soldiers to the Gallipoli peninsula until it was certain that the navy had failed. Asquith received periodic updates from the two service ministers about the changes being contemplated, but most members of the War Council were only dimly aware in mid-March that a major commitment of troops to the Gallipoli peninsula might soon take place.

Given the haphazard nature of Britain's strategic decision-making process in 1915, this is hardly surprising. Even after more than six months of war, the War Council was still providing only the loosest of oversight to the empire's military and naval operations. Churchill and Kitchener continued to run their respective services on a day-to-day basis with minimal interference from their Cabinet colleagues. This was an arrangement that suited Churchill well. It kept his colleagues from meddling in the navy's business, and gave him greater influence. Asquith and his ministers were also seemingly comfortable with this informal system, and were evidently in no hurry for change. But it was not well suited to the demands of modern mass warfare. The figure who saw this most clearly was Hankey, who, as Secretary to the CID, had been closely involved in the development of more efficient machinery for the management of government affairs before the war. On 16 March, as preparations geared up for a renewal of the naval offensive, and discussions took place behind the scenes for the commitment of troops, Hankey appealed to Asquith for greater government oversight of the Dardanelles campaign. His immediate concern was that the Dardanelles offensive was on the verge of escalating into a major combined operation, something that had not yet been discussed by the War Council. Hankey wanted to ensure that ministers were well informed on the subject before any major new commitments were undertaken. He had doubts about the whole enterprise, and warned the Prime Minister that the original justification for a combined operation was no longer valid. The Ottomans could no longer be taken by surprise, and had had several extra months to strengthen their defences. He also knew from personal experience the elaborate staff work needed to ensure the success of a major joint operation, and it appeared that the army and the navy were about to rush in without adequate preparation. He therefore urged Asquith to ensure that the War Council carefully questioned naval and military authorities about their plans. If the two services failed to work together efficiently 'it is conceivable', he warned, that 'a serious disaster might take place'.[1]

Hankey discussed his paper the next day with the Prime Minister, whose support would be essential if any action were to be taken. Asquith agreed to raise Hankey's specific concerns about the Dardanelles with the War Council when it met again in a few days, but applying the brakes at this stage was no easy matter.[2] With the navy gearing up for a major new offensive, and over 60,000 Allied troops now concentrated in Egypt and Lemnos, the campaign was fast developing a momentum of its own. Only one delay occurred around this time, and it was a brief one. On 16 March, Carden suffered a breakdown and announced that Admiral de Robeck was taking over command of the Allied fleet. The impact of this change was minimal. De Robeck was well acquainted with the plan for an expanded naval attack, and the change of command only pushed the start back by a day. No one in London seemed sorry to see Carden go. Churchill promptly wrote to the new Commander-in-Chief to confirm that he supported the plan that had been prepared under his predecessor's direction. 'If not', Churchill wrote, 'do not hesitate to say so. If so, execute them without delay and without further reference at the first favourable opportunity.'[3] De Robeck replied the following day that he was in full agreement with both the Admiralty's instructions and Carden's plan. His main objective, he informed the Admiralty, was to silence the Ottoman forts while simultaneously clearing a path through the minefields.[4] To achieve this, he proposed to employ eighteen of the capital ships under his command. His telegram affirming his commitment to the assault was dispatched to London on the morning of 18 March, even as the first British capital ships were entering the Straits to commence their attack.

The assault began with the four most powerful ships of the fleet—*Queen Elizabeth*, *Inflexible*, and the two British semi-dreadnoughts, *Lord Nelson* and *Agamemnon*—positioning themselves line abreast around 14,000 yards from their principal target, the Narrows forts.[5] From this position they began a deliberate, long-range bombardment at around 11:30. This division of the fleet, designated 'Line A', was accompanied by two pre-dreadnought battleships, *Prince George* and *Triumph*, whose job was to suppress the fire from the intermediate forts and mobile howitzers. The British ships remained outside the range of the Narrows forts, but from the moment they entered the Straits they came under heavy, and often accurate, fire from concealed Ottoman guns. Half an hour after the bombardment began, the four French battleships, designated 'Line B', passed through Line A to take up an even more exposed position, approximately 9,000–10,000 yards from the Narrows forts. The French ships soon came within range of the forts, whose fire was now added to that of the concealed guns. By 12:30, the enemy's fire was

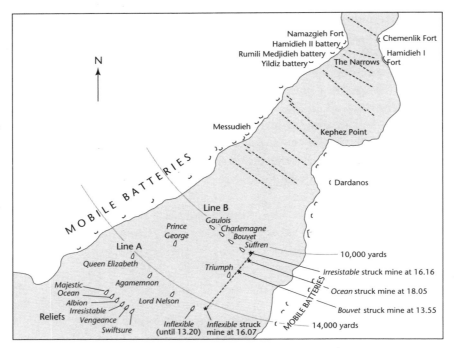

Map 6.1. The Dardanelles Bombardment, 18 March 1915.

beginning to take a toll. All the Allied ships were hit, some as many as ten to twelve times. *Queen Elizabeth*, for example, was hit five times by howitzers that day. Two shells hit the ship's armour and caused no damage, but the other three put holes in a funnel and the forecastle deck, destroying the ship's gunroom. *Inflexible*, the worst-hit British ship, suffered considerably more damage, being hit nine times by shells ranging from 4 to 13.9 inches.[6] With its forebridge ablaze, the battle cruiser was forced to fall out of line at 13:25, less than an hour and a half after the bombardment had commenced. The French squadron, which advanced as much as 5,000 yards further up the Straits, was subjected to heavier fire, and suffered even more. The battleships *Suffren* and *Gaulois* were both seriously damaged; the latter was badly holed below the waterline and for a time appeared to be in danger of sinking.

The Allied bombardment was also taking a toll on the enemy, although the extent of the damage to the Ottoman defences was hard to judge. Remarkably, given the high stakes involved, there were just two seaplanes available to the fleet that day for spotting and reconnaissance, and their work was impeded by the heavy smoke around the forts, which made it

Figure 6.1. French battleship *Gaulois*, badly damaged and in danger of sinking, awaiting rescue boats.

Getty Images

difficult to assess the effects of the bombardment. The two intermediate forts (Dardanos and Messudieh) ceased firing by 14:00 and appeared to be abandoned, but the Narrows forts, despite being hit numerous times, could not be silenced. The seaplane spotting for the battleship *Vengeance* reported, for example, that the battleship's shells were falling in the middle of the fort it was firing on, and caused no damage.[7] Even at a range of 9,000–10,000 yards, it was difficult to score a direct hit on the Ottoman guns, and nothing less would ensure they were permanently disabled. It was clear, however, that the forts had been hit numerous times, and at least some guns were out of action, even if only temporarily. Their rate of fire was seen to slacken by early afternoon, and de Robeck called for the minesweepers to begin their approach to the Kephez minefield. A fresh squadron of British pre-dreadnoughts was also brought in around this time to relieve the battered French squadron.

The battle had so far been inconclusive, with neither side able to gain a clear advantage, but the tide suddenly turned against the Allies at 13:55 when the French battleship *Bouvet* struck a mine as it began its return passage down the Straits. Allied sailors watched helplessly as the French ship sank in just a few minutes, with the loss of over six hundred of its crew. Unknown to the Allies, on the morning of 8 March the Ottoman minelayer *Nusret* had laid a fresh line of twenty-six contact mines in Erenköy bay, on the Asiatic side of the Straits, where the Allied battleships had frequently been seen to manoeuvre. Unlike the mines in the Narrows, which stretched in lines across the Straits, these ones were laid parallel to the coast. Until *Bouvet* went down, the Allies were unaware of their presence. The new line had not been spotted by aerial reconnaissance, and the British minesweepers had reported to de Robeck on the morning of 18 March that the waters below the Kephez minefield had been thoroughly swept. It was not immediately clear, there-fore, what had sunk the *Bouvet*. There were several possibilities: a floating mine, a torpedo fired from shore, or a magazine explosion caused by Ottoman gunfire all seemed just as likely as a moored mine, if not more so. The British battleships nevertheless continued their bombardment. The fleet's mine-sweepers, now en route to the Narrows, discovered several of the new Ottoman mines. Disaster followed soon after. At 16:07, the battle cruiser *Inflexible*, which had returned to its position in Line A, also struck a mine. Nine minutes later, the old battleship *Irresistible* suffered the same fate. Though badly damaged, *Inflexible* was able to remove itself to safety. *Irresistible* could not be saved, however, and the decision was promptly taken to abandon the ship. Once de Robeck realized that his losses were being caused by mines, he gave the order for the fleet to withdraw from the Straits. Minutes later, at 18:05, HMS *Ocean*, another British pre-dreadnought, also struck a mine. The damage was so bad that it, too, had to be abandoned.

The Allied naval attack of 18 March was, by any criteria, an unmitigated failure. By the end of the day de Robeck had lost fully a third of his fleet. Three capital ships had been sunk, and three others were so badly damaged that they would require weeks in the dockyards to repair. Other than the *Gaulois* and *Suffren*, whose damage was the result of gunfire, all the losses were caused by a single line of mines. The presence of a new and unde-tected minefield on 18 March can be blamed entirely on the failure of the

Figure 6.2. Sinking of HMS *Irresistible*.
Library of Congress

minesweeping flotilla, which demonstrated again its shocking inadequacy. To make matters worse, the fleet's heavy losses were not balanced by any notable successes. The Ottoman forts had been considerably knocked about by the fleet, and some guns were *temporarily* put out of action, but only one or two heavy guns had actually been destroyed. The batteries protecting the minefields and the howitzers that continually harassed the fleet had not been damaged at all in the attack. Most seriously, the Kephez minefield, the main obstacle to the fleet's advance, was untouched. The belated discovery of mines in the vicinity of the Allied fleet meant that minesweepers did not even attempt to penetrate the Narrows defences on 18 March. The Allies were therefore no closer to passing ships through the Straits at the end of the day than they had been at the beginning, although they were considerably poorer for having made the attempt.

News of the setback began to reach the Admiralty the following morning. De Robeck, believing that the area where his ships went down had been thoroughly swept for mines, mistakenly reported that his losses must have been caused by drifting mines, released by the enemy to float down the

Straits in the current, rather than by moored contact mines.[8] There could be no concealing the extent of his losses, but he optimistically reported that what remained of his fleet was 'ready for immediate action'. He warned, however, that the attack could not be renewed until means were found to deal with the threat from floating mines.[9] There was as yet no suggestion that the naval attack would not be resumed, and Churchill was eager that it should be. He informed the War Council of the fleet's losses later that day, and reassured his colleagues that there had been reports that the Ottomans were short of mines and ammunition. Fisher was evidently prepared to see the attack continue as well, although he warned that he had always expected to lose twelve battleships in the operation, a view he still held. Attention inevitably turned to the possibility of using troops to help the fleet get through. Hamilton, who had observed first-hand the attack of 18 March, told Kitchener that he did not believe the navy could force a passage on its own, and that any military action to see it through would have to be conducted on a large scale.[10] Kitchener read Hamilton's telegram to the War Council, and noted that the Allied troops and equipment at Lemnos would have to be sent to Egypt to be properly organized and loaded onto transports before they could be landed on a hostile shore. No formal decision was taken as to whether the army *would* be committed, but the idea seemed to enjoy broad support. Harcourt, who attended the meeting, wrote in his notes: 'We shall push on with the Dardanelles operation at almost any cost.'[11] Churchill was given approval to tell de Robeck that he could continue the naval attack at his discretion.[12]

While Churchill made arrangements to send four more pre-dreadnought battleships east to replenish de Robeck's fleet, Hankey made another attempt to ensure that no setbacks would be suffered due to poor staff work. He had little confidence that Kitchener would take the initiative, as the War Minister seemed content to leave the army's preparations in the hands of Hamilton and his small staff in the eastern Mediterranean. Hankey therefore urged Asquith to set up a joint army–navy technical committee—*without* either Kitchener or Churchill as members—to help plan the operation. He also wrote to Lloyd George to enlist his support, suggesting that Balfour might make a good chairman for the proposed committee. These were all good ideas, but without support from Kitchener nothing was likely to come of them, and nothing did.[13] The Admiralty and the War Office continued to take their own separate paths. For several days after de Robeck's failed attack, Churchill's attention was focused on renewing the naval offensive as soon as possible. He seems to have given little or no thought to the possibility of waiting until troops were ready to assist the fleet, which would have meant a delay of several weeks. The disaster of 18 March had undoubtedly unnerved him. Lord Esher recorded shortly afterward that 'Winston is very excited and "jumpy" about the Dardanelles; he says he will be ruined if the attack fails.'[14] But rather than slowing things down, as Hankey wanted, Churchill was determined to speed them along. He wrote to de Robeck on 20 March urging him to take action as soon as possible. 'It appears important', he wrote, 'not to let the forts be repaired or to encourage [the] enemy by an apparent suspension of the operations.'[15]

Churchill also set out to shore up support at home for the naval operation. He reassured Fisher on 20 March that Britain still had ample forces in home waters, lest the admiral become alarmed by the dispatch of additional pre-dreadnoughts to the east. He also emphasized that, despite the loss of several old ships, British casualties had so far been quite light, probably amounting to fewer than 150 sailors. If French losses are excluded, this estimate turned out to be accurate: only around fifty British sailors were killed in the attack. The important thing, Churchill told Fisher, was that most of the crews had survived, and were therefore available to man new warships about to enter service.[16] Churchill amplified on this idea a few days later, when he told the Cabinet that the loss of the British ships on 18 March had actually been a 'blessing in disguise', as the vessels were 'very old, [and would] have been laid up in a few months, as we want the crews for other new Dreadnoughts'.[17]

Everything appeared to be set for a renewal of the naval offensive, and as late as 21 March, de Robeck was moving ahead with preparations. The admiral had been shaken by his losses on the 18th, but he had written to Hamilton the next day that the fleet was 'getting ready for another "go" and [was] not in the least beaten or downhearted'.[18] Vice-Admiral Rosslyn Wemyss, in charge of the Allied base at Lemnos and the senior naval officer in the theatre, also favoured a prompt renewal of the offensive. According to Hamilton's account, Wemyss was 'clear that the Navy must not admit a check and must get to work again as quickly as they can'.[19] De Robeck wrote to the Admiralty on the 21st expressing his confidence that the fleet could dominate the forts and batteries guarding the Narrows once the bombardment was resumed. The only reason for delay was the urgent need to address the deficiencies of the minesweeping force. It was clear by now that it was pointless to risk ships silencing the Ottoman guns if the minesweepers could not immediately clear the Kephez minefields. De Robeck also had no intention of sending his fleet back into the Straits until he could be certain they would not encounter mines during the bombardment phase of the operation.[20] This task was entrusted to the energetic Keyes, who was also convinced that the attack must be renewed. 'I am spoiling to have at it again', the Commodore wrote to his wife on the 21st. 'Only this time', he continued, 'it must be an onslaught on the mine field—the forts we can always dominate—but the mine field is the devil—and I am making it my own!'[21] Most of the reservist trawler crews were now sent home, to be replaced by volunteers drawn from the unemployed crews of the two lost battleships. More importantly, the decision was finally taken to expand the minesweeping force by fitting destroyers as minesweepers. Keyes estimated that this could be completed by around 3–4 April.[22]

De Robeck's initial confidence was not shared by the generals. Hamilton had immediately informed Kitchener of his doubts as to the navy succeeding on its own, a view shared by General Birdwood, his principal subordinate, and General Braithwaite, his chief of staff. Did they reveal their doubts to de Robeck? Hamilton always maintained that he scrupulously adhered to his instructions from Kitchener not to interfere in the naval operation until the navy asked for help. When the generals arrived on the *Queen Elizabeth* on the morning of 22 March, Hamilton stated that they had previously 'agreed that, whatever we landsmen might think, we must leave the seamen to settle their own job, saying nothing for or against land operations or amphibious operations until the sailors themselves turned to us and said they had abandoned the idea of forcing the passage by naval operations alone'.[23] If this account is accurate, the decision to suspend the naval attack was purely a naval one. This is supported by Wemyss' memoirs, which suggest that he and de Robeck had both decided against a renewal of the attack as early as 19 March.[24] This does not appear to be entirely accurate, however. De Robeck's initial preparations for another assault and his optimistic reports to the Admiralty suggest that he had not, in fact, reached any firm decision in the first days following the attack.[25] Keyes was clearly under the impression at this time that de Robeck intended to resume the naval attack at the earliest opportunity.[26] But if this had been de Robeck's intention, he soon changed his mind. Hamilton stated that this change of heart was revealed at the beginning of the meeting on the 22nd. 'The moment we sat down', he wrote, 'de Robeck told us *he was now quite clear he could not get through without the help of all my troops.*'[27]

Figure 6.3. Commodore Roger Keyes, Vice-Admiral John de Robeck, General Sir Ian Hamilton, General Walter Braithwaite.

Australian War Memorial H10350

Kitchener had previously laid down that troops were only to be committed to the seizure of the peninsula if the navy was unable to get through on its own. Hamilton evidently thought this point had been reached, and he was ready to land his troops in force. De Robeck's views are less clear. According to Birdwood, the admiral was particularly concerned at the time about the danger posed by submerged torpedo tubes in the Narrows.[28] The general informed Kitchener on 23 March that de Robeck believed he *could* get through the Straits 'with further heavy loss, but only to arrive with little ammunition, and no object attained as regards getting transport through'.[29] De Robeck informed the Admiralty that the fleet might still force a passage through the Straits, but troops should be landed to protect its communications once it had reached the Sea of Marmara. This, he explained, would require the enemy's guns to be knocked out, otherwise the Straits might be sealed up behind the fleet. The guns could only be destroyed by troops, and since there was no realistic possibility of landing demolition parties so far inside the Straits, he concluded that the army would have to occupy the peninsula. He therefore proposed to suspend his offensive until the mine-sweeping problem had been solved and the army was ready to land in force. The earliest date for a combined offensive would be 14 April, which meant a delay of three full weeks. 'It appears better to prepare a decisive [combined] effort about the middle of April', he told the Admiralty, 'rather than risk a great deal for what may possibly be only a partial solution.'[30] Hamilton, who was justifiably alarmed by the prospect of sending troopships through the Straits if the Ottoman guns continued to fire, supported de Robeck's decision and immediately began planning the army's landings.[31]

Churchill was incensed that de Robeck was abandoning the original plan of a naval assault on the Straits. This was a valid concern, insofar as the War Council had not yet formally authorized a major combined operation. The decision should not have been de Robeck's to make. However, the War Council *had* left the renewal of the naval attack to the admiral's discretion, and de Robeck had good reason to wait. The admiral on the spot should not be blamed for the British government's inability to reach a clear decision as to how the operation would proceed. What really bothered Churchill, though, was not that de Robeck was proposing to involve the army, something he had already accepted in principle, but the delay it would entail. Churchill was willing to contemplate an occupation of the Gallipoli peninsula at some later date, but he wanted the naval offensive to continue while the army undertook its preparations. His reasons for immediate action were laid out in a lengthy telegram he drafted—but did not send—to de Robeck. His first point was that German or Austrian submarines could be dispatched to the eastern Mediterranean at any time, which would jeopardize the whole operation. He then pointed out that the commitment of troops would mean thousands of casualties, a much higher figure than would be suffered in a naval reverse. A naval offensive might lose ships, but ultimately it would economize on soldiers' lives. Churchill was still confident, moreover, that the naval offensive could succeed on its own. De Robeck's concerns about his line of communications were brushed aside. A naval breakthrough would have a 'supreme moral effect' on the enemy, Churchill wrote, 'provided it was strong enough to destroy the Turco-German vessels'. In fact, with the modern battle cruiser *Inflexible* undergoing repairs for the next few months, there was no certainty that the fleet *could* catch and destroy the *Goeben*. But Churchill insisted that the arrival of the fleet in the Sea of Marmara would probably lead to an immediate evacuation of the peninsula, and that its arrival at Constantinople might knock the Ottoman Empire out of the war entirely.[32]

Churchill went on to argue that even if his predictions were wrong, and the enemy's resistance did *not* collapse after the fleet broke through, troops could always be landed to occupy the peninsula at a later date. De Robeck, after all, had said the fleet *could* get through unaided. Churchill therefore wanted to resume the attack, which he predicted would take four to five days to complete, with the possible 'loss of 7 or 8 old ships'.[33] He proposed to send this telegram immediately, but he was blocked by the senior members of the Admiralty War Group, who discussed the situation that day. Fisher, Wilson, and Jackson all insisted that the final decision must rest with the commander on the spot. Churchill was indignant. 'For the first time since the war began', he wrote in his memoirs, 'high words were used around the octagonal table [in the First Lord's room, where the War Group met].' With the admirals lined up solidly against him, Churchill unwisely attempted to circumvent them by appealing to Asquith and Kitchener for support. If they could be persuaded to continue the operation, Churchill might have enough leverage to overrule the admirals, and the matter would not necessarily even need to be discussed by the War Council.

At first it seemed as if he might succeed. Kitchener also wanted to have the offensive resumed with as little delay as possible. He wrote to Hamilton on the 23rd that a postponement until 14 April was 'far too long'.[34] Kitchener also saw no reason for the navy to wait for the army. Another telegram drafted by the War Minister that day suggested that Hamilton might now contemplate immediate landings 'of considerable force' on the peninsula to destroy guns and forts. In other words, Hamilton would no longer be required to wait for the arrival of the 29th Division before landing his men in force. Like Churchill, Kitchener was concerned about the campaign losing momentum. 'It is important', he wrote, 'to keep up [both] the bombardment and all attempts to pass the narrows by ships.' And, again like Churchill, he still thought that a naval breakthrough would result in the withdrawal of Ottoman forces from the peninsula. 'Once ships are through', he concluded, 'the Gallipoli military position ceases to be of importance.'[35]

Asquith was also sympathetic to Churchill's position. 'I agree with Winston & K', he wrote to Venetia Stanley on 23 March, 'that the Navy ought to make another big push, so soon as the weather clears.'[36] A visit from Churchill the following day strengthened the Prime Minister's opinion. 'Winston thinks, & I agree with him', he told Stanley, 'that the ships, as soon as the weather clears, & the aeroplanes can detect the condition of the forts & the positions of the concealed guns ought to make another push: &

I hope this will be done.'[37] Churchill tried to use Asquith's support to overcome Fisher's resistance. He wrote to the First Sea Lord on 25 March to say
that the Prime Minister had 'seemed disappointed that we had not sent de
Robeck a definite order to go on with his attack at the first opportunity'.[38]
Churchill went on to repeat his previous arguments for a prompt renewal of
the offensive, but this had no effect. He was no more successful in his efforts
to win over de Robeck. Churchill had reluctantly agreed on the 23rd to scrap
his telegram insisting on the resumption of the naval attack, but the following day he sent the admiral a 'personal' telegram presenting his case and
seeking an explanation. Although this was not an official Admiralty telegram,
Fisher was not happy with this attempt to sway the Commander-in-Chief,
and he hinted that he would resign if the telegram was sent.[39] Churchill,
however, was undeterred and unrepentant. He assured Fisher the next day
that the Prime Minister supported his decision to send a 'personal' message
to de Robeck, as 'nothing wd be lost by a full interchange of views'.[40]

    Churchill's 'personal' telegram contained the same arguments for renew-
ing the offensive as his unsent message from the day before, but there was no
longer any suggestion that de Robeck was being *ordered* to renew the attack.
Churchill invited the admiral to say if he thought that the failure of the fleet
on 18 March had been 'decisive' and that 'the task [of forcing the Straits] is
beyond our powers'. This was probably an attempt to put the admiral on the
spot. 'What has happened since the 21st', he asked, 'to make you alter your
intention of renewing the attack as soon as the weather is favourable?'

> We have never contemplated a reckless rush over minefields or past undam-
> aged primary guns. But the original Admiralty instructions and telegram
> [of 14 March] prescribed a careful and deliberate method of advance, and I
> should like to know what are the reasons which in your opinion render this
> no longer possible, in spite of your new aircraft and improved methods of
> minesweeping. We know forts are short of ammunition. It is probable that they
> have not got many mines. You should be able to feel your way while at the
> same time pressing hard.[41]

De Robeck had a strong case and he held his ground. He replied on
26 March that he did not consider the recent failure to be decisive, but that
he had decided, *after* meeting with Hamilton on the 22nd, that a combined
operation would give him a better chance of success.[42] He followed this up
the next day with a more detailed message explaining the case for a suspension of the naval attack. He began by reaffirming his belief that he could
succeed in getting 'a portion' of his fleet through the Straits, and had only

changed his mind about renewing the attack as a result of his discussions with Hamilton. He then proceeded to give Churchill the fullest explanation the latter had yet received about the problems faced by the fleet. The most serious flaw with the original plan, de Robeck maintained, was the assumption that naval gunfire alone was sufficient to destroy the Ottoman forts. Any comparison with the German reduction of the Belgian forts at Antwerp was, he suggested, 'quite misleading'. The high velocity guns of the fleet were not well suited to attacking forts. The structural damage they caused was of little value unless the guns themselves were put out of action, which seldom happened. Even in the case of the outer forts, where the range had sometimes been as little as 700–800 yards, de Robeck noted that it had been almost impossible to score direct hits against individual guns. The most the fleet could hope to do was 'dominate' the forts, which meant that their guns were temporarily silenced while the enemy gunners took cover or removed debris and restored their guns to working condition. Permanent destruction of the guns would require the landing of demolition parties, which would be too dangerous so far inside the Straits.[43]

De Robeck also noted that dominating the enemy forts was only one part of the problem. The fleet still had to face torpedoes and mines. The former had not been a problem so far, but that might suddenly change, as the enemy was reportedly adding additional tubes. The mines were clearly a much greater threat than anyone had anticipated, and, while de Robeck and Keyes were seemingly confident that this problem could be solved by a reorganized minesweeping force, there could be no way of knowing if the new measures would be effective. De Robeck did not even mention the constant bombardment of warships and minesweepers by enemy howitzers, a problem that had by now been accepted as insoluble. This was such a formidable list of obstacles that de Robeck must have had doubts about his ability to force a passage unaided, even if he was not willing to reveal them to Churchill. De Robeck had advocated a combined operation to force the Straits even before relieving Carden, and he reached the obvious conclusion on 22 March—that a combined offensive stood a better chance of success than a renewal of the naval attack, which could easily result in another disastrous setback. Even if the naval offensive succeeded in reaching the Marmara, the fleet would still face serious challenges. The admiral told Churchill that he did not assume that the Ottomans would withdraw from the peninsula as soon as warships broke through the Narrows defences. If the enemy continued to defend the Straits, as he expected, the army's support would be vital. 'With Gallipoli

Peninsula held by our Army and [a naval] Squadron through [the] Dardanelles our success', he maintained, 'would be assured.'[44]

On the day this message arrived, Hankey visited Churchill at the Admiralty and found him not only suffering from laryngitis, but also 'very depressed about [the] Dardanelles'.[45] De Robeck's telegram demolished any chance of the naval offensive being renewed in the short term. And, contrary to the claims frequently made by his critics, Churchill could not simply overrule his naval advisers whenever he met opposition. The First Lord accepted this new setback with as much good grace as he could muster. He informed de Robeck that 'the reasons you give make it clear that a combined operation is now indispensable'. He also told the admiral, in what must have come as an unexpected vote of confidence, that he would retain command of the fleet even if Carden recovered from his illness. Churchill was now prepared to wait for the army, and took consolation from the fact that the projected start date for the new operation was little more than two weeks distant.[46] His attention also shifted back to the Borkum scheme. On 24 March, he drafted a memorandum outlining a major combined operation to take place sometime after 15 May. He proposed to land up to 12,000 troops on the island, following a preliminary bombardment by the navy's new monitors and other ships.[47] But even Churchill had to admit that none of this could be contemplated until the Dardanelles operation had been wound up.

The decision to launch a combined offensive on the Gallipoli peninsula had effectively been taken by the commanders on the spot, de Robeck and Hamilton. Having abandoned the naval offensive, there was no doubt in Churchill's mind that the new attack must go ahead. However, the occupation of the Gallipoli peninsula was never submitted to the War Council for approval. In fact, Asquith hinted to Venetia Stanley that he preferred not to involve this body. On the morning of 30 March, he recorded that he had 'had a small conclave here this morning—K, Winston, myself, & Hankey—to go over carefully & quietly the situation, actual and prospective, at the Dardanelles. There are risks, & it will in any event be an expensive operation, but I am sure we are right to go through with it.'[48] This short note is the only written record that the Prime Minister and his two service ministers had, on behalf of the government, decided 'quietly' among themselves to proceed with a combined military–naval assault to occupy the Gallipoli peninsula. Neither the Cabinet nor the War Council were given the opportunity to discuss whether the time had come to call off the operation.

The only politician on the War Council to question the wisdom of proceeding with a military operation was Arthur Balfour. 'As you know', he wrote to Churchill on 8 April, 'I cannot help being very anxious about the fate of any military attempt upon the Peninsula.'

> Nobody was as keen as myself upon forcing the Straits as long as there seemed a reasonable prospect of doing it by means of the Fleet alone:– even though the operation might cost us a few antiquated battleships. But a military attack upon a position so inherently difficult and so carefully prepared, is a different proposition: and if it fails we shall not only have to suffer considerably in men and still more in prestige, but we may upset our whole diplomacy in the Near East, which, at the present moment, seems to promise so favourably.[49]

There was little the Conservative politician could do to apply the brakes, however. He was not a member of the Cabinet, and if the War Council did not meet he had no forum in which to raise his concerns. Churchill, for his part, was determined to see the landings through. 'You must not be unduly apprehensive of the military operation', he replied to Balfour the same day. 'The soldiers think they can do it, & it was their influence that persuaded the Admiral to delay the renewal of his attack till their preparations were completed.' It is also clear from Churchill's response that he mistakenly assumed de Robeck would continue operations inside the Straits once the army was safely ashore. 'The military attack is in addition to, & not in substitution for, or abrogation from, the naval attack', he wrote. 'Both attacks naturally aid each other; & either by succeeding wd be decisive.'[50]

The strongest dissent from those in the know came from Fisher, who was notably absent from Asquith's 'conclave'. On 27 March, the First Sea Lord sent Churchill a memorandum insisting that 'before the final plunge is taken', the Admiralty should carefully review Hamilton's plans and obtain the views of the War Office on the operation's prospects. That such a review was not instituted as a matter of course says a great deal about the slapdash decision-making process in place at the time. Fisher naturally had concerns about the possibility of further heavy naval losses and also, after reading de Robeck's telegram, about the ability of the fleet to force a passage, but he still seems to have been primarily concerned about the drain of resources from the Grand Fleet, especially submarines and destroyers. He once again warned about the critical need to ensure that Britain maintained a large margin of superiority over the Germans in the North Sea theatre.[51] Churchill immediately agreed to ask Kitchener for the War Office's views, and reassured Fisher that there was 'no reason for anxiety'. But he also made clear his own position—that Britain was too heavily invested in the campaign to abandon it: 'We cannot go back now.'[52] Fisher replied that he was 'not blind to political necessity of going forward', but correctly pointed out that Hamilton's plans were still not known. The Admiralty could not even say if he contemplated a rapid occupation of the peninsula or a prolonged siege.[53]

Churchill had a different, and equally legitimate, concern about the land attack: what would the fleet do if the army failed to capture the high ground overlooking the Narrows? Even though de Robeck had stated that he believed the fleet, or some portion of it, *could* get through, his exposition of the difficulties gave Churchill good reason to question his willingness to launch another independent naval attack. The First Lord therefore fired off another 'private' telegram to de Robeck on 27 March asking his intentions if the army suffered a setback. Would he then consent to a renewal of the naval attack? Or did he regard the army's success as essential for the navy to force a passage?[54] De Robeck replied two days later that the navy would resume its advance as soon as the army was safely landed. But he was evasive as to what would happen if the army was held up. It was 'militarily unsound', he pronounced, to send a fleet into the Sea of Marmara until the Ottoman defences along the Straits were neutralized—a tacit rejection of the naval offensive as originally conceived. If the army were held up, he proposed that careful consideration would have to be given to whether the fleet could do more by remaining below the Narrows, with its communications secure, than by forcing a passage through the Straits and possibly finding itself cut off and isolated in the Marmara. De Robeck was unwilling to commit himself, and clearly preferred not to risk another naval attack. He nevertheless reassured Churchill that if it was 'found to be expedient' for the navy to force the Narrows alone, 'the Fleet will do so'.[55]

Churchill had enough confidence in Hamilton and the army to be uninclined, at this stage, to dwell on de Robeck's uncertain attitude, but Fisher's opposition was an ongoing concern. Not long after the naval offensive stalled, the First Sea Lord resumed his practice of expressing strong doubts to his closest confidants. He wrote to Jellicoe on 4 April that he had 'time for little else now but increasing anxiety over the Dardanelles situation'. Typically, he hinted at resignation, but held back, he claimed, on the grounds that 'No good purpose will be served' by doing so.[56] A few days before he had complained to Hankey about Churchill's practice of circumventing his naval advisers by marking his telegrams to de Robeck as 'private'. Fisher again suggested he would resign, and Hankey again advised him against it.[57] But one change had taken places since his campaign to sabotage the Dardanelles in mid-January: Fisher was now more willing to voice his concerns directly to Churchill. After 25 January, the First Lord could have been in no doubt as to the strength of Fisher's fears that the Dardanelles would fatally weaken the navy in home waters. And lest there be any doubt, Fisher continued to remind him. '*We cant send another rope yarn even to de Robeck!*', the First Sea Lord wrote to Churchill on 2 April. 'WE HAVE GONE TO THE VERY LIMIT!'[58] More ominously, Fisher complained a few days later that 'You are just simply eaten up with the Dardanelles and cant think of anything else! D—n the Dardanelles! they'll be our grave!'[59]

Churchill took Fisher's concerns about the strength of the Grand Fleet seriously, and was alarmed by the admiral's obvious lack of enthusiasm for the operation. But it was only when Fisher seemed to be obstructing his preparations that Churchill began to lose patience. He finally lost his temper when Fisher launched into an ill-considered tirade against de Robeck. The First Sea Lord wrote to Churchill on 10 April accusing the Commander-in-Chief of having recklessly endangered *Inflexible* in the attack of 18 March. Fisher maintained that the battle cruiser should have been 'kept out of danger as much as the "Queen Elizabeth"', which suggests that he was unaware that the new battleship had operated inside the Straits on several occasions, *with Admiralty approval*, and that both modern ships had been committed to 'Line A' throughout the day of the attack.[60] He nevertheless insisted that de Robeck be told that *Queen Elizabeth* should only be employed for indirect bombardment across the peninsula. Fisher followed up this message with an even stranger one the following day, addressed to both Churchill and Oliver. The First Sea Lord now railed against de Robeck because *Inflexible* had nearly foundered while being towed to Malta for repairs. Fisher felt that the Commander-in-Chief had chosen the wrong vessel to tow the battle cruiser, and accused de Robeck of an 'ominous want of judgment'. He then complained again about the employment of *Inflexible* inside the Straits on 18 March, allegedly 'against known Admiralty intentions'. He charged de Robeck with 'a disastrous want of judgment'. To avoid any further misjudgements, he insisted that de Robeck be told not to risk *Queen Elizabeth* inside the Straits, and to hold back both *Lord Nelson* and *Agamemnon* if older ships might be used in their place.[61]

Churchill attempted to placate Fisher by agreeing to send de Robeck instructions about the employment of *Queen Elizabeth*, but he was not convinced this was necessary, and he declined to impose any limitations on the use of the two semi-dreadnoughts. In a curious reversal of his usual role as 'meddler', Churchill told Fisher that 'at this critical moment' it would not 'be right to harass the Ad[mira]l by imposing restrictions on his use' of the older battleships. Nor did he agree that the towing of *Inflexible* pointed to poor judgement. If anything, Fisher's attack on de Robeck pointed to a lapse by Fisher, but Churchill was more concerned that this latest incident represented yet another act of obstruction by the First Sea Lord. His frustration is evident in his reply:

> Seriously my friend you are not a little unfair in trying to spite this operation by sidewinds & small points when you have accepted it in principle. It is hard on me that you shd keep on like this—every day something fresh: & it is not worthy of you or the great business we have in hand together.... It is not right now to make small difficulties or add to the burden wh in these times we have to bear.[62]

This obviously touched a nerve. Fisher retorted that 'Never in all my whole life have I ever before so sacrificed my convictions as I have done to please you! THAT'S A FACT!' Fisher was not suggesting by this that he was loyally supporting the operation, as Churchill expected of him. Rather, the point seems to have been that his opposition was so great that Churchill should be grateful for any support! Fisher went on to complain that the 'outside world' mistakenly believed he had pushed Churchill into the Dardanelles operation, rather than the reverse. 'So far as I know', Fisher wrote, 'the Prime Minister is the solitary person who knows to the contrary—I have not said one word to a soul on the subject except to Crease & Wilson & Oliver & Bartolome and you may be sure those 4 never open their mouth!' As an afterthought, he also admitted to having 'worked up Kitchener' through his military secretary, Colonel Fitzgerald.[63]

Fisher's indiscretions went much further than this, of course. He had complained to several others about being pushed into the Dardanelles campaign against his better judgement. In addition to Asquith, Kitchener, Fitzgerald, and the members of the Admiralty War Group, there was also Jellicoe, Hankey, and, either directly or indirectly, Lloyd George and Balfour. The admiral had also alerted Bonar Law. Before the naval operation was approved at the end of January, the circle of people who knew Fisher's opposition had spread to include Venetia Stanley and Frances Stevenson. In all likelihood, it extended far beyond this. In mid-May, Margot Asquith said to Fisher: 'You know, you have talked too much. All London knows you are against the Dardanelles expedition.' Fisher protested that this was 'a lie: I've seen no one, been nowhere. I'm far too busy.' Margot replied, 'But you've talked to a few—enough for all to know.'[64] This was hardly an exaggeration. In April, Fisher's opposition to the Dardanelles had, in fact, become public knowledge. The *Morning Post* published a devastating leader on the 23rd proclaiming that Churchill had not only ignored warnings about the need for troops at the Dardanelles, but had deliberately misrepresented the views of his naval advisers to the Cabinet:

> We understand that it was the opinion of our military and naval experts that the Straits could only be forced by a joint naval and military expedition acting in concert. This was the opinion of the Sea Lords of the Board of Admiralty, and it was also the opinion of the War Office. But it was not Mr. Winston Churchill's opinion. We understand that, against the opinion of his naval colleagues, he represented to the Cabinet that it was possible for the Navy alone to force its way through these narrow Straits. The experiment was made, and, as we know, it ended disastrously.

The newspaper called once again for members of the government to rein in their colleague and leave the naval side of the war in the hands of the admirals. There was 'no place', it charged, 'for a civilian Minister who usurps the functions of his Board, takes the wheel out of the sailor's hand, and launches ships upon a naval operation'.[65]

The driving force behind this new attack was Gwynne, who was more convinced than ever by April 1915 that Churchill must be removed from office. What made Gwynne a particularly dangerous critic was his access to inside information. Even though he did not name his sources publicly, his criticism of Churchill over the Dardanelles was too specific and well informed to be pure speculation. Gwynne confided on 12 April that the information about Churchill misleading the War Council had come to him from an 'authority that I can absolutely trust'.[66] Violet Asquith suspected that Fisher was behind it all, noting in her diary that he had been 'right & left giving the impression that he had been from the outset opposed to the Dardanelles, had fought it tooth & nail, and been overridden'.[67] There were also suspicions at the Admiralty that Fisher was directly responsible for the leak. Richmond told is wife that 'from his knowledge of Jacky he thinks the article is probably inspired by him and very likely written by [the well-known military writer] Spenser Wilkinson to whom J[acky] furnished the information'. Commodore Bartolomé, Churchill's naval secretary, suspected that Richmond had written the leader himself, something that the latter indignantly denied. According to Lady Richmond, her husband 'says he has never written to the papers at all, though he has often had much provocation to do so'.[68]

Fisher was, to be sure, a seasoned intriguer with a history of leaking information to journalists during his previous term as First Sea Lord and long before. But Gwynne and Fisher were unlikely confidants. Gwynne had used his newspaper to support Fisher's hated rival, Admiral Lord Charles Beresford, during the famous Fisher–Beresford feud a few years earlier. The editor had wanted Fisher driven from office in 1909–10, and he was no better disposed towards him during the war. When Fisher returned to the Admiralty in October 1914, Gwynne admitted privately that he was 'thoroughly miserable' at the prospect. He had hoped that Battenberg's resignation would lead to a strong Board of Admiralty that would curb 'Winston's activities and restor[e] some confidence to the Fleet....All I can do is to trust and pray that he [Fisher] may be a better man than I have ever thought he was.'[69] Gwynne felt constrained about criticizing Fisher in wartime, but his comments about the appointment in the pages of the *Morning Post* hardly constituted a ringing endorsement:

> We would have liked to be able to say that this change puts us completely at our ease: we regret that we cannot say so, because with the best will in the world we cannot obliterate the past. If Lord Fisher is to save the position he must act very differently from the manner in which he acted when last at the Board. But, being at war, he will have the less excuse—if not the less temptation—for bowing down to the political gods that be.[70]

Nor was Fisher one to forgive a grudge. He responded to Gwynne's public criticism by asking Churchill, 'Why don't we lock him up?'[71]

But even if Fisher was unlikely to have approached Gwynne himself, he had made his views so widely known by mid-April that there were many possible sources for the *Morning Post*'s criticisms.[72] Gwynne's confidants included Kitchener and Fitzgerald, both of whom were acquainted with Fisher's views *and* with the inner workings of the War Council. The editor was also close to Admiral Beresford, now a Conservative MP, who was

probably feeding Gwynne information about the Admiralty from his network of naval sources. By 1915, Beresford's animosity towards Fisher
embraced Churchill as well, and in mid-April, a week before Gwynne's first
leader on the Dardanelles, Beresford launched a personal campaign against
the Admiralty's leadership. His first shot was a private letter to the Prime
Minister criticizing the navy's recent record and insisting, among other
things, that it had been a mistake to launch a naval attack on the Dardanelles
before troops were available to support the fleet.[73] Beresford was convinced
that Churchill was to blame. He told Leo Maxse, editor of another
Conservative publication, the *National Review*, that:

> Churchill in one of his brainstorms, against the advice of the Admiralty, and,
> I believe, Kitchener, forced the naval attack. I am told that the Sea Lords
> implored him to do nothing of the sort until an army was landed. Churchill
> was asked how long that would take, and was informed, about eight weeks. He
> said 'Oh, we cannot wait such a time as that.' He then was requested anyway
> not to proceed until they could get the [anti-torpedo] nets out to the
> Dardanelles in order to capture the floating mines, a very easy proceeding, as
> there was a tide that would be certain to drive the mines into the nets. He
> asked how long this would take, and was informed six weeks. He said 'Oh, that
> would not do at all; the Fleet would be through long before that.' The result
> has been that in only attacking the outpost forts, we have lost three
> battleships . . .

'In my opinion', he concluded, 'Churchill is a serious danger to the State.
After Antwerp, and now the Dardanelles, the Government really ought to
get rid of him.'[74]

Beresford was wrong on virtually every detail, but Conservative leaders
were predisposed by now to accept that Churchill, impatient and domineering, routinely overrode his professional advisers. This was certainly the
view of Gwynne. However, his knowledge of the Admiralty's inner workings was also inaccurate in most respects. The newspaper editor believed, for
example, that the idea of a naval campaign had originated with Captain
Hall, the DNI. He told General Wilson on 12 April that the scheme had
subsequently been taken up by Churchill, 'having no military knowledge
whatever, but being at the same time a man of dramatic instincts who looks
upon every phase of this war as an opportunity for him to appear before the
footlights, he rushes the thing through'. The rest of Gwynne's account is
similar to Beresford's:

Crinolines [anti-torpedo nets] would take six weeks to make: then no crinolines. Floating mines could be stopped in some mysterious way of his own,
which he never divulged. A large force would take two months: another delay
in the dramatic coup. In vain Jackie and his Board protested against the supersession of the crinolines and the military force. He carried this precious
War Committee of the Cabinet with him, and I am told...that he gave the
Committee to understand that on this question the Board of Admiralty were
with him.[75]

General Wilson, to whom Gwynne confided this story, soon became an
important ally in the campaign against Churchill. Wilson, an Ulsterman, had
been a bitter critic of Churchill immediately before the war because of his
support for Irish home rule. His animosity abated briefly at the outset of
war, but by March 1915 he too had come to the conclusion that Churchill
should be removed from office.[76] On 18 March, the day de Robeck lost a
third of his fleet, Wilson recorded in his diary that he was 'beginning to
hope that the whole Dardanelles affair may prove a fiasco so that we may
try to get rid of Winston. I think it would be cheap.'[77] After news of the
naval setback reached him, he recorded that he could not 'help being
glad as it may teach the people at home to mistrust amateur strategy and
possibly...get Winston removed. With the best intentions in the world he
will do things which will make the victory of the Germans as certain as he
can.'[78] Wilson, one of the army's most 'political' generals, was serving at this
time with the BEF as a member of French's staff. His negative view of
Churchill was initially based on critical reports from Callwell and others at
the War Office. Wilson had close ties with leaders of the Conservative Party,
and his personal campaign against Churchill began on 27 March with a
letter to Bonar Law denouncing the Dardanelles campaign. 'I know enough
of the origination of the scheme', he wrote, 'to know that it was done in a
slap dash manner, without careful thought & preparation & without a clear,
a crystal clear, idea as to what it was we wanted to do and how it was we
were going to do it.'[79]

Wilson's fears were confirmed on a visit to London in April when he
met with Hankey. The War Council Secretary, who knew Fisher's views
better than anyone, informed the general that 'Winston alone [was] responsible for Dardanelles' and that the project had been 'opposed by [the] whole
of naval opinion' and was 'absolutely unthought out'. Hankey suggested,
moreover, that if the operation 'fails it will dégommé [a term used in the
British army at this time to refer to senior officers who were removed from

their posts] Winston'.[80] The following week Wilson met separately with Bonar Law and Lord Milner, another prominent Conservative, to press the case for removing Churchill from office. And on 16 April, he met with Gwynne.[81] The newspaperman subsequently incorporated Wilson's ideas into a letter he sent the Prime Minister on 22 April. This document denounced the Dardanelles campaign at considerable length on both strategic and political grounds, and put the blame for its failure squarely on Churchill's shoulders. 'I considered', Gwynne told Asquith, 'that the Antwerp expedition thoroughly justified the opinion' that Churchill did not belong at the Admiralty, 'and the recurrence [in the Dardanelles] of the same lack of study, the same desire to rush in without due preparation, and the same ignorance of strategic and tactical principles in the Dardanelles expedition confirm this opinion'.[82]

The same day, Beresford asked the Prime Minister in the House of Commons who had been responsible for the Dardanelles, and whether the failure to land troops at the outset had been a mistake.[83] Asquith easily side-stepped the question, and the criticism it implied, and probably had no idea that Gwynne and his allies were about to take their public campaign against the First Lord to a new level. The bombshell burst in the pages Morning Post the following day. Gwynne's outspoken attack in his leader of 23 April, titled 'The Dardanelles Blunder', was widely reported in the British and international press, and was soon being reported in German newspapers. On 24 April, readers of the Berliner Tageblatt, for example, were informed on the authority of the Morning Post that: 'The whole responsibility for the failure [at the Dardanelles] lies with Churchill since he insisted upon the attempted forcing through the fleet alone against the opinion of the experts.'[84] Fisher's opposition to the Dardanelles was therefore known not just to 'all London', as Margot Asquith had observed: thanks to Gwynne, it was known to all Berlin as well.

Predictably, the Liberal press offered a defence of Churchill. The Morning Post was denounced as 'unpatriotic' and castigated for 'encouraging the enemy'.[85] It was widely pointed out, moreover, that the newspaper had offered no evidence to back up its assertions, and that it expected readers to believe that Churchill, a relatively junior Cabinet minister, possessed virtually unlimited power over his colleagues. As the Northampton Mercury observed, Churchill was, according to the Morning Post, 'the supreme superman whom the Prime Minister and the Secretary of State for War and the First Sea Lord and the French Minister of Marine permit to commit what they know to be acts of folly. Does anybody really believe such nonsense?'[86] This was a valid point, but the attack on Churchill was, nevertheless, welcomed by many Conservatives, who were increasingly restive over the party truce that had been in place since the war began. William Joynson-Hicks, a Conservative backbencher who had once defeated Churchill in a by-election, praised the *Morning Post* in its letters page for having 'the courage to say in public *what all men are saying in private*, viz., that Mr. Churchill has in this matter overruled Lord Fisher, and overruled him to the grave detriment of the national interest':

> The truth is that Mr. Churchill has come to regard himself as omnipotent, largely from lack of criticism. Who is to blame for this unhealthy condition of affairs? Surely his Majesty's Opposition. We have been for the last nine months stupidly patriotic, or rather would I say that by our stupid acquiescence in what we believed to be wrong we have carried our so-called patriotism to the verge of treachery to our country. It is so easy to acquiesce and gain the applause of the unthinking for our 'patriotic' conduct. But surely patriotism demands the self-sacrifice of popularity; criticism, even though it be harsh, is, if genuine and honest, necessary to the welfare of this country. . . . This disastrous tenderness on our part allowed him to go on usurping the powers of the Sea Lords, the men who have made a life's study of naval strategy, while his has largely consisted of battles in Sidney-street, Whitechapel.[87]

By the beginning of May, the public controversy over the Dardanelles was straining the party truce.[88] And, unfortunately for Churchill, the story would not die. The subject was raised again by Beresford in the House of Commons on 4 May, and also by Frederick Kellaway, a Liberal backbencher. The former was easily rebuffed by Asquith. The latter, who cited the *Morning Post*'s allegations, bluntly asked Churchill 'whether Lord Fisher was consulted with regard to the March attack on the Dardanelles by the Fleet; and whether he expressed the opinion that the attack ought not to be made in the circumstances in which it was made?' Churchill's reply was curt and dismissive: 'The answer to the first part of the question is in the affirmative, and to the second part in the negative.' What particularly alarmed Kellaway was the fact that the *Morning Post*'s attacks had been reported in German newspapers.[89] The subject was raised once more in Parliament. On 13 May, Joynson-Hicks asked the First Lord 'whether Lord Fisher, in the course of the consultation regarding the March attack on the Dardanelles, expressed the view that it would be wiser to wait for the co-operation of a military force; and, if so, who overruled such advice?'

Churchill was more evasive on this occasion. 'I am sure this House will not approve of this kind of question', he declared, 'which is calculated to be detrimental to public interests of serious importance. The unity and integrity of the Board of Admiralty ought not in time of war to be impugned by any Member.'[90]

It was not just the Admiralty leadership that was being impugned, however. Gwynne's public attack called into question the ability of the Asquith government to manage the nation's war effort, something that reflected badly on all ministers. The *Spectator* made this point clearly on 1 May, noting that if Churchill had 'acted on his own initiative and did not obtain the full consent of his colleagues to his schemes before be put them into operation, then his colleagues should take stock of the whole position and proceed to appropriate action as soon as possible. If, however, they endorsed his proposals, then they are as responsible as he is.'[91] Lloyd George hardly needed to be reminded that Fisher's indiscretions were not just harmful to Churchill. 'We should have made Fisher and Wilson say what they thought in the war council', he complained to Margot Asquith. 'Now Fisher gasses about all over the place saying he was against this expedition—and he was, but he should have said so, neither he nor [Wilson] uttered.'[92]

There is no doubt, though, that Churchill suffered most from the *Morning Post*'s attacks, although he still felt the best course was not to respond publicly to the specific charges made against him. The frequent attacks were a source of considerable frustration, however. Riddell, the chairman of the Newspaper Proprietors' Association and a friend of Churchill, recorded in his diary at the end of April that: 'Winston is evidently very sensitive to criticism in the press although he says he disregards it.'[93] Churchill poured out his frustration to Riddell in his room at the Admiralty. His irritation stemmed in large measure from his absolute conviction that the charges against him over the Dardanelles were unfounded. 'I am not responsible for the expedition', he told Riddell, by which he meant that he was not *solely* responsible, as the press was alleging. 'The whole details were approved by the Cabinet and Admiralty Board', he explained. 'I do not shirk responsibility, but it is untrue to say I have done this off my own bat.' He was confident, moreover, that his tenure at the Admiralty had been a success. 'I have followed every detail [of naval operations] and I think I am the right man for the job', Riddell recorded him saying. 'Then he laughed, "In fact I think the country is damned lucky to have me here just now."'

It is also evident from Churchill's comments that he was looking forward to the time when he could refute the allegations against him not just over the Dardanelles, but also Antwerp, Coronel, and the loss of the three cruisers. 'I have a complete answer for them when the time comes', he asserted. Warming to the subject, he immediately launched into a rehearsal of his defence. Churchill also offered to show his friend 'the private files from which you will see my position is absolutely sound':

He then called in his secretary and told him to get the files which were locked up. When they came Winston went through them and pointed out the important telegrams, etc. As to the North Sea disaster [i.e. the loss of the three cruisers] it appeared that he had written a memorandum, I think on 18th September, saying that slow cruisers should not be used for patrol purposes. The disaster took place I think on the 22nd. As to the Coronel battle, Winston's instructions to Admiral Cochrane [sic] were disobeyed. Winston said, 'He is dead. One does not like to criticise a dead man, but as you have seen he disobeyed orders. He was warned and disregarded the warning.' The telegrams were expressed in remarkably clear language and seemed to betoken great knowledge of the situation. Winston is a wonderful person. The question is whether he has good judgment. As we were talking Fisher put his head into the room and said, 'A person of importance wishes to see you.' Fisher spoke very sharply and seemed to wish to get Winston away. However, he did not go, but went on to tell me that in the early days of the war he had a very difficult task to perform. Prince Louis was very lethargic and Sturdee was not a good Chief of Staff. He is a good fighting admiral but not a clever man. The North Sea disaster seems to have been due in a great measure to the delay in communicating Winston's orders. Winston rang for his secretary and handed him the files to be put away again. I could not help wondering whether Fisher's sudden appearance may not have been due to some communication from Masterton Smith [Churchill's private secretary] warning him that Winston was showing me these secret documents.[94]

The ongoing criticism of Churchill over the Dardanelles in early May prompted Riddell to offer on the 11th to publish a statement from Churchill 'as to [the] political reasons for [the] Dardanelles Expedition'. Riddell was a useful ally for the embattled First Lord, as he had become the principal liaison between the British press and the government. It must have been abundantly clear to Churchill by now that the persistent and escalating attacks by the Conservative press and opposition politicians was doing serious harm to his political position. He was therefore willing to take advantage of his friend's offer to help with damage control, and to this end prepared a statement defending his actions for Riddell to read to his fellow newspapermen.[95] But by now Churchill could have had little doubt that the only sure way to retrieve his reputation was to secure a military victory in the east—and this now depended on the operations that opened on the Gallipoli peninsula on the morning of 25 April.

7
Jacky Fisher's Crisis

The decision to land troops on the Gallipoli peninsula had been taken in a haphazard manner that reflected poorly on all concerned. Kitchener unilaterally committed the army to the operation before Hamilton even departed London for the eastern Mediterranean. In effect, he pre-delegated to his subordinate the authority to proceed with landings if the navy asked for assistance. De Robeck subsequently called for troops, without seeking permission from the Admiralty, because, although he would not admit it, he had lost faith in the naval offensive. Fisher had backed the admiral's decision not to renew the naval attack, but did not seem to realize that, in doing so, he was tacitly endorsing de Robeck's request for the army to occupy the Gallipoli peninsula. Churchill, who did understand the implications, acquiesced because he wanted to ensure that the naval offensive was eventually resumed. These measures were not considered by the full War Council, where the possibility of calling off the entire operation might have been raised by Balfour or Fisher. The decision to land troops was subsequently endorsed by just three ministers—Asquith, Kitchener, and Churchill.

Preparations for landing Allied forces on the Gallipoli peninsula proceeded just as the operation had been conceived: with only the barest oversight from the War Council. Asquith was in no hurry to bring members of his Cabinet together to discuss the change in plan. In the month following the collapse of the naval offensive he allowed Kitchener and Churchill a free hand. After the War Council of 19 March adjourned, the full body did not meet again until 14 May, eight weeks later. The Prime Minister convened only one other meeting to discuss the operation during this period. This was constituted as an 'informal meeting' of the War Council, and took place on 6 April. Once again, the gathering consisted of just the Prime Minister, Kitchener, Churchill, and Hankey. Neither the First Sea Lord nor the CIGS attended. This arrangement, which foreshadowed the later War Cabinet, evidently appealed to Asquith. It streamlined the decision-making process and avoided long and divisive debate amongst his ministers.[1] The discussion on 6 April, judging by Hankey's minutes, was brief. The two service ministers read out the most recent telegrams from their respective commanders in the eastern Mediterranean. Churchill then 'urged that the attack should be pressed home vigorously', and Kitchener 'agreed that the attack would have to be made'. Hankey was, to judge by the minutes, the only voice of caution. He warned that landing troops might be difficult, but Churchill disagreed. According to the official record, the First Lord 'anticipated no difficulty in effecting a landing'. The meeting adjourned shortly afterward.[2]

The Gallipoli campaign commenced on the morning of 25 April, when around 52,000 Allied troops were put ashore on the peninsula. One set of landings took place on Cape Helles, at the southern end of the peninsula, on five separate beaches (see Map 2.2). The other main landing took place approximately 15 kilometres to the north along the Aegean coast, slightly north of the Narrows, in the area that would become known as Anzac Cove. A diversionary landing was also undertaken by the French at Kum Kale, on the Asiatic side of the Straits. Hamilton planned for his forces on the peninsula to move rapidly inland and seize the critical high ground before moving on to capture the Kilid Bahr plateau, but this proved to be overly ambitious. The Ottomans were prepared for the landings and inflicted heavy casualties on the Allied troops, who were fortunate in most cases just to preserve their beachheads. Some commanders judged the situation to be so bad on the first days that they advised Hamilton to re-embark the troops. The general refused to contemplate withdrawal, however, and told his commanders to begin digging in. For several days the situation was precarious, but more troops were poured in by the Allies. It soon became clear that the Ottomans lacked the strength to drive the attackers back into the sea. It was equally clear, however, that the Allies were no better placed to move inland and take the high ground. The troops at Helles were able to consolidate their position, but their subsequent advance north towards Krithia made little progress and they suffered heavy casualties. The situation on the peninsula increasingly resembled that on the Western Front, with two entrenched armies facing one another, neither able to take the offensive without suffering prohibitive losses for little gain. By the end of the second week of the land campaign, Hamilton accepted that a stalemate had emerged. He informed de Robeck that the army had been 'checked'.

The admiral passed this unwelcome news to the Admiralty on 9 May. He now had to face the awkward question Churchill had raised in March: would the navy resume its offensive if the army failed? The First Lord's position was not difficult to predict. Before Churchill could raise the subject afresh de Robeck launched a pre-emptive strike, explaining why he was *against* a resumption of the naval campaign. His main concern was that the Ottoman defences could not be counted on to crumble simply because a fleet had passed through the Straits. This had always been a concern for naval leaders, but the army's recent experience had shown beyond doubt that the enemy was much more determined and resilient than the Allies had expected. This meant that there was a good chance the fleet would find itself in the Sea of Marmara with its communications cut off, and the army still unable to advance. If this happened, only a handful of smaller ships would be available outside the Straits to support the army's operations on the peninsula. The navy might also suffer a serious setback while passing through the Straits, which could jeopardize the army's entire position.[3]

Churchill remained open to the possibility of resuming the naval offensive, even though he now seemed to accept that an Ottoman collapse was far from certain. The alternative was for the navy to remain relatively idle, and that held little appeal. The day after de Robeck's telegram arrived, Churchill asked Jackson to prepare a memorandum on the difficulties the fleet would encounter if forced to withdraw from the Sea of Marmara while the defences along the Straits were still intact. The reply was not encouraging, and intentionally so. Jackson's memorandum explicitly built on his gloomy appreciation of 5 January, which had predicted that an attempt to rush the Straits would put nearly all of the first squadron of eight battleships out of action. Churchill was still thinking in terms of a slow and deliberate advance by the fleet into the Marmara, but Jackson's conclusions were based on the assumption that the Straits would be 'rushed' in both directions. The admiral probably adopted the worst-case scenario deliberately so as to make the memorandum as discouraging as possible. The only bright spot in his assessment was that the current would be working in the fleet's favour on the return trip, which would reduce the time ships were under heavy fire by around 30 per cent. This, he predicted, would decrease to four the number of battleships lost, as against the six he expected to lose on the passage into the Marmara. And these were only the losses from gunfire; Jackson was not prepared to estimate the number of ships that might be sunk by mines and torpedoes. If an attempt was made to rush a fleet of sixteen battleships through the Straits in both directions, Jackson concluded that only four badly damaged vessels would survive.[4]

Fisher was, by now, even more strongly against any attempt to renew the naval attack. On the morning of 11 May he sent for Hankey, who recorded in his diary afterward that the First Sea Lord had been 'in a great state of mind' because Churchill had proposed sending a 'private telegram which Fisher interpreted as leaving de Robeck an option to try if he thought fit. Fisher had declined to agree', his account continued, '& there had been a terrible row.'[5] Fisher might have taken some consolation from the fact that Churchill was prepared to defer to de Robeck, and did not appear to be *insisting* on a new naval attack. This had, after all, been Fisher's position on 22 March when he had stopped Churchill from ordering a renewal of the offensive. But Fisher was now firmly opposed to a renewal of the naval attack in *any* circumstances, whether de Robeck was willing or not. He therefore asked Hankey to prepare a memorandum clearly stating his new position.[6] This document was sent to Churchill later that day, with a covering note by Fisher declaring that it was 'essential that on so vital a point I should not leave you in any doubt as to my opinion'.[7]

Fisher's views were outlined clearly and forcefully in the memorandum Hankey had drafted for him:

> Although I have acquiesced in each stage of the operations up to the present, largely on account of considerations of political expediency and the political advantage which those whose business it is to judge of these matters have assured me would accrue from success, or even partial success, I have clearly expressed my opinion that I did not consider the original attempt to force the Dardanelles with the Fleet alone was a practicable operation.

The document went on to remind Churchill that Fisher had recently reaffirmed his position that additional resources could not be sent to the Dardanelles at the expense of the Grand Fleet 'without a grave risk in the principal theatre of the Naval war':

> I therefore feel impelled to inform you definitely and formally of my conviction that such an attack by the Fleet on the Dardanelles forts, in repetition of the operations which failed on 18th March, or any attempt by the Fleet to rush by the Narrows, is doomed to failure, and, moreover, is fraught with possibilities of disaster utterly incommensurate to any advantage that could be obtained therefrom.

Fisher maintained that recent operations had shown that there was no 'reasonable prospect' of knocking out the Ottoman guns; that it was 'not possible' to sweep the Narrows mines; and that there was no chance of keeping a fleet supplied if it did break through. 'I therefore wish it to be clearly understood', he concluded, 'that I dissociate myself from any such project.'[8]

Churchill was undoubtedly alarmed to receive such a strong protest. He reassured Fisher that he had no intention of attempting to 'rush' the Dardanelles, and correctly pointed out that he had not actually proposed to renew the naval offensive immediately. In fact, the only real difference between them—although one that Churchill deliberately downplayed—was that Churchill was unwilling to rule out the *possibility* that conditions *might* occur in which the naval attack should be renewed. He was more concerned, however, about Fisher's eagerness to disavow any responsibility for the campaign, which could easily turn into further obstruction. 'We are now committed', Churchill wrote, 'to one of the greatest amphibious enterprises of history. You are absolutely committed.' The situation was precarious, he reminded Fisher, with a 'great army hanging on by its eyelids to a rocky beach & confronted with the armed power of the Turkish Empire under German military guidance'. There was no choice, therefore, but to see it through to a successful conclusion. This, Churchill maintained, would 'require from us every conceivable exertion & contrivance'. His letter concluded with an appeal for Fisher's help: 'I beg you to lend your whole aid & good will; & ultimately then success is certain.'[9]

Hankey described Churchill's reply to Fisher as 'rather a slippery one', presumably having noted that it did not rule out the *possibility* of a new naval attack. Fisher was still not happy and the following day proposed to send a copy of his memorandum to Asquith. Hankey advised Fisher to go ahead, 'as it was absolutely necessary', he felt, 'to bring Churchill to his bearings'.[10] The document was sent that day, and Fisher asked that it be circulated to the War Council. He then wrote to Churchill that his 'unwilling acquiescence' in the Dardanelles campaign stopped short of another naval attack like the one on 18 March.[11] The First Lord complained to his private secretary, Masterton Smith, that Fisher was proposing to block *any* attempt by de Robeck to support the army's advance. But since Churchill was not ready to launch another naval attack, he proposed that the question should be left in the air until 'the moment arrives'.[12] In other words, he did not want to argue the matter unless and until a decision was actually required. Fisher was eager to press the issue, however, and reportedly 'had it out' with

Churchill the same day. Their meeting was evidently a productive one. According to Fisher's account, the First Lord agreed that there would be no renewal of the naval attack, and arranged to send *Queen Elizabeth* immediately to join the Grand Fleet. The damaged battle cruiser *Inflexible* was also to go to Jellicoe once its repairs were completed, and de Robeck was to receive two of the navy's new monitors in return.[13]

Asquith was eager to confirm that Churchill and Fisher had really patched up their differences, and sent Hankey to the Admiralty to check that the dispute had been resolved. Masterton Smith agreed that this was so, although he observed that Churchill had not necessarily promised to abandon the idea of a naval attack at some future date. Fisher, however, was clearly under a different impression, although he would soon be disillusioned. On the evening of the 12th, Kitchener visited the Admiralty to complain about the proposed withdrawal of the *Queen Elizabeth*. Fisher reacted angrily, telling the War Secretary that he would resign if the movement did not take place 'at full speed within 12 hours'. Fisher told Jellicoe the next day that the meeting between Kitchener and the Admiralty War Group 'broke up—in disorder!' Typically, Fisher exaggerated his role in this episode, suggesting that his threat of resignation was decisive in overcoming the determined opposition of both Kitchener and Churchill.[14] General Callwell, who accompanied Kitchener to the Admiralty for this meeting, recalled the incident differently:

> When we went across the road we found Mr. Churchill and Lord Fisher waiting in the First Lord's room. After some remarks by Mr. Churchill giving the *pros* and *cons*, Lord Fisher burst out that, unless orders were dispatched to the battleship without delay to 'come out of that', he would resign. The First Lord thereupon, somewhat reluctantly as it seemed to me, intimated that in view of the position taken up by his principal expert adviser, he had no option but to recall the vessel. Lord Kitchener demurred, but he demurred very mildly. There was no jumping up and going off in a huff. Some perfectly amicable discussion as to one or two other points of mutual interest ensued, and when we took our departure the Chief [Kitchener] was in the very best of humours and asked me if he had made as much fuss as was expedient under the circumstances.[15]

Fisher also became indignant that Churchill was wavering on his earlier commitment not to renew the naval offensive. He wrote to Asquith after the meeting to complain that the First Lord had told the Field Marshal ' "that in the event of the Army's failure, the Fleet would endeavour to force its way through", or words to that effect'. Moreover, he claimed that Churchill was endeavouring to transfer still more resources to the Dardanelles. Fisher concluded by warning Asquith *that I feel my time is short!*'[16]

Churchill, however, was not pressing for an immediate renewal of the naval assault. He sent a 'personal' telegram to de Robeck on the evening of the 13th saying that 'the moment for an independent Naval attempt to force the Narrows has passed and will not arise again under present conditions'. This may have been designed to mollify Fisher, but Churchill does appear to have been content for the moment that the navy should continue supporting the army's operations.[17] The more pressing problem was the fallout from the withdrawal of the *Queen Elizabeth*. Churchill attempted to defend the decision when the full War Council met on 14 May, for the first time in nearly two months. He noted that the troops in Gallipoli would be just as well supported by the two monitors being despatched to the theatre. Kitchener, according to one minister, was 'very angry'.[18] He read a statement to the War Council claiming that he had agreed reluctantly to the Dardanelles campaign only because he had been assured that the new battleship would guarantee the operation's success. He now suggested that naval leaders had misled him as to the power of the ship's guns, and that its withdrawal would deprive the army of vital support. These arguments were groundless. The *Queen Elizabeth* had never been assigned permanently to the eastern squadron, and its guns were not essential to the success of the army's operations. The battleship's main contribution was to have been the bombardment of the Ottoman forts from a greater distance than the other warships, and, in particular, its ability to fire across the peninsula. The removal of this ship would have no direct impact on the campaign unless the navy resumed its attempt to force the Straits, which was not then under consideration. Kitchener's concerns really stemmed from the impact the ship's withdrawal could have on British prestige. 'It would be taken as the first sign of the abandonment of the enterprise', he warned, 'and as the first of many withdrawals.' He feared that it might even involve the risk of a rising in Egypt.[19]

After the meeting adjourned, Churchill wrote to Asquith expressing his concerns about both Kitchener and Fisher. He feared that the War Minister would be tempted to 'punish' the Admiralty for withdrawing the *Queen Elizabeth* by withholding troops from Hamilton. But he was much more troubled by Fisher, who had bluntly stated during the meeting 'that he had been no party to the Dardanelles operations'.[20] Churchill insisted that Fisher could not so easily escape responsibility, since he had 'agreed in writing' to every order sent by the Admiralty. What really worried him, however, was what might happen if it became necessary to resume the naval offensive. The time might come, he warned Asquith, when de Robeck and Hamilton would 'wish & require to run a risk with the Fleet for a great and decisive effort'. Churchill feared that Fisher's hostility to the operation could jeopardize everything. He told Asquith that if the commanders on the spot advised action by the fleet, and if he agreed with them, 'I cannot undertake to be paralyzed by the veto of a friend who whatever the result will certainly say "I was always against the D[ardane]lles."'

> You will see that in a matter of this kind *someone* has to take the responsibility. I will do so—provided that my decision is the one that rules—& not otherwise.... But I wish now to make it clear to you that a man who says 'I disclaim responsibility for failure' cannot be the final arbiter of the measure wh[ich] may be found to be vital to success.[21]

Churchill was giving notice that he intended to overrule his chief professional adviser on an operational matter if he considered it necessary, on the advice of the commanders on the spot, to ensure the success of the Dardanelles campaign. He could have had no doubt that Fisher would immediately resign if this happened, but he was now so committed to the success of the Dardanelles campaign that he was willing to take exceptional political risks to see it though. If, as he believed, a naval attack led to victory, Fisher would clearly be in the wrong and Churchill could weather the political storm that would be created by the First Sea Lord's resignation. But since no such action was then in sight, Churchill was content to continue working with Fisher. Fisher was the fourth First Sea Lord to serve under Churchill since 1911. His resignation so soon after taking office would fuel doubts about Churchill's management of the Admiralty.

As troubled as he was by Fisher's recent behaviour, Churchill did not take seriously his continued threats to resign. When Violet Asquith asked him 'if he knew he was on the edge of a volcano in his relations with Fisher', Churchill 'said no—they had always got on perfectly loyal etc.' But Churchill was bad at reading people, as Violet knew well. 'Poor Winston', she wrote, 'there is a very naïve disarming trustfulness about him—he is quite insensitive to climatic conditions.'[22] Churchill also continued to overestimate his ability to 'manage' Fisher. Shortly after Churchill left the Admiralty, Violet recorded that he 'said quite ingenuously: "That's why I took him [i.e. Fisher]—because I knew he was old and weak—& that I should be able to keep things in my own hands." '[23] These were serious miscalculations. Fisher was neither as loyal nor as malleable as Churchill thought. Nor was the Dardanelles the only source of friction in their relationship. Fisher's irritation with Churchill's methods had been building for months. Crease recalled that 'Fisher became annoyed at Churchill's constant intervention in purely technical matters which should have been left for the Sea Lords and technical departments.' The admiral was also 'continually and increasingly irritated by the First Lord's methods in dealing with telegrams and in issuing often in his own name executive orders to the fleets, squadrons and ships'. Crease observed that Churchill typically drafted telegrams on the basis of the conclusions reached by the Admiralty's 'War Group'. These were not always shown to Fisher before being sent:

> Churchill had acquired habit of speaking and acting on behalf of the Board [of Admiralty] on his own responsibility, for his First Sea Lords had been of different calibre and temperament to Lord Fisher. In his eagerness to get on with the work he did not attach much importance to the form so long as the substance was secured. And no doubt he [Churchill] felt he was the best interpreter of the Admiralty instructions and views even in operational matters.... Most of his telegrams leave the idea that it was Mr. Churchill speaking and not the Board. Any naval officer seeing them will see the reasons for Lord Fisher's irritation, which was not decreased because as a rule there was nothing definite to which exception could be taken!... I had ample evidence of the irritation so caused, by the sulphurous... comments of Lord Fisher as he read his daily copies.

Crease also recalled that Fisher became increasingly irritated by Churchill's practice of seeking advice on the Dardanelles directly from Wilson and Jackson.[24]

On the evening of 14 May, following the stormy meeting of the War Council, Churchill and Fisher still appeared capable of working together amicably. They agreed to the dispatch of certain reinforcements to de Robeck's fleet and Fisher, as was his practice, left the Admiralty while Churchill continued working late into the night. When the First Sea Lord returned to the Admiralty early the next morning he discovered that Churchill had proposed to send additional forces to the Dardanelles beyond what had been agreed the evening before, including two submarines.[25] Churchill had left Fisher a note saying that these measures could be discussed before any action was taken, but Fisher was nonetheless indignant. According to Crease, this incident was what finally caused Fisher to carry through on his threat to resign.[26]

The admiral prepared a short letter to the First Lord announcing that he had 'come to the regretted conclusion I am unable to remain any longer as your Colleague'. He did not explain his reasons, on the dubious grounds that it was 'undesirable in the public interests to go into details'. All he would say was that he found 'it increasingly difficult to adjust myself to the increasingly daily requirements of the Dardanelles to meet yr views—As you truly said yesterday I am in the position of continually veto-ing yr proposals.—This is not fair to you besides being extremely distasteful to me.' A similar letter was also dispatched to the Prime Minister.[27] Fisher's previous attempt to take a stand had ended with the admiral being diverted from his path by Churchill and Asquith, much to his subsequent regret. Fisher had so little confidence in his ability to stand up to the appeals of the politicians that he now went to extraordinary lengths to avoid any contact with them. His letters to Churchill and Asquith stated that he was leaving 'at once' for Scotland 'so as to avoid all questionings', but this was a deliberate false trail. Fisher remained in London. He absented himself from the Admiralty, however, and avoided his official residence so as to create the impression that he had, in fact, left the capital.

Crease promptly passed Fisher's letter to Masterton Smith, telling him that Fisher ' "really meant it this time", and that nothing would persuade him to remain at the Admiralty working with Winston'.[28] Masterton Smith rushed to convey the news to Churchill, intercepting him in the Horse Guards' Parade on his return to the Admiralty after a meeting at the Foreign Office. Churchill later recalled that he did not yet take Fisher's threat seriously, but the gravity of the situation soon became evident when the First Sea Lord could not be located.[29] On the morning of 15 May, during the greatest war in modern times, the professional head of the Royal Navy did not want to be found. But the fact remained that, until his resignation was formally accepted, Fisher was still First Sea Lord. Asquith soon lost patience, telling Masterton Smith that 'it was a grave dereliction of duty for an officer, holding the foremost Naval place, in time of war, to desert the post assigned to him by the King and to be unavailable at such a time for the conduct of urgent and immediate naval business'.[30] The Prime Minister wrote a note ordering Fisher, in the King's name, to return to his post, and charged Masterton Smith with tracking down the wayward admiral to deliver it. The private secretary later reported to Asquith that he returned to the Admiralty and:

[A]t once spoke to Crease and made every effort in my power to discover Fisher's whereabouts—but without success. Bearing in mind Fisher's intimation

to Crease that he intended to leave for Scotland I had two copies made of your
minute of direction, of which I handed one to Crease and the other I gave to
a messenger with instructions to proceed to the railway station from which
the next fast train to Scotland was scheduled to leave, to wait on the platform
until the train left and to hand the letter containing this direction to Fisher
if he should be in the train. Needless to say the messenger's mission was
fruitless.

The Prime Minister also sent his own private secretary, Maurice Bonham
Carter, to scour the city for Fisher. The absurdity of these events was not lost
on him. Violet Asquith recorded that her father 'c[ou]ldn't help laughing at
[the] extraordinary comic aspects' of the situation.[31]

Fisher was eventually tracked down at the Charing Cross Hotel in central
London and brought to Downing Street that afternoon for a meeting with
Asquith. He informed both the Prime Minister and Lloyd George, whom
he met on the way, that he refused to work with Churchill any longer.
Violet Asquith recalled that her father's meeting with Fisher lasted about an
hour. When the admiral refused to withdraw his resignation, Asquith insisted
that he 'must do so in the proper way and put his reasons for doing so in
writing'.[32] Churchill, also, was eager to learn the specific reason for Fisher's
departure. He wrote to the admiral that day hoping to obtain an explanation
so that he might attempt to remedy Fisher's grievances and keep him at the
Admiralty. He first appealed to Fisher on grounds of friendship, noting that
he had taken a huge personal and political risk in appointing the admiral as
First Sea Lord against the opposition of both the King and the Prime
Minister. Churchill had told Riddell a few weeks earlier that ' "Fisher and
I have made an agreement. If we stand together my enemies are powerless."
He seemed very sure of Fisher.'[33] Churchill now reminded the admiral that
he had 'promised to stand by me and see me through'. Fisher, in his view,
was honour bound to support him, since Churchill's political enemies
would exploit the admiral's resignation to the fullest.

Churchill also appealed to Fisher's sense of duty. Resigning at this
moment, he wrote, would 'strike a cruel blow at the fortunes of the Army
now struggling on the Gallipoli peninsula' and would 'invest [the campaign]
with an air of disaster'. This, he maintained, would be 'profoundly injurious
to every public interest'.[34] But Fisher was determined this time not to give
in. He wrote to Churchill the following morning, reaffirming his decision
to resign, although he still did not furnish the clear explanation for which
Asquith had asked. He left no doubt, however, that the Dardanelles had

been the root cause. 'You are bent on forcing the Dardanelles', he wrote, 'and nothing will turn you from it—nothing. I know you so well!!' What did Fisher hope to gain by tendering his resignation? He told Churchill, 'You will remain and I shall go. It is better so.'[35] His real intentions, however, were exactly the opposite. He could not have predicted that his actions would precipitate the downfall of the Liberal government, but he undoubtedly knew that his resignation would cause a political crisis. And he had good reason to assume that, when the dust settled, Churchill would be gone from the Admiralty and he would remain. To ensure that a full-blown crisis did erupt, Fisher sent a cryptic communication to Bonar Law tipping off the leader of the Conservative Party to his resignation.[36]

Fisher's main concern throughout the following day, 16 May, was to ensure that he did not have to face either Asquith or Churchill before news of his resignation had spread too far for the government to conceal it. He instructed Crease to have Masterton Smith tell Churchill not to come see him, and belatedly proposed that the Second Sea Lord should take over his official duties.[37] Asquith attempted to use Reginald McKenna, a former First Lord of the Admiralty and a close friend of Fisher, as an intermediary, but this had no effect. The admiral insisted that he had, in fact, resigned, and asked McKenna 'to tell the Prime Minister distinctly and definitely that *I am no longer First Sea Lord. There is no compromise possible!*'[38] McKenna was probably a bad choice for this mission. He detested Churchill and shared Fisher's concerns about the Dardanelles. Later that day he described the naval offensive to Margot Asquith as 'impossible. We shall perhaps get 6 ships through, but we shall lose 20. . . . We shall have to send more ships till we are bled white. . . . I know you think it is mere prejudice on my part', he continued, 'but Winston is a real danger. . . . The public won't stand Fisher going and Winston remaining, of that I am quite sure.'[39] McKenna's visit to Fisher may, in fact, have only served to strengthen the admiral's resolve.

In the event, Asquith was unwilling to release Fisher from his duties until he received the admiral's 'precise grounds definitely formulated in writing'.[40] In the meantime, Churchill made another attempt to persuade Fisher to remain in office. He wrote to the admiral again on the 16th promising not to press him to send any more reinforcements to de Robeck, and reassuring him that there would be no attempt to rush the Narrows. It is probably no accident, however, that Churchill only ruled out a 'rush' through the Dardanelles, and made no mention of another attempt to pass through after a deliberate bombardment like the one on 18 March. No matter how badly

Fisher's resignation could hurt him politically, Churchill was still unwilling to rule out the *possibility* of resuming the naval offensive. He probably assumed Fisher would not notice this detail. To avert a crisis, he appealed again to Fisher not to jeopardize the campaign by resigning, especially as Italy, still a neutral state, appeared to be on the verge of entering the war on the side of the Allies. 'You must not act', he advised, 'so anyone can say you were unmindful of public interests and lives of soldiers and sailors.' But if Fisher really were determined to resign, Churchill insisted that he had a right to meet with the admiral first, 'if only for the purpose of settling what explanation to be offered to Parliament'.[41]

This letter also had no effect. Fisher replied with a short note declining to meet with Churchill. 'I could say nothing', he insisted, 'as I am determined not to.'[42] While Fisher waited for the crisis to escalate, he was dismayed by the lack of support from within the Admiralty. The other three sea lords, whose influence had been eclipsed since the outbreak of war by the new Admiralty 'War Group', expressed sympathy for Fisher's position, but in a joint letter to Churchill and Fisher they declined to follow Fisher's lead and resign in the face of a 'national crisis of the first magnitude'. In their view, there were no issues so great that they could not be settled through 'mutual discussion and concession'.[43] Admiral Wilson also wrote to Fisher, urging him to stay at his post. 'It would mean a great national disaster', he warned, 'and you have no right to consider your private feelings in the matter while the interests of the country are so much at stake as they are now.'[44]

Churchill took full advantage of these sentiments. He was able to persuade Wilson to take over from Fisher as First Sea Lord, and the rest of the Board of Admiralty agreed to remain at their posts. Churchill informed the Prime Minister of these arrangements on the evening of the 16th, and Asquith, who was content to see Churchill remain at the Admiralty, was evidently ready to accept them. It still seemed possible to keep the crisis at the Admiralty contained, and Churchill was confident that the reformed Board of Admiralty would settle matters. 'I only wish I could have put it in all the papers tonight', he remarked to Margot Asquith, 'just to dish Fisher.' Margot, who had a better grasp of how serious the situation still was, shot back: 'How can you be so childish?':

> There will be a tremendous outcry if Fisher goes. It is <u>all–important</u> to patch this up. For God's sake, hurry <u>nothing</u>, as it will only break the Government. You think you'll get on with Arthur Wilson? I give you 10 days, or at outside 12.

W[inston]. Why! I see him every day, and we get on very well.

M[argot]. He is more or less your guest now, but I'm pretty sure you would both hate each other very soon.[45]

Later that evening Churchill began preparing a statement to give the House of Commons the next day explaining the changes taking place, and defending the policies that led to his rupture with Fisher.

These plans were soon overtaken by events. Fisher wrote to Asquith the following morning, Monday the 17th, to say that he would definitely be leaving the Admiralty that day. He added a curious postscript claiming that he had 'not seen a single visitor of any kind since last Friday except McKenna as authorised by you'.[46] This may have been strictly true, but Fisher had indirectly warned Bonar Law of the trouble at the Admiralty. The admiral evidently did not want to be blamed for leaking his resignation to the opposition. He wrote to Asquith later the same day saying that Lord Esher had told him that 'it was common knowledge that I had left the Admiralty and that he knew of it yesterday [i.e. on the 16th]'. Presumably Fisher wanted to reassure Asquith that he was not the source of Esher's information.[47] And this was probably true. However, it was convenient to him that news was getting out, and that Esher could be blamed for the leak. But at the same time, Fisher was becoming concerned that if he was replaced by Wilson, as Churchill intended, Asquith might yet succeed in averting a full-blown crisis. He therefore wrote directly to Bonar Law, urging him in strong terms to take immediate action. 'This letter and its contents', he began, 'must not be divulged now or ever to any living soul.' Fisher insisted that Asquith must not be allowed to keep his resignation quiet. 'I must not see you', he told Law, 'but Parliament should not rise till the fact of my going is extracted. Lots of people must know.' To cover his own indiscretions, Fisher suggested that Law consult Esher, who could then be identified as the source of his inside information.

Fisher was no less determined that Churchill be forced from the Admiralty. The First Lord, he wrote, was a 'REAL DANGER'. 'Don't be cajoled *privately* by the P.M. to keep silence.'

> The danger is imminent and VITAL. I don't want to stay, but W.C. MUST go at all costs! AT ONCE...you must be most prudent and not give me away, but I feel bound to tell you as Leader of the Opposition, because *a very great national disaster is very near us in the Dardanelles! Against which I have vainly protested and did not resign long ago*...W.C. is a bigger danger than the Germans by a long way in what is just now imminent in the Dardanelles.[48]

In fact, Bonar Law had already moved to take advantage of the situation. He visited Lloyd George on the morning of the 17th to confirm Fisher's departure, and met with Asquith soon afterward. The timing could not have been worse for the Liberal government. Fisher's resignation coincided with another emerging crisis following sensational allegations in the Northcliffe press that Britain's recent offensive on the Western Front had failed because the BEF had not been adequately supplied with ammunition. The resulting 'shells scandal', combined with the crisis at the Admiralty, was too much for the Conservatives. Party leaders were no longer willing to stifle their criticisms of Asquith's ministry on patriotic grounds. The Prime Minister promptly agreed to enter into a coalition with the opposition parties, a development that took Churchill and many others by surprise. One of the Conservative leaders' conditions for coalition was that Churchill be removed from the Admiralty. Asquith was not disposed to argue.

The only question remaining, it seemed, was the fate of Fisher. With Churchill on the way out, the admiral no longer had any reason to resign. And since he had many supporters within the Conservative Party, the formation of the new government could only work in his favour. For a time, it seemed that he might be kept on as First Sea Lord. 'I think Jacky has triumphed', Harcourt wrote on the 18th.[49] But Fisher's prospects crumbled with surprising speed, and entirely from his own actions. His first misstep occurred on the afternoon of the 17th, as the composition of the new government was still being discussed. Decrypted German signals suggested that the German fleet was about to sail into the North Sea. Churchill was still First Lord when the news arrived, and he immediately rushed to the Admiralty. He was joined there by Vice-Admiral Sir Frederick Hamilton, the Second Sea Lord, who stood in for the absent Fisher, and two other members of the old War Group, Oliver and Wilson. Throughout the afternoon there appeared to be a possibility of a major fleet action. But Fisher, who technically remained First Sea Lord, was still determined to avoid meeting Churchill and obstinately refused to return to the Admiralty.[50] This may be because he correctly anticipated the German sortie was a false alarm, but his naval colleagues were nonetheless dismayed that he would refuse to take up his post with a great sea battle possibly imminent. Churchill, who still hoped to remain at the Admiralty with Wilson as his First Sea Lord, was quick to exploit this. He informed Asquith on the 20th that the three sea lords 'take a vy serious view of Lord Fisher's desertion of his post in time of war for what has now amounted to six days, during wh[ich] serious operations have been in progress'.[51] Fisher's mysterious absence from the Admiralty could not be kept quiet. *The Times* reported on 18 May that the 'fact that LORD FISHER was not in attendance, and that certain definite steps were apparently taken in his office yesterday afternoon, became known not only to all members of the immense Admiralty staff, but to many outside it'.[52]

Fisher's next misstep was more serious. With Churchill's departure from office seemingly settled, Fisher assumed his own position was secure and, consequently, overplayed his hand. Encouraged by his old friend Esher, Fisher now hoped to return to the Admiralty with his powers considerably strengthened.[53] He probably had his sights set on achieving a position analogous to Kitchener's at the War Office. Hankey records that, when he met the admiral on the 18th, Fisher complained that he no longer wished to devote 40–60 per cent of his energy to managing a First Lord, 'so he wants to be First Lord' himself.[54] The following day Fisher drafted his 'terms' for remaining in office. Churchill would have to be removed not just from the Admiralty, but from the Cabinet altogether. Balfour, who had angered Fisher by his support for the Dardanelles operation, and was now regarded as Churchill's likely successor, was not to become First Lord. Admiral Wilson, who was widely seen as a serious contender for the post of First Sea Lord, was to be banished from both the Admiralty and the War Council. The junior sea lords, who had declined to resign in support of Fisher, were all to be replaced. Fisher then demanded that he be given 'complete professional charge of the War at sea', including absolute control over fleet movements; the appointment of officers, 'of all ranks whatsoever'; and naval construction. He did not demand to be made First Lord, but insisted that whoever held the post should be 'absolutely restricted to policy and parliamentary procedure'. In effect, the First Lord would be reduced to the position of a parliamentary under-secretary.

Fisher's letter promised that if these conditions were met, he could 'guarantee the successful termination of the War'. He insisted, however, that his conditions 'must be published verbatim so that the Fleet may know my position'.[55] The letter was a colossal miscalculation. Hankey, who was increasingly frustrated with Fisher's erratic behaviour, was horrified when the First Sea Lord showed him his 'preposterous' set of terms. He warned the admiral that 'no self-respecting Minister would look at them'.[56] 'Lord Fisher madder than ever', he confided to his diary. Hankey was also concerned, with good reason, that Fisher, who was known for his vindictive streak, would immediately begin 'head hunting' if he returned to the Admiralty. Churchill had similar concerns, and warned Asquith that both the sea lords and 'many officers of the department who have been associated with me' were worried that their positions would become 'vy difficult' if Fisher returned.[57] Fisher ignored Hankey's warnings, however, and sent his letter to Asquith later that day. Any chance he had of returning to the Admiralty immediately disappeared.[58] The Prime Minister was 'greatly incensed' by Fisher's terms.[59] He complained to Lord Stamfordham, the King's private secretary, that the admiral's letter 'indicates signs of mental aberration!'[60] Asquith was even more dismissive when he spoke to Harcourt a few days later, describing Fisher as 'a raving maniac who ought not to be at large'.[61] Balfour, who had always been well disposed towards Fisher, wrote that 'I am afraid Jacky is a little mad.'[62] Hankey, like most who knew the full story, concluded 'that whatever happened he [Fisher] could not go back to the Admiralty'.[63]

In fact, there was no longer any chance of Fisher remaining First Sea Lord. Asquith would not have him, and even Conservative supporters like Bonar Law saw that he had committed a monumental error of judgement.[64] The general view, summed up by Hankey, was that 'Jackie had got megalomania.'[65] Fisher's position deteriorated even further in the days to come as more of his indiscretions came to light. Hankey recorded on the 19th that Fisher had been 'intriguing horribly' with both the Conservatives and Lord Northcliffe, the newspaper magnate.[66] Two days later, J. A. Spender, editor of the *Westminster Gazette*, revealed after dinner at 10 Downing Street that Fisher 'had been to him and was threatening a public attack on the Government & to state that the Grand Fleet was insufficient'. According to Hankey, who was present at the dinner, Spender 'really believed Fisher was a bit "off his balance"; McKenna agreed; and I could really not deny it'.[67] The following day, Fisher made a final attempt to discredit his main rival for the post of First Sea Lord, Arthur Wilson. He warned Bonar Law that Jellicoe and the whole Grand Fleet were opposed to Wilson's appointment. 'I can only hope that Jellicoe will not resign in consequence—that indeed would bring down the British Empire. *For the matter of that so will Sir A. Wilson if First Sea Lord!*'[68] But no one was listening any more. Later that day, Hankey persuaded Fisher to depart at last for Scotland, where he could do no further mischief. Asquith's letter accepting his resignation followed soon afterwards.

Churchill was every bit as determined as Fisher to remain at the Admiralty, but his efforts were no more successful. At first, he did not seem to realize how badly the formation of a coalition would hurt him. Lloyd George told Stevenson on 18 May that 'Churchill was taking his defeat very well. "I feel like a wounded man"', he reportedly told the Chancellor. '"I know I am hurt, but as yet I cannot tell how badly. Later on I shall know the extent to which I am damaged, but now I only feel the shock." '[69] By the following day, however, he had no illusions as to the seriousness of his situation. When he found that two of his closest colleagues, Lloyd George and Grey, had accepted his departure from the Admiralty with equanimity, Churchill 'completely los[t] his temper': '"You don't care ... what becomes of me", he admonished the Chancellor. "You don't care whether I am trampled under foot by my enemies. You don't care for my personal reputation..." '.[70] In desperation, he made a final attempt to persuade Fisher to remain with him at the Admiralty. On the evening of 19 May, Churchill dispatched George Lambert, a Liberal MP and the Civil Lord of the Admiralty, to offer Fisher, in his own words, 'a seat in the Cabinet if I would return as his First Sea Lord with him (Winston) as First Lord! I rejected the 30 pieces of silver to betray my country.'[71]

The main obstacle to Churchill remaining at the Admiralty was not Fisher, however, but the Conservative Party, which could barely conceal its glee at the prospect of ousting him. Ironically, Churchill had long been favourably disposed towards the idea of a coalition government, often to the dismay of his Liberal colleagues.[72] He does not seem to have realized the depths of the rival party's hostility towards him. Churchill had, of course, made a high-profile defection from the Conservatives to the Liberals early in his career. But Conservative animosity in 1915 was driven by Churchill's prominent role in the bitter political struggles of recent years, including the battle over House of Lords reform (the 'Peers vs the People') and, especially, over home rule for Ireland. Their distrust of Churchill had only increased since the outbreak of the war, fuelled by the attacks of the Morning Post. The belief that the First Lord rode roughshod over his professional advisers was gaining momentum in early May, as other newspapers began to speak out on the subject. The Spectator, for example, while acknowledging that the charges against Churchill were as yet unproven, maintained that there were many people 'who, though they have no personal feeling against Mr. Churchill, have come to regard him as a public danger'.[73] The Times, a Conservative paper owned by Lord Northcliffe, which had so far refrained from direct attacks on Churchill, began openly calling for his dismissal. 'What long ago passed beyond the stage of mere rumour', according to a leader on 18 May, 'is the charge, which has been repeatedly and categorically made in public, that the FIRST LORD OF THE ADMIRALTY has been assuming responsibilities and overriding his expert advisers to a degree which might at any time endanger the national safety.'

> When a civilian Minister in charge of a fighting service persistently seeks to grasp power which should not pass into his unguided hands, and attempts to use that power in perilous ways, it is time for his colleagues in the Cabinet to take some definite action. Such is the stage which they appear to have reached.[74]

Even Liberal newspapers began to echo the *Morning Post*'s criticisms. 'It had been an open secret for some time', the *Daily Chronicle* reported on 19 May, 'that Lord Fisher and Mr. Churchill...were at variance', primarily over the Dardanelles. 'It is universally admitted', the newspaper announced, 'that the original naval attack on the Dardanelles ought to have been supported by land operations on a large scale.'[75]

These criticisms found a receptive audience in the ranks of the Conservative Party, which was in no mood to be forgiving now that their adversary's star was falling. Asquith was the only possible source of salvation. Clementine Churchill wrote to the Prime Minister on 20 May imploring him to leave her husband at the Admiralty, with Wilson as First Sea Lord. 'If you throw Winston overboard you will be committing an act of weakness', she charged, 'and your Coalition Government will not be as formidable a War machine as the present Government.'[76] Asquith was not impressed. 'Clemmie...wrote me the letter of a maniac', he told Venetia Stanley.[77] Churchill also wrote to the Prime Minister the next day, lamenting the possibility that he would be removed from the Admiralty 'on mere uninformed newspaper hostility'. He followed with an emotional plea to accept the reconstituted Board of Admiralty he had proposed four days earlier. 'It is no clinging to office', he wrote, 'or to this particular office or my own interest or advancement wh[ich] moves me. I am clinging to my *task* & to my *duty*.' What seemed to bother Churchill most at this juncture was that he would not have the opportunity to defend his actions in public or to his new Conservative colleagues before he was forced from office. 'I can only look to you', he concluded. 'Let me stand or fall by the Dardanelles—but do not take it from my hands.'[78]

This missive was also misjudged. Churchill, in his desperation, continued to misread the political landscape. The Prime Minister had bigger concerns in the midst of this crisis than the fate of any one member of his Cabinet, particularly as many of them would have to vacate their posts to make way for Conservatives. Asquith might conceivably have made a stand on Churchill's behalf if the Liberal Party had demanded it, but this did not happen. On the contrary, Liberal backbenchers were disposed to blame Churchill for the crisis that had brought down the government. Asquith's private secretary, who was well placed to watch the crisis unfold, observed that 'Winston is without an inkling of what the [Liberal] party feels towards him.'[79] The Prime Minister told his daughter Violet that 'all the cream of the party...were in open revolt at the Coalition', which they blamed on the '2 Tories in the Cabinet W. & K. who had brought us to ruin as it was'.[80] It is only to be expected that Churchill's role in Fisher's resignation would engender resentment, but the party's misgivings ran much deeper. Churchill's close friendship with F. E. Smith, a prominent Conservative, his enthusiasm for coalition, and his support for conscription, the most illiberal of causes, all deepened the party's suspicions. Some Liberal MPs even suspected Churchill of involvement in the disclosures that had led to the 'shells scandal'. One wrote to Asquith stating that he and his colleagues would regard Churchill's 'presence in the [coalition] Government as a public danger'.[81]

Churchill had been viewed with misgivings within the Liberal Party long before the crisis of May 1915 raised fresh doubts about his loyalty. Within the anti-militarist 'radical wing' of the party, Churchill had been unpopular for his support of ever-increasing expenditure on naval armaments. But the problems ran deeper than this. The Liberal Party's rank and file had never warmed to Churchill, despite appreciating his many gifts. 'Though Winston inspired devotion in his personal friends', Violet Asquith noted in her memoirs, 'and in those who served him, he could not have been described as popular.'

> I was constantly aware of the hostility he seemed to provoke, quite unconsciously and unwittingly. Lord Beaverbrook has written that in the Conservative Party 'he was hated, he was mistrusted, and he was feared'. Among certain sections of our own party he was an object of vague suspicion. His successes were grudgingly conceded, while his failures were greeted with exultant Schadenfreude. Why was it, I wondered unceasingly. Most people recognized his genius. Were they jealous of it? Were they afraid of it? Or were they merely offended because they believed him to be insufficiently

interested in themselves and their opinions? In this belief they were, inciden-
tally, dead right. He was not interested. Nor did he seek to conceal his
indifference by any softening subterfuge. To save his life he could not have
pretended to an interest that he did not feel, nor would he have thought it
worth doing. He enjoyed the ovation of the crowd but he still ignored the
necessity of having a personal following.[82]

One of Churchill's few supporters on the Liberal backbenches, A. MacCallum
Scott, reached similar conclusions. 'Churchill's greatest weakness', he wrote
in a 1916 biography, 'lay in his lack of a personal following in any quarter of
the House.'

> His personal friends were few. He was not a man who encouraged intimacies.
> His brusqueness often verged on rudeness, and alienated many a well-wisher.
> Many members of the House had never exchanged words in conversation
> with him. Many Liberals had never ceased to distrust him, some because they
> regarded him as a political adventurer, others because they felt that, in spite of
> his rare intuition for the popular mind, he was essentially an aristocrat, and
> others, again, because they knew nothing of his personal qualities.... Thus it
> came about that, at the time when he most needed support, he stood alone.[83]

Churchill's isolation in May 1915 was painfully evident. 'It seems strange',
Frances Stevenson reflected, 'that Churchill should have been in politics all
these years, & yet not have won the confidence of a single party in the
country, or a single colleague in the Cabinet.'[84]

Churchill's supporters within the government were indeed few. Asquith
had told his wife in March that Churchill was 'far the most disliked man in
my Cabinet by his colleagues'. His strongest critic was Reginald McKenna,
whom Churchill had replaced as First Lord in 1911. Riddell noted during the
war that 'McKenna's animosity to Winston is one of the most virulent and
persistent hatreds I have ever known.'[85] After Churchill was forced from office
in 1915, Riddell speculated that McKenna might even have 'conspired with
Fisher to bring down Winston. He would have stopped at nothing—not even
at stabbing him in the back in a dark lane.'[86] Even Lloyd George, a friend and
sometimes close ally, was frequently exasperated by his colleague's behaviour.
He developed strong doubts about Churchill's judgement early in the war. In
September 1914, for example, he complained to Riddell, saying that 'he cannot
trust Winston—never knows what he may be up to and afraid to leave town
for long for fear Winston may bring forward some dangerous plan'.[87] And
shortly before Fisher's resignation he complained to Margot Asquith that
'Winston is a difficult fellow: he has not merely <u>bad</u> judgment but he has

none.'[88] Churchill had also managed to alienate Lord Kitchener. Harcourt recorded during the crisis that the War Minister was 'very angry at Churchill's interference in military affairs, his visits to Sir J. French & others at front and his system [of] secret correspondence thro' Jack Churchill with Sir Ian Hamilton at the Dardanelles. It is thought that if Churchill remains at the Admlty., Kitchener may go.'[89]

Churchill's role in provoking the political crisis also irritated his Cabinet colleagues. Earl Beauchamp, the First Commissioner of Works, reported that the 'feeling among his colleagues is that he [Churchill] is primary cause of trouble and should be first to go instead of others who will lose their seats in cabinet'.[90] Asquith really had little choice. Churchill's political enemies and many of his Liberal colleagues clamoured for his removal from the Admiralty, and not a single powerful voice was raised on his behalf. Asquith's patronage had been vital to Churchill's rapid rise within the Liberal Party, but even he was frustrated at times by Churchill's behaviour. 'Oh! he is intolerable!', Asquith had explained to Margot two months before: '*noisy*, long-winded and full of perorations.'[91] Churchill's desperate bid to remain at the Admiralty in May 1915 only succeeded in irritating the Prime Minister, who finally sent him 'a stern note to say that he must make up his mind that he must go'.[92]

A chastened Churchill replied that he would 'accept any office—the lowest if you like—that you care to offer me'.[93] He met with Asquith on 22 May to learn his fate. '[A] most painful interview to me', the Prime Minister wrote afterwards, 'but he was good & in his best mood. And it ended all right.' However, Churchill never forgave Asquith for forcing him to relinquish the Admiralty, even though the Prime Minister had genuinely done his best. Considering the forces arrayed against him, Churchill was fortunate to retain a seat in the Cabinet at all, albeit as Chancellor of the Duchy of Lancaster, a sinecure and the lowest post in the government. In the circumstances, this was more than he had any right to expect. 'I accept your decision', Churchill wrote to Asquith once his fate had been settled. 'I shall not look back', he added.[94] This could not have been further from the truth.

8

The Duchy of Lancaster Goes to War!

Churchill's dismissal from the Admiralty was received with widespread approval in the British press and throughout the Royal Navy. Even the King welcomed the idea of a coalition government. 'Only by that means', he wrote, 'can we get rid of Churchill from Admiralty . . . he is a real danger.'[1] At the offices of the *Morning Post*, H. A. Gwynne was elated. 'Thank heavens W. Churchill is going', he wrote to Lady Bathurst. 'That is the very best news I have heard for a very long day and I confess that I am very cock-a-whoop.'[2] Churchill was slow, however, to grasp the depth of the hostility towards him in May 1915. When the crisis broke, he naively thought that he could still win the support of senior Conservatives and retain his position at the Admiralty. Before the composition of the coalition ministry had been settled, he made a futile appeal to Bonar Law not to allow his party to be swayed by 'a newspaper campaign—necessarily conducted in ignorance and not untinged with prejudice'. Churchill defended his record at the Admiralty in a lengthy letter to the Conservative leader on 21 May. He pleaded for a chance to have all the facts placed before members of the new government so that he could be 'judged fairly, deliberately, and with knowledge'.[3] Bonar Law, a confidant of both Gwynne and Henry Wilson, sent back a terse note assuring Churchill that his departure from the Admiralty was 'inevitable'.[4]

Churchill had largely resisted the urge to respond to specific press criticisms during his time at the Admiralty, but he bitterly resented the Conservative newspapers—and the *Morning Post* in particular—for their part in driving him from office. The attacks he was subjected to for months before Fisher's resignation sprang from a mixture of press speculation, rumour, gossip, and deliberate falsehoods spread by Fisher to serve his own ends. But while they contained a mixture of truths, half-truths, and outright fabrications, the dominant themes were consistent: that Churchill, thinking himself another Napoleon or Marlborough, routinely ignored his naval advisers; that he was a reckless amateur with fatally flawed judgement; and that he was solely and personally responsible for the worst setbacks Britain suffered in the first year of the war. There was enough truth in these charges that his enemies saw no reason to question them. And they circulated for so long, and in so many different venues, that doubts increasingly emerged among those who were otherwise well disposed towards him.

As the strength of popular feeling against him began to sink in, Churchill's thoughts turned to Riddell's suggestion that he issue a statement to the press defending himself. Lloyd George dissuaded him from this step. 'There is no public insinuation up to present', the Chancellor pointed out, 'that the success of the Dardanelles operations is questioned. If you publish that, you will imply that it is.'[5] Churchill wisely abandoned the idea. Instead, he set his sights on persuading his new Conservative Cabinet colleagues that he had been treated unfairly by the press. On 19 May, while he still clung to the hope that he might remain at the Admiralty, Churchill sent Bonar Law a collection of Admiralty telegrams that he believed would prove he was not to blame for the loss of the three cruisers in September or for the dispositions that had led to the Battle of Coronel.[6] These were probably the same documents that he had shown to Riddell a few weeks earlier. Churchill wrote in a similar vein later that month to Lord Selborne, another of the new Conservative ministers. This time he also included telegrams to deflect criticism over his role in the British intervention at Antwerp.[7]

With the demands of running the Admiralty no longer claiming his full attention, Churchill had plenty of time on his hands to present his case to influential individuals. Over the next few months he showed his collection of exculpatory documents to people he hoped to win over. The list included Conservative politicians like Walter Long and Sir Edward Carson, influential figures like Lord Esher, and sympathetic journalists like C. P. Scott, editor of the *Manchester Guardian*.[8] But behind-the-scenes lobbying with confidential documents was hardly an efficient means to reverse popular opinion. In mid-September, Churchill asked Asquith to consider presenting to Parliament a selection of documents relating to Antwerp, Coronel, and the loss of the three cruisers. If it was not considered desirable for the government to release the documents in this manner, he suggested that he might still be allowed to issue a detailed personal statement addressing the charges that had been made against him during his time at the Admiralty.

'I am repeatedly made the object of vy serious charges in all these matters', he complained to the Prime Minister, 'wh have never been contradicted, & seem in some way to be confirmed by my leaving the Admiralty.'[9] Churchill immediately began editing these documents into a form suitable for publication, and let Asquith know he was willing to defer to his wishes or Balfour's about what material to include.[10] There was as yet no question of releasing information about the origins of the Dardanelles campaign. Churchill believed that those documents should eventually be published as well, but he was at least sufficiently self-aware to realize that it was not in the national interest to release detailed information about operations that were still in progress. None of this mattered, however, as Asquith declined to release *any* documents.

A victorious conclusion to the Gallipoli campaign would have provided the surest means to rehabilitate Churchill's reputation, but here, too, his hopes were frustrated. Asquith permitted Churchill to retain a seat on the coalition government's War Council, now renamed the Dardanelles Committee, but he no longer wielded anywhere near the same influence as when he was First Lord. 'It is a horrible experience', he confided to his friend Archie Sinclair, 'remaining here in the midst of things knowing everything, caring passionately, conscious of capacity for service, yet paralysed nearly always. It is like being in a cataleptic trance while all you value is being hazarded.'[11] In the months following his departure from the Admiralty, Churchill was oppressed by this feeling of powerlessness, which was made all the worse by his enforced inactivity. He took up oil painting to help occupy his unaccustomed free time, but he continued to brood on his dismissal from office and the continuing criticisms of his performance as First Lord. In one respect, however, Churchill was fortunate. His successor as First Lord, Arthur Balfour, was a strong proponent of the Dardanelles campaign. The government as a whole was initially reluctant to consider abandoning the peninsula, meaning the campaign might still be won.

Churchill naturally had strong opinions about the future of British grand strategy, and he lost no opportunity to press his ideas on his colleagues. The best course, he suggested in a memorandum in June, before the first meeting of the new Dardanelles Committee, was to stay on the defensive in the west. Rather than launch costly and futile attacks on strong German positions, the Germans should be allowed to exhaust themselves in attacks on the Allies. This was good advice, even if it was designed to ensure that resources would be available for the prosecution of the Gallipoli campaign. The surest way to wrap up Britain's commitments in the east, Churchill suggested, was to send large reinforcements to the theatre as soon as possible. Because the peninsula was so small, even minor advances there could be expected to produce major benefits, which was not the case on the Western Front. And as always, Churchill maintained that a decisive victory was within grasp. Once Allied forces reached the Kilid Bahr plateau, the forts protecting the Narrows could be neutralized. The fleet could then pass into the Sea of Marmara; the Turkish Navy would be destroyed; Russian troops would be free to attack Constantinople from the north; Bulgaria and the other Balkan states would enter the war; and the Ottomans would evacuate the Gallipoli peninsula. 'Where else', he asked his colleagues, 'in all the theatres of war can we look during the next three months for a decisive victory, or for results of this extraordinary character?'[12] He was equally optimistic in public. Speaking to his constituents in Dundee a few days later, he proclaimed, in a widely reported speech, that British forces were 'separated only by a few miles from a victory such as this war has not yet seen':

> When I speak of victory, I am not referring to those victories which crowd the daily placards of any newspapers, I am speaking of victory in the sense of a brilliant and formidable fact, shaping the destinies of nations and shortening the duration of the war. Beyond those few miles of ridge and scrub...lie the downfall of a hostile empire, the destruction of an enemy's fleet and army, the fall of a world-famous capital, and probably the accession of powerful Allies.[13]

One of the last acts of the Liberal War Council had been to send a telegram to Hamilton asking what additional forces he would require to secure victory.[14] He replied on 17 May, just as the government was dissolving, requesting two to four more divisions. The new government did not formally consider the matter for three weeks. The Dardanelles Committee met for the first time on 7 June, and the Cabinet decided two days later to send Hamilton three divisions of the 'New Armies'—the new formations raised by Kitchener since the start of the war. These were expected to reach the theatre around mid-July.[15] Churchill played a major role in persuading his colleagues to strengthen Hamilton's forces, but some members of the new government, notably Bonar Law, were unenthusiastic about the operation. The decision to send reinforcements did not signal the whole-hearted commitment to victory that Churchill wanted. The stress on Churchill around this time was immense. When the British journalist Ellis Ashmead–Bartlett, a war correspondent recently returned from Gallipoli, dined with Churchill on 10 June, he observed that the former First Lord:

> [L]ooked years older, his face was pale, his skin flabby and his eyes bloodshot. He seemed terribly upset and depressed. In fact it is obvious to me he has felt his fall keenly. He has come a colossal cropper and will never appear in history as a great statesman but only as an exceedingly clever politician.

Ashmead–Bartlett recorded that evening's events in his diary:

> At dinner the conversation was more or less general and I said nothing about the Dardanelles except to Mrs Winston next [to] whom I was sitting and to the Duchess of Marlborough. Winston was fairly quiet for some time, but then, unable to restrain himself, he suddenly burst forth on a tremendous discourse on the expedition and what might have been done addressed directly across the table in the form of a lecture to his mother, who I must say listened most attentively... Winston seemed unconscious at times of the limited number of his audience. He seemed determined to get this discourse off his chest at all events. He talked the most appalling nonsense about what the Fleet might have done on March 18th, but I had the heart at this stage [not] to interrupt him by recalling the actual facts. His great point was that the fight had never been fought through to a finish and that had it been, the Fleet could have got through.[16]

The journalist was certain that Churchill was deluding himself as to how close the fleet had come to success. Churchill did not appear, he noted, 'to realise that the fleet never reached the minefield or the concealed torpedo tubes, and that the guns of the forts were never permanently silenced'. Ashmead–Bartlett's understanding of the Allied naval attack of 18 March was informed by an official Ottoman report on the operation, which revealed that almost no damage had been done to the enemy's guns in the attack. Remarkably, he had been shown the report, while en route to the eastern Mediterranean, by the Turkish military attaché in Italy. According to his diary, this document confirmed 'my opinions that we were hopelessly underestimating our task, and that the attack on March 18th had never stood any chance of succeeding'.[17]

The two men discussed the campaign after dinner and into the early hours of the morning. Ashmead–Bartlett recalled that Churchill was determined that the offensive must be 'carried through at all costs, not only because he feels that strategically it must have a great effect on the war, but also because he knows it will mean his complete vindication and restore something of his old prestige, because the mistakes will be speedily forgotten in the final success'.[18] Sometime after midnight that evening, he wrote in his memoirs, 'Winston began once more to soliloquise on the past and on his own position, addressing his remarks half to himself and half to me.'

> He said, "I felt sure it could be done with the Fleet alone, and I am still convinced that it might have been. As long as we tried it with our old reserve ships it mattered little, because, even if they were lost, we were none the weaker. I told them over and over again, once an army was landed, it was quite another affair, and that they would be dragged into a great enterprise from which they could not withdraw."[19]

This would certainly explain Churchill's reluctance to employ the army until after the fleet had broken through the Straits, although whether he gave his colleagues such a clear warning on this is questionable. The journalist's diary records another, and less flattering, comment by Churchill that evening, one that Ashmead–Bartlett kept out of the published version. Complaining of the decision to call off the naval attack, Churchill reportedly charged that the ships 'ought to have gone on':

> What did it matter if more ships were lost with their crews? The ships were old and useless and the crews mostly old reservists. They were sent out there to die, it was their duty. That is what they were mobilised for.[20]

When the Dardanelles Committee met two days later, Churchill was having second thoughts about the wisdom of launching frontal attacks on the Ottoman lines from the existing Allied positions. He now threw his weight behind a recommendation by Ashmead–Bartlett that troops should be landed further north to capture the Bulair isthmus, at the base of the Gallipoli peninsula. Controlling this position, Churchill wrote, would allow the Allies to prevent the enemy supplying its army by land. And by passing submarines through the Straits into the Sea of Marmara, he predicted that the Ottomans could be denied supplies by sea as well. In time, the defenders could be starved out.[21] This idea gained support within the Dardanelles Committee, but was rejected by Hamilton and de Robeck. Hamilton and his subordinates preferred to develop a plan of their own for an offensive from the Anzac position. As more forces became available for the operation in the weeks that followed, the planned attack was expanded to include the landing of troops north of Anzac Cove at Suvla Bay. By the end of July, the operation had developed into a major offensive designed to seize the high ground opposite Anzac and Suvla, break through the Ottoman defences, and establish a new line across the peninsula.[22]

Churchill welcomed the decision for a major new offensive, although he was critical of his colleagues for not taking the steps necessary to launch it sooner. 'We have always sent two-thirds of what was necessary a month too late', he lamented in mid-July.[23] In the event, the new offensive did not begin till 6 August, and the results, as usual, fell far short of expectations. Fresh British divisions were successfully landed at Suvla Bay, but Allied planners had been far too optimistic about what they might hope to accomplish. The commanding general made little effort to seize the high ground before Turkish reinforcements arrived, and the intended break-out from Anzac failed to materialize. Within days the Allies faced strong opposition, and stalemate once again set in. The failure of the August offensive to achieve any of its wider objectives raised fresh doubts in London as to the future of the campaign and the wisdom of pouring additional men and equipment into this theatre. Even Churchill had to question the desirability of diverting more forces from the Western Front to Gallipoli. But he was not prepared to abandon the operation, and believed there was another potential solution at hand. On 21 August, he launched a fresh campaign to renew the naval offensive. Contrary to Churchill's original expectations, the Allied fleet had not resumed its operations in the Straits once the army had been established on the peninsula. Writing to Asquith, Balfour, and Kitchener, Churchill derided the idea that British naval losses on 18 March had been a 'stupendous event', given that Britain had lost only two old battleships and 'about 100 men'. With the army unable to neutralize the Ottoman forts, he urged that the naval attack should 'be resumed, pressed to a decision, and fought out, as it has never yet been'.[24]

Churchill had still not reconciled himself to the decision to break off the naval attack, and he was now confident that it could be renewed with every chance of success. Indeed, he believed that the Allies were in a stronger position than ever, since de Robeck had recently received the first of Britain's new big-gunned monitors. Churchill had high hopes that these ships would transform the situation. Their shallow draft would allow them to pass safely over the Turkish mines, and their 'blistered' hulls would protect them against Ottoman torpedo tubes inside the Straits and against German submarines, which were now operating in the region. He therefore proposed that another attempt be made by the fleet to neutralize the Turkish forts with naval gunfire while simultaneously sweeping the mines blocking the Narrows. After perhaps four or five days, he predicted that a combined force of monitors and submarines could break through to the Sea of Marmara.

Once there, Turkish forces in the peninsula would be cut off and Constantinople exposed to attack.[25] These conclusions may have been overly optimistic, but Churchill was not alone in thinking it was time the navy made another attempt. In the eastern Mediterranean, Commodore Keyes and other members of de Robeck's staff had reached the same conclusion.

Keyes in particular was seized by a determination to renew the naval offensive. By mid-August he had concluded that the situation on land would not improve, as the army lacked the resources to carry the campaign to a successful conclusion. And its difficulties would increase if the fighting carried on over the winter, as seemed likely. The heavy losses suffered in the bitter fighting on the peninsula had made a strong impression on Keyes. He estimated that nearly 26,000 casualties had been sustained in just the first ten days of the August offensive—all while the navy watched safely from the side lines. 'I hate it', Keyes told his wife, 'and feel all the time that we [i.e. the navy] could stop it all and win this great prize—I simply can't bear it.'[26] On 17 August he presented his case for a renewal of the naval attack to de Robeck. Like Churchill, Keyes was optimistic that indirect fire across the peninsula by the new monitors would improve the effectiveness of the Allies' bombardment. He also noted that the navy was much better equipped for aerial observation and minesweeping than had it had been in March. He was therefore certain of success, predicting that half of the Allied fleet could expect to reach the Sea of Marmara. This would make a winter campaign by the army unnecessary, and put 'an end to the terrible slaughter of our troops in the Peninsula'.[27]

Keyes found a sympathetic audience in Admiral Wemyss, the senior naval officer at Mudros, but the offensive could not be resumed without de Robeck's support—and he remained obstinately opposed to the idea.[28] Keyes was not easily dissuaded, however. The following month he sent the admiral a plan of attack that had been drafted by another member of his staff, Captain Godfrey.[29] This also failed to have any effect. After listening again to Keyes' pleas on 27 September, de Robeck told his chief of staff: 'well Commodore you and I will never agree on this subject—but there is no reason why we should not remain good friends'.[30] The ever-optimistic Keyes resumed his efforts in October, when he asked de Robeck to put the proposal to the Admiralty. He later told his wife that the admiral 'flatly refused' the suggestion: 'Said he did not believe in it, etc.' Keyes, whose faith in the operation never wavered, was by now losing confidence in de Robeck.

'He does not deserve to go down in history as the man who forced the Dardanelles', Keyes complained in mid-October, 'and I don't think he will. But I am sure it will be done.'[31]

Churchill's efforts in London to revive the naval offensive were no more successful. He presented his case to the Dardanelles Committee in late September, but the idea gained no support. Like Keyes, Churchill regarded de Robeck as the main obstacle. On 6 October he complained to Balfour that the admiral could not be expected to take an objective view. 'The naval attack' would undoubtedly be 'a great hazard', Churchill admitted. 'If it fails there is a heavy loss; if it succeeds he [de Robeck] would be stultified. Is it not natural [that de Robeck's] opposition to it should be deep-seated?'[32] But the question that increasingly occupied British leaders was not whether to renew the naval offensive, but whether to evacuate Allied forces from the peninsula altogether.

This subject was considered by the Dardanelles Committee on several occasions during October 1915. Lloyd George and Bonar Law were both persistent advocates of withdrawal, but Churchill remained steadfastly opposed to the idea. In late September, with no prospect of a fresh naval offensive in sight, he proposed that the best means of breaking the deadlock at Gallipoli would be a new land offensive, but on a much large scale than anything that had yet been attempted. On 21 September he contemplated landing ten British divisions on Turkey's Asiatic shore. This force, he suggested, could advance rapidly towards Chanak, on the Asiatic side of the Narrows, while a fresh attempt was made by forces at Anzac and Suvla to advance across the peninsula.[33] The obstacle to this proposal was that such a large force could only come at the expense of the Western Front. Churchill, who consistently advocated a strict defensive in the west, complained bitterly a week later when he learned the results of the latest offensive in France. On this occasion the British Army suffered nearly 50,000 casualties in order to make a modest advance that captured the village of Loos, which had no strategic significance. Churchill lamented that 'the same effort and expenditure which had given us Loos would have given us Constantinople and command of the Eastern world'.[34]

In early October, Churchill also suggested launching an offensive against the Ottoman Empire from the Anglo-French base at Salonika, where Allied troops had recently been despatched to aid Serbia. The French Army, he suggested, might go to the aid of the Serbs while British and Greek forces advanced eastward against Turkey and Bulgaria, which had recently

entered the war on Germany's side. There was increasingly an air of desperation surrounding Churchill's proposals. As Lloyd George commented,
'The Dardanelles has become an obsession with him. He is anxious to
achieve victory at all costs because he feels that failure will probably ruin
his career.'[35] His suggestions excited little interest among his colleagues. By
October, most ministers would have been happy to liquidate the Gallipoli
commitment if it had not been for the heavy casualties that were expected
during an evacuation. Kitchener initially predicted that losses might run as
high as 25,000.[36] Hamilton, hoping to kill the idea of evacuation, predicted
that Allied casualties might be 50 per cent, at least 50,000 men. Churchill
told his colleagues bluntly that 'he would be no party to our going unless
it was proved that there was no other course'.[37] He put his case against
evacuation to the Dardanelles Committee in a memorandum of 15 October.
'No more terrible decision than the evacuation of the Gallipoli peninsula
and the abandonment of the attempt to take Constantinople has been
wrung from a British Government', he maintained, 'since the loss of the
American colonies.' The government, in his view, first had to consider the
human and material sacrifice evacuation would entail, which he put as
high as 30,000 men, 'with hundreds of guns and vast accumulations of
stores'. The moral effect promised to be even more devastating. '[T]o
re-embark and row out of range under the full pressure of a victorious and
exulting army must be one of the most shocking tragedies of the war', he
insisted. British prestige in the Muslim world would collapse. Nor was that
all. Australia and New Zealand would always resent the fact that their sacrifices on the peninsula had been in vain. Russia would be deprived of vital
aid. The Balkans would be lost to the Allies. And the Ottomans would be
free to turn their efforts against the Russians in the Caucasus and the British
in the Middle East.[38]

This forceful appeal may have added to ministers' doubts about the wisdom of evacuation, but the question continued to dominate the government's deliberations. In London, the advocates of withdrawal were gradually
gaining the upper hand. Hamilton's removal from the command of the
Mediterranean Expeditionary Force (MEF) in mid-October deprived
Churchill of an important ally. He was immediately wary of Hamilton's
replacement, General Sir Charles Monro. His worst fears were confirmed at
the end of October, when Monro formally recommended evacuation.
Churchill now pinned his hopes on the influential Kitchener. The War
Minister had consistently opposed evacuation, telling the Dardanelles

Committee on one occasion that 'abandonment would be the most disas-trous event in the history of the Empire'.[39] He was therefore unwilling to accept Monro's advice, and decided he needed to visit Gallipoli to judge the situation there for himself. Churchill's hopes were also buoyed by Keyes' arrival in London. The indefatigable chief of staff had continued to lobby for the resumption of the naval offensive, and de Robeck, who remained opposed to the idea, generously permitted him to return to England to present his case directly to the Admiralty. The naval Commander-in-Chief made his own views clear, however, in a letter Keyes carried with him for Henry Jackson, the new First Sea Lord. 'In regard to his [Keyes'] proposals', de Robeck wrote, 'they would not lead to any result if we got through with a few ships. It most probably leads to a most colossal disaster!'[40]

Churchill was naturally eager to see Keyes during his visit, but Keyes tried at first to avoid him, as he felt a meeting 'would be very awkward'.[41] Churchill persisted, however, and the two men and their wives dined together on the evening of 4 November. Keyes had not been able to gener-ate much enthusiasm at the Admiralty for a renewed naval offensive, but Kitchener had been impressed by his arguments. According to Keyes' account of their dinner, Churchill 'said Lord K. was going out [to Gallipoli] pinning his faith in me and my scheme and he [Churchill] felt sure it would succeed'. The meeting evidently did not prove awkward after all. Keyes recorded that he 'couldn't help liking him [Churchill] more than ever…Of course his chief concern is the vindication of his policy, but he has a warm place in his very self centred heart for me!'[42] Keyes may also have learned that evening that Churchill's ability to influence the debate had received a serious blow a few days before.[43] On 28 October, Asquith announced his intention to dissolve the Dardanelles Committee and replace it with a smaller, and hopefully more efficient, 'War Committee', composed at first of just the Prime Minister and the two service ministers. The composition of the committee was subsequently expanded, but Churchill, who had hoped to be included, was left out.

His initial reaction was to resign from the government, as Asquith's pro-posed changes would deprive him of any meaningful input into the central direction of the British war effort. Since being forced from the Admiralty, Churchill had resisted the strong desire to take active part in the fighting in France, but only so that he might continue to have a role, even a minor one, in the oversight of the Dardanelles–Gallipoli campaign. But if that role were now denied to him, there was nothing holding him back from the front.

He began drafting his resignation letter to Asquith the day after the new committee was announced. '[I]t would not be right for me at this time to idle in a well paid sinecure', he wrote. 'Nor cd I conscientiously accept responsibility without any share of influence or power.'[44] He offered his resignation to Asquith on the 30th, but the Prime Minister was planning to address the Dardanelles campaign in a speech to Parliament and asked Churchill to stay on until after it had been delivered. Churchill agreed, believing that Asquith would use this opportunity to defend him against his critics. Hankey recorded in his diary that, on 1 November, Churchill asked for his help putting together 'his defence over the Dardanelles operations for the P.M. to deliver next day in Parliament. This I did. He was in a very excited state and told me he had only stayed in the Government for this.'[45]

Asquith's speech fell far short of what Churchill expected, but it nevertheless went some way towards exonerating the former First Lord of charges that he was solely responsible for launching the naval operation. 'People who think and say that that attack was initiated without due consideration, without a full review of all its Naval possibilities, are entirely mistaken', the Premier stated. The operation, he continued, 'was most carefully considered':

> It was developed in consultation between the Admiral on the spot and the War Staff of the Admiralty here, and before any final decision was taken it was communicated to the French Admiralty, who entirely approved of it, and agreed to take part in it, and it was—I am not using too strong a word—enthusiastically received and acclaimed by the illustrious Grand Duke who then commanded the Russian Armies, and who rightly thought that it would assist his operations in the Caucasus.
>
> The matter was carefully reviewed over and over again by the War Council, and…all the operations…were communicated to, and approved by, the Cabinet. In the circumstances of the case in which we then stood, the operation conceived was a purely Naval operation. We could not afford at that time—Lord Kitchener said, and we all agreed—any substantial Military support. It was, therefore, decided to make the attempt with the Naval Forces alone.
>
> I take my full share of the responsibility for the initiation of that operation—my full share. I deprecate more than I can say the attempt to allocate responsibility to one Minister or another, or to suggest that in a matter of this kind some undefined personality, of great authority and over-mastering will, controlled and directed the strategy of the operations. That is not the case. If anybody is responsible for the initiation of this enterprise in the Dardanelles, nobody is more responsible than I.

Asquith's emphasis on the collective responsibility of the government, and especially his assumption of a major share of any blame, could only help Churchill's position. But Churchill was still disappointed. He had expected the Prime Minister to offer a robust defence of his performance as First Lord, but Asquith had only alluded in passing to damning accusations in the press that Churchill had overridden his naval advisers and misled his Cabinet colleagues. The Prime Minister had not used any of the material Churchill had prepared. Indeed, he had not even mentioned him by name, referring to him only as 'some undefined personality'.

Churchill's formal resignation letter, dated 11 November, was written with publication in mind. It avoided any strong criticisms of the government's decision-making process and made only a passing reference to Churchill's period as First Lord. 'Time', he wrote, 'will vindicate my administration of the Admiralty.'[46] But Churchill had no desire to wait long for his vindication. In the first draft of his private resignation letter to Asquith the week before, he had written that the time had now come 'for the truth to be made public about the initiation of the Dardanelles expedition'.[47] He expanded on this following day. 'I cannot consent [any] longer to rest under the aspersions wh have been allowed to flourish without correction of any kind', he warned the Prime Minister. 'About this & other matters belonging to the past there can now no longer be any valid reason for secrecy; & I must claim from you full liberty to state my case to Parliament.'[48]

A resigning Cabinet minister was permitted to give Parliament an explanation for his break with the government, and Churchill took full advantage of this custom. His reasons for resigning as Chancellor of the Duchy of Lancaster were so straightforward, however, that his formal letter to Asquith required little elaboration. When Churchill began his resignation speech to the House of Commons on 15 November, he began by admitting that he had nothing to add on this point. His intention all along was to deal with criticisms of his administration of the Admiralty, and this subject occupied nearly his entire speech. He began by addressing the Battle of Coronel and the loss of the three cruisers the previous year. In neither case did he provide a detailed account of his involvement. He simply asserted that the charges against him were wrong, and that the publication of the relevant documents by the Admiralty would eventually vindicate him. He then moved on to a more elaborate defence of his role in the relief of Antwerp. On the origins of the British intervention he was on strong ground. The decision had been taken in principle by Kitchener and the French government before Churchill became involved. The despatch of the Royal Naval Division, which included among its officers the Prime Minister's son, had been sanctioned by both Kitchener and Asquith. The decision to send additional Allied forces to defend the city was taken in London during Churchill's absence. He was only informed of it afterwards. It was only when he addressed the decision to employ the naval brigades at Antwerp that Churchill faltered. He admitted that these troops were not highly trained, but suggested that they were employed because they were the best troops available, and because they were considered adequate in a static, defensive role.[49]

Churchill's defence of the Dardanelles followed. Since the Gallipoli campaign was still under way, he concentrated on the origins of the naval attack on the Straits. This still gave him plenty of scope to deal with the persistent criticism that he had forced the scheme through against the strong objections of Fisher and his other professional advisers. To make his case, Churchill outlined the genesis of the campaign in considerable detail, beginning with the Russian request at the beginning of January for a demonstration against the Ottomans. The original plan for forcing the Straits had been devised, he noted, by Admiral Carden, and was subsequently approved by Admiral Jackson. 'The coincidence of opinion between those two officers', he observed, 'both of the highest attainments and so differently circumstanced—one man on the spot, and the other the expert at the Admiralty, who was studying the Eastern theatre with the War Staff—the coincidence of opinion between those two made a profound impression on my mind.' Churchill also noted that both Fisher and Wilson initially supported the project, and had been present when it was submitted to the War Council on 13 January. Once tentative approval had been given, Carden's plan, he noted, 'was searchingly re-examined by the Admiralty War Staff and various gunnery experts whom we had at our disposal—the highest and best in the world—and a general consensus of opinion was established in its favour'. Churchill insisted, therefore, that 'this enterprise was profoundly, maturely, and elaborately considered, that there was a great deal of expert opinion behind it, that it was framed entirely by expert and technical minds, and that in no circumstances could it be regarded as having been undertaken with carelessness or levity'.[50]

These claims were essentially true: Churchill had not meddled in the details of the actual planning. But had he forced his naval advisers to go along with the project against their will, as his critics alleged? Churchill was in a position to state, probably with perfect honesty, that he believed Fisher supported the operation in its early stages. The admiral had, after all, remained silent at the War Council on 13 January, and had actively concealed his true feelings about the project until 25 January. Prior to this date, Churchill had reason to assume Fisher supported the scheme. But what about Fisher's dissent prior to the War Council's decision on 28 January to proceed with the operation? Churchill was able to make a strong case here as well. When the admiral finally came out against the operation on 25 January, he had not questioned the feasibility of the plan to force the Straits by ships alone. His main objection was to the reduction of the Grand Fleet—and, on this point, Churchill observed that the admiral's fears had not been justified by events. Fisher had revealed that he would have preferred a combined attack in conjunction with the army, but he did not warn Churchill, Asquith, or the War Council that an attack by the navy alone was likely to fail. At 'no time', Churchill maintained, 'did I receive from Lord Fisher any criticism of the definite method of attack proposed [to force the Dardanelles]'.

In hindsight, two things seem clear about the critical deliberations on 28 January. First, that Churchill genuinely assumed at the end of the day that he had secured Fisher's support, even if it had been given with reservations. Second, that Fisher had not conveyed effectively either the depth of his opposition or the reasons for it. The responsibility for this unsatisfactory state of affairs, Churchill maintained, rested entirely with Fisher. 'I am not going to embark upon any reproaches this afternoon', he told the House of Commons, as he launched into his reproach of Fisher, 'but I must say I did not receive from the First Sea Lord either the clear guidance before the event or the firm support after which I was entitled to expect.'

> If he did not approve the operation, he should have spoken out in the War Council. War is a hard and brutal job, and there is no place in it for misgivings or reserves. Nobody ever launched an attack without having misgivings beforehand. You ought to have misgivings before; but when the moment of action is come, the hour of misgivings is passed. It is often not possible to go backward from a course which has been adopted in war. A man must answer 'Aye' or 'No' to the great questions which are put, and by that decision he must be bound. If the First Sea Lord had not approved the operation, if he believed they were unlikely to take the course that was expected of them, if he thought they would lead to undue losses, it was his duty to refuse consent. No one could have prevailed against such a refusal. The operation would never have been begun.

There was a great deal of truth in this argument as well.

Having dealt with the origins of the naval attack, Churchill made two other important points about the original plan. The first was that, in launching the campaign, Britain had run no great risks with the navy. The two British battleships that were lost on 18 March, 'if they had not been employed at the Dardanelles, would have been rusting uselessly in our southern ports', he pointed out. Second, the naval plan did not necessarily commit Britain to land troops on the Gallipoli peninsula. This was an attempt to distance himself from the heavy losses being incurred in the land campaign. Churchill had not been the driving force behind the decision to land troops. 'That was a separate decision', he correctly noted, 'which did not rest with me or the Admiralty either in principle or in method.' Moreover, he pointed out that the original plan had called for the naval attack to be called off if it failed to progress. In other words, he had provided his colleagues with an 'exit strategy'. Churchill even hinted that, in hindsight, the attack should have been abandoned after the setback on 18 March. 'I cannot conceive', he stated, 'that anyone would have hesitated to face the loss of prestige in breaking off the attack on the Dardanelles' if it had been 'known what we now know of the course of the military operation.' This is probably true, but here Churchill was undoubtedly being disingenuous. He had been the most vigorous advocate of renewing the offensive after de Robeck's attack failed.

Churchill carefully avoided the question of whether the naval attack might have succeeded; in later years this would become the centrepiece of his defence. The dominant fact in November 1915 was that the naval attack *had* failed. In the middle of the war Churchill could hardly criticize the naval officers who had planned and carried out the operation, so he simply left the question alone. He admitted that he could not prove that 'the plan we adopted was the best plan that could have been adopted. No amount of argument will do that.' His main concern at this time, however, was only to discredit claims that the plan was so poorly thought out that its failure should have been obvious, and that he had misrepresented its prospects to the War Council. The reality, he insisted, was that he had recommended the scheme to his colleagues 'not as a certainty, but as a legitimate war gamble, with stakes that we could afford to lose for a prize of inestimable value... On that basis clearly understood it was accepted by all concerned.'[51] The accuracy of this statement is certainly open to dispute, since Churchill, while acknowledging the risks, had been prone to overstate the chances of success. But what bothered his audience at the time was the characterization of the Dardanelles offensive as a 'war gamble'. The point he had wanted to make was certainly legitimate: in wartime, *all* military operations contain an element of risk, since their outcome can never be absolutely certain. To his critics, however, he appeared to suggest that lives had been risked and lost in a reckless or frivolous spirit.

Churchill's resignation speech was generally well received by Parliament and the British press. The Conservative *Daily Mail*, for example, reported that MPs were 'thrilled' by Churchill's revelations. 'The speech received their close and absorbed attention', it continued, 'and though the House was conspicuously undemonstrative it was clear that it was sympathetic toward the young Minister who was defending himself with so much vigour and ability.'[52] Even the *Morning Post*, normally a harsh critic, noted that Churchill had 'gone out with a flare. Members were greatly impressed with the eloquence, the cleverness, even the audacity of the speech, and the Lobby rang with its praise.'[53] Churchill's decision to leave the Cabinet in order to serve in the army was universally applauded. 'The offer shows fine spirit', according to *The Times*, 'and, if it is accepted, we do not doubt that the Army will accord a warm welcome to a soldier who has proved his mettle in the field.'[54] On this point, even the *Morning Post* was eager to sound a positive note. 'No man of any strength of character could act otherwise', one article stated. 'Mr. Churchill has always shown gallantry in the field, and we trust that he will find in his regiment more useful as well as more congenial work than in the squalid labyrinth of Downing-street.'[55]

However, the substance of Churchill's speech received mixed reviews, especially from the Conservative press. *The Times* called it 'an undoubted Parliamentary triumph', and concluded that if Churchill's facts were accurate, then 'he must be completely absolved from the specific charges of independent action brought against him'. A perceptive editorial on 16 November suggested that the disasters attributed to Churchill could be blamed on 'want of co-ordination and supreme control in the Government to which we have pointed again and again as the root of all evil'.[56] The *Daily Mail*, another Northcliffe paper, accepted Churchill's account of Antwerp, and was open to the possibility that Fisher bore some of the blame for the mismanagement of the Dardanelles campaign.[57] The *Spectator*, on the other hand, considered the speech 'most regrettable', finding in it 'an admission, to our thinking, that he often assumed the functions of his expert advisers. Instead of seeking advice he gave it, and then held himself injured by the somewhat sultry silence or affronted hesitation that not unnaturally followed.'[58]

The *Morning Post* remained unrepentant, and continued to denounce Churchill in the harshest terms. Gwynne now seized upon Churchill's revelations about the decision-making process to heap scorn on Fisher for failing to make his views clear to Asquith or Churchill. 'All this does not very much surprise us', he wrote, 'because Lord Fisher was too old to be trusted to contest with vigour the will of so formidable and forceful a debater as his political colleague. So old a man should never have been appointed at such a crisis.'[59] But he made clear the following day that this did not diminish Churchill's culpability. 'Lord Fisher...was not responsible', Gwynne wrote on the 17th. 'He ought to have been, but he was not. His responsibility, together with the responsibility of the rest of his colleagues, had been filched from him long ago.'[60] All that the editor would concede was that the naval authorities had been involved in drafting the service's plans, but he was nonetheless adamant that Churchill, as the driving force behind them, was ultimately responsible for everything that followed. Nor could Gwynne resist closing with a fresh warning. 'As a field officer', he wrote, 'we are certain that [Churchill] will acquit himself with the dash, courage, and energy which are his best qualities; but his judgment is too erratic and fallible for high Staff command.'[61]

Gwynne would have been dismayed to learn that Churchill had asked to be appointed Governor General of British East Africa and Commander-in-Chief of the British forces fighting the Germans in this remote theatre.[62] When this idea was shot down, Churchill hoped, and for a time expected, to be put in command of a brigade on the Western Front, but this also fell through in the face of widespread criticism. In the event, he was made a lieutenant-colonel and placed in command of a battalion of the Royal Scots Fusiliers. As he began the transition into his new post, the future of the Gallipoli campaign continued to be hotly debated. The pressure to evacuate mounted steadily over the course of November, and Kitchener's visit to the theatre became the deciding factor. The War Minister had departed London hoping to prevent a withdrawal, but he changed his mind soon after arriving. '[W]ell', he told a dismayed Keyes, 'I have seen the place, it is an awful place, you will never get through!'[63] The commodore was crushed, having convinced himself that Kitchener would support a renewal of the offensive. In his diary he denounced the field marshal as 'an old scoundrel' and 'a vacillating old villain—incapable of making up his mind'.[64]

Keyes immediately redoubled his efforts to win over de Robeck, but he could make no headway. The admiral 'was more hopeless than ever', his chief of staff complained: he 'only saw the difficulties'.[65] With evacuation increasingly likely, Keyes could not help but feel that his service's honour was at stake. 'The Navy would go down in history utterly disgraced if we gave it up now without trying', he predicted.[66] In his opinion, since 18 March the eastern fleet had become 'a Commissariat Service, not a fighting force—and [de Robeck] appears to have no ambition beyond feeding the Army'.[67] To Keyes' relief, de Robeck was now on his way out. The strain of command had taken a toll on the admiral's health. He was replaced near the end of the month—although no one knew for how long—by Admiral Wemyss. The new Commander-in-Chief was hardly less horrified than Keyes at the prospect of an opposed evacuation. Kitchener's recommendation that Suvla and Anzac be abandoned spurred him to action. From that moment, Wemyss recorded in his memoirs, 'we realized that a crisis had been reached when definite action one way or another could no longer be postponed'.[68] With the support of Keyes and Godfrey, Wemyss made the case for a renewal of the naval offensive to the Admiralty in a lengthy telegram, despatched on 28 November. He reported that he was 'strongly of opinion' that the 'disaster' of evacuation should not be accepted without one final attempt to force the Straits. If the navy succeeded, he pointed out that the army could immediately exploit its success. And if it failed, the evacuation could still take place 'under no more adverse circumstances than at present'.[69]

Churchill, who was now serving in France, received a copy of Wemyss' telegram via Lord Curzon, the Lord Privy Seal, who was now the leading opponent of evacuation in the Cabinet.[70] The government remained divided, but Wemyss' last-minute intervention could not stop the drift towards evacuation. The Admiralty might have supported another attempt to force the Straits if pressed to do so by the army, but General Monro and his chief of staff were firmly convinced of the need to evacuate. Keyes complained, and with good reason, that the two men were 'obsessed with the idea that the only place to fight the Germans is in Flanders or France, [and] that men employed elsewhere are being wasted'.[71] But the general, like de Robeck, had legitimate doubts as to whether the passage of ships through the Straits would actually improve the army's position on the peninsula. '[E]ven if we open the Straits and appear off Constantinople and reduce it', he asked Wemyss and Keyes, 'what then?'[72] Monro's opposition was decisive. In early December, the Cabinet decided to begin the evacuation of the Anzac and Suvla positions that same month.

Despite fears that the Ottomans would inflict heavy casualties on Allied forces as they abandoned their defences and withdrew from the beaches, the operation was completed with a degree of skill that had so far been absent from the campaign. Over the course of 11 days, over 100,000 men and 300 guns were evacuated from Anzac and Suvla without *any* casualties being suffered. The deception measures employed to cover the operation were so effective that the Ottomans did not even realize an evacuation was under way until after it was over. The unexpected success of this withdrawal induced the Allies to evacuate the Helles position as well. Remarkably, despite having been fooled once, the enemy was again taken unawares. By 9 January 1916, the last 35,000 troops had been evacuated from the peninsula, bringing the Gallipoli campaign to a conclusion. Upon learning that the last soldiers had left the peninsula, Churchill, now commanding a battalion in Belgium, commented to his brother, 'Well it is all over now & as the Lokalanzeiger [a German newspaper] joyfully remarks "Churchill's dream of a victorious march on Constantinople is at an end".'[73] The land campaign had been far more costly than the naval campaign. Since the first troops were landed on 25 April, over 132,000 Allied soldiers had been killed or wounded in the fighting, and many more were incapacitated by disease and other causes. One authoritative study concludes that the overall casualty figures for the campaign may be as high as 390,000.[74]

9

Exile

The management of the British naval effort in the first nine months of the war had not created enough work to absorb all of Churchill's restless energy, and active service on the Western Front was no different. The former First Lord threw himself into his new responsibilities with vigour, and by all accounts proved himself a success. But after so many months at the top of the British war effort, the command of a single battalion—around 1,000 men at full strength—could only be anti-climactic. In his six months of active service, Churchill never overcame the feeling that his formidable talents were not being fully utilized for the benefit of the nation's war effort. Even the command of a brigade, a force of around 4,000 men, would have fallen far short of his expectations. And since there was clearly no longer any prospect of achieving high command in the army, Churchill had no interest in abandoning his political career, very much the opposite. He therefore retained his seat in Parliament while serving in Belgium, and had every intention of returning to Westminster at the first favourable opportunity. Active service was simply a means to an end. It would help him to rebuild his reputation, and, in time, provide a platform from which to launch his political comeback.

At the front, Churchill continued to brood on his dismissal from the Admiralty. 'Whenever my mind is not occupied by work', he confided to his wife in January 1916, 'I feel deeply the injustice with wh[ich] my work at the Admiralty has been treated. I cannot help it—tho I try.'[1] In fact, Churchill never wavered in his belief that the operation could have succeeded. Nor was he prepared to question his own role in conducting the offensive. If he made any mistakes, he was certain that they were minor. 'History will vindicate the conception' of the naval attack, he wrote to his brother Jack, '& the errors in execution will on the whole leave me clear.' The critical mistakes, in his view, were all made by others. 'If I have erred', he told Hankey in June 1915, 'it has been in seeking to attempt an initiative without being sure that all the means & powers to make it successful were at my disposal.'[2] Churchill's belief in the Dardanelles operation soon hardened to the point that it became virtually an article of faith. And the more blame that was heaped upon him, the less inclined he was to view the campaign objectively. His unwillingness to acknowledge the many obstacles to a successful resumption of the naval offensive suggests there was a strong element of self-delusion at work. This was certainly the impression of Ashmead-Bartlett when he discussed the campaign with Churchill again in mid-October 1915. 'I found Winston', the journalist wrote in his diary, 'to my disgust has learnt but little wisdom from his experience and had apparently taken but little to heart the lessons I had endeavoured to tell him.'

> I found him still full of his absurd ideas on the whole Expedition and still persisting in his statement that the Fleet alone might have forced the Narrows had it but been allowed to make another effort. . . . I left this interview with a deep impression on my mind, namely, that Winston knows nothing of modern warfare, that he jumps at the most absurdly erroneous conclusions, and that he suffers from extraordinary illusions.

In his memoirs, Ashmead-Bartlett added that the idea that the naval attack might have been renewed successfully had 'become a regular obsession—a fetish which had gained possession of his mind, blinding him to facts and filling his brain with illusions'.[3]

Churchill was especially bitter that his career and reputation had been so badly set back while nearly everyone else implicated in the Dardanelles failure continued to prosper. The 'damnable mismanagement wh[ich] has ruined the Dardanelles enterprise & squandered vainly so much life & opportunity cries aloud for retribution', he told Clementine, '& if I survive [the trenches], the day will come when I will claim it publicly'.[4] Churchill relished the idea that the responsible parties would all one day be exposed. 'Nothing now remains but to punish the guilty', he told Eva Keyes, '& for that the time is not yet come.'[5] The main culprits, in Churchill's eyes, were Kitchener and Asquith. The shortcomings of the Secretary of State for War were well known to his colleagues on the War Council, many of whom had wanted him removed from office, yet he retained his position in the new coalition government. What particularly rankled Churchill was that, in June 1915, Kitchener was awarded the Order of the Garter, another vote of confidence which could not help but reinforce the public impression that the War Minister was not held responsible for the failure at the Dardanelles. Churchill's principal complaint against Kitchener was his indecision over the release of troops during the naval phase of the campaign. His resentment towards Asquith, on the other hand, was driven primarily by a sense of personal betrayal. Churchill felt the Prime Minister had let him down badly, first by dismissing him from the Admiralty in May 1915, and then for not carrying through on his promise to give him the command of a brigade when he left the government. When Churchill later formulated his complaints against Asquith with respect to the Dardanelles, he invariably focused on the Prime Minister's want of resolve and control. Asquith, he complained to Lloyd George, was the only person who could 'have co-ordinated the naval and military action & given to the war-policy of the country the necessary guidance & leadership'.[6]

Churchill had a more ambivalent attitude towards Fisher, and never really understood what had caused the admiral's resignation. 'Fisher is a mystery', he confessed to Archie Sinclair. 'Was it a nervous breakdown or a coup d'etat? Or more likely than either both combined.'[7] Churchill's bitterness would have been considerably greater had he known the admiral's role in the press campaign against him and his list of 'terms' for staying at the Admiralty in May 1915. But what seemed to matter most to Churchill in the aftermath of the crisis that brought down the Liberal government was that Fisher had not been re-employed as First Sea Lord. The fact that Fisher was forced to share in the public blame for the navy's failures appears to have gone some way towards satisfying Churchill's sense of justice. He was incensed, therefore, when Asquith appointed Fisher chairman of the government's new Board of Invention and Research in July 1915. As long as Fisher was adrift in the wilderness Churchill was inclined to leave him alone, but his re-employment by the government, even in a relatively minor position, could be interpreted as a signal that his resignation had been justified. This threatened to shift all the blame for the breakdown at the Admiralty entirely on Churchill. Fisher's rehabilitation could only come at his own expense. He thought better of protesting to Asquith about Fisher's appointment. Instead, he complained to Balfour that the admiral's behaviour in May 1915 should disbar him from any further official appointments. Fisher, he noted, had deserted his post in wartime and refused the Prime Minister's direct order to return to duty. His return in any official capacity would be divisive within the Admiralty, he warned, and would encourage Fisher's supporters to lobby for his return. 'All this must be viewed', he concluded, 'in relation to a very old man, without the nerve to carry on war, not quite sane in moments of crisis, and perfectly unscrupulous.'[8]

There was little likelihood of Fisher returning to the Admiralty in 1915. Asquith and Balfour both knew his faults too well by now to contemplate restoring him to power. But by early 1916 Fisher's prospects were, nevertheless, improving. At the Admiralty, Balfour and Jackson were thought by many to lack the dynamism of their predecessors. There were growing concerns throughout the country that a more energetic leadership was needed for the navy. Fisher did everything in his power to foster these feelings, employing many of the same methods he had used the year before to undermine the Dardanelles project. He wrote to influential figures like Hankey and Jellicoe, denouncing the Admiralty for 'lethargy', 'inertia', and 'apathy'. And he warned Bonar Law, now a member of the government, that the Balfour–Jackson regime was 'jeopardizing the country'.[9] Once again, Fisher's indiscretions became widely known. Gwynne learned that Fisher, whom he characterized as 'notoriously a talker and a babbler of secrets', had been telling his friends that Jellicoe and other officers in the Grand Fleet had written to him to 'deplore the present inaction of the Fleet' and that Jellicoe attributed this lamentable state of affairs 'to the supineness of the [Balfour] Board [of Admiralty]'. Gwynne, echoing Margot Asquith's comments in April 1915, told Jellicoe that:

> The fact that Lord Fisher possesses letters of yours in this strain is known to everybody in London. The inference which he and his friends draw is that you and some of your admirals are sick of the present 'inaction' and would welcome the return of Lord Fisher as a sign that a more active and aggressive policy will follow his assumption of office.
>
> These letters of yours are, I am afraid, the chief factor in a press campaign which Lord Fisher has inaugurated with his accustomed skill. In these matters he is a consummate master as I know myself.[10]

Fisher also continued his practice of talking 'very big in his own room'. He could no longer threaten resignation if his demands were not addressed, but he could propose to make his concerns public in the House of Lords.[11] Fisher was encouraged in all this by his supporters in the press, which included powerful figures like Lord Northcliffe, C. P. Scott (editor of the *Manchester Guardian*), and J. L. Garvin (editor of the *Pall Mall Gazette* and the *Observer*). At the beginning of February 1916, Fisher's campaign seemed to be developing momentum. Churchill, who watched political developments carefully from Flanders, was alarmed. 'I cannot trust the PM not to put him back', he told his wife.[12]

Gwynne was even more alarmed than Churchill by the prospect of Fisher returning to office. He went on the offensive with a strong leader in the

Morning Post on 11 February, denouncing the press agitation for Fisher's recall. He later explained both his motives and his methods to Henry Wilson:

> Fisher started a very pretty little intrigue in the Press, his sole object being to return to power for the purpose—as he himself was silly enough to say—of smashing up the present Board. I got wind of it and came to the conclusion that Jacky should be smashed for all time. I therefore laid into him with a bludgeon instead of with a stick, and I think I have succeeded in smashing him into such small pieces that even his most devoted friends on the Press cannot reconstruct him again.[13]

The *Morning Post* published another damning attack the following day, along with a letter from three retired admirals praising the newspaper for its stand against Fisher.[14] Churchill watched the proceedings from the sidelines with evident satisfaction. 'I expect the old rogue will realise increasingly as time passes the folly of his action', he wrote to Clementine from the front.[15] In fact, Gwynne's attack on Fisher seems to have had the desired effect. Ian Hamilton informed Churchill on 16 February that: 'A week ago I think the old boy [Fisher] really thought he was going to carry the thing through, and come right out on top, but, suddenly, his main-stay, [the press baron Alfred] Harmsworth [Lord Northcliffe], has failed him, and in several of the papers belonging to that organization other ideas have been finding favour.' The result, Hamilton concluded, was that Fisher and his allies were 'all rather in the blues'.[16]

The sudden collapse of Fisher's press campaign strengthened the admiral's fears that he would be excluded from power as long as Asquith and Balfour remained in office. However, ousting them was no simple matter. The formation of a coalition government meant that there was no longer a strong opposition in Parliament on which he could draw for support. Fisher, in characteristic fashion, began looking for someone he could promote for the premiership. C. P. Scott, one of the admiral's strongest supporters, recorded with alarm at the end of February 1916 that Fisher 'lives in an atmosphere of intrigue in which he does not appear to play a very skilful part'. Scott was especially concerned in late February when he discovered Fisher had met with T. P. O'Connor, an Irish nationalist MP and journalist, 'in order', Scott recorded, 'to propound to him in all seriousness a wild idea which he had conceived of making [the Irish nationalist leader John] Redmond Prime Minister'. In his diary, Scott complained that he had to plead with O'Connor afterwards to keep secret Fisher's indiscretions about the state of the British Navy.[17]

Fisher was not alone, however, in lamenting the absence of any effective challenge to Asquith's coalition. There was a growing feeling in the press and amongst disgruntled MPs that the absence of an organized opposition in Parliament allowed the government too much freedom. When Churchill returned to London on leave in early March, some of his friends and supporters urged him to fill this void by leading an opposition group. Among those pushing Churchill forward were Scott and Garvin, both enthusiastic supporters of Fisher. Churchill lacked the political strength and popularity to set himself up as an unofficial leader of the opposition, but he was eager to take part in the upcoming debate on the annual navy estimates, which would allow him to defend his record at the Admiralty and contrast his administration favourably with his successors'. In this respect, Churchill's interests clearly aligned with Fisher's. Their mutual friends had been working for months to stage a reconciliation, and Churchill's visit to London was too good an opportunity to pass up. Fisher, who was the more calculating of the two men, clearly saw the personal advantage to be gained by cooperation with his old friend. It had been Churchill, after all, who had insisted on Fisher's recall to the Admiralty in 1914 against strenuous opposition. The admiral was again in need of a powerful patron, and he was happy to cast Churchill in that role if Churchill was willing to accept it.[18] He was fortunate that Churchill was not one to hold a grudge. Garvin had broached the subject of reconciliation with him at the end of 1915, and told Fisher afterwards that the former First Lord was 'willing to bury the hatchet'.[19]

Violet Bonham Carter (the former Violet Asquith) wrote in her memoirs that, 'There was a magnetic mutual attraction between these two and they could not keep away from each other for long.'[20] And so it was in March 1916. Fisher was invited to Churchill's home for lunch on the 4th, and the two men patched up their differences with astonishing speed. 'I had a lovely time with Winston!!!', Fisher enthused afterwards to his friend Robert Donald, editor of the *Daily Chronicle*. 'How always personal attacks rectify themselves.'[21] The two men were immediately back on intimate terms, and both seemed happy to put their differences over the Dardanelles behind them. The day after their reconciliation, Churchill met with Fisher again and read him the speech he proposed to make on the navy estimates. The old admiral was delighted with his friend's plans to criticize the Balfour Admiralty, which could only improve his own chances of being recalled to service. Fisher wanted to see as much pressure put on the government as possible. He pleaded with the former First Lord not to return to the front

when his leave was over. 'The reason the Government are strong', he proclaimed, 'is there is no opposition leader!' Churchill, he insisted, should '*Get
up every night and batter the box from the Opposition Bench!*'

> [It was n]o use your sending up one rocket and then going to have your head
> '*bashed in*' at the Trenches! Go the Whole Hog! *Totus Porcus!* . . . I repeat what
> I have said behind your back. *There is no one in it with you to conduct the War—
> And you can be Prime Minister* if you like![22]

Fisher's advice was entirely self-serving, but Churchill, who was uncertain at
first as to the wisdom of resigning his commission, was susceptible to Fisher's
cajolery after months of political exile. The idea of staging a triumphant
return to the House of Commons and rallying parliamentary opposition
behind him would have had a great appeal. According to C. P. Scott, by the
evening of 6 March Churchill had 'virtually decided' to leave the army.[23]

Figure 9.1. Churchill, March 1916, on leave from active service. Shown here leaving
his London home to make his disastrous speech to Parliament calling for the recall
of Lord Fisher to the Admiralty. He is followed by Clementine Churchill and Archie
Sinclair, his battalion's second-in-command (and a future leader of the Liberal party).
Topical Press Agency/Getty Images

Balfour's speech on the navy estimates the next day in the House of Commons was an uninspired performance—'dull, halting, unilluminating' was the verdict of one MP.[24] Churchill, who followed him in the debate, warned his audience at the outset that he intended 'to strike a jarring note, a note not of reproach, nor of censure nor of panic, but a note in some respects of warning'. The bulk of his speech dealt with the need to continue building new warships on a large scale so as to maintain Britain's margin of superiority over the German Navy. This was particularly important, he insisted, since it was impossible in wartime to be sure what was being built in German shipyards. There was nothing especially remarkable in this, but towards the end of his speech Churchill turned to a more controversial subject: the Balfour Admiralty's alleged lack of initiative. 'A strategic policy for the Navy, purely negative in character, by no means necessarily implies that the path of greatest prudence is being followed', he told the House of Commons. 'I wish to place on record that the late Board [of Admiralty] would certainly not have been content with an attitude of pure passivity during the whole of the year 1916.' His most serious charge against the Balfour–Jackson regime was its failure to deal effectively with German zeppelins, which had recently begun bombing British cities.

If Churchill had ended his speech here it might have been judged a modest success, but his well-placed criticisms were leading to a dramatic—and disastrous—conclusion: 'I have no doubt whatever', he continued:

> [W]hat it is my duty to say now. There was a time when I did not think that I could have brought myself to say it, but I have been away for some months, and my mind is now clear. The times are crucial. The issues are momentous. The Great War deepens and widens and expands around us. The existence of our country and of our cause depend upon the Fleet. We cannot afford to deprive ourselves or the Navy of the strongest and most vigorous forces that are available.

The only way to restore to the Admiralty the 'driving force and mental energy' it required, he declared, was to recall 'Lord Fisher to his post as First Sea Lord'.[25]

This proposal took nearly everyone by surprise. Hankey recalled that Fisher listened to the speech in the House of Commons' visitors' gallery with 'a face like an Indian Buddha'.[26] 'Splendid!!!', Fisher wrote to Churchill afterwards. 'I feel the good old times are back!'[27] The reaction in the House, however, was one of disbelief and amazement. Churchill had hoped that proposing Fisher's return to the Admiralty would demonstrate, in a seemingly disinterested manner, his willingness to put aside personal grudges for the good of the war effort. This was a colossal miscalculation, one of the worst Churchill would make in his long career. The government's supporters immediately went on the attack. Carlyon Bellairs, a Conservative MP and retired naval officer, declared that it was 'intolerable' that Churchill should demand of the Prime Minister, over the head of the current First Lord, the supersession of his naval advisers. This was, in his view, an unwarranted attack on Fisher's successor, Henry Jackson. Bellairs was followed by Admiral of the Fleet Sir Hedworth Meux, who was quick to point out that nobody had done more than Churchill to advertise Fisher's unsuitability for the position of First Sea Lord. When the two men were at the Admiralty together, Meux pointed out, 'they were at daggers drawn, and everybody at the Admiralty knew it':

> Are we to have all that over again? What did the late First Lord say about Lord Fisher when he made his exculpating speech in this House? Did he not say that he could not get proper guidance from Lord Fisher, and is that the man you want to bring back? Who has called for Lord Fisher? Has the House called for him? The Navy has not called for him.

Churchill's humiliation continued the following evening when Balfour rose again to speak. The First Lord, a skilled and experienced parliamentarian, launched into what the *Daily Mail* described as 'a crushing rejoinder to Mr. Churchill. For three-quarters of an hour his stinging phrases flew about the ears of Mr. Churchill, who sat in gloomy isolation in one corner of the Opposition front bench.'[28] Balfour deftly addressed the points raised by Churchill the day before, but was particularly scathing about the call for a change of leadership at the Admiralty, telling his listeners that he did not think Churchill had 'ever astonished' the House of Commons 'so much as when he came down to explain that the remedy for all our ills, as far as the Navy is concerned, is to get rid of Sir Henry Jackson and to put in his place Lord Fisher'. Churchill, he continued:

> [H]as never made the smallest concealment, either in public or in private, of what he thought of Lord Fisher. (Laughter.) Certainly the impression that we all had of what he thought of Lord Fisher was singularly unlike the picture that we should ourselves have drawn, uninspired, as to the character of a saviour of his country. (Laughter.)
>
> What did he say when he made what, at the time, we thought was his farewell speech—(renewed laughter)—when he exchanged a political for a military career? He told us that the First Sea Lord, Lord Fisher, did not give him, when he was serving in the same Admiralty with him, either the clear

guidance before the event or the firm support after it which he was entitled to expect.

Balfour went on to mock Churchill's implicit suggestion that Fisher 'could not be adequately trusted to do his work when he disapproved of the policy of the Government, but that he could be trusted to carry it out when he approved of it'. Why, he asked, would Churchill assume:

> [T]hat Lord Fisher would behave differently to me from the manner in which he declares Lord Fisher behaved to him? Is it my merit? (Laughter.) Am I more happily gifted in the way of working with people? (Laughter.) ... [Churchill], who could not get on with Lord Fisher—(laughter)—I won't say that Lord Fisher could not get on with him—(renewed laughter)—who, according to him, neither supported him nor guided him, is nevertheless the man who ought to be given as a guide and a support to anybody who happens to hold at this moment the responsible position of First Lord of the Admiralty! It is a paradox of the wildest and most extravagant kind.

'I should regard myself as contemptible beyond the power of expression', he concluded, 'if I were to yield an inch to a demand of such a kind, made in such a way. (Cheers.)'[29]

Balfour's devastating rebuke was delivered, according to the *Daily Mail*, to the 'obvious satisfaction' of the government front bench, and especially its Conservative members.[30] Asquith, who had done so much to advance Churchill's early career, told his wife that if he had not had a delegation to attend to, he would 'have given Winston 10 of the nastiest minutes of his life he was so *disgusted*'.[31] The Prime Minister was still angry the next day, complaining to C. P. Scott that Churchill's speech was 'a piece of the grossest effrontery.': According to Scott's diary, Asquith told him that when Fisher was appointed head of the Board of Invention and Research a few months earlier,

> both Churchill and his wife had been furious and denounced it as an outrage, so much so that Mrs. Churchill had almost cut him and his wife and would not speak to him. And now suddenly Churchill professed to have discovered Fisher's extraordinary merits and called for his reinstatement. It was a piece of 'impudent humbug'. Why when Churchill and Fisher were together they did nothing but quarrel and Fisher's resignations were a perpetual worry of his life. He had resigned 8 times before the last time. Then he actually deserted his post and went away at a time too of some anxiety....'He deserved to be shot', shouted Asquith, 'and in any other country he would have been shot.' This was known in the navy and his recall now would be deeply resented.[32]

Churchill's misjudged intervention in the navy estimates debate was a serious setback to his campaign to revive his political career. Not only did he alienate members of the government like Balfour and Asquith, who were generally well-disposed towards him, he raised fresh doubts throughout Whitehall and in the British press as to the soundness of his judgement. Even a close friend like Violet Bonham Carter was left dumbfounded. 'Could he possibly believe in the course which he was advocating?', she asked in her memoirs. 'It would be unlike him to swerve from his convictions... Yet if he believed in it he must surely be deranged.'[33]

Churchill immediately realized his mistake. The day of Balfour's speech, Bonham Carter found him alone at his mother's house looking 'pale, defiant, on the defensive'. She later recalled 'the pain of the talk that followed'. 'I saw at once', she observed, that 'he realized that he had hopelessly failed to accomplish what he had set out to do. His lance was broken.'[34] Fisher and C. P. Scott continued to encourage Churchill to resign his commission and return to Parliament. Despite his recent setback, Churchill was inclined to follow their advice. He wanted nothing more by now than to be back at the centre of events. But he was dissuaded from resignation by his wife and a handful of others, including Asquith. Bonham Carter records that the Prime Minister spoke to Churchill at length about his plans, and reminded him that his late father, Lord Randolph Churchill, had irretrievably destroyed his political career by a poorly thought-out resignation. When Churchill naively spoke of his supporters who looked to him to lead an opposition, Asquith bluntly pointed out that: 'At the moment you have none who count at all.'[35] Asquith was hardly a disinterested observer—he had a vested interest in reducing opposition in Parliament, not encouraging it—but this was, nonetheless, excellent advice. Churchill wisely chose to return to the army when his leave expired, but his heart was not in it. The only real question to be settled, from his perspective, was when and how to make his exit. An opportunity presented itself in early May when his battalion was amalgamated with another. Command of the new unit passed to the other battalion's colonel, who was senior to Churchill. Churchill's services were therefore not immediately required by the army, giving him a convenient opportunity to return full time to politics.

Only a handful of Churchill's most loyal supporters welcomed his reappearance in the House of Commons. The Dardanelles campaign was frequently thrown in his face in the months that followed. During a debate on 9 May on the extension of conscription to Ireland, for example, Churchill was interrupted by an Irish Nationalist MP who shouted 'What about the

Dardanelles?', a challenge that would be repeated many times in the years to come.[36] Churchill was also dismayed to discover that Conservative newspapers were quick to raise the Dardanelles campaign when they wished to undermine his position. In October 1916, when it was rumoured that Churchill was intriguing against General Sir Douglas Haig, French's replacement as Commander-in-Chief of the BEF, the *Daily Mail* denounced him as 'a megalomaniac politician' who, in the Dardanelles campaign, had 'risked the fate of our Army in France and sacrificed thousands of lives to no purpose'. As First Lord, the newspaper charged, Churchill had 'just intelligence enough to know that Antwerp and Constantinople were places of importance and yet was mad enough to embark on adventures in both places with forces and methods that were insanely disproportionate to the enterprises on which our unfortunate sailors and soldiers were launched in each case'.[37]

Churchill was 'deeply hurt' by the *Daily Mail*'s attack.[38] Incidents like this only reassured him that he had been right to return to London to concentrate on reviving his political career. In this respect, his timing was propitious. At the end of April 1916, the Allied failure at Gallipoli was overshadowed by a new disaster in the east. An Anglo-Indian Army at Kut Al Amara in Mesopotamia surrendered to the Ottomans following a prolonged siege. Around 13,000 soldiers were taken prisoner after a relieving force failed to reach the garrison, and the British public was outraged. Under strong pressure in the House of Commons, the Asquith government agreed the following month to publish official papers relating to the humiliation in Mesopotamia. This decision inevitably raised new demands for the release of documents relating to the Dardanelles. The subject was mooted in the House of Commons on 1 June by Sir Henry Dalziel, a dissident Liberal MP who had been prominent among those encouraging Churchill to lead the opposition to the government. He may, in fact, have been raising the subject on Churchill's behalf. Dalziel called for both the publication of documents and a formal enquiry into failure at the Dardanelles, even though it might damage the reputations of some of the statesmen involved in launching the operation. He professed, however, to have no idea what view Churchill might take on this issue. Churchill, who immediately followed Dalziel in the debate, made the most of this opportunity to press his case. He did not admit, however, that he was motivated by the desire to clear his own name. Instead, he suggested that the release of papers was desirable insofar as it would protect ministers, past and present, from accusations that 'they were in some way trying, by delaying the publication of the Papers, to shield themselves, and to allow the whole burden of blame to fall upon the military or naval commanders at the scene of action'. Churchill averred that he, personally, would be happy to see everything published. 'I make absolutely no stipulation of any kind', he announced.[39]

Bonar Law, speaking on Asquith's behalf, announced that the government had decided to submit papers on the Dardanelles campaign to Parliament as soon as possible. He promised, moreover, that no documents would be held back except those that might reveal information of value to the enemy. 'It is quite obvious', he stated, 'that, if a story is to be told, then the whole of it should be told.'[40] Churchill was elated. The government was now formally committed to disclosing documents on the Dardanelles, and he was hopeful that his exoneration was now just a matter of time. When C. P. Scott visited Churchill afterward, he was 'in a frivolous mood':

> He marched up and down the room descanting on the fix the Dardanelles papers would put various eminent persons into—Jackson, Kitchener, Balfour all 'up to the neck' in the business—and doubting whether Asquith when he came to see them would venture on publication, yet how after giving his promise could he avoid it?[41]

Churchill naturally hoped to take control of the process and immediately suggested to Asquith that he and Hankey should be delegated the task of selecting the papers to be published.[42] But Churchill so clearly had his own agenda that the Prime Minister was not about to allow this. The task was assigned instead to the ubiquitous Hankey, who could be counted on to protect the current government's interests.

Churchill's main concern in the following weeks was to ensure the publication of every document he deemed critical to his defence. And so great was his faith in his case that he never sought to suppress a single record. A dispute immediately arose over the publication of the War Council minutes. These had not been formally circulated to ministers when they were made, and Churchill had probably only recently become aware of them. He was naturally eager to ensure they were published, since they clearly established that the entire War Council had backed the Dardanelles scheme. They also showed that he had fought with Kitchener to secure the release of troops at an early date. Hankey, however, was firmly opposed to this course of action. He advised Asquith that it would not be in the public interest to publish the minutes of the War Council verbatim, and complained that it would be 'a difficult and laborious task' for anyone to prepare a sanitized digest. His own view, moreover, was 'that the War Committee proceedings ought to be regarded as just as confidential and personal as those of the Cabinet, and ought not to be published at all'.[43] But his objections went much further than this. He felt strongly that it would be a mistake to publish *any* documents before the end of the war, a view shared by Balfour. The Secretary to the War Council sent a lengthy memorandum to Asquith on 5 June encouraging him to abandon the idea of publication. His main objection was that a great many documents would have to be excluded so as not to reveal too much to the enemy about Allied diplomacy and strategic decision-making. It would be a mistake, for example, to disclose that the Allies had planned to give Constantinople to the Russians, or that Churchill had intended naval operations along the German coast and in the Baltic. 'The story that can be told... at present will be so incomplete', he warned, 'that I would submit it should not be told at all. A half story will give rise to an infinity of personal bickerings and complaints, and friction concerning persons still engaged in conduct of war.'[44]

Asquith was unwilling to go back on his promise to Parliament, however, and a frustrated Hankey had no choice but to begin the task of compiling and editing documents for publication.[45] The fate of the War Council minutes still remained to be settled, however. Churchill sent a strong appeal to Asquith a few days later, but the Prime Minister sided with Hankey. Churchill was informed that the full publication of these records would set a bad precedent, making it difficult for the government to resist demands for the disclosure of more records of ministerial deliberations. The effect would be to stifle free discussion in future meetings, as ministers would have 'to worry about their remarks being liable to publication'.[46] Churchill wrote to Asquith on 22 June pleading with him not to allow these documents to be suppressed.[47] By now, he would have been happy to see even a summary of the War Council meetings published. Asquith was evidently willing to consider this option, although Churchill was not informed that this possibility was under consideration. Hankey went to the considerable trouble of preparing a digest of the War Council's deliberations over the Dardanelles, although whether it would be deemed suitable for publication remained uncertain.[48]

There was one other unexpected development that Churchill had to deal with in June 1916: the death of Lord Kitchener. On the evening of 5 June, the cruiser HMS *Hampshire*, which was carrying the War Minister on an official mission to Russia, struck a German mine and sank off the Scottish coast. Kitchener, along with Fitzgerald and most of the ship's crew, was killed. Churchill was in Hankey's office going through War Council documents the next morning when Masterton Smith telephoned from the Admiralty to inform Hankey of the loss. The Secretary to the War Council took care not to reveal anything to Churchill, as he did not yet know whether the news was to be kept secret.[49] 'I endeavoured to preserve a perfectly calm demeanour at this shocking news', he wrote in his memoirs, 'in order that my visitor might not guess that anything sensational had happened, and I tried to reply to Masterton Smith as though our conversation were on some routine matter. Churchill must have recognized some unexpected quality in my voice, for he pricked up his ears and asked if there was any news. I refused to be drawn. I am not sure he ever quite forgave me.'[50] Churchill remained in the dark until later that day. Ian Hamilton and Churchill were alone together at the latter's home 'when suddenly we heard someone in the street crying out Kitchener's name. We jumped up and Winston threw the window open. As he did so an apparition passed beneath us', Hamilton recalled. 'I can use no other word to describe the strange looks of this newsvendor of wild and uncouth aspect. He had his bundle of newspapers under his arm and as we opened the window was crying out, "Kitchener drowned! No survivors!"'[51]

In light of this unexpected news, both Hamilton and Churchill would have to reconsider how they planned to defend themselves over the Dardanelles and Gallipoli campaigns. Kitchener had already been regarded as a great hero before his death. The British public, devastated by his loss, would react badly to anyone who sought to shift the blame for these failures onto the shoulders of a dead idol who could no longer defend his reputation. Hamilton was under an even greater handicap in this respect than Churchill. The general hoped to receive another command during the war. He could not afford to alienate opinion in the British Army, where Kitchener's reputation was jealously guarded after his death. If Hamilton had any doubts as to the wisdom of criticizing Kitchener, they were soon dispelled by Callwell, who had been assigned by the War Office to work with Hankey in the selection of documents for publication. Callwell confided to Hamilton that it would be 'quite impossible' to publish all the available documents 'because they must give away Lord K if the story is fairly told. The tragedy of the "Hampshire" simply precludes publication at present.'[52] Hamilton explained to Churchill several months later that he had concluded it was in his own best interest not to make any criticisms of

Kitchener whatsoever, even though his defence depended upon it. 'I came to the conclusion', he wrote, 'I should be utterly done for during my life-time if any act of mine were to draw out a Government defence of Kitchener. Once my defence becomes looked upon as an attack on a dead hero it would be better for my reputation to lose than to win.'[53]

The War Office was not the only department opposed to the publication of documents. Officials at the Admiralty and Foreign Office made it clear to Hankey that they were strongly against the idea as well. So many documents would have to be excluded on security grounds that nothing would remain, as one of Hankey's assistants observed, but 'a barren and emasculated collection of papers [that] would give no satisfaction to the House'.[54] The Secretary to the War Committee conveyed these objections to the Prime Minister, but even though Asquith's inclination was 'to publish as little as possible', he still insisted that something would have to be produced to satisfy Parliament.[55] The objections continued to pour in, however. In early July, Hankey persuaded Asquith to refer the matter to the War Committee for a decision.[56] By now, Churchill realized that something was amiss. He told Riddell on 7 July that his position 'in the country will be very different' when the Dardanelles papers were finally published, but that he now feared that the government would renege on its pledge. Privately, he speculated that Asquith had only agreed to publish documents 'because he knew that I had a murderous case against Kitchener...My documents would have been most useful and effective weapons to destroy Kitchener's influence and the P.M. could have cast the responsibility for publication upon me.'[57] He also suspected that Hankey was using his influence behind the scenes to prevent publication. Shortly after Asquith's promise to Parliament, Hankey had innocently revealed to Churchill his arguments against publication. This did not go over well. 'He became quite furious', Hankey recalled, 'and asked where he came in.'

> 'Whenever I open my mouth in Parliament' he said 'some-one shouts out that I am the man who let us in for the Dardanelles mistake, and the papers are perpetually repeating it. My usefulness in Parliament is entirely ruined until my responsibility is cleared on the subject. No doubt it is very convenient for members of the present Government to leave their responsibility on my shoulders' &c &c. All entirely selfish.[58]

On 8 July, an increasingly frustrated Churchill wrote again to Asquith, who had not yet replied to his letter of 22 June, seeking an assurance that the government intended to fulfil its pledge. If this was not forthcoming, he proposed to raise the issue in Parliament.[59] It had now been nearly six weeks since Asquith had made his pledge, and a decision could not be long delayed. The subject was discussed by the War Committee three days later. Hankey had prepared a long memorandum for ministers in which he forcefully and persuasively set out the case against publication.[60] This had the desired effect: the decision was taken not to proceed. Lloyd George told Riddell afterward that he had been the only member of the committee to speak in favour of publication, on the grounds that 'you must treat public servants fairly, that Winston was a great public servant and that he was being unfairly treated. The Committee would not budge.'[61] Hankey believed his memorandum had been decisive in killing the project, as did others. 'All the afternoon', he wrote, 'I was being rung up from different departments by people thanking me for managing this.'[62]

All that remained to be settled was whether something should be substituted for the publication of documents. One possibility was the confidential release of documents to Parliament, followed by a secret debate. The other idea to emerge was a parliamentary commission to examine the secret evidence and issue a report suitable for publication. Churchill learned from Lloyd George that the latter was under consideration, and he did not like the idea. He felt strongly that the government must adhere to its pledge to publish documents, which he believed would be in his own best interest. To Lloyd George, who had replaced Kitchener as Secretary of State for War, Churchill protested that the real issue was not the damage that might be done to British interests, which he thought was negligible, but the injury that would be sustained by the government. This being the case, he suggested that 'the government desire not unnaturally to substitute for a publication of authentic documents on which the nation could judge, a secret inquiry of indefinite duration by a body selected by themselves'.[63]

This was not entirely true, as there were many legitimate diplomatic and security concerns in the way of a full disclosure of documents. But even Hankey was willing to admit in his diary that he did not 'know how the P.M.'s reputation could have been saved' if the Dardanelles documents had been published.[64] In any event, Churchill could not understand why Asquith and Bonar Law had voluntarily pledged to publish in the first place, since the content of the documents was already known to them. The objections now being raised to their publication should have been foreseeable.[65] Asquith informed Churchill of the decision against publication on 12 July, and Churchill protested against the abandonment of a formal pledge to

Parliament. He urged the Prime Minister to reconsider, assuring him that any material unsuitable for release could easily be excised from documents before publication.[66] Asquith, who was already uneasy about renouncing his pledge to Parliament, hesitated. Hankey feared that he intended to take the issue back to the War Committee for reconsideration.[67] But the strength of opposition in Whitehall was so great by now that there was no longer any prospect of the documents appearing, and even Churchill was willing to concede privately that there 'are many good arguments in the public interest against publishing'.[68]

Asquith announced the decision not to release papers on either the Dardanelles or Mesopotamia on 18 July, telling the House of Commons that the Admiralty, War Office, and Foreign Office were unanimously against publication at the present time, and that so many important documents would have to be held back that the results could only be 'incomplete and misleading'.[69] The coalition government was already under intense pressure from many directions over its conduct of the war, and this decision was badly received by the House. Demands were immediately made to establish a select committee of the House of Commons to examine the evidence. Hankey was against the idea, mainly on the grounds that it would involve an immense amount of work for himself and numerous others, whose attention should be concentrated instead on the war effort. Asquith assured the Secretary to the War Committee the next day that he would resist pressure for a select committee, and asked him to gather historical precedents to bolster the case against such an expedient. Hankey and his staff were already at work on this task, and armed the Prime Minister for a debate on the subject the next day.[70] But when Asquith rose to speak on 20 July he announced, to Hankey's dismay, that two special commissions would be established, one to examine the Mesopotamian disaster and the other to consider the Dardanelles.[71] These bodies, he announced, would meet in secrecy to examine all the available evidence. This was not the course Churchill would have chosen, but in the short term it was his best and only chance to restore his reputation. He was determined from the outset to make the most of it.

10

The Dardanelles Commission I
The Preliminaries

The Dardanelles Commission was formally constituted by Parliament through the Special Commissions (Dardanelles and Mesopotamia) Act, 1916, to examine the origins and execution of the naval campaign and the conduct of the military offensive on the Gallipoli peninsula. Its first chairman was Evelyn Baring, 1st Earl of Cromer, a Liberal peer who had served with distinction as Britain's Consul-General of Egypt until his retirement in 1907. Cromer's appointment would have come as welcome news. He was a friend of Churchill's mother and had advised the young Churchill on his book *The River War* (1899). The seventy-five-year-old statesmen's health was not up to the task, however. After a chance encounter in August, Churchill reported that Cromer 'looked so ill & old that I hardly recognised him'.[1] Cromer himself realized how much strain the job would put on him. 'I know it will kill me', he admitted, 'but young men are giving their lives for their country, so why should not I who am old?'[2] He died in January 1917, just four months into the Commission's deliberations. His successor was William Pickford, a law lord. In a break with usual practice, the other members of the Commission were not all parliamentarians. Thomas Mackenzie and Andrew Fisher, respectively the New Zealand and Australian High Commissioners in London, were both appointed. The Australian government, which viewed the enquiry as an unnecessary distraction in the midst of a great war, insisted that Fisher, a former Prime Minister, was not acting as the official representative of the Australian government. To ensure a fair hearing for the military and naval figures who came before the Commission, two retired officers were also included: Admiral Sir William May (who had once served under Fisher as Second Sea Lord) and Field Marshal William Nicholson (Baron Nicholson), a former CIGS. The remaining members were drawn from the House of Commons: Frederick Cawley (Liberal), James Clyde (Liberal Unionist), Stephen Gwynn (Irish Nationalist), and Walter Roch (a Welsh Liberal MP). The secretary was E. Grimwood Mears, a barrister, who agreed to serve in exchange for a knighthood. Churchill judged it to be 'a pretty good commission'.[3]

The weeks leading up to the enquiry were hectic ones for Churchill. He continued hunting down official documents to bolster his case and painstakingly prepared a written statement outlining his part in launching and managing the naval operation. This was designed to provide a far more elaborate defence than the one he had presented to Parliament in November 1915, when the campaign was still in progress. Churchill had been unable then to reveal much about how the operation had been prepared. His main concern at that time was to contest the idea popularized in the press that he had consistently acted against the advice of Admiral Fisher and other naval authorities. Because the Dardanelles Commission was reviewing documents in secret, Churchill could now submit the full record for judgement, and he was determined to leave nothing out that might vindicate him. In early August, he enlisted Alexander MacCallum Scott, a Scottish Liberal MP and journalist, to assist him with the presentation of his defence.[4] Besides being one of Churchill's few supporters on the Liberal backbenches, Scott had the distinction of being the author of two biographies of Churchill. The first had been published in 1905, when its subject had not yet achieved Cabinet rank. The second, *Winston Churchill in Peace and War*, appeared in mid-1916, shortly before the Commission was formed. It offered a sympathetic treatment of Churchill's record at the Admiralty, and in particular his role in the inception of the Dardanelles campaign.[5] In addition to Scott, who scrutinized early drafts of his defence, Churchill consulted a number of others, most notably his close friend F. E. Smith, the Attorney General (and a prominent Conservative), who offered legal advice. He also worked closely with Ian Hamilton and a various officials involved in preparing evidence for the enquiry, including Hankey, Callwell, and Graham Greene, the Permanent Secretary at the Admiralty.

Collaboration with Fisher was bound to be problematic. There is no evidence that Churchill resented Fisher for manipulating him into his disastrous speech in March, but he had good reason to be wary about again associating himself closely with such a volatile and controversial figure. Clementine Churchill, who had few illusions about the admiral, consistently urged her husband to be cautious. Riddell recorded in July that 'Mrs. Winston...said in Winston's presence that she has warned W. against him [Fisher]—that he is treacherous—that he has turned on Winston once and may do so again.'[6] Churchill probably had these entreaties in mind when the admiral unexpectedly approached him in August for help in preparing his case for the Commission. The politician replied that he felt great 'diffidence in doing what you ask of me'. He suggested that it would be better for Fisher to prepare his own defence in the first instance and then bring it to Churchill for discussion.[7] There was an obvious disadvantage to collaborating with Fisher. Churchill would be forced to gloss over, ignore, or condone the admiral's erratic behaviour as First Sea Lord, thereby abandoning one of his strongest defences. It would have been difficult, and probably unwise, however, for Churchill to refuse the admiral's request, since it would allow him to shape Fisher's case to conform to his own. Churchill was also anxious to avoid an open clash with Fisher at the enquiry, which would inevitably weaken his position and overshadow his carefully constructed defence. No one would benefit from a renewal of their feud except the other members of the former Liberal government. Churchill, according to Fisher, said '<u>he knows</u> that the one thing relied on by the officials in authority is that the Dardanelles Enquiry will "<u>fizzle out</u>" as a personal battle between Winston & myself! <u>& he is determined that no single word shall escape him to my detriment</u>!!!!'[8]

Fisher was also eager to avoid a clash. The first draft of his case for the Commission was evidently couched in such flattering terms that Churchill soon put aside any misgivings about assisting him.[9] When the two met on the evening of 10 August, Churchill expounded at length about how Fisher should frame his evidence for the Commission. The old admiral was delighted, telling Churchill the next day that his presentation had been 'most convincing'. 'Impossible for me to equal it!', he enthused. Nor was he inclined to try. He urged Churchill to summon a shorthand writer and repeat everything he had said to Fisher the previous evening. As an incentive, he assured Churchill that he hoped to bring out in his evidence 'how you fought for me and how I reciprocated your affection!'[10] Churchill did not accept this invitation to dictate Fisher's statement for him, but he continued to consult and advise him in the weeks that followed. The admiral's best line of defence, he suggested on 16 September, was to maintain that he had always been against the Dardanelles operation, but had supported the project in its early stages because of the strong political arguments in its favour; because the idea enjoyed definite support both within the Admiralty and from the admiral on the spot; and out of personal loyalty to Churchill.

This line of defence would clearly benefit Churchill, who badly wanted to dispel the widespread idea that he had ignored Fisher's advice and overruled his naval advisers. Fisher's explicit support on these points would be invaluable. Churchill, in return, tacitly agreed to support Fisher's other proposed line of defence: that he had 'loyal[ly] and resolute[ly]' supported the operation right 'up to the point where the Admiral on the spot pulled up'. Churchill proposed that Fisher should take the position that he had resigned in May only because he could no longer give his wholehearted support to the operation.[11]

This version of events involved considerable distortion of the truth. Fisher's support for Churchill could hardly be described as 'loyal'. But neither wanted to see the Commission probe into their turbulent personal relations, so they agreed to maintain a façade of harmony. Thus, an early draft of Fisher's written submission to the Commission proclaimed that, from 28 January onward, 'Lord Fisher's sole duty was to see that the Government plan was carried out as successfully as possible with the available means, and no one has ever suggested for one moment that Lord Fisher failed in this in any respect.' Churchill's consent was assured by Fisher's statements that 'Mr. Churchill had the whole naval opinion at the Admiralty as well as the naval opinion at the Dardanelles with him—Lord Fisher was the only dissentient.'[12] Fisher faithfully adhered to this position in the various drafts of his written statement and in his evidence to the Commission, but other aspects of his defence were changed in the weeks leading up to his testimony.

In the earliest drafts of his case, the admiral had maintained that his principal objection to the Dardanelles operation was the diversion of naval resources from the North Sea. He only resigned, he claimed, when this drain 'became so great as to jeopardise the major operations of the Fleet'. He also suggested that his reluctance to resign earlier stemmed from concerns about the fate of the large naval construction programme he initiated after returning to the Admiralty. It was not 'in the public interest', he averred, 'to resign until he could see it well on its way to completion'.[13] Fisher was undoubtedly sincere when he claimed that he was heavily invested in the construction of new ships for the navy, a task he thought himself uniquely capable of achieving. Indeed, there is evidence to suggest that this massive building project had preoccupied him to the point that it overshadowed his other duties. According to Masterton Smith, 'Fisher was not interested in naval operations. He never was. He was chiefly concerned with constructional work. That was the arrangement between him and Winston. Fisher made the ships in the one room and Winston used them in another.'[14] Crease, who worked closely with Fisher, shared this view. After the war he recalled that, when Fisher returned to the Admiralty in 1914, he 'devoted himself largely to the task of ordering and supplying new ships of all kinds and materials that were badly wanted, and Mr. Churchill left him alone in this work in which he was deeply interested'.[15] In 1930, a decade after Fisher's death, Churchill offered a similar judgement. 'Fisher', he wrote, 'brought to the Admiralty an immense wave of enthusiasm for the con-struction of warships....To build warships of every kind, as many as possible and as fast as possible, was the message, and in my judgement the sole mes-sage, which he carried to the Admiralty.' Churchill also hinted that he, rather than Fisher, had assumed responsibility for 'the war in general and...the need of making British naval supremacy play its full part in the struggle'. Fisher provided 'an impetus intense in its force', he observed, 'but mainly confined to the material sphere'.[16]

This implicit division of labour would certainly help to explain the admiral's seeming disengagement at times from the Dardanelles campaign. Fisher's testimony to the Dardanelles Commission confirms that he was often detached from planning and operations. When he was unable to answer detailed questions from the commissioners about the effects of naval gunfire on the Turkish forts, for example, Fisher explained that he had been 'tremendously busy' at this time 'over getting this Armada ready. I do not mean to say I did not give my best attention to this thing, but I had a multitude of other things to do.' He was not familiar with all the details of the operation, he admitted, because:

> I went on the principle that we had a splendid fellow as chief of the War Staff, Admiral Oliver. He had splendid people to consult with, Sir Henry Jackson, Sir Arthur Wilson, and other people, and I went on the principle of 'Do not keep a dog and bark yourself, too!' I thought 'these chaps have got this in hand; I will leave it to them until some big point comes such as when they begin to weaken improperly or vitally the Grand Fleet...'[17]

It also seems that Fisher, at seventy-four, lacked the energy to keep a firm hand on all aspects of Admiralty business. Richmond was not the only one to note that the admiral was often tired. Churchill confided to Riddell in July 1916 that Fisher, though a 'man of genius', 'can only work for three or four hours' in a day.[18]

Fisher's defence for the Dardanelles Commission drew heavily on Churchill's advice, but some differences naturally emerged. When the admiral proposed at one point to include in his statement some material to which Churchill objected, Churchill sent an intermediary, the MP Edward Goulding, to dissuade him. Goulding recorded afterwards that Fisher 'was reasonable, promising what I asked that he would not produce certain documents which would call for retaliation on W's part. Of course he is not too happy as he sees the prospect of his recall no brighter.'[19] Fisher also made important changes to his testimony on the advice of J. L. Garvin, who suggested that Fisher's case would be 'more strongly constructed on a different basis altogether'. The journalist advised Fisher to recast his evidence to show that his main concern about the Dardanelles was that it made such heavy demands on British resources that it would jeopardize 'what Lord Fisher thought was a far greater thing—the Baltic project', which 'had been the real focus of Lord Fisher's purposes as the Admiralty'.[20]

Fisher had made no direct reference to the Baltic in his first drafts, possibly because it had not, in fact, been his primary concern. But Garvin's suggestion obviously appealed to him, presumably because it would enable him to claim that he had been committed to bold offensive action rather than the passive strategy outlined in his memorandum of 25 January. To strengthen this claim, Fisher doctored the evidence he planned to submit. The 'armada' of 612 warships, initiated after Fisher's recall at the end of October 1914, had been ordered over a period of seven months, and was intended mainly for the North Sea and the strengthening of Jellicoe's Grand Fleet. Ruddock Mackay's biography of Fisher, published in 1973, revealed that the admiral sought to mislead the Commission. Fisher had convened a meeting at the Admiralty on 3 November 1914 to expedite the construction of a relatively modest force of twenty new submarines. In 1916, he altered the minutes of this meeting to suggest that all 612 vessels in his armada had been authorized at this one meeting, just days after returning to office; that he had placed orders for them at the conclusion of the meeting; and that the ships were 'intended for great projects in the Baltic and North Sea'. It is not clear whether the falsified version of this document was submitted to the Dardanelles Commission, although it was subsequently printed in Fisher's memoirs, published in 1919.[21]

Garvin did not feel that this new line of defence would be detrimental to Churchill in any way. And Churchill saw no reason to object to Fisher making the 'Baltic project' a central part of the case he put before the Commission. But this is not to say that he believed it, or that it was necessarily accurate. Churchill had strong doubts on this point. He wrote in 1930 that he did not accept that the admiral was ever serious about the Baltic scheme, as he had never 'framed a definite or coherent plan of action'. 'Still less', Churchill continued, 'do I believe that he had the resolution which . . . would inevitably have been required' to see it through. The admiral was 'very old', Churchill stated, and 'where naval fighting was concerned he was more than usually cautious'. In his view, Fisher's real policy was the one enshrined in his memorandum of 25 January—the maintenance of the distant blockade, a predominantly passive strategy. Fisher talked 'vaguely and impressively' about a British naval expedition into the Baltic, primarily, Churchill suggested, 'with a view to staving off demands which he knew I would make upon him...to use the naval forces more directly in the main shock of war'.[22]

It is impossible to say whether Fisher had been serious about mounting an expedition to the Baltic in 1915. The admiral never asked the naval staff to study the operation, which suggests that he did not intend to see it through. On the other hand, the lack of consultation could be a sign that he was serious. Fisher was notoriously secretive. He may have eschewed formal planning in order to prevent leaks about an operation in which he placed great hopes. There is no way of knowing. As historian Andrew Lambert has noted, 'Fisher took his plans to the grave.' The claims made by the admiral in his memoirs were, nevertheless, widely accepted prior to Mackay's biography, which sided firmly with Churchill's interpretation. Fisher's Baltic plan, Mackay concluded, was 'little more than a talking point, useful for warding off Churchill's most dangerous and unpromising projects'.[23] More recently, however, historians have treated the Baltic scheme as a serious proposition. In support, they point to the detailed plans drawn up during Fisher's previous tenure as First Sea Lord and the large programme of specialized naval construction he initiated in 1914–15. Fisher's 'armada' included shallow draught battle cruisers and monitors particularly suited for operations in the Baltic, along with 260 motorized and armoured landing craft that might have been intended for combined operations along the Pomeranian coast or elsewhere in the Baltic. It seems unlikely that Fisher intended to send the Grand Fleet into the Baltic while the German High Seas Fleet remained afloat, but he could have contemplated using a custom-built squadron of fast vessels. Even the *threat* of a British naval expedition to the Baltic might have achieved Fisher's goals if it induced the Germans to take risks with their fleet in the North Sea.[24] But in 1916 none of this mattered to Churchill. He was happy with the broad case Fisher intended to make to the Commission. It did not matter if the admiral embellished his reasons for opposing the Dardanelles, as long as he agreed that he had given the scheme his genuine support.[25]

Churchill was still confident that he would be absolved from blame for the Dardanelles once it was known that, contrary to hostile press reports and uninformed gossip, he had received consistent support from both his professional advisers and his colleagues on the War Council. Given that Churchill's political fortunes had already hit bottom, his position was bound to improve so long as the Commission was prepared to spread the blame around to some extent. But Churchill had higher expectations. He believed that once the evidence was examined by an impartial body, Asquith and Kitchener would be the ones singled out for censure. Churchill's former colleagues, who had so far escaped public criticism, realized that his rehabilitation might come at their expense. When Lloyd George suggested to Hankey that he should represent the War Council at the Dardanelles Commission, the latter was horrified. He recorded in his diary that he 'alarmed' Lloyd George 'by reminding him of his part in it [the inception of the Dardanelles campaign], & asking him how he would like me to say it all at the C[omit]tee'.[26] Hankey, who had witnessed the muddled decision-making that led to the campaign, had no doubt the investigation would reveal that there was plenty of blame to go around. He told his wife that the idea of being 'tortured in the witness box for weeks' filled him 'with horror!...How am I to avoid slaughtering the reputations of the P.M., K., Winston, Jackie and others who have been my friends I can't conceive.'[27]

Hankey, nevertheless, accepted the task of preparing the government's case for presentation to the Commission. 'Then began', he wrote in his memoirs, 'one of the most dreary tasks that has ever fallen to my lot.' By September, he estimated that he had devoted 174 hours to this project, all at the cost of his attention to the war effort.[28] Hankey's main objective was to shield the reputations of the former members of the War Council, and in particular Asquith, to whom he remained devoted. During August and early September 1916, the Secretary to the War Committee compiled a detailed and formidable defence of the late Liberal government's war management, and coached individual ministers on their testimony to the Commission. Liberal ministers clearly realized that they would all be dragged down together if they began to indulge in mutual recriminations, and Hankey's efforts ensured that everyone would remain on the same page. What mattered most to Churchill was that there would be no concerted attempt by his former colleagues to scapegoat him. When Hankey's written submission was complete, Asquith allowed him to send an advance copy to Churchill, who considered it 'very satisfactory from my point of view'.[29] The Secretary to the War Committee had, in fact, met with Churchill on more than one occasion, and was careful to include material that was important to his defence.

Hankey studiously avoided controversy and presented the broad outlines of the War Council's deliberations in a matter-of-fact manner, based on the minutes he had kept. As the documentary record was far from complete, Hankey also provided background to the Council's deliberations in order to supply important context and present the government's decisions in the most favourable light. In recounting the War Council's deliberations on 13 January, for example, when Churchill first raised the idea of a naval assault on the Dardanelles, Hankey emphasized the urgent Russian request for a diversion, the widespread concern at the time about the fate of Serbia, and the need to provide military backing for British diplomacy in the Balkans. All of this was intended to bolster the impression that, in January 1915, *some* action in the east had been both essential and unavoidable. On the critical meetings of 28 January, where the Dardanelles operation received final approval, Hankey's account was favourable to Churchill. He emphasized that there was no hostile criticism of the plan other than that implied by Fisher when he stated that Asquith knew his opinion and rose to leave the room. Hankey noted that Churchill's plan had been prepared by the naval officer on the spot; that it had the support of both the French and the Russians; that Churchill had warned the Council that losses must be expected; and that the most difficult part of the operation would come when the fleet attempted to pass the Narrows.[30]

Hankey's memorandum went on to outline how the decision had been taken to land troops on the Gallipoli peninsula. A joint operation could not have been launched at the beginning of the naval campaign, he noted, because Kitchener had insisted that no troops were available to cooperate with the fleet. Concern for the fate of Serbia had led to growing support for an expedition to Salonika, and, when this fell through, an informal meeting of the War Council decided, on 16 February, to divert troops from this project to support the Dardanelles operation. Hankey also recorded Churchill's disclaimer of responsibility for any military failure during his struggle with Kitchener over the release of the 29th Division.

He concluded his written evidence by considering a question that would inevitably be raised by the Commission: why had the operation not been called off once the naval attack had clearly stalled? This was not easy to answer, as the question had never been explicitly discussed at the War Council. Hankey noted the importance that ministers, and especially Kitchener, had placed on maintaining British prestige. But instead of revealing that the War Minister had effectively decided this issue on his own without reference to the War Council, Hankey maintained that ministers had been influenced by many of the same political and military factors that had induced them to attempt the naval attack in the first place: the ongoing stalemate in the west, the desire to rally Balkan states to the Entente, the possibility of bringing Italy into the war, and the growing threat to Serbia. He also suggested that Russia was still a dominant consideration—not because a successful campaign would have opened up a secure supply route through the Black Sea, or because it was hard pressed on the Caucasian front, but because a decision to call off the campaign so soon after promising Constantinople to St Petersburg would have had a disastrous impact on Anglo-Russian relations.[31]

The Dardanelles Commission was ready to begin its work in mid-September. Rather than trying to tackle everything at once, it planned initially to concentrate on the events up to mid-May 1915.[32] Churchill's first written submission for the Commission in September 1916 dealt only with this period. He prepared both a general statement of his case and a large selection of official documents to support it, over a hundred printed pages in total. His main concerns going in were whether he would be allowed to attend all of the Commission's meetings and call his own witnesses.[33] Cromer informed him on 20 September, two days into the Commission's deliberations, that it had been decided that all sessions were to be held in secret. Churchill could not attend, except to give evidence. The chairman sought to placate Churchill by assuring him that all the testimony would be printed, and that, when appropriate, transcripts would be confidentially supplied to witnesses who had already been examined. Individuals could ask to be recalled if they wished to address the testimony offered by other witnesses.[34] Cromer wrote again, the following day, to inform Churchill that he would be supplied with a copy of the evidence Hankey had provided to the Commission on the 19th, although he naively suggested that it probably did not contain 'much that would be of use to you'.[35]

Hankey's testimony to the Commission on 19 September began with a fresh wrangle over his War Council minutes, which the government had decided to withhold from the commissioners. Hankey recalled afterwards that: 'They talked big about their powers, and were apparently discussing whether, in the event of continued refusal, they should send someone to the Tower—though whether it was to be the Prime Minister, the War C[omit]tee, the Cabinet or me, I don't know!'[36] Hankey later brokered a compromise by which Cromer alone would be allowed to see a copy of the minutes so that he might confirm that Hankey's evidence accurately reflected their contents.[37] Despite getting off to a bad start, Hankey made a favourable impression during his two days of testimony. He was by now thoroughly conversant with the official documents and had no trouble fielding questions. The commissioners were eager to determine what information the War Council had before it when the decision was taken to launch the naval attack. They particularly wanted to know whether it had sought corroboration of the views presented by Churchill from either Fisher or Wilson, who usually attended these meetings, or by consulting independent experts. Hankey admitted that ministers had relied almost entirely on Churchill for their information on naval matters. The First Lord, he explained, 'used to act as spokesman of his Department as a rule', although he quickly added that the views Churchill expressed 'would certainly be pointed by remarks from the others [i.e. Fisher and Wilson], I should say, speaking from memory'.[38]

The commissioners clearly wanted to establish whether Churchill had withheld critical information from the War Council, and Hankey took care not to incriminate the former First Lord. Throughout his testimony he maintained that the War Council had not heard any adverse opinions about the Dardanelles from naval sources, even from Fisher. The First Sea Lord had *implied* dissent on 28 January, to be sure, but 'he did not definitely say that he disagreed with the thing'.[39] Hankey also observed that Churchill had elucidated the navy's proposals at considerable length, including the potential risks and drawbacks. 'He fully explained the plan', Hankey recalled. 'He explained it in very great detail. There he was standing up at the end of a long table with a map and the members [of the Council] crowding round him....He was reading from a document and explaining the whole thing in detail. It was most exhaustively explained.'[40] But it was nevertheless clear that Fisher had had strong reservations about the Dardanelles operation when the War Council met on 28 January, and the commissioners could not understand why his views had not been discussed. They knew Fisher had articulated his case against the operation in his memorandum of 25 January, although they had not yet seen a copy of the document. When asked if the War Council should have been given this memorandum and Churchill's reply, Hankey obfuscated. 'I do not know that I have ever seen them', he replied, 'so I really cannot express an opinion upon them.'[41] Of course, Hankey knew Fisher's memorandum well—he had helped Corbett draft it!

Fisher's silence at the meeting of 28 January was especially perplexing. If the First Sea Lord disagreed with a proposed naval operation, surely he had a duty to speak up. Fisher always maintained, however, that he was not actually a member of the War Council, and only attended in his capacity as an expert adviser. Thus he spoke only when his opinion was explicitly sought. Was this really the case? Hankey did not think so. He believed that Fisher and Wilson both had the right to present their unsolicited views, and he said so to the Commission.[42] The real mystery, however, was why the War Council never asked Fisher to present his views, especially after the incident when he left the Cabinet table with the intention of resigning. Hankey observed that this episode had made it 'fairly clear that he [Fisher] did not agree' with the proposed operation. Pickford pressed Hankey for an explanation. 'Did anybody ever ask what [Fisher's opinion] was?', he enquired:

HANKEY: 'No, nobody ever did. . . .'
PICKFORD: 'But the other members of the War Council showed no curiosity about the matter at all?'
HANKEY: 'No.'

Pickford was incredulous. 'What was the use of these naval experts attending the Council', he wondered, 'if their opinion was never asked on purely naval matters?'[43]

At the conclusion of his first day's evidence, Hankey felt that he had 'acquitted [him]self well', although he admitted that the Commission had uncovered 'all the weak points!'[44] He subsequently wrote to Fisher to assure him that he had said nothing that would injure his friend, with one possible exception. He warned the admiral that he had admitted, under cross-examination, that it *was* normally the custom for professional advisers to speak at meetings of the CID, and that their silence was usually taken to indicate consent.[45] Hankey had done his best to protect his friend's interests, but his first loyalty was to Asquith and the government, and it was undoubtedly to their advantage for the Commission to think that the politicians had innocently assumed Fisher would have volunteered his views if they were sufficiently important. In the event, Fisher was under no illusions as to where Hankey's priorities were. 'Hankey is to be the first witness', he had told a friend, '& of course all he says will be what Asquith tells him to say.'[46]

Churchill was called to give evidence on 28 September and 4 October.[47] The first day of testimony was taken up by a detailed statement outlining his case, periodically interrupted by questions from the commissioners. He began by declaring that he took full responsibility for everything done by the Admiralty during his administration. 'I have no complaint to make', he said, 'in regard to any officer serving under the Board of Admiralty, whether ashore or afloat. On the contrary, I am here to defend those by whose professional advice I was guided.'[48] He then outlined, for the Commission, the main points he intended to establish, followed by an overview of Admiralty administration during the opening months of the war. Once these preliminaries were out of the way, he began laying out the evidence to support his main arguments. The first point to establish was that he had always been aware that a joint naval–military attack was the ideal means to put pressure on Turkey. This, he pointed out, was the course he had proposed in 1914. The idea had not been pursued either then or in January 1915, however, because Kitchener maintained that the necessary troops were not available. Churchill then turned to his second point, that the decision to prepare a naval attack had been necessitated by urgent military and diplomatic considerations in the east, and especially the pressing appeal to aid the Russians. On these matters, Churchill's argument closely—and no doubt deliberately—mirrored the one expounded by Hankey on behalf of the government as a whole.

With his third point, Churchill came to the crux of his defence: that he had not unduly interfered in the Admiralty's planning process. The basic plan for an assault on the Dardanelles, he insisted, had been developed by Carden and his staff. Prior to this, Churchill had assumed that troops would be necessary to ensure the operation's success. It was Carden's 'novel' proposal for a gradual advance through the Straits, he insisted, that had led him to reconsider. The subsequent planning at the Admiralty had been undertaken, he assured the Commission, 'in the regular way' by the naval war staff, assisted by Admiral Jackson, and with oversight from the First Sea Lord. Churchill shrewdly emphasized the fact that Jackson and Oliver had both been closely involved in the planning process from the outset:

If the detailed plans set forth by the present First Sea Lord and Chief of Staff are foolish and incompetent, if they reveal ignorance of the simplest propositions of modern naval gunnery, if they were wholly visionary and unpracticable [sic], then that professional authority is rightly overturned. But if it is not overturned, then it must be accepted. And if it is accepted I have a right to say that I had unimpeachable expert authority for the statements I made to the War Council.

The Commission would find it difficult, as Churchill knew, to denounce the naval plan for the Dardanelles without criticizing the judgement of the two highest naval officers then serving at the Admiralty, something not lightly done in wartime.[49]

The commissioners interrupted Churchill to question him on one detail he had skipped over: how his naval advisers at the Admiralty had felt about Carden's proposal. It might be true that Jackson and Oliver had worked to develop the plan, but the Commission wanted to know whether Churchill had compelled them to do so against their own judgement. The documentary evidence on this point was virtually non-existent. Churchill maintained that, in conversation, Jackson and Oliver had both spoken favourably to him about Carden's proposal, and may also have done so at a meeting of the Admiralty War Group.[50] It was on this basis, he claimed, that he had written to Carden on 5 January asking him to draw up concrete plans for forcing a passage through the Straits. Jackson's memorandum of the same date showed that the admiral did not approve of an attempt to *rush* a fleet through, but Churchill maintained that he did not see this document until several days after he asked Carden to draw up plans. 'I remember thinking', he stated, 'well that is less favourable than the impression I had from the conversation.'[51] He pointed out, however, that Jackson stated on 15 January that he concurred in Carden's detailed plan to force a passage by extended operations. This, he felt, was more impor-tant than Jackson's early reservations about an attempt to *rush* the Straits—a course that had been rejected.

Fisher's opinion of the Carden proposal was also difficult to pin down, as he had not at any time put his views in writing. Churchill maintained, however, that the First Sea Lord had given him no reason to think he opposed the idea: 'I consider that he assented at this stage; we met every day and discussed the thing.'[52] Churchill insisted, probably with complete sincerity, that when he took the Dardanelles project to the War Council on 13 January he had done so in good faith, honestly believing that he had the willing support of his principal naval advisers: 'When I unfolded my case to the Council, I turned to my right and to my left [where Fisher and Wilson were seated], and they often pointed my remarks by assent and by additional observations which do not appear in the [written] record.' It was only much later in the month, Churchill stated, that he became aware of Fisher's misgivings.[53]

Churchill went on to outline his remaining arguments. His fourth point was that the War Council, which had ample opportunity to question Fisher and Wilson, had unanimously backed the proposal to attack the Dardanelles. They had approved Carden's plan, and so had the responsible authorities in France. His next point was that Fisher and Wilson had both assented to the War Council's final decision on 28 January to approve the Dardanelles project. He admitted that Fisher was 'not personally in favour of the operation', but he stressed that the admiral had nevertheless agreed to it—a statement he knew Fisher would support. He then turned to the reasons for Fisher's misgivings about the enterprise, emphasizing that the admiral had never told him or the Prime Minister that he objected to the naval operation on technical grounds. His dissent had stemmed entirely from his concerns about Britain's margin of safety in the North Sea. Churchill insisted: 'If Lord Fisher had said: "What is the good of trying to force the Dardanelles; they will put mines in the channel and they will bring out the howitzers and shoot at you while you are shooting at the forts, and this scheme of Admiral Carden's is all wrong"; that would have been different.'[54] But Fisher had not made these points, and the concerns he did express had not been justified by events. Despite the movement of ships to the eastern Mediterranean, Britain's position in home waters had never been in jeopardy.

Churchill concluded with three final points. The first was that Fisher had assented to all the operational orders sent to the Mediterranean fleet. At no point in the proceedings had Churchill overruled him. He clearly wanted to give Fisher no opportunity to avoid his personal responsibility for how the operation had been managed. He was also eager to establish that the other members of the War Council had not been passive spectators in the decision-making process. On the contrary, he maintained that *they* were primarily responsible for the decision to land troops on the Gallipoli peninsula. The naval attack, as originally conceived, did not inevitably commit the government to undertake a major commitment of land forces—this was an entirely separate decision. The naval offensive, Churchill insisted, could have been halted at any time 'with little damage to our prestige'. This was certainly true, although Churchill conveniently sidestepped the fact that he had been in favour of using troops if and when it became necessary.[55] The important thing, however, was to establish that he had not foisted the land campaign on a reluctant or uninformed War Council, as some of his detractors had suggested. Churchill was careful, of course, to soften his implicit criticism of Kitchener by paying generous tribute to the late field marshal. The implication was clear, however: something had gone badly wrong with the government's decision-making machinery. 'What appears to me extraordinary', he said:

> [W]as that while there had been such long and searching discussions about the naval attack, there never was, so far as I am aware, any formal discussion or decision, either by the War Council or the Cabinet, upon the far more serious question of the landing of an army to storm the Gallipoli Peninsula. Up to a point no one would hear of a military attempt, and any preparations for it, even contingent or hypothetical, were scouted. But after a point it seemed to have been automatically decided. I presume the agreement of the Admiral and General on the spot was accepted by those responsible at home.[56]

Churchill did not deny his share of the War Council's collective responsibility for the decision to land troops, but there was no doubt in his mind that Kitchener and Asquith were mainly to blame. And he gave the Commission enough hints that they might be expected to reach the same conclusion.

Churchill's opening presentation took around five and a half hours, which, according to one source, 'proved too much for poor Cromer who has taken to his bed'.[57] The Commission only reassembled to question Churchill on his evidence a week later. Fisher's role in the decision-making process was clearly still a source of confusion—as it remains a century later. The commissioners may have been sceptical of Churchill's account, or they may have been genuinely perplexed by the admiral's chaotic behaviour. In the event, Churchill avoided saying anything under cross-examination to undermine Fisher's argument that he had had reservations about the Dardanelles operation from the outset. The challenge Churchill faced, therefore, was to convince the Commission that he had been unaware of Fisher's misgivings until 25 January. He must have realized that the idea of the First Sea Lord concealing his views on such an important matter from both the First Lord of the Admiralty and the War Council would seem implausible on its face. But it was essentially true. Churchill made the case as best he could, even hinting at one point that Fisher may have supported the idea at first. In response to questions from Pickford, he stated: 'My feeling is that [Fisher] was very much impressed by Carden's plan for the first ten days or fortnight, and then he began to revise his opinion upon it.'

PICKFORD: 'Did he ever say, "No, I do not think it ought to be done"?'
CHURCHILL: 'No, at no time did he demolish the Carden plan.'
PICKFORD: 'I am speaking now of before the 13th [of January]. Did he ever before that meeting [of the War Council] say, "I do not think that a naval operation alone ought to be undertaken"?'
CHURCHILL: 'No, not to the best of my recollection.... he never criticised the practicability of the operation.'[58]

The other challenge for Churchill was to explain why he had persisted with the Dardanelles scheme after he learned of Fisher's objections. On this question he adhered to the defence outlined in his opening statement: that Fisher had never challenged the plan on its merits, so he had no reason to think it would not succeed; and that he was right to do so, as the concerns Fisher raised about British security in home waters were unfounded. But the commissioners were still not satisfied. They called on Churchill to explain why Fisher's concerns had not been brought to the attention of the War Council on 28 January to inform its deliberations before a final decision was reached. This went right to the heart of the persistent allegations that Churchill had overruled Fisher and then concealed the admiral's views from his political colleagues.

Churchill had several explanations. First, he downplayed the extent of Fisher's opposition, suggesting that when he met with Fisher and Asquith on the morning of 28 January the admiral's reservations about the Dardanelles offensive were 'not very vehement'.[59] Second, he maintained that the admiral had the right to voice his views or circulate his memorandum if he had really wished to oppose the operation, but he had chosen not to do so. Third, Fisher had definitely agreed to put aside his doubts and support the operation. According to Churchill's testimony, at the end of the meeting in the Prime Minister's room he was under the impression that Fisher's opposition 'was not very deep, though he did not like the thing. But he did not think it could not be done. I thought he agreed to put it through.' This still did not seem to square with Fisher's abrupt departure from the table when the subject was subsequently raised at the War Council. Churchill admitted he had been surprised by Fisher's action, but he reassured the Commission that the matter had soon been resolved. He recounted that when the Council's meeting concluded, he:

> [T]hought I must come to a clear understanding with Lord Fisher, and he came to see me in my room. Then I had a talk with him and we discussed the thing, and, of course, I urged him strongly—you can put that on to me—to go ahead with it. It could not possibly be done unless he was willing to do it— not merely to say: 'Oh, you may do it', but unless he was willing to do it himself it could not be done—nothing could be done. He said, 'All right, I will', and then we went down to the second meeting of the War Council, Admiral Oliver being with us at that time, and I announced on behalf of the united Board that we would put the thing through subject to the right to break it off.[60]

Churchill emphasized that Fisher had not been overruled. He had *explicitly* agreed to support the operation, and in doing so had committed himself to seeing it through. Churchill also drew attention to Fisher's support, and even enthusiasm, for the operation in mid-March, when he had agreed to the intensification of the naval attack, while ignoring the admiral's complaints and obstruction at other times. Raising these incidents would not, in any event, have helped his case. He needed the Commission to believe Fisher's support had been genuine, even if it had been given with reluctance. The First Sea Lord, he asserted at one point, had 'fought the thing out up to the battle of the 18th with growing resolution'.[61]

The commissioners probed one other apparent inconsistency in Churchill's defence: why had the First Lord been so confident in launching a purely naval operation in January, but later insisted so strongly on the necessity of providing soldiers? Historians have often treated Churchill's determination in February to have troops on hand as a tacit admission that he knew from the outset that a purely naval assault was unlikely to succeed. In fact, as Churchill explained, there was no contradiction. His initial confidence in the naval operation was based on the assumption that troops were not essential to secure the passage of the fleet through the Straits. This was, in his view, a worthwhile objective in itself, as British warships in the Marmara would, at the very least, be able to destroy the *Goeben* and *Breslau*. And Churchill had warned the War Council that there were limits to what a purely naval victory might achieve. There was no guarantee, for example, that unarmoured warships would be able to use the Straits if the enemy did not abandon the peninsula. However, there was still a possibility of achieving far-reaching political effects if the fleet got through. Ottoman resistance might crumble rapidly, or Italy and the Balkan states might be induced to join the Allied cause, as had nearly happened, it seemed, after the success of the initial bombardment. Churchill had, therefore, been eager to proceed with the operation as a purely naval affair. Troops were desirable, in other words, but not essential: worthwhile results could be obtained without them. But once the possibility of an army appeared, he insisted that he would have been foolish not to pursue it. An army on the spot would ensure that a naval victory was immediately exploited and major results achieved, far beyond the destruction of enemy warships.

Churchill's argument with Kitchener about the release of the 29th Division was therefore not about ensuring the navy could get through, as many commentators assume, but whether Britain would be in a position to obtain the full benefits of a naval victory afterwards. Throughout his testimony, Churchill drew a distinction between the original decision to have troops on hand in the eastern Mediterranean to exploit a naval success, and the subsequent decision to land soldiers once the naval advance was suspended. Although he had supported the latter decision, he continued to point out that it had meant a far more onerous commitment of lives and resources, as the land operation could not easily be broken off if it did not succeed. With this in mind, he stressed that he was not solely responsible for the land campaign. He also hinted at a breakdown in the decision-making process that was beyond his control. And if his recommendations had been followed in mid-February, he pointed out, the army could have been landed around the time the naval operation had to be called off, which would have greatly increased its chances of success. But Kitchener had refused to make a decision on the 29th Division, meaning a delay of three weeks, during which the Ottomans had ample time to prepare. Churchill reminded the commissioners at every opportunity that he had gone on record that he could not be held responsible for any military failures that occurred because of Kitchener's indecision.[62]

By the end of his second day of testimony, Churchill had laid out a formidable defence of his actions as First Lord of the Admiralty. But how well would it stand up under scrutiny? The principal naval figures involved in the origins of the Dardanelles campaign gave their testimony in the week that followed, and commissioners naturally wanted to see whether they would corroborate Churchill's account of the decision-making process at the Admiralty. The first thing the Commission tried to establish was whether Carden's proposal had received general support when it reached the

Admiralty, as Churchill claimed. Given that the attack had conclusively failed, naval officers were naturally wary about admitting they had been in favour of it. But they generally supported the picture that had been painted by Churchill. Bartolomé, Churchill's naval secretary, stated at the outset of his evidence that he 'was in favour of the gradual bombardment of the forts', although only, he maintained, so long as the attack could be cancelled if it did not succeed. He confirmed, moreover, that the Admiralty's plans for the operation had been drawn up by the naval staff.[63] Oliver, the chief of staff, also acknowledged that he had initially supported Carden's plan. Asked by Admiral May if he considered himself responsible for the decision to make the attack, Oliver responded unambiguously: 'Yes, I consider I have got responsibility. If I thought the First Lord and the First Sea Lord were bent on doing something which appeared to me highly imprudent, I should have my opinion recorded that I was not in agreement with it.' Later, Pickford asked him if the entire War Group had agreed to attempt Carden's plan. 'To the best of my recollection', Oliver replied, 'yes.'[64]

Admiral Wilson was somewhat more difficult to pin down. He claimed that he had always been 'moderately adverse' to the operation, but admitted that he had not opposed it on naval grounds. 'I thought it was a possible success', he stated:

> [A]nd, of course, it was a very big prize to work for, and the risks were not great provided we were prepared to leave off when we saw we could not get through. In fact, the risk was really very little more than the loss of prestige, which always attaches to a failure, but I did not expect it would be anything serious.[65]

Wilson testified that his main objection to the Dardanelles operation was that it would tie up resources he wanted to see used in naval operations closer to home, such as an assault on the German or Belgian coasts. He clearly had no objections to inshore operations and coastal bombardments in principle. And when Carden's proposal first arrived at the Admiralty, he confirmed that he had agreed it was worth examining further.[66] Admiral Jackson, now the First Sea Lord, was rather more evasive in his testimony. He insisted that he had been strongly opposed from the outset to any attempt to force the Dardanelles without an army, as demonstrated by his memorandum of 5 January. And he denied having stated any other view in conversation with Churchill. 'I have always stuck to that Memorandum', he maintained. 'I have never changed that opinion, and I have never given anybody any reason to think I did.'[67] But the awkward fact remained that he had written on 15 January that, after examining Carden's plan, he concurred in it. Under questioning by Nicholson, it became clear that Jackson was not distinguishing between an attempt to *rush* the Straits and Carden's plan for a systematic bombardment of the enemy's defences. He had undoubtedly opposed the former on 5 January, but under questioning he conceded that he had, in fact, been willing to support at least the first stage of Carden's proposed operation, the bombardment of the outer forts.

This was not the unqualified backing Churchill hoped for, but the testimony of Admiralty officials, who had every reason to distance themselves from the Dardanelles, showed that there *was* early support at the Admiralty for launching a gradual and systematic naval assault on the Ottoman defences, provided always that it could be called off it did not succeed. These naval witnesses also confirmed that Fisher had not actively opposed the scheme in its early stages.[68] Indeed, they could not definitely say what Fisher's views on the operation had been, although Bartolomé and Jackson recalled that their *impression* at the time was that the First Sea Lord disliked the idea.[69] Fisher himself appeared before the Commission on 11 October, the tenth day of proceedings. His testimony kept to the lines he had previously agreed with Churchill, although he spoke rather more freely at times than he probably intended. Cromer recounted to Lloyd George afterwards that Fisher had said to the Commission 'that Winston came there all bluster and flurry, or words to that effect, [and] that Fisher looked round at the shorthand writer and said "You are not taking that down are you?" "Yes" replied the shorthand writer. "Good God!" said Fisher, throwing up his hands in alarm.'[70] For the most part, however, the admiral was careful to support his former chief. 'You had no objection', Pickford asked, 'to the experiment suggested by Mr. Churchill on the strength of Admiral Carden's opinion, being tried?'

FISHER: 'That is right, only I always had the feeling that there would be a loss of ships, and I wanted to have them to lose in the decisive theatre.'
PICKFORD: 'Still you did not object to the experiment being tried?'
FISHER: 'No.'[71]

The admiral also confirmed that the naval staff had supported the operation. Churchill's view at the time, Fisher recalled, was that the First Sea Lord was the only one at the Admiralty against the Dardanelles scheme. 'I am perfectly certain', he stated, 'and I cannot help saying that I more or less had that [same] view [about the naval staff's support for the project]—that I was the only one who stood out against it.'[72] Fisher maintained that he had made his dislike of his project known to his subordinates, but admitted that he had not given the proposal much personal attention. 'To a large extent', he said, 'having expressed my indisposition to have much to do with it, I more or less left it alone. Sir Henry Jackson was a very able man, and so was Admiral Oliver, and I more or less stood aside. I backed it up in every possible way as far as executive work was concerned.'[73]

When the commissioners pressed Fisher to explain his actions on 28 January, the admiral continued to support Churchill as best he could. At the meeting that morning with Churchill and Asquith, he recalled that, at the end of the discussion, the Prime Minister had declared: 'I am going to give my decision. I am the arbitrator.... "Zeebrugge will not be done; the Dardanelles will go on."' According to Fisher, Asquith 'got up then and walked away, and we followed him'.[74] The admiral testified that he accepted this decision, even though he did not like it. But when the commissioners turned to the War Council that followed, Fisher made it clear that he had not really accepted the Prime Minister's verdict. Roch pressed the admiral to explain the apparent contradiction in his testimony: 'You say that at the interview with the Prime Minister you did not contemplate resignation, or did not mention it?'

FISHER: 'No.'
ROCH: 'Why was it you did subsequently?'
FISHER: 'When the Prime Minister said that the thing was to be gone on with, or words to that effect, then I got a sudden feeling, "this thing has come to a point now; I will be off".'
ROCH: 'You did not look upon the morning's decision as completely decisive?'
FISHER: 'No; I thought one would have time to think it over. I did not think it would be gone on with at the meeting.'[75]

The Commission also struggled to understand why, if his views were so strong, Fisher had not voiced them to the full War Council. The admiral continued to assert that he believed he had only two choices when he disagreed with his political chief at the War Council: to remain silent or to resign. And he insisted that he would have done nothing to contradict Churchill in front of his colleagues. 'I had a very great regard for him', he maintained. 'The things he did were splendid in conjunction with me, so I did not want to leave him in the lurch.'[76] Of course, having his First Sea Lord resign in the middle of a War Council would have been at least as damaging to Churchill as an open expression of dissent from the admiral during the Council's meeting. In any event, the commissioners may have accepted this as Fisher's genuinely held view, but they had trouble accepting that loyalty to Churchill should have been his overriding concern. 'You did not feel', Roch asked, 'that the other members of the War Council [who] had to bear the responsibility for the decision were entitled to know how strong your opposition was?' 'No', Fisher replied, 'I do not think I did.'[77]

The other mystery that continued to defy solution was why no one on the War Council had invited the admiral to give his views. Fisher was adamant that ministers were aware that he was opposed to the Dardanelles offensive. 'Why they all jolly well knew', he exclaimed. 'Everyone knew; even the charwomen at the Admiralty knew it. It was obvious by the tone of my remarks and the way I talked at each of these meetings.'[78] Fisher even suggested that the reason for their silence was that they did not want to give him an opportunity to express an adverse opinion to an operation they were in favour of. 'They knew the situation', he asserted, 'and they might not have wanted to embarrass matters.'[79]

At different points in his testimony Fisher provided three reasons he had been against the Dardanelles operation: that he had doubted the operation would succeed without troops; that he was worried about the impact that naval losses in the Mediterranean would have on Britain's margins in home waters; and that the operation would consume resources essential for his Baltic project. The commissioners were clearly sceptical about Fisher's new claim about the Baltic, no hint of which had appeared in the massive documentation submitted by Hankey or Churchill, or in any previous testimony. In response to questions from Pickford, Fisher stated that he would have supported the Dardanelles offensive if troops had been provided. Did this mean, Pickford asked, that Fisher believed a combined operation against the Ottomans would not have interfered with his Baltic plans? 'That is right', Fisher replied.

PICKFORD: 'Was Admiral Wilson also working in the direction of that Baltic scheme?'
FISHER: 'No, he did not know anything about it; it was a most secret thing; in fact, it is a secret now, as far as that goes.'
PICKFORD: 'And, as I understand, a thing which ought to be still kept secret?'
FISHER: 'Yes, it ought to be still kept secret. I really did not go into the whole details of the thing, even with Mr. Churchill.'[80]

The admiral testified, however, that Churchill was generally aware of his Baltic plans. He claimed to be puzzled, therefore, that Churchill had submitted in evidence Fisher's memorandum of 25 January (which had stressed the importance of not taking risks with Britain's naval superiority), but had not included 'the second part of it'—Fisher's 'Baltic memorandum'.[81] This was a reference to the memorandum prepared by Corbett in December 1914 suggesting a possible future campaign in the Baltic. The admiral was obviously eager to provide some concrete support for his assertion that he had been animated by the desire to take action in the Baltic. But this involved misrepresenting the so-called 'Baltic memorandum' as an integral part of the case he put to Asquith and Churchill against the Dardanelles in January 1915, which it was not. Fisher had not included the Baltic memorandum when he sent his memorandum to Asquith on 25 January, nor had he included it with the copies he had subsequently sent to Balfour, Lloyd George, and Bonar Law.

After completing his testimony, Fisher sent a letter to Cromer elaborating on some of the points he had made under examination. He concluded with an unqualified endorsement of the former First Lord: 'Mr. Churchill is quite correct', he proclaimed. '*I backed him up till I resigned*. I would do the same again! He had courage and imagination! *He was a war man!*'[82] Fisher was upbeat after his testimony. 'I just finished Dardanelles!', he wrote to Garvin. '4 hours!...The shorthand writer collapsed! So did the Committee! I enjoyed it awfully! So did they!'[83] Churchill was also pleased. 'Fisher's evidence is great fun', he later commented to Asquith, 'and he did his best to atone.'[84] The testimony of the former First Sea Lord and his naval advisers would go a long way towards discrediting the idea that Churchill had routinely ignored or overruled Admiralty officials. There had been at least cautious support for Carden's proposal when it reached the Admiralty in early January, and no one had been overruled. Churchill's argument that he had been unaware of Fisher's strong opposition until late in the month was probably starting to seem plausible.

The naval witnesses had consistently represented Churchill as being far more optimistic than his advisers about the prospects of a purely naval assault on the Dardanelles, which was undoubtedly true. But had he concealed the views of his naval advisers when he presented the operation to the War Council? This was one of the most damning allegations circulating in the press and in Westminster. Only Fisher and Wilson were in a position to judge. When asked if Churchill was 'in any way misrepresenting the state of facts' by presenting the operation 'in a sanguine way', Fisher did not hesitate to support his friend and ally: 'No', he replied, 'I do not think so.'[85]

Wilson, however, was probably a more reliable witness. Admiral May asked him if Churchill's representations to the War Council on 13 and 28 January had accurately reflected the concerns that had been expressed within the Admiralty. 'No', he replied. 'I think he rather passed over them. He was very keen on his own views.' This was especially the case on the 28th, when he thought 'the First Lord ignored the difficulties very much'.[86] Pickford picked up on this point at the end of Wilson's testimony. In what way, he asked, had Churchill failed to represent the potential difficulties to the War Council? 'In the first place', Wilson responded:

> [H]e kept on saying he could do it without the Army; he only wanted the Army to come in and reap the fruits, I think, was his expression; and I think he generally minimised the risks from mobile guns, and treated it as if the armoured ships were immune altogether from injury. I do not mean to say he actually said they were immune, but he minimised the risk a great deal.[87]

Wilson's testimony on this subject clearly made a stronger impression on the Commission than Fisher's.

11

The Dardanelles Commission II
The Naval Staff under Scrutiny

As the Dardanelles Commission worked to reconstruct Churchill's role in the decision-making process at the Admiralty, it also investigated whether there had been good reasons in January 1915 to think that Carden's plan to force a passage through the Straits was feasible. The naval attack had ultimately failed for two reasons: the fleet's guns were unable to knock out the Turkish shore defences; and the minesweepers could not clear a path through the minefields. From the vantage point of October 1916 it was clear that naval planners had underestimated these obstacles going into the campaign. Curiously, the Commission showed little interest in the failure of Allied minesweeping. On the few occasions when this problem was raised, discussion quickly turned to other subjects. The failure either to foresee this problem or to solve it prior to 18 March reflected poorly on the navy's staff work, both in the fleet and at the Admiralty. Naval officers were only too happy not to dwell on this issue. The gunnery question, on the other hand, was examined repeatedly and in depth. The driving force behind this enquiry was Field Marshal Nicholson, who clearly felt that the naval campaign could have been avoided altogether if the naval staff had bothered to consult gunnery experts at the War Office. Nicholson rejected the widespread idea that the destruction of Belgian forts at Liège, Namur, and Antwerp by German howitzers early in the war was reason to think that Turkish forts could be demolished by naval gunfire. In his view, the high velocity naval guns, with a relatively flat trajectory, had never had much chance of destroying the enemy's defensive fortifications—and this, in his opinion, should have been determined before the operation was launched.

Churchill wisely refused to be drawn on these questions in his own testimony, insisting that he had left technical matters like this to the appropriate experts on the naval staff. And this is probably true. Churchill had certainly been impressed by the rapid fall of the Belgian forts in 1914, but what seemed to influence him the most in January 1915 was that the heavy guns of the fleet had greater range than the guns in the Turkish forts, so that the ships could fire at little risk to themselves. There is no evidence that he gave the subject much thought beyond this. 'I did not make the plan', he reminded the Commission. 'My personal opinion on the gunnery has no virtue in it at all.'[1] All he could do was reassure the Commission that the matter had been thoroughly examined by qualified people. Nicholson was not convinced on this point, however. He grilled Admiralty officials about how they had reached their conclusions, and which authorities, if any, had been consulted. It did not take long to establish that army experts had not been asked for advice. Nor had the Admiralty sought the views of Admiral Limpus, who had been the British naval adviser to the Ottomans before the war. In fact, the efficacy of naval gunfire against forts had barely been investigated at all. Oliver, Jackson, and other senior naval officers at the Admiralty generally assumed that their own knowledge and experience was sufficient to enable them to form valid opinions on this subject. When Rear-Admiral Thomas Jackson, the Director of Naval Operations (DNO), was asked which experts should have been consulted, he replied that he did 'not think there was any necessity to consult any particular person; it was more a question of individual opinion'.[2]

As Chief of the War Staff, Oliver would have been responsible for ensuring that the subject was properly studied, and his testimony was not at all reassuring. He stated that he had been advised by two figures: Rear-Admiral Thomas Jackson, who was described as a gunnery expert on his staff, and the Director of Naval Ordnance, Rear-Admiral Morgan Singer. According to Oliver's evidence, the latter was 'frequently asked . . . for information about ammunition and the performance of guns'. But Oliver admitted that he could not remember ever asking Singer his opinion as to the feasibility of destroying the Turkish forts by naval gunfire.[3] Oliver's credibility received a blow when Singer was examined a few days later. The Director of Naval Ordnance was generally held to be the Admiralty's main authority on matters relating to gunnery, but he insisted that he had not been involved in planning the Dardanelles operation. 'You were not consulted', Cromer asked, 'by either the First Sea Lord or the First Lord or by any other responsible authority as to the possibility of knocking these forts to pieces?' When Singer answered 'No', Cromer continued in disbelief: 'You were not consulted at all?'

SINGER: 'No.'
CROMER: 'Not by Admiral Oliver?'
SINGER: 'No.'
CROMER: On no occasion?
SINGER. 'No. . . . The operations were over by time I knew anything about them.'[4]

The admiral went on to state that, if he had been consulted, he would have advised against the operation. Pickford obviously shared Cromer's bewilderment. To ensure there was no misunderstanding, he read to Singer the portions of Oliver's testimony in which he claimed to have discussed various gunnery matters with the Director of Naval Ordnance. Singer maintained that he could not recall any such conversations.[5]

Oliver's standing took another hit when Thomas Jackson was summoned by the Commission the following week to explain his part in the planning process. The commissioners thought they would be questioning the naval staff's leading gunnery expert, but Jackson insisted at the beginning of his testimony that he was *not* 'an official adviser at the Admiralty on gunnery matters'. 'Not at all?', asked Cromer. 'No', he replied. Jackson suggested, moreover, that he had been much too busy at that time to be diverted from his regular duties to planning the Dardanelles offensive. Cawley asked Jackson directly if he had been consulted by Oliver or anyone else as to the feasibility of forcing a passage through the Straits:

JACKSON: 'No.'
CAWLEY: 'You do not remember giving any opinions about it?'
JACKSON: 'No.'
ROCH: 'Had you anything to do with the Dardanelles operations at all?
JACKSON: 'Nothing whatever.'[6]

After a few more desultory questions, Jackson was dismissed.

The army witnesses called by the Commission reinforced the perception that the Admiralty had not properly investigated the problem of reducing forts with naval guns. Callwell, who had served as Kitchener's DMO, confirmed that the views of the general staff had never been officially sought, 'although there was ample leisure', he stated, 'for the subject to have been gone into thoroughly'.[7] He asserted, moreover, that if the subject *had* been examined jointly by qualified staff officers from the Admiralty and the War Office, the operation would not have been recommended.[8] Nor had anyone on the naval staff asked for his opinion, despite his previous study of the subject. In fact, he had only learned of the proposed naval operation 'gradually and more or less casually'.[9] His opinion at the time, he testified, had been against the attack.[10] This is corroborated by his correspondence with General William Robertson, then French's chief of staff in the BEF, in March 1915. Callwell wrote on the 18th—without knowing of the fleet's heavy losses that day—that the navy's slow progress was showing the Admiralty 'what I told Winston five months ago when the undertaking was first mooted—that they do not understand using their guns against the land. They have not the right ammunition and if they had it they would not know how to make the most of it.' Robertson, who would become CIGS at the end of 1915, agreed. 'I have never thought that the Fleet would get through the Dardanelles', he told Callwell, 'and do not think so now. To my mind such an attempt is a ridiculous farce, and we all know the accuracy of the sailors' shooting.'[11]

Two other gunnery authorities were invited that day specifically to comment on whether an 'expert artillerist' would have considered a naval attack on the Dardanelles defences to be a 'reasonable undertaking'. The first, Major-General T. E. Hickman, then commanding the army's Plymouth Garrison, offered a blunt and devastating critique. The navy, he asserted, should have expected to encounter a variety of defences along the Straits, some of which would be concealed from direct view. Most of the enemy's guns could only be disabled by a direct hit, he noted, which would be difficult to achieve and would require a massive expenditure of ammunition. Howitzers, designed for high-angle firing, were much more effective for this task than naval guns, he noted, because their shells had a greater angle of descent, allowing them to penetrate the overhead protection provided for personnel and ammunition. They might also be expected to destroy some guns without necessarily achieving a direct hit. But all this assumed that the targets were visible to the gunners, which was not always the case. Naval guns, he pointed out, were not designed for indirect fire. Their relatively flat trajectory would prevent them from hitting guns or forts that could not be observed, especially if protected by hills or promontories. It made sense, he suggested, to assume that many of the enemy's mobile guns and howitzers would be located where they could not be touched by naval gunfire.[12]

These views were confirmed later that day by another expert witness, Brigadier-General Sir George Aston, a Royal Marine Artillery officer and former member of Admiral Henry Jackson's staff.[13]

Churchill had not expected naval gunnery to occupy so much of the Commission's attention, and the poor showing by Oliver and other Admiralty witnesses undoubtedly came as an unpleasant surprise. It would be difficult for anyone to blame Churchill for faulty staff work at the Admiralty or in the fleet, given the prevailing view that Churchill already interfered too much in technical matters best left to the professionals, but serious failures by the naval staff would, nevertheless, reflect badly on him. Churchill received another blow the day after Hickman, Callwell, and Aston testified, when the *Daily Mail* attacked him over alleged intrigues against Douglas Haig. MacCallum Scott recorded afterwards that Churchill was 'crushed & overwhelmed by the odium which he feels the public attach to him for the whole Gallipoli affair'. He was also 'very nervous about the Dardanelles Commission of Inquiry & fears all is not going well for him there'. Scott noted that his friend had asked him 'eagerly for any expressions of opinion which may have been let fall by any of the members'.[14]

On 17 October, the beleaguered Churchill appealed again to Cromer for the right to examine witnesses himself. The recent article in the *Daily Mail* entitled him to this privilege, he claimed, because it 'shows very clearly the kind of attack to which I am exposed and from which I have every right to defend myself before the Commission'. Witnesses had often been asked about matters they were not competent to address, Churchill complained, and their answers were sometimes open to challenge. Unless these individuals were subjected to a rigorous cross-examination, the Commission would be in no position to 'do justice to the Admiralty case'.[15] Cromer gave in. Churchill was given permission to examine witnesses himself, a privilege accorded to no one else during the course of the Commission's investigations. Mears, the secretary, informed him, however, that the only issue commissioners desired additional evidence on was whether the gunnery problem had been properly studied by the Admiralty.[16]

MacCallum Scott was alarmed to discover that Churchill considered testifying himself on this question. And to make matters worse, he was not convinced by the evidence Churchill had to offer, noting that he could not show that the Admiralty's gunnery specialists had been consulted *before* the operation was approved.[17] To establish his case, Churchill proposed to call six witnesses, including several, like Oliver, who had already given evidence. To avert any more missteps by the chief of staff, Churchill wrote to the admiral with advice on how to frame his testimony. Since it was already established that Oliver had not consulted any acknowledged gunnery experts, he would have to argue that he, like 'other Naval officers of high standing', was fully qualified to form a judgement on questions involving naval gunnery. Churchill also urged him to claim that he had frequently consulted with Bartolomé, who could be regarded as 'a gunnery specialist of a very high order', and that he had worked closely with Henry Jackson. The broad argument that Churchill proposed was that Oliver's plan had been sound, so far as reducing the Turkish forts was concerned. The attack had failed as a result of what he termed 'incalculable' factors: the strength of the enemy's resistance, the difficulty of sweeping the minefields, and the impact of mobile Turkish guns. It was precisely because these things could not be calculated, Churchill proposed, that the Admiralty had only committed itself to a gradual advance that could be called off if necessary.[18]

Churchill's reappearance before the Commission on 24 October got off to a bumpy start. Prior to the meeting, he had submitted a new selection of documents relating to the relief of Antwerp in 1914. The recent attack by the *Daily Mail* had invoked both Antwerp and the Dardanelles as proof of Churchill's bad judgement, and he probably hoped the Commission would clear him of blame for both operations. But Cromer and the other members were not interested. The scope of their investigation was quite wide enough already, and they had no desire to broaden it further purely for the sake of Churchill's political reputation. Before Churchill was allowed to summon his first witness, the chairman announced that the Antwerp documents would not be admitted as evidence. Churchill did his best to justify himself, insisting that Antwerp *was* relevant, as were the loss of the three cruisers in 1914 and the Battle of Coronel, because they related to the wider question of how he had exercised his initiative as First Lord—an issue on which a great deal of prejudice had grown up. But the Commission's job was not to evaluate Churchill's overall performance as First Lord of the Admiralty. Cromer remained firm this time, and administered a mild rebuke. 'Our opinion', he asserted, 'is that, as far as that is concerned, we are going to wipe it entirely out from our memories: We have nothing whatever to do with Antwerp or the [Battle of] Coronel.'[19]

The first witness Churchill called that day was Arthur Wilson, who appears, like Oliver, to have been coached beforehand. Churchill had no trouble extracting what he wanted from Wilson on the subject of naval gunnery. The admiral stated that he did not adhere dogmatically to the view that it was *always* a bad idea for ships to attack forts, the position Fisher had taken before the Commission. In many cases, he suggested, it could be done, and in some instances it was virtually a necessity. Moreover, the problem of attacking forts from the sea and the use of indirect fire *had* been studied by the navy before the war. These issues were also frequently discussed by the Admiralty's War Group. In other words, naval officers were not rank amateurs compared to their army counterparts when it came to modern gunnery. Naval guns had become so accurate and powerful, he claimed, that forts *could* be effectively bombarded by warships. In a memorandum submitted to the Commission beforehand, Wilson countered some of the technical arguments put forward by Hickman. The general had dealt with the problem of reducing the Dardanelles forts in an abstract manner, without detailed knowledge of the forts themselves. This allowed Wilson to make one telling point: the Turkish forts and their guns were not as well protected from direct fire as Hickman assumed. On the contrary, their high parapets made them good targets for high velocity naval guns.[20] This conclusion was supported, he believed, by the fleet's early success against the outer Dardanelles forts.

Wilson went on to argue that fleet had only failed to reduce the inner forts because the enemy's mobile guns and howitzers had interfered with their firing and prevented the sweeping of the minefields. The implication of this was that, in a straight duel between ships and forts, Allied ships *would* have prevailed. But, of course, they had not. So what had gone wrong? Churchill and Wilson were both happy to characterize the fire from mobile guns and howitzers as an 'incalculable' factor, thereby excusing the naval staff of any serious failure in not foreseeing its effects. Hickman's memorandum, on the other hand, reasonably suggested that the problem was such an obvious one that it could and should have been foreseen.

After Churchill finished leading Wilson through his evidence, the commissioners took over the questioning. Their main interest, it seems, was to establish whether Oliver had properly investigated the gunnery problem. Wilson was seemingly unprepared for this line of questioning. He stated that Oliver had conferred with Rear-Admiral Singer, but began backtracking after Cromer read out Singer's statements that he had not been consulted. Wilson defended the chief of staff as best he could. There was no reason, he asserted, for Oliver to ask Singer his view on the Dardanelles plan, as he was merely the head of a department, and it was important to maintain secrecy.

Singer would only have been consulted on technical details, and matters such as the availability of ammunition, but not on the plan itself. When asked who should have been consulted, Wilson replied that the two best experts available at the Admiralty were Fisher and himself, both of whom had offered their opinions. This revelation probably came as a surprise in view of Fisher's previous admission that he had not been involved in the planning process. It must have struck the Commission as curious that no one, including Oliver or Churchill, had thought to mention any of this before. Wilson maintained, however, that he and Fisher had discussed the problem 'from various points 100 times. The things were constantly under discussion.' But he hesitated to commit himself as to what Fisher had actually thought of the idea: 'I do not think he ever expressed an opinion against the practicability; but like everybody else, he had certain doubts.'[21]

The commissioners did not press Wilson to elaborate, and were probably sceptical by now of his reliability on this subject. Wilson's credibility as a gunnery expert was challenged by Nicholson. He shared the views presented by Hickman, and was unwilling to accept that naval guns were now nearly as accurate as land guns. The field marshal castigated Wilson at one point for his unfamiliarity with gunnery during the siege operations in the Russo-Japanese War (1904–5), and determined to extract an admission from the admiral that he was not qualified to judge the effects of naval gunfire on land fortifications:

NICHOLSON: 'If a landsman is going to attack ships, he obviously would consult a naval officer. Similarly when a naval officer or the naval authorities are going to attack forts, would it not be advisable for them to consult experts as regards the construction of forts?'
WILSON: 'I do not see why you should when you have seen the forts yourself.'
NICHOLSON: 'You think a naval officer knows all about a fort?'
WILSON: 'He does not know all about it, but he knows enough.'
NICHOLSON: 'Would you say that a military officer who casually visits a ship knows all about it?'
WILSON: 'But a ship is very much more complicated than a fort.'
NICHOLSON: 'Is it?'
WILSON: 'Yes.'
NICHOLSON: 'It is possible. It is a mere matter of opinion perhaps and not a matter of fact, is it? You are not an expert on fortification, are you?'
WILSON: 'I went through a course of fortification in my youth.'

Given that Wilson was now seventy-four, this could hardly have inspired confidence. Still, he was unwilling to back down in the face of Nicholson's questioning, and stuck to his views in the best tradition of the British amateur. On being pressed further, he maintained that he knew 'a little' about fortifications, having visited a great many and from reading about them. 'I do not think', he concluded, 'there is anything very mysterious in the Turkish forts, certainly.'[22]

Vice-Admiral Sir Reginald Bacon, who commanded the navy's Dover Patrol, was an altogether more effective witness. Bacon was well acquainted with the technical aspects of modern gunnery and possessed extensive practical experience from his command's frequent bombardments of enemy defences along the Belgian coast. Unlike Wilson, he had no trouble holding his ground under examination by Nicholson. Bacon argued that the idea of ships neutralizing the Turkish forts would not have seemed absurd in January 1915. The critical condition for success along the Belgian coast, he asserted, was that the guns of the fleet must be able to outrange the guns of the forts. As long as the fleet could remain at a safe distance from its target, it would just be a matter of time until the enemy's fortifications were neutralized. The only other necessity was good weather to allow for efficient spotting. All the conditions for success were therefore present in the Dardanelles operation, and he saw no reason why Carden's plan should not have been adopted. The problem posed by mobile guns and howitzers was simply brushed aside. These might be 'most unpleasant', he admitted, but they would 'never sink a good battleship and from the fighting point of view there was little reason to pay any attention to these guns'. He took a similarly cavalier view of the enemy's minefields, declaring that these would have 'worried me very little'.[23]

Bacon's testimony, like Wilson's, nicely reinforced the argument Churchill wanted to make—that the navy's confidence in neutralizing the Turkish forts had not been misplaced. But Hickman's testimony had, nevertheless, revealed the gaping flaw in the argument: the forts did not represent the whole of the enemy's defences. The naval experts clearly preferred to focus on the one area in which the fleet had achieved some undoubted success—the silencing of the forts by gunfire—and ignored the two areas in which they had utterly failed—destroying concealed guns and howitzers and clearing the minefields.

Churchill's main witness on his second day as an examiner, 25 October, was Oliver, who did his best to mitigate the damage from his previous testimony. As Churchill had suggested, he argued that he had not needed advice from the Director of Naval Ordnance about anything other than minor technical details, as he was well qualified to form his own conclusions on general gunnery issues. Oliver outlined for the Commission his previous gunnery experience and asserted that he had been closely involved in planning bombardments in the first months of the war. Moreover, he had frequently discussed the subject with Bartolomé, whom Churchill described as 'one of the best gunnery officers in the Service', and with Henry Jackson. Churchill did not want the commissioners to miss this point. 'You were in close touch with Jackson?', he asked. 'Yes', Oliver answered. 'He worked in a room near mine and I had frequent conversations with him and I saw all his work, which was done with the greatest care and exactitude.'[24] Best of all, from Churchill's perspective, Oliver confirmed that he and Jackson had been 'in general agreement' about the Dardanelles plan.[25] As Jackson had previously depicted himself as a firm and consistent sceptic, Churchill came back to this point at the end of his examination:

CHURCHILL: 'Did Admiral Jackson ever express any opinion to you against this operation...?'
OLIVER: 'We often discussed the Dardanelles—very frequently.'
CHURCHILL: 'Would you gather he was for or against it; can you give us his general opinion—whether he was for or against it?'
OLIVER: 'I should say he was for it.'[26]

Notably, neither Churchill nor any of the commissioners were interested in asking Oliver if he had sought or received advice from Admiral Wilson on either gunnery or fortifications.

Churchill did not limit himself to the gunnery question. He also used Oliver's testimony to strengthen his case that Fisher had given his willing support to the Dardanelles operation when it was first proposed. Since submitting his evidence on the origins of the naval offensive, Churchill had learned, probably from Oliver himself, that the chief of staff possessed two documents linking Fisher to the early preparations for the attack. The first was the minute, dated 12 January, in which the First Sea Lord had urged that the *Queen Elizabeth* be included in Carden's fleet. The second was the minute by Churchill the same day, calling for Oliver and the naval staff to begin drawing up plans for a naval assault on the Straits. Churchill had marked the minute to both Fisher and Oliver, but had not included it in his evidence for the Commission. After reviewing his copy of the minute, he probably concluded that it might be taken to imply that he had issued instructions on his own authority and without support from his advisers. But he had since learned that Oliver's copy of the minute had a green tick by Fisher's name on the list of recipients, indicating the admiral had seen and, presumably, approved the instruction to begin active planning. These two documents, Churchill told the Commission, constituted definite written evidence of Fisher's explicit support for the project *before* it was taken to the War Council on 13 January.

Churchill also used his witnesses to score other points off Fisher and Jackson. Oliver and Wilson both went on record, for example, saying that they had never been concerned that the movement of ships to the Dardanelles was jeopardizing Britain's position in home waters, further bolstering Churchill's argument that he had been right to disregard Fisher's warnings about the strength of the Grand Fleet.[27] Bartolomé was brought back for further questioning as well, although not, it seems, because he had anything new to offer, but because he had been a genuine supporter of the Carden plan from the outset. Churchill wanted to leave no doubt as to this officer's views. Bartolomé affirmed that, as Churchill's naval secretary, he had been present at all discussions about the Dardanelles (and therefore would have known if there had been any statements of opposition by members of the War Group); that he was, in fact, a gunnery officer (a reasonable precaution lest Oliver's testimony on that point be in doubt); that he had thought the original scheme had a 'very good' chance of succeeding (to remind the Commission that the proposal had had genuine naval supporters); and that he would have informed Churchill of his doubts if he had had any (to establish that Churchill had not intimidated his advisers into compliance).[28]

Churchill's star witness, however, was Captain Reginald Hall, the DNI, who had not yet appeared before the Commission. Hall testified that the Naval Intelligence Division (NID) was well supplied with information about the fortifications lining the Dardanelles, including the presence of mobile guns and howitzers. This was presumably meant to reassure commissioners on two points: that naval plans had been based on more than the observations of officers on the spot; and that the Admiralty had been aware of the concealed armament the fleet would encounter. But Churchill was most interested in convincing commissioners that the Ottoman forts were running out of ammunition when the naval assault was called off. In his first appearances before the Commission, Churchill had revealed that the Admiralty had obtained 'absolutely reliable' intelligence on 12 March that the enemy was short of shells, although for security reasons he could not reveal the source of this information.

Hall now confirmed that this was the case. And, like Churchill, he interpreted the decrypted German telegram to mean that the enemy's situation would have been critical around the time the naval assault was called off.

Churchill could not have hoped for a more cooperative or helpful witness than Hall. When asked if the Admiralty had been justified in acting with 'great confidence' in pressing its attack in mid-March, the DNI replied, 'Oh yes, absolutely.' Admiral de Robeck had previously told the Commission that he had not shared the Admiralty's opinion that the enemy was near the end of its ammunition, but the DNI stated that, with the information available to him on 18 March, he was in a better position than de Robeck to judge the situation.[29] Moreover, the Ottomans' shortage of ammunition had been confirmed by other sources. However, when Churchill prompted him for details, Hall revealed that his optimistic conclusions were based on just two informants. One, presumably a Turkish agent, had reported his opinion in July 1915, based on the views of 'several' unnamed Turks, that a continuation of the naval attack after 18 March would have succeeded. The DNI's second source, a non-Turkish informant who had 'never failed me yet', had reported that the forts were practically out of ammunition on 19 March, and 'there was only one line of mines to get through'.[30] This was hardly a firm basis on which to assert that the Turks were nearly out of ammunition. And the fact that all ten lines of mines inside the Narrows were obviously still intact on 19 March should have been enough to discredit Hall's second source.

Hall was also happy to speculate, for Churchill, about the political effects of the Allied fleet breaking into the Sea of Marmara. He testified that, by early March, the Ottomans were in a state of near panic over the naval attack. There was no doubt in his mind that a British breakthrough would have produced an immediate revolution in Constantinople. 'We had direct evidence', Hall stated:

> [T]hat the [Ottoman] Government was preparing to shift to Asia Minor, and the archives had already started to go over. Undoubtedly as the bombardment went on there was panic in Constantinople, and the better families were preparing to pack up and to go over into Asia Minor rather than stay there. We had undoubted evidence on that from a number of good sources.[31]

Of course, this was also speculative. The sources Hall cited might just as easily, and probably more accurately, have been interpreted as a sign that the Ottomans meant to continue fighting if the Allied fleet reached the Sea of Marmara. The relocation of a state's archives hardly constitutes evidence of an impending revolution or imminent collapse of morale.[32] But Hall, to Churchill's undoubted pleasure, took an optimistic view. He affirmed that the naval offensive had been on the verge of success when it was called off, and that if it had been continued the Ottoman Empire would certainly have been knocked out of the war.

After allowing Churchill to examine witnesses over the course of two consecutive days, the Commission recalled him as a witness on the third day. Most of the session was taken up by another lengthy statement. Churchill examined the conflicting testimony on naval gunnery and offered a final summing up of his case in light of the evidence gathered by the Commission since its deliberations began. Despite Scott's misgivings, Churchill provided a masterful defence of the naval staff's handling of the gunnery issue. If the Commission accepted the evidence of Hickman and Singer, then it must conclude, he insisted, that the plans developed by Carden, Jackson, Oliver, and the naval staff were 'not merely unsound but ignorant and incompetent'. It was 'inconceivable', he proclaimed, 'that officers of the standing of the present First Sea Lord and the chief of staff should have prepared plans of this detailed character, and all the time have felt that they were nonsensical and absurd'.[33] In fact, the naval staff *had* badly underestimated the problems posed by the enemy's mobile guns and the obstacles to effective minesweeping—but it would not be easy for the Commission to say so.

Churchill also explained that the navy had experimented before the war with indirect fire at extreme ranges and with firing at land targets. The results in both cases confirmed the accuracy of naval gunnery. Further evidence on this point was provided after the war began by the bombardments along the Belgian coast and the plans drawn up for attacking fortified islands along the German coast. All of this had convinced Churchill that Carden and the naval staff were justified in thinking the Dardanelles forts might be knocked out by naval gunfire. There was evidently some doubt in his mind, however, as to whether the frequent analogy between the Dardanelles defences and the Belgian forts was entirely defensible, and he carefully qualified his position. What had impressed him most about the German attacks in Belgium—and he reminded the Commission that he had seen the results in Antwerp at first hand—was their devastating impact on the defenders' morale. The Belgians' 'hearts were absolutely broken' he recalled, 'by the sudden collapse of these famous forts one after another, and the feeling that they were in contact with an irresistible force'. Churchill explained that he had expected the systematic destruction of the Dardanelles forts to have the same effect on Ottoman morale. It was only in this sense, he concluded, that he would have invoked the Belgian analogy.[34]

Churchill continued to treat the Turkish forts as the main obstacle to the passage of the fleet. His statement glossed over the problems created by the enemy's mobile guns and howitzers, although he did briefly address the failure of British minesweeping. The problem here, he noted, had been the use of slow trawlers with reservist crews, who had been unable to achieve the desired results. But this did not necessarily mean that the minefield could not have been swept, he argued. The earliest attempts to clear mines had been called off without having suffered heavy casualties, which meant that there was no telling what might have been accomplished if a more determined effort had been made. Better results would undoubtedly have been achieved, he maintained, if the minesweepers had been manned entirely by regular naval personnel.[35] This may have been true, but the small force of slow trawlers allocated to the task was still unlikely to have succeeded. And other awkward questions remained unanswered. Why were these problems not foreseen by Carden and his staff, or by the Admiralty, before the attack began? Why were the deficiencies of the minesweeping force not identified and remedied before 18 March? And would a reorganized sweeping force have succeeded when the batteries protecting the minefields could not be silenced? Churchill did not address—and was not asked to comment on—any of these issues.

The balance of Churchill's statement provided a detailed reiteration and defence of the main arguments he had presented in his initial testimony. The most damaging allegation against him had always been that he had ignored or overruled naval advisers who had been solidly against the scheme from the beginning. Churchill undoubtedly took satisfaction in pointing out that this was not the picture painted by Admiralty officials themselves. Fisher, supposedly a harsh critic who had resisted from the outset, declared that he had willingly gone along with the proposal despite his reservations. Moreover, when Fisher did eventually raise objections, he had not done so on technical grounds. All this was supported by naval witnesses. Not a single officer suggested that Fisher had actively opposed the operation in its early stages. Nor had Wilson expressed any dissent. Best of all, from Churchill's perspective, Oliver and Bartolomé both made it clear that they had supported the operation. Only Jackson's position remained problematic. To support his claims that Jackson had backed the operation, Churchill relied heavily on the admiral's memorandum of 15 January in which he expressed his concurrence in Carden's proposals. Oliver's testimony that Jackson had supported the plan undoubtedly helped as well. But the commissioners were still not sure what to make of Jackson's more critical memorandum of 5 January. Churchill reassured them that this document had not been ignored. Jackson had only advised against an attempt to *rush* a fleet through the Dardanelles, and this advice had been heeded. At no point had Churchill or anyone at the Admiralty or in the fleet advocated taking battleships through unswept minefields.

Churchill was therefore in a strong position to claim that there had been enough professional support for Carden's plan to justify preparations for a naval assault on the Dardanelles. The process could have been stopped by Fisher at any time merely by withdrawing his support, but the admiral had not done so. Instead, he had agreed on 28 January to support the operation, making him jointly responsible for what followed. From then until 22 March, Churchill maintained that there had been no sharp division of opinion within naval circles. He then turned to the decision to employ the army on the peninsula. Little evidence had been taken on this point, as the Commission had decided to scale back the first phase of its investigation to focus on events leading up to the suspension of the naval attack in March, rather than the landing of troops in April. Churchill, nevertheless, rehearsed his argument that he could not be held responsible for any failures incurred on land. If his advice had been followed, troops might have been landed in March, either in conjunction with the navy's operations or immediately following their suspension. In either case, the assault would have stood a better chance of success than the one launched on 25 April.

By the end of his third additional day of testimony Churchill could hardly deny that he had been granted a full hearing. He had now appeared on five of the Commission's first sixteen days of hearings, far more than any other witness. And he was pleased with the results. His concerns of the previous week all but disappeared. 'I am slowly triumphing in this Dardanelles Commission,' he wrote afterwards to his friend Major Edward Spiers, a British Army officer in France, 'and bit by bit am carrying the whole case. I am really hopeful that they will free me from the burden wh[ich] cripples my action.'[36] He was particularly pleased with Hall's evidence, which he described to Asquith as 'a plum'. The commissioners had been so impressed by it, he claimed, 'that I was forced to defend myself for not overruling all the naval people both here and on the spot and ordering the renewal of the fight after the 18th'.[37] Churchill also enthused about Bacon's expert testimony, which he thought had 'demolished' the damaging technical arguments put forward by Hickman.[38] His optimism was largely justified. The only real disappointment during these three days had been Admiral Wilson, who had not acquitted himself well during cross examination—and not just on gunnery matters. When the commissioners' questioning had turned to Wilson's early opinions about the naval offensive, the admiral's testimony had become vague and confusing, although it is difficult to say whether he was being evasive, or simply struggled to articulate his views effectively. At the end of Wilson's testimony, the commissioners had had to recall Churchill as a witness to interpret parts of the admiral's evidence for them! But Wilson's missteps were not necessarily detrimental to Churchill.

Churchill had also reversed much of the damage done by Oliver's original testimony and ensured that the commissioners heard a coherent and persuasive (albeit selective) rebuttal of Hickman's arguments. There were still holes in the Admiralty case, of course, but poor staff work would not necessarily be held against Churchill either. If there was anything for him to worry about at this stage, it was the effect of Henry Jackson's testimony. However, he was evidently not alarmed about this. He told Asquith that 'We have got him [Jackson] tighter than anybody else on paper.... I gather the Commission were very unfavourably impressed by his efforts to wriggle out' of his written support for Carden's plan on 15 January.[39] And it is true that Jackson had come across as cagey. But the concerns raised in his memorandum of 5 January were not easy to disregard. Churchill made a strong case that he had the support of his professional advisers when he took the Dardanelles plan to the War Council, but had he faithfully represented their concerns to his political colleagues? There was no evidence for the allegations made the previous year by the *Morning Post* that Churchill had deliberately misrepresented Fisher's views, but had he been too optimistic in presenting the Admiralty's position? There were certainly grounds to think that, in his eagerness to obtain approval for the operation, he had not really taken his advisers' concerns on board. 'You know what Winston is', remarked Herbert Creedy, the Permanent Under-Secretary at the War Office. 'At a conference he talks everyone else into a jelly and then goes away saying that everyone agreed with him.'[40] The Commission was probably undecided about Churchill's contribution to the War Council, however, as it was still gathering evidence on the government's decision-making process. Some key politicians had not yet testified, including Asquith and Lloyd George, and no final verdict would be possible until their statements had been collected and weighed.

12

The Dardanelles
Commission III

An Instalment of Fair Play

The Dardanelles Commission questioned all the surviving members of the War Council over the course of its first five weeks. The first to give evidence was Sir Edward Grey, who had retained the post of Foreign Secretary in Asquith's coalition government. He was followed at intervals by six others: Churchill; Arthur Balfour, the current First Lord of the Admiralty; Lord Haldane, the former Lord Chancellor, who had been driven from office in May 1915 for his alleged German sympathies; Lord Crewe, the Liberal government's Secretary of State for India; David Lloyd George, the former Chancellor of the Exchequer, who had succeeded Kitchener as Secretary of State for War a few months earlier; and finally Asquith, who was still Prime Minister when he testified. Some of the subjects the Commission probed were relatively straightforward, such as the Russian request for a diversion in January 1915, the functions of the War Council, and its relationship to the Cabinet. There was also little difficulty settling why the War Council had not simply postponed the naval offensive until troops were available to support it, which commissioners clearly felt was the right and obvious course to have taken. The politicians explained that this was never considered an option because Kitchener, whose word on such matters was always considered final, had asserted there were no soldiers available. On this question, as on all others, ministers stuck to the brief submitted by Hankey, ensuring a strong degree of uniformity in their testimony.

Some issues were not easily resolved, however, and most of them involved Lord Fisher. The former First Sea Lord repeated throughout his testimony that he felt constrained from speaking at the War Council unless asked to by the politicians. The only options open to him when he disagreed with Churchill, he maintained, had been either silence or resignation, since it would have been inappropriate to contradict his political chief at the Council table. Hankey had disputed this view at the opening of the Commission's hearings, and every politician who followed emphatically rejected Fisher's defence. One after another, ministers and ex-ministers insisted that the expert advisers who attended the War Council had every right to speak without an explicit invitation; and, moreover, that they were *expected* to offer their opinions, especially if they felt they had something important to say. If Churchill was not accurately representing Admiralty opinion, Balfour remarked, this would only 'throw a greater obligation on the other members of the Admiralty present to express their views'.[1] Haldane was openly contemptuous of Fisher's defence, which had been mirrored by Admiral Wilson in his testimony. 'I do not know what exaggerated views of loyalty may have been in their minds', Haldane stated, 'but apart from those views I should have called that grievous timidity and contrary to their duty.' 'I am perfectly certain', he continued, echoing the views of his colleagues, 'that if Lord Fisher had said to the Prime Minister: "Do you wish me to speak?" he would have said: "I most certainly do", and we all did. We all looked upon him as there to take counsel with us.'[2]

Fisher's habitual silence at the War Council made it easier for ministers to dodge responsibility for approving a naval operation that did not have the full support of the First Sea Lord, but the commissioners correctly surmised that the politicians were not entirely in the dark as to his views. The admiral's cryptic remarks at the War Council on 28 January, followed by his departure from the table and discussion with Kitchener, seemed to show that Fisher's opposition to the scheme was—or should have been—known to all. However, by the end of the investigation, commissioners might have been excused for wondering if these incidents had actually taken place. Grey, the first to be questioned about them, testified that he did not recollect Fisher's remarks that day. Grey had forgotten so many details that commissioners probably did not think much of it, but other witnesses professed ignorance as well. Balfour stated, 'I do not remember the incident at all.' He claimed that he had only heard the story after the Commission had commenced its work.[3] Haldane told a similar story. 'I have not the slightest recollection of it', he stated. Lloyd George said that the incident 'made no impression on my mind at all. I have heard of it since, but I have forgotten all about it.'[4] Asquith could not recall Fisher's departure either. 'I do not remember it at all', he claimed. 'I never noticed it.' Nor had Kitchener, who worked with him closely, mentioned it to him afterwards.[5] The only ministers who admitted remembering this episode were Churchill and Lord Crewe, although the latter maintained that he had not known at the time why Fisher left the table.[6]

If Fisher's actions that day had gone largely unnoticed, ministers could claim they had reasonable grounds for not pressing him to voice his objections. However, they all admitted knowing by 28 January that Fisher disliked the proposed operation. This had not generally been regarded as cause for alarm, they suggested, because they, like Churchill, did not believe Fisher objected to the plan on its technical merits. So why, then, did they think he disliked it? Balfour suggested that Fisher was afraid of losing old battleships and upsetting the naval balance in the North Sea—a natural inference from Fisher's memorandum of 25 January, which Balfour had studied carefully. This was also the position taken by Churchill. Asquith, who would presumably have drawn the same conclusion from Fisher's memorandum, appears to have tailored his testimony to agree with Fisher's. He asserted that the admiral disliked the plan because he had his heart set on a major operation in the Baltic.[7] Lloyd George and Crewe also suggested that Fisher objected because he preferred to act elsewhere, not because he thought the operation was doomed to fail. After studying Fisher's memorandum, Balfour had concluded—like Churchill and Asquith—that the loss of old battleships in the Mediterranean would *not* jeopardize Britain's naval supremacy in home waters. None of the other politicians elaborated on why they were unworried by Fisher's opposition, but their testimony suggests that they thought they knew Fisher's objections and did not regard them as decisive. This provides a plausible explanation as to why the admiral was not asked on 28 January to state his views. What seems to have mattered most to ministers was that, by the end of the day, Fisher had agreed to put aside his reservations and support the naval attack.

The other mystery the Commission struggled to solve was how the naval attack had escalated into a land campaign on the Gallipoli peninsula. Why had the assault on the Straits not simply been called off when the fleet's progress had stalled, as the original plan had envisioned? And who was responsible for the decision to commit troops? Hankey's minutes showed that the War Council had not reached any decision on 19 March about using the army, or even discussed the pros and cons of doing so. The Council had then lapsed into abeyance for eight weeks, during which time the navy's offensive was suspended and the army launched its campaign. But there was no record of how the decision had been taken, or by whom. Churchill's position was that the government had gradually drifted into the campaign without ever pausing to examine the potential consequences. He was careful, however, not to criticize Asquith for failing to keep a firm hand on the decision-making process. If anyone was to- be blamed he implied that it was Kitchener, who had jealously guarded his control over all matters involving the army. The Prime Minister took a different perspective, however. He admitted that the War Council had never been consulted, and that the decision had been 'very slowly arrived at', but he was naturally eager to dispel any hint of 'drift', which would imply a want of control on his part. He argued instead that the decision to land troops was based on the recommendations of the responsible commanders on the spot, de Robeck and Hamilton, and that their advice was subsequently confirmed by authorities at the Admiralty and the War Office. There was no need to bring the matter to the War Council, therefore, because the subject *had* received proper consideration, and all that remained was for the army to carry out the operation.[8]

The commissioners were uncomfortable with the idea that such a momentous decision had been taken without careful consideration by either the War Council or the Cabinet, but every witness confirmed that had been the case. Political oversight was undoubtedly lacking. Other than Asquith and Churchill, the members of the War Council could only speculate for the Commission as to when and how the final decision had been reached. Haldane, for example, said he *thought* 'there had been a change of opinion. We [the other members of the War Council] heard of it afterwards....I observed that with a good deal of concern.' His assumption at the time, he stated, was that the operation must have been recommended by Churchill, Kitchener, and their respective advisers, and approved by the Prime Minister.[9] Lloyd George painted a similar picture. It was 'quite true', he agreed, that the government had simply 'drifted into' the land campaign.[10] He pointed out that the War Council had not provided careful and regular management of land and sea operations, which were left largely in the hands of Kitchener and Churchill, subject to the 'supreme authority' of the Prime Minister. When asked about the decision to commit troops, Lloyd George did not hesitate to identify Kitchener as the responsible party. 'Is it right to say', Cawley asked, 'that Lord Kitchener decided we should attack the Dardanelles [with the army], and that he did it alone?' 'Unless Lord Kitchener did', Lloyd George replied, 'I do not know who did.'[11] When

Churchill was questioned again several weeks later, the Commission raised the issue one last time in hopes of clearing up the conflicting testimony. Churchill now attempted to distance himself from the term 'drifted', probably to avoid causing offence to Asquith. 'I cannot say that at any moment was there any drifting', he insisted. But when pressed to clarify his views, he confirmed that, after the naval failure on 18 March, the use of troops had never—contrary to Asquith's testimony—been put to the Cabinet.[12]

Kitchener's role in the decision-making process was difficult to pin down. He was frequently criticized for his reluctance to share information with his colleagues and his failure to use the army's general staff effectively, but his role in the inception of the naval offensive received little attention and did not appear to be controversial. Neither Hankey nor the politicians so much as hinted that Kitchener had opposed the plans for a naval operation at the Dardanelles, although it was noted that he had protested strongly against the withdrawal of the *Queen Elizabeth* in May 1915. Colonel Fitzgerald, Kitchener's military secretary, was the only person at the War Office in whom Kitchener regularly confided his views, and he had been lost with the *Hampshire*. Callwell, the former DMO, testified that he had no idea what Kitchener's views had been when the offensive was first proposed, although his impression later, he told the Commission, was that the field marshal had disliked the operation.[13] Lieutenant-General Sir James Wolfe-Murray, the former CIGS, could offer no insight at all. He maintained that he had not been 'intimately acquainted' with Kitchener's views, and had barely been consulted about the Dardanelles.[14] No other witness was called from the War Office in the first phase of the investigation, and the Commission had no reason to question whether Kitchener had opposed the Admiralty's plan for an assault by the navy alone. This changed suddenly in late November 1916, when Sir George Arthur, Kitchener's former personal private secretary, surprised the Commission with a memorandum detailing a conversation in which the War Minister had allegedly recounted his early views on the navy's plan.

'Lord Kitchener told me', Arthur wrote, 'and told me very distinctly' that he had 'protested vigorously' against the naval plan when he was first invited to a conference at the Admiralty to discuss the subject with Churchill.[15] According to Arthur, Kitchener said he had told Churchill that no operation against the Dardanelles should be undertaken without 'very strong and very carefully prepared support from and co-operation with the Army'.

Churchill allegedly replied that the presence of the *Queen Elizabeth* would completely transform the situation, making a previously impossible operation 'now comparatively easy, or, at any rate, wholly practicable'. When Kitchener continued to protest, he was challenged, Arthur claimed, on the grounds that he had no expert knowledge of the new dreadnought's capabilities and could not therefore appreciate its enormous 'destructive powers'. The War Minister was reportedly still not satisfied, however, and renewed his objections. Arthur stated that Kitchener had been 'sure that he voiced all military opinion' when he presented his objections, and that 'he said also that his inevitable uneasiness would have been considerably diminished had he been able to satisfy himself that the First Lord's confidence both in the "Queen Elizabeth" and in the success of his plan was wholly and whole-heartedly shared by his chief Naval advisers'.[16]

Churchill was livid when a copy of Arthur's statement reached him. He protested immediately to Mears, the Commission's secretary, that no such meeting had taken place; that Kitchener had never expressed these views, either at the War Council or in private conversation; and that there was abundant evidence—including testimony by Asquith and Fisher—to show that the War Minister *had* supported the naval operation when it was proposed. The only explanation he could offer was that Arthur was reporting comments made by Kitchener in May 1915, when he was angry about the withdrawal of the *Queen Elizabeth*. But he objected strongly to drawing conclusions about Kitchener's opinions in January 1915 from an unverifiable statement about a conversation at some unnamed date about an undocumented meeting at another unnamed date. Churchill was suspicious, moreover, that Arthur's evidence was part of a plot within the War Office to discredit him. He had always known that any perceived attack on Kitchener might result in a backlash from the field marshal's supporters, but he thought this document went beyond simple retaliation. Churchill blamed Kitchener's associates for having fuelled the persistent press criticism of him over the Dardanelles as far back as April 1915. One source for Churchill's suspicions was MacCallum Scott, who had written that, while Churchill was still First Lord, the rumour 'was passed from mouth to mouth on the alleged authority of a colleague in the Cabinet' that he had ' "tricked the Cabinet into the Dardanelles affair" '.[17] 'It is hardly conceivable', Churchill now wrote to the Commission's secretary, that press criticisms 'would have been maintained with so much confidence if they had not been founded and nourished on statements purporting to emanate from the highest authority of the character of those now brought before the Commission by Sir George Arthur'. He continued:

> I cannot believe that Lord Kitchener himself had anything to do with the circulation of such untruthful and unfounded allegations, but that they have been made from time to time by persons in his entourage has long been suspected by me and this suspicion cannot but be confirmed by Sir George Arthur's statement.[18]

The commissioners could not have welcomed this distraction. They had already ceased taking evidence on the inception of the naval campaign and were working on their interim report. Arthur's allegations were too important to ignore, however, and he was summoned to give evidence on 1 December—with Churchill present for cross-examination. The commissioners had trouble concealing their scepticism about Arthur's story. His claims were contradicted by the mass of written evidence they had collected, and his oral testimony was too vague to inspire much confidence. Some members of the Commission were troubled, moreover, by the timing of Arthur's revelations, and he was pressed to explain why he had waited so long to submit a statement. It emerged under questioning that he had been encouraged by Sir Reginald Brade, the Permanent Under-Secretary of State for War, and Major-General Sir Stanley von Donop, the War Office's Master General of the Ordnance. This may have given weight to Churchill's claims that he was the victim of a War Office conspiracy. If officials there had set out to concoct a plausible account of Kitchener's opposition to the Dardanelles, Arthur's statement is precisely the sort of document they might have produced—one that projected backwards from the one piece of reliable evidence in their possession, Kitchener's May statement on the *Queen Elizabeth*. Commissioners were further frustrated by Arthur's inability to provide additional details about his conversation with Kitchener. He was unwilling even to commit himself as to when the discussion took place. He agreed that it had *probably* occurred in mid-May 1915, around the time the War Minister was indignant about the withdrawal of the *Queen Elizabeth*, but he was not prepared to swear to it. Nor could he confirm the date of Kitchener's alleged meeting with Churchill, although he suggested it was probably in mid-January. However, when Churchill produced documents showing that Kitchener actively supported the naval operation around that time, Arthur said he could not rule out a date in February.[19] His credibility was further shaken when he admitted that Kitchener almost never discussed war-related matters with him.

The Commission clearly attached little weight to Arthur's statement, which allowed Churchill to exercise considerable restraint in his cross-examination. He even made a point of telling Arthur that he did not doubt his veracity or good faith, which was probably not altogether true. The commissioners seemed inclined to think that, insofar as Arthur's statement could be taken as accurate, Kitchener's remarks must have been the product of his anger over the *Queen Elizabeth*, and should not be treated as a reliable record of what had transpired several months earlier. Churchill adopted the same perspective. His main concern was to demonstrate for the Commission that the facts allegedly stated by Kitchener could not be true. This was a relatively easy task, given Kitchener's support for the operation at the War Council on 13 January, and his well-known appeal to Fisher to agree to the operation on the 28th.

After demonstrating the unreliability of Arthur's statement, Churchill, at his own request, was recalled as a witness. He proposed that the only possible date for Arthur's alleged conference at the Admiralty was 12 January. No thought had been given to the use of the *Queen Elizabeth* before the 12th, he pointed out, and by the 13th Kitchener was on record as a willing supporter of the operation. Churchill assured the Commission that he had absolutely no recollection of any conference or informal discussion with Kitchener like the one described by Arthur. He found an ally in Nicholson, whose scepticism seems to have mounted throughout the hearing. The latter interjected at one point, probably for the benefit of his fellow commissioners, that if Kitchener had really been eager for a joint operation, he had obviously gone to some lengths to conceal this. Had he not, the field marshal asked, repeated ad nauseam to Hamilton and others that he 'had no intention whatever of using the army on any large scale on the Dardanelles? ... Yet we are told here [by Arthur] that he made this protest. The things are perfectly incompatible, are they not?'[20]

Two other witnesses were also summoned from the War Office to give evidence on Kitchener's early views about the Dardanelles. Both appeared on 4 December, without Churchill being present. The first, von Donop, stated that he had only been told of the Dardanelles operation on 17 February, two days before the bombardment began, so he, like Arthur, had no direct knowledge of Kitchener's perspective in January. Von Donop testified that he had himself been sceptical about the prospects of a purely naval operation when first told of it, but he was cautious when asked about Kitchener's opinion. His *impression*, he stated, was that the Secretary of State was 'very doubtful' about the operation and the views expressed by the Admiralty. He admitted, however, that Kitchener had made no attempt to secure expert opinion on the gunnery issue from him or anyone else at the War Office.[21] Von Donop was followed by Creedy, Kitchener's departmental private secretary, who stated at the outset that he had not been consulted by his chief about the Dardanelles. When asked about Kitchener's initial views on the operation, he recalled that the War Minister had been generally in favour of a diversion in the east; that he was enthusiastic about the benefits that would flow from success; and that he 'welcomed the idea of the diversion being a purely naval one, because he was rather at his wits' end to find troops'.[22] However, he added that, in mid-January, Kitchener had been particularly impressed by the Admiralty's claims for the power of the *Queen Elizabeth*, and that while he had hoped for the best, he had doubts that it was practicable.[23]

None of this was particularly damaging to Churchill. According to Arthur, Kitchener had bluntly stated his opposition to a naval attack at the beginning of the planning process, an allegation that would only reinforce the popular view that Churchill had recklessly brushed aside warnings and forced the operation on his ignorant or unwilling colleagues in the War Council. But Arthur's statement was hardly flattering to Kitchener. It suggested he had meekly supported a major operation he believed was likely to fail. Von Donop and Creedy, on the other hand, took more balanced and moderate positions. They credited Kitchener with enough scepticism about the operation to protect his professional reputation, but did not suggest that Churchill had actively misled him. Fortunately for Churchill, the Commission was more comfortable with this version than the more sensational one offered by Arthur.[24] Arthur's bombshell therefore did little to dampen Churchill's spirits. 'Everything I hear about the Dardanelles Commission encourages me', he wrote to Archie Sinclair at the end of November. 'The interim report cannot now be long delayed and I have good hopes that it will be a fair judgment.'[25]

The Commission's first report *was* delayed, however, in part because Asquith's coalition government collapsed in early December. Lloyd George, whose resignation precipitated Asquith's fall from power, emerged from the resulting wreckage as the leader of a new coalition government. Over the course of a few days, Britain's political landscape was dramatically altered. Lloyd George's break with Asquith split the Liberal Party. About a third of its MPs patriotically supported the new wartime Prime Minister, while the remainder loyally followed Asquith into opposition. The new coalition government was therefore dominated by the Conservatives. Churchill had high hopes at first that his friend and former colleague would offer him a place in the Cabinet, but he was disappointed. Conservative opinion was still very much against him, and Lloyd George was in no position to press for Churchill's inclusion in the government.[26] The new Prime Minister was sympathetic, though, and let Churchill know via Riddell that he hoped to bring him into the government in some capacity once the report of the Dardanelles Commission had been published.[27] In the meantime, Churchill remained out of office. The only bright spot on the horizon was that the interim report of the Dardanelles Commission must appear soon, and he was still confident it would absolve him of blame.

Churchill had waited so long for vindication, and his expectations for the Commission were so high, that he was bound to be disappointed. Lloyd George sent him an advance copy of the report shortly after it was completed on 12 February 1917. The document consisted of a majority report signed by nine of the Commission's ten members, along with minutes by Fisher and Mackenzie outlining their dissent on certain points, and a detailed minority report by the tenth member, the Welsh Liberal MP Walter Roch. Churchill and Asquith were both dismayed that the reports did not include the evidence on which the Commission's conclusions were based. Instead, commissioners constructed a narrative of the main events that included short excerpts—'clippings and snippings', in Churchill's words—from the documents and statements provided by witnesses. The majority report was by no means hostile to Churchill, however. Indeed, he was only singled out for criticism on one point: pressing the original Dardanelles plan on the War Council on the basis of what it described as 'a certain amount of half-hearted and hesitating expert opinion'.[28] But the damage here was not as bad as it might have been. The report largely accepted Churchill's account of the decision-making process at the Admiralty, noting that no member of the naval staff had 'dissented from the bombardment of the outer forts. Their concurrence was not apparently very cordial', it was stated; 'at the same time there can be no doubt that it was given.'[29]

This was certainly less than Churchill had hoped for, but it still explicitly refuted one of the most damaging allegations that had been repeatedly made against him. He was bothered, however, by the evidence the commissioners used to illustrate this part of their narrative. Churchill had presented a strong case that his naval advisers had backed the operation when it was first discussed at the Admiralty, but the strength of his argument was not reflected in the 'clippings and snippings' selected for the report. The most damaging piece was a statement by Henry Jackson to the Commission that he had not considered a purely naval assault on the Dardanelles to be 'a feasible operation'. The report stated that Jackson believed 'it would be a mad thing to do'.[30] This implied that the admiral had clearly warned of failure. Churchill later complained about the prominence the press gave to this line. 'I expect [it] has been quoted more widely than any of the sober conclusions of the Commission. It has run from one end of the country to the other.'[31] The problem here was that Jackson's words referred specifically to the idea of a *rush* through the Straits, not the careful and progressive advance that was actually adopted. The report's handling of Bartolomé's evidence was similarly misleading. The naval secretary was quoted as saying that Admiralty officials felt 'there should be no question of what is known as forcing the Straits'. Bartolomé had subsequently clarified to the Commission that, by 'forcing' the Straits, he had meant 'a deliberate rush', but this was omitted from the report, once again creating the impression that naval opinion was against *any* attack.[32] The report also ignored explicit statements of support for the initial operation by Oliver, Bartolomé, and Wilson.

The rest of the report was generally favourable. Churchill undoubtedly benefited from the Commission's suggestion that his failure to represent naval opinion accurately to the War Council would not have mattered if the decision-making process as a whole had not been dysfunctional. Thus, while Churchill had an obligation to ensure that the full range of Admiralty opinion was known to the War Council, this responsibility was shared with the Prime Minister and the other members of the Council, who should have taken steps to make sure that they were fully informed. Churchill scored another significant victory when the Commission criticized Fisher and Wilson for not making their opinions known. 'We have not the least doubt', the report stated, 'that the attitude which they adopted at the War Council was dictated by a strong sense of duty. But we have no hesitation in recording our opinion that it was a mistaken sense of duty.'[33] Better still, from Churchill's perspective, the Commission agreed with him that Fisher and Wilson had not opposed the naval attack for technical reasons, but because they would have preferred other operations in different theatres. There was therefore nothing in the report to sustain the damaging claims that Churchill had overruled his professional advisers and concealed their strong and explicit objections from his colleagues on the War Council. At worst, the

Commission implied that Churchill had been over-optimistic about the prospects of the naval attack and let his enthusiasm get the better of him. 'We have not the least doubt', the report stated, 'that, in speaking at the Council, Mr. Churchill thought that he was correctly representing the collective views of the Admiralty experts. But, without in any way wishing to impugn his good faith, it seems clear that he was carried away by his sanguine temperament and his firm belief in the success of the undertaking which he advocated.'[34]

The issue that seemed most to bother commissioners about the inception of the Dardanelles operation was that it was not planned from the outset as a combined operation, which everyone involved, including Churchill, knew would offer the best chance of success. This failure was ascribed mainly to Kitchener, who had denied that troops were available, and, to a lesser extent, to the other members of the War Council, who had not challenged him. 'Had this been done', they stated, 'we think that it would have been ascertained that sufficient troops would have been available for a joint naval and military operation at an earlier date than was supposed.'[35] Churchill also had the satisfaction of seeing the Commission confirm that Kitchener *had* initially supported the project. Sir George Arthur's evidence to the contrary was explicitly rejected.[36]

In the Commission's view, the critical point in the inception of the naval campaign had been the War Council of 13 January. The need to provide a diversion for the Russians was not so great, it maintained, that the politicians did not have time to investigate both the availability of troops and the technical feasibility of an assault by ships alone. The underlying assumptions were that a combined operation could have been launched, and that the impracticability of an assault by the navy alone could have been predicted. Of course, the feasibility of the naval operation *had* been studied by the Admiralty after 13 January. Naval planners still failed to predict how difficult it would be to clear the minefields or spot the fall of shot inside the Straits. The report did not dwell on these specific problems, however. Commissioners may have been reluctant in wartime to highlight the failure of the navy's staff work, but it seems their main concern was the concealed guns and howitzers lining the Straits. This obstacle, in their view, could have been predicted if army experts had been consulted in the early stages of the planning process. The Commission also sided with the army's witnesses over the general utility of naval guns against land targets, and rejected the frequently drawn analogy between the Belgian and Ottoman forts.

The Commission's verdict on the decision to use the army was another substantial success for Churchill, who was widely regarded as being solely responsible for the land campaign—and the heavy casualties it produced. The report treated this as another failure of the decision-making process as a whole. It suggested that the original plan for a probing attack by the navy, one that could be easily discontinued, began to break down on 16 February when it was decided to begin assembling troops in the vicinity of the Dardanelles. From this point on, in the Commission's opinion, there could have been no withdrawal without a loss of prestige. The War Council should therefore have accepted that there was no option but to press ahead vigorously with a joint operation. This was not done, however, and the main obstacle was undoubtedly Kitchener. The War Minister was censured for his decision to withhold the 29th Division, which put back the land campaign by more than three weeks. 'This delay', the Commission charged, 'gravely compromised the probability of success of the original attack made by the land forces, and materially increased the difficulties encountered in the final attack some months later.' This and other mistakes by Kitchener were attributed to the War Minister's unwillingness to make proper use of the general staff, 'with the result that more work was undertaken by him than was possible for one man to do, and confusion and want of efficiency resulted'.[37]

This was a serious blow to Kitchener's reputation, but a bigger question remained: why had his colleagues not kept him under control? The Commission blamed Asquith, who alone was in a position to ensure effective political oversight of the nation's war-making machinery. The Cabinet, in its opinion, had delegated the supervision of the British war effort to the War Council, but that body had not fulfilled its proper function because the Prime Minister had favoured a more informal system in which the coordination of the fighting services and the broad outlines of British grand strategy remained in the hands of himself and the two service ministers. It was this loose system of political control that had allowed the nation to drift into a major land campaign without a thorough examination by the responsible civil authorities. The commissioners were particularly critical of Asquith for not calling a meeting of the War Council between 19 March and 14 May, thereby ensuring that the decisions to abandon the naval offensive and use the army were neither discussed nor approved by the government. The Commission charged that Asquith should have brought the subject to the War Council, and that when he failed to do so, the other members of the Council should have pressed for a meeting. The report concluded that 'this was a serious omission'.[38]

The minority report by Roch—contemptuously dubbed 'Mr. Cockroach' by Churchill[39]—was a curious document in that its author did not reach conclusions markedly different from those of his colleagues. The most important thing from Churchill's perspective was that Roch gave slightly more weight than the other commissioners to the naval experts' initial reservations about the Dardanelles operation. Roch's narrative also included excerpts from Jackson's memorandum of 5 January and details of Fisher's near-resignation on 28 January. But his report was not especially hostile either. Like his colleagues, Roch concluded that 'Mr Churchill failed to present fully to the War Council the opinions of his naval advisers, and that failure was due to his own strong personal opinion in favour of a naval attack.'[40] Roch also drew attention to the haphazard nature of the decision-making process as a whole. He was especially critical of the War Council for not properly investigating the plans for a naval offensive after 13 January; for not calling on army authorities to offer an opinion as to its feasibility; and for not meeting to consider the use of troops after the abortive naval attack on 18 March. However, these failures were implicitly attributed to Asquith.

Churchill was unsure at first what to make of the Commission's Report. The document was generally favourable to him, and would undoubtedly help to shield him from charges that he had brazenly overruled his naval advisers and misled his colleagues. Furthermore, there could be little doubt after reading the report that Churchill was not personally responsible for everything that had gone wrong. But the report had not completely cleared him of wrong-doing either. There was no way of predicting how it would be received when it was released to the press and public. He therefore had good reason to be nervous. Hankey recorded in his diary that he briefly discussed the report with Churchill on 16 February. 'He said he was satisfied', the Secretary wrote, 'but the tone of his voice indicated disappointment.'[41] Churchill sought the opinion of George Riddell, who was in a good position to judge how the press would react. Riddell reassured him that 'he had come well out of the inquiry, but that the documents would be damaging to Asquith and Kitchener'. Riddell was more candid—and more accurate—when he discussed the report with Lloyd George later the same day: 'It is not good for Winston', he stated, 'but it is bad for Asquith and Kitchener. Winston does not come out of it white or black. He comes out grey.'[42]

The only person singled out for credit in the report was Hankey, whose detailed statement of the government's case had greatly simplified the commissioners' work. Hankey nevertheless complained that they had produced 'a very unfair document & much too hard on Asquith, dwelling insufficiently on the difficulties of the times & the tiresome personalities whom Asquith had to handle'.[43] At the same time, the former Secretary to the War Council must have been relieved that the Commission had not looked too closely at his own role in the decision-making process. Hankey was always alarmed by suggestions that he was anything but an impartial civil servant, even though he had, on numerous occasions, used his position to sway members of the War Council. Charles à Court Repington, the influential military correspondent of *The Times*, had noted perceptively a few months earlier that Hankey 'was too much in the position of military adviser to the Prime Minister especially at the beginning of the war. "Hankey is a very nice fellow & a very able fellow" he said "but the thing is wrong in principle, and we shall have to clear it up at the end of the war."'[44] Given the emphasis of the report on systemic failures, Hankey worried 'that the papers may try and treat me as mixed up in the defects of the Asquith War Council'. And he was under no illusions as to the shortcomings of the decision-making machinery in the early months of 1915, although he did not consider himself responsible for them. In the event that he was criticized in the press, 'I have my defence', he recorded, 'having both orally & in writing warned Asquith of the trouble he was laying up for himself by his rather easy & slipshod or, perhaps I should say, unsystematic methods.'[45]

Asquith hoped to block publication of the Dardanelles Report once he saw its contents, but this was hardly realistic. Lloyd George was not about to pass up an opportunity to embarrass the former Prime Minister and damage his chances of returning to office. Asquith was still leader of the Liberal Party, and Lloyd George was eager to thwart what he saw as 'an organized attempt to re-establish the Asquith legend'. The Prime Minister felt strongly, moreover, that Asquith deserved to be censured. He told Riddell, 'with great emphasis: If the truth were told and if we lived in other times there is no doubt that Asquith would be shot or beheaded. It is a serious statement to make but it is a true one. If you examine the actual conduct of affairs you cannot point to one thing that Mr. A. did for the war.'[46] This was a sentiment shared by other members of the new government, who were also eager to keep Asquith out of office. According to Hankey:

> [T]he War Cabinet, obviously delighted because it hits Asquith hard, decided to publish [the Dardanelles Commission Report] immediately... They were most vindictive & unpleasant, especially Ll. George & Curzon, in their observations about Asquith—who is a bigger man than any of them—and though they themselves are guilty of many of the lapses for which Asquith is blamed: e.g. they know less about the plans of our generals in Mesopotamia, Egypt & France than Asquith knew of the Dardanelles. Perhaps one day they themselves will get it 'in the neck'. I shall not be sorry...[47]

The Commission's report was published on 8 March, which allowed time for the excision of several paragraphs considered unsuitable for publication. Some newspapers, conditioned by years of tight government censorship, questioned the wisdom of releasing so much information in wartime about the British strategy and operations, but the contents of the report were all the more eagerly covered by the press for this reason. The overwhelming consensus was that the Commission had revealed a shocking lack of political oversight and control by Asquith's first wartime administration. The verdicts on Churchill's role in the inception of the naval offensive varied widely. At one extreme was the *Manchester Guardian*. The Liberal newspaper dealt at length with the ramifications of the report for Churchill, and took a wholly positive view. The former First Lord had long been the 'popular scapegoat' for the Dardanelles failure, it noted, 'but no one can read this report without acknowledging that an injustice has been done him'. Churchill's only failure, it suggested, had been his impatience, which had undoubtedly created 'a great deal of mischief'. But even here there was a silver lining: his eagerness to strike at the enemy 'looks almost like a virtue side by side with the slowness of others'. The newspaper concluded that Churchill *had* been properly supported by expert naval opinion; that his advisers had *not* actively opposed the operation; and that Fisher's main objection to the scheme was that it would interfere with another operation that he favoured. Moreover, it suggested that the naval attack might have succeeded if it had been renewed after 18 March.[48]

This was a reasonable interpretation of the report's findings, and the *Guardian* was not the only newspapers to conclude that Churchill had largely been vindicated. The *Observer*, for example, stated that the report cleared him 'from the overwhelming obloquy which was so long heaped upon him alone, and he comes out of the case better than his colleagues'. The former First Lord had understood the deadlock on the Western Front, it declared, and 'saw that the one and only chance of an early decision lay in the idea of "Victory via Constantinople". Thoroughly backed by a united Government', it concluded, 'that plan would have won.'[49] But such views were not universally shared. At the other end of the spectrum was the *Morning Post*, which denounced both Churchill and Fisher in harsh terms. The politician's 'folly was unrestrainable', it charged. He had taken too much power into his own hands and appointed an old, weak, and subservient First Sea Lord who could not control him.[50] The *Daily Mail* was even more critical, although it spread the blame around rather more widely than the *Morning Post*. Northcliffe, its owner, had been a driving force behind the formation of the Lloyd George coalition a few months earlier, and he clearly relished the opportunity to demonstrate that he had been right to bring down the Asquith ministry. The Dardanelles Report, the *Daily Mail* declared, was 'a scathing denunciation' of what it dismissively labelled the 'Old Gang'. The paper condemned everyone involved in the Dardanelles. It sub-headlines proclaimed: 'Mr. Asquith Wobbled', 'Lord Kitchener Did Not Realise the Facts and Ignored his Staff', 'Mr. Churchill Misled Everybody', and 'Lord Fisher and Other Experts Sat Mum'.

The Commission's Report confirmed all of the paper's worst prejudices about Churchill. Every criticism in the document was eagerly seized upon, and he was denounced in the same harsh language as Asquith and Kitchener. 'Mr. Churchill was guilty in the first degree', it declared:

> He misrepresented the experts and interfered in matters of which, as a laymen, he knew nothing. He telegraphed to Admiral Carden, commanding in the Mediterranean, in terms which plainly suggested the answer which he required from that officer. He then encouraged Admiral Carden to proceed with the insane enterprise by telling him that 'high authorities' concurred, when, according to the evidence, he had only succeeded in obtaining 'a certain amount of half-hearted and hesitating expert opinion' in favour of his 'gamble'. He dazzled everyone concerned with his pictures of the great political and military results which would follow a successful attack on Constantinople, but he never produced, nor ordered his experts to produce, a plan which would make success possible.[51]

This was hardly a fair representation of the conclusions drawn by the Dardanelles Report. And it is absurd to suggest that Churchill had not asked his experts for a workable plan. But the *Daily Mail's* bias against Churchill was by now deeply ingrained. *The Times*, Northcliffe's other newspaper, did considerably better. Its leader on 9 March observed that there was 'not much credit here for anyone concerned'. Mr. Churchill, it conceded, 'was at least consistent in his purpose when all the rest were vacillating'. However, 'it was the consistency of a dangerous enthusiast, who sought expert advice only where he could be sure of moulding it to his own opinion, and unconsciously deceived both himself and his colleagues about the real character of his technical support'. This was not a charitable reading of the report, but it was probably not far from the truth.[52]

On balance, the Dardanelles Report improved Churchill's standing in the eyes of the British public. It was now difficult to sustain charges that he alone was responsible for the disaster. Even the hypercritical *Daily Mail* had heaped blame in roughly equal measure on Asquith, Kitchener, and Fisher. The report also challenged the popular view of Churchill as a reckless amateur who had brushed aside Fisher's clear warnings of disaster and pressed an impossible scheme on his helpless colleagues. And a careful reading of the document would shift most of the blame for the land campaign from Churchill to Kitchener. These were all points Churchill had been arguing for nearly two years, and he could now claim validation from a respected parliamentary commission. His reputation was bound to improve. But the Dardanelles Report had not cast Churchill in the same light in which he saw himself: as the vital driving force behind a campaign that could have achieved a great victory if not for the mistakes and vacillation of others. The best Churchill could have hoped for was that the Dardanelles Enquiry would identify him as the one reliable cog in a dysfunctional decision-making machine, but the Commission suggested instead that his idiosyncrasies were an integral part of the system's flaws. And this was obvious to his critics, whose low opinion and distrust of Churchill was largely unaffected by the Dardanelles Report. Many of those who accepted that his responsibility for the Dardanelles disaster might have been exaggerated still found ample reasons to dislike him, whether it was for his pre-war position on Irish home rule, the defeat at Antwerp, or something else. But the real obstacle to Churchill's rehabilitation was that the Dardanelles Report offered such a mass of detail about his part in the process—much of which pointed to undeniable mistakes and miscalculations—that his enemies saw no reason to question their entrenched views about his responsibility for the Dardanelles.

The *Daily Mail*'s coverage of the Dardanelles Report showed Churchill how far he still had to go. His first reaction was to take the offensive against Northcliffe. In the week before Britain entered the war, the press baron had strongly opposed the despatch of the BEF to France,

and Churchill assumed this knowledge would damage Northcliffe's standing with the British public if it were revealed. He told Riddell on 10 March
that he was planning an attack. This would have been disastrous for Churchill,
and Riddell was able to talk him out of it. But he did not abandon the idea
completely.[53] 'Some day I will make it public', Churchill told MacCallum
Scott a few days later. 'I am keeping it in reserve for a big occasion. It will
knock him out.'[54] Churchill also complained to Lloyd George about the
excision of material from the published version of the Dardanelles Report,
which he felt had been detrimental to his interests. Two changes particularly
concerned him. First, his letter to Callwell in September 1914 had been
removed. This document, he claimed, had 'proposed to take the exact
course for which the Government is censured for not adopting, viz the
examination of an amphibious surprise attack on Gallipoli by representatives of the joint Staffs of the Admiralty and the War Office'. Second, he
objected to the 'complete suppression' of Hall's evidence to the Commission
about Ottoman ammunition shortages and the likelihood of a revolution
at Constantinople.[55]

The editing of the report was raised in Parliament a few days later. The
government agreed to set up a small committee, including Churchill and
Asquith, to review the excisions that had been made and, where possible, to
draft an alternative version suitable for publication.[56] Most of the changes
Churchill wanted were agreed and ready for publication within a few days.[57]
But the real challenge facing him was the parliamentary debate on the report
set for 20 March. Riddell, probably fearing that Churchill would launch into
an intemperate attack on the Commission, advised him 'to treat the matter
in a very dignified way'. The 'public will not occupy themselves on this
post-mortem for long', he told Churchill, and your 'proper course was to
make moderate, helpful, well thought out speeches concerning the war'.[58]
This was good advice, and Churchill was careful to moderate his criticisms.
He began by stating that he did not agree with all of the Commission's conclusions, but that he nevertheless welcomed the report as 'an instalment of
fair play'. It was clearly a relief that he would no longer have to bear the full
weight of public disfavour for the Dardanelles campaign. 'The burden that
I have hitherto borne alone is now shared', he observed, 'with the most
eminent men which this country has produced within the lifetime of a
whole generation in Parliament, in the Army, or the Fleet.'[59]

Churchill did not directly criticize the report's conclusions, although he
complained at length about the decision to include only a small selection of

the evidence the Commission had evaluated. Many of the short statements embedded in the narrative had been taken out of context, he complained, and this created a misleading impression of the opinions held by his naval advisers, especially in the case of Jackson and Bartolomé. Churchill provided an alternative selection of evidence that painted a different picture, all of which had been available to the Commission but was not included in the report:

> When I spoke before I said that Sir Arthur Wilson's opinion was that we should attack the outer forts, and that our future progress would depend upon the degree of the Turkish resistance. Sir Arthur was asked, 'Was this a fair account of your view?' and he said, 'Yes; I think it expresses my opinion fairly well.' Admiral Oliver stated that the whole War group was agreed to begin the attack on the outer forts and consider from the results derived from it how much further it could be pressed. Admiral de Robeck, who comes into the story at a later stage, a brand new admiral, not involved in any way, with a free hand and a clean slate, after being given the command, is asked by me specifically, pointedly, directly, 'Are you in full agreement with the Admiralty telegrams and Admiral Carden's replies thereto; and do you consider that, after separate and independent judgment, that they are wise and practicable? If not, do not hesitate to say so.' To which he replied, 'He was in full agreement, and that the Admiralty telegrams expressed his intentions exactly, and that he would attack at the first favourable opportunity.'[60]

Churchill also questioned the wisdom of relying on statements taken long after the event by individuals who had a vested interest in dissociating themselves from an operation that had failed. He particularly deplored the decision to exclude from the report the detailed plans and memoranda prepared by Carden, the naval staff, and Jackson in January–February 1915. These provided a better guide, in his view, to the opinions held by naval figures at the time.

All this was meant to dispel the impression that Churchill had received little in the way of genuine support for the Dardanelles plan when he took it to the War Council on 13 January. Churchill dismissed the idea that he could have adopted the scheme if his naval advisers had really been opposed. It was 'a most humiliating reflection' on the navy's leaders, he maintained, to suggest that they were unable or unwilling to stand up against an operation they disliked:

> Here are at least six of the most important Admirals and Admirals of the Fleet in the Royal Navy, three of whom have held the position of First Sea Lord,

covering in the aggregate, I suppose, nearly ten years. One of them is the Chief of Staff to-day. Both of the others have held important commands afloat. Some of them are men with reputations for strength of personality, and whose reputation for having strong and formidable personalities is almost world-wide. We are invited to believe that here is a plan to which they were all averse, which was full of errors, tactical errors, which the Commission could easily find out. Yet not one of those Admirals, not one of these great officers we are invited to believe, had the gumption to put his finger on a defect in the plan, and not one of them had the manhood to stand up and say to the First Lord, 'I, for one, will have nothing to do with it.' If that were true, it would constitute a most humiliating reflection. Further, we are asked to believe that they carried their subservience to such a point that not merely did they say 'We will acquiesce, we will stand aside, we make no protest', but that they actually carried their subservience to such a point as to repress their views in these long, technical, elaborate Staff plans which were the basis for our action.[61]

Churchill went on to challenge the assumption underlying the report that the naval operation had been not just a failure but a disaster. The ships that were lost were soon to be scrapped and were of no use in the North Sea theatre, he reminded his audience. And the loss of life had been slight—only sixty-one British officers and men were killed on 18 March. The number lost over the course of the naval attack amounted to just 350 sailors and marines. This, he pointed out, was 'only about a third of what is lost on the Western Front on an ordinary day when nothing is going on'. It was important, he maintained, to 'observe a sense of proportion in these terrible matters'.[62] The losses were justified, moreover, in view of their results—the Russians obtained much-needed relief, Bulgaria temporarily dropped its hostile stance, Serbia was saved from imminent defeat, and Italy was won over as an ally. All this was achieved even though the operation failed. Success would have produced far greater results, and he maintained that victory *could* have been achieved. He hinted that there was more information to support this view than the Commission could include in its report. More, in fact, than the Commission had even been told. And he was confident that it would one day be revealed that the Ottomans' defences were on the point of breaking when the attack was called off. 'When this matter is passed in final review before the tribunal of history', he concluded, 'I have no fear where the sympathies of those who come after us will lie. Your Commission may condemn the men who tried to force the Dardanelles, but your children will keep their condemnation for all who did not rally to their aid.'[63]

This was a masterful performance. The *Manchester Guardian*'s London correspondent called the speech 'a great triumph of Parliamentary oratory'. By the end of the speech, Churchill's standing in the House of Commons had perceptibly improved. 'I think it is fair to say', the *Guardian*'s correspondent continued, 'that no one could have got up with fewer friends than Mr. Churchill on this question, and no one could have sat down with more.'[64] The parliamentary correspondent for the *Observer* also sensed that Churchill's fortunes were at last on the rise. 'Here unquestionably was the turning-point of the struggle', he judged, 'and perhaps a decisive point at the same time in Mr. Churchill's personal career.'[65] The Dardanelles Report was never going to win over his most devoted critics, but Churchill had been a controversial figure for so long that opinion would always be polarized. What mattered to Churchill in 1917 was that the Dardanelles Commission raised doubts about the narrative his political enemies had created in April 1915, a narrative in which he alone had led Britain to disaster. For nearly two years, the story of Churchill as the dangerous amateur who ran roughshod over his professional advisers and deceived his political colleagues had been largely uncontested. With the publication of the Dardanelles Report, public opinion began to shift in Churchill's favour. His friends and supporters in the press were again free to champion his cause and proclaim his merits. And, most importantly, the first signs of a counter-narrative were beginning to emerge, one in which the Dardanelles was a viable operation that might have succeeded.

The Dardanelles Report did not restore Churchill's reputation to anything like its former position, but it refurbished it to the point that Lloyd George could contemplate bringing him into the government. Only one obstacle remained, but it was a serious one. Conservative opinion was solidly against the idea. Lloyd George was naturally wary about alienating the party on whose support he depended. For months, Churchill waited uneasily on the sidelines. He periodically rose in Parliament to criticize the government, so as to demonstrate his potential to cause trouble. But he said nothing so damaging that he would alienate Lloyd George and destroy his chances of returning to office. In mid-July, Lloyd George was ready to risk the wrath of his Tory colleagues.[66] Without warning, Churchill was given the post of Minister of Munitions, albeit without a seat on the War Cabinet, the successor to the old War Council. The appointment was accompanied by firm promises from Lloyd George that the new minister would confine himself to his departmental duties and not meddle in his colleagues' business.

Predictably, there was a howl of protest from the Conservative Party and press.

No one was more outraged than Gwynne at the *Morning Post*. 'It is an appalling disaster', he wrote to Bathurst, 'greater I think than has fallen on us during the whole of the war.'[67] Churchill's appointment to office required him to stand for re-election in his Dundee constituency, and the Conservatives, despite their misgivings, showed their loyalty to the coalition government by not opposing this. Gwynne was so upset, however, that he began gathering funds to back his own candidate in the by-election. Finding a suitable individual to run was difficult, however. 'I see all the good men are away', he complained, 'and only the scum of military age are left.' He briefly contemplated standing himself, but was persuaded that there was little chance of success.[68] In the end, Churchill's sole opponent in the by-election was a prohibitionist candidate. The new minister won the contest easily.

13

The Cabinet Minister as Censor

The Official Histories

The interim report of the Dardanelles Commission may have jump-started Churchill's political revival, but it had not completely exonerated him of wrong-doing. Nor did he feel that justice had been done. The Dardanelles campaign remained a serious blot on his reputation in the years to come. The Commission's report provided as much ammunition to his critics as to his friends, and his enemies continued to cite the campaign as proof of his recklessness, poor judgement, and unfitness for high office. Moreover, Churchill's political future was hardly secure. His improved fortunes after mid-1917 depended, to an uncomfortable degree, on Lloyd George's patronage. Churchill had good reason to worry about his long-term prospects. The Conservative Party remained hostile, the Liberal Party was in disarray, and the British public was wary. Churchill badly needed to change public perceptions about the Dardanelles campaign to rescue his reputation. In early 1917, the immediate obstacle to overcome was still the Dardanelles Commission, which now turned its attention to the conduct of the army's campaign on the Gallipoli peninsula. The Commission's first report had already blamed Kitchener for the decision to launch the land offensive, which took much of the pressure off Churchill. But the public still tended to elide the navy's attack in the Dardanelles and the army's much costlier failure at Gallipoli. Churchill recognized the importance of distancing himself from the latter and, ideally, of decoupling the two campaigns entirely. In a pair of statements drafted for the Dardanelles Enquiry in February 1917, he sought to reinforce the idea that, as Chancellor of the Duchy of Lancaster, he had been a marginal figure who bore no special responsibility for the disaster at Gallipoli. He maintained that he had used what little influence he had to press for the vigorous prosecution of the campaign, and painted himself as a prophet whose warnings went unheeded.[1]

Churchill offered the Commission several explanations for the failure on the peninsula, the most important of which was the delay in sending Hamilton reinforcements after his first attack in late April broke down. This, he suggested, was the result of the political crisis in mid-May. Asquith had delayed sending Hamilton more men, Churchill asserted, first because he was distracted by the challenges of forming a new government, and then by the need to convince his Conservative partners to support a campaign that many of them disliked. This resulted in the loss of several critical weeks, which put off Hamilton's next offensive by a full month, and allowed the enemy time to bring in substantial reinforcements. When the army struck at Anzac and Suvla in August, it did so without any pronounced numerical advantage over the defenders. Churchill took care, however, not to imply any criticism of his friend and ally Hamilton, whose reputation he was eager to salvage. The general had not been given an impossible task, Churchill insisted, but he had been consistently denied the resources he needed to secure victory. Reinforcements had arrived late; his formations were kept under strength; many of his troops were not well trained; and some of his subordinate commanders were incompetent. And yet, despite these severe handicaps, Churchill held that Hamilton had nearly succeeded in securing victory on several occasions. Responsibility for defeat therefore rested with the government, Kitchener, and the War Office.[2] These were the themes Churchill reinforced when he was questioned by the Commission again on 26 and 28 March 1917.

The Commission completed its final report in December 1917, but publication was delayed until November 1919, by which time the war had been won and interest in the campaign was beginning to wane. Churchill emerged from this new document unscathed. He might have been legitimately criticized for his part in launching the Gallipoli campaign—he had, after all, enthusiastically pushed for the build-up of troops in the theatre—but the commissioners were more interested in establishing why operations on land had ultimately failed. Most of the blame was assigned to Kitchener. The Report charged that the War Minister should have known by February 1915 that large-scale military operations in the east were a possibility, and that he failed to ensure that the general staff did its job properly. The War Office had an obligation to study the problem of capturing the peninsula before any decision was taken, the Commission pointed out, and this was not done. Consequently, neither Kitchener nor the War Council understood the problems that would be encountered or the resources necessary to ensure success. Kitchener himself had been overly optimistic, especially about the resistance to be expected from the Ottomans. These initial miscalculations were compounded by the government's delay in sending Hamilton reinforcements, the War Office's failure to divert sufficient resources to the theatre, and mistakes by subordinate commanders, especially during the August offensive. Hamilton himself was criticized for not impressing on Kitchener and authorities in London the full extent of the difficulties he faced, although this was a relatively mild rebuke. The commissioners placed the blame for the campaign's failure on decision-makers in London. It was collective blame, however, and Churchill was not personally criticized.[3]

Churchill's political career was given a fresh boost at the end of the First World War by Lloyd George's invitation to remain in his coalition government as Secretary of State for War and Air. One advantage to being inside the government was that he was able to influence how the Dardanelles would be treated in official publications. The most important of these were the Official Military Histories of the Great War, which ultimately comprised 29 volumes published between 1920 and 1948. This series was produced by the Historical Section of the CID, whose director from 1919 on, Brigadier-General Sir James Edmonds, had served on Haig's staff during the war. The project, approved by the Cabinet in late 1915, was designed to produce authoritative histories based on official documents unavailable either to the public or to non-official historians.[4] The first volume to be completed was the initial instalment of the history of British naval operations by Sir Julian Corbett, who had been working on the project since 1916. Corbett was a respected naval historian with no obvious bias against Churchill, but Churchill was, nevertheless, alarmed by the idea of anyone producing an official *narrative* account of naval operations during his tenure as First Lord. The last thing he wanted was a repetition of the Dardanelles Commission's interim report, whose narrative was supported, in his view, by a narrow and misleading selection of evidence. Churchill had argued in 1917 that the only fair way to deal with such a complex and controversial subject as the Dardanelles was to publish a 'full and fair selection of authentic documents...just as they were written before the event'. And when Corbett's work came into view in early 1919, Churchill argued that the planned official histories should be scrapped altogether.

Instead, he proposed that the government publish collections of official documents, with only as much commentary added as was necessary to 'make the account fully intelligible. It will then be for the public at large and for unofficial historians to draw their own conclusions and express them at their discretion. Let the public have the facts', he concluded, 'whatever they are.'[5]

Hankey, a friend and supporter of Corbett and the driving force behind the official histories, outlined the problems with Churchill's proposals a few months later in a memorandum for the Cabinet. The first difficulty was practical: there were far too many official documents relating to the conduct of the war at sea to publish anything more than a small selection. That, he pointed out, was why it had been decided to employ historians—to distil the massive documentary record into a form suitable for public consumption. The second problem was financial. Producing a collection of documents for publication would mean additional costs. And because the government had already signed contracts with a commercial firm to publish Corbett's history, penalties would be incurred there as well. Finally, pledges had been given in Parliament that a series of official histories would be published. Hankey was keen to ensure the publication of Corbett's work in its existing form, and Churchill seems to have received little or no support from his Cabinet colleagues. In the end, he backed down. His main concern, as Hankey learned from Corbett, was the treatment of the Battle of Coronel. What Churchill wanted, it seems, was an account that explicitly cleared him of blame for the loss of Cradock's squadron. And Corbett was willing to meet most of his concerns. The historian revised his manuscript in the summer of 1919 to address Churchill's objections, going so far as to insert, verbatim, three telegrams and minutes Churchill wanted to see published, relating both to Coronel and the loss of the three cruisers in 1914.[6]

This did not settle the matter, however. The Admiralty immediately objected to the publication of the documents Corbett had inserted to mollify Churchill. The manuscript had been cleared for publication by the Admiralty before Churchill began pressing for changes, and naval officials objected to adding new material that would reveal 'controversies and cross-currents within the Admiralty connected with action which was taken in the name of the Board'.[7] The Admiralty, in other words, wanted its internal decision-making process to remain a black box, while Churchill insisted that, since he had been publicly attacked for his part in the process, he had a right to insist on the publication of documents that would refute the charges against him. Hankey prepared a new memorandum for the Cabinet warning that it might have to decide between the Admiralty and Churchill. And he suggested that the government might need to reconsider the policy of publishing official histories of the war, since more such controversies were bound to arise as new volumes were completed.[8] However, the dispute over Corbett's history was resolved shortly afterward, and without Cabinet intervention. Churchill proposed a compromise by which one of the three documents he wanted published would be dropped, and the other two moved from the main text to an appendix. This was accepted by the Admiralty, and the Cabinet approved the first volume of the naval history for publication.[9]

Churchill also took an interest in the work of a special committee set up by the Admiralty in March 1919 to examine and report on the Dardanelles campaign. The committee, chaired by a naval officer, Commodore F. H. Mitchell, was made up of representatives from all three armed services (a separate air force had been established in 1918). Ian Hamilton hoped this investigation would produce 'a straight and strong report saying the Dardanelles could easily have been forced', but he was disappointed.[10] The committee's terms of reference made it clear that its purpose was only to draw practical lessons from the campaign so that the services might better prepare for similar operations in the future. Criticism was to be avoided.[11] In April 1919, members of the committee travelled to Turkey, now a defeated power occupied by the Allies, to examine the Ottoman defences and interview participants from the other side of the campaign. Their 530-page report, known, after the chairman, as the Mitchell Report, contained a wealth of technical detail about the enemy's defences, the damage inflicted to forts and guns during the campaign, and other aspects of the British operations, but it deliberately avoided the sorts of broad judgements about the campaign for which Hamilton had hoped.[12] Churchill was ambivalent about the final product. The report, he told Masterton Smith in September 1920, was 'not in all respects unsatisfactory'. The best feature, from his perspective, was the conclusion, based on interviews with Turkish authorities, that the Dardanelles forts had been down to two days' supply of ammunition for their heavy guns when the naval assault was called off in March. Churchill was also particularly struck by the committee's opinion that the various elements of the enemy's defences—mines, forts, minefield batteries, and howitzers—were mutually dependent, and that if any one of these had been disabled the whole system would have collapsed. Since the report suggested that the forts might have been overcome, Churchill was encouraged in his conviction that a continuation of the naval assault would have been successful.[13]

The report was less satisfactory in other respects. Churchill was clearly surprised to read—probably for the first time—a full and detailed account highlighting the inadequacy of the fleet's minesweepers and aircraft. The only answer to these shortcomings, he suggested, was 'that we sent all we could lay our hands on'. The committee also failed to reach any verdict on how close the naval attack had come to success. The Ottomans and Germans interviewed by the committee offered a wide variety of opinions. Some felt that a renewal of the attack might have succeeded, as ammunition would have run out after two more days of heavy fighting. Others noted that the Allied failure on 18 March had strengthened the defenders' morale and improved public confidence. The personnel manning the forts were reportedly confident that another naval attack would have failed, although the officers interviewed were uncertain on this point. Some commanders, including Djevad Pasha, the Ottoman Army commander, stated that the Allied fleets probably could have forced a passage through the Straits. On the other hand, Enver Bey, chief of staff to the German admiral, Souchon, maintained that the minefield would have been sufficient to block the fleet's advance, even if the forts had been silenced. Nor was there agreement on what would have happened if the fleet had reached the Sea of Marmara. Some speculated that the Ottoman position on the Gallipoli peninsula would have become untenable and revolution would have erupted at Constantinople. But others suggested that the Straits would have remained impassable for supply ships and the Allied fleet would have found its line of retreat cut off.[14]

Churchill's main concern about the Mitchell Report was that it should not be released to the public. Like the Dardanelles Commission Report, it contained much information that could be used against him. If the Admiralty intended to publish, Churchill told Walter Long, the Conservative First Lord, then all the relevant documents must be published with it to ensure the full story was told. But there was never any intention to publish the Report, as Churchill probably knew. Nor was he in a position to stop the document being circulated confidentially within the navy, although this did not stop him from trying. Churchill advised Long to withhold the Report from the service, expressing concern that it would vindicate the senior officers who had called off the naval offensive in March 1915. This decision, he suggested, had stemmed from the same 'negative attitude of mind' in the service that had led to the 'melancholy' failures in the Battle of Jutland, and it was not in the navy's interest to foster these attitudes.[15] Long was unmoved. The distribution of the Report, he told Churchill, was 'surely a technical question' to be decided by the naval staff, and he refused to interfere.[16] The full report was issued to the fleet as a confidential book in April 1921.

The official history of Australia's participation in the Gallipoli campaign represented a different challenge for Churchill. The British had no say in what the Australian government published, and Churchill could not exercise any direct influence over official historians in Australia or any of the British Dominions. When Australian authorities approached the War Office in 1921 for access to British Army war diaries, Churchill, still Secretary of State for War, was happy to provide copies at no cost, but he took the opportunity to send the Australians a memorandum instructing them on the 'precautions' that should be taken in an official history when it came to 'the publication of certain undesirable matter'.[17] This document explained that official narratives 'should be without criticism, and particularly without remarks on commanders still living'. Where matters had to be dealt with that had become controversial, it recommended that original documents should be presented without comment. This was, in fact, the approach Edmonds favoured for the British official histories. Churchill had criticized Corbett's naval history for 'its awful flatness and sterility', but he was happy to see an official history take this form, at least when dealing with operations with which he was associated.[18] The War Office memorandum also noted that drafts of the British histories were routinely circulated to the officers involved for comment, to ensure that no injustices were done to individuals. And, as an additional safeguard, final manuscripts were scrutinized by both the CIGS and the Secretary of State for War.[19]

The first volume of the Australian official history, *The Story of ANZAC*, was published in 1921. The author, Charles Bean, was a respected journalist who had been attached to the Australian Imperial Force (AIF) throughout the conflict as a war correspondent. Bean drew on the extensive records he had compiled during the war, including detailed diaries and contemporary interviews with participants, and a vast store of official documents, to create a colourful, detailed, and, above all, nationalistic account of the Australian experience.[20] *The Story of ANZAC* transcended the usual limitations of official history. It not only became a key text in the creation of the 'Anzac

Legend', it was also instrumental in popularizing the idea that, for Australians, the Gallipoli campaign represented the 'birth of a nation'. Churchill had probably been more concerned about what the Australian history would say about Hamilton than about himself, but Bean devoted a chapter to the naval offensive to force the Dardanelles—and condemned Churchill for instigating the land campaign. However, this chapter, in contrast to the rest of the book, was prepared without access to official records. The British had shared neither the evidence taken by the Dardanelles Commission nor the Mitchell Report with the Australians, forcing Bean to rely on a handful of published sources. He drew heavily, therefore, on the two reports of the Dardanelles Commission and such memoirs as appeared immediately after the war, particularly those by Jacky Fisher and Ian Hamilton. Bean was not disposed to interpret these sources charitably. After spending more than four years with the AIF, he had evidently absorbed the disparaging views of Churchill common within the Australian Army's upper echelons. Major-General Brudenell White, one of highest ranking Australian officers at Gallipoli, had told Bean in 1915, for example, that Churchill was 'responsible for the deaths of at least 25 per cent of the men who have fallen at Gallipoli—almost as directly responsible as if he had shot them. Well what happens to him—a man like that ought to be hanged as surely as any criminal.' Bean assured White at the time that Churchill had 'wrecked his career', but he clearly sympathized with the general's views. 'You cannot pretend', he wrote afterwards in his diary, 'that these ministers act with responsibility—not even the legal responsibility attaching to a trustee.'[21]

Bean's chapter on the origins of the naval offensive cast Churchill in a particularly unfavourable light. The former First Lord, the Australian wrote (in terms that would not have been permitted in a British official history), had been 'possessed of a brilliant, restless intellect, and a passion for adventure'. Furthermore, he 'possessed one of those headstrong natures whose thoughts are fathered by their wishes. He was restlessly eager to attempt his great stroke.' Churchill's fatal miscalculation, Bean asserted, was thinking that the demolition of the Belgian forts by German howitzers in 1914 had demonstrated that modern naval guns could reduce the Ottoman forts lining the Dardanelles. Once imbued with this conviction, Churchill had obtained the assent of his naval advisers, even 'though at first almost to a man they disliked the idea of a purely naval attack'. Why had the War Council agreed to the operation? On this question Bean ignored the findings of the Dardanelles Commission, which had stressed the government's collective failure to examine its expert advisers and faulted Asquith for losing control over the decision-making process. Instead, Bean concluded that Asquith and Kitchener had simply been overwhelmed by Churchill's enthusiasm. '[B]etween these two minds', he asserted, 'both possessing stability, there was a third, unceasingly active and almost boyishly impetuous. Kitchener gave at times a grudging assent, at other times an eager one, to the prospects which Churchill's optimism sketched out for him.'[22] Bean also ignored the Commission's conclusions about the origins of the land campaign, where blame had been placed squarely on Kitchener's shoulders. The decision to commit troops was treated as the inevitable result of the equally inevitable failure of the naval campaign. Everything therefore stemmed from Churchill's original advocacy of a naval attack. Bean's chapter on the Dardanelles concluded: 'So, through a Churchill's excess of imagination, a layman's ignorance of artillery, and the fatal power of a young enthusiasm to convince older and more cautious brains, the tragedy of Gallipoli was born.'[23]

Churchill was stung by this sharp criticism, but there was little he could do except register a protest in his memoirs, where he expressed his 'hope that the Australian people... will not rest content with so crude, so inaccurate, so incomplete and so prejudiced a judgment, but will study the facts for themselves'.[24] The British official history of the Gallipoli campaign might easily have been just as bad for Churchill. In 1923, the task of preparing these volumes was assigned to Lieutenant-General Sir Gerald Ellison, who had served on Hamilton's staff after August 1915 as Deputy Quartermaster-General. Ellison was convinced that the Gallipoli campaign never stood any chance of success, and, like Bean, he maintained that the blame for launching it rested entirely with Churchill. Moreover, Ellison intended to use his position as official historian to advance his strong personal views. His chief objective was to challenge Churchill's account of the campaign's origins in the second volume of his memoirs, which had been published in 1923. 'The whole trend of Churchill's "World Crisis"', Ellison complained to his superiors, 'is to attribute the failure of the Gallipoli campaign to the vacillation and shortcomings on the part of Lord Kitchener, who is no longer alive to answer strictures on his conduct and to explain the motives for his actions.'[25] As one historian has noted, Ellison's antipathy towards Churchill 'developed into an almost personal crusade'.[26]

None of this was known to Churchill. And if it had been, he was in no position to do anything about it. The Lloyd George coalition had collapsed in October 1922 when the Conservatives withdrew their support. Churchill was again forced out of office. A month later, he lost his seat in Parliament, and would not be re-elected to the House of Commons for another two years. This was a turbulent period in British politics, and another low point in Churchill's career. The rift between Lloyd George and Asquith split the Liberal Party and destroyed its prospects of forming another government. With the Liberals in disarray, popular support for the Labour Party surged. In 1924, Ramsay MacDonald formed a minority Labour government with the support of Asquith's Liberals. Churchill's political future was once more uncertain, and he was certainly in no position to influence the direction of the official histories. He was fortunate, therefore, that both Hankey and Edmonds, the Director of the CID's historical section, were out of sympathy with Ellison's approach. Edmonds believed strongly that the official histories should avoid controversy. Above all, individuals should not be explicitly criticized. And in the case of campaigns in subsidiary theatres, official historians were to confine themselves to detailing operations. 'Questions of policy', Edmonds told Ellison, 'should be touched on very lightly if at all.'[27]

Ellison submitted his first draft chapters for approval in mid-1924, and quickly discovered that his trenchant criticisms of Churchill were not welcome. When Edmonds and Ellison were unable to agree on what material should be included in the volume, the latter decided to go over Edmonds' head by submitting his drafts directly to the Sub-Committee of the CID for the Control of the Official Histories, which oversaw the work of the Historical Committee. This body met in December 1924, and Hankey, whose support was essential, sided with Edmonds. The Secretary to the War Council noted that Ellison had 'so far written quite a different book from what had been asked to produce. It was, he considered, out of perspective.' Hankey also knew that Churchill, recently returned to office as Chancellor of the Exchequer, had learned that Ellison intended to criticize him. He had been tipped off a few weeks earlier by Hamilton, who suggested that if he 'were to glance at the History as written up to date, you would get rather a startler'.[28] Churchill immediately obtained a draft from Hankey, who would have had no difficulty predicting his reaction.[29] There was no need for Churchill to get involved, however. The controlling committee concluded that Ellison would have to accept substantial changes to his manuscript or be replaced.[30] The historian was unwilling to compromise and agreed to step down.

This was not the end of the problem for Churchill, as Ellison was still eager to publicize his views on the Gallipoli campaign. When Ellison's relations with Edmonds first began to sour, Hamilton had suggested that he might one day produce his own unofficial history of the campaign.[31] The idea must have appealed to Ellison, because in 1926 he published *The Perils of Amateur Strategy: As Exemplified by the Attack on the Dardanelles Fortress in 1915*. Free from official oversight, Ellison denounced the whole decision-making system. And there were many legitimate criticisms to be made. Ellison was correct in arguing that reforms were necessary, as Hankey himself had pointed out in 1915. The first report of the Dardanelles Commission, which Ellison drew on heavily for support, revealed numerous problems that could have been avoided if the politicians had provided better oversight and worked more effectively with their professional advisers. But Ellison had a more radical overhaul in mind. In his view, strategy should be placed *entirely* in the hands of military professionals. 'Politics and strategy are radically and fundamentally things apart from one another', he asserted. 'Strategy begins where politics ends.' Politicians were amateurs when it came to military matters, he argued, and they should not be permitted to interfere in things they did not fully understand. His harshest criticisms were reserved for Churchill, who was accused of overruling his professional advisers, promoting a naval operation that was 'unsound in the last degree', and leading Britain into a military campaign that was doomed to fail.[32] Ellison maintained that, as First Lord, Churchill had 'acted . . . as though the office of Lord High Admiral had been revived in his own person':

> He seemed to imagine that he was at liberty to pick and choose his advisers as he liked. If one Admiral did not agree with him, he looked for some other who did. Even so, he accepted only so much of the advice proffered as suited him.[33]

The most serious failure of the British decision-making machinery in wartime, he concluded, was that it allowed strategy to be decided by politicians like Churchill.

Ellison's successor on the Gallipoli official history, Brigadier-General Cecil Aspinall-Oglander, had also served on Hamilton's staff during the campaign. Like Ellison, he believed that he had an obligation to point out where mistakes had been made. Aspinall tended to be critical of Hamilton's leadership throughout the campaign, believing the general had been naively optimistic and insufficiently forceful in representing his needs to London.

He also did not hesitate to point out mistakes by Hamilton's subordinates when he thought criticism was warranted. But Aspinall differed sharply from Ellison in believing that the Gallipoli campaign *had* stood a reasonable chance of success. The main obstacle to victory in his view was not the mistakes made by senior officers in the MEF, but decisions by the British government that had deprived Hamilton of the resources necessary to do the job. In view of the shortage of men and ammunition available to Britain in 1915, Aspinall felt it had been a mistake to attempt major offensives both on the Western Front and at Gallipoli. Moreover, it was clear in hindsight that any offensive on the Western Front at this stage of the war was bound to fail. If the resources used there had been committed instead to the campaign in the east, Aspinall believed that decisive results might have been obtained.[34] This was essentially the same argument Churchill had made to the Dardanelles Commission. And as Chancellor of the Duchy of Lancaster, he *had* consistently advocated a defensive posture in the west in order to bolster offensive capabilities in the east.

Aspinall's approach inevitably raised protests from Edmonds, who objected, among other things, to his subordinate's criticisms of senior commanders. Their differences came to a head in March 1928. Edmonds complained that Aspinall's draft chapters contained 'certain phrases and adjectives which want toning down as they hardly fit in with the dignity of an official narrative'. He felt that Aspinall's criticisms created 'a thread of unkindliness, almost ill-bred innuendo', which would tend to prejudice readers. In his opinion, 'unpleasant facts' should be 'merely recorded without rubbing them in'.[35] This view was generally shared, moreover, by the War Office and the Foreign Office, which both insisted on substantial revisions. Aspinall, like his predecessor, decided to go over Edmonds' head—and he found a powerful ally at the Treasury. Churchill had returned to Parliament in the 1924 General Election, rejoined the Conservative Party, and been appointed Chancellor of the Exchequer by Stanley Baldwin, a position he still occupied in 1928. Churchill had favoured Edmonds' approach to official history when confronted with potentially critical works like those by Corbett and Bean, but he was eager to champion Aspinall's more opinionated method when that author wished to expound positions favourable to him. He therefore invited himself to the meeting of the CID's Committee of Control on 9 March, when the differences between Aspinall and Edmonds were due for consideration.

Edmonds began the discussion by expressing his concern that Aspinall had been 'a little unkind' to senior commanders. It was important, he maintained, to avoid the sort of criticisms that had been levelled against the more outspoken Australian official history. The right approach, in his view, was to 'hint' at criticism 'rather than to state it baldly....We did not, he considered, want everybody to see the trouble we had had and the mistakes we made.' Churchill, always mindful of Hamilton's reputation, was disposed to agree— to a point. He was generally content to let readers draw their own conclusions from the evidence, provided it was accurately presented. But he was uneasy about the idea of downplaying or concealing errors. The purpose of an official history, he maintained, was to identify mistakes, not hide them: 'What we did not want to do was to make the same mistakes again', he stated, 'or that our children should make them.' But Churchill's main concern was Edmonds' insistence that the Gallipoli history should be simply an operational record written without reference to events in other theatres. The main value of Aspinall's work for Churchill was in highlighting the relationship between Gallipoli and the Western Front, and the consequences of failing to prioritize one over the other:

> He [Churchill] argued that when you are writing a special monograph on one campaign, to say you should write it without being allowed to make even the most indirect reference or the most restricted reference to the setting of that campaign in relation to the general issue, was absolutely indefensible and absurd. You could not lay down such a principle as that: it would make the story unintelligible. The one excuse in this case, for instance, for leaving the troops in the Gallipoli Peninsula so cruelly ill-supplied with reinforcements and ammunition was the dire and bitter need in France. That was the defence for Lord Kitchener. But it was also perfectly legitimate to show the relative value which could have been derived from the use of those troops in one theatre or another.

If Aspinall's treatment of this problem were 'censored out of the official history', Churchill charged that 'it would be an atrocious falsification of the true presentation of the case'. Moreover, when this censorship became known to the public, as it surely would, the whole work would be devalued. He continued:

> Why should it be wrong to say that they had only 50,000 shell or whatever it was, and advanced four miles on the Gallipoli Peninsula at the same time that the other people [on the Western Front] with 1,000,000 shell advanced only half a mile? Why should not these important considerations be placed together

as an indication that it would have been at that moment a more fertile application of our force? The whole ghastly error which lay at the root of this story and of our war conduct was the inability of the military and naval authorities to distinguish between the main and the decisive theatre.... And to smudge over that lesson in our history, written in blood and disaster, would be to render the greatest disservice to future students of war. For his own part he could not conceive why these passages should be struck out.[36]

Churchill's forceful intervention on Aspinall's behalf achieved its purpose: Edmonds and the War Office both backed down. The controlling committee's meeting of 9 March ended with an agreement that Aspinall would work with Edmonds to revise his manuscript, although few changes were actually made.[37] The first volume of the Gallipoli official history, published in 1929, was all that Churchill could have hoped for. Aspinall made his position clear in his preface, stating that there was 'abundant proof' victory could have been achieved in the east. On at least three occasions during the campaign, including the naval attack on 18 March, he believed that 'the issue hung in the balance'. And he went on to cite the judgement of the German official account of the campaign that 'Mr. Churchill's bold idea was decidedly not a fine-spun fantasy of the brain.'[38] Near the end of the volume Aspinall outlined his case that the fatal mistakes were those made by authorities in London, who deprived Hamilton of the resources he needed for the sake of the Western Front. 'Here undoubtedly was the crux of the whole situation', he concluded. There could be:

> [L]ittle question that, in view of the shortage of men and ammunition it was wrong to embark [on the Gallipoli operations], and to proclaim that they must be carried through, unless it was first decided that they were of such supreme importance, that, till success was achieved, the peninsula must be regarded as the decisive theatre of war. This was the acid test.... With barely enough ammunition for one theatre, an offensive campaign was sanctioned in two, and both ended in failure.

To illustrate his point, Aspinall contrasted Hamilton's offensive on 6–8 May with French's near-simultaneous attack on 9 May at Aubers Ridge in France, both of which failed. Hamilton had employed 20,000 troops and expended around 18,500 rounds of ammunition. French had used a larger force, around 30,000 troops, with another 25,000 in reserve, and fired 80,000 rounds in a single day. Around 11,000 casualties were suffered in the attack in France, and not a yard of ground was taken. The Germans did not even have to divert reserves to this sector of the front to repel the attackers.

Aspinall pointed out that if Hamilton's resources had been added to the attack on Aubers Ridge, the results would have differed little. But if the men and ammunition used by the BEF in its attack had been available in Gallipoli, Hamilton's army might have advanced across the peninsula and allowed the fleet to reach Constantinople.[39]

The second volume of the Gallipoli official history, published in 1932, was another strong endorsement of Churchill's view. In the volume's epilogue, Aspinall described the campaign as one of the 'world's classic tragedies. The story is a record of lost opportunities and eventual failure...There is little doubt to-day that the idea of forcing the Straits with a view to helping Russia, eliminating Turkey from the war and rallying the Balkan States to the side of the Entente, was one of the few great strategical conceptions of the World War.'[40] The implications for Churchill's reputation were not lost on reviewers. The sub-headlines for Compton Mackenzie's review in the *Daily Mail* proclaimed 'Mr. Churchill Vindicated' and 'Might Have Ended War in 1915'.[41] Churchill therefore achieved a considerable measure of success in shaping how the Dardanelles campaign would be presented in the British official histories, which in turn helped him to shape public perceptions of the campaign. As a Cabinet minister, he used his influence to make uncritical works like Corbett's naval history more complimentary to himself, and to ensure that favourable interpretations like Aspinall's were not censored or emasculated before publication. He also benefited considerably from the British government's policy of avoiding controversy and criticism in its official war histories, which ensured that Ellison's damning attack was denied the weight and authority that typically attached to government publications. Churchill's only notable misfortune in this respect was Bean's official history, which he was powerless to influence. But the damage here was mitigated by the fact that this work was not widely read outside Australia.

14

The Battle of the Memoirs

The British official histories helped to undermine the popular perception of the Dardanelles and Gallipoli campaigns as unadulterated
disasters, but the biggest influence on public sentiment in the decades
following the war was the flood of memoirs by Churchill and other prominent figures associated with the operations. The first on the scene was Lord
Fisher, who published in late 1919. Churchill and Fisher had remained on
good terms since coordinating their evidence for the Dardanelles
Commission in 1916, but Churchill must still have felt some apprehension
in the weeks before publication. The admiral's behaviour was, after all,
unpredictable at the best of times, and he was in a unique position to harm
Churchill's reputation. And as the first excerpts from Fisher's memoirs were
being prepared for serialization in *The Times* in October 1919, Hamilton
warned Churchill that he *should* be concerned. After Fisher's resignation in
1915, Hamilton revealed, the admiral had told Hamilton's wife that he 'had
some fine things in his diary about you and me which would be printed in
America if they were not printed here'.[1] In the event, there was no cause for
alarm. Fisher was still committed to his truce with Churchill. His disjointed
and rambling volume of recollections (*Memories*) proclaimed that readers
who expected 'to see Sport and that I am going to trounce Mr. Winston
Churchill... are woefully mistaken'.[2]

The admiral's harshest words were directed at the 'stupidity of Lord
Cromer' and others who had faulted him for not voicing his views at the
War Council. Otherwise, Fisher stuck to the version of events he had presented to the Dardanelles Commission three years before. In the single
chapter devoted to the Dardanelles, he claimed that, in early 1915, he had
been committed to launching a great operation in the Baltic, and had initiated the construction of a 'great armada' of new warships for this purpose
in early November 1914, only days after his appointment as First Sea Lord.

These claims were supported by doctored versions of the official memoranda detailing the new warships started during his tenure at the Admiralty.[3] This deception, as noted in Chapter 10, was only uncovered by Fisher's biographer in 1973.[4] Elsewhere in this chapter, Fisher included an excerpt from the War Council minutes for 28 January that were misleadingly edited to suggest that a great armada intended specifically for the Baltic had previously been sanctioned by both Churchill and Lloyd George.[5] However, none of this was inherently damaging to Churchill. '[I]t seems', Hamilton wrote, 'that after all the old boy is not going to be nasty about you.'[6]

The following year, Ian Hamilton published his two-volume *Gallipoli Diary*.[7] This was not actually a diary, as its title suggested, but a memoir written in diary form. Hamilton had been widely blamed for the army's failure on the peninsula, and was not given another senior command for the duration of the war, even though he was largely absolved of responsibility by the Dardanelles Commission in 1917. He was therefore every bit as eager as Churchill to clear his reputation, and the two men continued to coordinate their efforts after the war. Churchill went over drafts of *Gallipoli Diary* for his friend in late 1919, and was pleased with the results. The volumes argued that Britain's eastern strategy *was* a worthwhile endeavour, one that could have produced decisive results and had, in fact, come close to victory. The challenge for Hamilton was to shift the responsibility for failure from himself to authorities in London—but without explicitly criticizing Lord Kitchener, who continued to be held in high regard by the British public. Hamilton made his point indirectly by reprinting his frequent telegrams home requesting more men, munitions, and supplies.[8]

The general also went out of his way to praise Churchill, casting his friend as a far-sighted and capable leader whose removal from the Admiralty in May 1915 had been a devastating blow to the campaign's prospects. 'What a tragedy', Hamilton wrote, 'that his nerve and military vision have been side-tracked: his eclipse projects a black shadow over the Dardanelles.' Nor was Hamilton's praise for Churchill confined to the Dardanelles. He suggested that his friend's intervention in Antwerp in 1914 had been a 'brilliant effort of unaided genius' that had prevented the Germans from capturing Calais. 'Any comfort our people may enjoy from being out of cannon shot of the Germans', he wrote, 'they owe it to the imagination, bluff and persuasiveness of Winston and to [the] gallant Naval Division.'[9] Hamilton also got in a few jabs at Fisher, noting, for example, that as Commander-in-Chief of the MEF he could only hope for assistance from the Admiralty if the request were seen by Churchill: 'if it falls into the hands of Fisher it fails', Hamilton recorded, 'as the sailors tell me he is obsessed by the other old plan and grudges us every rope's end or ha'porth of tar that finds its way out here'.[10]

It would be Churchill's memoirs, however, that would have the biggest impact on popular perceptions of the Dardanelles. Churchill had been waiting since 1915 for the opportunity to present his complete case to the British public, and the lifting of wartime restrictions allowed him to begin laying the groundwork for his memoirs in late 1919. The project promised to be lucrative as well. By early 1921, Churchill had secured massive advances totalling £27,000 (equivalent to around £1.2 million today).[11] He had no contractual obligation to print official documents in this work, but he firmly believed that these were the best answer to the criticisms that had been levelled against him. He planned from the outset to print a large selection of the minutes, memoranda, and telegrams he had drafted during his period as First Lord. However, he could not be certain when he embarked on this project that the government would not intervene to prevent the publication of official and secret material. The possibility of government intervention had also been a concern for Hamilton while he was preparing *Gallipoli Diary*. As a precaution, he had written to Churchill to ask him, in his capacity as Secretary of State for War, to approve the disclosure of official documents.[12] Churchill did not feel he could personally give permission on behalf of the War Office, although he tacitly encouraged Hamilton to proceed without formal sanction, noting that he did 'not see any reason why you should not publish' or why 'any serious objection could be entertained'.[13] Hamilton's memoir printed numerous official telegrams, most of them verbatim, and no official objections were ever raised.

Gallipoli Diary, like Fisher's memoirs, established an important precedent for the publication of confidential wartime material. The admiral had also quoted extensively from official documents, including Hankey's jealously guarded War Council minutes, and the Admiralty in particular was upset about the extent of his unauthorized revelations. According to the DNI, Fisher should not have 'disclosed matters which it is of such paramount importance to preserve secret'.[14] The Board of Admiralty concluded, however, that no action should be taken against the admiral, as this would only draw unwanted attention to his indiscretions.[15] Other memoirs published immediately after the war—including volumes by Jellicoe, French, Robertson, and Callwell—also revealed information that was considered secret, and no action was taken against any of these authors either. This suited Churchill nicely. The more classified material that entered the public domain, the stronger his own claim to publish official documents.

The government was seemingly content to drift along without any settled policy on this issue, although, in January 1922, a former parliamentary secretary to the wartime Ministry of Shipping forced the Cabinet's hand by seeking formal approval to publish two of his own Cabinet memoranda.[16] An adverse decision would have been a serious blow to Churchill's plans, and he admitted afterwards that he had watched the Cabinet discussion that day 'with some anxiety'.[17] However, his colleagues were 'generally' sympathetic to the idea that ministers should be allowed to publish wartime documents to defend themselves against unfair public criticism. Lloyd George, the Prime Minister, was hardly a disinterested party. He had recently been offered an advance of £50,000 for his own memoirs, and it was thus not in his interest to close the door on the publication of official wartime documents.[18] Nor were ministers unaware that Churchill would take full advantage of a favourable ruling, as he was then unhappy about a recent book by Lord Esher, which contained an unflattering and inaccurate account of the origins of his mission to Antwerp in 1914.[19] The Cabinet decided to set up a committee to establish a set of rules for future guidance, although this body never actually met.[20] For Churchill, the Cabinet's 'general sympathy' amounted to a tacit acceptance of his right to quote official documents in self-defence. On this basis, he evidently decided it was safe to include confidential material in his memoirs without first obtaining formal permission.

Churchill originally planned to publish two volumes covering his time as First Lord of the Admiralty and Chancellor of the Duchy of Lancaster, which would allow him to conclude the work with the decision to evacuate the Gallipoli peninsula in late 1915. However, these were not to be straightforward memoirs. He intended to supplement his 'personal narrative' with historical material on the origins of the war and with accounts of events and operations in which he had been only peripherally involved.[21] But the books could not be produced quickly, as Churchill held high office from the end of the war until October 1922, first as Secretary of State for War and Air and then, from February 1921 on, as Colonial Secretary. Compiling the necessary documentation for the volumes was not difficult, however. Churchill already possessed a large collection of official and unofficial records from his time in office, and to these were added the documents he had collected while preparing his evidence for the Dardanelles Commission. As a minister of the crown and former First Lord, Churchill had little difficulty gaining access to additional material held by the Admiralty and the Cabinet Office. And he did not hesitate to call on officials across Whitehall for assistance, which was usually forthcoming. He submitted queries and circulated draft chapters to former colleagues at the Admiralty, including Oliver and Bartolomé; to Edmonds and Aspinall-Oglander at the CID's Historical Office; and to officials like Sir James Headlam-Morley, the historical adviser to the Foreign Office, who provided Churchill with extensive material on the diplomatic background to the war. When Churchill wanted information on the policy of the Greek government in 1915, he wrote directly to Eleftherios Venizelos, the former Greek Prime Minister. And to ensure the books' technical accuracy, he took on a naval adviser, Vice-Admiral Thomas Jackson, a former DNO and DNI, who was then on half-pay.[22]

The first volume of Churchill's memoirs was published in the United States, Canada, Britain, and Australia in April 1923 as *The World Crisis*, after first being serialized by *The Times* in Britain and by several Canadian newspapers.[23] It attracted widespread interest and became an immediate best-seller in Britain. Although this volume only covered events up to the end of 1914, Churchill was already laying the groundwork for his treatment of the Dardanelles campaign in his second volume. This meant demolishing the popular idea that the early defeats Churchill presided over—Antwerp, the loss of the three cruisers, and the Battle of Coronel—established a pattern of domineering behaviour and poor judgement on his part that would resurface later with the Dardanelles. These early episodes therefore received careful attention, albeit with mixed results. Churchill was in a strong position to defend his part in the loss of Cradock's squadron, since the mistakes made by the Admiralty could be attributed, for the most part, to poor staff work, where the main culprits were Battenberg and Sturdee, then Chief of the Admiralty War Staff. But Churchill unwisely glossed over these mistakes and placed virtually all the blame on Cradock.[24] His criticisms were largely justified, but Churchill's ungenerous treatment of a gallant admiral who had been killed in action after seeking out and engaging a superior force did him little credit, and elicited protests from naval officers eager to defend Cradock's reputation.

Churchill's treatment of Antwerp was more successful.[25] He carefully laid out the strategic context for the decision to attempt to hold the city, making it appear a logical and worthwhile endeavour. More importantly for his own reputation, he was able to show that he had not foisted the idea of sending Allied troops on unwilling or uninformed colleagues, as his critics alleged. The plan to raise a large Anglo-French force for the city had preceded Churchill's mission, and was supported by British and French military leaders, including Kitchener. Churchill also included the text of his telegram to the War Minister from Antwerp on 3 October 1914, in which he instructed that the Admiralty should be ordered to send the two naval brigades to Antwerp *minus recruits*.[26] Finally, he made a persuasive case that the decision to prolong Antwerp's defence had produced important (albeit unintended) benefits, even though the city had ultimately fallen to the Germans. By delaying the release of the large German forces around Antwerp, Churchill maintained that the enemy had been prevented from capturing the Channel ports. 'I cannot feel', he concluded, 'that I deserve the reproaches and foolish fictions which have been so long freely and ignorantly heaped upon me.'[27] His treatment of the loss of *Aboukir, Cressy,* and *Hogue* was even more effective, as he was able to reproduce his clear warning about the unnecessary risks being run by these ships. The allegation that he had overruled his advisers and sent the ships to their certain doom clearly could not be sustained. Unlike Antwerp and Coronel, which are still cited as evidence of Churchill's bad judgement and interference, the loss of the three cruisers is now largely forgotten.

Churchill was the first major British politician to publish his war memoirs, and each succeeding volume of *The World Crisis* was prominently reviewed in the British press. The first instalment made a strong and generally favourable impression. The *Observer*, for example, described it as 'the best book about the war by any leading figure in it, at home or abroad. Amongst the shoal of other narratives and apologies on the British side, it is like a whale amongst the minnows, and some of his most confident and vehement critics—especially in the Antwerp business—are sent to the bottom by the whacks of his tail.'[28] Churchill's decision to include a large selection of official documents added considerably to the book's impact. The *Manchester Guardian* noted that Churchill had 'carried off a trunkful of Admiralty archives, and here they are the "exhibits" in court, with Mr. Churchill saying blandly, "You may not believe me, but here are the documents; what do you say to these?"'[29] But Churchill's publication of confidential records, which far exceeded that by any other public figure to date, also provoked controversy. Questions were immediately raised in

Parliament both as to the propriety and the legality of an ex-Cabinet minister publishing—and profiting from—the publication of restricted information. The matter was raised on several occasions from February to April 1923, and suggestions were made in the House of Commons that Churchill should be investigated for breaching the Official Secrets Act; that some of the profits from *The World Crisis* should be paid to the Treasury or donated to charity; and that the government should take steps to prevent the further publication of official documents.[30]

Churchill initially brushed these complaints aside on the dubious grounds that the material he covered in his first volume had already been 'fully dealt with' in Corbett's official history. But this hardly addressed the ethical and legal considerations being discussed in Parliament. Bonar Law, the Conservative Prime Minister, was not mollified.[31] He suggested in the House of Commons that Churchill might have breached his Privy Councillor's oath by publishing confidential documents, a charge that Churchill considered 'crude and uncalled for'.[32] But when he learned that the Cabinet was setting up a new committee to consider the publication of official material, Churchill realized he had to take the issue seriously. The second volume of *The World Crisis* was due to be published later that same year, and a government ban on the publication of official documents at this stage would be disastrous. His first step was to coordinate his efforts with Lloyd George, who had signed a lucrative contract before leaving office to publish his own memoirs. At the end of February, Churchill protested to the former Prime Minister that it was 'far too late in the day for the Government to draw up a new strict code of rules applicable to the war period. The position is governed by the precedents which, for good or ill, have been established.'[33] Churchill proposed that Lloyd George appeal to Hankey along these lines.

Churchill laid out his case a few days later in a long letter to Bonar Law. His principal defence was that he was not the first to print secret documents. Fisher and Hamilton had both done so in their memoirs. And so had Sir George Arthur and Charles Bean. The former's biography of Lord Kitchener included, among other documents, excerpts from a Cabinet memorandum penned by Churchill; the latter's official history quoted verbatim not only Admiralty telegrams drafted by Churchill but also private letters written by Churchill to French. The memoirs of other admirals and generals, even though not quoting directly from official documents, had also revealed secret information. In no instance had the government of the day taken action, he correctly pointed out, and it could not be claimed that he had broken any rules. What really mattered, however, was whether he would be allowed to *continue* publishing official documents. Churchill's case here rested on the fact that this type of material had previously been used to attack him without any official sanctions against the authors. It would be unfair, he argued, to deprive him of the right to defend himself 'after every naval or military personage concerned has had fullest latitude conceded to him'. This was an exaggeration, although it certainly was true that Churchill had been more heavily criticized than any other wartime minister. He could reasonably claim therefore that it was 'only by publishing certain documents and telegrams which I have written myself and for which I bear the prime responsibility, that I can deal with the lies and fictions which have ruled for so long and which I have borne all these years without making any reply, while every other version has been put before the public'.[34]

Hankey confirmed that these claims, though sometimes exaggerated, were generally accurate. He also reminded the Prime Minister that previous Cabinets had always decided not to interfere with the publication of confidential wartime material. Hankey, who may already have been contemplating his own memoirs, seems to have been sympathetic to Churchill's position. He suggested, however, that the government might want to establish a policy for future guidance, in which case Churchill's letter should be circulated to ministers for consideration before any decision was taken.[35] In the event, nothing appears to have come from this proposal. Bonar Law was by now seriously ill and Stanley Baldwin succeeded him as Prime Minister in May, by which time the parliamentary controversy over divulging government documents had largely subsided. Churchill therefore saw no need to modify the second volume of *The World Crisis*, covering the year 1915, and it was published as planned in October 1923. In his preface, he rehearsed his case for publishing official documents, saying it was 'absurd' to suggest that they must be withheld, 'or that obligations of secrecy are violated by their disclosure in good faith'.[36] Churchill sent a copy of the book to Hankey, who noted in his reply that the new volume had led to further grumbling about his lavish use of official documents. 'I wonder', Hankey noted ruefully, 'if, another time, you could not get formal authority to use them! But I expect you weighed all this [before publishing].'[37]

Most of the second volume of *The World Crisis* was taken up with the Dardanelles and Gallipoli campaigns. Churchill's case here closely paralleled the one he had presented to the Dardanelles Commission six years before, and in places he incorporated his written statements for the Commission directly into his text. At the same time, he attempted to correct what he regarded as the main deficiency of the Commission's interim report—the suggestion that his naval advisers did not wholly support the naval offensive when he took the project to the War Council on 13 January. The commissioners had seemingly disregarded the evidence that tended to support Churchill's version of events, and he sought to rectify this by stating that, at every step in the process, his advisers were informed and supportive. Thus, he claimed that his initial telegram to Carden on 3 January was sent 'with the active agreement of Lord Fisher' and after consultation with Henry Jackson. On 5 January, he reported that Carden's proposal was 'viewed with favour both by Admiral Oliver, the Chief of the Staff, and by Sir Henry Jackson'. And he wrote that Fisher saw (and therefore implicitly approved) his telegram of 5 January to Carden asking for a detailed plan to be drawn up. Up to this point, he claimed, the First Sea Lord had expressed no opinion on the technical merits of the scheme, but he nevertheless 'seemed at this time not merely to favour the enterprise in principle, but to treat it almost as a matter practically decided'.[38]

Churchill also mistakenly claimed that he had read out Carden's telegram of 5 January to a meeting of the War Council that afternoon, when 'the question of an attack on Turkey and a diversion in the Near East was one of the principal subjects discussed'. According to Churchill's account, 'Every one seemed alive to all its advantages, and Admiral Carden's telegram . . . was heard with extreme interest.'[39] In fact, there was no War Council that day. This passage may have been a deliberate deception on Churchill's part, as one writer recently suggested.[40] It was certainly to his advantage to suggest that he had political backing for the project at this early date. On the other hand, it is possible that Churchill was mistakenly referring to a Cabinet meeting the following day or the War Council of 7 January.[41]

When Churchill came to the plan Carden submitted to the Admiralty on 11–12 January, he wrote that Fisher and Oliver both 'seemed favourable to it'. Churchill may have been overstating his case, although it is only fair to note that there is no documentary evidence to contradict his claims. And even if he did exaggerate the support he received, he was probably correct in saying that none of his leading naval advisers explicitly warned him against the project. 'No one', he stated, 'of the four or five great naval authorities, each with his technical staff who was privy said,

"This is absurd. Ships cannot fight forts", or criticised its details. On the contrary, they all treated it as an extremely interesting and hopeful proposal; and there grew up in the secret circles at the Admiralty a perfectly clear opinion favourable to the operation.' This was demonstrated, he argued, by the War Staff's suggestion that the *Queen Elizabeth* be added to Carden's fleet.[42]

Fisher's death in 1920 gave Churchill greater freedom to reveal the admiral's erratic behaviour as First Sea Lord, but in the main he treated the admiral gently. He may have calculated that readers would be more impressed by magnanimity towards a departed colleague than by criticism, although it is just as likely that he was animated by a lingering affection for his friend. Whatever the reason, Churchill's case did not depend on scapegoating Fisher. And destroying the credibility of someone he had gone to such lengths to appoint as First Sea Lord was not necessarily in his own best interest either. Churchill was, nevertheless, eager to refute persistent claims that Fisher had warned him the naval attack was doomed. He printed the admiral's memorandum of 25 January, but also included his detailed response, showing that Fisher's concerns about the strength of Jellicoe's fleet in the North Sea were unjustified. He then turned to the idea that he had worn down opponents of the project by his enthusiasm and persuasiveness. Churchill was ready to admit to himself that it had been a mistake to pressure Fisher to agree to the project on 28 January, as the admiral had never really given the offensive his full support in the months that followed.[43] But he was still committed to the position he had taken at the Dardanelles Commission, that Fisher had thrown himself behind the offensive '*totus porcus*'. Churchill therefore argued that he had been justified in proceeding with the operation despite Fisher's obvious reservations. He pointed out, first, that the admiral had been unable to counter his arguments in favour of the operation. And he suggested that it was reasonable to press for the adoption of a scheme in which he and others believed. The position of First Sea Lord inevitably involved great pressure, he reminded his readers, especially in wartime. Fisher had a duty to stand up against an operation if he truly did not believe in it, and he had not done so. Nor did he need to resign, or even threaten to resign, to get his way. He could have scuttled the naval operation at any time during the planning stage simply by refusing to sign the necessary orders.[44]

It was only when Churchill turned to Fisher's behaviour around the time of his resignation that he intimated the admiral was not fit to hold his position. The First Sea Lord, he recorded, was under 'considerable strain' by May 1915. 'His seventy-four years lay heavy upon him.' To illustrate this point, Churchill recalled that when he had to visit Paris shortly before the political crisis erupted, Fisher, who remained in London, 'had shown great nervous exhaustion. He had evinced unconcealed distress and anxiety at being left alone in sole charge of the Admiralty. There is no doubt that the old Admiral was worried almost out of his wits by the immense pressure of the times.'[45] Fisher's instability was obvious to Clementine Churchill, who lunched with the admiral while her husband was in Paris. She recalled years later that she found Fisher afterward 'lurking in the passage':

> She asked him what he wanted, whereupon, in a brusque and somewhat incoherent manner he told her that, while she no doubt was under the impression that Winston was conferring with Sir John French, he was in fact frolicking with a mistress in Paris! Clementine was much taken aback, but treated this interesting piece of information with the scorn it deserved. 'Be quiet, you silly old man', she said, 'and get out.'[46]

Churchill must have also heard disquieting accounts of Fisher's behaviour from Admiralty officials. An early draft of this chapter stated that during Churchill's absence from the Admiralty, Oliver 'had found difficulty in securing from him [Fisher] the necessary signatures for such action as had to be taken. On more than one occasion his Confidential Secretary (Captain Crease) had written the essential initials himself.'[47]

Churchill had fewer reservations about criticizing de Robeck's decision to call off the naval attack after 18 March. The admiral's action had been perfectly reasonable. He had, after all, lost around a third of his fleet for no appreciable gain; the naval offensive would have to be delayed for several weeks anyway to allow for the minesweepers to be reorganized; and a substantial body of troops would soon be available. Everything pointed towards a suspension of the fleet's offensive, but Churchill was not prepared to admit this. His entire defence rested on the idea that the naval offensive could have succeeded, and was on the verge of success when it was called off. He had thoroughly convinced himself by now that the navy *would* have broken through the enemy's defences if de Robeck had but resumed the offensive. He therefore attempted to convince readers that de Robeck not only made the wrong decision, but that he made it for the wrong reasons. De Robeck's telegram of 27 March outlining his reasons for suspending the naval attack was printed in full, but Churchill did not examine the merits of de Robeck's case. Instead, he suggested that the admiral had called things off because he was temperamentally incapable of facing further losses. According to Churchill, de Robeck acted from an irrational attachment to the old ships under his command, which he regarded as 'sacred':

> The discredit and even disgrace of casting away a ship was ingrained deeply by years of mental training and outlook. The spectacle of this noble structure . . . foundering miserably beneath the waves, appeared as an event shocking and unnatural in its character. . . . Admiral de Robeck was saddened and consternated to the foundations of his being [by the losses of 18 March].[48]

Churchill insisted that these losses were relatively trivial, amounting to fewer than thirty British lives and 'two or three worthless ships'. And this assessment is not altogether wrong. But the question facing de Robeck in March 1915 was whether the resumption of the naval offensive stood a better prospect of success if supported by troops. The admiral reached the obvious conclusion that it would, but Churchill implied that, in doing so, de Robeck cast away a golden opportunity and must share responsibility for the casualties later suffered by the army.

While de Robeck bore the brunt of Churchill's displeasure, the admiral's decision not to renew the naval offensive was treated as symptomatic of a wider failure within the upper ranks of the Royal Navy. The service was divided, Churchill maintained, into two schools of thought during the war. The first, which included senior figures like de Robeck and Jellicoe, was wanting in initiative and fighting spirit. Members of this group, branded the 'negative school' of admirals, were reluctant to run risks and lose ships, preferring to maintain a passive strategy at sea while the army secured victory on land at great cost. The ascendency of this school within the navy led to failure at the Dardanelles, indecision at the Battle of Jutland, and near disaster from German submarines in 1917. The second school of thought, which Churchill described approvingly as the 'forward school', was eager to take bold offensive measures to weaken the enemy using the navy's 'surplus' forces. This group was represented by officers like David Beatty, who commanded the Battle Cruiser Force (and later the entire Grand Fleet), and by Commodore (later Rear-Admiral) Roger Keyes, who had championed a renewal of the Dardanelles offensive and later led the famous Zeebrugge raid. Churchill proclaimed that these figures represented the 'true war spirit of the Navy'.[49]

Churchill's case—that the naval offensive could have succeeded—rested on three interlocking arguments. The first was that naval gunfire could have neutralized the enemy forts. Churchill naturally wanted to dispel the idea that he had pressed for a naval assault because he naively and mistakenly believed that the Turkish forts could be as easily destroyed as the Belgian defences had been the previous year. To support this argument, he reproduced the memorandum Sir Arthur Wilson had submitted to the Dardanelles Commission in 1916 to rebut the gunnery evidence from army witnesses. This allowed him to develop a persuasive case that the fleet's guns could have accomplished their objectives—all that was needed was sufficient ammunition and effective aerial spotting. However, Churchill did not consider how, even if the forts were silenced, the other obstacles blocking the fleet's advance would have been overcome. He brushed this problem aside by developing his second argument, borrowed from the Mitchell Report, that all aspects of the Ottoman defences—forts, mines, field guns, and howitzers—were 'mutually dependent'. 'So long as all four factors stood together', he asserted, 'the defences constituted a formidable obstruction. But not one could stand by itself, and if one were broken down, its fall entailed the collapse of the others.'[50] This reduced Churchill's problem to manageable proportions by allowing him to focus on the area where the fleet had the best prospects of success.

His third argument was that the forts' heavy guns were critically short of ammunition. Churchill had believed this to be true in 1915, and used Captain Hall's testimony to make this case to the Dardanelles Commission in 1916. In his memoirs, he backed up his claim with figures taken, without attribution, from the Mitchell Report, a highly confidential *post-war* document from which he should not have been quoting. The Mitchell Committee's sources included a variety of Turkish and German authorities, although they did not agree on the number of rounds available after the attack of 18 March. Churchill cautiously estimated that the Ottomans possessed around forty to sixty rounds for their heaviest guns (35.5 cm). He also noted that the enemy's smaller guns and howitzers had reportedly used about half their ammunition, although he admitted that they were better stocked than their heavier counterparts. On the basis of the estimates compiled by the Mitchell Committee, Churchill concluded that the forts could only have sustained their resistance for two more days of heavy fighting.[51] Thus, de Robeck only had to go on attacking and the enemy's forts would have soon fallen silent, which in turn would have allowed the minefields to be cleared. This conclusion was bolstered by the interviews the Mitchell Committee conducted after the war with Turkish and German officers. However, as noted in Chapter 13, their opinion was about evenly split as to the likelihood of the fleet breaking through the Narrows. Churchill manipulated this evidence to paint a more optimistic picture. He excluded, for example, much of the testimony that did not support his position. He cited the views of all five of the informants who predicted a naval victory, but only two of the five who thought it unlikely.[52] He also printed the favourable conclusions of one Turkish officer about whom the Mitchell Committee had concluded that 'no weight can be given to his opinions'.[53] This created the impression that the balance of opinion was markedly in Churchill's favour. Furthermore, he quoted from interviews in the Mitchell Report suggesting that the passage of the fleet into the Sea of Marmara would have forced the Ottomans to abandon the Gallipoli peninsula and, in Souchon's opinion, would have sparked a revolution at Constantinople.

In addition to the Mitchell Report, Churchill supported his case for renewing the naval offensive by citing the views of a German officer, Major Franz Carl Endres, who had been chief of staff for the First Turkish Army. Churchill sent Endres a questionnaire through a friend on the Inter-Allied Commission of Control in Berlin, and was so pleased with the answers that they were printed at length in *The World Crisis*, even after Edmonds informed him that Endres had not actually served at Gallipoli.[54] But it is easy to see why Churchill could not resist publishing this material. Endres confidently pronounced that the 'situation was most critical for the Turks immediately after March 18....If on the 19th or 20th a fresh attack with all available forces had been made, it would probably have succeeded.' He also confirmed Churchill's estimate of the ammunition situation, stating that 'supply was so short that it would not have sufficed for a second engagement on a large scale'.[55]

Churchill could never hope to prove conclusively that a renewed naval offensive would have succeeded, and he acknowledged in 1923 that his case was necessarily speculative. He nevertheless marshalled the evidence with considerable skill and made out a persuasive argument that it *might* have succeeded, which was the best he could hope to accomplish in the circumstances. When he subsequently turned to the origins of the land campaign, he sought to deflect criticism in a number of ways. First, by emphasizing the chaotic and haphazard decision-making system that had led to the army's commitment. The land offensive had never received the full and careful consideration that such a major campaign required, and for this he suggested that 'there can be no defence except human infirmity'. In other words, the government had simply drifted into the land operations: '[S]o obliquely were [the] issues presented, so baffling were the personal factors involved, that the War Council were drawn insensibly and irresistibly into the gulf.'[56] Second, Churchill attempted to shift responsibility for this unhealthy state of affairs to Asquith and Kitchener. Although he did not openly attack either one, his narrative made it clear that the Prime Minister had failed to impose order on the decision-making process, and that Kitchener had marginalized both the War Council and the general staff at the War Office. This allowed Churchill to depict himself, to some extent, as the victim of a dysfunctional process he could not control. This point was nicely reinforced by his account of his clash with Kitchener over the release of the 29th Division. It did not hurt his case that the Dardanelles Commission had already publicly censured the field marshal for this delay.

The fighting on the Gallipoli peninsula occupies several chapters of *The World Crisis*, and, not surprisingly, Hamilton's reputation emerges without a scratch. Churchill's account of the land campaign emphasized the difficulties the general faced and the inadequate resources devoted to the theatre, while largely ignoring Hamilton's mistakes and shifting the blame for operational failures to subordinate commanders like the much-maligned Lieutenant-General Sir Frederick Stopford.[57] And, like Hamilton in *Gallipoli Diary*, Churchill argued that the land campaign had come close to success on more than one occasion. Thus, from the climax of the naval assault until the final evacuation of the Gallipoli peninsula, the war in the east was characterized as a succession of 'fatal missed chances'. 'One sees in retrospect', he concluded, 'at least a dozen situations all beyond the control of the enemy, any one of which, decided differently, would have ensured success.'[58] Failure arose, in Churchill's account, from a combination of bad luck, misplaced priorities, and mistakes by commanders on the spot, rather than from any fundamental flaw in the underlying strategy.

The second volume of *The World Crisis*, like the first, was generally well received by the press and public. Churchill had the satisfaction of seeing his case widely disseminated and his documents, if not always his interpretations, frequently cited. Until the British archives for the First World War were opened to historians in the late 1960s, *The World Crisis* and the Dardanelles Commission Report were virtually the only public sources of documentation about the origins of the Dardanelles offensive. Churchill continued to gather information about the Ottoman side of the campaign in the years that followed, although not all of it was to his liking. Shortly after publication, he received a letter from Otto Liman von Sanders, the

German general who had commanded the Ottoman Army during the Gallipoli campaign. Liman disagreed with the main arguments in *The World Crisis* about the prospects of the naval offensive. He predicted that a renewed attack after 18 March would have failed, since the minefield was still intact and the forts and minefield batteries still had 'plentiful provisions of ammunition':

> Nobody can of course express with a full certainty, if an early third or fourth attack by the Fleet would have had better chances of success, as the heavy batteries built deeply into the ground would have only had left trifling provisions of munitions. But undoubtedly all field batteries of the 3rd Army Corps which were available in any way, were drawn on the heights west of the Straits and defended the mining barrage with all their might.

Liman noted next that, even if the fleet had reached the Sea of Marmara, it would still have had to overcome the German–Ottoman fleet before it could attempt to reach Constantinople. And an Allied victory in the Marmara would still not have ended the fighting. Constantinople was also well protected, as 'all possibly feasible means of defence' had been prepared for the 'most remote possibility' of a British breakthrough. 'I can express this certainly with the utmost assurance', he added, 'as I had arranged everything myself.' Finally, Liman maintained that the Ottoman Empire would not have been knocked out of the war by the appearance of an enemy fleet at Constantinople. 'There could be no danger of a revolution', he asserted. 'The strong bodies of troops [defending the capital] were quite reliable and in safe hands. It is undoubtedly true that there were also at Constantinople nervous and unfaithful people who wrote or talked about coming disturbances, but these individuals were without any power.'

The only encouraging note in the general's letter was the opinion that victory might more easily have been achieved on land. 'Often', he wrote, 'the decision hung indeed on a knife's edge.'[59] But this was probably small consolation to Churchill, who could not have been happy to have his arguments about the naval offensive disputed by such an eminent and well-placed German officer. Liman intimated that he would be happy to communicate further with Churchill on this subject, but Churchill did not take up the offer. He was undoubtedly relieved to discover two and a half years later that one of Liman's staff officers, Carl Mühlmann, took a more sanguine view of the fleet's chances. In early 1927, Edmonds alerted Churchill to Mühlmann's volume on the Dardanelles campaign in the official German history of the war.[60] This account stated that, at the end of

18 March, 'Most of the Turkish ammunition had been expended.' Mühlmann recorded that 271 shells were available for the heaviest (35.5 cm) Ottoman guns, around 50 rounds per gun, which accorded with the figures in the Mitchell Report that had provided the basis for Churchill's estimate of 40–60 rounds per gun. But the German account added a new twist. Mühlmann suggested that there was an even more serious shortage, specifically of long-range high explosive shells, the only type of shell that was effective against armoured warships. One fort was down to just ten rounds, he claimed, and another to seventeen. In addition, he noted that the Ottomans had, by this time, depleted their reserve of mines.[61] This was more to Churchill's liking, as it suggested the ammunition shortage was even more serious than he originally thought.

Churchill put this new information to use in 1930, when he was commissioned to write a series of articles for *Colliers* in the United States on the 'Crucial Crises of the War'. One instalment was devoted to the Dardanelles campaign, and Churchill used the opportunity to recast his case for a resumption of the naval attack in much stronger terms than he had employed in *The World Crisis*.[62] On the basis of Mühlmann's new evidence, Churchill proclaimed that, after the attack of 18 March 'the door [of the Straits] was open . . . We had only to resume a gradual naval advance and bombardment to discover the wonderful truth that they had, in fact, scarcely any more ammunition. We now know what we could have so easily found out then, that for the heavy guns which alone could injure the armoured ships, they had not twenty rounds apiece.' He also suggested, rather more spuriously, that the enemy's minefields no longer constituted a serious obstacle. If de Robeck had made another attempt to sweep the channel, Churchill wrote, he would have discovered that 'there were no more mines'. This implied that the minefields had somehow disappeared following the British attack, which was certainly not the case. Churchill subsequently indicated that he was referring to *reserves* of mines, which might have been used to replenish swept mines, but this would not have been apparent to most of his readers.[63] The Kephez minefield actually remained a formidable obstacle after 18 March, as Churchill would have known from the Mitchell Report. The Mitchell Committee's investigation found that, on 18 March, the Allied fleet faced 344 mines in 11 lines, and revealed that this number had subsequently *increased*. Drawing on Turkish sources, it reported that two short new lines were added 'very soon' after the attack of 18 March; two 'deep minefields' were laid in May and June against submarines, and another in August; and two more lines were provided against ships in September and December 1915, raising the total to 512 mines in 18 lines.[64] Churchill, however, was eager to paint a different picture. To this end, he reproduced a passage from Aspinall's official history suggesting that the enemy's minefields were in a bad state when the naval attack was called off:

> Of the nine [sic] rows of mines many had been in position for six months, and a large proportion of these were believed to have sunk to such a depth that ships would not have touched them. For the rest, many were of the old patterns and not at all trustworthy, and owing to the shortage of numbers they were at an average ninety yards apart, more than three times the beam of a ship.[65]

This picture was reinforced later in the article when Churchill asserted that, after 18 March, the power of the 'Turkish forts *and minefields* . . . to stop the advance of the armoured ships was gone'.[66]

This new article also provided Churchill with an opportunity to strengthen the idea that the successful passage of the Straits would have meant the collapse of Ottoman resistance. He did this by arguing that a naval breakthrough would have caused the enemy to abandon the Gallipoli peninsula and driven the Ottoman government out of Constantinople. Three sources are cited to back up this claim. The first is a statement attributed to Liman that: 'If the Straits had fallen the Turkish military forces would have retired across the Bosphorous into Asia Minor.' 'No one', Churchill asserted, 'can dispute the authority of Liman von Sanders.' The other sources were the American ambassador at Constantinople, Henry Morgenthau, and the German ambassador, both of whom recorded plans to move the Sultan and the government to Asia Minor if the fleet broke through. Morgenthau went even further and suggested that there would have been a revolution in Constantinople and the city would have surrendered immediately to the British fleet. Churchill clearly wanted readers to take these statements as fact rather than speculation. He therefore described his sources as 'unchallengeable authorities', and immediately moved on to discuss the immense advantages that would have accrued from an Allied victory—the war would have ended in 1915, saving millions of lives on both sides of the conflict, and the Bolshevik seizure of power in Russia would have been averted! But this line of causality hinged on an Ottoman collapse flowing inevitably from the entry of an Allied fleet into the Sea of Marmara. Furthermore, the *evacuation* of the government is not the same as *capitulation*.

Churchill depended on his readers not looking critically at his evidence or his argument. He was well aware, moreover, both from Liman's private letter of 1923 and the general's earlier memoirs, that this 'indisputable' source did *not* believe that a naval breakthrough would have led to an Ottoman collapse.

This new treatment of the Dardanelles differed from *The World Crisis* in two other notable ways. First, Churchill elaborated on his argument that if any one aspect of the Ottoman defences had broken down, the whole system would have collapsed. The flaw in his logic now became clear. Churchill assumed that the mobile guns and howitzers protecting the minefields could have been located and destroyed by naval gunfire once the heavy guns in the forts were neutralized. But, as Churchill himself noted, the enemy's 'mobile armament' was 'hidden in ravines, in groves, in marshes, behind hummocks, here, there and everywhere, in every unexpected corner and valley'.[67] These guns were very difficult to locate, and even harder to hit with low trajectory naval guns. By 18 March, de Robeck had accepted that this problem was insoluble. Churchill did not realize—or was not prepared to admit—that putting the Ottoman forts out of action would not have made any appreciable difference to the volume of fire that could be brought to bear on Allied minesweepers.

Second, Churchill sharpened his criticisms of de Robeck, who had died in 1928. In *The World Crisis* the admiral was castigated mainly for his sentimental attachment to old warships. Churchill now suggested that this state of mind was a by-product of de Robeck's intellectual shortcoming. De Robeck, he wrote, was not 'a man of exceptional force of intellect', nor was he 'among the leading minds in the naval service':

> Above all, like so many pre-war Admirals, he had not studied the art of war very deeply.... The larger issues of war in general or of the Great War itself were to a serious extent beyond his compass. He had not ever received any training comparable to that of a General Staff officer. He never revealed any of that capacity for seeing the whole vast problem of the war in its true proportion, and for balancing effectively one set of risks against another. To him the care of his ships was a scared trust.

This flaw resulted, according to Churchill, in de Robeck recoiling from any further operations in the Strait after 18 March. 'He just sat down and watched', Churchill complained, 'or fetched and carried the Army to and fro, waiting there, a passive spectator, month after month, until finally the whole enterprise ended in a complete disaster.'[68]

The following year, Churchill's American and British publishers decided to produce a single-volume abridged edition of *The World Crisis*.[69] Churchill took advantage of this opportunity to make changes and small additions to the original text. Most of the new material from the *Colliers* article did not make it into the revised edition of the book, with one notable exception. The section describing the shortage of ammunition for the enemy's heavy guns and the virtual disappearance of the mine obstacle was incorporated directly into the new text, while the less persuasive evidence Churchill had previously relied on—the Mitchell Report and the Endres' questionnaire— was dropped.[70] A large audience was therefore exposed to Churchill's more dramatic, but less reliable, claims. The one-volume edition of *The World Crisis* was published in 1931 in the United States, Britain, and Canada, and even greater exposure was achieved for the new account when George Newnes produced an illustrated version of *The World Crisis* in 1933–4 (as *The Great War*). This work initially appeared in magazine format in 26 biweekly instalments, with average sales of over 43,000 copies. Unsold copies were subsequently bound to produce 3,000 collections. In addition, both the one-volume and illustrated editions were widely translated. The first edition of *The World Crisis* had been published during the 1920s in France, Germany, and Italy. Over the next decade, the revised editions were published in Denmark, Norway, Sweden, Japan, Czechoslovakia, and Yugoslavia.[71] Curiously, however, when Odhams published a cheap edition of *The World Crisis* in 1939, Churchill incorporated some of the new material from the 1931 abridged edition, but not the passages relating to the Ottoman ammunition shortage, which remained unchanged from the 1923 edition.[72]

The World Crisis was, in every sense, a triumph for Churchill. His decision to turn his personal memoir into a quasi-history of the First World War had been shrewd. The books appealed to a wider audience than the standard political memoir, while his personal role in the higher direction of the war and access to official documents set his work apart from the run-of-the-mill general histories of the war. This, along with his widely acknowledged skill with the pen, allowed him to present his case to an unusually large audience—and make a great deal of money in the process!

Churchill was fortunate, moreover, that he avoided becoming embroiled in controversy with any of his former colleagues in the Liberal government. The first ex-minister to publish his memoirs after Churchill was Edward Grey (now Viscount Grey of Fallodon) in 1925. Although Grey dealt only briefly with the Dardanelles, he decisively rejected the idea that Churchill

was solely responsible for initiating the campaign, and asserted that success
had been possible. 'The real defence' of the operation, he wrote, 'was that it
very nearly did succeed as planned.' Grey also defended Churchill over
Antwerp, noting that Churchill was responsible for the decision to travel
to the city, but also that this movement 'was part of a concerted plan, and
not the mere madcap exploit of passion for adventure, which it was for
some time afterwards assumed to be'.[73] Asquith's memoirs followed in 1928.
The former Prime Minister's name was not widely associated with the failure at the Dardanelles, but he had been tarred with the same brush as
Churchill in the Dardanelles Commission Report, and he saw the advantage
of mirroring Churchill's broad defence when he came to address the campaign. Asquith's account focused on the critical meetings of 28 January.
'I assert unhesitatingly', he wrote, 'that at this time the whole of our expert
naval opinion was in favour of a naval operation.' He acknowledged that
Fisher had disliked the idea, but pointed out that the admiral's opinion, 'as
he told me that same morning, was not based upon the technical or strategic demerits of a Dardanelles operation, but upon the fact that he preferred
another and totally different objective in the Baltic'.[74] Lloyd George, the last
to publish, in 1933, also treated Churchill leniently. 'The Dardanelles failure',
he wrote, 'was due not so much to Mr. Churchill's precipitancy as to Lord
Kitchener's and Mr. Asquith's procrastination.'

> Mr. Churchill's part in that unfortunate enterprise had been worked out by
> him with the most meticulous care to the last particular, and nothing had been
> overlooked or neglected as far as the naval operations were concerned. The
> fatal delays and mishandlings had all been in the other branch of the Service.
> It is true that the conception of a one-sided Naval operation without simul-
> taneous military action was due to Mr. Churchill's impetuosity, but both the
> Prime Minister and Lord Kitchener were equally convinced that it was the
> right course to pursue.[75]

The naval memoirs published during this period also strengthened
Churchill's position. In this respect, he benefited from certain prominent
figures, notably Carden, de Robeck, and Henry Jackson, deciding not to
put forward their cases in print. Only two admirals associated with the
campaign published memoirs. The first, Rosslyn Wemyss, had succeeded de
Robeck as Commander-in-Chief of the Anglo-French naval forces at the
Dardanelles, and later served as First Sea Lord. Wemyss was hardly an
admirer of Churchill during the war. After Churchill's forced departure
from the Admiralty in May 1915, he had written that Churchill's 'name will

be handed down to posterity as that of a man who undertook an operation of whose requirements he was entirely ignorant'.[76] When it was rumoured that Lloyd George might reappoint Churchill as First Lord at the end of the war, Wemyss, then First Sea Lord, told Beatty that he would resign immediately 'on the grounds that I could not work with a man whose presence at the Admiralty I should consider a national danger'.[77] But his attitude towards Churchill softened somewhat after the war. When he met Churchill at a party in 1920, he wrote that: 'Winston was most captivating and extremely agreeable. The fact of the matter is that whatever disabilities he may have he is clever and imaginative.'[78] In his memoirs, published in 1924, Wemyss concluded that the idea of forcing the Straits was sound. Churchill's only mistake, in his opinion, was not directing 'all his talents and great energies' towards securing the troops to make it a combined operation from the outset. '[W]ho shall blame him', Wemyss asked, 'for this conception which, if properly carried out, would have led to such brilliant results?'[79] More importantly, Wemyss recounted his strong conviction in late 1915 that the evacuation of the peninsula would be a 'disastrous mistake'. He argued that the fleet stood a good chance of success if it had attempted once more to force a passage through the Dardanelles. Wemyss' verdict on Churchill was mixed, to be sure, but his vigorous advocacy of renewing the naval offensive added weight to Churchill's argument that naval success had been possible—all that was missing were the right men in charge.

Roger Keyes' *Naval Memoirs*, published in 1934, was a veritable windfall for Churchill. Keyes shared none of Wemyss' reservations about the naval offensive. He had been dismayed in March 1915 by the decision to suspend the naval attack; he believed the offensive could have been successfully renewed as early as April; he was appalled by the navy's relative inactivity after the army landed; and he had pressed hard for a fresh naval assault in late 1915 as an alternative to evacuation. Best of all, from Churchill's perspective, Keyes' opinions carried considerable weight. As chief of staff to Carden, de Robeck, and Wemyss, he obviously knew the campaign inside and out and was well qualified to address technical matters. Moreover, his famous Zeebrugge raid in 1918 had made him a popular hero. Keyes had gone on to a successful post-war career in the navy, rising to Admiral of the Fleet in 1930. In short, he was Churchill's perfect witness, not least because he was eager for Churchill's advice and approval when he came to write his memoirs. Keyes had provided feedback on drafts of *The World Crisis*, and the politician was only too happy to return the favour when Keyes turned to him for help in 1933. Their collaboration went smoothly. Keyes reassured Churchill at the outset that he planned to shape his account of the Dardanelles campaign to reinforce Churchill's main arguments in *The World Crisis*. Churchill had no cause to interfere with the book's contents. The only subject he seems to have had strong feelings about at this time was the treatment of Fisher.

Keyes' own animosity towards Fisher extended back to the pre-war period, and one of the questions on which he sought Churchill's advice was how to treat the former First Sea Lord. 'I want you to help me to put that old villain in his proper place in History', Keyes told his friend in November 1933.[80] Churchill had treated Fisher with great restraint over the years, but he was evidently no longer in a mood to be magnanimous. In 1927, Asquith had sent Churchill a copy of Fisher's ultimatum from May 1915 calling for Churchill's expulsion from both the Admiralty and the Cabinet, and by 1933 Churchill must have had some inkling of the extent of Fisher's animosity towards him when he resigned. Looking back, what bothered him most was that Fisher had not given the Dardanelles operation his full support after agreeing to it. And it must have rankled that he had upheld Fisher's claims to the contrary at the Dardanelles Commission and later in *The World Crisis*. 'It is a pretty poor game', Churchill told Keyes, 'when you have agreed to go with your chief into what is practically a battle, simply to wait about for an opportunity when things look black to ruin it all by desertion, and try to ride off by throwing the blame on him. This is what [Fisher] did, and what will damn him before history.'[81]

The other issue Churchill wanted to set straight was Fisher's supposed Baltic strategy. Churchill had supported these claims during the Dardanelles Commission as part of his bargain with Fisher, and he was unhappy that they had gained wide acceptance following the publication of Fisher's memoirs. Churchill had attempted to contest these claims when they were repeated in Bacon's biography of Fisher, published in 1929.[82] He published a moderate article in response, suggesting that the admiral had never really been serious about this project, but the idea did not go away. Churchill therefore proposed that Keyes should discredit the whole idea of a Baltic strategy by declaring, from the perspective of a former Director of Plans at the Admiralty, that such a scheme would never have survived the scrutiny of the Plans Division. But he also wanted Keyes to suggest that Fisher never actually meant to carry out the operation. 'If this was really Fisher's obsession', Churchill wrote, 'it would be pitiful that the fate of the Dardanelles campaign should have turned upon such moonshine.'

> I cannot help feeling from my knowledge of these matters that more practical and more personal motives animated and influenced the old admiral. He hated the Dardanelles but he was equally committed to it. Merely to turn back and desert the plan by itself was impossible. Naturally he laid the stress of these vague remote operations in the Baltic as the alternative which explained his action, though he would never have to carry it out.

Churchill next proposed that Keyes denounce Fisher's ultimatum to Asquith in May 1915 as evidence of the admiral's 'excitement, hysteria, megalomania'. These views were not only 'true and right', Churchill maintained, but also 'necessary in the public interest'. But he did not want Keyes to feel pressured to adopt his opinions: 'on no account', he concluded, 'write anything you do not feel the truth of'.[83]

In the event, Keyes passed quickly over Fisher's Baltic strategy in his memoirs. He took the position—which had also been suggested to him by Churchill—that no such operation was feasible as long the German fleet remained afloat and had access to the Baltic through the Kiel Canal, which had been the case throughout the war. But he did not express any view as to whether Fisher seriously intended to take such a risk.[84] His only explicit criticism appeared when he reached the admiral's resignation in May, where he recorded his opinion that the naval offensive at the Dardanelles would have succeeded 'if that wonderful old man had devoted all his fierce, ruthless energy towards supporting, instead of thwarting, the prosecution of [the] operation.... The forts at the Narrows would have crumbled...had Lord Fisher worked with Winston Churchill to that end.'[85] Readers were left in no doubt that Keyes had nothing but admiration for the former First Lord. 'Personally', he wrote, 'I think Winston Churchill's name will always be honoured in history for his great strategic effort.' Churchill had been right, Keyes maintained, to insist that de Robeck renew the naval attack after 18 March. And he proclaimed with conviction that the attack would have succeeded:

> I wish to place on record that I had no doubt then, and I have none now—and nothing will ever shake my opinion—that from the 4th April, 1915, onwards, the Fleet could have forced the Straits, and with losses trifling in comparison with those the Army suffered, could have entered the Marmora with sufficient force to destroy the Turco-German fleet. This operation would have cut the communications—which were sea-borne—of any Turkish armies either in

Gallipoli or on the Asiatic side, and would have led immediately to a victory decisive upon the whole course of the War.[86]

Keyes' case for renewing the naval attack rested on his conviction that the only serious obstacle was the enemy's minefields. He pointed out that by far the worst damage had been inflicted by a single line of undetected mines. If not for this misfortune, Allied losses would have been relatively light. The injury caused by concealed howitzers and mobile artillery during nearly seven hours of continuous firing on 18 March was 'simply negligible', he concluded, amounting to just six men killed and less than a dozen seriously wounded. The Narrows forts had wrought more substantial damage, and the French ships had suffered particularly badly, with the *Gaulois* nearly lost, but Keyes nonetheless believed that experience that day showed that the forts could be neutralized by naval gunfire.[87] All that was required to get the fleet through, therefore, was an efficient minesweeping force, and Keyes was confident that such a force was available by early April. After the setback on 18 March, efforts were stepped up to convert the fleet's River-class destroyers into minesweepers. These vessels, capable of sweeping at 14–20 knots, proved to be far more efficient than the slow trawlers previously used. Eight of these destroyers were ready by 4 April, and within two weeks another eight were available, along with eight fast 'fleet sweepers' belatedly sent from home waters.[88] Keyes' optimism about the ability of this force to sweep a channel for the fleet was shared by one of the officers involved in the reorganization of the minesweepers, who wrote in 1965 that the new force 'was capable of leading the fleet through the Narrows without undue loss.... There was really nothing to stop the fleet forcing the Straits, and a glorious opportunity was missed.'[89]

Churchill's amateur status and obvious bias had always detracted from his ability to make a case for the renewal of the naval offensive on technical grounds, which made Keyes a formidable ally. The admiral's opinions are frequently dismissed now as the dangerous and erratic by-product of his naive optimism and recklessly aggressive spirit, but these defects were not widely appreciated in the 1930s. When Churchill reviewed Keyes' memoirs in the *Daily Mail*, he highlighted the admiral's absolute conviction that the Straits could have been forced by the fleet alone. The fact that Keyes strongly believed this in 1915 strengthened Churchill's case that he had been right to insist that the attack be renewed and pressed with vigour. Nor could Churchill resist restating his argument that it was now well known that, when the attack was called off, the enemy had 'only *a few* rounds of armour-piercing shell left for their heavy guns' and no reserve of mines.[90] But what is perhaps most interesting about Churchill's review is that the defensive tone that pervaded his earliest speeches and writings about the Dardanelles had been replaced by a more assertive posture. 'All the poor loyal unthinking, uninstructed politicians and people at home rejoiced when the mad adventure at the Dardanelles was finally abandoned', he reproved:

> They acclaimed the evacuation as if it were a victory, and turned with pathetic, purblind confidence to the measureless slaughters and agonies of the barbed wire on the Western Front. They and their feeble guides had their way, and plodded on with patient hearts and closed minds through years of hideous waste and carnage to a victory so long delayed, so dearly purchased, that it has proved in the aftermath almost indistinguishable from defeat.[91]

That Churchill was now willing to go on the offensive was a sign of his confidence that the tide of public opinion had turned in his favour.

15

From Millstone to Myth

'The Great Movement of Opinion'

Public opinion towards the Dardanelles campaign went through a gradual transformation during the interwar period, although the process was never as fast or as complete as Churchill would have liked. Speaking at an ANZAC Day luncheon in London in 1921, Churchill observed—with some justification—that popular views were beginning to shift in his favour. 'I await with calmness', he stated, 'the great movement of opinion which is taking place.'[1] The publication of *The World Crisis* in 1923 accelerated the trend towards a more favourable view of the campaign, and Churchill increasingly found himself swimming with the popular current rather than against it. There were still writers critical of the campaign and Churchill's role in it, but moderate or favourable opinions were found with growing frequency in the memoirs, official histories, and other war books of the interwar period. The nature of public criticisms of Churchill over the Dardanelles also changed after the war. For years, the strongest attacks on Churchill for his role in launching the campaign had originated with his Conservative opponents, who were generally less interested in the accuracy of their charges than their usefulness for denigrating a political opponent. But, by late 1923, Churchill was drifting away from the Liberals and towards the Conservative Party, which he finally rejoined in 1924. In the process, the Dardanelles ceased to be a bludgeon wielded by the Conservatives against Churchill. In March 1924, the Conservative *Daily Mail* published a leader that signalled a new approach. In a sharp reversal of its wartime position, the newspaper lamented that Churchill had been made a 'scapegoat for half the mistakes of the German War'. Allied intervention at Antwerp was now credited with saving the Channel ports in 1914, and it was accepted that Churchill had been acting in accordance with professional advice when he initiated the Dardanelles campaign. 'It is not fair or just', the newspaper pronounced, 'to condemn a statesman because he was wrongly advised by his experts, and Mr. Churchill can be acquitted of an excessive share of responsibility for the Dardanelles action.'[2]

But the Dardanelles failure was so useful a weapon against Churchill that it was appropriated almost immediately by the Labour Party, an up-and-coming force in British politics whose members were often offended by Churchill's virulent anti-Socialism. 'Now that the facts are becoming known' about the Dardanelles, Churchill noted in 1924, 'there is a great change in educated public opinion, and only the Socialists continue to excite prejudice for purely political reasons.'[3] This manifested itself with particular force in late 1923 when Churchill stood for election in Leicester. Labour supporters disrupted his campaign speeches with taunts about the Dardanelles. But Churchill was quick to lash back. The press recorded his reaction to one heckler who shouted 'What about the Dardanelles?':

> 'What do you know about that?' promptly declared Mr. Churchill. 'You throw that retort out without having given consideration to the question. The Dardanelles might have saved millions of lives.'

More than once during the campaign Churchill was forced off script to defend his wartime record, and he refused to concede any ground to the hecklers. 'Don't imagine I am running away from the Dardanelles', he told one audience defiantly: 'I glory in it.'[4] Churchill subsequently lost the election, but his Labour opponents must have sensed that public opinion was turning in Churchill's favour with respect to the Dardanelles, and this line of attack gradually gave way to others.

The shift in public perceptions of the Dardanelles gained momentum in the late 1920s, fuelled by the growing revulsion against the heavy losses suffered by the army on the Western Front. The British people took an increasingly critical view of the war in the decade after the Armistice. British war literature was still dominated by patriotic, triumphalist, and heroic themes, but the wave of anti-war books that began to appear towards the end of the 1920s—in particular Remarque's hugely popular *All Quiet on the Western Front*—also found a large and receptive audience in Britain.[5] Post-war disillusionment also began to eat away at the reputation of Britain's wartime generals, who had once been virtually immune to public criticism.

By the late 1920s, more and more writers were questioning the wisdom of costly offensives like the Somme and Passchendaele, which had incurred massive casualties for little apparent gain.

Churchill had been critical of the army's offensive strategy on the Western Front practically from the outset. Once deadlock had set in, he consistently advocated a defensive posture in the west. In the second volume of *The World Crisis*, Churchill criticized the generals for launching unsuccessful offensives in France in 1915, although his main concern at this time, it seems, was to show that men and material squandered in the west would have been better employed in the east. It was only in the third volume of *The World Crisis*, published in 1927, that Churchill unleashed his full case against the generals. He was particularly critical of Allied strategy in 1916–17, when the army's leaders launched major offensives against strongly defended German positions, offensives that lasted for months despite their meagre results. Churchill charged that the Somme Offensive of 1916, which dragged on for nearly 5 months and resulted in over 600,000 British and French casualties, 'was from beginning to end a welter of slaughter'.[6] Worse, the campaign had produced no strategic benefits. In a chapter titled 'The Blood Test', Churchill challenged the view propagated by the generals and their supporters (including Edmonds in the official histories) that German casualties in 1916–17 were at least as heavy as Britain's. In fact, as Churchill demonstrated, the British had invariably suffered heavier losses.[7] The army, in other words, was not even winning the battle of attrition. 'If we lose three or four times as many officers and nearly twice as many men in our attack as the enemy in his defence', Churchill asked, 'how are we wearing him down?'[8]

While Churchill tempered many of his criticisms of Haig and other leading generals in *The World Crisis*, Lloyd George's influential memoirs, which outsold even Churchill's, were uniformly damning.[9] The former Prime Minister condemned his military advisers in the harshest terms for their bloody and unimaginative Western Front strategy. And Churchill was quick to endorse this view. His articles in the 1930s are littered with evocative references to the generals' 'senseless butcheries' and 'ghastly crimes' like the Battle of Passchendaele.[10] Many historians and commentators on the war came to share this disparaging opinion of Britain's wartime generals, the most prominent being Captain Basil Liddell Hart and Major-General J. F. C. Fuller. The prolific Liddell Hart was particularly useful to Churchill. Not only did he develop and popularize a devastating critique of British generalship, he also praised the strategic logic behind the Dardanelles campaign. 'The fault was not in the conception', he wrote in his popular history of the war, 'but in the execution.'[11] This perspective stemmed, in large measure, from his belief that Britain should never have committed a mass army to the Western Front. Instead, the government should have stuck to the traditional 'British way of warfare', utilizing the nation's predominant sea power to wear down the enemies' strength through peripheral operations—like the Dardanelles—and economic pressure. Britain's deadliest weapon in the war, in his view, had been the economic blockade of Germany, not the BEF.[12] Critiques like these added considerable weight to Churchill's argument that the Dardanelles had been a bold, imaginative, and *viable* alternative to the futile slaughter on the Western Front.

The public's increasing disillusionment with Britain's wartime generals gradually spread to encompass its admirals, and Churchill had a hand in this as well. While praising figures like Beatty and Keyes in *The World Crisis*, he had been critical of others, like Jellicoe and de Robeck, and implied that the officer corps as a whole was intellectually deficient. Churchill conceded that British naval officers were well trained in the technical aspects of their profession, but suggested that their education was so narrowly focused that they were generally ill-equipped to deal with broad strategic issues. The implication, of course, was that properly trained and intellectually capable officers would have embraced Churchill's offensive proposals rather than constantly blocking them. Churchill was helped by the fact that the admirals' wartime record was undeniably a mixed one. The navy was divided after the war by its controversial failure to secure a decisive victory over the German fleet at the Battle of Jutland, but its reputation suffered even more from its failure to counter the German submarine offensive until the shipping situation became critical in 1917. Notably, these were purely *naval* failures. Unlike the Dardanelles, the blame could not be passed to civilian leadership. On the contrary, Lloyd George's memoirs revealed that the Admiralty had resisted the implementation of convoy—the measure that eventually neutralized the attack on British trade—and alleged that Lloyd George had had to force this step on a reluctant Jellicoe, then Britain's First Sea Lord.

Churchill naturally seized on this episode to buttress the idea that the admirals were just as error-prone and unimaginative as the generals, and, more importantly, that civilian leaders were sometimes justified in overruling their professional advisers. 'The astonishing fact', he wrote in a 1931 article in *The Daily Telegraph*, 'is that the politicians were right, and that the Admiralty authorities were wrong.'

The politicians were right upon a technical, professional question ostensibly quite outside their sphere, and the Admiralty authorities were wrong upon what was, after all, the heart and centre of their own peculiar job. . . . British politicians . . . asked all kinds of questions. They did not always take 'No' for an answer. They did not accept the facts and figures put before them by their experts as necessarily unshakable. They were not under moral awe of professional authority, if it did not seem reasonable to the lay mind.[13]

★★★★

The shift in public opinion in favour of the Dardanelles in the late 1920s did not translate into immediate political gains for Churchill. On the contrary, his political fortunes entered a decade-long slump just as a more favourable consensus on the campaign was beginning to emerge. Churchill ceased to be Chancellor of the Exchequer in 1929 when the Labour Party returned to power, and he subsequently broke with his party's leaders over their intention to give home rule to India. When the Conservatives entered into a 'National' coalition government in 1931—a coalition they dominated—Churchill was excluded from office. He remained a backbench MP for most of the decade, a period often referred to as his 'wilderness years'. And controversy continued to follow him. During the 1920s, he was widely criticized for Britain's intervention in the Russian Civil War; his belligerence during the Chanak Crisis of 1922, which nearly embroiled Britain in a new war with Turkey and brought down the Lloyd George coalition; and for his provocative role in the British general strike of 1926. In the 1930s, his hardline position on India (he denounced Gandhi at times with as much vehemence as Hitler) and his support for Edward VIII during the abdication crisis raised fresh doubts about his judgement and reliability. Even his early calls for rearmament were not initially well received by a British public eager to avoid another war.

The Dardanelles campaign was therefore not the most serious obstacle Churchill faced as he tried to revive his political career for the second time. It was possible to take a positive view of the Dardanelles and still regard Churchill himself with disdain. By the mid-1930s, there were plenty of other reasons to question his judgement. To his critics and political opponents, the failed naval campaign was simply one in a long line of missteps and miscalculations demonstrating his unsuitability for high office. Even his friends acknowledged that, for all his great gifts, his judgement sometimes failed him. Lord Birkenhead (formerly F. E. Smith), one of Churchill's closest friends, once commented that 'When Winston is right he is unique.

When he is wrong—Oh My God!'[14] Lloyd George, a perceptive critic who was well acquainted with Churchill's strengths and weaknesses, made a similar judgement in his memoirs. His view when he assumed the premiership in 1916, he wrote, was that Churchill would be a valuable addition to his War Cabinet on account of his 'fertile mind, his undoubted courage, his untiring industry, and his thorough study of the art of war'. But he also felt that Churchill needed close supervision, especially in wartime. By bringing him into the War Cabinet, Lloyd George calculated that his colleague's 'more erratic impulses could have been kept under control and his judgment supervised and checked, before plunging into action. Men of his ardent temperament and powerful mentality need exceptionally strong brakes.'[15]

Lloyd George's memoirs also suggested an explanation for Churchill's unreliability. His 'mind was a powerful machine', the ex-premier wrote, 'but there lay hidden in its material or its make-up some obscure defect which prevented it from always running true.... When the mechanism went wrong, its very power made the action disastrous.'[16] Lloyd George had been even more critical of Churchill in the first draft of this passage, but Hankey prevailed on him to tone down his remarks after he vetted the manuscript on behalf of the government. Churchill was 'rather down on his luck' at the time, Hankey noted, and Lloyd George's blunt criticism 'will hit him dreadfully. It will always be quoted against him if he is ever in, or aspires to get into, office again.'[17] Lloyd George agreed to soften his criticism, and revised the offending passage to suggest he was only recording the opinion of Churchill's wartime critics, not his own.

Churchill's standing with the public gradually improved, however, as Europe moved closer to a new war. As the historian Robert Rhodes James famously noted in 1970, if Churchill's story had ended in 1938 or 1939 he would have been judged a failure, for, despite his great gifts and early successes, he had not lived up to his full potential. His career until this time had been marked by repeated setbacks and crushing disappointments.[18] This was a provocative judgement in 1970, when the Churchill Legend was well entrenched, but it would hardly have surprised anyone in the 1930s, when many felt that Churchill's political career had entered into a state of terminal decline. A critical biography published in 1931 by Victor Wallace Germains, *The Tragedy of Winston Churchill*, made much the same point as Rhodes James. In 1914, Germains noted, Churchill had seemed a 'natural successor' to Asquith: 'Yet for lack of the right balance of cool-headedness and judgement, all these advantages were thrown away.' Churchill's career since 1914, he argued, had been 'the tragedy of the brilliant failure, who has repeatedly seen men whom he secretly despises pass him on the road to office and power'. When he turned to Churchill's future, Germains made two notable predictions. First, that Churchill would fail to 'command the confidence of the genuine Conservative'. Second, that the Dardanelles was an insurmountable impediment to Churchill's future prospects. '[T]he ghosts of the Gallipoli dead will always rise up to damn him anew in times of national emergency', Germains wrote. 'Neither official historians, nor military hack writers, will ever explain away or wipe out the memory of the Dardanelles.'[19]

Germains' second prediction, unlike his first, proved to be wide of the mark. The rise of Hitler gave Churchill an opportunity to reinvigorate his failing political career. While successive British governments pursued a policy of appeasement towards Nazi Germany and implemented a modest rearmament programme—policies popular at first with the British public—Churchill warned that Hitler was driving Europe towards war and called for

Figure 15.1. General Sir Ian Hamilton, Winston Churchill, and Admiral of the Fleet Sir Roger Keyes at The Royal Naval Volunteer reserve and Royal Naval Division Association reunion at Crystal Palace, London on 11 June 1938.
Topfoto

a more vigorous British response. His criticisms of government policy hardly endeared him to his party's leaders, and were not always well received by the British public. But his dire prognostications became harder and harder to dismiss. Germany's occupation of Bohemia and Moravia in the spring of 1939 and the subsequent collapse of the Munich Agreement shocked the British public. It was obvious that Neville Chamberlain, Britain's Prime Minister from 1937 on, had been duped. Hitler was not merely seeking redress for moderate and legitimate grievance, as Chamberlain thought. In fact, the German dictator harboured a vast annexationist programme that could only be fulfilled by war, as Churchill had been saying for years. Churchill's stature rose steadily as Hitler's duplicity and true ambitions were exposed. The British government frantically switched gears during the final months of peace as it attempted to contain and deter Germany by forging new alliances and hastening British rearmament. But even while adopting Churchill's prescription for averting war, Conservative leaders still viewed him warily. It was only when war was declared on Germany on 3 September 1939 that Chamberlain gave in to public pressure and invited him into the government as First Lord of the Admiralty.

Churchill's stock continued to rise during the so-called 'Phony War'. He was virtually the only national leader untainted by association with the now-discredited policy of appeasement. The controversial episodes that punctuated his career were not forgotten, but he had undoubtedly been right about Hitler, and in the early months of the Second World War that was what mattered most to the British people. And, in contrast to Chamberlain, Churchill looked and sounded like a war leader. His speeches demonstrated an understanding of modern war that, once again, was in short supply in the British government. It was widely acknowledged that the Prime Minister had done his best to avert war, but his commitment to peace, once widely admired, increasingly seemed naive. People questioned whether he possessed the ruthlessness, determination, and fighting instincts needed in a life-or-death struggle against Hitler's Germany.[20] Churchill's strong record of opposition to Hitler, his inspiring public speeches, and his successful leadership of the Royal Navy during the early months of the war marked him out as an obvious successor to Chamberlain.[21] They also helped reassure the public about his record in the last war.

The qualitative surveys of public opinion compiled by the Mass Observation organization provide an interesting snapshot of public opinion during this part of the war. Notably, the Dardanelles and Gallipoli were seldom mentioned in connection with Churchill. When they were, opinion was mixed. One diarist recorded that 'plenty of people say [Churchill] mismanaged the whole show badly last time, evidencing Antwerp & Gallipoli'.[22] Another noted a conversation with an acquaintance who had 'not forgiven Churchill for what he calls his blunder over the Dardanelles in the last "do"'. But he also noted that the individual in question 'does not like Churchill and that's a rarity nowadays for practically everyone lauds him to the skies'.[23] The continuing relevance of the Dardanelles was questioned by Annie Elliott, a Lancashire housewife, who wrote in November 1939 that the war had transformed her opinion of Churchill.'Never liked Churchill after Gallipoli', she recorded, 'but can't help admiring him now.'[24] And several respondents felt that the Dardanelles was actually a mark in Churchill's favour. The best informed of these was Adelaide Poole, a retired nurse in Sussex, who wrote in September 1939 that 'Churchill is the one genius in the Cabinet, and his genius is tempered by vast experience and the wisdom of age.'

> Churchill is muzzled now [that] he is in the Cabinet unless, or until, he resigns. Many blame him for Gallipoli but all books written by those on the inside from Hamilton to Bartlett show how near it came to being a magnificent success, if only it could have been carried out with the same genius which suggested it. But from first to last it was muddled by the men in command out there.[25]

There were probably more concerns about Churchill's judgement in the corridors of power than among the general public at this time. Britain's opposition parties, many Conservatives, members of the royal family, and much of Whitehall continued to view him with suspicion even after the Second World War began. He was still regarded by many as something of loose cannon—a dynamic, inspiring, and sometimes brilliant figure, to be sure, but also reckless, unreliable, and, above all, prone to serious errors of judgement. The Conservative Party, moreover, had never quite forgiven Churchill for his defection to the Liberals in 1904. His persistent criticisms of the party's leaders and policies during the 1930s only underscored doubts about his loyalty.[26] When Churchill began to promote Allied operations in Scandinavia as a means to deny Germany access to essential supplies of Swedish iron ore, critics immediately compared the idea to Gallipoli. John Colville, a private secretary to Chamberlain (and later a strong admirer of Churchill), wrote in his diary that the Scandinavian scheme, 'instigated by Winston', was 'dangerously reminiscent of the Gallipoli plan'.[27] Henry Channon, a parliamentary private secretary to the Undersecretary of State for Foreign Affairs (and a staunch Chamberlainite) recorded that he was 'appalled by the plan to send an expeditionary force to Sweden, for it is clear that the same brain who conceived the Dardanelles Campaign is responsible for this wild enterprise'.[28] These complaints were not entirely fair, as Churchill's Scandinavian project actually enjoyed a broad measure of support from military and naval authorities at the time, but any peripheral operation associated with Churchill was bound to elicit disparaging comparisons to Gallipoli at this stage of the war, especially from those already inclined to be critical.

But while some waited anxiously for history to repeat itself, Churchill took great care to ensure that it did not. He showed far more restraint in 1939–40 than in 1915 when it came to pressing his ideas on reluctant naval advisers. One of those who noted the change was Roger Keyes. As Churchill approached the end of his second tenure at the Admiralty, the admiral remarked that 'the iron of Gallipoli had entered into [Churchill's] soul', meaning that his friend's fall from power and public disgrace over the Dardanelles had sapped his willingness to take bold risks.[29] This was not entirely fair, however. As First Lord in 1939–40, Churchill's determination to take the war to the enemy and adopt offensive measures was as great as ever. Soon after returning to the Admiralty, he began pressing his naval advisers to project British naval power into the Baltic, an impracticable scheme carried over from the previous war. And in early 1940, after his Baltic scheme failed to gain traction, he focused his attention on naval and military operations in Norway and Sweden, and other schemes, such as the mining of the Rhine. All that had changed in 1940 was that Churchill was more willing to accept 'No' for an answer, which was fortunate for all concerned, since his proposals for offensive action met with much the same opposition as in the First World War.

Britain's First Sea Lord in September 1939 was Admiral Sir Dudley Pound, who had first encountered Churchill in 1917 as a captain in the Admiralty's newly established War Plans Division. One of his first tasks then had been to comment on Churchill's latest proposals for operations along Germany's North Sea coast, proposals that were once again rejected by the naval staff as dangerous and impracticable. As First Sea Lord during the next war, Pound had the task again of deflecting Churchill from unworkable schemes. This was a time-consuming and wearying assignment, but Pound handled it with skill and tact. He rarely presented Churchill with a flat 'no', and instead tirelessly argued the technical obstacles until the First Lord moved on to something new.[30] It helped, of course, that Churchill was eager to avoid a clash. His expulsion from the Admiralty had, as Keyes suggested, left a deep mark. The Churchill of 1915 had used every resource at his disposal to overcome or sidestep professional resistance to his schemes. He staked his political future on the Dardanelles offensive with little thought to the personal consequences because he had believed it was the right and necessary thing to do. This willingness to accept responsibility, while admirable in some ways, also reveals the young politician's impetuosity and political naiveté.

The Churchill of 1939–40 was more mature—and more calculating. Above all, the Dardanelles had taught him the folly of launching a major operation with only grudging and half-hearted support from his naval advisers. His only chance of surviving another high-profile naval failure was to ensure that his service advisers were firmly with him. Churchill had come to realize the importance, from a political perspective, of not setting himself up as an easy scapegoat if things went wrong. And he had a better understanding of the limits of his powers as First Lord of the Admiralty. In June 1915, a month after being forced from office, Churchill had already concluded that his biggest mistake with the Dardanelles project had been 'in seeking to attempt an initiative without being sure that all the means & powers to make it successful were at my disposal'.[31] He made the same point in the second volume of his Second World War memoirs, published in 1949, where he noted that the Dardanelles, 'a supreme enterprise', had been 'cast away, through my trying to carry out a major and cardinal operation of war from a subordinate position. Men are ill-advised to try such ventures. This lesson had sunk into my nature.'[32] And indeed it had.

The Norwegian campaign of April–May 1940 was a turning point in Churchill's career. His standing with the British public had improved dramatically in the space of just a few years, but another humiliating setback so early in the war might have been disastrous to his prospects—and the Norwegian campaign had all the makings of a humiliating setback. German forces inflicted a series of embarrassing defeats on the Allies throughout the campaign, defeats made all the more painful by the theatre's maritime character. That the Germans could land troops along the Norwegian coast in the face of Britain's superior sea power reflected badly on all concerned. As First Lord of the Admiralty, Churchill might easily have been singled out for the blame. He even gave critics a hostage to fortune by telling the House of Commons soon after the German invasion that 'Herr Hitler has committed a grave strategic error in spreading the war so far to the north.'[33] In fact, once the Germans had established themselves throughout the country, the situation quickly went from bad to worse for the Allies, whose efforts to expel the German invaders ended in failure. By the start of May, the situation had deteriorated to the point that British troops in central Norway had to be evacuated.

The parallels with Gallipoli, another peripheral campaign that ended in defeat and evacuation, were all too obvious. Norway could easily have been branded another Churchillian disaster. And some historians, impressed by the superficial similarities between the two campaigns, have indeed jumped to the conclusion that Churchill—showing the same defects in judgement and character that produced failure in 1915—was responsible for virtually everything that went wrong in the campaign. But this was not the view generally taken in 1940. The defeat in Norway focused the British public's attention on what was now perceived to be the biggest issue facing the country: Neville Chamberlain's suitability as war leader. The Prime Minister's reputation, already tarnished by the failure of appeasement, took a severe beating as Britain suffered its first serious defeat in the war. The public's sense of frustration is captured by contemporary Mass Observation reports. One respondent, Daidie Penn, articulated a common view:

> [It is useless] to go on under our present leadership. I think that Mr. C[hamberlain] is sincere enough in his statements he makes—I think he speaks the truth as far as a politician ever <u>does</u> speak the truth—but he hasn[']t the vision—the competence or the driving power to deal with opponents like the Germans and I maintain that if he persists in office—it will be the end of the war for us—however long it may drag on. He is damaging what reputation we had the whole world over by his incompetence—his fumbling—he should retire.[34]

'Chamberlain must go', another diarist wrote on 28 April. 'We want a man of fury, devilish cunning & energy.'[35]

With Chamberlain's support crumbling, Churchill was the figure most widely thought to possess the qualities the British public was looking for. 'Haven't we, can't we, find more men of Churchill's breed?', one Mass Observation respondent asked. Another noted that: 'Nearly everyone I speak with suggests Churchill for premier.' And Churchill was undoubtedly the main beneficiary of the public's growing disenchantment with Chamberlain. On 4 April, just days before the German invasion of Norway, Chamberlain had boasted that he was 'ten times as confident of victory' as when the war started, and suggested that Hitler, by delaying his offensive in the west so long, had 'missed the bus'. These ill-judged statements came back to haunt him during the evacuation from Norway. When he defended his conduct of the campaign in the House of Commons, he was taunted with cries of 'missed the bus'. Churchill's more recent, but equally flawed, prediction that Hitler had made 'a grave strategic error' in invading Norway was seemingly forgotten. Rather than calling for the First Lord's removal, the public wanted to see him given more control over the military direction of the war. Chamberlain bowed to this sentiment in April by appointing Churchill to preside over the government's Military Co-ordination Committee, which was charged with providing the War Cabinet with unified military advice from the three fighting services. The appointment was generally well received, although not everyone was eager to increase Churchill's power. Hankey (now Baron Hankey), who had been appointed Minister without Portfolio in Chamberlain's War Cabinet, shared Lloyd George's view that Churchill required close supervision in wartime. He told Colville on 17 April that he was 'a little worried by Winston's determination to direct the war: he remembers, he says, the operations at the Dardanelles all too clearly. He is going to warn the P.M.'[36]

Public and political frustration with Chamberlain's leadership reached a peak during the parliamentary debate on the Norwegian campaign on 7–8 May, when the Prime Minister came under heavy fire from both sides of the House. One of the most dramatic interventions on the first day of the debate—and the only one to invoke the memory of the Dardanelles—came from Keyes, who had entered Parliament before the war as an MP for Portsmouth. Keyes, wearing the full dress uniform of an Admiral of the Fleet, denounced the government for bungling the campaign. He was animated, in part, by a personal grievance. His proposal personally to lead a naval attack on the German forces holding the important Norwegian port of Trondheim had been summarily rejected by the Admiralty. 'I was foolish enough to think that my suggestions might be welcomed', he informed the House, 'but I was told it was astonishing that I should think that all these suggestions had not been examined by people who knew exactly what resources were available, and what the dangers would be.' The parallels with Gallipoli struck Keyes particularly hard. Defeat could have been avoided in Norway, he argued, if only the Admiralty and the War Cabinet had acted with speed and vigour. Failure, in his view, stemmed from the same causes that had brought disaster in 1915: the government's want of boldness and initiative. But he did not hold Churchill personally responsible for this state of affairs. On the contrary, he maintained that the only way to avoid further setbacks and possibly retrieve the situation was to give Churchill still more power. 'I am longing to see proper use made of his great abilities', Keyes announced. In 1915, he recalled, Churchill had 'had many enemies, who discredited his judgment and welcomed his downfall'. But this was no longer the case, he stated. Churchill now had the confidence of the War Cabinet, the navy, 'and indeed of the whole country, which is looking to him to help to win the war'.[37]

The onslaught against Chamberlain continued the following day, with prominent figures like Lloyd George and Leo Amery calling for the Prime Minister's resignation. Churchill stoutly defended the government's record in Norway and announced that he accepted his full share of responsibility for recent defeats. By loyally supporting his beleaguered chief, who had done so much to thwart his ambitions in the 1930s, Churchill—who had often been suspected of excessive ambition and disloyalty—further increased his own stature and, ironically, hastened Chamberlain's departure. After two days of bitter attacks in the House of Commons, Chamberlain's position had clearly become untenable. On 10 May 1940, Churchill became Prime Minister and Minister of Defence in a new all-party government. The change in his fortunes seems to have astonished even him, especially in light of his close association with the Norwegian campaign and its parallels to Gallipoli. '[I]t was a marvel', he wrote in a draft of his Second World War memoirs 'I really do not know how...I survived and maintained my position in public esteem while all the blame was thrown on poor Mr. Chamberlain.'[38] Churchill undoubtedly believed that 'poor Mr. Chamberlain' got exactly what he deserved, but this probably did not make his surprise any less genuine.

Churchill assumed the premiership just as Britain's fortunes were about to reach their lowest ebb, and his reputation as a war leader ultimately rests on his remarkable performance in 1940. It would be difficult to exaggerate just how desperate Britain's position was to become within just a few weeks. By June, German forces had overrun France and the Low Countries, robbing Britain of its only major continental ally. Hitler's ally, Fascist Italy, joined the war against Britain just as France collapsed. A neutral Soviet Union was actively supplying the German war machine with raw materials. In the Far East, Japan waited for the right moment to strike. Britain's strategic situation could hardly have been worse. The Germans now possessed air and naval bases across the English Channel in occupied France. The small British Army had been rescued from Dunkirk, but in a terrible state—most of its equipment and weapons had to be left behind. In the short term, the British would be hard-pressed just to withstand a German invasion. The choice confronting Churchill's new government in June 1940 was whether to make peace with a brutal and treacherous enemy or to continue a war that, by almost any criteria, was unwinnable. Churchill, a gambler by nature, intuitively made the right choice—he believed that Britain must continue fighting. And he was able to carry the rest of his government and the British people with him. The gamble paid off. In the months that followed, Britain prevailed over the German Air Force in the Battle of Britain, thwarted Hitler's invasion plans, and endured the horrors of the 'Blitz', the bombing campaign against its major cities. And through all this Churchill established his enduring claim to greatness.

Popular legend has it that Churchill's heroic leadership and inspiring speeches were instrumental in sustaining British morale through the worst months of the war, and there is more than a little truth in this, although the British people were never as united as the legend suggests. Nor did Churchill enjoy anything like universal support, even at the height of his popularity. His standing fluctuated during the war with the ups and downs of Britain's military fortunes, and he famously lost the General Election of 1945. But he *was* a genuinely popular wartime leader from start to finish. The British people responded to his defiant, heroic rhetoric, and embraced the suggestion in his famous speech that they were playing a part in their nation's 'finest hour'. The narrative he constructed in the summer of 1940 continues to resonate. 'The central and founding myth of [Britain in] World War II', according to cultural historians Graham Dawson and Bob West, 'is of a nation *united* through idolatry for its totemic leader, Churchill. All other mythic aspects of the war are subordinated to this one, that had its genesis in May 1940, and is reproduced to this day.'[39] It is hardly surprising that the popular British memory of the war has been constructed around the idea of a small state heroically defying the unstoppable Nazi war machine, then at the height of its power, thereby laying the foundations for Germany's ultimate defeat—and saving Western civilization in the process. Churchill's inspiring rhetoric and resolute leadership in the summer of 1940 are a vital and integral part of this story.

The myth-making started not long after Churchill came to power. In the aftermath of the Dunkirk evacuation, public opinion turned even more sharply against Chamberlain and the so-called 'Men of Munich'.[40] Popular sentiment was both captured and enflamed by the book *Guilty Men*, a widely read polemic that condemned everyone associated with appeasement and pre-war rearmament. The authors, three Beaverbrook journalists, charged that the devastating military defeats of May–June 1940 stemmed directly and inevitably from the complacency and incompetence of the men who had led Britain through the 1930s. The book was a huge success. Published in early July 1940, only a month after Dunkirk, it went through 21 impressions and had sold 200,000 copies by the end of the year.[41] Churchill, who had warned of the dangers of appeasement and been excluded from power, is the only major figure to emerge from the tract with his reputation enhanced. Thus began the rewriting of the history of the 1930s to fit the myths of 1940. The public's support for appeasement, and Chamberlain's overwhelming popularity at the time of Munich, were conveniently forgotten. In the new narrative, Churchill had been ignored and kept out of power by lesser men. His campaign against Indian home rule was pushed far into the background, and his sometimes spotty record as an anti-appeaser—he had, for example, taken a conciliatory stance towards Italy during the Abyssinian Crisis—was ignored and eventually forgotten. Before long, Churchill was being remembered and celebrated as almost the sole voice against appeasement in the 1930s, giving his assumption of power in 1940 an aura of inevitability.

The foundations of the Churchill Legend were firmly established by 1945. The prestige he gained during the Second World War easily survived his defeat in the General Election. The rest of the world was surprised and perplexed by the verdict of the British electorate, but his stature was barely diminished, even in his own country. The British people drew a distinction between Churchill the war leader and Churchill the party politician. Rejection of the latter did not necessarily mean a repudiation of the former. The Churchill Legend, firmly rooted in the myths of 1940, prospered and grew in the decades after the war. To Churchill's heroic defiance of Hitler and inspiring speeches could be added his successful management of the British war effort, his skilful handling of Britain's allies, and his early perception of a Soviet threat. By 1947, Churchill's reputation as a wise but too often unheeded prophet had gained a fresh boost from his 'Iron Curtain' speech in Fulton and the onset of the Cold War.[42] The historian John Ramsden, in his masterful study *Man of the Century*, has shown how Churchill worked assiduously after the war to foster and shape his legend. As in the

1920s, he relied mainly on his pen to influence popular opinion. His Second World War memoirs, published in six volumes from 1948 to 1953, were a publishing sensation, eclipsing sales of *The World Crisis* by a wide margin. But this time, his fame and prestige ensured him a receptive audience. Churchill laid out his case in *The Second World War* with great skill and unrivalled authority. By the late 1950s, his version of the war's origins, controversies, and outcome, and his own contribution to victory, had gained wide acceptance. Along the way, his cemented his reputation not just as a great war leader, but as a great man.

And what about the Dardanelles? Public interest in the battles and controversies of the First World War faded rapidly with the onset of Hitler's war. Churchill's attention was also focused elsewhere. His Second World War memoirs contained only a few passing references to the 1915 campaigns that had once consumed so much of his energy. By the late 1940s, his legacy rested on his record since 1933, and this is naturally what he focused on as he set out to craft his reputation for posterity. But he also had the luxury of being able to ignore the Dardanelles after 1945 because it was seldom invoked by his critics, and, more to the point, because his version had finally gained the upper hand. From Churchill's perspective, the battle over the memory of the Dardanelles during the interwar period had effectively ended in a draw. Public opinion had shifted considerably from where it started in 1915, due in no small part to Churchill's own tireless efforts to shape popular views. And this, in itself, was a notable victory, not least because it cleared the path for his return to power in 1939–40. However, opinion towards the campaign was still divided when Britain went to war again. It was only over the course of the Second World War that the tide of popular opinion turned perceptibly in Churchill's favour.

The shift was both gradual and subtle. The Dardanelles campaign was not much in the public eye during the war, and what attention it received was usually connected with Churchill in one way or another. As his prestige soared, popular writers and biographers readily adopted uncritical or pro-Churchill views of the campaign. And this trend continued after the war. Churchill's representation of the offensive as an imaginative idea that might have saved millions of lives steadily gained ground. In 1956, the first major book on the campaign since the 1930s was published by Alan Moorehead, an Australian expatriate and renowned war correspondent for the British press during the Second World War. Moorehead, who had previously written a short biography of Churchill, embraced the Churchillian perspective of the Dardanelles. The campaign, he wrote, was 'no longer a blunder or a reckless gamble; it was the most imaginative conception of the war, and its potentialities were almost beyond reckoning'. He went on to suggest that the case for the campaign had been conclusively settled in the 1930s, by which time, he claimed, 'no serious student now questioned the wisdom of the Allies going to the Dardanelles'.[43] The book, simply titled *Gallipoli*, was a huge critical and popular success. Moorehead was awarded a £1,000 literary award and gold medal by the *Sunday Times*, and became the inaugural recipient of the Duff Cooper Memorial Prize. The latter award allowed the recipient to nominate the presenter, and Moorehead chose Churchill himself, now approaching his eighty-second birthday. Churchill had stepped down as peacetime Prime Minister the year before, and was no longer a frequent public speaker, but he accepted this invitation and presented Moorehead with the award at the Savoy Hotel in London on 28 November 1956. According to Moorehead's biographer, Churchill took the opportunity to wish the writer 'a much greater success with the book than he had had with the campaign'.[44]

Churchill's role in the Dardanelles also received generous praise from Clement Attlee—the leader of the opposition, leader of the Labour Party, former Prime Minister, and veteran of the Gallipoli campaign. In November 1954, Attlee gave the welcome address when members of both Houses of Parliament assembled in Westminster Hall to honour Churchill on his eightieth birthday. He stated that the Dardanelles offensive had been 'the only imaginative strategic idea of the war. I only wish you had had full power to carry it to success.'[45] Attlee's generous tribute and Moorehead's laudatory book represent the high-water mark for the Churchillian version of the Dardanelles. But there was more going on by the mid-1950s than just the growing acceptance of the Dardanelles as a worthwhile concept spoiled by poor execution. The campaign was also being recast to fit the Churchill Legend. Looking back through the lens of 1940, admiring writers easily discerned signs of Churchill's future greatness in his early years and in all facets of his life. The so-called Siege of Sidney Street in 1911, for example, once widely accepted as evidence of Churchill's questionable judgement, was reimagined as a colourful but essentially harmless episode that demonstrated little more than an unconventional personality. His record in the First World War was rewritten at the same time to emphasize his genius for war and previously underappreciated contributions to the Allied victory. The new narrative credited the defence of Antwerp with

Figure 15.2. Sir Winston Churchill presenting the inaugural Duff Cooper Memorial Prize to Alan Moorehead for his book *Gallipoli*. The ceremony took place at the Savoy Hotel, London on 28 November 1956, two days before Churchill's 82nd birthday.
Moorehead family collection

saving the Channel ports; it praised Churchill for practically inventing the tank, which might have broken the deadlock on the Western Front if used properly; and, of course, it lauded the Dardanelles as a missed short cut to victory.

Popular opinion towards the Dardanelles concept remained broadly favourable through the 1960s. This can be attributed in part to the enduring strength of the Churchill Legend, which was given fresh impulse by Churchill's death in January 1965. As the British people mourned the loss of their great wartime Prime Minister, and world leaders lined up to praise his memory, the time was hardly ripe for criticism. At the same time, the Churchillian view of Gallipoli was being reinforced by the growing perception of the First World War as a great national tragedy. The strong anti-war sentiment of the 1960s fuelled a sense of disillusionment that went far beyond anything experienced in the 1930s. The conflict came to be regarded by a new generation as the embodiment of futility and horror. Britain's generals completed their transformation from national heroes into 'butchers' and 'donkeys' who had callously despatched a generation of Britons to senseless and brutal deaths on the Western Front. As Brian Bond has noted, this 'ultra-critical view' of the Western Front and British generalship 'gained a powerful hold on public opinion' in the 1960s and 1970s.[46] Churchill had been one of the earliest critics of British generalship, but he had never expressed views this extreme. However, the trend tended to reinforce rather than diminish the allure of the Dardanelles as a creative alternative to the Western Front.

Churchill also emerged largely unscathed from the memoirs of Maurice Hankey, the last major figure involved in the inception of the Dardanelles to go into print. His two-volume account of the First World War, *The Supreme Command*, had actually been completed in 1943 but official restrictions on the release of confidential information—restrictions that Hankey himself had a hand in establishing, and that Churchill was evidently happy to enforce—delayed publication until 1961.[47] These books recounted in detail for the first time the muddled deliberations of the War Council, and made clear that the British machinery for coordinating military and naval operations had been severely flawed in the early stages of the war. All this implicitly shifted blame for the Dardanelles and Gallipoli to Asquith. His criticisms of Churchill were actually relatively mild. There were, in fact, few prominent writers condemning Churchill during the 1960s, and many, like Basil Liddell Hart, now Britain's pre-eminent military writer, were quick to praise him. In an influential essay on Churchill as a military strategist published in 1969, Liddell Hart again presented Churchill as a far-sighted exponent of a traditionally British maritime strategy during the First World War. The Dardanelles represented the epitome of the 'indirect approach' in strategy that Liddell Hart championed in his own work. 'On the retrospective view of history', he wrote, 'it seems shocking, and historically ironical, that Churchill should have been shelved and his career nearly wrecked after he had made such signal contributions to Britain's war effort.' Even more ironic, in his view, was that Churchill's record in the First World War had been frequently, and in his opinion unfairly, disparaged, while his strategy in the Second World War, which Liddell Hart regarded as much less successful, had been widely praised.[48]

However, from the mid-1960s onwards, historians began to reassess the Dardanelles from a more detached perspective than had been possible thirty or forty years earlier. The year 1965 saw the publication of two important new works, a major history of Gallipoli by Robert Rhodes James and the second volume of *From the Dreadnought to Scapa Flow*, a monumental multi-volume history of the Royal Navy in the First World War by the pre-eminent naval historian of the era, Arthur J. Marder. Both authors avoided either the uncritical praise or unqualified condemnation that marked so much of the earlier literature, and both succeeded, to a large degree, in setting aside the Churchill of myth and legend to engage with Churchill as an historical actor. The publication of the third volume of Churchill's official biography in 1971, the first in the series written by Martin Gilbert, represents something of a watershed. Gilbert's detailed treatment of the Dardanelles took a predictably pro-Churchill perspective, but it was distinguished from previous academic works on this subject by its unprecedented use of archival sources. Every account of the Dardanelles published up to the late 1960s had relied on the documents reproduced in *The World Crisis* and the Report of the Dardanelles Commission, supplemented by a handful of memoirs and official histories. In other words, for half a century the verdicts offered on Churchill's role in the Dardanelles had been based on a small and incomplete body of documentary evidence—a body of evidence, moreover, that was used to support both extreme praise and extreme criticism. Gilbert, however, not only had full access to Churchill's own extensive collection of unpublished papers, he was also able to utilize the full range of British official records, which had been opened to the public only a few years earlier and were still largely untapped by historians of the First World War.

The infusion of new evidence into the debate in the 1970s did nothing to help reconcile opposing views about Churchill and the Dardanelles. Opinion not only remained divided, it continued to fracture along the same fault lines established in the 1920s. The opening of the archives coincided, however, with a resurgence of critical opinion towards Churchill's role in the campaign. Notably, this shift was not driven by a renewed public interest in the campaigns and controversies of the First World War, but by the growing dissatisfaction among historians with orthodox views towards Britain's involvement in the Second World War. As a new generation of scholars threw themselves into the challenge of demythologizing and historicizing Hitler's war, Churchill's record inevitably came under close scrutiny. And his reputation could only be diminished by matching the inflated claims made for him—and sometimes by him—against the documentary record. The Dardanelles was by now firmly embedded in the Churchill Legend as early evidence of the exceptional skill he would demonstrate as war leader and strategist in 1940–45. But it could just as easily support a counter-narrative in which Churchill was in fact a dangerous amateur strategist responsible for many of the worst decisions of the Second World War. This view has gained ground since the 1970s, and is sometimes pushed to great lengths. One recent study of the Second World War, for example, describes Churchill as 'the man who by his political actions between 1919 and 1929 contributed in very large measure to Britain being unready for [the Second World War], and who by his flights of fancy, his unwillingness to trust professionals and his unshakeable belief that he knew better than anyone else how this nation's efforts should be directed, was very nearly responsible for losing it'.[49]

It is hardly surprising that the success—and excesses—of the Churchill Legend would eventually give rise to a counter-legend. The Dardanelles and Gallipoli campaigns have been accorded a prominent place in both because they seem to offer a key to understanding and evaluating Churchill's leadership in the Second World War. In other words, the Dardanelles matter because they can be used to establish a *pattern* of behaviour, whether of recklessness or genius. But the explanatory power of the Dardanelles for Churchill's leadership in the Second World War is easily exaggerated. The Norwegian campaign of 1940, for example, has been particularly susceptible to what might be termed a process of 'Gallipification'. A plausible and attractive case can be made that the defeats of April 1940 stemmed from the same root cause—that is, Churchill—that produced disaster in 1915. And there are enough surface similarities between the two campaigns to make comparison difficult to avoid. But the assumption that the Allied defeat in Norway can be explained simply as a Churchillian fiasco produces a skewed version of the campaign. Every mistake and misjudgement at sea, and many of those on land, have been attributed by some writers entirely to Churchill's interference in operations, his impatience, and his poor strategic judgement. Every error, however, small, has been treated as a major factor in the Allied defeat. Churchill himself is often credited with the power to override both his naval advisers and the members of Chamberlain's War Cabinet. Other decision-makers are pushed into the background or simply ignored. The reality, of course, is more complicated, just as it was in 1915. Many of the worst errors attributed to Churchill in Norway can be traced back to others, including Pound, Chamberlain, and Lord Halifax, Britain's Foreign Secretary. Most of the mistakes Churchill made had little bearing on the overall course of the campaign. And far from being a virtual dictator, Churchill saw his advice frequently rejected by the War Cabinet and the chiefs of staff.[50]

Gallipoli is also an unreliable guide to Churchill's part in the Anglo-American debates over the opening of a Second Front in 1942–4. American leaders suspected at the time that Churchill's preference for a peripheral strategy in the Mediterranean could be traced back to his experiences in the First World War—which was partially true—and to the legacy of Gallipoli in particular. British Field Marshal Sir John Dill reported from Washington in 1942 that General George C. Marshall, the US Army Chief of Staff, had recently been studying *Soldiers and Statesmen*, the memoirs of Sir William Robertson, Britain's CIGS during the First World War. Robertson was a fervent Westerner, a critic of the Dardanelles, and no fan of Churchill. Marshall evidently shared Robertson's view that the diversion of Allied resources into peripheral campaigns had been a mistake, and he was eager to avoid a repetition in the current war. General Sir Alan Brooke, Britain's current CIGS, noted that Churchill's 'hackles were up over [Marshall's] reference to the Dardanelles'.[51] But Churchill's strong interest in the Balkans in 1943–4 fuelled American suspicions that he was not really interested in American plans to launch a massive cross-Channel invasion of France. And it is true that Churchill was never enthusiastic about the idea. General Eisenhower later recalled that he had once 'jokingly asked the Prime Minister, "now you're not trying to get over into the Balkans just to prove that you were right in World War I?" '

> 'Look, I'll admit that the Gallipoli concept was a brilliant one in view of the conditions in France at that time. And only bad management elsewhere defeated your objective. But we're fighting another war, not that one.' He just laughed and said, 'You know better than that.'[52]

The Soviets also suspected that Churchill's views on the Second Front could be traced back to the Dardanelles. Prior to Churchill's visit to Moscow in August 1942, Ivan Maisky, the Soviet ambassador to London, informed Stalin that the British Prime Minister's aversion to a Second Front stemmed primarily from his lack of confidence in the ability of the British Army to beat the Germans. But there was also, he suggested, a 'purely personal' consideration at work. 'In the previous war', he wrote, 'Churchill was the architect of the Dardanelles Operation, which left an indelible mark in his mind.' The ambassador pointed out that Churchill had also been responsible for a string of defeats in the current war: Norway, Greece, Libya, Crete, and Singapore. This had 'impacted the prime minister's psychology, making him unsure about his abilities'.[53] In fact, Churchill's self-confidence was as robust as ever in 1942. In suggesting otherwise, Maisky appears to have been influenced by Lloyd George. The former Prime Minister had told him the previous week that Churchill had developed 'some sort of *inferiority complex* when it comes to offensive operations. He was "bruised" already in the last war by the Dardanelles.' The result of his more recent failures, Lloyd George concluded, was that Churchill had come to fear offensive operations.[54]

After the war, American historians were more inclined than their British counterparts to see Churchill's experiences in the First World War as a key to understanding the Anglo-American strategic debates of 1942–4. One of the earliest and most influential exponents of this view was the American military historian Trumbull Higgins, who published two popular studies of Churchill as a strategist. The first, *Winston Churchill and the Second Front*, appeared in 1957. In this volume, Higgins proposed that the Dardanelles campaign had been the product of Churchill's preference for a traditional British maritime strategy—a strategy that Churchill mistakenly believed had been a success in the First World War. When he adopted the same approach in the Second World War, the result, according to Higgins, was the dissipation of Allied strength in peripheral theatres that could not produce decisive results. The cross-Channel attack favoured by American leaders, who saw the inherent advantages of a more direct 'Western' strategy, was needlessly delayed until 1944. These themes resurfaced in 1963 when Higgins published *Winston Churchill and the Dardanelles*. Although nominally a study of Churchill as a strategist in the early years of the First World War, the subtext was clear: Churchill's baggage from the earlier conflict had diverted the Allies from the superior strategy proposed by American generals in the Second World War. 'The danger', Higgins wrote, 'of allowing the personal engagement of Winston Churchill to predominate over the judgment of the professionals in matters of strategy or even of tactics would again be witnessed in a long series of dangerous and unnecessary offensives in and about the Mediterranean between 1940 and 1942, scratch and largely nugatory operations, which only through good fortune did not collectively amount to more than the 250,000 Allied casualties of the Dardanelles expedition.'[55]

The problem with this analysis is the assumption that Churchill's views in either conflict can be reduced to those of a stereotypical 'Easterner'. The label is a clumsy one at the best of times, and is certainly not a good fit for Churchill during the First World War. His natural inclination in 1914 was to focus on Germany rather than the Ottoman Empire. Moreover, he was an early and enthusiastic supporter of the decision to raise a mass British Army for service on the Continent, which put him at odds with members of the Liberal government who initially favoured the sort of limited maritime strategy Higgins attributed to Churchill. The decision to attack the Dardanelles in 1915 was essentially opportunistic, a chance to utilize forces not being employed in the main theatre to achieve useful ends on the periphery. Churchill's support for an eastern strategy strengthened and expanded in 1915 as Britain's commitment of resources and prestige escalated, but it receded just as quickly once Gallipoli had been evacuated. All this has been obscured, however, by the grandiose claims Churchill himself made after the war for the potential of the Dardanelles, which has tended to focus attention on this campaign and the strategic imperatives as Churchill saw them in 1915. But this hardly represents the whole of Churchill's development as a strategist in the First World War. In 1916–17, his attention swung back to the idea of turning the German flank in the north by using British and Allied naval forces in the North Sea and the Baltic. In the final years of the war he continued to believe that Germany was the main enemy; that the outcome of the war would ultimately be decided on land; and that Britain must contribute a vast army to the common cause. As Minister of Munitions in 1917–18, Churchill's attention was concentrated on the Western Front, although he deprecated costly offensive battles like the Somme and Passchendaele. He nevertheless expected victory to be achieved in the west. To this end, he advocated a defensive posture while the Allies gathered strength for an overwhelming offensive in 1919 or 1920.[56] There *are* continuities in Churchill's strategic views from one war to the next, but they are not to be found in the application of a simple east versus west model.

Only in Australia has the Dardanelles–Gallipoli campaign continued to be a subject of strong interest in its own right, and this has produced a distinctively Australian Churchill counter-legend. Australia's tragic-heroic sacrifices at Gallipoli and the popular ANZAC legend it gave birth to have become firmly established as part of Australia's foundational mythology. Charles Bean's judgement that the campaign was the product of a fundamentally misconceived strategy devised and implemented by Churchill has coloured the views of generations of Australians. Bean himself, it should be noted, was unconvinced by the defence Churchill mounted in the 1920s. In a revised edition of *The Story of ANZAC* published in 1933, he was one of the first writers to challenge the idea that the Ottomans were critically short of ammunition in March 1915. He correctly pointed out that the enemy was only short of shells for its heaviest guns, and that the British themselves had a limited supply of ammunition for a renewed attack. The decisive factor for the fleet, he rightly stated, was that, on 19 March, the Ottoman minefields and mobile batteries were virtually untouched. The new edition therefore concluded that both the naval attack and the land campaign that followed still appeared 'as rash to-day as they did, to those who bore the consequences, in 1915'.[57]

Churchill's reputation in Australia was further damaged during the Second World War by the traumatic events of February 1942, when the British and Commonwealth forces defending Singapore surrendered to the Japanese. Churchill's eagerness to use Australian soldiers to fight the Germans and Italians in North Africa contrasted badly with his reluctance to commit British forces to the defence of Australia before the Pacific War and during the critical early months of the conflict. Churchill firmly believed at the time and afterwards that this was the right decision. In 1941–2 Germany still posed a mortal threat to Britain, but even if Singapore fell, as it did, the Japanese were unlikely to attempt an invasion of Australia. The situation there could always be retrieved, he felt, by a last-minute diversion of British forces to the Far East or, more realistically, by American intervention. Britain's belated and inadequate efforts to defend Singapore, the key to its defences in the Far East, were, nonetheless, a severe blow to Australians during the war, and left a bad taste afterwards. David Day, an Australian historian, has labelled this the 'Great Betrayal', an inflammatory charge that was controversially taken up in 1992 by Australia's then-Prime Minister.[58] Churchill's association with both Gallipoli and Singapore naturally fostered the view in Australia that he was not just a bad strategist—that largely went without saying—but that he also had a cavalier attitude towards Australia's security and was willing to squander the lives of its soldiers. These negative stereotypes of Churchill were reinforced by a popular Australian television mini-series aired in 1984, *The Last Bastion*, in which the actor playing Churchill blames the failures of 1915 on Australian soldiers: 'If they had got on with Gallipoli in the Last War we would have swept the Dardanelles.' The problem with Australians, he added, was that 'You can't breed a decent race out of convicts and Irishmen.'[59]

The possibility that Churchill's actions in two world wars stemmed from an underlying contempt for Australians was given credibility by a comment Churchill reportedly made to his doctor in January 1942—not published until 1966, but frequently repeated since—that 'the Australians came of bad stock'.[60] In the *Great Betrayal*, Day dismisses the idea that this might have been simply 'an off-hand comment in a fit of anger'. Rather, echoing *The Last Bastion*, he asserts that the aristocratic Churchill 'could not prevent himself being dismissive of a country established originally as a convict colony and subsequently settled by large numbers of working-class Irishmen'.[61]

There is increasingly little common ground in the twenty-first century between the Churchill Legend and the most virulent strains of the counter-legend. Churchill's merits as a strategist in the Second World War are no longer even relevant to many of his critics, for whom any claims to greatness on Churchill's part are undercut by racist attitudes, unredeemed imperialism, and a bloodthirsty nature. As one such critic wrote recently, any evaluation of Churchill today must recognize that he was 'a chemical weapons enthusiast and unreconstructed racist who cut a swath of suffering and death across three continents'.[62] Given how often Churchill is denounced today on the Internet as a genocidal mass-murderer, the rights and wrongs of the Dardanelles campaign is perhaps the least of the challenges his legacy faces. Nevertheless, interest in Gallipoli and the Dardanelles has not disappeared, although it remains polarized along familiar lines. However, there is little in the way of serious debate. The myths and legend of the Dardanelles have largely taken on a life of their own, with the pro- and anti-Churchill camps tending to gravitate towards the version that best suits their predilections. The only really notable contribution to our understanding of the naval campaign in recent years has been the scrutiny of Turkish archives, which seems to point conclusively to the Ottomans having a much greater stock of ammunition available after 18 March 1915 than Churchill and many historians have suggested.[63] This revelation further undermines Churchill's argument that the fleet was on the verge of complete victory, but it has had no impact on popular perceptions of the campaign, or Churchill's part in it. Indeed, other than specialist military and naval historians, it seems that barely anyone has noticed.

Conclusion

What about the Dardanelles?

If the Dardanelles is to figure in the wider appreciation of Churchill's legacy, a century's worth of clutter needs to be stripped away. The same is true, of course, if we simply wish to understand the campaign on its own terms. The greatest obstacle has always been the desire to find simple explanations for complex events. These campaigns do not lend themselves to the kinds of black-and-white judgements and sweeping generalizations that are, admittedly, the most satisfying. If we wish to address, for example, a seemingly straightforward question such as whether 'the concept' behind the offensive was sound, it helps to be clear as to which iteration of 'the concept' we mean. The original plan was to force a passage through the Dardanelles by ships alone, but within weeks this had transformed into a naval attack on the Straits to be followed by the landing of troops to 'reap the fruits' of a naval victory. Subsequently, and for a brief period, it was intended to launch coordinated attacks by the two services to occupy the Gallipoli peninsula and force a passage through the Straits more or less simultaneously. It then became a land campaign that, if successful, would have allowed a *subsequent* naval advance through the Dardanelles. Thus, there were four distinct variants of the concept: an attack by the navy alone; by the navy then the army; by the navy and army together; and by the army then the navy. There is also the question of what all this was meant to accomplish. At times the naval offensive was conceived primarily as a means to destroy the two modern German warships that had been absorbed into the Ottoman Navy. Later, it came to be viewed as an opportunity to knock the Ottoman Empire out of the war, or even as a launching pad for an Allied offensive against Austria-Hungary. Different views on these goals were held concurrently by different actors, and virtually everyone's views changed over time.

The one indisputable fact in all this is that the campaign ended in failure. No Allied fleet ever reached the Sea of Marmara. Indeed, no fleet ever got as far the Kephez minefield guarding the Narrows. Was success ever a possibility? The simple answer is yes, although even this is not straightforward. What might have worked at one time would not necessarily have succeeded at another. It is generally agreed that a surprise attack by the army and the navy together *probably* would have succeeded if it had been launched before the Ottoman defenders were fully prepared. The massive Allied Army hopelessly bogged down on the peninsula in November 1915 might, in other words, have achieved complete success if it had been landed, instead, in February. But this is not what was attempted. In January 1915 this was not even considered an option. And by March it was already too late—the best, if not the only, shot at victory had, by then, passed. From this point on, it was consistently a case of 'too little, too late'. The window of opportunity was a narrow one.

If success was not inconceivable under any circumstances, the obvious question is whether the earliest iteration of the British plan could have succeeded, that is, an assault by ships alone. This seems unlikely. The counterfactual argument constructed by Churchill, in which the enemy was critically short of ammunition and victory easily within grasp, greatly oversimplifies the problems facing the Allied fleet in March 1915. The Ottoman forts were not the only obstacle to the fleet's advance, and not even the main obstacle. Even if the heaviest Ottoman guns had suddenly ceased firing, which seems unlikely, the minefields were still intact and protected by a network of batteries and howitzers that were—and would remain—largely immune to naval gunfire. Keyes' counterfactual argument, which posited a revamped and efficient minesweeping force clearing the way for a rapid advance through the Narrows sometime after April, is perhaps slightly more realistic, but still downplays the heavy fire from the forts and mobile batteries. And both scenarios consider only the problem of getting ships through the Dardanelles. It does not automatically follow, as Churchill claimed, that there would have been a revolution in Constantinople, that Ottoman resistance would have crumbled, or even that the Gallipoli peninsula would have been evacuated. These outcomes always represented the best-case scenario. Churchill never really came to terms with the possibility that an Allied fleet that reached the Sea of Marmara might be too weak to overawe the Ottoman capital, or even to destroy the enemy fleet. It seems likely that the Ottomans would, in fact, have kept fighting. The worst-case scenario, as Jackson pointed out on 5 January, was a depleted and battered fleet, short of ammunition and fuel, eventually fighting its way back through the Straits having accomplished virtually nothing.

But it must be remembered that a key component of the original British plan was that it could be called off if it did not go as well as expected. The worst-case scenario could, in theory, have been avoided, provided British leaders were willing to cut their losses. It was on this basis alone that sceptics like Jackson were prepared to endorse the original plan, and that the politicians eagerly accepted it. Viewed from this perspective, the naval assault emerges in a better light. Churchill's original proposal was, as he often claimed, a relatively low-risk venture, since Britain *could* afford to lose a few pre-dreadnought battleships without jeopardizing its position in the North Sea. The chances of complete success may have been slim, but this is more obvious in hindsight than it could have been at the time. Churchill and his colleagues on the War Council were overly impressed by political calculations and the many intangible factors that would come into play, such as the state of Ottoman morale and the willingness of the Balkan states to join the fighting. But these things could not be predicted beforehand, and if everything went in the Allies' favour, the pay-off was potentially huge. For this reason, Churchill and the War Council were prepared to contemplate an operation that was rightly regarded at the time as an experiment, confident that the technical obstacles identified by the naval professionals would lead, at worst, to stalemate, light losses, and an embarrassing withdrawal, not to heavy naval losses and humiliating failure—and certainly not to a protracted and costly land campaign.

The assumption that the naval attack could easily be called off was at once the greatest strength and the greatest weakness of the original plan. At best, it was naive. It is difficult to contemplate Churchill, of all people, calmly accepting failure. When the point was reached on 18 March that the naval offensive had clearly miscarried, he was the strongest advocate of resuming the attack at the earliest opportunity, with or without troops. Churchill's natural combativeness, combined with an awareness that a prominent naval defeat would hurt him personally, practically guaranteed that he would try to keep going. Other members of the War Council were also reluctant to accept the verdict of 18 March as final. They had, after all, agreed to the operation knowing that some ships would probably be lost. The time had, therefore, not necessarily come to abandon the attack. But another important factor in the minds of most decision-makers through all this was the impact of failure on Britain's prestige in the east. This was a concern from the moment the operation was launched. The ministers who approved the naval attack in January accepted, rather too optimistically, that they would be willing to abandon the operation completely at the first serious setback. But the importance they attached to ensuring success gradually transformed the original idea of an 'experiment' into something more in the nature of a 'commitment'. And this, in turn, led to the tacit abandonment of the original plan, the one in which operations could be easily called off. Once troops were allocated to the theatre in mid-February, escalation, rather than withdrawal, became the most likely response to a naval setback.

The tendency towards escalation was present almost from the beginning. The decision to have a substantial body of troops in the eastern theatre to exploit a naval victory turned a limited-liability naval operation into something, in Churchill's words, 'far more momentous and far reaching in its scope & irrevocable in its character'.[1] Who was responsible for this gradual escalation? Churchill tried to disavow personal responsibility on more than one occasion, suggesting that Kitchener had been the driving force, and that it was up to the War Council to provide oversight. And to a point he is correct. Churchill was only the First Lord. He could not and did not control everything. He was probably correct, moreover, in suggesting that his colleagues did not really appreciate how the fundamental character of the operation would be altered by the commitment of troops. At the same time, he was not the helpless spectator he sometimes made himself out to be. He may have warned his colleagues about the dangers of escalation, as he later told Ashmead-Bartlett, although there is no contemporary evidence to corroborate this. However, we know that he was present at the meeting where the decision was taken to have troops on hand, and there is no reason to think he spoke out against it. He was eager in the weeks that followed to build up the largest force possible, as evidenced by his dispute with Kitchener over the release of the 29th Division. But he did not initiate the abandonment of the original plan, and he does seem to have adhered longer than most to the idea that the campaign should, if possible, be a purely naval affair, with troops only brought in later to exploit the fleet's successes.

The pressure to find troops for the operation originated with Fisher and members of the naval staff, but their methods proved to be their undoing. They privately voiced their concerns to Hankey, who also saw the advantages of a combined operation. And he used his influence behind the scenes to persuade Asquith and possibly other members of the War Council to release troops to support the naval attack. But at this stage—mid-February—the politicians remained cautious. They only contemplated soldiers as a means to exploit a naval victory, not to launch a genuine combined operation. Most importantly, this was Kitchener's view. The War Council's commitment of troops therefore produced what was probably the worst possible result. It did nothing to improve the fleet's chances of breaking through the Straits, while making the eventual escalation into a land campaign far more likely. Once Allied troops began to arrive in Egypt and Lemnos, the temptation to use them to retrieve a faltering naval campaign became overwhelming. This was the perspective of the admirals on the spot, Carden and de Robeck, of Fisher and Jackson at the Admiralty, of Kitchener, and, it seems, of most members of the War Council. Kitchener and Churchill both seem to have realized early on that this might happen. But the pros and cons were never properly thrashed out in the War Council; there were no staff talks between the Admiralty and War Office; and no contingency plans were drawn up by the general staff. The government never even took a formal decision to land troops on the peninsula, although there does appear to have been implicit support from ministers.

The suspension of the naval attack after 18 March demonstrates that it was not difficult, after all, to halt the naval operation at short notice. But no serious thought was given at the time to the possibility of abandoning this theatre entirely, as the original plan had envisioned. The subsequent campaign on the Gallipoli peninsula is often treated as the inevitable result of the original decision to force a passage through the Straits, and it is true that the army would not have been employed but for the previous decision to attempt a naval assault. However, as Churchill noted in November 1915, 'Naval operations did not necessarily involve military operations. This was a separate decision, which did not rest with me or the Admiralty.'[2] By April 1915, however, a land campaign stood little chance of success. The Ottomans were, by now, well prepared to defend the peninsula, and too few resources were committed by the Allies to make the initial attack a success. The responsibility for launching the Gallipoli operation with little consideration and insufficient forces rests primarily with Kitchener, who alone had the power to initiate the land campaign. Churchill's responsibility for the commitment of the army was slightly more than that of other Cabinet ministers, since he was better informed of Kitchener's intentions than they were, but he did not irrevocably commit the government to launching a major land campaign.

Churchill was therefore responsible in January 1915 for convincing the War Council to approve a naval offensive that we know had little chance of success. Those who blame him for everything that followed generally assume that he was solely responsible for the original idea of an attack by ships alone; that he forced the scheme on reluctant naval advisers who warned of failure; and that the War Council was actively misled about professional opinion. In this version of events, admirals and ministers alike were simply victims of Churchill's Dardanelles obsession. These charges need to be considered carefully. The initiative behind a purely naval attack did come from Churchill. If he had not raised the idea, no one else would have. But the proposal for a step-by-step advance was not his—this plan originated with Carden and his staff. If the admiral did not really think the idea was practicable, he could have killed the project at the outset simply by predicting prohibitive losses. Instead, he calculated optimistically that the fleet 'Might do it all in a month about.'[3] Responsible figures at the Admiralty might have stopped the project when Carden's plan arrived in London, but they did not. One need only recall the fate of Churchill's Borkum proposal to see how easily his initiatives could be blocked. In the case of the Dardanelles, however, there is no contemporary record of strong and clearly expressed dissent from anyone in the initial stages, including Fisher. Even the testimony provided later to the Dardanelles Commission tends to confirm a broad measure of cautious support for the initial proposal. The final Admiralty orders drawn up by Oliver and the naval staff weeks later were also confident, predicting that the fleet could probably advance by 'perhaps a mile a day, perhaps more, perhaps less'.[4] Churchill could, therefore, legitimately claim that what he promoted was, in fact, a 'service plan'.

The common view that Churchill forced the naval attack on unwilling advisers originated with Fisher, and was popularized in the first instance by Gwynne. Fisher's motives are obscure. It appears that the admiral was not paying close attention when the possibility of a naval attack on the Dardanelles was first raised; that he gave it some degree of backing on 12–13 January because his principal advisers, on whom he relied, expressed their support; and that within a week of taking the project to the War Council he had developed strong regrets. He later exaggerated his previous efforts to halt the plan, depicting himself as the victim of political forces he could not control, and of a First Lord who would not listen. The evidence suggests, however, that he wanted his naval colleagues to think he had been overruled so that they would not suspect that he had meekly submitted to a plan in which he no longer believed. When Fisher did come out openly against the Dardanelles project on 25 January, he undermined his case by focusing on the risk to Britain's naval margins in the North Sea. This fear was not shared by others at the Admiralty or in the War Council, and Churchill had no difficulty brushing these concerns aside. If Fisher thought the naval attempt was doomed to fail, he could have stopped it. But considerable momentum had developed behind the project by then, and he needed to say clearly and forcefully that it was likely to fail, which he did not do. When the project continued, he immediately resumed his efforts to undermine it by telling friends and supporters that he was, and had always been, against the idea, which gave rise to speculation and gossip that Churchill, whose forcefulness was well known, had overruled him and everyone else at the Admiralty. This story was not, on the face of it, implausible, especially in light of earlier accusations that Churchill frequently exceeded his authority as First Lord. These rumours eventually found an outlet in the British press, and for a century have been at the heart of the case against Churchill.

In fact, naval leaders were not consistently and uniformly opposed to the Dardanelles operation. Two members of the Admiralty war group—Oliver and Bartolomé—always believed the operation was worthwhile, and acknowledged as much to the Dardanelles Commission. And the opposition from Fisher and Jackson was, at best, inconsistent. The fleet's early success in neutralizing the outer defences appears, for a time, to have won over the sceptics. Churchill was not necessarily exaggerating when he suggested in his memoirs that, if the Dardanelles Commissioners had 'taken the expert evidence on the feasibility of ships attacking forts in the first week of March, 1915 . . . they would have been impressed by the robust character of naval opinion on these questions'.[5] The admirals were not desperately applying the brakes to the operation and looking for a way out, as might be expected if they were certain of failure. Churchill did not, for example, have to pressure anyone to intensify the naval attack in mid–March, when the fleet's progress had stalled. And the growing desire in early February to commit troops for follow–up operations—a desire that Churchill shared—did not mean that troops were considered essential to get ships through the Straits. The main concern at the time was to ensure the fleet's communications after it got through. The despatch of troops to the theatre was initially spurred, in other words, by naval leaders' expectations of success rather than of failure.

The other charge frequently levelled against Churchill is that he concealed the concerns of his naval advisers from the War Council in order to secure approval. There is some truth in this. By January 1915, Churchill was convinced that many worthwhile and promising offensive schemes had been rejected merely because doubts had been raised. He was therefore quick to gloss over potential difficulties that might result in this latest proposal for action being casually rejected, as he saw it, before its merits could be fully appreciated. In the process, he painted an overly optimistic picture of the operation's prospects, thereby reducing the likelihood that it would be carefully scrutinized by the War Council. Churchill was temperamentally predisposed to ignore or downplay potential difficulties once he had set his heart on a particular course of action. This trait was exacerbated by an inflated confidence in his own judgement. Once committed to a project, Churchill was reluctant to abandon it. To make matters worse, he could be resentful of criticism and was quick to marginalize or dismiss subordinates who might stand in his way. Churchill valued compliance highly in an adviser, which was an important factor in the disastrous decision to recall Fisher.

Churchill's effectiveness as First Lord of the Admiralty in 1914–15 was compromised by these aspects of his personality, but the impact of such aspects on the inception of the Dardanelles campaign should not be exaggerated. The proposal Churchill took to the War Council on 13 January 1915 had cautious backing from his principal naval advisers, provided it could be called off at an early stage. And this is how he presented it to his fellow politicians. He did not dwell on potential difficulties, but he had addressed many of the concerns previously raised by Jackson. There was to be no reckless 'rush' through mined waters, and the attack could be broken off if it proved more difficult than expected. It was not until later in the month that a measure of real opposition began to emerge. Only then did Churchill's reluctance to listen to unwelcome advice became a serious problem. He continued to insist on moving ahead with the scheme even after he knew it was not wholeheartedly supported by the First Sea Lord. But even then, Churchill did not conceal from his fellow politicians that the operation involved risks, that ships would undoubtedly be lost, and that the operation might conceivably fail.

Churchill's eagerness to press ahead with the Dardanelles offensive was not the sole reason the operation was approved, as Bean and others have suggested. His powers of persuasion were formidable, but he never dominated the strategic decision-making process by sheer force of personality. His Cabinet colleagues frequently challenged his proposals and rejected his advice. Churchill's exaggerated optimism over the Dardanelles operation was just one of many things wrong with Britain's machinery for the higher direction of the war in January 1915. At the Admiralty, the Dardanelles scheme did not receive the rigorous study it required, as the Dardanelles Commission later revealed. The naval war staff were overly optimistic about the ability of naval guns to reduce the Ottoman forts, and, more importantly, assumed that these would be the main obstacle to the fleet. Far too little attention was given to the enemy's concealed field guns and howitzers and the problem of sweeping the minefields, which proved to be the most formidable obstacles to the fleet's advance. Nor did the Admiralty seek advice from gunnery or fortification experts in the army, who might have predicted some of the obstacles the fleet would encounter. The other problem at the Admiralty was Fisher, who did not use his advisers effectively or give the naval staff clear guidance. Most seriously, he failed to communicate clearly with the First Lord and the War Council. Things might have turned out very differently if he had been willing to voice his objections on 12 and 13 January, although it is not clear whether Fisher actually had strong doubts at that time. But it is certainly not the case that Churchill deliberately silenced his naval advisers at the War Council in order to have his way. And Fisher's claim that he believed he could only speak when invited to do so must be taken with a healthy dose of scepticism. The admiral chose to remain silent, it seems, because he lacked confidence in his ability to defend his views from challenge by Churchill or other politicians. Churchill's determination to appoint him First Sea Lord in 1914 was a serious error of judgement.

These problems at the Admiralty were compounded by the shortcomings of the War Council, which never provided the close and regular oversight of the war effort that many expected of it. During the first year of the war, Britain's machinery for coordinating the two fighting services remained informal and amateurish. As Hankey pointed out with increasing urgency, the British system, such as it was, was not suited to the demands of modern global warfare. The Prime Minister was the only one who could have imposed greater order and efficiency on the system, but he preferred to leave strategy and operations in the hands of the two service ministers, with himself as coordinator and arbitrator. When the War Council *was* involved in strategic decision-making, it was seldom effective. There was nothing to stop the politicians from seeking Fisher's independent views when the Dardanelles operation was first proposed or before a final decision was taken, but they preferred not to do so. No detailed appreciation was ever drawn up by either the Admiralty or the War Office for circulation to ministers. Even Kitchener, who might have probed the technical aspects of the Admiralty's proposal, was disinclined to do so. If the War Council was less informed about the potential risks than it should have been, this was largely by its own choice. These problems became worse once the decision was taken to support the naval offensive with troops. Kitchener, as War Minister, was virtually a law unto himself. He was reluctant to share military information with his political colleagues; he was not subjected to close oversight by the War Council; and he largely ignored his own general staff. The War Council was effectively sidelined when the final decision about using the army had to be taken—Asquith simply stopped calling meetings for eight critical weeks. Furthermore, Kitchener's preparations for an invasion left much to be desired. He did not seek approval or guidance from his colleagues on the War Council, and he bypassed the general staff, effectively delegating the detailed planning for the operation to Hamilton and the men on the spot.

The most extreme views about Churchill's role in the Dardanelles—that the concept was brilliant and could have succeeded, or that it was an obviously hopeless idea forced on helpless advisers and politicians—both break down under scrutiny. The inception of the Dardanelles campaign highlights both Churchill's strengths and his weaknesses as war leader. On the plus side, he realized early on the futility of large offensives on the Western Front and tried to exploit Britain's strategic flexibility by launching peripheral operations where better results might be obtained at a lower cost. The original plan for the Dardanelles—as an experimental attack with surplus warships that would be called off if things went badly—began as an imaginative, low-risk venture. It had enough support from his professional advisers, moreover, that Churchill *was* probably justified in taking the proposal to the War Council. But this must be balanced against a formidable list of weaknesses. To begin with, the idea of an attack by ships alone was never likely to succeed. This was not obvious at first, even to many high-ranking naval officers, but Churchill undoubtedly underestimated the practical difficulties that stood in the way of this and other offensive schemes he promoted. The methods he employed to see the project through were a much greater problem. The Dardanelles campaign highlights Churchill's habitual overconfidence; his impatience and willingness to run unnecessary risks; his tendency to disregard or downplay professional advice he did not like; and his readiness to escalate Britain's commitment in the east after there were clear signs that the naval offensive had irretrievably broken down.

When everything is taken into consideration, the Dardanelles naval offensive was launched because Churchill and his professional advisers underestimated the obstacles the Allied fleet would encounter; because Churchill and other members of the War Council believed little risk was involved as long as the operation could be called off; and because none of the principal actors foresaw the dangers of escalation. The latter miscalculation was by far the most serious. If the attack had been abandoned in mid-March, by which time the Fleet had ceased to make any meaningful progress, there would have been no perception that Britain had sustained a serious defeat. Even the losses of 18 March hardly qualified as a disaster. It was clear by then, however, that the Ottoman defences had been underestimated, and that continuing the offensive *would* involve serious risks. The offensive should have been broken off then. The greatest harm to British interests was caused by the protracted and brutal land campaign. The Gallipoli operations formed no part of Churchill's original proposal. The First Lord, like everyone else, failed to anticipate the strong pressures to escalate Britain's eastern commitment once the campaign got under way. And he was admittedly more often to be found applying the accelerator than the brakes. But the drift from a limited naval commitment to a major combined undertaking was driven by Kitchener more than anyone, and was facilitated by a flawed decision-making process at the highest levels.

Given how much of the immediate responsibility for the costly Gallipoli campaign rightfully attaches to the Secretary of State for War, it is curious that Churchill should have become the main political casualty of the Dardanelles–Gallipoli operations. However, Churchill was a controversial politician, and Kitchener a popular hero. The latter's shortcomings as War Minister were well known to his Cabinet colleagues, but not to the general public. When Kitchener was attacked by Northcliffe's *Daily Mail* in May 1915 for his role in the 'shells scandal', the public rallied to his defence. Historian J. Lee Thompson noted that: 'An affronted nation condemned the press lord and all his works and rose in fervent defense of Kitchener. *Daily Mail* circulations and advertising plummeted and papers were burned in the street and at the stock exchange.'[6] This is in stark contrast to the reaction to repeated attacks on Churchill in the *Morning Post*, which produced a perfunctory defence at first from the Liberal press, but generated no public backlash against the Conservative newspaper. On the contrary, Gwynne's

charges were increasingly repeated in other newspapers in the months that
followed and were eventually raised in Parliament.

Churchill was always going to be associated in the public mind with the
failure at the Dardanelles. He was the head of the navy when the operation
was launched, and it was widely known that he had been the one to set
events in motion. He also closely associated himself with both operations in
the months and decades that followed, as he strove to defend and rebuild his
reputation. But beyond this, it must be noted that Churchill was marked out
for sole blame at an early stage by hostile elements in the British press and
by the Conservative Party. His removal from the Admiralty and Fisher's
resignation in May 1915 seemed to confirm charges that the politician could
not work with his naval advisers, but they also reinforced the perception
that his personal responsibility for both the Dardanelles and Gallipoli overshadowed that of his colleagues. Most of the ministers who had been
involved in launching the campaign were unaffected by the political crisis
that resulted. When the dust settled, Asquith was still Prime Minister,
Kitchener was still Secretary of State for War, and Lloyd George was head of
the new Ministry of Munitions. Churchill's embarrassing demotion to the
Chancellorship of the Duchy of Lancaster was widely perceived as a sign of
his colleagues' disapproval. But members of the Liberal government were
well aware of their own part in launching these operations, and were not
looking to scapegoat Churchill. If Asquith had not agreed to a coalition in
May 1915, Churchill might have remained in office and weathered the
storm. The rapid collapse of his political position, his isolation even within
his own party, and ongoing criticism in the press created such strong
momentum against Churchill that he was fortunate ever to recover.

The gradual improvement in his reputation during and after the First
World War owes a great deal to Churchill's own tireless efforts to shape
public perceptions of the Dardanelles campaign. Beginning with his 1915
resignation speech, he hammered away at the many exaggerated and inaccurate criticisms that had been made against him. He skilfully used the
Dardanelles Commission to build a comprehensive case for his defence,
neutralize potential enemies, and start spreading blame to other members of
the former government. But somewhere along the way, he realized that
quibbling with his critics over details was unlikely to get him very far. What
he needed was to offer the public a new narrative to supplant the one his
enemies had created in 1915. The most potent antidote to the anti-Churchill
myths that threatened to drag him down proved to be a robust counter-myth.

With *The World Crisis*, Churchill launched a remarkably successful campaign to convince the public that the Dardanelles was actually a brilliant concept that had come close to success. Over the course of a decade, Churchill laid the foundations of an alternative history of the campaign, one constructed from a mixture of truths, half-truths, and dubious assertions.

Churchill would later say of his Second World War memoirs that 'This is not history, this is my case.'[7] The same applies with even greater force to *The World Crisis*. In the preface to the second volume, he acknowledged that he did not approach his subject as an historian. 'It is not for me', he wrote, 'with my record and special point of view to pronounce a final conclusion.' The book, he suggested, was only 'a contribution to history'.[8] When he began work on *The Second World War* in the 1940s, Churchill was already looking ahead to his legacy. He sought to establish the Churchill Legend on a firm foundation for posterity. In *The World Crisis*, however, he was still writing as a politician. His goals were more prosaic. He wanted to further his political career. He therefore crafted a plausible and seductive counter-narrative, one in which he had nothing to apologize for. His single-minded focus on the Dardanelles and his overbearing manner were transformed into virtues. In the process, Churchill laid the foundations for a popular and enduring myth: that the Ottoman forts were nearly out of ammunition, the minefields were falling apart, the Ottoman Empire was on the verge of collapse, Russia could have been saved from defeat, and the war might have been shortened by years, with millions of lives spared. Churchill reinforced these themes at every opportunity in his journalistic writing and speeches. The myth took root, in part, because it found support in the British official histories and numerous memoirs and histories published in the interwar period. But also because it held a strong appeal to a British public becoming disillusioned with the cost and conduct of the First World War.

Churchill was unable to expunge the shadow of the Dardanelles before the start of the Second World War, but he nevertheless succeeded in reducing it to manageable proportions. In May 1940, when the stakes were at their highest, the legacy of the Dardanelles did not block his rise to power. The British people readily accepted him as war leader. And when the fighting was over, they celebrated his legacy. Churchill was quick to capitalize on this reversal of his fortunes. After 1945, he deployed the same skills as self-propagandist he had developed in the 1920s, and this time with even greater success. His version of the Dardanelles, which blended myth with history, was easily absorbed into the Churchill Legend that emerged from the Second World War. And this, from Churchill's perspective, was exactly how it should be. In 1914 he had been confident that he would emerge from the First World War hailed by his countrymen as a great leader, strategist, and statesman. The Dardanelles campaign demonstrated that, despite his many gifts, he was none of these things in 1915. Churchill's refusal to accept this verdict ensured that he would have another chance to prove himself. In 1940 he was ready.

Notes

WINSTON CHURCHILL AND THE DARDANELLES: A RIDDLE WRAPPED IN MYTHS INSIDE A LEGEND

1. A. J. P. Taylor, *English History 1914–1945* (Oxford: Oxford University Press, 1965), 4.
2. Speech, House of Commons, 23 January 1948, *Winston S. Churchill: His Complete Speeches* [hereafter cited as *Complete Speeches*], ed. Robert Rhodes James (8 vols, New York: Chelsea House, 1974), VII:7587. On the 'Churchill Legend', see, in particular, John Ramsden, *Man of the Century: Winston Churchill and His Legend since 1945* (New York: Columbia University Press, 2003); David Reynolds, *In Command of History* (London: Allen Lane, 2004).
3. This label is, admittedly, anachronistic. The Conservatives were popularly known at this time as Unionists, stemming from the alliance of traditional Conservatives and 'Liberal Unionists' in their opposition to Irish Home Rule after 1886. As the term Unionist fell into disuse in the 1920s and is now largely forgotten, Conservative will be used here instead.
4. Probably the worst offenders in this respect is Tom Curran's *The Grand Deception* (Newport, NSW: Big Sky Publishing, 2015).
5. Margot Asquith diary, 16 May 1915, *Margot Asquith's Great War Diary, 1914–1916: The View from Downing Street*, ed. Michael and Eleanor Brock (Oxford: Oxford University Press, 2014), 174.
6. C. P. Scott notes, 22 November 1916, in Randolph S. Churchill and Martin Gilbert, *Winston S. Churchill* [Churchill's official biography, cited hereafter as *WSC*] (8 vols and 13 companion books, London: Heinemann, 1966–88), III/2:1583.
7. George Riddell diary, 7 July 1916, Lord Riddell papers, British Library, Add MS 62978.
8. There is an interesting parallel to Churchill's aggressive response to recurring allegations that he had behaved dishonourably during his escape from captivity in the Boer War. See Celia Sandys, *Churchill: Wanted Dead or Alive* (Edison, NJ: Castle Books, 2005), 104–15.

CHAPTER I

1. Matthew S. Seligmann, 'The Anglo-German Naval Race, 1898–1914', in *Arms Races in International Politics*, ed. Thomas G. Mahnken, Joseph A. Maiolo, and David Stevenson (Oxford: Oxford University Press, 2016), 21–40.
2. Crease, 'General Remarks', The National Archives [TNA], Kew, ADM 1/28268.
3. Winston S. Churchill (hereafter WSC) to Clementine Churchill, 28 July 1914, *Speaking for Themselves*, ed. Mary Soames (Toronto: Stoddart, 1998), 96.
4. Violet Asquith diary, *Champion Redoubtable: The Diaries and Letters of Violet Bonham Carter 1914–1945*, ed. Mark Pottle (London: Weidenfeld & Nicolson, 1998), 25; see also Violet Bonham Carter, *Winston Churchill as I Knew Him* (London: Eyre & Spottiswoode, 1965), 361, where the wording is altered slightly to make the statement more benign. Churchill's seemingly light-hearted attitude could and did cause offence. Pamela McKenna, the wife of Reginald McKenna, a Liberal Cabinet minister and Churchill's predecessor as First Lord, was appalled in January 1915 when she heard Churchill refer to the conflict as 'This delicious war'. Riddell diary, 14 January 1915, Add MS 62975.
5. Margot Asquith diary, 10 January 1915, *WSC*, III/1:400; *Margot Asquith's Great War Diary*, 144.
6. David French, 'The Rise and Fall of Business as Usual', in *War and the State: The Transformation of British Government, 1914–1919*, ed. Kathleen Burk (London: George Allen & Unwin, 1982), 7–31.
7. 'Great Britain and Germany: Dreadnoughts at Outbreak of War', 1 October 1914, Churchill papers, Churchill College Archives Centre, Cambridge, CHAR 2/105/11.
8. Matthew S. Seligmann, 'Failing to Prepare for the Great War? The Absence of Grand Strategy in British War Planning before 1914', *War in History* (forthcoming).
9. David G. Morgan-Owen, 'An 'Intermediate Blockade'? British North Sea Strategy, 1912–1914', *War in History*, 22, no. 4 (2015), 478–502.
10. WSC to Battenberg, 17 February 1913, ADM 116/3412.
11. Ibid.
12. See Shawn Grimes, *Strategy and War Planning in the British Navy, 1887–1918* (London: Boydell Press, 2012), 182–4.
13. Asquith to Venetia Stanley, 24 December 1914, in *H. H. Asquith: Letters to Venetia Stanley*, ed. Michael and Eleanor Brock (Oxford: Oxford University Press, 1982), 338.
14. *The Jellicoe Papers*, ed. A. Temple Patterson (2 vols, London: Navy Records Society, 1966–8), I:36, 40–1.
15. Grimes, *Strategy and War Planning*, 187–9.
16. WSC to Asquith, 31 July 1914, ADM 137/452; *WSC*, III/1:6–7.
17. WSC to Battenberg and Sturdee, 9 August 1914, *WSC*, III/1:24–6; Grimes, *Strategy and War Planning*, 193–4.
18. Richmond diary, 9 August 14, Richmond papers, National Maritime Museum, RIC/1/9; *Portrait of an Admiral*, ed. Arthur J. Marder (Cambridge, MA: Harvard University Press, 1952), 96–7.

19. WSC memorandum, 19 August 1914, *WSC*, III/1:45–6; Harcourt diary, 20 August 1914, Harcourt papers, Bodleian Library.

20. Lady Richmond diary, 10 August 1914, RIC 1/16.

21. Wake report, ADM 137/452; Grimes, *Strategy and War Planning*, 189.

22. Jellicoe to WSC, 30 September 1914, *Jellicoe Papers*, I:71–2.

23. Richmond diary, 12 August 1914, RIC/1/9; *Portrait*, 98.

24. Ibid.

25. Lady Richmond diary, 23 August 1914, RIC 1/16.

26. Lady Richmond diary, 18 August 1914, RIC 1/16.

27. Report by Jellicoe, 24 September 1914, *Jellicoe Papers*, I:69.

28. WSC to Asquith, Grey, and Kitchener, 25 August 1914, *WSC*, III/1:53; Harcourt diary, 2 September 1914; undated memorandum, CHAR 13/27.

29. *Jellicoe Papers*, I:69. Churchill revived this idea later in the war, when he contemplated the United States Navy forming part of the combined Allied fleet. See Christopher M. Bell, *Churchill and Sea Power* (Oxford: Oxford University Press, 2012), 80–2.

30. Richmond notes around this time that Admiral Sturdee complained to him that 'Winston & the soldiers are at him because the Fleet is "doing nothing"—that he is making a "negative" use of the Fleet.' Richmond diary, 13 September 1914, RIC/1/9; *Portrait*, 107.

31. Clementine Churchill to WSC, *c.*19 September 1914, *Speaking for Themselves*, 104–5.

32. Ibid.

33. Richmond diary, 24 October 1914, RIC/1/10; *Portrait*, 121; *WSC*, III/1:216.

34. Balfour to Sandars, 22 September 1914, Sandars papers, Bodleian Library, MS Eng Hist, c.766.

35. Winston S. Churchill, *The World Crisis* (5 vols, New York: Scribners, 1963–4), I:253; see also Viscount Grey, *Twenty-Five Years: 1892–1916* (2 vols, Toronto: Ryerson Press, 1925), II:68–70.

36. Speech of 11 September 1914, National Liberal Club, London, *Complete Speeches*, III:2331.

37. Richmond diary, 20 August 1914, RIC/1/9; *Portrait*, 100. In her diary, Margot Asquith recorded her husband telling her that Clementine Churchill 'said some time ago that inventing uniforms was one of Winston's chief pleasures and temptations'. Entry for 17 February 1915, *Margot Asquith's Great War Diary*, 149; *WSC*, III/1:524.

38. Harcourt diary, 5 October 1914.

39. WSC to Asquith, 5 October 1914, *WSC*, III/1:163.

40. Sir Edward Grey to Sir Francis Bertie, 4 October 1914, *WSC*, III/1:162.

41. WSC to Asquith, 5 October 1914, *WSC*, III/1:163.

42. Asquith to Venetia Stanley, *WSC*, III/1:166.

43. Bonham Carter, *Winston Churchill*, 335. Clementine has similarly commented on Churchill's sense of proportion when he had contemplated leaving the Admiralty a few weeks earlier. 'Great & glorious as have been the achievements

of our army', she wrote, 'it is only a small one, 1/8 of the allied forces—Whereas you rule this gigantic Navy which will in the end decide the War.' Letter of *c.*19 September 1914, *Speaking for Themselves*, 104–5.

44. Asquith to Stanley, 6 October 1914, *WSC*, III/1:172–3; Harcourt diary, 6 October 1914.

45. Asquith to Stanley, 7 October 1914, *Asquith: Letters*, 266; *WSC*, III/1:177–8; Earl of Oxford and Asquith, *Memories and Reflections 1852–1927* (2 vols, Toronto: McClelland & Stewart, 1928), II:54–5.

46. Bridgman to Sandars, 26 November 1914, MS Eng Hist c.767. Sandars promptly passed this information to H. A. Gwynne, editor of the *Morning Post*, without revealing his source, along with the observation that, 'It will not take much to get Churchill out of the Admiralty.' Sandars to Gwynne, 27 November 1914, H. A. Gwynne papers, Imperial War Museum.

47. Fisher to Reginald McKenna, 16 May 1915, *WSC*, III:442. Emphasis in original.

48. WSC to Jellicoe, 8 October 1914, Jellicoe papers, British Library, Add MS 48990; *Jellicoe Papers*, I:74; *WSC*, III/1:180–2.

49. 21 September 1914, *Complete Speeches*, III:2337.

50. *WSC*, III:84–5.

51. HC Deb., 7 March 1916, vol. 80, c. 1425.

52. WSC to Bonar Law, 21 May 1915, *WSC*, III/2:922–4.

53. 'The Conduct of the War at Sea', *Candid Quarterly Review*, February 1915, 210. Bowles reportedly issued a pamphlet that made similar claims about the loss of the cruisers. Churchill, *World Crisis*, I:353; *WSC*, III/2:1174, n. 2.

54. Julian S. Corbett, *Naval Operations* (3 vols, London: Longmans, 1920–3), I:172–7, 441; Arthur J. Marder, *From the Dreadnought to Scapa Flow* (5 vols, Oxford: Oxford University Press, 1961–71), II:55–7.

55. Marder, *Dreadnought*, II:116–18.

56. Harcourt diary, 4 November 1914.

57. A. J. A. Morris (ed.), *The Letters of Lieutenant-Colonel Charles á Court Repington CMG Military Correspondent of The Times 1903–1918* (Stroud: Sutton Publishing for the Army Records Society, 1999), 41.

58. Gwynne to Bathurst, 13 October 1914, Glenesk-Bathurst papers, University of Leeds Library, MS/DEP/1990/1/2288; *The Rasp of War: The Letters of H.A. Gwynne to the Countess Bathurst, 1914–1918*, ed. Keith M. Wilson (London: Sidgwick & Jackson, 1988), 39.

59. Douglas Jerrold, *The Royal Naval Division* (London: Hutchinson, 1923), 39.

60. Gwynne to Bathurst, 13 October 1914, MS/DEP/1990/1/2288; *Rasp of War*, 39.

61. 'The Antwerp Blunder', *Morning Post*, 13 October 1914, 6.

62. 'Secret of Britain's Antwerp Expedition: It was Churchill's Own Personally Conceived Idea, Carried Out against Kitchener's Advice', *New York Times*, 23 October 1914, 2.

63. Riddell diary, 22 October 1914, Add MS 62974.

64. Undated Buckmaster memorandum, TNA, HO 139/5; Buckmaster to Churchill, 13 October 1914, CHAR 13/45/66.
65. Gwynne to Buckmaster, 14 October 1914, HO 139/5; *Rasp of War*, 41.
66. Ibid.
67. Edward Marsh to Buckmaster, 18 October 1914, HO 139/5.
68. Riddell diary, 22 October 1914, Add MS 62974.
69. Harcourt diary, 13 November 1914; Riddell diary, 6 December 1914, Add MS 62974.
70. Gwynne to Buckmaster, 20 October 1914, HO 139/5 A48/1.
71. 'The Man at the Wheel', *Morning Post*, 23 October 1914, 6; see also Gwynne to Bathurst, 22 October 1914, MS/DEP/1990/1/2292; *Rasp of War*, 45: 'What has happened is that Winston Churchill has practically taken command of the Board of Admiralty and the *Navy is being run by a civilian instead of by naval experts.*'
72. Selborne, HL Deb., 11 November 1914, vol. 18, cc. 37–40; Bonar Law, HC Deb., 11 November 1914, vol. 68, cc. 17–18.
73. Asquith, HC Deb., 11 November 1914, vol. 68, cc. 26–7.
74. The full text of the press release was subsequently published in Rear-Admiral Sir Douglas Brownrigg, *Indiscretions of the Naval Censor* (New York: Doran, 1920), 23–31.
75. Ian Buxton, *Big Gun Monitors*, 2nd edn (Barnsley: Seaforth Publishing, 2008), 93–6; Corbett, *Naval Operations*, I:213–25.
76. WSC to Fisher, 11 December 1914, Fisher papers, Churchill College Archives Centre, Cambridge, FISR 1/16; WSC to Fisher, 21 December 1914, *Fear God and Dread Nought*, ed. Arthur J. Marder (3 vols, London: Jonathan Cape, 1952–9), III:105. Graham Clews, *Churchill's Dilemma: The Real Story behind the Origins of the 1915 Dardanelles Campaign* (Santa Barbara, CA: Praeger, 2010), 26–8.
77. WSC to Bayly, 21 January 1915, CHAR 8/182.
78. Burney to WSC, 8 November 1914, FISR 1/16.
79. Asquith to Stanley, 24 December 1914, *Asquith: Letters*, 338.
80. See, for example, the memorandum by Lord Stamfordham, 27 October 1914, *WSC*, III/1:2201.
81. Asquith to Stanley, 27 October 1914, *Asquith: Letters*, 287.
82. Lady Richmond diary, 11 November 1914, RIC 1/16.
83. Dumas diary, 1 November 1914, Dumas papers, University of Leeds Library.
84. Lady Richmond diary, 17 November 1914, RIC 1/16.
85. Fisher–Corbett memorandum, 'On the Possibility of Using our Command of the Sea to Influence More Drastically the Military Situation on the Continent', December 1914, ADM 116/3454; *WSC*, III/1:284–7; Donald M. Schurman, *Julian S. Corbett, 1854–1922* (London: Royal Historical Society, 1981), 159–60.
86. Fisher–Corbett memorandum, 'On the Possibility of Using our Command of the Sea', December 1914, ADM 116/3454.
87. Schurman, *Corbett*, 160; Grimes, *Strategy and War Planning*, 205–6.

88. See David Morgan-Owen, 'Cooked Up in the Dinner Hour? Sir Arthur Wilson's War Plan, Reconsidered', *English Historical Review*, 130, no. 545 (August 2015), 898–903.

89. Oliver unpublished memoirs, Oliver papers, National Maritime Museum, OLV/12; Admiral Sir William James, *A Great Seaman: The Life of Admiral of the Fleet Sir Henry F. Oliver* (London: Witherby, 1956), 138. Hankey was also dismissive of Fisher's Baltic scheme: Ruddock Mackay, 'Hankey on Fisher's Baltic "Chimera"', *Mariner's Mirror*, 82, no. 2 (May 1996), 211–13.

90. War Council minutes, 1 December 1914, *WSC*, III/1:290.

91. Callwell to Henry Wilson, 2 December 1914, Henry Wilson papers, Imperial War Museum, HHW 2/75/17.

92. WSC memorandum, 2 December 1914, ADM 137/452; *WSC*, III/1:2913.

93. Balfour to Hankey, 5 December 1914, *WSC*, III/1:297.

94. Memorandum by Arthur J. Balfour to Hankey, 3 December 1914, ADM 116/1350; Marder, *Dreadnought*, I:184–5; Grimes, *Strategy and War Planning*, 198.

95. WSC to Fisher, 21 December 1914, *WSC*, III/1:323–4; *Fear God and Dread Nought*, III:105.

96. WSC to Fisher, 22 December 1914, *WSC*, III/1:325–6.

97. Asquith to Stanley, 24 December 1914, *WSC*, III/1:333; *Asquith: Letters*, 338.

98. WSC to Asquith, 29 December 1914, and memorandum, 31 December 1914, *WSC*, III/1:343–5, 347–9.

99. Ibid.

100. Hankey memorandum, 28 December 1914, *WSC*, III/1:337–43.

101. Lloyd George memorandum, 31 December 1914, *WSC*, III/1:350–6.

102. Asquith to Stanley, 30 December 1914, *WSC*, III/1:345–6.

103. On Balfour's views, see Balfour to Hankey, 2 January 1915, Stephen Roskill, *Hankey: Man of Secrets*, (3 vols, London: Collins, 1970–4), I:150–1.

CHAPTER 2

1. Asquith to Stanley, 17 August 1914, *Asquith: Letters*, 171; Asquith, *Memories and Reflections*, II:32; Harcourt diary, 17 August 1914; see also Warren Dockter, *Churchill and the Islamic World* (London: I.B. Tauris, 2015), 70–1.

2. WSC to General Sir Charles Douglas, 1 September 1914, in Churchill, *World Crisis*, I:531–2.

3. Colonel M. Talbot minute, 5 September 1914, TNA, WO 106/1463; *WSC*, III/1:91–2; *WSC*, III:203.

4. Callwell memorandum, September 1914, WO 106/1463; *WSC*, III/1:81–3.

5. WSC to Kerr, 4 September 1914, *WSC*, III/1:83–4; Churchill, *World Crisis*, I:532–3.

6. WSC to Grey, 6 September 1914, *WSC*, III/1:95.

7. Harcourt diary, 30 October 1914.

8. War Council meeting, 25 November 1914, TNA, CAB 22/1.

9. WSC to Asquith, 31 December 1914, *WSC*, III/1:346.

10. Fisher to Hankey, 2 January 1915, CAB 63/4; Robin Prior, *Gallipoli* (New Haven, CT: Yale University Press, 2009), 12.

11. Fisher to WSC, 3 January 1915, *WSC*, III/1:367; *Fear God and Dread Nought*, III:117–18.

12. *Fear God and Dread Nought*, III:117–18; Fisher to Hankey, 2 January 1915, CAB 63/4.

13. WSC to Fisher, 4 January 1915, *WSC*, III/1:371; *Fear God and Dread Nought*, III:121; see also Churchill, *World Crisis*, II:91, where the latter part of this statement is omitted.

14. Kitchener to WSC, 2 January 1915, *WSC*, III/1:360–1; Churchill, *World Crisis*, II:86–7, where Churchill states that Kitchener made similar statements when they discussed this subject at length at the Admiralty.

15. WSC to Fisher, Wilson, and Oliver, 3 January 1915, *WSC*, III/1:365–6.

16. WSC to Jellicoe, 4 January 1915, Add MS 48990; *Jellicoe Papers*, I:118–19; *WSC*, III/1:367–8.

17. Keyes to WSC, 4 January 1915, *The Keyes Papers*, ed. Paul G Halpern, (3 vols, London: Navy Records Society, 1979–81), I:69–70; Clews, *Churchill's Dilemma*, 68.

18. WSC to Fisher, 23 December 1914, *WSC*, III/1:326–7.

19. WSC to Carden, 3 January 1915, *WSC*, III/1:367.

20. A recent example is Tom Curran, 'Who was Responsible for the Dardanelles Naval Fiasco?', *Australian Journal of Politics & History*, 57, no. 1 (March 2011), 33.

21. Dardanelles Commission, Churchill testimony, 4 October 1916, Q. 1261–4, CAB 19/33.

22. Dardanelles Commission, Carden testimony, 6 October 1916, Q. 2556–6, CAB 19/33.

23. Lady Richmond diary, 3 January 1915, RIC/1/17.

24. Fisher to Balfour, 4 January 1915, Balfour papers, British Library, Add Mss. 49712.

25. Carden to WSC, 5 January 1915, *WSC*, III/1:380.

26. Jackson memorandum, 'Note on Forcing the Passage of the Dardanelles and Bosphorous by the Allied Fleets, in Order to Destroy the Turko-German Squadron and Threaten Constantinople without Military Co-operation', 5 January 1915, ADM 137/1089.

27. WSC to Carden, 6 January 1915, *WSC*, III/1:381.

28. Harcourt diary, 6 January 1915.

29. Bayly to Admiralty, 8 January 1915, ADM 137/1089.

30. War Council minutes, 7 January 1915, *WSC*, III/1:384–90. Emphasis in original.

31. War Council minutes, 8 January 1915, *WSC*, III/1:393–4.

32. War Council minutes, 8 January 1915, *WSC*, III/1:395.

33. WSC to French, 11 January 1915, *WSC*, III/1:401.

34. Jellicoe to WSC, 8 January 1915, *WSC*, III/1:397–8.
35. WSC to Jellicoe, 11 January 1915, Add MS 48990; *Jellicoe Papers*, I:122–4; *WSC*, III/1:402–4.
36. WSC to Jellicoe, 11 January 1915, Add MS 48990.
37. Richmond diary, 4 January 1915, RIC/1/12; *Portrait*, 134–5.
38. Lady Richmond diary, 4 January 1915, RIC/1/17. Richmond later attempted to sabotage the Borkum project by denouncing it to Callwell, when the latter was sent by Kitchener to the Admiralty to make enquiries about it. Lady Richmond diary, 6 January 1915, RIC/1/17.
39. Lady Richmond diary, 5 January 1915, RIC/1/17.
40. Lady Richmond diary, 9 January 1915, RIC/1/17.
41. Lady Richmond diary, 14 January 1915, RIC/1/17; Oliver made similar remarks in his unpublished memoirs.
42. Carden to WSC, 11 January 1915, *WSC*, III/1:405–6.
43. Churchill, *World Crisis*, II:95.
44. Fisher to Oliver, 12 January 1915, *WSC*, III/1:405–6; Robin Prior, *Churchill's 'World Crisis' as History* (London: Croom Helm, 1983), 55, 58–60; Clews, *Churchill's Dilemma*, ch. 8.
45. Jackson to Oliver, 15 January 1915, ADM 137/1089.
46. Geoffrey Penn, *Fisher, Churchill and the Dardanelles* (Barnsley: Leo Cooper 1999), 124–6.
47. WSC to Fisher and Oliver, 12 January 1915, Churchill, *World Crisis*, II:102–3.
48. WSC to Fisher and Oliver, 20 January 1915, CHAR 2/74/45–6; *WSC*, III/1:432–3; WSC to Kitchener, 20 January 1915, *WSC*, III/1:433; also WSC draft message to the Russian Grand Duke Nicholas, 19 January 1915, *WSC*, III/1:430–1.
49. Churchill, *World Crisis*, II:116.
50. E.g. Michael Howard, 'Churchill and the First World War', in *Churchill*, ed. Robert Blake and William Roger Louis (New York: Norton, 1993), 132, 137.
51. The principal exceptions are Robin Prior and Graham Clews.
52. CHAR 8/134, Prior, *Churchill's 'World Crisis'*, 47.
53. War Council, 13 January 1915, *WSC*, III/1:409.
54. Lord Hankey, *The Supreme Command* (2 vols, London: Allen & Unwin, 1961), I:265–6.
55. War Council, 13 January 1915, *WSC*, III/1:410; Grey, *Twenty-Five Years*, II:75–6. There was never, Grey recalled, any possibility that the Dardanelles operation would have been planned from the outset as a joint military and naval operation. '[I]f this had been proposed the operation would never have been agreed to.'
56. David French, 'The Origins of the Dardanelles Campaign Reconsidered', *History*, 68, no. 233 (June 1983), 210–24.
57. War Council, 13 January 1915, *WSC*, III/1:411. Emphasis in original.
58. WSC to Fisher and Oliver, 13 January 1915, CHAR 2/74/42–44; *WSC*, III/1:412–13.

59. Richmond diary, 16 January 1915, RIC/1/12; *Portrait*, 135–6; also Lady Richmond diary, 14 January 1915, RIC/1/17.

60. Admiralty Confidential Book (CB) 1550, 'Report of the Committee Appointed to Investigate the Attacks On and the Enemy Defences of the Dardanelles Straits' (cited hereafter as 'Mitchell Report'), 1919, 23–4, ADM 186/600.

61. Jackson memorandum, 15 January 1915, *WSC*, III/1:419–21.

62. Mitchell Report, 73–8.

63. Prior's calculations, also based on the figures in the Mitchell Report, are in Prior, *Gallipoli*, 39–41.

64. Oliver memorandum, 25 January 1915, *WSC*, III/1:450–1.

65. WSC to Carden, and WSC to Asquith, Kitchener, and Grey, both 25 January 1915, *WSC*, III/1:449–50.

66. WSC to the Comte de Saint-Seine, 16 January 1915, *WSC*, III/1:421–2; Saint-Seine to Augagneur, 19 January 1915, George H. Cassar, *The French and the Dardanelles* (London: Allen & Unwin, 1971), 53–4; WSC to Grand Duke Nicholas, 19 January 1915, Churchill, *World Crisis*, II:113–14.

67. Cassar, *French and the Dardanelles*, 54–6.

68. WSC to Grey, 24 January 1915, *WSC*, III/1:447.

69. Cassar, *French and the Dardanelles*, 59, 251–2.

70. WSC to Grey and Kitchener, and Grey to WSC, 26 January 1915, CHAR 2/74/54.

CHAPTER 3

1. Fisher to WSC, 18 January 1915, FISR 16/6; *WSC*, III/1:428.

2. Fisher to Jellicoe, 19 January 1915, Add MS 49006; *Jellicoe Papers*, I:125; *WSC*, III/1:429–30.

3. In his memoirs, Hankey later recorded, that 'Fisher knew that I invariably reported our conversations to Asquith, and I was the means of arranging at least one interview between them. But I could never induce him to speak his mind at the Council.' *Supreme Command*, I:313.

4. Asquith to Stanley, 20 January 1915, *WSC*, III/1:431–2.

5. Hankey to Balfour, 21 January 1915, *WSC*, III/1:437.

6. Fisher gives the date of his discussion with Fitzgerald as 19 January. Dardanelles Commission, Fisher testimony, 11 October 1916, Q. 3088, CAB 19/33.

7. Stevenson diary, 21 January 1915, *Lloyd George: A Diary by Frances Stevenson*, ed. A. J. P. Taylor (London: Hutchinson, 1971), 23.

8. Richmond diary, 19 January 1915, RIC/1/12; *Portrait*, 137; Lady Richmond diary, 17 January 1915, RIC/1/17.

9. J. A. Spender, *Life, Journalism and Politics*, (2 vols, London: Cassell, 1927), II:70–1.

10. Dardanelles Commission, Asquith testimony, 31 October 1916, Q. 5838, CAB 19/33.

11. Hankey, *Supreme Command*, I:313.

12. Fisher to WSC, 20 January 1915, FISR 1/18.

13. WSC to Fisher, 20 January 1915, *WSC*, III/1:433–4; Churchill, *World Crisis*, II:149–50; Fisher to WSC, 20 January 1915, *WSC*, III/1:435.

14. Fisher to Jellicoe, 21 January 1915, Add MS 49006; *WSC*, III/1:436.

15. Fisher to WSC, 23 January 1915, *WSC*, III/1:442–3.

16. Fisher to WSC, 25 January 1915, *WSC*, III/1:451.

17. 'Memorandum by the First Sea Lord on the Position of the British Fleet and its Policy of Steady Pressure', 25 January 1915, *WSC*, III/1:452–4.

18. Corbett diary, 26 January 1915, Corbett papers, National Maritime Museum, CBT/43/14.

19. WSC to Asquith, Kitchener and Grey, 25 January 1915, and Oliver memorandum, CHAR 2/74/53; *WSC*, III/1:450–1.

20. WSC to Fisher, 26 January 1915, FISR 1/18; *WSC*, III/1:458.

21. Fisher to Churchill, 28 January 1915, *WSC*, III/1:460.

22. Fisher to Asquith, 28 January 1915, *WSC*, III/1:461.

23. Churchill to Fisher, 28 January 1915, FISR 1/18; *WSC*, III/1:462.

24. Fisher to Asquith, and Fisher to Churchill, 28 January 1915, *WSC*, III/1:460–1.

25. WSC to Jellicoe, 26 January 1915, Add MS 48990; *Jellicoe Papers*, I:128–30.

26. WSC memorandum, 27 January 1915, Churchill, *World Crisis*, II:157.

27. Asquith to Stanley, 28 January 1915, *WSC*, III/1:462.

28. Ibid.

29. War Council minutes, 28 January 1915, *WSC*, III/1:463.

30. Hankey's minutes of the meeting do not mention this incident, so the timing is uncertain. It is generally accepted, however, that it occurred near the beginning.

31. Dardanelles Commission, Fisher testimony, 11 October 1916, Q. 3140, CAB 19/33.

32. Lord Fisher, *Memories* (New York: George H. Doran, 1920), 71.

33. Asquith to Stanley, 28 January 1915, *WSC*, III/1:462.

34. War Council minutes, 28 January 1915, *WSC*, III/1:463–4. Asquith also saw the value of opening up communications with Russia through the Black Sea. See Nicholas Lambert, *Planning Armageddon* (Cambridge, MA: Harvard University Press, 2012), 331–8. It is an exaggeration, however, to claim on this basis that economic considerations were the '*principal* justification for the inception of the Dardanelles campaign' (p. 336, emphasis added).

35. War Council minutes, 28 January 1915, *WSC*, III/1:463–4.

36. Ibid.

37. Dardanelles Commission, Churchill testimony, 28 September 1916, Q. 1190, CAB 19/33.

38. War Council minutes, 28 January 1915, *WSC*, III/1:469.

39. Fisher to Lloyd George, 29 January 1915, Lloyd George papers, Parliamentary Archives, C/4/11/3.

40. Lloyd George to Fisher, 30 January 1915, FISR 1/18.

41. Balfour draft memorandum, 'Notes on Lord Fisher's Mem. of Jan. 15', 1 February 1915, Add Mss. 49712.

42. Fisher to Bonar Law, 31 January 1915, Bonar Law papers, House of Lords Records Office, BL/36/2/57; Robert Blake, *The Unknown Prime Minister* (London: Eyre & Spottiswoode, 1955), 236–7; Ruddock F. Mackay, *Fisher of Kilverstone* (Oxford: Clarendon Press, 1973), 489.

43. Fisher to Bonar Law, 15 March 1915, BL/36/6/29.

44. Hankey's biographer states that this document was circulated on 24 January, although Hankey implies in his memoirs that this occurred in mid-February. Roskill, *Hankey*, I:154; Hankey, *Supreme Command*, I:279–80; CHAR 2/74/114.

45. Hankey memorandum, 'Attack on the Dardanelles', 2 February 1915, CAB 24/1.

46. Corbett diary, 4 February 1915, CBT/43/14.

47. Corbett to Hankey, 4 February 1915 (circulated to the War Council on 5 February), CHAR 2/89/3.

48. Corbett diary, 2 March 1915, CBT/43/14.

49. Cassar, *French and the Dardanelles*, 59–63; Paul G. Halpern, *The Naval War in the Mediterranean* (Annapolis, MD: Naval Institute Press, 1987), 60.

50. Naval Staff History CB 1553: *History of British Minesweeping in the War*, December 1920, 25.

51. Enclosure to Captain-in-Charge, Naval Base, Lowestoft to Rear-Admiral Nicholson, 'Report of Naval Operations against Zeebrugge on 23rd November 1914', 24 November 1914, ADM 137/1007; Rear-Admiral Stuart Nicholson, 'Preliminary Report on Bombardment of Zeebrugge', 24 November 1914, ADM 137/1007; Len Barnett, 'Royal Naval Gunnery and Minesweeping at the Dardanelles, February to March 1915' (self-published), 17–18.

52. Carden to Admiralty, 10 January 1915, ADM 137/96.

53. *History of British Minesweeping in the War*, 11–13; 'Taffrail' (Captain H. Taprell-Dorling), *Swept Channels: Being an Account of the Work of the Minesweepers in the Great War* (London: Hodder & Stoughton, 1935), 17.

54. *History of British Minesweeping in the War*, 12–13; Admiral Viscount Jellicoe, *The Grand Fleet* (New York: Doran, 1919), 19, 170; Corbett, *Naval Operations*, II:17.

55. Oliver minute, 30 December 1914, ADM 1/8407/492.

56. Undated paper on *Ark Royal*, TNA, AIR 1/361; Stephen Roskill (ed.), *Documents Relating to the Naval Air Service* (London: Navy Records Society, 1969), 201–4.

57. Oliver to WSC, 16 January 1915, AIR 1/361. Churchill approved this request the following day. I am grateful to Alex Howlett for drawing my attention to this file.

58. Oliver memorandum, 2 February 1915, CHAR 2/74/55; *WSC*, III/1:478–80.

59. Admiralty orders, 5 February 1915, ADM 137/1089; *WSC*, III/1:485–90; Churchill, *World Crisis*, II:appendix II.

60. Richmond diary, 9 February 1915, RIC/1/12; *Portrait*, 140.

61. Asquith to Stanley, 9 February 1915, *WSC*, III/1:498.

62. Bonham Carter, *Winston Churchill*, 353.

63. Sir Charles Hobhouse diary, 16 February 1915, *Inside Asquith's Cabinet*, ed. Edward David (London: John Murray, 1977), 222. Emphasis added. The estimate of two to three weeks is confirmed by Harcourt in his diary for the same date.

CHAPTER 4

1. War Council, 13 January 1915, *WSC*, III/1:407–9.
2. Asquith to Stanley, 21 January 1915, *WSC*, III/1:437; George H. Cassar, *Asquith as War Leader* (London: Hambledon Press, 1994), 62–4.
3. War Council subcommittee, 28 January 1915, *WSC*, III/1:465.
4. Lloyd George to WSC, 29 January 1915, *WSC*, III/1:472.
5. Fisher to Lloyd George, 10 February 1915, C/4/11/5.
6. Hankey, *Supreme Command*, I:276–7; Cassar, *Asquith*, 64–5.
7. Hankey, *Supreme Command*, I:277–9.
8. Asquith to Stanley, 9 and 10 February 1915, *WSC*, III/1:499–500.
9. Hankey to Balfour, 10 February 1915, *WSC*, III/1:500.
10. Jackson memorandum, 'Attack on Constantinople', 15 February 1915, ADM 137/1089; CHAR 2/82/1; *WSC*, III/1:506–12; Churchill, *World Crisis*, II:178.
11. Richmond memorandum, 'Remarks on Present Strategy', 14 February 1915, RIC/1/12; *Portrait*, 142–5.
12. Fisher to Richmond, 15 February 1915, RIC/1/12; *Portrait*, 145; Lady Richmond diary, 16 February 1915, RIC/1/17.
13. *Portrait*, 145.
14. Asquith to Stanley, 13 February 1915, *Asquith: Letters*, 429–30; *WSC*, III/1:512.
15. War Council, 16 February 1915, Hankey, *Supreme Command*, I:281; *WSC*, III/1:516.
16. Violet Asquith diary, entry for 22 February 1915, written 22–3 May 1915, *Champion Redoubtable*, 25.
17. WSC to Kitchener, 18 February 1915, *WSC*, III/1:518–19. Emphasis added.
18. Lord Esher diary, 16 February 1915, *WSC*, III/1:516.
19. War Council, 19 February 1915, *WSC*, III/1:527–34.
20. Corbett, *Naval Operations*, II:144–9; Mitchell Report, 33–4.
21. WSC memorandum, 23 February 1915, *WSC*, III/1:547.
22. Corbett, *Naval Operations*, II:155–6.
23. WSC to Carden, 24 February 1915, ADM 137/109; *WSC*, III/1:550.
24. Released by the Office of the Chief Censor, Admiralty, 20 February 1915, 2 p.m., ADM 137/109; 'Dardanelles Shelled', *The Times*, 22 February 1915, 8; Hankey, *Supreme Command*, I:282–3.
25. Lady Richmond diary, 20 February 1915, RIC/1/17; Fisher to Jellicoe, 22 February 1915, *WSC* III/1:544.
26. Stevenson diary, 15 May 1915, *Lloyd George*, 50.
27. Hankey, *Supreme Command*, I:282–3; Hankey to Lord Esher, 15 March 1915, *WSC*, III/1:700.
28. 'Dardanelles Attacked', *The Times*, 22 February 1915, 6.

29. Curran, *Grand Deception*, 86; Curran, 'Who was Responsible?', 25.
30. Curran, *Grand Deception*, 89, 260.
31. War Council, 24 February 1915, *WSC*, III/1:555–61.
32. Balfour memorandum, 24 February 1915, *WSC*, III/1:561–3.
33. WSC memorandum, 25 February 1915, *WSC*, III/1:563–4; Churchill, *World Crisis*, II:185.
34. Asquith to Stanley, 26 February 1915, *WSC*, III/1:577.
35. War Council, 26 February 1915, *WSC*, III/1:573. Emphasis added.
36. Asquith to Stanley, 26 February 1915, *WSC*, III/1:577.
37. War Council, 26 February 1915, *WSC*, III/1:567–77.
38. Asquith to Stanley, 26 February 1915, *WSC*, III/1:578.
39. WSC to John Churchill, 26 February 1915, *WSC*, III/1:580.
40. Corbett, *Naval Operations*, II:160.
41. WSC to John Churchill, 26 February 1915, *WSC*, III/1:580.
42. Carden to WSC, 27 February 1915, *WSC*, III/1:584.
43. WSC to Grand Duke Nicholas, 27 February 1915, *WSC*, III/1:584.
44. WSC note for War Council, 27 February 1915, *WSC*, III/1:587.
45. WSC to Grey, and WSC to Fisher, Oliver, and Jackson, both 28 February 1915, *WSC*, III/1:591.
46. Corbett, *Naval Operations*, II:163–8; Mitchell Report, 36.
47. Corbett, *Naval Operations*, II:178–82; Mitchell Report, 42–3.

CHAPTER 5

1. Harcourt diary, 2 March 1915.
2. Sir Frederick Hamilton to his son, 1 March 1915, Hamilton papers, National Maritime Museum, Greenwich, HTN 120; Prior, *Gallipoli*, 63.
3. Lady Richmond diary, 1 March 1915, RIC/1/17.
4. Lady Richmond diary, 4 March 1915, RIC/1/17; Prior, *Gallipoli*, 63.
5. Callwell to Robertson, 1 March 1915, Field Marshal Sir William Robertson papers, Liddell Hart Centre for Military Archives, King's College, London.
6. Hankey memorandum, 'After the Dardanelles: The Next Steps', 1 March 1915, CAB 63/3; *WSC*, III/1:593–602.
7. Sir Francis Elliot to Grey, 1 March 2015, *WSC*, III/1:603.
8. Bonham Carter, *Winston Churchill*, 368–9.
9. Harcourt diary, 2 March 1915.
10. War Council minutes, 3 March 1915, *WSC*, III/1:610–18.
11. WSC to Jellicoe, 9 March 1915, *WSC*, III/1:656.
12. Morgan-Owen, 'Cooked Up in the Dinner Hour?', 37–8.
13. Fisher to WSC, 3 March 1915, *WSC*, III/1:622.
14. *Portrait*, 145. Richmond and Corbett both strongly opposed the idea. Richmond memorandum, 'Considerations affecting the Dispatch of "Queen Elizabeth" Class to the Baltic', 6 March 1915, *Portrait*, 145–7; Corbett diary, 6 March 1915, CBT/43/14.

15. Jellicoe to WSC, 6 March 1915, *WSC*, III/1:649.
16. WSC to Jellicoe, 9 March 1915, *Jellicoe Papers*, I:150–1; *WSC*, III/1:656.
17. WSC to Grey (unsent), 6 March 1915, *WSC*, III/1:645.
18. *WSC*, III:329.
19. Churchill to Kitchener, 4 March 1915, Churchill, *World Crisis*, II:195.
20. Edward J. Erickson, *Gallipoli: The Ottoman Campaign* (Barnsley: Pen & Sword, 2010), 13–16.
21. Carden to Admiralty, 7 March 1915, ADM 137/109.
22. Mitchell Report, 83.
23. Roger Keyes, *The Naval Memoirs of Admiral of the Fleet Sir Roger Keyes* (2 vols, London: Thornton Butterworth, 1934–5), I:204; Keyes to his wife, 8 March 1915, *Keyes Papers*, I:102–3; H. A. Jones, *The War in the Air*, vol. 2 (Oxford: Clarendon Press, 1928), 17–18.
24. Mitchell Report, 48.
25. R. D. Layman, *Naval Aviation in the First World War: Its Impact and Influence* (Annapolis, MD: Naval Institute Press, 1996), 143.
26. Mitchell Report, 52–3.
27. Keyes to wife, 2 July 1915, *Keyes Papers*, I:153.
28. Carden to WSC, 6 March 1915, *WSC*, III/1:646.
29. Keyes, *Naval Memoirs*, I:210–11.
30. Mitchell Report, 54–5.
31. Keyes to his wife, 8 March 1915, *Keyes Papers*, I:103–4; Keyes, *Naval Memoirs*, I:207–8.
32. Carden to WSC, 10 March 1915, ADM 137/109; *WSC*, III/1:661.
33. Kitchener to Maxwell, 20 February 1915, CHAR 2/88/1.
34. Carden to Maxwell, 23 February 1915, CHAR 13/54/80; George H. Cassar, *Kitchener's War* (Potomac Books, 2004), 294.
35. Maxwell to Kitchener, 24 February 1915, CHAR 2/88/2.
36. Birdwood to Kitchener, *c.*4 March 1915, Cassar, *Kitchener's War*, 309; Trumbull Higgins, *Winston Churchill and the Dardanelles* (London: Heinemann, 1963), 111–12.
37. Birdwood to Kitchener, 5 and 6 March 1915, *WSC*, III/1:637–8 and 643.
38. Birdwood to Kitchener, 4 March 1915, *WSC*, III/1:625–6; Corbett, *Naval Operations*, II:185–6.
39. Corbett, *Naval Operations*, II:176.
40. Kitchener to Birdwood, 4 March 1915, *WSC*, III/1:632.
41. War Council, 10 March 1915, *WSC*, III/1:665.
42. Jackson to Oliver, 11 March 1915, ADM 137/109; *WSC*, III/1:676–7; Churchill, *World Crisis*, II:213–14.
43. Churchill, *World Crisis*, II:218–20.
44. WSC to Carden, 11 March 1915, in Churchill, *World Crisis*, II:220; *WSC*, III/1:677.
45. Minute to WSC from unidentified member of the naval staff, 25 February 1915, AIR 1/361.

46. WSC to Carden, 8 March 1915, ADM 137/109.
47. Carden to Admiralty, 9 March 1915, AIR 1/361.
48. Admiralty to Carden for Commanding Officer, *Ark Royal*, 12 March 1915, ADM 137/109. The first elements of the new RNAS squadron did not reach the theatre until 24 March, and were not operational until 29 March. Hugh Popham notes that, prior to the squadron's arrival, an aerodrome was 'scratched out of the vineyards' on the island of Tenedos by 'Clark-Hall and the men of the *Ark Royal* with indentured Greek labour'. Hugh Popham, *Into Wind: A History of British Naval Flying* (London: Hamish Hamilton, 1969), 28.
49. Kitchener to Hamilton, 13 March 1915, *WSC*, III/1:684–6; Hankey, *Supreme Command*, I:290–1.
50. Kitchener to WSC, 12 March 1915, *WSC*, III/1:681; see also Churchill, *World Crisis*, II:216, where it is dated 13 March.
51. Neither Churchill nor Hamilton mention this conversation in their respective memoirs or in their testimony to the Dardanelles Commission, but Hamilton recounted it to Hankey soon afterwards. Hankey diary, 12 March 1915, Hankey papers, Churchill College Archives Centre, Cambridge, HNKY 1/1; Hankey, *Supreme Command*, I:290.
52. Hall memoirs, Hall papers, Churchill College Archives Centre, Cambridge, HALL 3/5. See also Admiral Sir William James, *The Eyes of the Navy* (London: Methuen, 1955), 62–3, and Patrick Beesly, *Room 40: British Naval Intelligence 1914–18* (London: Hamish Hamilton, 1982), 81. This incident is also recounted in Curran, *Grand Deception* (pp. 118–19) where the author appears to suggest that Hall's account, as quoted in Churchill's official biography, was fabricated by Martin Gilbert. However, Gilbert does acknowledge that Hall's memoir is his source (albeit without providing a proper reference to it). Ironically, Curran cites James' account as proof of Gilbert's alleged mistake, without realizing that James based his account on the same unpublished source!
53. WSC to Carden, 13 March 1915, ADM 137/109; *WSC*, III/1:687.
54. Fisher to Jellicoe, 15 March 1915, *WSC*, III/1:701.
55. Carden to WSC, 13 March 1915, *WSC*, III/1:687.
56. WSC to Carden, 13 March 1915, ADM 137/109; *WSC*, III/1:687–8.
57. Keyes to his wife, 9 March 1915, *Keyes Papers*, I:105.
58. Von Usedom dispatch (decrypted and translated), n.d., CAB 45/215.
59. Carden to Admiralty, 14 March 1915, ADM 137/109; *WSC*, III/1:693; Churchill, *World Crisis*, II:220.
60. WSC to Carden, 15 March 1915, ADM 137/109; also *WSC*, III/1:694–5, where it is misdated 14 March.
61. WSC to Kitchener, 14 March 1915, *WSC*, III/1:694.
62. Fisher to WSC, 15 March 1915, *WSC*, III/1:698–9.
63. WSC to Fisher, 15 March 1915, FISR 1/18; *WSC*, III/1:699.
64. Keyes *Naval Memoirs*, I:216–17.
65. Carden to Admiralty, 14 March 1915, ADM 137/109; *WSC*, III/1:695–6. This is also the conclusion reached by Keyes, *Naval Memoirs*, I:217.

66. Mitchell Report, 51–9.
67. WSC to Carden, 15 March 1915, ADM 137/109.

CHAPTER 6

1. Hankey to Asquith, 16 March 1915, CAB 63/3; Hankey diary, 16 March 1915, HNKY 1/1; Hankey, *Supreme Command*, I:291–2.
2. Hankey diary, 17 March 1915, HNKY 1/1; Hankey, *Supreme Command*, I:292.
3. WSC to de Robeck, 17 March 1915, ADM 137/109; *WSC*, III/1:706.
4. De Robeck to WSC, 18 March 1915, ADM 137/109; *WSC*, III/1:706–7.
5. *Lord Nelson* and *Agamemnon* were designed and laid down before HMS *Dreadnought*, but were completed after it, making them technically not *pre*-dreadnought battleships.
6. Captain R. F. Phillimore Report: 'Damage Done to "Inflexible" by Shell-Fire March 18th 1915', 25 March 1915, ADM 137/39; Mitchell Report, 82.
7. HMS *Ark Royal*, Report of Operations, 18 March 1915, ADM 137/39; Corbett, *Naval Operations*, I:219; Jones, *War in the Air*, II:21.
8. See also de Robeck to Hamilton, 19 March 1915, in Ian Hamilton, *Gallipoli Diary* (2 vols, New York: George H. Doran, 1920), I:40: 'How our ships struck mines in an area that was reported clear and swept the previous night I do not know, unless they were floating mines started from the Narrows!'
9. De Robeck to Admiralty, 19 March 1915, *WSC*, III/1:708–9.
10. Hamilton to Kitchener, 19 March 1915, CHAR 2/88/11; *WSC*, III/1:710.
11. Harcourt diary, 19 March 1915.
12. De Robeck to Admiralty, 19 March 1915, *WSC*, III/1:708–9.
13. Hankey diary, 19 March 1915, HNKY 1/1; Hankey to Asquith, 20 March 1915, CAB 63/3; Hankey to Lloyd George, 19 March 1915, *WSC*, III/1:716–17; Hankey, *Supreme Command*, I:293–4.
14. Esher diary, 20 March 1915, *WSC*, III/1:719.
15. Admiralty to de Robeck, 20 March 1915, *WSC*, III/1:719.
16. WSC to Fisher, 20 March 1915, FISR 1/18; *WSC*, III/1:718.
17. Harcourt diary, 23 March 1915.
18. De Robeck to Hamilton, 19 March 1915, Hamilton, *Gallipoli Diary*, I:40; Keyes, *Naval Memoirs*, I:260.
19. Hamilton, *Gallipoli Diary*, I:39.
20. De Robeck to Admiralty, 21 March 1915, *WSC*, III/1:720.
21. Keyes to his wife, 21 March 1915, *Keyes Papers*, I:113.
22. Hamilton, *Gallipoli Diary*, I:48; Keyes, *Naval Memoirs*, I:257.
23. Hamilton, *Gallipoli Diary*, I:41.
24. Admiral of the Fleet Lord Wester-Wemyss, *The Navy in the Dardanelles Campaign* (London: Hodder & Stoughton, 1924), 43.
25. De Robeck told Churchill a few days later that he had changed his mind about renewing the naval attack on 22 March. De Robeck to WSC, 27 March 1915, *WSC*, III/1:751–2; Churchill, *World Crisis*, II:249–50.

26. Keyes, *Naval Memoirs*, I:262; Hamilton, *Gallipoli Diary*, I:42.
27. Hamilton, *Gallipoli Diary*, I:41.
28. Philip Magnus, *Kitchener: Portrait of an Imperialist* (London: Murray, 1958), 327.
29. Birdwood to Kitchener, 23 March 1915, Magnus, *Kitchener*, 327; Clews, *Churchill's Dilemma*, 276.
30. De Robeck to Admiralty, 23 March 1915, *WSC*, III/1:723–4; Churchill, *World Crisis*, II:236.
31. Hamilton, *Gallipoli Diary*, I:41–2.
32. WSC to de Robeck (draft, unsent), 23 March 1915, *WSC*, III/1:724–6; Churchill, *World Crisis*, II:237–8.
33. Churchill, *World Crisis*, II:237–8.
34. Kitchener to Hamilton, 23 March 1915, CHAR 2/88/11.
35. Kitchener to Hamilton, draft, 23 March 1915, *WSC*, III/1:727.
36. Asquith to Stanley, 23 March 1915, *WSC*, III/1:726.
37. Asquith to Stanley, 24 March 1915, *WSC*, III/1:731.
38. WSC to Fisher, 25 March 1915, *WSC* III/1:741; Churchill, *World Crisis*, II:257.
39. Fisher minute, *WSC*, III/1:728, n. 2.
40. WSC to Fisher, 25 March 1915, *WSC* III/1:741; Churchill, *World Crisis*, II:257.
41. WSC to de Robeck, 24 March 1915, *WSC*, III/1:728–30.
42. De Robeck to Admiralty, 26 March 1915, *WSC*, III/1:747.
43. De Robeck to WSC, 27 March 1915, *WSC*, III/1:751–2; Churchill, *World Crisis*, II:249–50.
44. Churchill, *World Crisis*, II:249–50.
45. Hankey diary, 27 March 1915, HNKY 1/1.
46. WSC to de Robeck, 27 March 1915, *WSC*, III/1:753.
47. WSC memorandum, 24 March 1915, *WSC*, III/1:732–8.
48. Asquith to Stanley, 30 March 1915, *WSC*, III/1:761.
49. Balfour to WSC, 8 April 1915, Add Ms 49694; *WSC*, III/1:779.
50. WSC to Balfour, 8 April 1915, Add Ms 49694; *WSC*, III/1:780.
51. Fisher memorandum, 27 March 1915, FISR 1/18; *WSC*, III/1:754–5.
52. WSC to Fisher, 28 March 1915, *WSC*, III/1:756.
53. Fisher to WSC, 28 March 1915, FISR 1/18; *WSC*, III/1:757–8.
54. WSC to de Robeck, 27 March 1915, *WSC*, III/1:755–6.
55. De Robeck to WSC, 29 March 1915, *WSC*, III/1:759.
56. Fisher to Jellicoe, 4 April 1915, *WSC*, III/1:769.
57. Hankey diary, 29 March 1915, HNKY 1/1; *WSC*, III/1:760.
58. Fisher to WSC, 2 April 1915, *WSC*, III/1:764.
59. Fisher to WSC, 5 April 1915, *WSC*, III/1:770.
60. This was pointed out by Churchill in his reply the same day. FISR 1/19.
61. Fisher to WSC, 10 April 1915, and Fisher to WSC and Oliver, 11 April 1915, FISR 1/19; FISR 16/6; *WSC*, III/1:787, 791.
62. WSC to Fisher, 11 April 1915, FISR 16/6; *WSC*, III/1:792.
63. Fisher to WSC, 12 April 1915, FISR 16/6; *WSC*, III/1:794. Fisher told Hankey a few days later that he had threatened to resign rather than agree to *Queen*

Elizabeth and the two semi-dreadnoughts of the Lord Nelson class being allowed inside the Straits. Hankey diary, 15 April 1915, HNKY 1/1; Hankey, *Supreme Command*, I:302.

64. Margot Asquith diary, 13 May 1915, *Margot Asquith's Great War Diary*, 170; *WSC*, III/1:871.

65. 'The Dardanelles Blunder', *Morning Post*, 23 April 1915, 6.

66. Gwynne to Wilson, 12 April 1915, Gwynne papers; *Rasp of War*, 76.

67. Violet Asquith diary, *Champion Redoubtable*, 51.

68. Lady Richmond diary, 28 April 1915, RIC/1/17.

69. Gwynne to Maxse, 2 November 1914, Leopold Maxse papers, West Sussex Records Office, MSS 469, f. 584; *Rasp of War*, 47.

70. 'The Admiralty', *Morning Post*, 31 October 1914, 6.

71. Fisher to Churchill, undated, CHAR 13/28/96.

72. *Rasp of War*, 11.

73. Beresford to Asquith, 15 April 1915, Asquith papers, Bodleian Library, MS Asquith 27; *WSC*, III/1:798.

74. Beresford to Maxse, 17 April 1915, MSS 470, f. 148.

75. Gwynne to Wilson, 12 April 1915, Gwynne papers.

76. Keith Jeffery, *Field Marshal Sir Henry Wilson: A Political Soldier* (Oxford: Oxford University Press, 2006), 134.

77. Wilson diary, 18 March 1915, Henry Wilson papers, Imperial War Museum, HHW 1/24.

78. Wilson diary, 20 March 1915, HHW 1/24.

79. Wilson to Bonar Law, 27 March 1915, BL/36/6/67.

80. Wilson diary, 3 April 1915, HHW 1/24.

81. Wilson diary, 16 and 18 April 1915, HHW 1/24.

82. Gwynne to Asquith, 22 April 1915, MS Asquith 27; *Rasp of War*, 84; Wilson diary, 21 April 1915, HHW 1/24.

83. HC Deb., 22 April 1915, vol. 71, cc. 398–9.

84. *Berliner Tageblatt*, 24 April 1915, 2.

85. 'Liberals Defend Churchill: Tory Section of the London Press Accused of Playing Politics', *New York Times*, 30 April 1915, 2.

86. *Northampton Mercury*, 30 April 1915.

87. 'Mr. Churchill and the Opposition', *Morning Post*, 26 April 1915, 6 (emphasis added).

88. One Tory backbencher wrote confidentially to Bonar Law to enquire if Joynson-Hicks' 'sharp criticism' of Churchill in the *Morning Post* meant that the 'party truce' was no longer being observed. Herbert Nield to Law, 26 April 1915, BL/37/1/61. Unfortunately, I have been unable to locate a copy of Law's reply.

89. HC Deb., 4 May 1915, vol. 71, c. 969.

90. HC Deb., 13 May 1915, vol. 71, c. 1794.

91. 'Cabinet Responsibility', *Spectator*, 1 May 1915, 4.

92. Margot Asquith diary, 8 May 1915, *Margot Asquith's Great War Diary*, 169; *WSC*, III/2:849–50.

93. Riddell diary, 29 April 1915, Add MS 62975.
94. Ibid.
95. Riddell diary, 11 May 1915, Add MS 62975. Riddell claimed in his diary that Churchill prepared a statement and delivered it to Riddell, although he does not say whether he conveyed its contents to his fellow newspapermen.

CHAPTER 7

1. Asquith considered continuing this arrangement, with himself as de facto Minister of Defence, during the formation of the first coalition government. According to Stamfordham, the old War Council would be replaced by a smaller body consisting of Asquith, Kitchener, and Balfour, the new First Lord, with Hankey as secretary. Peter Fraser, *Lord Esher: A Political Biography* (Barnsley: Pen & Sword, 2013), 283–4. Asquith also briefly considered the same arrangement in October 1915.
2. Informal War Council meeting, 6 April 1915, *WSC*, III/1:774; Hankey, *Supreme Command*, I:300.
3. De Robeck to WSC, 9 May 1915, *WSC*, III/2:855–6.
4. WSC to Jackson, 10 May 1915, and Jackson memorandum, 'Note on the Passage of the Dardanelles from the Sea of Marmara in Case such an Operation was Necessary by a Fleet in the Near Future, in Order to Obtain Supplies, &c.', 11 May 1915, ADM 137/154; *WSC*, III/2:856–8.
5. Hankey diary, 11 May 1915, *WSC*, III/2:858.
6. Ibid.
7. Fisher to WSC, 11 May 1915, *WSC*, III/2:859.
8. Fisher to WSC, 11 May 1915, FISR 1/19; *WSC*, III/2:859–61; Churchill, *World Crisis*, II:354–7.
9. WSC to Fisher, 11 May 1915, FISR 1/19; *WSC*, III/2:862; Churchill, *World Crisis*, II:357–8.
10. Hankey diary, 12 May 1915, *WSC*, III/2:864.
11. Fisher to Asquith and Fisher to WSC, 12 May 1915, MS Asquith 27; FISR 1/19; *WSC*, III/2:868, 870.
12. WSC to Masterton Smith, 13 May 1915, *WSC*, III/2:869.
13. Hankey diary, 12 May 1915, *WSC*, III/2:864; on the movement of *Inflexible*, see Fisher to Jellicoe, 13 May 1915, *WSC*, III/2:869. Fisher told Jellicoe that he had resigned on the 12th over the Dardanelles, but had relented when Asquith stepped in. This is not substantiated by any source, and appears to be another instance of Fisher exaggerating his opposition for the benefit of a sympathetic audience.
14. Fisher to Jellicoe, 13 May 1915, *WSC*, III/2:869. In a subsequent account of this incident, Fisher claimed that, after announcing his intention to resign if the *Queen Elizabeth* were not immediately recalled, Kitchener 'got up from the table and he left!' Fisher to Cromer, 11 October 1916, Fisher, *Memories*, 57.
15. Charles E. Callwell, *Experiences of a Dug-Out* (London: Constable, 1920).

16. Fisher to Asquith, 13 May 1915, FISR 1/19; *WSC*, III/2:870.
17. WSC to de Robeck, 13 May 1915, ADM 137/154; *WSC*, III/2:872.
18. Harcourt diary, 14 May 1915.
19. War Council, 14 May 1915, *WSC*, III/2:874–83.
20. Ibid.
21. WSC to Asquith, 14 May 1915, *WSC*, III/2:884–5.
22. Violet Asquith diary, 15 May 1915, *Champion Redoubtable*, 52.
23. *Champion Redoubtable*, 54; see also Bonham Carter, *Winston Churchill*, 343.
24. Crease, 'General Remarks', ADM 1/28268.
25. WSC to Fisher, 14 May 1915, CAB 1/33; *WSC*, III/2:885–7.
26. Admiral Sir R. H. Bacon, *The Life of Lord Fisher of Kilverstone* (2 vols, Garden City, NY: Doubleday, Doran & Co., 1929), II:254–5; see also Crease to Jellicoe, 17 May 1915, *Jellicoe Papers*, I:160–1; Crease, 'General Remarks', ADM 1/28268.
27. Fisher to WSC, 15 May 1915, *WSC*, III/2:887; Fisher to Asquith, 15 May 1915, MS Asquith 27; FISR 1/19; Bacon, *Fisher*, II:256.
28. Masterton Smith to Asquith, 6 November 1923, MS Asquith 18.
29. Churchill, *World Crisis*, II:373–4.
30. Masterton Smith to Asquith, 6 November 1923, MS Asquith 18.
31. Violet Asquith diary, 15 May 1915, *Champion Redoubtable*, 50–1; Asquith to Fisher, 15 May 1915, *WSC*, III/2:888.
32. Violet Asquith diary, 15 May 1915, *Champion Redoubtable*, 51; David Lloyd George, *War Memoirs* (6 vols, London: Ivor Nicholson & Watson, 1933–6), I:226–7.
33. Riddell diary, 15 April 1915, Add MS 62975.
34. WSC to Fisher, 15 May 1915, FISR 1/19; *WSC*, III/2:888–9.
35. Fisher to WSC, 16 May 1915, FISR 1/19; *WSC*, III/2:891–2.
36. Blake, *Unknown Prime Minister*, 243.
37. Fisher to Crease, 16 May 1915, *WSC*, III/2:891.
38. Fisher to McKenna, 16 May 1915, *WSC*, III:442.
39. Margot Asquith diary, 16 May 1915, *Margot Asquith's Great War Diary*, 173.
40. McKenna to Fisher, 16 May 1915, *WSC*, III:442.
41. WSC to Fisher, 16 May 1915, FISR 16/6; *WSC*, III/2:892–3.
42. Fisher to WSC, 16 May 1915, FISR 1/19; *WSC*, III/2:893–4.
43. Hamilton, Tudor, and Lambert to WSC and Fisher, 16 May 1915, FISR 1/19; *WSC*, III/2:896–7.
44. Wilson to Fisher, 16 May 1915, FISR 1/19.
45. Margot Asquith diary, 16 May 1915, *Margot Asquith's Great War Diary*, 174.
46. Fisher to Asquith, 17 May 1915, MS Asquith 27; FISR 1/19; *WSC*, III/2:900.
47. Fisher to Asquith, 17 May 1915, MS Asquith 27.
48. Fisher to Law, 17 May 1915, BL/37/2/34; Blake, *Unknown Prime Minister*, 243–5; Mackay, *Fisher*, 498.
49. Harcourt to Esher, 18 May 1915, *WSC*, III:452; Harcourt diary, 18 May 1915.
50. Bacon, *Fisher*, II:265–7; Crease, 'Notes for Fisher's Biographer', *c.*1923, ADM 1/28268.

51. WSC to Asquith, 20 May 1915, MS Asquith 14; *WSC*, III/2:920.

52. 'Unrest at the Admiralty', *The Times*, 18 May 1915, 9.

53. Esher to Fisher, 16 and 20 May 1915, FISR 1/19. On Esher's influence, see Mackay, *Fisher*, 499–501.

54. Hankey diary, HNKY 1/1; Hankey, *Supreme Command*, I:316. Asquith also believed that Fisher wished to become First Lord, 'a position corresponding to K.'s in War Office'. Margot Asquith diary, 17 May 1915, *Margot Asquith's Great War Diary*, 175.

55. Fisher to Asquith, 19 May 1915, MS Asquith 27; FISR 1/19; *WSC*, III/2:906–7.

56. Hankey diary, 19 May 1915, HNKY 1/1; Mackay, *Fisher*, 502.

57. WSC to Asquith, 20 May 1915, *WSC*, III/2:920.

58. This was also the term Asquith used in his memoirs. For over a decade Churchill remained unaware of Fisher's specific terms for remaining in office. When Asquith sent him a copy of Fisher's letter in 1927, Churchill concluded that Fisher had 'used the uncertain course of events at the Dardanelles as a means of making a bid for the supreme naval power'. Asquith, *Memories and Reflections*, II:111–13.

59. Hankey diary, 19 May 1915, HNKY 1/1; Mackay, *Fisher*, 502; Corbett diary, 22 May 1915, CBT/43/14.

60. Stamfordham to King George V, *WSC*, III:453.

61. Harcourt diary, 25 May 1915.

62. Balfour to Selborne, 20 May 1915, Add MS49708, ff. 249–50; Mackay, *Fisher*, 504.

63. Hankey diary, 19 May 1915, HNKY 1/1; Mackay, *Fisher*, 502.

64. R. J. Q. Adams, *Bonar Law* (Stanford, CA: Stanford University Press, 1999), 184; Margot Asquith diary, 17 May 1915, *Margot Asquith's Great War Diary*, 175.

65. See also Asquith, *Memories and Reflections*, II:111–13.

66. Hankey diary, 19 May 1915, HNKY 1/1.

67. Ibid., 21 May 1915, HNKY 1/1. This is probably the same incident Churchill later related to Sir George Riddell: 'Winston said that Alfred Spender had come to him in a state of terrible alarm to tell him that Fisher had conducted himself in a most extraordinary fashion at an interview he had had with him when he said, "*I will tell the Germans. I will tell the people of this country the disposition of our Fleet.* I will get up in the House of Lords and tell the facts. I will not submit to this state of things any longer!"' Riddell diary, 6 July 1915, Add MS 62976. Riddell excised the italicized words from the published version of his diary. *Lord Riddell's War Diary 1914–1918* (London: Ivor Nicholson & Watson, 1934), 111–12.

68. Fisher to Bonar Law, 22 May 1915, *WSC*, III/2:931.

69. Stevenson diary, 19 May 1915, *Lloyd George*, 52.

70. Ibid.

71. Fisher to Law, BL/27/2/34; Blake, *Unknown Prime Minister*, 243–5. This is corroborated by Hankey's diary for 19 May 1915, HNKY 1/1; see also Hankey, *Supreme Command*, I:316; and Fisher to Law, 22 May 1915, *WSC*, III/2:931.

72. E.g. Asquith to Stanley, 9 February 1915, and commentary, *Asquith Letters*, 420–3; Cecil Black to Churchill, 26 May 1915, *WSC*, III/2:955; Margot Asquith diary, 21 April 1915, *Margot Asquith's Great War Diary*, 167.
73. 'Cabinet Responsibility', *Spectator*, 4.
74. 'Unrest at the Admiralty', *The Times*, 9.
75. 'A Coalition Ministry', 19 May 1915, *Daily Chronicle*, 1.
76. Clementine Churchill to Asquith, 20 May 1915, MS Asquith 27; *WSC*, III/2:921.
77. Asquith to Stanley, 22 May 1915, *WSC*, III/2:932.
78. WSC to Asquith, 21 May 1915, MS Asquith 14; *WSC*, III/2:925.
79. Bonham Carter, *Winston Churchill*, 406.
80. Violet Asquith diary, *Champion Redoubtable*, 54. Lloyd George spoke in similar terms. 'Well!', he exclaimed to Margot Asquith, 'It is the 2 Tories in our Cabinet that brought this about—K. and Winston.' Margot Asquith diary, 19 May 1915, *Margot Asquith's Great War Diary*, 177. See also 'Creating a Cabinet: Position of Mr. Churchill', *The Times*, 24 May 1915, 7.
81. W. M. R. Pringle to Asquith, 20 May 1915, *WSC*, III/2:919; Mark Bonham Carter to Violet Asquith, 20 May 1915, *Champion Redoubtable*, 56; A. MacCallum Scott, *Winston Churchill in Peace and War* (London: Newnes, 1916), 148.
82. Bonham Carter, *Winston Churchill*, 330–1.
83. Scott, *Winston Churchill*, 143–4.
84. Stevenson diary, 19 May 1915, *Lloyd George*, 52.
85. Riddell diary, 31 October 1914, Add MS 62974.
86. Riddell diary, 22 May 1915, Add MS 62975.
87. Riddell diary, 21 September 1914, Add MS 62974.
88. Margot Asquith diary, 8 May 1915, *Margot Asquith's Great War Diary*, 168; *WSC*, III/2:849.
89. Harcourt diary, 18 May 1915, apparently recording information obtained from Lord Esher.
90. Stamfordham to George V, in Fraser, *Esher*, 283.
91. Margot Asquith diary, 7 March 1915, *Margot Asquith's Great War Diary*, 152; *WSC*, III:329.
92. Stevenson diary, 24 May 1915, *Lloyd George*, 52.
93. WSC to Asquith, 21 May 1915, MS Asquith 14; *WSC*, III/2:926.
94. WSC to Asquith, 21 May 1915, MS Asquith 14; *WSC*, III/2:927.

CHAPTER 8

1. George V to Queen Mary, 19 May 1915, *WSC*, III/2:911.
2. Gwynne to Bathurst, 18 May 1915, MS/DEP/1990/1/2326; *Rasp of War*, 92.
3. WSC to Bonar Law, 21 May 1915, *WSC*, III/2:922–4.
4. Bonar Law to WSC, 21 May 1915, *WSC*, III/2:924.
5. Stevenson diary, 19 May 1915, *Lloyd George*, 52.
6. WSC to Bonar Law, 19 May 1915, BL/37/2/30; *WSC* III/2:908.

7. WSC to Selborne, 29 May 1915, *WSC* III/2:964.
8. WSC to Long, 15 September 1915, and Esher to WSC, 21 October 1915, *WSC* III/2:1175 and 1232; WSC to Carson, 4 September 1915, CHAR 21/37; C. P. Scott diary, 1 October 1915, *The Political Diaries of C.P. Scott, 1911–1928*, ed. Trevor Wilson (Ithaca, NY: Cornell University Press, 1970), 140–1.
9. WSC to Asquith, 15 September 1915, MS Asquith 28; CHAR 13/53/22–3; *WSC* III/2:1174–5.
10. WSC to Asquith, 23 September 1915, CHAR 13/53/39–40; *WSC* III/2:1185–6.
11. WSC to Archibald Sinclair, 30 July 1915, *Winston and Archie*, ed. Ian Hunter (London: Politico's, 2005), 18.
12. WSC memorandum: 'A Note on the General Situation', 1 June 1915, *WSC* III/2:977–83; Churchill, *World Crisis*, II:403–10.
13. Speech of 5 June 1915, Dundee, *Complete Speeches*, III:2379–80.
14. War Council, 14 May 1915, *WSC*, III/2:879–80.
15. Robert Rhodes James, *Gallipoli* (New York: Batsford, 1965), 215–16.
16. Ashmead-Bartlett diary, 10 June 1915, Ashmead-Bartlett papers, Institute of Commonwealth Studies, ICS 84/A/11; see also Ellis Ashmead-Bartlett, *The Uncensored Dardanelles* (London: Hutchinson, 1928), 121–4. Ashmead-Bartlett also described his meeting with Churchill that evening in his testimony to the Dardanelles Commission, where he stated that Churchill 'was in a terrible state about the whole thing. He was so nervous and excited about it, you could hardly get him to be coherent on the question. He had no clear view in his mind as to what should be done at this date.' Dardanelles Commission, Ashmead-Bartlett testimony, 3 May 1917, Q. 26794, CAB 19/33.
17. Ashmead-Bartlett diary, 28 March 1915, ICS 84/A/11; Fred and Elizabeth Brenchley, *Myth Maker: Ellis Ashmead-Bartlett, the Englishman who Sparked Australia's Gallipoli Legend* (Milton, Qld: Wiley, 2005), 56.
18. Ashmead-Bartlett diary, 10 June 1915, ICS 84/A/11; Brenchley, *Myth Maker*, 107.
19. Ashmead-Bartlett, *Uncensored Dardanelles*, 121–4.
20. Brenchley, *Myth Maker*, 108; Ashmead-Bartlett diary, 10 June 1915, ICS 84/A/11.
21. WSC to Asquith, Balfour, Bonar Law, and Curzon, 11 June 1915; Dardanelles Committee, 12 June 1915, *WSC* III/2:1003–8, 1012.
22. Rhys Crawley, *Climax at Gallipoli* (Norman, OK: University of Oklahoma Press, 2014), 31–45.
23. Untitled WSC memorandum, July 1915, *WSC* III/2:1088–95; Churchill, *World Crisis*, II:445–6.
24. WSC to Asquith and Balfour, 21 August 1915, CHAR 2/88; *WSC* III/2:1151–5.
25. *WSC* III/2:1151–5.
26. Keyes to his wife, 16 August 1915, *Keyes Papers*, I:176–87.
27. Keyes to de Robeck, 17 August 1915, *Keyes Papers*, I:188–91.
28. Wemyss to Keyes, *c.*20–30 August 1915, Keyes papers, British Library, Add 82403.

29. Godfrey to Keyes and Godfrey memorandum, 13 September 1915; Keyes to de Robeck, 23 September 1915; *Keyes Papers*, I:194–204.
30. Keyes to his wife, 27 September 1915, *Keyes Papers*, I:206.
31. Keyes to his wife, 12 October 1915, *Keyes Papers*, I:210; see also Keyes, *Naval Memoirs*, I:438, where the criticisms of de Robeck are omitted.
32. WSC to Balfour, 6 October 1915, *WSC* III/2:1204.
33. *WSC* III:540.
34. C. P. Scott diary, 1 October 1915, *Political Diaries*, 140–1; *WSC* III; 540–1.
35. Riddell diary, 2 October 1915, Add MS 62976; also C. P. Scott diary, 26 October 1915, *Political Diaries*, 148–9.
36. Dardanelles Committee, 11 October 1915, *WSC* III/2:1213.
37. Dardanelles Committee, 7 October 1915, *WSC* III/2:1209.
38. WSC memorandum, 'Dardanelles', 15 October 1915, *WSC* III/2:1220–4.
39. Dardanelles Committee, 11 October 1915, *WSC* III/2:1213.
40. De Robeck to Jackson, 30 October 1915, *Keyes Papers*, I:232.
41. Keyes diary, 3 November 1915, *Keyes Papers*, I:221.
42. Keyes diary, 4 November 1915, Keyes papers, Add MS 82447; *Keyes Papers*, I:228.
43. Keyes does not mention in his diary that Churchill imparted this information during their meeting, but implies in his memoirs that he did. Keyes, *Naval Memoirs*, I:456.
44. WSC to Asquith, 29 and 30 October 1915, *WSC* III/2:1244; CHAR 2/67/50–1.
45. Hankey diary, 1 November 1915, HNKY 1/1; *WSC* III:562.
46. WSC to Asquith, 11 November 1915, MS Asquith 14; *WSC* III/2:1249–50.
47. WSC to Asquith (unsent draft), 29 October 1915, *WSC* III/2:1244.
48. WSC to Asquith, 30 October 1915, CHAR 2/67/50.
49. Speech of 15 November 1915, *Complete Speeches*, III:2390–403.
50. Ibid., III:2390–403.
51. Ibid., III:2400.
52. 'Thrilled Members', *Daily Mail*, 16 November 1915, 5.
53. 'Political Notes', *Morning Post*, 16 November 1915, 8.
54. 'Mr. Churchill's Resignation', *The Times*, 13 November 1915, 9.
55. 'The Need for an Opposition', *Morning Post*, 15 November 15, 6.
56. 'Mr. Churchill's Defence', *The Times*, 16 November 1915, 9.
57. 'Peeps at the Truth', *Daily Mail*, 16 November 1915, 4.
58. *Spectator*, 20 November 1915, 15.
59. 'Mr. Churchill's Apologia', *Morning Post*, 16 November 1915, 6.
60. 'Civilian Control in War', *Morning Post*, 17 November 1915, 6.
61. 'Mr. Churchill's Apologia', *Morning Post*, 6.
62. Hankey diary, 6 November 1915, HNKY 1/1; *WSC* III:563–6.
63. Keyes diary, 18 November 1915, *Keyes Papers*, I:244; Keyes, *Naval Memoirs*, I:461.
64. Keyes diary, 24 November 1915, *Keyes Papers*, I:254–5.
65. Keyes diary, 18 November 1915, *Keyes Papers*, I:245–6.
66. Keyes diary, 19 November 1915, *Keyes Papers*, I:247.

67. Keyes diary, 18 November 1915, *Keyes Papers*, I:245–6.
68. Wemyss, *Dardanelles Campaign*, 212.
69. Wemyss to Admiralty, in Keyes, *Naval Memoirs*, I:473–5; Wemyss, *Dardanelles Campaign*, 216–20.
70. Curzon to WSC, 30 November 1915, *WSC* III/2:1294–5.
71. Keyes to Oliver, 29 November 1915, Keyes papers, Add Ms 82848, f. 8; *Keyes Papers*, I:261.
72. Keyes to Oliver, 30 November 1915, Keyes papers, Add Ms 82848, f. 9; *Keyes Papers*, I:262; Wemyss also records this remark in his memoirs: *Dardanelles Campaign*, 227.
73. WSC to Jack Churchill, 14 January 1916, *WSC* III/2:1373.
74. Prior, *Gallipoli*, 242.

CHAPTER 9

1. WSC to Clementine Churchill, 10 January 1916, *WSC*, III/2:1366.
2. WSC to Jack Churchill, 14 January 1916, and WSC to Hankey, 2 June 1915, *WSC*, III/2:984 and 1373. Churchill's letter to his brother goes on in a similar vein: 'My one fatal mistake was trying to achieve a g[rea]t enterprise without having the plenary authority wh[ich] c[oul]d so easily have carried it to success.'
3. Ashmead-Bartlett diary, 15 October 1915, ICS 84/A/11; Ashmead-Bartlett, *Uncensored Dardanelles*, 257. He made virtually identical comments to the Dardanelles Commission. Ashmead-Bartlett testimony, 3 May 1917, Q. 26866, CAB 19/33.
4. WSC to Clementine Churchill, 10 January 1916, *WSC*, III/2:1366.
5. WSC to Eva Keyes, 14 December 1915, *WSC*, III/2:1328–9.
6. WSC to Lloyd George, 11 July 1916, CAB 17/132.
7. WSC to Sinclair, 9 June 1915, *WSC*, IV/1:5.
8. WSC to Balfour, 9 July 1915, *WSC*, III/2:1083. See also WSC's unsent letter to Asquith, 8 July 1915, *WSC*, III/2:1081–2; and Riddell diary, 6 July 1915, Add MS 62976.
9. Fisher to Bonar Law, 7 January 1916, FISR 1/21.
10. Gwynne to Jellicoe, 7 February 1916, Gwynne papers. Jellicoe assured Gwynne that he had 'never written any letter to Fisher deploring inaction of the fleet', and 'doubt[ed] whether any other officer in fleet has done so'. Jellicoe to Gwynne, 12 February 1916, Gwynne papers.
11. Fisher to Jellicoe, 8 February 1916, *WSC*, III:701.
12. WSC to Clementine Churchill, 2 February 1916, *WSC*, III:699.
13. Gwynne to Henry Wilson, 17 February 1916, HHW 2/82/27. See also Gwynne to Lady Bathurst, 16 February 1916, MS/DEP/1990/1/2365: 'One day when I see you', he wrote, 'I will tell you the true story of his filthy intrigue.'
14. *WSC*, III/2:1421.

15. WSC to Clementine Churchill, 13 February 1915, *WSC*, III/2:1421.
16. Hamilton to WSC, 16 February 1916, Ian Hamilton papers, Liddell Hart Centre, 8/1/16.
17. C. P. Scott diary, 29 February–3 March 1916, *Political Diaries*, 186.
18. *WSC*, III:709.
19. Garvin to Fisher, 25 December 1915, *WSC*, III/2:1344; 'Mr. Churchill and Lord Fisher', *The Observer*, 12 March 1916, 9. The article is attributed to a 'Political Correspondent', but the author was likely Garvin himself.
20. Bonham Carter, *Winston Churchill*, 343.
21. Fisher to Donald, 9 March 1916, Robert Donald papers, Parliamentary Archives, DON/4/13.
22. Fisher to WSC, 6 March 1916, CHAR 2/72; *WSC*, III/2:1439.
23. C. P. Scott diary, 6 March 1916, *Political Diaries*, 187–8.
24. A. MacCallum Scott diary, 7 March 1916, A. MacCallum Scott papers, University of Glasgow, MS Gen 1465/7.
25. HC Deb., 7 March 1916, vol. 80, cc. 1420–30; *Complete Speeches*, III:2405–11.
26. Hankey diary, 7 March 1916, HNKY 1/1. A. M. Scott recorded in his diary that 'Lord Fisher in the Gallery smiled sardonically.' Scott diary, 7 March 1916, MS Gen 1465/7.
27. Fisher to WSC, 7 March 1916, CHAR 2/72; *WSC*, III/2:1443.
28. 'A Cruel Exposure', 9 March 1916, *Daily Mail*, 5.
29. Ibid.; HC Deb., 8 March 1916, vol. 80, cc. 1570–5.
30. 'A Cruel Exposure', *Daily Mail*, 5.
31. Margot Asquith to Balfour, *WSC*, III/2:1443–4.
32. C. P. Scott diary, 8 March 1916, *Political Diaries*, 191–2.
33. Bonham Carter, *Winston Churchill*, 448.
34. Ibid., 452.
35. Ibid., 454.
36. HC Deb., 9 May 1916, vol. 82, cc. 500–1. Churchill replied: 'I am afraid I should be out of order if I were to deal with that matter.'
37. 'Politicians and Casualties', *Daily Mail*, 13 October 1916, 4.
38. A. M. Scott diary, 20 October 1916, MS Gen, 1465/7.
39. HC Deb., 1 June 1916, vol. 82, cc. 2972–6.
40. Ibid., c. 2977.
41. C. P. Scott diary, 5 June 1916, *Political Diaries*, 212.
42. WSC to Asquith, 2 June 1916, CHAR 2/74; *WSC*, III/2:1510.
43. Hankey to Asquith, 5 June 1916, CAB 17/132.
44. Ibid.
45. Hankey to Foreign Office, War Office, and Admiralty, 7 June 1916, CAB 17/132.
46. WSC to Asquith, 8 June 1916, and Hankey to WSC, 19 June 1916, CAB 17/132; CHAR 2/72; *WSC*, III/2:1515 and 1518.
47. WSC to Asquith, 22 June 1916, CAB 17/132; *WSC*, III/2:1520.
48. Hankey memorandum, 30 June 1916, CAB 17/132.

49. Hankey diary, 6 June 1916, HNKY 1/1.
50. Hankey, *Supreme Command*, II:505; Roskill, *Hankey*, I:279–80.
51. General Sir Ian Hamilton, *Listening for the Drums* (London: Faber & Faber, 1944), 254.
52. Callwell to Hamilton, 5 July 1916, CHAR 2/74; *WSC*, III/2:1525.
53. Hamilton to WSC, 11 November 1916, Ian Hamilton papers, 8/1/16.
54. Storr to Hankey, 15 June 1916, CAB 17/132.
55. Hankey, undated minute, CAB 17/132; Hankey diary, 6 June 1916, HNKY 1/1.
56. Hankey to Asquith, 5 July 1915, CAB 17/132.
57. Riddell diary, 7 July 1916, Add MS 62978.
58. Hankey diary, 5 June 1916, HNKY 1/1; Hankey, *Supreme Command*, II:518.
59. WSC to Asquith, 8 July 1916, CHAR 2/74; *WSC*, III/2:1527.
60. CID Paper G-74: Hankey memorandum, 'The Presentation to Parliament of Papers in Regard to the Military Operations in Mesopotamia and the Dardanelles', 8 July 1916, CAB 17/132.
61. Riddell diary, 16 July 1916, Add MS 62978.
62. Hankey diary, 11 July 1916, HNKY 1/1.
63. WSC to Lloyd George, 11 July 1916, CAB 17/132.
64. Hankey diary, 11 July 1916, HNKY 1/1.
65. WSC to Lloyd George, 11 July 1916, CAB 17/132.
66. WSC to Asquith, 13 July 1916, CHAR 2/74; *WSC*, III/2:1527–8.
67. Hankey to Robertson, 15 July 1915, CAB 17/132.
68. WSC to John Churchill, 15 July 1916, *WSC*, III/2:1530.
69. HC Deb., 18 July 1916, vol. 84, cc. 850–2.
70. Hankey diary, 19 July 1916, HNKY 1/1; Hankey, *Supreme Command*, II:520.
71. HC Deb., 20 July 1916, vol. 84, cc. 1236–9.

CHAPTER 10

1. WSC to Fisher, 4 August 1916, FISR 1/23; *WSC*, III/2:1541.
2. Roger Owen, *Lord Cromer: Victorian Imperialist, Edwardian Proconsul* (Oxford: Oxford University Press, 2004), 388.
3. WSC to Seely, 13 August 1916, *WSC*, III/2:1542. The Dardanelles Commission has received relatively little scholarly attention. The best accounts are provided by Jenny Macleod, *Reconsidering Gallipoli* (Manchester: Manchester University Press, 2004), ch. 1, and Tim Travers, *Gallipoli 1915* (Stroud: Tempus, 2001), ch. 11. However, both focus on the land campaign. Curran, *The Grand Deception*, nominally devotes a chapter to the earlier work of the Dardanelles Commission, but this is largely confined to the interim report rather than the process that produced it.
4. A. M. Scott diary, 9 August 1916, MS Gen 1465/7.
5. When Churchill learned that Newnes was contemplating a biography, he nominated Garvin to write it. He was, nevertheless, pleased with Scott's work, which he provided feedback on prior to publication. Riddell diary, 1 July

1915, Add MS 62976; WSC to Clementine Churchill, 3 and 6 April 1916, *WSC*, III/2:1479.

6. Riddell diary, 7 July 1916, Add MS 62978.
7. WSC to Fisher, 1 August 1916, *WSC*, III/2:1540.
8. Undated letter (September 1916), Fisher to George Lambert, FISR 15/2.
9. WSC to Fisher, 4 August 1916, FISR 1/23; *WSC*, III/2:1541.
10. Fisher to WSC, 11 and 16 August 1916, CHAR 2/72; *WSC*, III/2:1541 and 1544.
11. WSC to Fisher, 16 September 1916, *WSC*, III/2:1558–9.
12. Undated draft of Fisher evidence, ADM 116/3454.
13. Ibid.
14. Riddell diary, 10 March 1917, Add MS 62979.
15. Crease, 'General Remarks', ADM 1/28268.
16. Winston Churchill, 'Lord Fisher and His Biographer', in *Great Contemporaries* (rev. edn, London: Thornton Butterworth, 1938), 338.
17. Dardanelles Commission, Fisher testimony, 11 October 1916, Q. 3151, CAB 19/33.
18. Riddell diary, 7 July 1916, Add MS 62978.
19. Goulding to Garvin, 8 October 1916, Garvin papers, Harry Ransom Center, University of Texas at Austin.
20. Undated memorandum, FISR 5/32 and 16/6. Although unsigned, the document was almost certainly written by Garvin. See also Mackay, *Fisher*, 459.
21. Mackay, *Fisher*, 460–2. The doctored document is not included among the evidence collected in the Dardanelles Commission papers (CAB 19/28–32), so it is possible that Fisher may not have submitted it.
22. Churchill, *Great Contemporaries*, 338–9.
23. Mackay, *Fisher*, 459–64.
24. Grimes, *Strategy and War Planning*, 204–11; Andrew Lambert, '"The Possibility of Ultimate Action in the Baltic": The Royal Navy at War, 1914–1916', in *Jutland: World War I's Greatest Naval Battle*, ed. Michael Epkenhans, Jörg Hillmann, and Frank Nägler (Lexington, KY: University Press of Kentucky, 2015), 90–3, 113; Andrew Lambert, 'An Edwardian Intellectual at War: Julian Corbett, Plans, Strategy and Official History' (forthcoming).
25. While Fisher undoubtedly altered documents to support his case, there is no foundation for Nicholas Lambert's claim that Churchill forged documents for the Dardanelles Commission. Lambert, *Planning Armageddon*, 296. This allegation seemingly rests on the mistaken assumption that Churchill's collusion with Fisher over certain aspects of their evidence implicates Churchill in Fisher's tampering with documents. There is no evidence Churchill was involved in this, or was even aware of it. The allegation is not supported by the documents Lambert cites in his supporting footnote, which show only that the two men made some effort to coordinate their testimony.
26. Hankey diary, 21 July 1916, HNKY 1/1; Hankey, *Supreme Command*, II:522.
27. Hankey to Lady Hankey, 20 July 1916, Roskill, *Hankey*, I:291.

28. Hankey diary, 24 and 26 July 1916, HNKY 1/1; Hankey, *Supreme Command*, II:522–3.
29. WSC to F. E. Smith, 8 September 1916, CHAR 2/74; *WSC*, III/2:1551.
30. Hankey, 'Notes for Evidence', September 1916, CAB 19/29.
31. Ibid.
32. The terminal date of the first phase was later altered to 23 March 1915, although Churchill did not learn this until 24 October: Dardanelles Commission, Churchill testimony, 24 October 1916, Q. 4650.
33. WSC to Cromer, 12 August 1916, CHAR 2/74; *WSC*, III/2:1542.
34. Cromer to WSC, 20 September 1916, CHAR 2/74; *WSC*, III/2:1560.
35. Cromer to WSC, 21 September 1916, CHAR 2/74; *WSC*, III/2:1561. Hankey was actually the Commission's second witness. The first, General Monro, had to be examined out of sequence because he was about to depart for India when the Commission began its work.
36. Hankey diary, 19 September 1916, HNKY 1/1; Roskill, *Hankey*, I:299.
37. Hankey, *Supreme Command*, II:524; Dardanelles Commission, Hankey testimony, 27 September 1916, CAB 19/33.
38. Dardanelles Commission, Hankey testimony, 19 September 1916, Q. 525.
39. Ibid., Q. 526.
40. Ibid., Q. 568.
41. Ibid., Q. 464.
42. Ibid., Q. 630–1.
43. Ibid., Q. 616–17, 630–1.
44. Hankey diary, 19 September 1916, HNKY 1/1.
45. Hankey to Fisher, 28 September 1916, FISR 1/23; HNKY 5/2.
46. Fisher to George Lambert, September 1916, FISR 15/2.
47. Churchill's official biographer mistakenly suggests that Churchill only appeared before the Commission once, on 28 September. In fact, he appeared six times before the end of 1916, and twice in 1917. *WSC*, III:809 and IV:2.
48. 'Statement by Mr. Churchill upon the Dardanelles Operations to the End of the First Phase', CAB 19/28; WSC III/2:1562–3.
49. Dardanelles Commission, Churchill testimony, 28 September 1916, Q. 1106, CAB 19/33.
50. Ibid., Q. 1130–6.
51. Ibid., Q. 1130. Churchill was relying here on memory. The minutes on Jackson's memorandum in ADM 137/1089 establish that Churchill saw the document on 6 January.
52. Dardanelles Commission, Churchill testimony, 28 September 1916, Q. 1146.
53. Ibid., Q. 1153, 1177. See also Q. 1499 on 4 October 1916.
54. Dardanelles Commission, Churchill testimony, 28 September 1916, Q. 1189. See also his response to Q. 1521 on 4 October 1916.
55. Dardanelles Commission, Churchill testimony, 28 September 1916, Q. 1047–8.
56. Ibid., Q. 1201.

57. Masterton Smith to Fisher, 30 September 1916, FISR 1/23.
58. Dardanelles Commission, Churchill testimony, 4 October 1916, Q. 1546–9. See also Q. 1381 and 1499.
59. Dardanelles Commission, Churchill testimony, 4 October 1916, Q. 1413.
60. Ibid., Q. 1536. See also Q. 1189, 28 September 1916.
61. Dardanelles Commission, Churchill testimony, 4 October 1916, Q. 1560.
62. E.g. Dardanelles Commission, Churchill testimony, 4 October 1916, Q. 1251.
63. Dardanelles Commission, Bartolomé testimony, 5 October 1916, Q. 1580–5, 1687–8.
64. Dardanelles Commission, Oliver testimony, 5 October 1916, Q. 1829, 1916.
65. Dardanelles Commission, Wilson testimony, 5 October 1916, Q. 1926.
66. Ibid., Q. 1951.
67. Dardanelles Commission, H. Jackson testimony, 6 October 1916, Q. 2075.
68. Dardanelles Commission, Bartolomé testimony, 5 October 1916, Q. 1593–5 and 1675–6.
69. Ibid., Q. 1592 and 1675; Dardanelles Commission, H. Jackson testimony, 6 October 1916, Q. 2150.
70. Riddell diary, 14 October 1916, Add MS 62978.
71. Dardanelles Commission, Fisher testimony, 11 October 1916, Q. 3378–9; see also Q. 3123–4.
72. Dardanelles Commission, Fisher testimony, 11 October 1916, Q. 3383–4.
73. Ibid., Q. 3202.
74. Ibid., Q. 3241–4.
75. Ibid., Q. 3269–71.
76. Ibid., Q. 3122.
77. Ibid., Q. 3262.
78. Ibid., Q. 3121.
79. Ibid., Q. 3263–8. Fisher wrote to Clyde the following day to reinforce this point. FISR 1/24.
80. Dardanelles Commission, Fisher testimony, 11 October 1916, Q. 3365–76.
81. Ibid., 11 October 1916, Q. 3090.
82. Fisher to Cromer, 11 October 1916, FISR 1/23; printed with Fisher's testimony in CAB 19/33. Fisher also sent copies to both Churchill and Asquith.
83. Fisher to Garvin, 11 October 1916, Garvin papers.
84. WSC to Asquith, 28 October 1916, CHAR 2/74; *WSC*, III/2:1579; also Goulding to Garvin, 29 October 1916, Garvin papers.
85. Dardanelles Commission, Fisher testimony, 11 October 1916, Q. 3391.
86. Dardanelles Commission, Wilson testimony, 5 October 1916, Q. 2016.
87. Ibid., Q. 2036.

CHAPTER 11

1. Dardanelles Commission, Churchill testimony, 4 October 1916, Q. 1457.
2. Dardanelles Commission, T. Jackson testimony, 18 October 1916, Q. 4414.

3. Dardanelles Commission, Oliver testimony, 5 October 1916, Q. 1861–4.
4. Dardanelles Commission, Singer testimony, 12 October 1916, Q. 3921–7.
5. Ibid., Q. 3978–83.
6. Dardanelles Commission, T. Jackson testimony, 18 October 1916, Q. 4428–30.
7. Callwell memorandum, 'Summary of Proposed Evidence of Major-General Charles Callwell', CAB 19/28.
8. Ibid.; Dardanelles Commission, Callwell testimony, 12 October 1916, Q. 3539–42.
9. Callwell memorandum, 'Summary of Proposed Evidence'.
10. Dardanelles Commission, Callwell testimony, 12 October 1916, Q. 3520.
11. Callwell to Robertson, 18 March 1915, and Robertson to Callwell, 19 March 1915, Robertson papers.
12. Hickman memorandum, 'Attack of Forts by Ships', 9 October 1916, CAB 19/29; Dardanelles Commission, Hickman testimony, 12 October 1916.
13. Jackson's testimony could be taken to imply that Aston was still advising Jackson in January 1915, but Aston explained at the start of his testimony that he had left Jackson's staff in August 1914 and was no longer at the Admiralty when the Dardanelles operation was being planned. Dardanelles Commission, Jackson testimony, Q. 2136, and Aston testimony, 12 October 1916, Q. 3803.
14. A. M. Scott diary, 20 October 1916, MS Gen 1465/7.
15. WSC to Cromer, 17 October 1916, CHAR 2/74; *WSC*, III/2:1574.
16. A. M. Scott diary, 20 and 21 October 1916, MS Gen 1465/7.
17. Ibid., 21 October 1916, MS Gen 1465/7.
18. WSC to Oliver, 19 October 1916, OLV/5.
19. Dardanelles Commission, Churchill testimony, 24 October 1916, Q. 4646–9.
20. 'Remarks by Admiral of the Fleet Sir Arthur Wilson on the Paper and Evidence of Major-General Hickman', 23 October 1916, CAB 19/32.
21. Dardanelles Commission, Wilson testimony, 24 October 1916, Q. 4748–9.
22. Ibid., Q. 4792–9.
23. Dardanelles Commission, Bacon testimony, 24 October 1916; undated memorandum, 'Statement of Admiral Bacon', CAB 19/28.
24. Dardanelles Commission, Oliver testimony, 25 October 1916, Q. 5193–206.
25. Ibid., Q. 5207.
26. Ibid., Q. 5320–1.
27. Dardanelles Commission, Wilson testimony, 24 October 1916, Q. 4730, and Oliver testimony, 25 October 1916, Q. 5269.
28. Dardanelles Commission, Bartolomé testimony, 24 October 1916.
29. Dardanelles Commission, de Robeck testimony, 10 October 1916, Q. 2757–8, and Hall testimony, 24 October 1916, Q. 4942–3.
30. Dardanelles Commission, Hall testimony, 24 October 1916, Q. 4924–7.
31. Ibid., Q. 4904–6.
32. Prior, *Gallipoli*, 249–50.
33. Dardanelles Commission, Churchill testimony, 27 October 1916, Q. 5353.
34. Ibid., Q. 5369.
35. Ibid., Q. 5364–9.

36. WSC to Spiers, 27 October 1916, *WSC*, III/2:1578; see also Hankey's diary for 27 October 1916, HNKY 1/1.
37. WSC to Asquith, 28 October 1916, CHAR 2/74; *WSC*, III/2:1578–80. This is not recorded in the Commission's official minutes, although comments along these lines may have been made privately after the formal testimony had concluded—or Churchill may simply have been embellishing.
38. *WSC*, III/2:1578–80.
39. Ibid.
40. Riddell diary, 21 July 1916, Add MS 62978.

CHAPTER 12

1. Dardanelles Commission, Balfour testimony, 13 October 1915, Q. 4202.
2. Dardanelles Commission, Haldane testimony, 18 October 1915, Q. 4595–600.
3. Dardanelles Commission, Grey testimony, 26 September 1916, Q. 853; Dardanelles Commission, Balfour testimony, 13 October 1915, Q. 4179, 4237.
4. Dardanelles Commission, Lloyd George testimony, 30 October 1916, Q. 5548.
5. Dardanelles Commission, Asquith testimony, 31 October 1916, Q. 5841–43B.
6. Dardanelles Commission, Churchill testimony, 28 September 1916, Q. 1190; Dardanelles Commission, Crewe testimony, 27 October 1916, Q. 5442–3.
7. Dardanelles Commission, Asquith testimony, 31 October 1916, Q. 5784.
8. Ibid., Q. 5883–5.
9. Dardanelles Commission, Haldane testimony, 18 October 1916, Q. 4515–23.
10. Dardanelles Commission, Lloyd George testimony, 30 October 1916, Q. 5573.
11. Ibid., Q. 5558, 5581, 5585.
12. Dardanelles Commission, Churchill testimony, 25 November 1916, Q. 6051–65.
13. Dardanelles Commission, Callwell testimony, 12 October 1916, Q. 3568. But see also Callwell to Brade, 4 July 1916, where he suggests that Kitchener had not approved of the Admiralty's plan and only accepted it 'more or less under protest'. CAB 17/132; *WSC*, III/2:1523–5.
14. Dardanelles Commission, Murray testimony, 10 October 1916, Q. 2596–7, 2601–5.
15. Sir George Arthur memorandum, 25 November 1916, CAB 19/28; *WSC*, III/2:1585.
16. Sir George Arthur memorandum, 25 November 1916, CAB 19/28; cf. Sir George Arthur, *Life of Lord Kitchener*, (3 vols, London: Macmillan, 1920), III:105, 208–9.
17. Scott, *Winston Churchill*, 125.
18. WSC to Mears, 29 November 1916, CHAR 2/74; *WSC*, III/2:1586–8.
19. Dardanelles Commission, Arthur testimony, 1 December 1916, Q. 6176–8.
20. Dardanelles Commission, Churchill testimony, 1 December 1916, Q. 6205.
21. Dardanelles Commission, von Donop testimony, 4 December 1916.
22. Dardanelles Commission, Creedy testimony, 4 December 1916, Q. 6292–3.
23. Ibid., Q. 6294–7.

24. The first historian to treat Arthur's claims seriously was Cassar, *Kitchener's War*, 125–8. Clews, *Churchill's Dilemma* (pp. 104–6) disputes Cassar's interpretation, but Curran accepts it: *Grand Deception*, 58–9.

25. WSC to Sinclair, 29 November 1916, *WSC*, IV/1:34; *Winston and Archie*, 41–2.

26. Richard Toye, *Lloyd George and Churchill* (London: Pan Macmillan, 2008), 171–2.

27. Riddell diary, 10 December 1915, *The Riddell Diaries 1908–1923*, ed. J. M. McEwen (London: Athlone Press, 1986), 179.

28. *Lord Kitchener and Winston Churchill: The Dardanelles Part I, 1914–15* [cited hereafter as Dardanelles Report] (London: The Stationery Office, 2000), 156.

29. Ibid., 67.

30. Ibid., 65.

31. HC Deb., 20 March 1917, vol. 91, c. 1793.

32. Dardanelles Commission, Bartolomé testimony, 5 October 1916, Q. 1587–9; Dardanelles Report, 66; HC Deb., 20 March 1917, vol. 91, cc. 1787–8.

33. Dardanelles Report, 103. Andrew Fisher and Mackenzie both dissented from this conclusion.

34. Dardanelles Report, 105.

35. Ibid., 156.

36. Ibid., 58–60, 157.

37. Ibid., 126–7, 159–60.

38. Ibid., 160.

39. Riddell diary, 14 February 1917, Add MS 62979.

40. Roch report, 22 December 1916, Dardanelles Report, 211.

41. Hankey diary, 16 February 1917, HNKY 1/1; Roskill, *Hankey*, I:359.

42. Riddell diary, 15 February 1917, Add MS 62979.

43. Hankey diary, 15 February and 10 March 1917, HNKY 1/1.

44. Hankey diary, 28 September 1916, HNKY 1/1.

45. Hankey diary, 16 February 1917, HNKY 1/1; Roskill, *Hankey*, I:359.

46. Riddell diary, 15 February 1917, Add MS 62979.

47. Hankey diary, 16 February 1917, HNKY 1/1.

48. 'The Dardanelles Report', *Manchester Guardian*, 9 March 1917, 4; see also 'The Dardanelles Debate', *Manchester Guardian*, 21 March 1917, 4.

49. 'The Moral of the Dardanelles, *The Observer*, 11 March 1917, 6.

50. 'The Report of the Dardanelles Commission', *Morning Post*, 9 March 1917, 6.

51. 'A Damning Report', *Daily Mail*, 9 March 1917, 4.

52. 'The Dardanelles Report', *The Times*, 9 March 1917, 9.

53. Riddell diary, 10 March 1917, Add MS 62979.

54. A. M. Scott diary, 14 March 1917, MS Gen 1465/8.

55. WSC to Lloyd George, 10 March 1917, CHAR 2/97; *WSC*, IV/1:42–3.

56. HC Deb., 14 March 1917, vol. 91, c. 1095.

57. Swinton to WSC, 15 March 1917, CHAR 2/97; Hankey diary, 18 March 1917, HNKY 1/1; 'Dardanelles "Secrets" Disclosed', *Manchester Guardian*, 20 March 1917, 5.

58. Riddell diary, 10 March 1917, Add MS 62979.
59. HC Deb., 20 March 1917, vol. 91, cc. 1785–6.
60. Ibid., cc. 1794–5.
61. Ibid., cc. 1797–8.
62. Ibid., cc. 1800–1.
63. Ibid., cc. 1797–8.
64. 'Our London Correspondence', *Manchester Guardian*, 21 March 1917, 4.
65. 'From the Cross Benches: A Parliamentary Observer', *The Observer*, 25 March 1917, 10.
66. On Lloyd George's relationship with Churchill and his appointment as Minister of Munitions, see, in particular, Toye, *Lloyd George and Churchill*, 171–83.
67. Gwynne to Bathurst, 20 July 1917, MS/DEP/1990/1/2406.
68. Gwynne to Bathurst, 27 July 1917, MS/DEP/1990/1/2407.

CHAPTER 13

1. WSC memorandum, 'The Second Phase', February 1917, CHAR 2/98.
2. WSC memorandum, 'The Third Phase', February 1917, CHAR 2/98. Neither of these documents is to be found in the bound volumes of evidence collected by the Commission, which suggests that Churchill did not formally submit them. In his oral testimony in March 1917, Churchill referred only to the collection of *documents* he submitted relating to the second and third phases, and these *are* present in the Commission's records. Dardanelles Commission, Churchill testimony, 26 and 28 March 1917, CAB 19/33. Both written statements were typeset in June at the Foreign Office, however, which implies that they were seen by the Commission.
3. Dardanelles Commission Final Report, 4 December 1917, CHAR 2/101.
4. Andrew Green, *Writing the Great War* (London: Frank Cass, 2003), 1–20; Macleod, *Reconsidering Gallipoli*, 57–65; David French, 'Sir James Edmonds and the Official History: France and Belgium', in *The First World War and British Military History*, ed. Brian Bond (Oxford: Oxford University Press, 1991), 69–86.
5. GT 7087: WSC memorandum, 'Official Histories', 8 April 1919, CAB 24/77; Schurman, *Corbett*, 199.
6. GT 8019: Hankey Cabinet memorandum, 'Official Naval History of the War', 19 August 1919, CAB 24/87; Corbett minute, 25 August 1919, ADM 116/2067; Schurman, *Corbett*, 200.
7. Admiralty Board memorandum, 'Naval History of the War', ADM 167/59; Board minute 1042, 6 November 1919, ADM 167/56.
8. CP 9: Hankey Cabinet memorandum, 'Official Histories', 28 October 1919, CAB 24/92.
9. Admiralty Board minute 1048, 10 November 1919, ADM 167/56; CP 202: Hankey Cabinet memorandum, 'Publication of the First Volume of the Official Naval History of the War', 26 November 1919, CAB 24/94; Cabinet minutes, 5 December 1919, CAB 23/37; Green, *Writing the Great War*, 7–9.

10. Hamilton to WSC, 24 August 1920, CHAR 2/110; see also Hamilton to WSC, 8 April 1919, Ian Hamilton papers, 13/24.

11. Admiralty memorandum, 'Terms of Reference for the Committee on the Attacks Delivered on and the Enemy Defences of the Dardanelles Straits', 21 March 1919, ADM 116/1713.

12. Hamilton to WSC, 23 August 1919 and 24 August 1920, CHAR 2/106/32–3 and CHAR 2/110/153–6.

13. WSC to Masterton Smith, 20 September 1920, CAB 1/33; CHAR 2/111/25–7. See also Churchill to Keyes, 25 March 1923, *Keyes Papers*, II:87–8: 'on the whole', he wrote, 'I do not think ill of the report'.

14. Mitchell Report, 70–3, 84–7.

15. WSC to Long, 9 November 1920, CHAR 2/111/57–8.

16. Long to WSC, 15 November 1920, CHAR 2/111/64.

17. WSC to Lord Forster (Governor-General of Australia), 25 May 1921, ADM 116/2413.

18. WSC to Masterton Smith, 22 June 1921, CHAR 2/115/77.

19. WSC to Lord Forster, 25 May 1921, ADM 116/2413.

20. Macleod, *Reconsidering Gallipoli*, 65–80.

21. Bean diary, 2 November 1915, Australian War Memorial, AWM38 3DRL606/19/1, p. 44; Ross Coulthart, *Charles Bean: If People Really Knew* (Sydney: HarperCollins, 2014), 165.

22. C. E. W. Bean, *Official History of Australia in the War of 1914–1918*, vol. 1, *The Story of ANZAC*, 2nd edn (Sydney: Angus & Robertson, 1933), 168–75.

23. Ibid., I:201.

24. Churchill, *World Crisis*, II:117.

25. Green, *Writing the Great War*, 94–6.

26. Ibid., 95.

27. Edmonds to Ellison, 8 October 1923, Ellison papers, National Army Museum, 1987-04-35-297.

28. Hamilton to WSC, 20 November 1924, Ian Hamilton papers, 13/24.

29. Daniel to Marsh, 25 November 1924, CHAR 2/140.

30. Sub-Committee on Control of the Official Histories (COH), conclusions of second meeting, 3 December 1924, CAB 16/53.

31. Hamilton to Ellison, 1 August 1924, 1987-04-35-301.

32. Gerald Ellison, *The Perils of Amateur Strategy* (London: Longmans, Green, & Co., 1926), xix, 100.

33. Ibid., 51.

34. Macleod, *Reconsidering Gallipoli*, 81–5; Green, *Writing the Great War*, 100–3, 120–3.

35. Edmonds to Edward Marsh, 6 March 1928, CHAR 2/162/39.

36. COH, conclusions of fifth meeting, 9 March 1928, CAB 16/53.

37. Green, *Writing the Great War*, 132–3; Macleod, *Reconsidering Gallipoli*, 84–5.

38. C. F. Aspinall-Oglander, *Military Operations: Gallipoli* (2 vols, London: William Heinemann, 1929–32), I:viii–ix; cf. Carl Mühlmann, *Der Kampf um die Dardanellen 1915* (Oldenburg: Stalling, 1927), 61.

39. Aspinall-Oglander, *Military Operations*, I:354–5.
40. Ibid., II:479.
41. Compton MacKenzie, 'Official History of Gallipoli', *Daily Mail*, 25 April 1932, 6.

CHAPTER 14

1. Hamilton to WSC, 10 October 1919, CHAR 2/106.
2. Fisher, *Memories*, 63.
3. Ibid., 95–7.
4. Mackay, *Fisher*, 460–2.
5. Fisher, *Memories*, 90; cf. War Council minutes, 28 January 1915, *WSC*, III/1:464–5. The minutes show that Churchill proposed at this meeting to *begin* the construction of 'two light cruisers' (actually, battle cruisers) for possible use in the Baltic. Fisher changed 'two light cruisers' to 'cruisers, &c, &c', and indicated that this meant his full 'armada' of 612 vessels. The implication is that this 'armada' for the Baltic was already under construction and had previously been approved by the Chancellor.
6. Hamilton to WSC, 15 October 1919, CHAR 2/106.
7. Hamilton, *Gallipoli Diary*.
8. An excellent overview of Hamilton's memoirs is provided by Macleod, *Reconsidering Gallipoli*, 176–203.
9. Hamilton, *Gallipoli Diary*, I:242. This despite Churchill advising Hamilton against 'a eulogy of my work at Antwerp', on the grounds that it would be 'better to deal with one picture at a time'. WSC to Hamilton, 24 September 1919, Ian Hamilton papers, 13/24.
10. Hamilton, *Gallipoli Diary*, I:44. Hamilton wrote in similar terms to WSC on 29 June 1923: 'The Admirals on the spot not only felt no real drive from Fisher, but they got always a hearty kick if they asked even for an old bit of rope unless there was a likelihood of the request coming up to you.' CHAR 8/44.
11. *WSC*, IV:754. I have used the conversion rate provided by David Lough in *No More Champagne: Churchill and His Money* (London: Head of Zeus, 2015), 134.
12. Hamilton to WSC, 30 August 1919, CHAR 2/106.
13. WSC to Hamilton, 24 September 1919, Ian Hamilton papers, 13/24.
14. Director of Naval Intelligence (DNI) minute, October 1919, ADM 167/58.
15. Board of Admiralty minute 1016, 23 October 1919, ADM 167/57.
16. Cabinet 6 (22), 30 January 1922, CAB 23/29.
17. WSC to Clementine Churchill, 4 February 1922, *WSC*, IV/3:1753.
18. Peter Fraser, 'Cabinet Secrecy and War Memoirs', *History*, 70, no. 230 (October 1985), 401.
19. Cabinet 6 (22), 30 January 1922, CAB 23/29; H. A. L. Fisher diary, 30 January 1922, *WSC*, IV/3:1749. Martin Gilbert states that Churchill forced the discussion on this issue specifically to allow him to publish documents to refute Esher's recent accusations, but the Cabinet minutes and Churchill's account for

his wife are both clear about the initiative coming from a former parliamentary secretary, Chiozza Money, who asked Austen Chamberlain to raise the issue on his behalf. *WSC*, IV:757. This error is compounded in Curran's account by that author's mistaken attribution of Gilbert's words to Churchill, which strengthens the impression that Churchill was the one who raised this subject. Curran, *Grand Deception*, 198.

20. Cabinet 6 (22), 30 January 1922, CAB 23/29; John F. Naylor, *A Man and an Institution: Sir Maurice Hankey, the Cabinet Secretariat and the Custody of Cabinet Secrecy* (Cambridge: Cambridge University Press, 1984), 69.

21. Churchill's original conception of the work is outlined in the prospectus he prepared on 6 January 1921. CHAR 8/41.

22. WSC to Jackson, 22 July 1921, CHAR 8/40; *WSC*, IV:755.

23. Ronald I. Cohen, *Bibliography of the Writings of Sir Winston Churchill* (3 vols, London: Thoemmes Continuum, 2006), II:1331–41.

24. My treatment of Churchill's coverage of this and other episodes in *The World Crisis* draws on and invariably benefits from Robin Prior's ground-breaking and insightful analysis in *Churchill's 'World Crisis'*. For Coronel, see pp. 9–15.

25. Here Churchill drew on two articles he had published on Antwerp in the *Sunday Pictorial* in 1916:'Antwerp:The Story of its Siege and Fall' (19 November) and 'How Antwerp Saved the Channel Ports' (26 November), in *The Collected Essays of Sir Winston Churchill*, ed. Michael Wolff (4 vols, London: Library of Imperial History, 1976), I:172–82.

26. Churchill, *World Crisis*, I:374. Emphasis added.

27. Ibid., I:388.

28. 'The World Crisis', *The Observer*, 15 April 1923, 12.

29. 'Mr. Churchill on the War', *Manchester Guardian*, 10 April 1923, 9.

30. E.g. HC Deb., 19 March 1923, vol. 161, cc. 2086–7; HC Deb., 12 April 1923, vol. 162, cc. 1299–300; HC Deb., 25 April 1923, vol. 163, cc. 434–6.

31. WSC to Masterton Smith, 21 February 1923, and Patrick Gower to Masterton Smith, 26 February 1923, *WSC*,V/1:30–1.

32. WSC to Lloyd George, 28 February 1923, Lloyd George papers, LG/G/4/4/4.

33. Ibid.

34. WSC to Bonar Law, 3 March 1923, *WSC*,V/1:32–4.

35. Hankey to Bonar Law, 8 March 1923, *WSC*,V/1:37–9.

36. Churchill, *World Crisis*, II:viii.

37. Hankey to WSC, 4 November 1923, CHAR 8/45. In fact, Churchill *did* ask for permission before publishing the third volume of *The World Crisis* in 1927. As a member of Baldwin's government at the time, it would have been impolitic not to ask for approval—and he was probably confident that it would be given! WSC to Baldwin, 18 November 1926, CHAR 8/204; WSC to William Bridgeman, 13 November 1926, CHAR 8/204; Naylor, *Man and Institution*, 118.

38. Churchill, *World Crisis*, II:90–2.

39. Churchill, *World Crisis*, II:91.

40. Curran, *Grand Deception*, 51–2.

41. Harcourt diary, 6 January 1915. Harcourt's page of notes on this meeting reveals that Fisher was present, which would have given the meeting the character of a War Council. Another possibility, suggested by Clews, is that Churchill was thinking of an informal dinner that day at the Admiralty, attended by the Prime Minister. Clews, *Churchill's Dilemma*, 72.

42. Churchill, *World Crisis*, II:95–6.

43. Prior, *Churchill's 'World Crisis'*, 76–7; WSC to Garvin, 21 September 1916, Garvin papers.

44. Churchill, *World Crisis*, II:164.

45. Ibid., II:353–4.

46. Mary Soames, *Clementine Churchill* (London: Cassell, 1979), 120; see also *WSC*, III:419.

47. CHAR 8/149; Prior, *Churchill's 'World Crisis'*, 136–7.

48. Churchill, *World Crisis*, II:248–9.

49. Ibid., II:155, 541–3.

50. Ibid., II:262–3.

51. Ibid., II:263–5, 268–9.

52. Ibid., II:271–4; cf. Mitchell Report, 70–1, 84–7. Prior provides a detailed analysis of Churchill's account. *Churchill's 'World Crisis'*, 117–18.

53. Mitchell Report, 86; Prior, *Churchill's 'World Crisis'*, 118.

54. Arthur Bertie to WSC, 25 June 1923, CHAR 8/44.

55. Churchill, *World Crisis*, II:274–6.

56. Ibid., II:171.

57. The best analysis is provided by Prior, *Churchill's 'World Crisis'*, chs 8–10.

58. Churchill, *World Crisis*, II:545–6.

59. Liman von Sanders to Dr Hermann Bücher, 8 November 1923; a translated copy was sent to Churchill by Major Norman Holden on 27 November, CHAR 8/45. Liman had expressed similar views a few years earlier in his memoirs, *Fünf Jahre Türkei* (Berlin: Scherl, 1919), 65–6.

60. Edmonds to Marsh, 21 February 1927, CHAR 8/208/64.

61. Mühlmann, *Der Kampf um die Dardanellen 1915*, 74.

62. Winston S. Churchill, 'The Prize of Constantinople', *Daily Telegraph*, 1 July 1930, reprinted in *Collected Essays*, I:282–7. *Colliers* published this series in six instalments. In Britain, the *Daily Telegraph* printed them as twelve articles. Cohen, *Bibliography*, II:1369–70.

63. Churchill, *Collected Essays*, I:283–4.

64. Mitchell Report, 485–6.

65. Churchill, *Collected Essays*, I:284; Aspinall-Oglander, *Military Operations*, I:105–6. Everything in this passage is contradicted by the Mitchell Report (pp. 485–6).

66. Churchill, *Collected Essays*, I:284–5. Emphasis added.

67. Ibid., I:278.

68. Ibid., I:281–3.

69. Cohen, *Bibliography*, I:266–70.

70. Winston S. Churchill, *The World Crisis* (abridged and revised edition, Toronto: Macmillan, 1931), 414–16. This important change was first noted in Edward J. Erickson, 'One More Push: Forcing the Dardanelles in March 1915', *Journal of Strategic Studies*, 24, no. 3 (September 2001), 158–76.

71. Cohen, *Bibliography*, I:270–86.

72. The only post-war edition to print Churchill's modified argument was a 1992 Scribner's reprint of the original one-volume edition.

73. Grey, *Twenty-Five Years*, II:79–83.

74. Asquith, *Memories and Reflections*, II:106–7.

75. Lloyd George, *War Memoirs*, I:233–4.

76. Wemyss, *Dardanelles Campaign*, 136.

77. Marder, *Dreadnought*, V:200.

78. Wemyss to his wife, 16 May 1920, Wemyss papers, Churchill College Archives Centre, WYMS 7/12.

79. Wemyss, *Dardanelles Campaign*, 257.

80. Keyes to WSC, 5 November 1933, CHAR 2/203/21.

81. WSC to Keyes, 11 August 1933, CHAR 2/203/15.

82. Bacon, *Fisher*, II:181–98.

83. WSC to Keyes, 29 December 1933, CHAR 2/203/31.

84. Keyes, *Naval Memoirs*, I:183.

85. Ibid., I:340.

86. Ibid., I:186.

87. Ibid., I:249–53.

88. Captain L. A. K. Boswell, 'The Naval Attack on the Dardanelles, 1915', *Journal of the Royal United Service Institution*, 110, no. 638 (May 1965), 147; 'History of British Minesweeping in the War', 13.

89. Boswell, 'Naval Attack', 147; Mitchell Report, 14-16. Marder concludes, on the basis of Boswell's evidence, that a renewed attack after 4 April would have had a '50–50 chance of success'. Arthur J. Marder, *From the Dardanelles to Oran* (London: Clarendon Press, 1974), 23–6.

90. Winston S. Churchill, 'Ships *Could* have Forced the Dardanelles', *Daily Mail*, 2 October 1934, in *Collected Essays*, I:335. Emphasis added.

91. Churchill, *Collected Essays*, I:336.

CHAPTER 15

1. 'The British Failure at Gallipoli', *Manchester Guardian*, 26 April 1921, 7.

2. 'Mr. Churchill', *Daily Mail*, 18 March 1924, 8.

3. WSC to Viscount Halifax, 9 May 1924, CHAR 2/133/21.

4. 'Mr. Churchill's Opinion of Dr. Addison', *Manchester Guardian*, 28 November 1923, 10; 'Glories in Gallipoli', *Daily Mail*, 28 November 1923, 10.

5. Brian Bond, *The Unquiet Western Front: Britain's Role in Literature and History* (Cambridge: Cambridge University Press, 2002), 27–40.

6. Churchill, *World Crisis*, III:196.

7. Prior, *Churchill's 'World Crisis'*, ch. 12 provides a detailed critique of Churchill's figures and concludes that he successfully made his case. This verdict is supported by subsequent studies. See Robin Prior, '"The Blood Test": Churchill Writing on the Battle of the Somme', *Finest Hour*, no. 172 (spring 2016), 32–5.

8. Churchill, *World Crisis*, III:42.

9. Ian Beckett, 'Frocks and Brasshats', in *First World War and British Military History*, ed. Bond, 102–3; Ian F. W. Beckett, *The Great War 1914–1918* (Harlow: Longman, 2001), 463–4; Bond, *Unquiet Western Front*, 44–5.

10. Winston Churchill, 'Lloyd George's War Memoirs: Volume III', *Daily Mail*, 21 September 1934, and Winston Churchill, 'Lloyd George: The War Leader', *News of the World*, 18 February 1936, *Collected Essays*, III:98, 267.

11. B. H. Liddell Hart, *History of the First World War* (London: Pan, 1970), 135 (first published 1930 as *The Real War*).

12. Hew Strachan, 'Liddell Hart, Cruttwell, and Falls', in *First World War and British Military History*, ed. Bond, 43–53.

13. Reprinted in Churchill, *Thoughts and Adventures* (London: Thornton Butterworth, 1932), 130. Churchill returned to this theme in the 'Introduction' to E. L. Spears' *Prelude to Victory*, published September 1939. 'Generals are not always right', he wrote, 'and politicians are not always timid and weak. On many occasions during the War the military men were proved to be wrong, and the strategy of statesmen proved to be right.' Churchill, *Collected Essays*, I:491.

14. Robert Rhodes James, 'Churchill the Parliamentarian, Orator, and Statesman', in *Churchill*, ed. Blake and Louis, 503.

15. Lloyd George, *War Memoirs*, III:1067.

16. Ibid., III:1071.

17. Hankey to Lloyd George, 16 April 1934, Naylor, *Man and Institution*, 119; Toye, *Lloyd George and Churchill*, 296–7.

18. Robert Rhodes James, *Churchill: A Study in Failure* (London: Weidenfeld & Nicolson, 1970), 348–9.

19. Victor Wallace Germains, *The Tragedy of Winston Churchill* (London: Hurst & Blackett, 1931), 277–8.

20. David Dutton, *Neville Chamberlain* (London: Arnold, 2001), 57–63; Carla Pass, 'The Lasting Legacy of Munich: British Public Perceptions of Neville Chamberlain during the Phoney War', MA thesis, Dalhousie University, August 2014.

21. The reception and impact of Churchill's wartime speeches is often exaggerated, however. An important corrective to the established view is provided by Richard Toye, *The Roar of the Lion: The Untold Story of Churchill's World War II Speeches* (Oxford: Oxford University Press, 2013).

22. H. Dent diary, 1 May 1940, Mass Observation Archive, 5057.

23. C. W. Smallbones diary, 13 April 1940, Mass Observation Archive, 5201.

24. Annie Elliott diary, 12 November 1939, Mass Observation Archive, 5306.

25. Adelaide R. Poole diary, 21 September 1939, Mass Observation Archive, 5399.

26. Conservative views of Churchill during this period are well covered in Andrew Roberts, 'The Tories versus Churchill during the "Finest Hour"', in *Eminent Churchillians* (London: Phoenix, 1994), 137–210.

27. John Colville diary, 1 January 1940, *The Fringes of Power: 10 Downing Street Diaries 1939–55* (New York: W. W. Norton, 1985), 63.

28. Channon diary, 10 January 1940, *Chips: The Diaries of Sir Henry Channon*, ed. Robert Rhodes James (London: Weidenfeld & Nicolson, 1967), 231.

29. HC Deb., 7 May 1940, vol. 360, c. 1129.

30. Bell, *Churchill and Sea Power*; Graham Clews, 'Churchill and the Phoney War: A Study in Folly and Frustration', PhD thesis, University of New South Wales, 2016, ch. 2.

31. WSC to Hankey, 2 June 1915, *WSC*, III/2:984.

32. Winston Churchill, *Second World War* (6 vols, London: Cassell, 1948–53), II:15.

33. Speech of 11 April 1940, House of Commons, *Complete Speeches*, VI:6209.

34. Daidie Penn diary, 6 May 1940, Mass Observation Archives, 5396, Pass, 'Lasting Legacy', 114.

35. John Thornley diary, 28 April 1940, Mass Observation Archives, 5212, Pass, 'Lasting Legacy', 111.

36. Colville diary, 17 April 1940, *Fringes of Power*, 104.

37. HC Deb., 7 May 1940, vol. 360, cc. 1125–30.

38. Reynolds, *In Command of History*, 126.

39. Graham Dawson and Bob West, 'Our Finest Hour? The Popular Memory of World War II and the Struggle over National Identity', in *National Fictions: World War Two on Film and Television*, ed. Geoff Hurd (London: British Film Institute, 1984), 8–13.

40. Dutton, *Chamberlain*, ch. 3.

41. John Stevenson, 'Introduction' to 'Cato', *Guilty Men* (London: Penguin, 1998), xv.

42. Churchill actually titled his Fulton speech 'The Sinews of Peace', but this is now all but forgotten.

43. Alan Moorehead, *Gallipoli* (London: Hamish Hamilton, 1958), 364–5.

44. Ann Moyal, 'Alan Moorehead's Gallipoli', 16 May 2015, <http://www.aspistrategist. org.au/alan-mooreheads-gallipoli/> (accessed 18 July 2016).

45. *WSC*, VIII:1074. See also Lord Attlee, 'The Churchill I Knew', in *Churchill by His Contemporaries: An Observer Appreciation* (London: Hodder & Stoughton, 1965), 15.

46. Bond, *Unquiet Western Front*, ch. 3; see also Alex Danchev, ' "Bunking" and Debunking: The Controversies of the 1960s', in *The First World War and British Military History*, ed. Bond, 263–88.

47. Beckett, 'Frocks and Brasshats', 92; Curran, *Grand Deception*, 211–12.

48. Basil H. Liddell Hart, 'The Military Strategist', in A. J. P. Taylor, Robert Rhodes James, J.H. Plumb, B.H. Liddell Hart, Anthony Storr, *Churchill: Four Faces and the Man* (London: Book Club Associates, 1969), 153–202.

49. Gordon Corrigan, *Blood, Sweat and Arrogance and the Myths of Churchill's War* (London: Phoenix, 2006), 477.

50. Bell, *Churchill and Sea Power*, ch. 6.

51. Major-General Sir John Kennedy, *The Business of War* (London: Hutchinson, 1957), 254.

52. Dwight D. Eisenhower and Alistair Cooke, *General Eisenhower on the Military Churchill* (New York: Norton, 1970), 51.

53. Maisky to Stalin, 6 August 1942, in Anatoli Filev, 'New Documents about Winston Churchill from Russian Archives', *International Affairs* (Moscow), 47, no. 5 (2001), 132–3; *The Maisky Diaries*, ed. Gabriel Gorodetsky (New Haven, CT: Yale University Press, 2015), 458. I am grateful to Martin Folly for bringing these references to my attention.

54. Maisky diary, 30 July 1942, *Maisky Diaries*, 455.

55. Higgins, *Winston Churchill and the Dardanelles*, 184.

56. Bell, *Churchill and Sea Power*, ch. 2.

57. Bean, *Story of ANZAC*, I:vii.

58. David Day, *The Great Betrayal* (New York: Norton, 1989); Augustine Meaher IV, *The Road to Singapore: The Myth of British Betrayal* (Australian Scholarly Publishing, 2010), 29–31.

59. *The Last Bastion*, written and produced by David Williamson.

60. Lord Moran, *Winston Churchill: The Struggle for Survival 1940–1965* (London: Constable, 1966), 21.

61. Day, *Great Betrayal*, 241, 355. The IMDB page for *The Last Bastion* lists David Day as a 'consultant historian' for the series. <http://www.imdb.com/title/tt0087590/fullcredits?ref_=tt_ov_st_sm> (accessed 19 July 2016).

62. Amanda Taub, 'Bernie Sanders Has a Winston Churchill Problem', 12 February 2016, <http://www.vox.com/2016/2/12/10979266/bernie-sanders-churchill> (accessed 18 July 2016).

63. Travers, *Gallipoli 1915*, 31–2; Erickson, 'One More Push', 158–76; Erickson, *Gallipoli*.

CONCLUSION

1. Draft statement for the Dardanelles Commission, 8 September 1916, *WSC*, III/2:1554–5.

2. Speech of 15 November 1915, House of Commons, *Complete Speeches*, III:2390–403.

3. Carden to WSC, 11 January 1915, *WSC*, III/1:405–6.

4. Oliver memorandum, 2 February 1915, CHAR 2/74/55.

5. Churchill, *World Crisis*, II:194.

6. J. Lee Thompson, *Politicians, the Press, and Propaganda: Lord Northcliffe and the Great War, 1914–1919* (Kent, OH: Kent State University Press, 1999), 59.

7. Robert Blake and W. Roger Louis, 'Introduction', *Churchill*, ed. Blake and Louis, 4.

8. Churchill, *World Crisis*, II:vii.

Select Bibliography

ARCHIVAL SOURCES

The National Archives, Kew, London

ADM 1   Admiralty and Secretariat Papers
ADM 116   Admiralty and Secretariat Cases
ADM 137   Historical Section: Records used for Official History, First World War
ADM 167   Board of Admiralty Minutes and Memoranda
ADM 178   Admiralty: Papers and Cases, Supplementary Series
CAB 1   Cabinet Office: Miscellaneous Records
CAB 16   Committee of Imperial Defence Ad Hoc Subcommittees
CAB 19   Special Commissions to Enquire into the Operations of War in Mesopotamia (Hamilton Commission) and in the Dardanelles (Cromer and Pickford Commission): Records
CAB 21   Cabinet Office Registered Files
CAB 22   War Council and Successors: Minutes and Papers
CAB 23   War Cabinet and Cabinet: Minutes
CAB 24   War Cabinet and Cabinet: Memoranda
CAB 45   Committee of Imperial Defence, Historical Branch and Cabinet Office, Historical Section

Australian War Memorial, Canberra

AWM 38   Official History, 1914–18 War: Records of C. E. W. Bean, Official Historian

Electronic Databases

Mass Observation Archives

Personal Papers

Ashmead-Bartlett, Ellis, *Institute of Commonwealth Studies*
Asquith, Herbert Henry (Earl of Oxford and Asquith), *Bodleian Library, Oxford*
Balfour, Arthur J., *British Library*
Bathurst, Countess, *University of Leeds Library*
Battenberg, Prince Louis, *University of Southampton Library, Archives and Manuscripts*
Beaverbrook, Lord (William Maxwell Aitken), *House of Lords Records Office*

Churchill, Sir Winston S., *Churchill College Archives Centre, Cambridge*
Corbett, Sir Julian, *National Maritime Museum*
De Robeck, Admiral Sir John, *Churchill College Archives Centre, Cambridge*
D'Eyncourt, Sir Eustace Tennyson, *National Maritime Museum*
Donald, Sir Robert, *Parliamentary Archives*
Dumas, Admiral Philip W., *University of Leeds Library*
Ellison, Gerald, *National Army Museum*
Esher, Viscount, *Churchill College Archives Centre, Cambridge*
Fisher, Admiral of the Fleet John Arbuthnot (Lord Fisher of Kilverstone), *Churchill College Archives Centre*
Garvin, James L., *Harry Ransom Center, University of Texas at Austin*
Greene, Sir William Graham, *National Maritime Museum*
Gwynne, Howell Arthur, *Imperial War Museum*
Hall, Admiral Sir William Reginald, *Churchill College Archives Centre*
Hamilton, Admiral Sir Frederick Tower, *National Maritime Museum*
Hamilton, General Sir Ian, *Liddell Hart Centre for Military Archives*
Hankey, Maurice (1st Baron Hankey), *Churchill College Archives Centre*
Harcourt, Sir Lewis, *Bodleian Library, Oxford*
Jackson, Admiral Sir Henry, *National Maritime Museum* and *National Museum of the Royal Navy*
Keyes, Admiral of the Fleet Roger (Lord Keyes of Zeebrugge), *British Library*
Kitchener, Field Marshal Lord, *The National Archives.*
Law, Andrew Bonar, *House of Lords Records Office*
Liddell Hart, Sir Basil, *Liddell Hart Centre for Military Archives*
Limpus, Admiral Sir Arthur Henry, *National Maritime Museum*
Lloyd George, David, *House of Lords Records Office*
Maxse, Leopold J., *West Sussex Records Office*
Northcliffe, Viscount (Alfred Harmsworth), *British Library*
Oliver, Admiral Sir Henry, *National Maritime Museum*
Oliver, Vice-Admiral R. D., *National Maritime Museum*
Richmond, Admiral Sir Herbert, *National Maritime Museum*
Riddell, George, *British Library*
Robertson, Field Marshal Sir William, *Liddell Hart Centre for Military Archives*
Roskill, Captain Stephen S., *Churchill College Archives Centre*
Sandars, John, *Bodleian Library, Oxford*
Scott, Alexander MacCallum, *University of Glasgow*
Spender, J. A., *British Library*
Strachey, John St Loe, *Parliamentary Archives*
Wemyss, Admiral of the Fleet Rosslyn Erskine (1st Baron Wester Wemyss of Wemyss), *Churchill College Archives Centre*
Williamson, Captain Hugh, *Churchill College Archives Centre*
Wilson, Field Marshal Sir Henry, *Imperial War Museum*

Published Sources

Published Primary Sources

Bonham Carter, Mark and Mark Pottle (eds). *Lantern Slides: The Diaries and Letters of Violet Bonham Carter, 1904–1914*. London: Weidenfeld & Nicolson, 1996.

Brock, Michael and Eleanor (eds). *H. H. Asquith: Letters to Venetia Stanley*. Oxford: Oxford University Press, 1982.

Brock, Michael and Eleanor (eds). *Margot Asquith's Great War Diary, 1914–1916: The View from Downing Street*. Oxford: Oxford University Press, 2014.

Colville, John. *The Fringes of Power: 10 Downing Street Diaries 1939–55*. New York: W. W. Norton, 1985.

David, Edward (ed.). *Inside Asquith's Cabinet*. London: John Murray, 1977.

Gilbert, Martin (ed.). *The Churchill War Papers*. 3 vols, New York: Norton, 1993–2001.

Gorodetsky, Gabriel (ed.). *The Maisky Diaries*. New Haven, CT: Yale University Press, 2015.

Halpern, Paul G. (ed.). *The Keyes Papers*. 3 vols, London: Navy Records Society, 1979–81.

Langworth, Richard (ed.). *Churchill by Himself*. New York: Public Affairs, 2008.

McEwen, J. M. (ed.). *The Riddell Diaries 1908–1923*. London: Athlone Press, 1986.

Marder, Arthur J. (ed.). *Portrait of an Admiral*. Cambridge, MA: Harvard University Press, 1952.

Marder, Arthur J. (ed.). *Fear God and Dread Nought*. 3 vols, London, Cape, 1952–9.

Patterson, A. Temple (ed.). *The Jellicoe Papers*. 2 vols, London: Navy Records Society, 1966–8.

Pottle, Mark. *Champion Redoubtable: The Diaries and Letters of Violet Bonham Carter 1914–1945*. London: Weidenfeld & Nicolson, 1998.

Ranft, B. McL. (ed.). *The Beatty Papers*. 2 vols, Aldershot: Ashgate for the Navy Records Society, 1989–93.

Rhodes James, Robert (ed.). *Chips: The Diaries of Sir Henry Channon*. London: Weidenfeld & Nicolson, 1967.

Rhodes James, Robert (ed.). *Winston S. Churchill: His Complete Speeches*. 8 vols, New York: Chelsea House Publishers in association with R. R. Bowker Company, 1974.

Riddell, Lord. *Lord Riddell's War Diary 1914–1918*. London: Ivor Nicholson & Watson, 1934.

Roskill, Stephen (ed.). *Documents on the Royal Naval Air Service*. London: Navy Records Society, 1969.

Soames, Mary (ed.). *Speaking for Themselves*. Toronto: Stoddart, 1998.

Taylor, A. J. P. (ed.). *Lloyd George: A Diary by Frances Stevenson*. New York: Harper & Row, 1971.

Wilson, Keith M. (ed.). *The Rasp of War: The Letters of H. A. Gwynne to the Countess Bathurst, 1914–1918*. London: Sidgwick & Jackson, 1988.

Wilson, Trevor (ed.). *The Political Diaries of C. P. Scott, 1911–1928*. Ithaca, NY: Cornell University Press, 1970.

Memoirs

Bacon, Admiral Sir Reginald. *The Dover Patrol*. 2 vols, New York: Doran, 1919.

Bacon, Admiral Sir Reginald. *From 1900 Onward*. London: Hutchinson, 1940.

Bayly, Lewis. *Pull Together: The Memoirs of Admiral Sir Lewis Bayly*. London: Harrap, 1939.

Bonham Carter, Violet. *Winston Churchill as I Knew Him*. London: Eyre & Spottiswoode, 1965.

Brownrigg, Rear-Admiral Sir Douglas. *Indiscretions of the Naval Censor*. New York: Doran, 1920.

Callwell, Sir Charles E. *Experiences of a Dug-Out*. London: Constable, 1920.

Churchill, Winston S. *The World Crisis*. Abridged and revised edition, Toronto: Macmillan, 1931.

Churchill, Winston S. *The Second World War*. 6 vols, London: Cassell, 1948–53.

Churchill, Winston S. *The World Crisis*. 5 vols, New York: Scribners, 1963–4.

Dewar, Kenneth. *The Navy from Within*. London: Gollancz, 1939.

Fisher, Lord. *Memories* and *Records*. New York: George H. Doran, 1920.

Grey of Fallodon, Viscount. *Twenty-Five Years: 1892–1916*. Toronto: Ryerson Press, 1925.

Hamilton, Ian. *Gallipoli Diary*. 2 vols, New York: George H. Doran, 1920.

Hamilton, Ian. *Listening for the Drums*. London: Faber & Faber, 1944.

Hankey, Lord. *The Supreme Command*. 2 vols, London: George Allen & Unwin, 1961.

Jellicoe, Admiral Viscount. *The Grand Fleet*. New York: George H. Doran Co., 1919.

Kennedy, Major-General Sir John. *The Business of War*. London: Hutchinson, 1957.

Keyes, Roger. *The Naval Memoirs of Admiral of the Fleet Sir Roger Keyes*. 2 vols, London: Thornton Butterworth, 1934–5.

Liman von Sanders, Otto. *Five Years in Turkey*. Annapolis, MD: United States Naval Institute, 1927.

Lloyd George, David. *War Memoirs*. 6 vols, London: Ivor Nicholson & Watson, 1933–6.

Oxford and Asquith, Earl of. *Memories and Reflections 1852–1927*. Toronto: McClelland & Stewart, 1928.

Robertson, Sir William. *Soldiers and Statesmen 1914–1918*. New York: Scribners, 1926.

Samson, Charles. *Fights and Flights*. London: Ernest Benn, 1930.

Scott, Admiral Sir Percy. *Fifty Years in the Royal Navy*. New York: Doran, 1919.

Spender, J. A. *Life, Journalism and Politics*. 2 vols, London: Cassell, 1927.

Sueter, Murray F. *Airmen or Noahs*. London: Sir Isaac Pitman & Sons, 1928.

Wester-Wemyss, Admiral of the Fleet Lord. *The Navy in the Dardanelles Campaign*. London: Hodder & Stoughton, 1924.

Books

Adams, R. J. Q. *Bonar Law*. Stanford, CA: Stanford University Press, 1999.

Arthur, Sir George. *Life of Lord Kitchener*. 3 vols, London: Macmillan, 1920.

Ashmead-Bartlett, Ellis. *The Uncensored Dardanelles*. London: Hutchinson, 1928.

Ashplant, Timothy G., Graham Dawson, and Michael Roper (eds). *Commemorating War: The Politics of Memory*. London: Transaction Publishers, 2004.

Aspinall-Oglander, C. F. *Military Operations: Gallipoli*. 2 vols, London: William Heinemann, 1929–32.

Bacon, Admiral Sir Reginald H. *The Life of Lord Fisher of Kilverstone*. 2 vols, Garden City, NY: Doubleday, Doran & Co., 1929.

Bean, C. E. W. *Official History of Australia in the War of 1914–1918*, vol. 1, *The Story of ANZAC*, 2nd edn. Sydney: Angus & Robertson, 1933.

Beckett, Ian F. W. *The Great War 1914–1918*. Harlow: Longman, 2001.

Beesly, Patrick. *Room 40: British Naval Intelligence 1914–18*. London: Hamish Hamilton, 1982.

Beireger, Eugene Edward. *Churchill, Munitions and Mechanical Warfare: The Politics of Supply and Strategy*. New York: Peter Lang, 1997.

Bell, Christopher M. *Churchill and Sea Power*. Oxford: Oxford University Press, 2012.

Benbow, Tim. *British Naval Aviation: The First 100 Years*. Aldershot: Ashgate, 2011.

Ben-Moshe, Tuvia. *Churchill: Strategy and History*. Boulder, CO: Lynne Rienner Publishers, 1991.

Best, Geoffrey. *Churchill: A Study in Greatness*. London: Hambledon & London, 2001.

Best, Geoffrey. *Churchill and War*. London: Hambledon & London, 2005.

Black, Nicholas. *The British Naval Staff in the First World War*. Woodbridge: Boydell Press, 2009.

Blake, Robert. *The Unknown Prime Minister*. London: Eyre & Spottiswoode, 1955.

Blake, Robert and William Roger Louis (eds). *Churchill*. New York: Norton, 1993.

Bond, Brian (ed.). *The First World War and British Military History*. Oxford: Oxford University Press, 1991.

Bond, Brian. *The Unquiet Western Front: Britain's Role in Literature and History*. Cambridge: Cambridge University Press, 2002.

Bond, Brian. *Britain's Two World Wars against Germany*. Cambridge: Cambridge University Press, 2014.

Brenchley, Fred and Elizabeth Brenchley. *Myth Maker: Ellis Ashmead-Bartlett, the Englishman who Sparked Australia's Gallipoli Legend*. Milton, Qld: Wiley, 2005.

Brodhurst, Robin. *Churchill's Anchor*. Barnsley: Leo Cooper, 2000.

Buxton, Ian. *Big Gun Monitors*, 2nd edn. Barnsley: Seaforth Publishing, 2008.

Callwell, Sir Charles E. *The Dardanelles*. Boston, MA: Houghton Mifflin, 1919.

Cassar, George H. *The French and the Dardanelles*. London, Allen & Unwin, 1971.

Cassar, George H. *Kitchener: Architect of Victory*. London: William Kimber, 1977.

Cassar, George H. *Asquith as War Leader*. London: Hambledon Press, 1994.

Cassar, George H. *Kitchener's War*. Washington: Potomac Books, 2004.

'Cato' (Michael Foot, Peter Howard, and Frank Owen). *Guilty Men*. London: Penguin, 1998.

Charmley, John. *Churchill: The End of Glory*. London: Hodder & Stoughton, 1993.

Chatterton, E. Keble. *Dardanelles Dilemma*. London: Rich & Cowan, 1935.

Churchill, Randolph S. and Martin Gilbert. *Winston S. Churchill*. 8 vols and 13 companion books, London: Heinemann, 1966–88.

Churchill, Winston S. *Thoughts and Adventures*. London: Thornton Butterworth, 1932.

Churchill, Winston S. *Great Contemporaries*, rev. and expanded edn. London: Thornton Butterworth, 1938.

Churchill, Winston S. *The Collected Essays of Sir Winston Churchill*, ed. Michael Wolff. 4 vols, London: Library of Imperial History, 1976.

Clews, Graham. *Churchill's Dilemma: The Real Story behind the Origins of the 1915 Dardanelles Campaign*. Santa Barbara, CA: Praeger, 2010.

Coates, Tim (ed.). *Lord Kitchener and Winston Churchill: The Dardanelles Commission Part I, 1914–15*. London: The Stationery Office, 2000.

Corbett, Julian S. *Naval Operations*. 3 vols, London: Longmans, 1920–3.

Corrigan, Gordon. *Blood, Sweat and Arrogance and the Myths of Churchill's War*. London: Phoenix, 2006.

Coulthart, Ross. *Charles Bean: If People Really Knew*. Sydney: HarperCollins, 2014.

Crawley, Rhys. *Climax at Gallipoli*. Norman, OK: University of Oklahoma Press, 2014.

Curran, Tom. *The Grand Deception*. Newport, NSW: Big Sky Publishing, 2015.

Day, David. *The Great Betrayal*. New York: Norton, 1989.

D'Este, Carlo. *Warlord: A Life of Winston Churchill at War, 1874–1945*. New York: Harper, 2008.

Dockter, Warren. *Churchill and the Islamic World*. London: I.B. Tauris, 2015.

Dutton, David. *Neville Chamberlain*. London: Arnold, 2001.

Eade, Charles (ed.). *Churchill by His Contemporaries*. London: Hutchinson, 1953.

Eisenhower, Dwight D. and Alistair Cooke. *General Eisenhower on the Military Churchill*. New York: Norton, 1970.

Ellison, Sir Gerald. *The Perils of Amateur Strategy*. London: Longmans, Green, & Co., 1926.

Erickson, Edward J. *Gallipoli: The Ottoman Campaign*. Barnsley: Pen & Sword, 2010.

Forrest, Michael. *The Defence of the Dardanelles: From Bombards to Battleships*. Barnsley: Pen & Sword, 2012.

Fraser, Peter. *Lord Esher: A Political Biography*. Barnsley: Pen & Sword, 2013.

Freedman, Lawrence, Paul Hayes, and Robert O'Neill. *War, Strategy and International Politics*. Oxford: Oxford University Press, 1992.

French, David. *British Strategy and War Aims*. London, London: Allen & Unwin, 1984.

Freudenberg, Graham. *Churchill and Australia*. Sydney: Pan Macmillan Australia, 2006.

Germains, Victor Wallace. *The Tragedy of Winston Churchill*. London: Hurst & Blackett, 1931.

Gough, Barry. *Historical Dreadnoughts*. Barnsley: Seaforth Publishing, 2010.

Green, Andrew. *Writing the Great War*. London: Frank Cass, 2003.

Gretton, Vice-Admiral Sir Peter. *Former Naval Person*. London: Cassell, 1968.

Grimes, Shawn. *Strategy and War Planning in the British Navy, 1887–1918*. London: Boydell Press, 2012.

Grove, Eric. *The Royal Navy*. New York: Palgrave Macmillan, 2005.

Halpern, Paul G. *The Naval War in the Mediterranean*. Annapolis, MD: Naval Institute Press, 1987.

Halpern, Paul G. *A Naval History of World War I*. Annapolis, MD: Naval Institute Press, 1995.

Hart, Peter. *Gallipoli*. New York: Oxford University Press, 2011.

Hazareesingh, Sudhir. *In the Shadow of the General: Modern France and the Myth of De Gaulle*. Oxford: Oxford University Press, 2012.

Hazlehurst, Cameron. *Politicians at War July 1914 to May 1915*. London: Jonathan Cape, 1971.

Higgins, Trumbull. *Winston Churchill and the Second Front*. Oxford University Press, 1957.

Higgins, Trumbull. *Winston Churchill and the Dardanelles*. London: Heinemann, 1963.

Hill, J. R. *The Oxford Illustrated History of the Royal Navy*. Oxford: Oxford University Press, 1995.

Hough, Richard. *Former Naval Person*. London: Weidenfeld & Nicolson, 1985.

Hunt, Barry. *Sailor–Scholar: Admiral Sir Herbert Richmond, 1871–1946*. Waterloo: Wilfrid Laurier University Press, 1982.

Hyatt, A. M. J. (ed.). *Dreadnought to Polaris*. Toronto: Copp Clark, 1973.

Inglis, K. S. *C. E. W. Bean, Australian Historian*. St Lucia, Qld: University of Queensland Press, 1970.

James, Admiral Sir William. *The Eyes of the Navy*. London: Methuen, 1955.

James, Admiral Sir William. *A Great Seaman: The Life of Admiral of the Fleet Sir Henry F. Oliver*. London: Witherby, 1956.

Jeffery, Keith. *Field Marshal Sir Henry Wilson: A Political Soldier*. Oxford: Oxford University Press, 2006.

Jerrold, Douglas. *The Royal Naval Division*. London: Hutchinson, 1923.

Jones, H. A. *The War in The Air*, vol. 2. Oxford: Clarendon Press, 1928.

Lambert, Nicholas. *Planning Armageddon: British Economic Warfare and the First World War*. Cambridge, MA: Harvard University Press, 2012.

Layman, R. D. *Naval Aviation in the First World War: Its Impact and Influence*. Annapolis, MD: Naval Institute Press, 1996.

Liddell Hart, B. H. *The British Way in Warfare*. London: Faber & Faber, 1932.

Liddell Hart, B. H. *A History of the World War*. London: Pan, 1970.

McCarthy, Dudley. *Gallipoli to the Somme: The Story of C. E. W. Bean*. London: Cooper, 1983.

Mackay, Ruddock F. *Fisher of Kilverstone*. Oxford: Clarendon Press, 1973.

Macleod, Jenny (ed.). *Gallipoli: Making History*. London: Frank Cass, 2004.

Macleod, Jenny. *Reconsidering Gallipoli*. Manchester: Manchester University Press, 2004.

Macleod, Jenny (ed.). *Defeat and Memory*. Basingstoke: Palgrave Macmillan, 2008.

Macleod, Jenny. *Gallipoli*. Oxford: Oxford University Press, 2015.

Magnus, P. *Kitchener: Portrait of an Imperialist*. London: Murray, 1958.

Marder, Arthur J. *From the Dreadnought to Scapa Flow*. 5 vols, Oxford: Oxford University Press, 1961–71.

Marder, Arthur J. *From the Dardanelles to Oran*. London: Clarendon Press, 1974.

Masefield, J. *Gallipoli*. London: Heinemann, 1916.

Maurer, John H. (ed.). *Churchill and Strategic Dilemmas before the World Wars*. London: Frank Cass, 2003.

Meaher, Augustine, *The Road to Singapore: The Myth of British Betrayal*. Melbourne: Australian Scholarly Publishing, 2010.

Miller, Geoffrey. *The Millstone*. Hull: University of Hull Press, 1999.

Moorehead, Alan. *Gallipoli*. London: Hamish Hamilton, 1956.

Moran, Lord. *Winston Churchill: The Struggle for Survival 1940–1965*. London: Constable, 1966.

Moseley, S. A. *The Truth about the Dardanelles*. London: Cassell, 1916.

Moyal, Ann. *Alan Moorehead: A Rediscovery*. Canberra: National Library of Australia, 2005.

Murfett, Malcolm H. (ed.). *The First Sea Lords: From Fisher to Mountbatten*. Westport, CT: Praeger, 1995.

Naylor, John F. *A Man and an Institution: Sir Maurice Hankey, the Cabinet Secretariat and the Custody of Cabinet Secrecy*. Cambridge: Cambridge University Press, 1984.

Nevinson, H. W. *The Dardanelles Campaign*. London, 1918.

North, J. *Gallipoli: The Fading Vision*. London: Faber & Faber, 1936.

Offer, Avner. *The First World War: An Agrarian Interpretation*. Oxford: Clarendon Press, 1991.

Penn, Geoffrey. *Fisher, Churchill and the Dardanelles*. Barnsley: Leo Cooper 1999.

Popham, Hugh. *Into Wind: A History of British Naval Flying*. London: Hamish Hamilton, 1969.

Prior, Robin. *Churchill's 'World Crisis' as History*. London: Croom Helm, 1983.

Prior, Robin. *Gallipoli*. New Haven, CT: Yale University Press, 2009.

Prior, Robin. *When Britain Saved the West: The Story of 1940*. New Haven, CT: Yale University Press, 2015.

Puleston, Captain W. D. *The Dardanelles Expedition: A Condensed Study*, 2nd edn. Annapolis, MD: United States Naval Institute, 1927.

Ramsay, David. *'Blinker' Hall: Spymaster*. Stroud: Spellmount, 2008.

Ramsden, John. *Man of the Century: Winston Churchill and His Legend since 1945*. New York: Columbia University Press, 2003.

Reynolds, David. *In Command of History*. London: Allen Lane, 2004.

Reynolds, David. *From World War to Cold War: Churchill, Roosevelt, and the International History of the 1940s*. Oxford: Oxford University Press, 2006.

Rhodes James, Robert. *Gallipoli*. New York: Batsford, 1965.

Rhodes James, Robert. *Churchill: A Study in Failure*. London: Weidenfeld & Nicolson, 1970.

Roberts, Andrew. *Eminent Churchillians*. London: Phoenix, 1994.

Rodger, N. A. M. *Naval Power in the Twentieth Century*. London: Macmillan, 1996.

Roskill, Stephen. *Hankey: Man of Secrets*. 3 vols, London: Collins, 1970–4.

Roskill, Stephen. *Churchill and the Admirals*. London: Collins, 1977.

Rudenno, Victor. *Gallipoli: Attack from the Sea*. New Haven, CT: Yale University Press, 2008.

Sandys, Celia. *Churchill: Wanted Dead or Alive*. Edison, NJ: Castle Books, 2005.

Schurman, Donald M. *Julian S. Corbett, 1854–1922*. London: Royal Historical Society, 1981.

Scott, A. MacCallum. *Winston Churchill in Peace and War*. London: Newnes, 1916.

Soames, Mary. *Clementine Churchill*. London: Cassell, 1979.

'Taffrail' (Captain H. Taprell-Dorling). *Swept Channels: Being an Account of the Work of the Minesweepers in the Great War*. London, Hodder & Stoughton, 1935.

Taylor, A. J. P., Robert Rhodes James, J. H. Plumb, Basil Liddell Hart, and Anthony Storr. *Churchill: Four Faces and the Man*. London: Book Club Associates, 1969.

Thompson, J. Lee. *Politicians, the Press, and Propaganda: Lord Northcliffe and the Great War, 1914–1919*. Kent, OH: Kent State University Press, 1999.

Toye, Richard. *Lloyd George and Churchill*. London: Pan Macmillan, 2008.

Toye, Richard. *The Roar of the Lion: The Untold Story of Churchill's World War II Speeches*. Oxford: Oxford University Press, 2013.

Travers, Tim. *Gallipoli 1915*. Stroud: Tempus, 2001.

Usborne, C. V. *Smoke on the Horizon: Mediterranean Fighting 1914–1918*. London: Hodder & Stoughton, 1933.

Van der Vat, Dan. *The Dardanelles Disaster*. London: Duckworth Overlook, 2009.

Van Hartesveldt, Fred R. *The Dardanelles Campaign, 1915: Historiography and Annotated Bibliography*. Westport, CT: Greenwood Press, 1997.

Wallin, Jeffrey D. *By Ships Alone: Churchill and the Dardanelles*. Durham, NC: Carolina Academic Press, 1981.

Wilkinson, Nicholas. *Secrecy and the Media: The Official History of the United Kingdom's D Notice System*. London: Routledge, 2009.

Winter, Dennis. *Making the Legend: The War Writings of C. E. W. Bean*. St Lucia, Qld: University of Queensland Press, 1992.

Articles and Chapters

Attlee, Lord. 'The Churchill I Knew', in *Churchill by His Contemporaries: An Observer Appreciation*. London: Hodder & Stoughton, 1965, 14–35.

Barnett, Len. 'Royal Naval Gunnery and Minesweeping at the Dardanelles, February to March 1915' (self-published).

Barnett, Len. '"Trial and Error": The Royal Navy and Mine Countermeasures 1904–1914', <http://www.barnettmaritime.co.uk/Trial.pdf> (accessed 23 March 2016).

Beaumont, Joan. 'Gallipoli and Australian National Identity', in *Culture, Place and Identity*, ed. Neil Garnham and Keith Jeffery. Dublin: University College Dublin Press, 2005, pp. 138–51.

Bell, Duncan S. A. 'Mythscapes: Memory, Mythology, and National Identity', *British Journal of Sociology*, 54, no. 1 (March 2003), 63–81.

Boswell, Captain L. A. K. 'The Naval Attack on the Dardanelles, 1915', *Journal of the Royal United Services Institute*, 110, no. 638 (May 1965), 144–7.

Callahan, Raymond. 'What about the Dardanelles?', *American Historical Review*, 78, no. 3 (June 1973), 641–8.

Capern, Amanda L. 'Winston Churchill, Mark Sykes and the Dardanelles Campaign of 1915', *Historical Research*, 71, no. 174 (February 1998), 108–18.

Curran, Tom. 'Who was Responsible for the Dardanelles Naval Fiasco?', *Australian Journal of Politics & History*, 57, no. 1 (March 2011), 17–33.

Dawson, Graham. 'The Theory of Popular Memory and the Contested Memories of the Second World War in Britain', in *Myths, Gender and the Military Conquest of Air and Sea*, ed. Silke Wenk, Herbert Mehrtens, and Katharina Hoffmann. Oldenburg: BIS Verlag, 2012, 205–20.

Dawson, Graham, and Bob West. 'Our Finest Hour? The Popular Memory of World War II and the Struggle over National Identity', in *National Fictions: World War Two on Film and Television*, ed. Geoff Hurd. London: British Film Institute, 1984, pp. 8–13.

Dawson, R. MacGregor. 'The Cabinet Minister and Administration: Winston S. Churchill at the Admiralty, 1911–15', *Canadian Journal of Economics and Political Science*, 6, no. 3 (August 1940), 325–58.

Erickson, Edward J. 'One More Push: Forcing the Dardanelles in March 1915', *Journal of Strategic Studies*, 24, no. 3 (September 2001), 158–76.

Filev, Anatoli, 'New Documents about Winston Churchill from Russian Archives', *International Affairs* (Moscow), 47, no. 5 (2001), 131–5.

Finney, Patrick. 'The Ubiquitous Presence of the Past? Collective Memory and International History', *International History Review*, 36, no. 3 (2014), 443–72.

Fraser, Peter. 'Lord Beaverbrook's Fabrications in Politicians and the War, 1914–1916', *Historical Journal*, 25 (1982), 147–66.

Fraser, Peter. 'Cabinet Secrecy and War Memoirs', *History*, 70, no. 230 (October 1985), 397–409.

French, David. 'The Origins of the Dardanelles Campaign Reconsidered', *History*, 68, no. 233 (June 1983), 210–24.

Gedi, Noa and Yigal Elam, 'Collective Memory: What Is It?', *History and Memory*, 8, no. 1 (June 1996), 30–47.

Lambert, Andrew. ' "This Is All We Want": Great Britain and the Baltic Approaches 1815–1914', in *Britain and Denmark: Political, Economic and Cultural Relations in the 19th and 20th Centuries*, ed. J. Sevaldsen. Copenhagen: Museum Tusculanum Press, 2003, pp. 147–69.

Lambert, Andrew. 'The German North Sea Islands, the Kiel Canal and the Danish Narrows in Royal Navy Thinking and Planning, 1905–1918', in *The Danish Straits and German Naval Power 1905–1918*, ed. Michael Epkenhans and Gerhard P. Groß. Potsdam: Militärgeschichtliches Forschungsamt, 2010, pp. 35–62.

Lambert, Andrew. ' "The Possibility of Ultimate Action in the Baltic": The Royal Navy at War, 1914–1916', in *Jutland: World War I's Greatest Naval Battle*, ed. Michael Epkenhans, Jörg Hillmann, and Frank Nägler. Lexington, KY: University Press of Kentucky, 2015, pp. 79–116.

Lambert, Andrew. 'An Edwardian Intellectual at War: Julian Corbett, Plans, Strategy and Official History' (forthcoming).

Layman, Richard D. 'HMS Ark Royal: 1914–1922', *Cross and Cockade*, 18, no. 4 (winter 1987), 145–57.

Mackay, Ruddock. 'Hankey on Fisher's Baltic "Chimera" ', *Mariner's Mirror*, 82, no. 2 (May 1996), 211–13.

Macleod, Jenny. 'General Sir Ian Hamilton and the Dardanelles Commission', *War in History*, 8, no. 4 (November 2001), 418–41.

McEwan, J. M. ' "Brass-Hats" and the British Press during the First World War', *Canadian Journal of History*, 18 (April 1983), 43–67.

Meaher, Augustine. 'Australia as Victim: Keating and the Betrayal Myth', *Australian Studies*, 20 (2007), 351–74.

Morgan-Owen, David G. 'An 'Intermediate Blockade'? British North Sea Strategy, 1912–1914', *War in History*, 22, no. 4 (2015), 478–502.

Morgan-Owen, David G. 'Cooked Up in the Dinner Hour? Sir Arthur Wilson's War Plan, Reconsidered', *English Historical Review*, 130, no. 545 (August 2015), 865–906.

Mount, Ferdinand, 'Churchill Capsized: The Dardanelles Campaign was Fatally Misjudged', *The Spectator*, 264 (14 April 1990), 8–11.

Moyal, Ann. 'Alan Moorehead's Gallipoli', 16 May 2015, <http://www.aspistrategist. org.au/alan-mooreheads-gallipoli/> (accessed 19 July 2016).

Nykiel, Piotr. 'Minesweeping Operation in the Dardanelles (February 25–March 17, 1915)'. Çanakkale Araştırmaları Türk Yıllığı, 2 (March 2004), 81–115.

Nykiel, Piotr. 'Was it Possible to Renew the Naval Attack on the Dardanelles Successfully the Day after the 18th March?'. <https://www.academia.edu/165783/Was_it_ Possible_to_Renew_the_Naval_Attack_on_the_Dardanelles_Successfully_the_ Day_After_18th_March> (accessed 19 July 2016).

Paget, Gregory. 'The November 1914 Straits Agreement and the Dardanelles–Gallipoli Campaign', *Australian Journal of Politics & History*, 33, no. 3 (December 1987), 253–60.

Prior, Robin. ' "The Blood Test": Churchill Writing on the Battle of the Somme', *Finest Hour*, no. 172 (spring 2016), 32–5.

Quinault, Roland. 'Churchill and Australia: The Military Relationship, 1899–1945', *War and Society*, 6, no. 1 (May 1988), 41–64.

Reguer, Sara. 'Churchill's Role in the Dardanelles Campaign', *British Army Review*, no. 108 (December 1994), 70–80.

Richter, Heinz. 'The Impact of the Confiscation of the Turkish Dreadnoughts and of the Transfer of *Goeben* and *Breslau* to Constantinople upon the Turkish Entry into WWI', *Çanakkale Araştırmaları Türk Yıllığı*, 11, no. 15 (2013), 1–16.

Seligmann, Matthew S. 'The Anglo-German Naval Race, 1898–1914', in *Arms Races in International Politics*, ed. Thomas G. Mahnken, Joseph A. Maiolo, and David Stevenson. Oxford: Oxford University Press, 2016, pp. 21–40.

Seligmann, Matthew S. 'Failing to Prepare for the Great War? The Absence of Grand Strategy in British War Planning before 1914', *War in History* (forthcoming).

Stubbs, John O. 'Beaverbrook as Historian: "Politicians and the War, 1914–1916" Reconsidered', *Albion*, 14, no. 3/4 (autumn 1982), 235–53.

Sumida, Jon. 'Churchill and British Sea Power, 1908–29', in *Winston Churchill: Studies in Statesmanship*, ed. R. A. C. Parker. London: Brassey's, 1995, pp. 5–21.

Wallin, Jeffrey D. 'Politics and Strategy in the Dardanelles Operation', in *Statesmanship*, ed. Harry V. Jaffa. Durham, NC: Carolina Academic Press, 1981, pp. 131–55.

Theses

Clews, Graham. 'Churchill and the Phoney War: A Study in Folly and Frustration', PhD thesis, University of New South Wales, 2016.

Pass, Carla. 'The Lasting Legacy of Munich: British Public Perceptions of Neville Chamberlain during the Phoney War', MA thesis, Dalhousie University, 2014.

Photographic Acknowledgements

Australian War Memorial: 6.3; Mary Evans Picture Library: 2.3; Getty Images: 6.1, 9.1; Topham Picturepoint: 1.1, 2.2; TopFoto: 15.1; Library of Congress: 1.2, 1.3, 1.5, 1.6, 1.7, 2.1, 4.3, 6.2; Author's collection: 1.4; National Library of France: 4.1, 5.1; National Museum of the Royal Navy: 4.2; Moorehead family collection: 15.2.

Picture Credits

Index